ANCIENT
INDIAN HISTORICAL TRADITION

ANCIENT INDIAN HISTORICAL TRADITION

F.E. PARGITER

MOTILAL BANARSIDASS PUBLISHERS
PRIVATE LIMITED • DELHI

4th Reprint: Delhi, 2016
First Edition: London, 1922

ISBN: 978-81-208-1486-8 (Cloth)
ISBN: 978-81-208-1487-5 (Paper)

Also available at:
MOTILAL BANARSIDASS
41 U.A. Bungalow Road, Jawahar Nagar, Delhi 110 007
8 Mahalaxmi Chamber, 22 Bhulabhai Desai Road, Mumbai 400 026
203 Royapettah High Road, Mylapore, Chennai 600 004
236, 9th Main III Block, Jayanagar, Bengaluru 560 011
8 Camac Street, Kolkata 700 017
Ashok Rajpath, Patna 800 004
Chowk, Varanasi 221 001

MLBD Cataloging-in-Publication Data
Ancient Indian Historical Tradition
Religious Tradition, Reinterpretation and Response
George D. Bond
Includes Conclusion, Bibliography and Index
ISBN : 978-81-208-1486-8(Paper)
ISBN : 978-81-208-1487-5(Cloth)
I. Ancient II. Indian
III. Historical Tradition IV. Pargiter, F.E.

Printed in India

by RP Jain at NAB Printing Unit,
A-44, Naraina Industrial Area, Phase I, New Delhi–110028
and published by JP Jain for Motilal Banarsidass Publishers (P) Ltd,
41 U.A. Bungalow Road, Jawahar Nagar, Delhi-110007

PREFACE

THE views about ancient India now held by scholars are based upon an examination of the Veda and Vedic literature, to the neglect of Purāṇic and epic tradition; that is, ancient Indian history has been fashioned out of compositions, which are purely religious and priestly, which notoriously do not deal with history, and which totally lack the historical sense. The extraordinary nature of such history may be perceived, if it were suggested that European history should be constructed merely out of theological literature. What would raise a smile if applied to Europe has been soberly accepted when applied to India. This contrast is full justification for a consideration of what historical tradition has to tell us, and the results obtained from an examination of Purāṇic and epic tradition as well as of the Rigveda and Vedic literature are set out in the following pages.

Nothing herein has been the outcome of preconceived ideas, speculation, or haste. It began with a study of the epics and Purāṇas for geographical information about ancient India thirty years ago, during the translation of the Mārkaṇḍeya Purāṇa, in order to elucidate its geographical chapters. Geography included political divisions, and led to an examination of ancient kingdoms, and so on to their dynastic genealogies and traditions—subjects that were generally regarded as of little or no historical value, and were practically neglected. With no views about ancient Indian historical tradition, and a desire merely to see whether there was any substance in it, it was collected, compared, and studied, and inferences were drawn therefrom, revised continually with fresh material, and discarded freely if they proved untenable—which is simply the scientific process of collecting and testing facts copiously before forming any opinion or theory. At length some substance and order seemed to manifest themselves, and certain results gradually took shape; and some of these have been published in the *Journal of the Royal Asiatic Society* during the last fourteen years. These results developed with further study in various directions, especially on the religious side, and all have been revised and recast repeatedly, as their mutual relations became more complex, with fresh material from all sources.

The outcome of all these inquiries is set out here. No conclusion is put forward but what is based upon definite statements, and the authorities for every statement are cited. The results are totally different from the views now held by scholars as noticed above; yet there is nothing in them, as far as I am aware, really inconsistent with the most ancient book we possess, namely, the Rigveda, and they throw much new light thereon, and on all problems concerning ancient India. It remains however to be seen how far Professor M. Bloomfield's recent book, *Rig-Veda Repetitions*, which should lead to some solid chronological results, will support what tradition indicates regarding the order of rishis.

No pains have been spared to verify the references and make them complete and accurate. Unfortunately a few errors escaped notice in the proof-reading, and a considerable number of typographical blemishes have crept into the finally printed page, mostly the loss of diacritical marks which have failed or broken off in the printing, such as the stroke over the capital palatal sibilant, and the long mark over capital vowels. All these are exhibited in the list of Corrigenda at the end. I trust there are none others overlooked, yet feel sure that, if there are any, whether in the text or in the map, they can be readily corrected, and will not create any doubt as to what is intended.

My sincere thanks are given to the University of Oxford and the Government of India for generous help towards lightening the cost of this book for the benefit of readers.

OXFORD,
March, 1922.

TABLE OF CONTENTS

LIST OF ABBREVIATIONS

Ag	Agni Purāṇa.
Bd	Brahmāṇḍa Purāṇa.
Bhāg	Bhāgavata Purāṇa.
Br	Brahma Purāṇa.
Brāhm	Brāhmaṇa.
Bṛhadd	Bṛhaddevatā.
BV	Brahmavaivarta Purāṇa.
DKA	'Dynasties of the Kali Age.'
Gar	Garuḍa Purāṇa.
Hv	Harivaṁśa.
JAOS	Journal of American Oriental Society.
JASB	Journal of Asiatic Society of Bengal.
JRAS	Journal of Royal Asiatic Society.
Kūr	Kūrma Purāṇa.
Lg	Liṅga Purāṇa.
Mārk	Mārkaṇḍeya Purāṇa.
Mat	Matsya Purāṇa.
MBh	Mahābhārata.
Pad	Padma Purāṇa.
Raghuv	Raghuvaṁśa.
Rām	Rāmāyaṇa.
Rigv	Rigveda.
SBE	Sacred Books of the East.
Śiv	Śiva Purāṇa.
Up	Upaniṣad.
Vā	Vāyu Purāṇa.
Vām	Vāmana Purāṇa.
Var	Varāha Purāṇa.
Vedārth	Vedārthadīpikā.
Viṣ	Viṣṇu Purāṇa.
VN	Vṛhannāradīya Purāṇa.

Other abbreviations are readily intelligible.

CHAPTER I

GENERAL SURVEY OF ANCIENT INDIAN HISTORICAL TRADITION

यो विद्याच्चतुरो वेदान्साङ्गोपनिषदो द्विजः ।
न चेत्पुराणं संविद्यान्नैव स स्याद्विचक्षणः ॥
इतिहासपुराणाभ्यां वेदं समुपबृंहयेत् ।
बिभेत्यल्पश्रुताद्वेदो मामयं प्रहरिष्यति[1] ॥

THE brahman, who may know the four Vedas with the Aṅgas and Upaniṣads, should not really be (regarded as) having attained proficiency, if he should not thoroughly know the Purāṇa. He should reinforce the Veda with the Itihāsa and Purāṇa. The Veda is afraid of him who is deficient in tradition,[2] (thinking) 'he will do me hurt'.

Our knowledge of the most ancient times in India rests mainly on tradition. We know from the evidence of language that the Aryans entered India very early, and established themselves ultimately throughout North India and in the north-west of the Dekhan, so that the history of those times is bound up closely with the Aryan conquest. The Purāṇas, the Mahābhārata and in a minor degree the Rāmāyaṇa profess to give accounts from tradition about the earliest occurrences. The Vedas, the Brāhmaṇas and other brahmanic literature supply information also. The oldest of these, the Rigveda, contains historical allusions, of which some record contemporary persons and events, but more refer to bygone times and persons and are obviously based on tradition. Almost all the information therefore comes from tradition.

[1] Vā *1*, 200–1. Pad v, *2*, 50–2. Śiv v, *1*, 35. MBh has the two verses separately, the first (modified) in i, *2*, 645, and the second in i, *1*, 260.

[2] *Śruta* here means 'tradition', see chap. II.

Ancient India has bequeathed to us no historical works. 'History is the one weak spot in Indian literature. It is, in fact, non-existent. The total lack of the historical sense is so characteristic, that the whole course of Sanskrit literature is darkened by the shadow of this defect, suffering as it does from an entire absence of exact chronology.'[1] This is especially true of the brahmanic literature, for it has been truly said, 'That the Vedic texts, the Saṁhitās and the Brāhmaṇas, are not books of historical purpose is notorious,' nor do they deal with history.[2]

The evidence in the Rigveda, whether contemporary notices or matter concerning the past borrowed from tradition, consists of statements more or less isolated; they are merely allusions and make up no connected account. Even the contemporary notices, though having all the trustworthiness of first-hand evidence, yet fix little or nothing definitely of themselves, because they have no certain chronological setting with reference to other events. The same remarks hold good for the brahmanical literature later than the Rigveda. This may be illustrated by the contemporary information about king Sudās in the Rigveda.

It tells us of his battle with the ten kings, but that event cannot be assigned to any definite time unless we know when he lived; and there is the widest difference, whether it took place (as scholars believe at present) when the Aryans were in the Panjab conquering their way into India, and was a battle between them and the hostile races who opposed their eastward advance; or whether it took place (as tradition indicates) long after the Aryans had established themselves in N. India, and was a battle between Sudāsa (Sudās), king of North Pañcāla, and other Aryan and non-Aryan kings who opposed his westward conquests. There is nothing in the Rigveda to fix his position chronologically, but there are plain statements in the genealogies and tradition which assign him a definite place in the scheme of Aryan expansion in North India.

Even contemporary historical notices in the Rigveda therefore remain chronologically vague, and by themselves yield little information that can be co-ordinated for historical purposes. Statements of an historical kind in the Vedic literature become serviceable, if they can be linked up with other statements from elsewhere, and

[1] Macdonell, *Sanskrit Literature*, p. 10.

[2] Professor Keith, JRAS, 1914, pp. 739, 1031 note; 1915, p. 143 note.

that can be only from tradition. It is tradition that gives many of them a chronological position; hence the soundness and force of the counsel given in the verses prefixed to this chapter are manifest. Tradition therefore becomes all-important. It is the only resource, since historical works are wanting, and is not an untrustworthy guide. In ancient times men knew perfectly well the difference between truth and falsehood, as abundant proverbs and sayings show. It was natural therefore that they should discriminate what was true and preserve it; and historical tradition must be considered in this light. This will be noticed farther on.

The Aryans could not have established themselves in India without long and arduous warfare. Among the hostile races who possessed the country before them were not only rude tribes but also communities in a higher state of civilization (chapter XXV). The Aryans not only subdued them, but also gradually cleared much of the country of the forests which occupied a large portion of its surface, so as to render it fit for themselves, their cattle and their cultivation.

Their wars, their conquests and the founding of new kingdoms all implied that there were victorious kings, whose lineage and exploits would have been sung in many a kṣatriya ballad.[1] With their territorial expansion their religion naturally extended its sphere. Political supremacy fostered religious ascendancy, and rishis[2] and munis, protected and favoured by royal power and Aryan prestige, spread and propagated their doctrines and observances, not only in the countries conquered, but also in the surrounding regions beyond the actual Aryan sway. Thus they gradually brought the alien peoples and tribes under the influence of Aryan beliefs and customs. This process has prevailed to the present day, and along with it another process must have been going on also, which likewise has continued to the present day, namely, the Aryans met with religious practices and beliefs among the peoples whom they ruled over or came into lasting contact with, and have assimilated some of them gradually, thus modifying their own religion to a certain extent.

Their victorious career must have given rise to abundant tradition of all kinds, warlike, religious and peaceful, and tradition must have grown with their expansion and the length of their occupa-

[1] So MBh i, 1, 220–5 (10 verses).
[2] This word is Anglicized throughout.

tion. Naturally it was impossible to remember all the accumulated traditions, much dropped out, and only what was important or specially interesting to kings, priests and people was preserved. Consequently the principal matters that would have survived would be (speaking generally) the genealogies of great dynasties, ballads and stories about famous kings and eminent rishis, and accounts of the chief popular religious beliefs and observances. Kings and rishis therefore were the prominent figures, and it is mainly with them that ancient traditions deal.

There was, however, the widest difference between kings and rishis. Kings occupied settled countries and towns. The rishis were not confined to any place, but wandered into woods and hills and wilds to practise asceticism and a religious life in order to form and enhance their sacred character. The conditions of a king's life were fixed. The rishi was independent; spiritual eminence being his aim, he sought out when young the teaching of a distinguished preceptor and, when he had completed his novitiate, was free to establish his hermitage where he pleased or to seek the patronage of some king who might welcome his ministrations. The kings inherited the throne of celebrated ancestors, whose memory and fame they cherished with pride and sought to emulate. The rishis came from well-known families indeed, but that birthright merely entitled them to acquire religious lore, and their advancement depended wholly on their own faculties. To maintain their lineage and dynasties was the natural and ardent wish of kings; hence the great desire that is often mentioned among kings to have sons. Rishis perpetuated their sacred lore and fame through their disciples, among whom might be their own sons if capable.

One indication of this difference is the fact that, while kings are treated genealogically, brahmanic succession is reckoned by the line of teaching as shown in the lists of religious teachers set out in the Bṛhadāraṇyaka Upaniṣad,[1] Satapatha Brāhmaṇa,[2] &c.[3] Marriage alliances were matters of high importance with kings and are often noticed. As regards rishis, though the names of the wives of certain have been preserved, yet very little is ever said about their marriages except when they married princesses; and strange stories are told about rishis, which indicate that their

[1] ii, 6; iv, 6; vi, 5. [2] x, 6, 5, 9.
[3] Macdonell and Keith, *Vedic Index*, ii, p. 236.

marital relations were not seldom erratic and their lineage by no means pure.[1]

The result is displayed in the epics and Purāṇas on the one side and in the Vedic literature on the other. Sacred lore is the subject of that literature, and references to secular matters are generally incidental for the purpose of illustrating some religious point. The ancient portion of the Purāṇas consists largely, as will be shown in chapter III, of the royal genealogies and kṣatriya ballads and tales, while most of their teaching on religious matters was added by brahmans in later times. Dynastic accounts and heroic tales were the principal subjects of the kṣatriya record. Royal genealogies are found in thirteen Purāṇas, the epics and the Harivaṁśa; but brahman genealogies hardly exist and are most meagre. The former give long lists of kings, but among rishi families it is rare to find more than three or four descents remembered, and the longest rishi pedigree is that of Vyāsa's family with six descents. Further it is noteworthy that, in cases where a king became a brahman, his kṣatriya descent is given fairly fully, but the succeeding brahman pedigree stops short or is dissipated into a mere list of gotra names, as is especially noticeable in the famous case of Viśvāmitra.[2]

Such were the widely different conditions of kings and rishis. The secular business of kings, their wars and exploits, naturally had little interest for rishis, who dwelt apart from the world and were affected little and only indirectly by political changes. On the other hand, though eminent rishis commanded veneration from kings and their services were at times keenly solicited and handsomely rewarded, yet the religious doctrines of the rishis lay generally outside the purview of kings, unless they were *brahmaṇya*, 'brahmanically-minded'. Such was the attitude of the people also at large.

The foregoing considerations show that there must have been abundant tradition about kings and their exploits, and also much tradition about rishis and their doings; but it is obvious that in such different conditions the traditions about kings and those about rishis must have been correspondingly separate, that is, there must

[1] Sörensen's Index to the MBh *re* Droṇa, Kṛpa, Vyāsa, &c. Vedic Index ii, 84, 259.

[2] Vā *91*, 96–103. Bd iii, *66*, 68–75. Br *10*, 57–63. Hv *27*, 1460–8; *32*, 1767–72. MBh xiii, *4*, 248–59.

have been two great streams of distinct tradition, kṣatriya tradition and brahmanic tradition. It is absurd to suppose that all the genuine kṣatriya tradition has been lost or utterly corrupted, and that the traditions which we have now are spurious. If the brahmans could and did preserve their religious compositions with the most scrupulous care and fidelity, it is absurd to suppose the opposite about kṣatriya tradition, when (as will be shown in chapter II) there were men whose business it was to preserve such tradition. The general trustworthiness of tradition is the fact demonstrated, wherever it has been possible to test tradition by the results of discoveries and excavations, and we should distrust scepticism born of ignorance. The position now is this—there is a strong presumption in favour of tradition; if any one contests tradition, the burden lies on him to show that it is wrong; and, till he does that, tradition holds the field.

The distinction between kṣatriya and brahmanic tradition is very important. It is entirely natural, and there would be matter for wonder if it had not existed, because the Vedic literature confines itself to religious subjects, and notices political and secular occurrences only incidentally so far as they had a bearing on the religious subjects; and it is absurd to suppose that that literature contains all the genuine tradition that existed about political and secular occurrences, such as those involved in the Aryan conquest of North India and those revealed partially in the Rigveda. The very fact that that literature deals almost exclusively with brahmanic thought and action implies that there must have been a body of other tradition dealing with the kṣatriyas and the great part that they played during that conquest and in the political life that was the outcome of it.[1] The distinction existed from the earliest times, until the original Purāṇa was compiled and passed into the custody of the Purāṇic brahmans, as will be explained in chapter II. It is strikingly illustrated in two ways, first, by comparing the notices of kings and rishis in the epic and Purāṇic literature and in the Vedic literature, and secondly, by the difference between the two kinds of tradition. The former is discussed here, and the latter will be dealt with in chapter V.

Famous kings in the epics and Purāṇas were Māndhātṛ, Hariścandra, Sagara, Bhagīratha, Daśaratha and Rāma of Ayodhyā;

[1] The brahmans of course magnified their part therein, Macdonell and Keith, *Vedic Index*, ii, 5–6, 91.

Śaśabindu and Arjuna Kārtavīrya among Yādavas; Duṣyanta, Bharata, Ajamīḍha, Kuru and Santanu among Pauravas; Jahnu and Gādhi of Kānyakubja; Divodāsa and Pratardana of Kāśi; Vasu Caidya of Cedi and Magadha; Marutta Āvīkṣita and Tṛṇabindu of the Vaiśāla kingdom; and Uśīnara and Śivi of the Panjab Ānavas.[1] All were great monarchs, some of them great conquerors, and many (it is said) great sacrificers. The Rigvedic canon was not closed till after their times, because it contains a hymn by Devāpi, brother (or cousin) of king Śantanu; yet none of those kings are mentioned in the hymns except Bharata,[2] Śantanu,[3] apparently Ajamīḍha[4] and Māndhātṛ,[5] and possibly Rāma,[6] while x, *134* is attributed to Māndhātṛ, and in x, *179*, verse 1 is assigned to Śivi and verse 2 to Pratardana.

This difference is the more remarkable, because those kings did not all miss laudation for want of rishis. The Vasiṣṭhas were hereditary priests of Ayodhyā, and various members of their family are mentioned in close connexion with Hariścandra, Sagara and Daśaratha. Arjuna Kārtavīrya was favoured by Datta Ātreya.[7] Marutta Āvīkṣita had Saṁvarta Āṅgirasa for his priest,[8] and a Vasiṣṭha was minister to Kuru's father Saṁvaraṇa.[9] It can hardly be supposed that none of those rishis was capable of composing a hymn, nor that no rishis existed who might have celebrated the others of those kings. The absence of laudation is particularly noticeable in the case of Bharata. He is the only one of those great kings who is really extolled in Vedic literature, and yet no contemporary hymn in his honour exists. He reigned in central Madhyadeśa and seems to have been eminently *brahmaṇya*; and some of his descendants, Gārgyas, Sāṅkṛtyas and others, became brahmans, as will be shown in chapter XXIII.

On the other hand, the kings who are lauded in the Rigveda are hardly known to kṣatriya fame. Some, such as Vadhryaśva, Divodāsa, Sṛñjaya, Sudās, Sahadeva and Somaka are mentioned as kings in the North Pañcāla genealogy,[10] but nothing particular is

[1] See chap. IX and the table of genealogies in chap. XII.
[2] vi, *16*, 4 &c. [3] x, *98*, 1 &c. [4] iv, *44*, 6.
[5] Called Mandhātṛ in Rigv i, *112*, 13: viii, *39*, 8; *40*, 12.
[6] x, *93*, 14.
[7] Vā *94*, 10–11. Mat *43*, 15. Hv *33*, 1852–3. Pad v, *12*, 118–19, &c.
[8] Vā *86*, 9–11. Bd iii, *61*, 5–7. Bhāg ix, *2*, 26.
[9] MBh i, *173*, 6615–19.
[10] Table of genealogies in chap. XII. JRAS 1918, pp. 229 f.

recorded in the epics and Purāṇas about any of them except Somaka, and the story told of him is not creditable.[1] Others again such as Abhyāvartin Cāyamāna, Śrutarvan Ārkṣa, Plāyogi Āsaṅga and Svanaya Bhāvya, are absolutely unknown to the genealogies, the epics and the Purāṇas. The explanation of this difference is that the hymns celebrate, not the really great kings, but those who specially favoured and enriched poetical rishis. The praise is no measure of the king's greatness or fame, but rather the rishi's grateful laudation of the king's dignity and generosity. A king, though undistinguished, who secured the services of a poetical rishi and rewarded him liberally, might naturally obtain such praise.[2]

Similar remarks hold good with regard to the rishis celebrated in the Rigveda and in the epics and Purāṇas, though the difference is naturally not so wide, because the latter in praising them approximate to Vedic matter. Great rishis mentioned in the latter were Ṛcīka, Jamadagni and his son Rāma among the Bhārgavas; the Vasiṣṭhas of Triśaṅku and Hariścandra, of Sagara and of Kalmāṣapāda, all of Ayodhyā, and also Parāśara; Datta and Durvāsas of the Ātreyas; Bṛhaspati, Saṁvarta, Dīrghatamas and Bharadvāja among the Āṅgirasas; the first and great Viśvāmitra and Agastya: yet no hymns are attributed to some of them, and the portions attributed to others are meagre. Dīrghatamas, Parāśara, Bharadvāja, Agastya, Viśvāmitra, Atri and Vasiṣṭha are credited with many hymns, yet these names appear to be merely gotra and not personal names except the first two. On the other hand many rishis, to whom numerous hymns are ascribed, such as Madhucchandas, Kaṇva, Medhātithi, Kakṣīvant, Gṛtsamada, Vāmadeva and Asita, are mentioned in the epics and Purāṇas, though little definite is said about them. The majority of reputed authors are unknown to those works.

The Vedic literature gives us notices of ancient times from the brahmanic and religious points of view, and kṣatriya tradition enables us to picture ancient India and its political conditions from the kṣatriya standpoint. The kṣatriyas manifestly played the most important part in the Aryan conquest of India, and if we wish to discover and estimate what their position and achievements were, it is essential to study their traditions, for, as will be shown, the Purāṇic genealogies, and they alone, give an account how the Aila

[1] MBh iii, *125*, 10422; *127*, 10470 to *128*, 10499.
[2] See *Vedic Index* ii, 82, Gifts to brahmans.

race dominated all the regions to which we assign the Aryan occupation, while the brahmanic literature contains no inkling whatever of that great transformation.

Vedic literature not only lacks the historical sense as pointed out above (p. 2), but is not always to be trusted in matters that concerned brahmanical claims and pretensions. The greatest brahmanical book is the Rigveda. It is a compilation of hymns composed by many authors and is arranged according to certain principles. It must manifestly have been compiled and arranged by some one or more persons, yet Vedic literature says absolutely nothing about this. The brahmans cannot have been ignorant about it, for they preserved it and its text with unparalleled care; they certainly did not accept and venerate this canon blindly upon uncertain authority, and they must have known who compiled it and established its text.[1] This is made clearer by another fact, namely, that Vedic literature professes to know and declares the names of the authors of nearly all the hymns and even of single verses, yet it ignores all knowledge of the person or persons who afterwards compiled and arranged those hymns. To suppose that, when it preserved the earlier information, it was ignorant of the later work in so vital a matter is ridiculous. Plainly therefore Vedic literature has deliberately suppressed all information on these matters.

Epic and Purāṇic tradition unanimously and repeatedly declares that the Veda was 'arranged' by the great rishi, Parāśara's son Kṛṣṇa Dvaipāyana, who was consequently renowned by the name Vyāsa.[2] Yet Vedic literature is remarkably reticent about him, for the Vedic Index mentions no such Kṛṣṇa, no Dvaipāyana, and the only Vyāsa noticed is *Vyāsa Pārāśarya,* and all it says about him is that this 'is the name of a mythical sage who in the Vedic period is found only as a pupil of Viṣvaksena in the Vaṁśa (list of teachers) at the end of the Sāmavidhāna Brāhmaṇa and in the late Taittirīya Āraṇyaka.'[3] The Mahābhārata and Purāṇas are full of Vyāsa and habitually refer to him as 'Vyāsa', and it is incredible

[1] We might as well suppose that we do not know who translated the Bible into German, or who gave us the English Bible.

[2] e.g. MBh i, *63,* 2417; *105,* 4236. Vā *60,* 11–12. Viṣ iii. *4,* 2. Kūr i, *52,* 10. Acknowledged in the brahmanical Śānti-parvan, MBh xii, *342,* 13025, 13119.

[3] *Vedic Index* ii, p. 339.

that all they say about him is pure fiction. It is beyond doubt that the Vedic literature has deliberately ignored him; there is a conspiracy of silence in it both about the compilation of the Rigveda and about the pre-eminent rishi who is declared to have 'arranged' it. The reason is patent. The brahmans put forward the doctrine that the Veda existed from everlasting, hence to admit that any one had compiled or even arranged it struck at the root of their doctrine and was in common parlance, 'to give their whole case away.'

These considerations show how little trust can be placed in the Vedic literature as regards any matter which the brahmans found awkward for their pretensions. When they suppressed facts of the greatest moment, it was a light thing to distort smaller matters.[1]

Historical tradition in the Vedic literature has one great merit over that in the epics and Purāṇas, namely, that that literature has been very carefully preserved and what it contains now is what it contained when it was composed, so that its statements are statements of that time. Hence there is a strong presumption that its statements being ancient are nearer accuracy than statements in the epics and Purāṇas which were not so scrupulously preserved. But the presumption is seriously weakened by three well-known facts, (1) that literature deals with religious matters and is not of historical purpose nor does it deal with history (p. 2); (2) the brahmans, its authors, lacked the historical sense; and (3) they lived in secluded hermitages, and so lacked clear knowledge. The first two of these facts have been discussed above, and the third will be noticed more fully in chapter V, but one illustration of it may be mentioned here. The brahmanical story of Śunaḥśepa[2] speaks of the most famous city Ayodhyā as a village (*grāma*)![3]

With such grave defects the presumption virtually disappears, and two instances may be cited in which the brahmanical books are wrong, both taken from that story, which affords special opportunities for testing brahmanical accuracy. It says that the sacrifice of Śunaḥśepa was a rājasūya, and the first Viśvāmitra is there styled *Bharata-ṛṣabha*. Now the sacrifice was not a rājasūya, because Hariścandra had been reigning then some twenty-five years, the real rājasūya took place early in his reign, and the sacrifice

[1] They did misrepresent, cf. *Vedic Index* ii, 256.

[2] Aitareya Brāhm vii, *3*, 1 f. Śāṅkhāyana Śr Sūtra xv, 17–25.

[3] JRAS, 1917, p. 52, note.

of Śunaḥśepa was merely the belated fulfilment of a special vow. The appellation *Bharata-ṛṣabha*, 'leader of the Bharatas,' was impossible, because the Bharatas were Viśvāmitra's descendants and had not come into existence then, as will be shown in chapter IX.[1] Statements in Vedic literature therefore, though ancient, may be incorrect, and, if wrong originally, no amount of careful preservation can make them true. Besides, priestly tampering must not be forgotten, as shown above with regard to Vyāsa.

Though historical works about ancient India are wanting, yet tradition has handed down fairly copious genealogies of the ancient dynasties. These state the succession of kings, and in that way are historical. They are almost the only historical data found in Sanskrit books as regards ancient political development; and the lists of teachers in professed chronological order set out in some brahmanical books supply evidence as regards brahmanical succession. The genealogies form the basis by which the investigation of tradition for historical ends may be tested. They supply the best chronological clue, for the Vedic literature, as shown above, is not a sure guide in historical matters.

Great importance has been attached to historical statements in the Vedic literature, even when not contemporaneous and when based on tradition, and epic and Purāṇic tradition has been discredited, however numerous and clear may be its statements about any particular matter. Such exaltation of Vedic literature and depreciation of epic and Purāṇic tradition has led to surprising conclusions. Tradition in many passages tells of an early and well-known king of Ayodhyā named Satyavrata Triśaṅku, who was the subject of a famous contest between Vasiṣṭha and Viśvāmitra,[2] and the Taittirīya Brāhmaṇa (i, 10, 6) merely names an obscure religious teacher Triśaṅku (who belonged to a far later time); yet it has been said, 'The confusion of the chronology in the tales of Triśaṅku is a good example of the worthlessness of the supposed epic tradition'.[3] An apt parallel to the two Triśaṅkus occurs in Saul king of Israel and Saul (Paul) the religious teacher; yet would any one say—the confusion of the chronology in the tales of Saul is a good example of the worthlessness of the supposed historical books of the Old Testament?

[1] JRAS, 1917, pp. 57, 64. The rājasūya, MBh ii, *12*, 491–5.
[2] Chap. XVIII. JRAS, 1913, pp. 888 f.; 1917, pp. 37–40.
[3] *Vedic Index* i, 331.

Exaltation of Vedic literature has drawn historical conclusions even from its silence. It is not of historical purpose and does not deal with history (p. 2), hence its silence about historical points is of no significance, and to draw historical conclusions from its mere silence is astonishing. Two illustrations of this may be adduced.

First, it is said with reference to Yayāti, 'There is no trace whatever of his connexion with Pūru, as in the Epic, the tradition of which must be deemed to be inaccurate'.[1] Would any one argue—there is no trace whatever in the Book of Psalms of David's connexion with Solomon, as in the historical books of the Old Testament, the statement of which must be deemed to be inaccurate?

A few words may be said about the argument from silence, and the second example will illustrate them. Some matter, say *A*, is mentioned, and nothing is said about another matter, say *B*; and the question is, whether the silence regarding *B* proves anything against it. If *B* is closely connected with or directly related to *A*, it would naturally arise with *A*, and we should expect to hear of it along with *A*, so that, if it is not mentioned, the silence is strange and is cogent evidence against *B*. But if *B* is apart from *A* and has no concern with it, there is no reason why it should ordinarily be mentioned with *A*, so that the silence is natural and indicates nothing. The criterion is, whether in the particular circumstances silence is unnatural or not. If unnatural, it is significant; if natural, it has no significance in this respect.

The second illustration is this. The epics and Purāṇas repeatedly declare that the first Viśvāmitra was a king who became a brahman, but 'there is no trace of his kingship in the Rigveda'; and, though it is supported even by brahmanical books such as the Nirukta and the Aitareya and Pañcaviṁśa Brāhmaṇas, yet the conclusion has been drawn, 'that there is no real trace of this kingship of Viśvāmitra: it may probably be dismissed as a mere legend, with no more foundation at most than that Viśvāmitra was of a family which once had been royal. But even this is doubtful'.[2] Now, after Viśvāmitra had renounced his kṣatriya status and kingdom and become a brahman, neither he nor his descendants had any motive to refer to that discarded past in any Vedic hymns, which he or they may have composed as rishis in circumstances that had

[1] *Vedic Index* ii, 187. [2] *Ibid.* ii, 311–12.

nothing to do with that past and were alien to it, while other rishis had no concern with it. It would have been surprising if his kingship had been mentioned in such circumstances, and it is entirely natural that there should be no mention of it in the Rigveda. The non-mention of it there is not only no reason for discrediting the tradition but it is in exact keeping with what would be expected if the tradition were true. The tradition therefore stands unshaken.[1]

The foregoing considerations suggest some remarks on the way in which ancient Indian historical tradition should be treated. It is not to be put aside as wholly unworthy of attention, nor is it to be summarily explained by prima facie comments. The former course is not criticism but is mere prejudging the matter, and the latter is superficial observation. It is not to be interpreted by way of personification and allegory, as that the story of Rāma's doings in S. India and Ceylon represents the spread of Aryan civilization in the south. That is akin to euhemerism, and shirks real examination by suggesting a specious theory. Nor is it to be scrutinized for defects and discrepancies and so promptly discredited. All human testimony is liable to error, and tradition is human testimony concerning the long past: hence it is not to be discarded simply because it contains discrepancies. Ancient Indian historical tradition must be examined and weighed with the aid of all information available and of experience and common sense. It was preserved by the sūtas or bards and when collected into the Purāṇa soon passed into the hands of the Purāṇic brahmans, as will be shown in the next chapter. The attitude of the latter to ancient matters differed from that of the former, and changed still more as time went on through the causes that will be explained in chapter V, taking more and more a brahmanical colouring, so that generally the more brahmanical a statement is, the later or less trustworthy it is. This will appear, for instance, from the variations in the descriptions of the Dānavas, Daityas and Rākṣasas.[2] The older accounts treat them as men, the late brahmanical as demons.

Hitherto opinions about ancient India have been based on a study of the Veda and Vedic literature without much regard for historical tradition outside that. Historical tradition yields very different conclusions. To make the former the chief and authoritative basis

[1] JRAS, 1913, 887–8.

[2] See Prof. E. W. Hopkins, *Epic Mythology*, pp. 38–52.

of historical reconstruction is much the same as to write European history mainly from theological works—an undertaking that would not receive a moment's acceptance; yet that is how ancient India has been treated, and the results have been regarded with satisfaction. Vedic literature is not authoritative in historical matters (except where it notices contemporary matters), and conclusions drawn from it are not criteria for estimating the results yielded by historical tradition in the epics and Purāṇas. Those results are set out in the following pages and must be judged independently on their own merits. I have not drawn information from Buddhist and Jain literature, because it is of no real help: it is religious, does not deal with history any more than Vedic literature, and having diverged from the main course of Indian religion had largely lost touch with ancient tradition.

In the following chapters I endeavour to deal fully with ancient Indian historical tradition, basing my statements always on definite statements in Sanskrit books and citing those authorities; and no statements are made without such support.[1] The chief authorities are the Purāṇas and the Mahābhārata, and less reliably the Rāmāyaṇa; and as the first are continually mentioned, the word is Anglicized as Purana. Among the Puranas is reckoned the Harivaṁśa which is really a Purana. The Puranas are cited by name,[2] and the Mahābhārata in the Calcutta edition.[3] References are cited as copiously as possible, so that all passages may be combined and receive due consideration, because, when tradition is dealt with, the quantity and character of the statements about any particular matter are important in the way of evidence. The same matter or person has often to be noticed in different aspects or connexions, and cross-references have been given as far as practicable, yet it is impossible in the early pages to particularize later pages. A copious index is added, which will aid comparison, so that all the information on any particular subject may be collected, and the book serve as a compendium of ancient historical tradition.

[1] Sanskrit passages have not been quoted except rarely when essential, because of the great cost of printing.

[2] The editions cited are these: Vāyu, Matsya, Brahma and Padma, *Ānandāśrama*. Kūrma, Mārkaṇḍeya, Varāha and Vṛhannāradīya, *Bibliotheca Indica*. Agni, Liṅga, Garuḍa and Viṣṇu, *Jīvānanda Vidyāsāgar's*. Brahmāṇḍa and Bhaviṣya, *Śrī-Veṅkaṭeśvara*. Bhāgavata, *Gaṇapata-Kṛṣṇājī*.

[3] Including the Harivaṁśa. The Rāmāyaṇa in the Bombay edition.

CHAPTER II

TRADITION, ITS PRESERVERS AND THE ORIGIN OF THE PURANAS

THE Vāyu and Padma Puranas tell us how ancient genealogies, tales and ballads were preserved, namely, by the *sūtas*, and they describe the sūta's duty. Their statements are different versions of the same original. The Vāyu (*1*, 31–2) says[1]—'The sūta's special duty as perceived by good men of old was to preserve the genealogies of gods, rishis and most glorious kings, and the traditions of great men, which are displayed by those who declare sacred lore in the Itihāsas and Puranas.' The Padma (v, *1*, 27–8) says similarly,[2] but in a later and inferior version—'This is the sūta's duty from primaeval time as perceived by good men, to compose the genealogies of gods, rishis and most glorious kings and the eulogies of great men, who are seen as declarers of sacred lore in the Itihāsas and Puranas.' In the Vāyu's statement *śruta* obviously means 'tradition' and not 'celebrated', as the corresponding word *stuti* in the Padma version shows, and the meaning 'celebrated' yields poor sense. The sūtas would have, as bards have generally, preserved ballads and songs as well as genealogies. *Śruta* here does not mean 'sacred tradition', but simply 'tradition', for it is often used so in the Puranas, as will be shown. *Stuti* in the Padma would generally mean a 'ballad in praise of', and eulogies of and ballads about great men of the past would naturally be one subject of tradition.[3] Eulogistic ballads are found, as those

1 Sva-dharma eva sūtasya sadbhir dṛṣṭaḥ purātanaiḥ
devatānām ṛṣīṇāṁ ca rājñāṁ câmita-tejasām
vaṁśānāṁ dhāraṇaṁ kāryaṁ śrutānāṁ ca mahātmanām
itihāsa-purāṇeṣu diṣṭā ye brahma-vādibhiḥ.

Ye appears to refer to *vaṁśa* and *śruta*, and to be in the masc., in agreement with *vaṁśa*; but it might refer to *mahātmanām*.

2 Eṣa dharmas tu sūtasya sadbhir dṛṣṭaḥ sanātanaḥ
devatānām ṛṣīṇāṁ ca rājñām amita-tejasām
tad vaṁśa-kāraṇaṁ * kāryaṁ stutīnāṁ ca mahātmanām
itihāsa-purāṇeṣu dṛṣṭā ye brahma-vādinaḥ
* Some copies read *dhāraṇaṁ* as in Vā.

3 Cf. MBh xiii, *104*, 5104. *Stuti-Purāṇa-jña*, xii, *53*, 1898.

in praise of Arjuna Kārtavīrya,[1] Alarka,[2] Devāvṛdha[3] and others. Further the word *brahma* in both versions does not necessarily mean Vedic or brahmanic lore, but means Puranic lore, both because of the subjects mentioned and because the Puranas assert themselves to be *brahma*[4] and place themselves on an equality with the Veda, as will be shown at the end of this chapter. The Vāyu's statement is the older and appears to be the more trustworthy version, yet both come to practically the same effect for the present purpose.

The sūta mentioned here is not the caste that was described as the offspring of a kṣatriya father and brahman mother;[5] that was a later application of the term. This sūta was a bard, like the māgadha, and the origin of both is placed in the time of a primaeval king Pṛthu, son of Vena.[6] It is explained by a fable, which says the first sūta and māgadha came into existence at his sacrifice, and gives a fanciful explanation of the names. What is noteworthy is that the story says Pṛthu assigned the Anūpa (or Sūta) country to the sūta and Magadha to the māgadha;[7] and this discloses that the māgadhas were really inhabitants of Magadha and the sūtas inhabitants of the Anūpa country which appears to mean Bengal here, or of the Sūta country, the district east of Magadha. The story clearly distinguishes between these sūtas and the later class sprung from kṣatriya fathers and brahman mothers which also was called sūta, and explains that the latter received this name because they observed the same duty as the original sūtas, while they were also allowed two other *inferior* occupations, namely, secondly, employment with a kṣatriya in connexion with chariots, elephants

[1] Bḍ iii, *69*, 19 f. Vā *94*, 19 f. Mat *43*, 23 f. Br *13*, 170 f. Pad v, *12*, 125 f.

[2] Bḍ iii, *67*, 70–1. Vā *92*, 66–7. Br *11*, 51–3. Hv *29*, 1588–90.

[3] Vā *96*, 13–16. Br *15*, 41–44.

[4] *Param brahma sanātanam*, Bḍ i, *1*, 11. *Brahma-vidyā*, Pad iv, *110*, 400. Cf. *brahma sanātana*, Bḍ ii, *26*, 65. Vā *55*, 68. See Vā *1*, 196.

[5] Manu x, 11, 17. MBh xiii, *48*, 2571–3: &c.

[6] The whole account is narrated in Vā *62*, 137–48, and Bḍ ii, *36*, 158–73. Less fully in Vā *1*, 33–8: Pad ii, *27*, 65–86; v, *1*, 29–35: Br *4*, 60–8: Hv *5*, 324–9. Noticed, Kūr i, *1*, 6; *14*. 12: Śiv vii, *56*, 30–1: MBh xii, *59*, 2233–4: Br *2*, 24–5; Hv *2*, 78: Ag *18*, 15–16.

[7] Vā *62*, 147. Bḍ ii, *36*, 172. MBh xii, *59*, 2234. Br *4*, 67. Hv *5*, 325. Pad v, *1*, 31. But Pad ii, *27*, 86–7, says wrongly Mahodaya to the sūta, māgadha and vandin, and Kaliṅga to the cāraṇa. Mahodaya = Kānyakubja, Pad v, *35*, 1, 193. Rām (ed Gorr.) i, *35*, 5, 35.

and horses, and lastly, medicine.[1] The original sūtas seem to have been gradually superseded by the latter class.

The sūtas are often classed with māgadhas and vandins, even in descriptions of ancient times,[2] and distinctions are sometimes made between these three classes. One statement makes the sūta a *paurāṇika*, the māgadha a genealogist (*vaṁśa-śaṁsaka*), and the vandin a eulogist (*stāvaka*).[3] Another makes the two latter eulogists and says much the same of the sūta also.[4] A third passage says that from Pṛthu's time the sūtas and māgadhas, who both came into existence then, were royal panegyrists, and they and the vandins awakened the king in the morning with their blessings.[5] The Mahābhārata has other expressions.[6]

The distinction between the original sūtas and māgadhas and the two later mixed castes which were dubbed sūta and māgadha is clearly noticed in the Kauṭilīya Arthaśāstra. When dealing with *pratiloma* offspring it says that the offspring of a vaiśya and women of the two higher castes are the *māgadha* and *vaidehaka*; and that of a kṣatriya and a brahman woman is the *sūta*.[7] Then it adds, 'But the sūta who is mentioned in the Puranas is different, and so also is the māgadha *who is mentioned there*, from brāhmaṇa-kṣatriya offspring by a *real* distinction':[8] that is, in the Puranas the sūta

[1] The passages in second note above, collated, run thus—

yac ca kṣatrāt samabhavad brāhmaṇyāṁ hīna-yonitaḥ
sūtaḥ pūrveṇa sādharmyāt tulya-dharmaḥ prakīrtitaḥ
madhyamo hy eṣa sūtasya dharmaḥ kṣatrôpajīvanam
ratha-nāgâśva-caritaṁ jaghanyaṁ ca cikitsitam.

So used, MBh xiv, *72*, 2087. Cf. Manu x, 47. This statement helps to elucidate the brahmanical information about the sūta in the *Vedic Index*.

[2] Hv *107*, 5964; *113*, 6324. MBh viii, *1*, 12.

[3] Garga Saṁhitā, Goloka-khaṇḍa, *12*, 36. Quoted in Indian Antiquary, 1893, vol. xxii, p. 253, note: and the commentator on Rām ii, *6*, 6 says the same.

[4] Pad ii, *27*, 71–2, and 85–6. MBh iii, *256*, 15325: xiv, *64*, 1896: xv, *23*, 624.

[5] Bḍ ii, *36*, 172–3. Vā *62*, 148. Cf. MBh iii, *235*, 14750: xv, *38*, 1061: Rām ii, *65*, 1–4.

[6] MBh xiii, *48*, 2571–3.

[7] Book iii, chap. 7 (p. 165). See Manu x, 11, 16 f. MBh xiii, *48*, 2571 f.; *49*, 2622–3.

[8] Ibid. line 7—Paurāṇikas tv anyas sūto māgadhaś ca brahma-kṣatrād viśeṣataḥ. R. Shama Sastri translates this thus, 'But men of the names, Sūta and Māgadha, celebrated in the purāṇas, are quite different and of greater merit than either Brahmans or Kṣatriyas'—where the last assertion is surely staggering. *Brahma-kṣatra* means sometimes brahmans and

is different from the sūta who is the offspring of a brahman woman by a kṣatriya, and the māgadha from the māgadha who is the offspring of a kṣatriya woman by a vaiśya. Here the Paurāṇika sūta and māgadha are clearly distinguished from the *pratiloma* sūta and māgadha; and the reference to them as *Paurāṇika* plainly suggests that they were only known from the Puranas in Kauṭilya's time and had ceased to exist then, in the fourth century B.C.

A remote antiquity was thus assigned to the original sūtas, who were royal and other bards and held an honourable position; and that is true because bards existed in various countries in the earliest times and were highly esteemed. It was thus their duty to preserve the genealogies of gods, rishis and famous kings and the ballads about celebrated men[1]—which were all matters of ancient tradition; and this statement of their duty refers obviously to the earliest times before the Purana was compiled, because there would have been no genealogies or ballads to collect and fashion into the Purana, unless they had been preserving such ancient traditions all along. The genealogies of kings and rishis are referred to as really existing and as well known to those who were learned in ancient lore.[2] The sūta had no duty with regard to the Vedas.[3]

Tradition is cited by various expressions. *Smṛta*, 'remembered,' is the most common, and often has little force, but sometimes its use is emphatic, as in the statements that Viśvāmitra was remembered as having had the (kṣatriya) name Viśvaratha,[4] and that Śukra-Uśanas had the name Kāvya.[5] Similarly *anuśuśruma*, 'we have heard it handed down,' occurs fairly often.[6] Abundant is the

kṣatriyas', e.g. MBh xii, *65*, 2430; Mat *47*, 32; *273*, 61, 63; Vā *99*, 443, 446; Br *45*, 35; *123*, 6: and with reference to the Aila race which being kṣatriya gave rise to kṣatriyan brahmans and brahmans, Mat *50*, 88; Vā *99*, 278. Sometimes it means a blending of the two, as where kṣatriya kings became brahmans, e.g. Vā *57*, 121 (cf. Mat *143*, 37); Hv *27*, 1469; *32*, 1773; Br *10*, 63: or where a brahman became practically a kṣatriya, like Rāma Jāmadagnya, Vā *65*, 94; Bd iii, *1*, 98.

1 So the sūta is called *vaṁśa-kusala*, Vāyu *4*, 2.

2 MBh iii, *200*, 13482–5; *88*, 8329–30.

3 Vā *1*, 33. Pad v, *1*, 29.

4 Br *10*, 56: Hv. *27*, 1459; *32*, 1766.

5 Vā *65*, 75. Other instances, Mat *49*, 75–6; Vā *99*, 190–1; Hv *20*, 1081–2; Bd ii. *32*, 122.

6 e.g. Vā *62*, 174; *96*, 123. Bd ii, *36*, 201; iii, *71*. 124. Hv *1*, 47. Br *4*, 95. MBh i, *94*, 3740: xii, *227*, 8267.

use of the phrase *iti naḥ śrutam*,[1] 'so we have heard,' or shortly *iti śrutam*,[2] and its equivalent occurs often, *iti śrutiḥ*,[3] 'such is the tradition,' where *śruta* and *śruti* refer to secular tradition.

Śruti generally means 'sacred text' or 'sacred tradition', but in the Puranas very often means ordinary tradition and not sacred tradition, because the phrase *iti śrutiḥ* occurs too often to be a clerical mistake, and because matters on which it is cited do not appear to be mentioned or even alluded to in the Vedic literature. For instance, the Vāyu (*88*, 28) says, 'Bṛhadaśva's son was Kuvalāśva, such is the *śruti*'; and both the Brahma (*8*, 68) and Harivaṁśa (*15*, 802) say, one of king Sagara's two wives brought forth a gourd (out of which developed 60,000 sons), such is the *śruti*: but these citations are wholly unknown to Vedic literature.[4] Again the Matsya (*47*, 186) says that Ḍevayānī was born from Kāvya, such is the *śruti*, and the Rāmāyaṇa says of king Asita of Ayodhyā (called Bāhu in the Puranas), 'his two wives were with child, such is the *śruti*,'[5] though Vedic literature knows nothing about either statement.

Those notices refer to genealogical matters,[6] and *śruti* is found used similarly regarding other matters. Thus the Padma (v, *11*, 69–71) quotes a long-enduring *śruti*, that a son who goes to Gayā will please his seven paternal ancestors and also others of his maternal grandfathers. The Brahma (*175*, 35) declares Umā is queen of the three worlds and mother of the world, such is the well-known *śruti*. The former is not known to Vedic tradition, nor apparently is the latter.

The phrase *iti śrutiḥ* is also the authority adduced for many statements of various kinds, which do not appear to come from sacred tradition, such as these: that Viṣṇu is infinite;[7] that the Purana should be heard daily;[8] that Yayāti attained to heaven

[1] Vā *2*, 15; *62*, 192; *65*, 42; *88*, 153; *90*, 3, 10, 24; *95*, 2; *99*, 175. Other Puranas similarly.

[2] Vā *94*, 51, &c. Cf. Mat *35*, 4.

[3] Vā *18*, 3, 11, 14; *59*, 73; *65*, 43; *83*, 127; *85*, 7; *88*, 28, 182; *89*, 8, 15; *92*, 70; *94*, 4; *99*, 200, 231. Mat *35*, 5; *36*, 2. Br *7*, 6. Hv *10*, 619. Kūr i, *22*, 24. Pad iv, *17*, 70; *111*, 35. Lg i, *27*, 50. Bḍ in various passages, that correspond to those cited from Vā, reads *iti śrutaḥ* or *viśrutaḥ* instead, e.g. iii, *63*, 29, 182; *64*, 8, 15; *67*, 74: but in iii, *1*, 43 it has *iti śrutiḥ*. Its variations are probably editorial.

[4] Not found in *Vedic Index*.

[5] Rām i, *70*, 30; ii, *110*, 18.

[6] So also many of the references in third note above.

[7] Mat *247*, 39.

[8] Pad iv, *111*, 35.

a second time;[1] that there is no unrighteousness greater than theft;[2] and others.[3]

This meaning of *śruti* does not, I believe, occur in later brahmanic additions nor in the latest Puranas that are frankly sectarian. In passages enunciating purely brahmanic matter, which are later additions, *śruti* appears in its ordinary brahmanic sense and is generally restricted to 'sacred text or tradition',[4] as for instance in the brahmanic māhātmya of the river Godāvarī called Gautamī Gaṅgā,[5] and when it is contrasted with *smṛti*,[6] and in other brahmanic passages;[7] also it is used at times with the word *Veda*, seemingly as meaning sacred tradition.[8] Sometimes its precise import is not quite clear.[9]

Similar remarks apply to the word *śruta* in such connexions, where it has its brahmanic sense generally.[10] *Iti naḥ śrutam* is then applied to late mystic doctrine.[11] *Śrutam* and *iti śrutam* are used sometimes in tales and fables about tīrthas in order apparently to give them a semblance of ancient tradition,[12] just as Veda-vids are cited as vouching for the sanctity of tīrthas on the Godāvarī;[13] and it is even asserted that that river was celebrated by rishis in the Veda as well as in the Purana.[14] *Iti śrutaḥ* is similarly used in this latter way.[15]

The use of *śruti* for ordinary tradition is thus well-established in the earlier parts of the Puranas and especially in those containing kṣatriya tradition. When there was need to distinguish Vedic

1 Mat *35*, 5.   2 Lg i, *90*, 12.

3 MBh viii, *33*, 1394 : xiii, *155*, 7267. Mat *111*, 6; *247*, 7, 8, 39, 44. Lg i, *90*, 14–15. Var *13*, 10. Vā *53*, 108. Bd ii, *24*, 133. Br *213*, 32. Hv *42*, 2226.

4 So defined, Mat *145*, 32 : Vā *59*, 31 : Bd ii, *32*, 35. *Śruti-vettā purohitaḥ*, Mat *230*, 9.

5 Br *161*, 15, 33, 35; *174*, 4, 5.

6 Vā *59*, 51. Bd ii, *32*, 56. Mat *52*, 12; *144*, 7; *145*, 52. Pad iv, *17*, 25 : vi, *250*, 55; *256*, 6; *280*, 35–6.

7 e.g. Br. *221*, 170; *223*, 56. Pad i, *51*, 50 : vi, *277*, 49.

8 Br *175*, 78. *Purāṇaṁ Veda-śruti-samāhitam*, Br *213*, 167 and 31 (where for *deva* read *Veda*). Vā *100*, 33 has *Vede śrutau Purāṇe ca*, but Bd iv, *1*, 30 for *śrutau* reads *smṛtau*.

9 e.g. Mat *95*, 2; Br *75*, 21.

10 e.g. Vā *91*, 104. Bd iii, *66*, 76. Pad v, *19*, 337; *49*, 105. So *śrutavant*, Br *224*, 33; *226*, 28.

11 e.g. Lg ii, *52*, 1.   12 e.g. Br *111*, 85; *113*, 18; *164*, 41.

13 Br *99*, 1; *101*, 1; *152*, 1; *164*, 53–4.   14 Br *174*, 29.

15 Lg i, *29*, 46 : ii, *8*, 8. Pad vi, *224*, 42, 43; *238*, 7.

tradition, it was cited as *Vaidikī śruti*;[1] and so also Vedic gāthās[2] and Vedic mantras[3] were distinguished from ordinary gāthās and Puranic mantras by the same epithet. Sometimes the word *laukika* was added to distinguish ordinary or popular matters from Vedic, as in the cases of dharma,[4] vidyā[5] and śabda.[6]

The phrase *iti śrutaḥ* is common.[7] The words *śrūyate*[8] and *śrūyante*[9] are used of tradition. This use of *śrūyate* is set against *śrūyate* in brahmanical works; thus, it is often used in the Vedārthadīpikā and always of statements quoted from Vedic literature, but never, I believe, of non-sacred tradition, which is cited simply as an 'itihāsa', or by the word *smaryate* in its notice of Rigveda i, 65.

The Vāyu, Brahmāṇḍa and Viṣṇu give an account, how the original Purana came into existence;[10] and the Bhāgavata also gives an account,[11] which however is different and, being late and untrustworthy, need not be noticed. Those three Puranas say—Kṛṣṇa Dvaipāyana divided the single Veda into four and arranged them, and so was called Vyāsa. He entrusted them to his four disciples, one to each, namely Paila, Vaiśampāyana, Jaimini and Sumantu.[12] Then with tales, anecdotes, songs and lore that had come down from the ages he compiled a Purana,[13] and taught it and the Itihāsa to his fifth disciple, the sūta Romaharṣaṇa or Lomaharṣaṇa.[14]

[1] Vā *30*, 4. Bḍ ii, *13*, 4. Mat *19*, 3; *142*, 9; *248*, 1. Pad v, *10*, 37; *13*, 319. Var *17*, 23. Kūr i, *1*, 91. Similarly *Ātharvaṇī śruti*, Viṣ vi, *5*, 65.

[2] Br *120*, 3. [3] Mat *70*, 54. Pad vi, *233*, 80.

[4] Br *220*, 206. [5] Br *95*, 27. [6] Pad vi, *281*, 25. Cf. Br *130*, 7.

[7] e.g. Vā *88*, 206; *89*, 12. Bḍ ii, *30*, 39: iii, *63*, 206; *64*, 12. Br *13*, 155. Hv *33*, 1845. Cf. MBh xii, *20*, 614.

[8] Bḍ ii, *36*, 207, 209: iii, *69*, 16. Mat *10*, 1; *19*, 12. Pad v, *8*, 1; *27*, 5. Br *214*, 3. Var *37*, 7. MBh i, *223*, 8098: iii, *121*, 10291: xii, *33*, 1184. Hv *192*, 11098.

[9] Vā *24*, 3; *57*, 121; *94*, 16. Mat *143*, 37. MBh i, *66*, 2570: xii, *227*, 8267.

[10] Bḍ ii, *34*, 12–16. Vā *60*, 12–16. Viṣ iii, *4*, 7–10.

[11] Bhāg xii, *7*, 4–7.

[12] Cf. MBh i, *63*, 2418: xii, *342*, 13025–7; *329*, 12337–8.

[13] Bḍ ii, *34*, 21; Vā *60*, 21; and Viṣ iii, *6*, 16 say—

ākhyānaiś câpy upākhyānair gāthābhiḥ kalpa-jôktibhiḥ*
purāṇa-saṁhitāṁ cakre purāṇârtha-viśāradaḥ

* where Viṣ reads *kalpa-śuddhibhiḥ* and Vā *kulakarmabhiḥ*. Cf. also Vā *103*, 51; *104*, 20.

[14] Bḍ ii, *34*, 16 and Vā *60*, 16: Viṣ iii, *4*, 10 similarly but showing it is late because it makes the sūta a *mahā-muni*. Also Kūr i, *52*, 13.

After that he composed the Mahābhārata.[1] The epic itself implies that the Purana preceded it. It says that Vyāsa, just after he had composed it, declared that he had already made the Itihāsas and Puranas manifest.[2] It also asserts that a Vaiṣṇava may gain the same merit by listening to it that is gained by listening to the eighteen Puranas [3]—a statement which (however much we discount the number eighteen) would hardly have suggested itself, if the epic was believed to be prior to all the Puranas. The epic has also borrowed from the Puranas,[4] more often I think than they cite it.

This account mentions the materials[5] from which the Purana was compiled. As explained above, the sūtas had from remote times preserved the genealogies of gods, rishis and kings, and traditions and ballads about celebrated men, that is, exactly the material—tales, songs and ancient lore—out of which the Purana was constructed. Whether or not Vyāsa composed the original Purana or superintended its compilation, is immaterial for the present purpose. What is important is that there was abundant tradition of various kinds, which could and would naturally have been used in its construction, and of the very kinds that went to its construction. The ancient tales were topics of real interest to kings, people and rishis, as both the epics and the Puranas by their very structure proclaim, and they were also matters to which men of intelligence gave their attention.[6] Allusions in the Veda itself show the same.[7] It would be quite natural that, after the religious hymns were formed into the Veda, the ancient secular tales and lore should have been collected in a Purana.

What the next development of the Purana was is described in the Brahmāṇḍa and Vāyu, and similarly though less fully in the Viṣṇu.[8] Romaharṣaṇa made that *Purāṇa-saṁhitā* into six versions and taught

[1] Mat *53*, 70 says—

> aṣṭādaśa Purāṇāni kṛtvā Satyavatī-sutaḥ
> Bhāratâkhyānam akhilaṁ cakre tad-upavṛṁhitam

where the mention of eighteen Puranas accords with a later theory, see the end of this chapter. Cf. Viṣ iii, *4*, 5.

[2] MBh i, *1*, 54–64. Cf. viii, *34*, 1498.

[3] MBh xviii, *6*, 304.

[4] e.g. MBh i, *65*, 2560; *196*, 7265: v, *179*, 7073: xiii, *84*, 3990. Also third note above.

[5] The terms used are considered in chap. III.

[6] Mat *53*, 63 and 73.

[7] e.g. i, *112*, *116* and *117*: x, *39*.

[8] Bd ii, *35*, 63–70 and Vā *61*, 55–62, which have a common text. Viṣ iii, *6*, 17–19. Ag *270*, 10–13. The two former texts collated suggest the following version :—

them to his six disciples, Ātreya Sumati, Kāśyapa Akṛtavraṇa, Bhāradvāja Agnivarcas, Vāsiṣṭha Mitrayu, Sāvarṇi Somadatti, and Suśarman Śāṁśapāyana. Three of them, Kāśyapa, Sāvarṇi and Śāṁśapāyana, made three separate saṁhitās, which were called by their names. Romaharṣaṇa's saṁhitā and those three were the 'root-compositions' (*mūla-saṁhitā*). They consisted of four divisions (*pāda*) and were to the same effect but differed in their diction. All except Śāṁśapāyana's contained 4,000 verses.

Those versions do not exist now;[1] still some of those persons, besides Romaharṣaṇa, appear as inquirers or narrators in some of the Puranas and also in the Mahābhārata.[2] Thus Sāvarṇi,[3] Kāśyapeya[4] and Śāṁśapāyana[5] appear in the Vāyu and Brahmāṇḍa, which are two of the oldest Puranas and were one originally. The passages in which those persons appear may be remnants of those old Puranas incorporated in these two, especially as Śāṁśapāyana not seldom appears without announcement. Moreover these two Puranas alone have the old fourfold division spoken of in the above

ṣaṭśaḥ kṛtvā mayâpy uktam Purāṇam ṛṣi-sattamāḥ
Ātreyaḥ Sumatir dhīmān Kāśyapo hy Akṛtavraṇaḥ
Bhāradvājo 'gnivarcāś ca Vāsiṣṭho Mitrayuś ca yaḥ
Sāvarṇiḥ Somadattis tu Suśarmā Śāṁśapāyanaḥ
ete śiṣyā mama proktāḥ Purāṇeṣu dhṛta-vratāḥ
tribhis tatra kṛtās tisraḥ saṁhitāḥ punar eva hi
Kāśyapaḥ saṁhitā-kartā Sāvarṇiḥ Śāṁśapāyanaḥ
māmikā ca caturthī syāc catasrā mūla-saṁhitāḥ*
sarvās tā hi catuṣpādāḥ sarvāś caikârtha-vācikāḥ
pāṭhântare pṛthag-bhūtā veda-śākhā yathā tathā
catuḥ-sāhasrikāḥ sarvāḥ Śāṁśapāyanikām ṛte
Lomaharṣaṇikā mūlā tataḥ Kāśyapikâparā
Sāvarṇikā tṛtīyâsau ṛju-vākyârtha-maṇḍitā
Śāṁśapāyanikā cânyā nodanârtha-vibhūṣitā
sahasrāṇi ṛcām aṣṭau ṣaṭ śatāni tathaiva ca
etāḥ pañcadaśânyāś ca daśânyā daśabhis tathā.

Where * Vā reads *sā caiṣā pūrva-saṁhitā.*

[1] Mat calls itself a *Purāṇa-saṁhitā* (*290*, 20); so Viṣ (i, *1*, 30, 34) and Lg (i, *1*, 11, 13). *Ādi-Purāṇas* are referred to, Mat *164*, 16; Pad v, *36*, 14.

[2] Akṛtavraṇa, iii, *115*, 11027 f., &c.

[3] Vā *21*, 1.

[4] *Kāśyapeyaḥ sanātanaḥ*, Vā *7*, 1: *Kāpeyaḥ saṁśayāyati*, Bḍ ii, *6*, 1. Read in both *Kāśyapaḥ Śāṁśapāyanaḥ*?

[5] As inquirer, Vā *49*, 97; *56*, 1–2; *57*, 86, 88; *60*, 33; *62*, 1; *65*, 1; *71*, 2; *72*, 24; *89*, 16: and Bḍ ii, *15*, 1; *19*, 99; *28*, 2; *30*, 1, 5; *34*, 34; *36*, 1: iii, *1*, 1. As narrator, Vā *103*, 67. Read probably *Śāṁśapāyana* in Vā *69*, 34.

passage,[1] and their four *pādas* are called *Prakriyā*, *Anuṣaṅga*, *Upodghāta* and *Upasaṁhāra*.[2] The others have either no divisions, as the Matsya[3] and Brahma, or have a different number with other terms than *pāda*, as the Viṣṇu and Padma, Kūrma and Harivaṁśa.

After the original Purana was composed, by Vyāsa as is said, his disciple Romaharṣaṇa taught it to his son Ugraśravas,[4] and Ugraśravas the sauti appears as the reciter in some of the present Puranas;[5] and the sūtas still retained the right to recite it for their livelihood.[6] But, as stated above, Romaharṣaṇa taught it to his six disciples, at least five of whom were brahmans. It thus passed into the hands of brahmans, and their appropriation and development of it increased in the course of time, as the Purana grew into many Puranas, as Sanskrit learning became peculiarly the province of the brahmans,[7] and as new and frankly sectarian Puranas were composed. How they dealt with these subjects is explained thus—'Wise men, extracting valuable matters everywhere from the multitude of ancient stories (*or* the Puranas), have described things in many ways in various Puranas.'[8] This also acknowledges that the Puranas grew up in various localities.

This account of the origin of the Purana is supported by copious direct allusions to ancient tradition in the Puranas. These might be cited from many Puranas, but will be taken here chiefly from the Vāyu and Brahmāṇḍa, which have the oldest version in such traditional matters, and also from the Matsya, Brahma and Harivaṁśa, which have the next best versions.

There are many allusions to matters that were handed down from very ancient times, long before the original Purana was

[1] Vā *32*, 67:

catuṣpādam Purāṇaṁ tu Brahmaṇā vihitam purā.

[2] Vā says these are the four pādas (*4*, 13; *103*, 44–5). Bḍ is plainly so divided. The pādas in the Vā are (1) ch. 1–6; (2) ch. 7–64; (3) ch. 65–99; and (4) ch. 100–112: but *58*, 126 suggests that its Anuṣaṅga ended there once.

[3] Mat appears to have a memory of it, since for *avāpodghāta* read probably *atrôpodghāta* (last line).

[4] Bḍ iv, *4*, 67. Pad v, *1*, 2, 14. MBh i, *5*, 863, 867.

[5] Hv *1*, 11, 16. Pad v, *1*, 11 f. BV i. *1*, 2 f. MBh i, *4*, 851 f.

[6] Kūr i, *14*, 15.

[7] Mat *164*, 16 refers to the Adi-purāṇas and Vedas being recited by brahmans. Lg i, *39*, 61 says the Itihāsas and Puranas became separate *kāla-gauravāt*.

[8] Pad vi, *219*, 37.

compiled, such as old songs (*gāthās*) sung by Yayāti,[1] and songs eulogizing the famous kings, Māndhātṛ,[2] Arjuna Kārtavīrya (p. 16), Alarka (p. 16), Rantideva,[3] Nṛga,[4] and others.[5]

That there were men whose business it was to know the ancient genealogies and tales is proved by various expressions often met with, for nothing less than this can be implied by the frequent references to them as authoritative exponents of ancient events and by the many terms used to describe them. Thus, first, as regards ancient tradition generally, we find the term *purā-vid*, designating those who sang an ancient genealogical verse about the famous Yādava king Śaśabindu,[6] those who sang the songs of the *pitṛs*,[7] and others.[8] Its use was extended to later minstrels in additions made to the Puranas, and so the Vāyu in its description of the dynasties of the Kali age applies it to those who sang about the last Paurava king,[9] the Mahābhārata to those who sang about gifts,[10] and the late Bhāgavata to those who sang about Kṛṣṇa.[11]

Other terms, such as *purāṇa-jña*,[12] *purāṇa-vid*,[13] *paurāṇika*,[14] and *purāṇika*,[15] often mean merely 'one who knows the Purana (or

[1] Bḍ iii, *68*, 96–103. Vā *93*, 94–101. Br *12*, 39–46. Hv *30*, 1638–45. Viṣ iv, *10*, 8–15. Lg i, *67*, 15–24. MBh i, *75*, 3173–7; *85*, 3510–15: vii, *63*, 2299–2300: xii, *26*, 780–3. Maṭ *34*, 10–12.

[2] Bḍ iii, *63*, 69–70. Vā *88*, 67–9.

[3] MBh vii, *67*, 2369–73.

[4] MBh iii, *88*, 8329–30.

[5] e.g. Aitareya Brāhm viii, *4*, 21. Śatapatha Brāhm xiii, 5, 4, 3 f. quotes many. MBh v, *101*, 3515.

[6] Vā *95*, 19: where Bḍ (iii, *70*, 20), Mat (*44*, 19) and Pad (v, *13*, 4) have equivalent expressions.

[7] Bḍ iii, *19*, 9. Vā *83*, 10.

[8] MBh i, *121*, 4692. Also Raghuv. xviii, 23. Vedārth on Rigv iii, *53* quotes an itihāsa declared by purā-vids.

[9] Vā *99*, 278 with the significant word *vipra*.

[10] MBh xiii, *62*, 3136.

[11] Bhāg xii, *2*, 33.

[12] Mat *55*, 3; *273*, 38 (with *śrutarṣi*); end, 11, 17. Pad iv, *102*, 41; *109*, 26, 29; *110*, 397, 461 (with *dvija*), &c.; *111*, 1, 3, 7, &c. Applied to Romaharṣaṇa, Vā *101*, 70: Bḍ iv, *2*, 69. *Itihāsa-purāṇa-jña*, Pad v, *18*, 50.

[13] Mat *60*, 1. Pad iv, *111*, 46, 50. Perhaps Br *121*, 1: MBh ii, *40*, 1472.

[14] Bḍ iii, *63*, 69, 168. Vā *88*, 67, 168. Pad iv, *110*, 419, 462 (with *dvija*), &c.; *111*, 6, 49, 50: vi, *81*, 43. MBh i, *51*, 2021. Applied particularly to Romaharṣaṇa, Vā *45*, 71; *65*, 15; *101*, 72; &c.: Bḍ iv, *2*, 71: Pad i, *1*, 12: and so called *Paurāṇikottama*, Vā, *1*, 15: Lg i, *71*, 6; *99*, 3: &c. *Paurāṇika* also his son, Mat *114*, 3: MBh i, *1*, 2; *4*, 851–2: &c.

[15] Pad iv, *111*, 5.

Puranas)' and are found so used;[1] as also the precise expressions, *Purāṇa-vettṛ*,[2] *Purāṇa-vācaka*,[3] and others.[4] But at other times *purāṇa-jña*, *purāṇa-vid* and *paurāṇika* imply more and can only mean 'one who knows the ancient tales'. Thus, as regards *purāṇa-jñas*, vaṁśa-vids are cited as quoting an old verse sung by purāṇa-jñas as older authorities about Māndhātṛ[5]; paurāṇikas are cited as quoting an old verse sung by purāṇa-jñas about Datta Ātreya;[6] and a verse about king Devāvṛdha is repeated as well known from a genealogy recited by purāṇa-jñas.[7] This term is applied even to maharṣis,[8] when it cannot reasonably mean merely 'knowing the Purana'.[9] Similarly *purāṇa-vid janas* are quoted as singing a song about Rāma Dāśarathi of Ayodhyā,[10] about king Rantideva,[11] and about king Vyuṣitāśva of Ayodhyā,[12] and others.[13] *Paurāṇika* generally refers to the Puranas and means 'one who knows the Puranas',[14] yet it appears sometimes to mean 'those who know the purāṇas or ancient stories',[15] as in the old kṣatriya ballad about king Satyavrata Triśaṅku, in which the Vāyu and Brahmāṇḍa quote verses more ancient than themselves as having been recited by *paurāṇika janas*.[16]

Paurāṇa often means 'ancient',[17] but sometimes 'belonging to, connected with or mentioned in the Purana (or Puranas)'.[18] The

[1] Especially where the context shows a brahman is meant.
[2] Mat *16*, 9 (a brahman); *265*, 2.
[3] Mat, end, 22–3. Pad iii, *25*, 32.
[4] Pad iv, *110*, 398, 463; *111*, 28. Br *174*, 4.
[5] Vā *88*, 69. Distinguished perhaps from the Paurāṇikas of verse 67.
[6] Vā *70*, 76–7. Bd iii, *8*, 83.
[7] Vā *96*, 13. Bd iii, *71*, 14. Mat *44*, 57. Br *15*, 41. Hv *38*, 2010. Lg i, *60*, 5. Pad v, *13*, 42.
[8] Hv *202*, 11445. Pad v, *37*, 3. So Vasiṣṭha, Pad iv, *111*, 9. To *surarṣis*, MBh xiii, *16*, 1054.
[9] Parāśara is called *itihāsa-purāṇa-jña*, Viṣ i, *1*, 4—apparently by an anachronism.
[10] Bd iii, *63*, 192. Vā *88*, 191. Br *213*, 152. Hv *42*, 2352.
[11] MBh vii, *67*, 2369.
[12] MBh i, *121*, 4692.
[13] e.g. MBh vii, *57*, 2203.
[14] See sixth note above. MBh vi, *12*, 483.
[15] Sūtas, MBh i, *214*, 7777.
[16] Vā *88*, 114. Bd iii, *63*, 113; see *8*, 83–4. JRAS, 1913, p. 897.
[17] e.g. kavis, MBh i, *74*, 3024: Vasiṣṭha, v, *107*, 3773: vṛtti, xv *26*, 677: &c. So also purāṇa rishis, Hv *59*, 3291.
[18] e.g. MBh i, *2*, 543; *223*, 8097–8: xii, *349*, 13525.

word *purātana* is used, denoting sometimes men not really ancient, such as the brahmans who treated of the dynasties of the Kali age[1] not earlier than about the sixth century B.C., but sometimes men more ancient as those who sang about Saśabindu[2] and Alarka.[3]

The way in which these terms are introduced shows that they do not refer to the present Puranas and hardly even to the original Purana, but more probably to ancient minstrels, because no songs could have been handed down unless there had been a succession of minstrels, as is natural; and the verses that are quoted are scraps of song, evidently the remains of larger ballads, for there are always pieces of ancient poetry surviving.

Next, as regards genealogical lore, expressions are used, which prove that genealogies were specially studied, just as the Veda and other subjects were studied. Thus *vaṁśa-vid*[4] occurs, denoting 'one who had acquired knowledge of genealogies', just as plainly as *Veda-vid*[5] meant 'one who had learnt the Veda', and *Vedānta-vid*,[6] *yoga-vid*[7] and even *saṅkhyā-vid*,[8] besides many similar expressions which imply thorough knowledge.[9] Vaṁśa-vids are mentioned as quoting from more ancient purāṇa-jñas (p. 26), and in particular Soma-vaṁśa-vids[10] are referred to. The character of these men is emphasized by the superlative *vaṁśa-vittama*,[11] showing that there were men specially learned in genealogies, just as *Veda-vittamas*[12] are alluded to; and these special genealogists were ancient and are cited as earlier authorities by *paurāṇikas*.[13]

[1] *Vipraiḥ purātanaiḥ*, Mat *50*, 88; *271*, 15.

[2] Bḍ iii, *70*, 20: where Vā (*95*, 19) uses *purā-vid*.

[3] Bḍ iii, *67*, 70. Br *11*, 51. Hv *29*, 1588. Cf. Vā *92*, 66.

[4] Vā *88*, 69. Lg i, *65*, 1. Also *vaṁśa-kuśala*, Vā *4*, 2.

[5] Very common, e.g. Vā *66*, 39. Bḍ iii, *3*, 38. Mat *72*, 44; *96*, 21. MBh xii, *344*, 13241.

[6] Mat *274*, 37.

[7] Vā *83*, 98–9. Bḍ iii, *19*, 66. Br *234*, 2; *238*, 2. Lg i, *8*, 86; *9*, 62. Pad v, *36*, 5.

[8] Mat *142*, 15. Vā *57*, 20; *70*, 46.

[9] e.g. *Ṛgveda-vid* and *Sāma-vid*, Mat *274*, 39. *Yajur-vid*, Mat *58*, 35; *93*, 129; *274*, 39. *Mantra-vid*, Mat *93*, 41; *102*, 2: *240*, 27; Lg i, *25*, 16. Also *brahma-vid*, *sūtra-vid*, *nyāya-vid*, &c.

[10] Vā *99*, 432. Bḍ iii, *74*, 245. Mat *273*, 53.

[11] Vā *88*, 169. Bḍ iii, *63*, 169.

[12] Br *85*, 2. Pad v, *29*, 11: vi, *248*, 23 (ironical?). So also *brahma-vittama*, Pad v, *26*, 35: Vā *71*, 48: Lg ii, *55*, 26.

[13] See second note above.

The same fact is proved by the word *cintaka,* which in *vaṁśa-cintaka* [1] proves that men did give thought to ancient genealogies, just as it shows in *Veda-cintaka* [2] that men gave thought to the Veda, as is well known. Similarly are used the terms *vaṁśa-purāṇa-jña* [3] and *anuvaṁśa-purāṇa-jña,*[4] meaning either 'one who knew the genealogies and Purana', or better 'one who knew the ancient tales connected with the genealogies'. It thus appears that ancient genealogies and tales were matters of study as well as the Veda, but the brahmans, with the growing pretensions of their caste and doctrines, and through the political vicissitudes that befell North India, exalted the Vedic literature to the undue depreciation of non-religious lore.

In this connexion two expressions may be noticed, which occur rarely, yet seem to indicate that genealogies were not accepted blindly but were scrutinized in order to ascertain the true or most trustworthy version. One is *icchanti,* which appears to mean 'men prefer', 'men approve', as if the statement to which it is applied was approved after inquiry; [5] and it is used somewhat similarly elsewhere.[6] The other is *śaṁsanti,* which does not mean 'extol' in the passages where it occurs, because Antara (Uttara, Uttama) is unknown otherwise, but it appears to mean 'men announce', in an emphatic way as if settling some difference of opinion.[7]

The genealogists and students of ancient tales are often mentioned without any allusions to their status, and are sometimes called by the general word *jana* [8] added to the various appellations mentioned above; but at other times the description 'brahmans' (*dvija,*[9]

[1] Br *8,* 77. Hv *15,* 812.
[2] Vā *83,* 100. Cf. MBh xii, *344,* 13241.
[3] Vā *88,* 171. Bḍ iii, *63,* 171. [4] Lg i, *69,* 5.
[5] Bḍ iii, *70,* 16. Vā *95,* 15. Br *15,* 1. Hv *37,* 1969:—

Vārjinīvatam icchanti Svāhiṁ svāhāvatāṁ varam.

Also Hv *37,* 1977: but cf. Br *15,* 9; Mat *44,* 17 and Lg i, *68,* 23. Cf. apparently *iṣṭa* in Vedārth on Rigv ii, *29.*

[6] Cf. Vā *32,* 37; *66,* 39; *76,* 21. Bḍ iii, *3,* 38; *12,* 23: Pad iv, *100,* 123.

[7] Bḍ iii, *70,* 23. Mat *44,* 22. Br *15,* 5. Hv *37,* 1973. Also Vā *95,* 22 (cf. Lg i, *68,* 26, confusedly):—

Śaṁsanti ca purāṇajñāḥ Pārthaśravasam Antaram.

[8] e.g. Vā *88,* 69, 114, 168, 191. MBh i, *121,* 4692; vii, *67,* 2369.

[9] e.g. Vā *88,* 67; *96,* 13; and Bḍ iii, *63,* 69; *71,* 14; as regards *paurāṇikas* and *purāṇa-jñas.*

vipra,[1] and even *śrutarṣi*[2] and *maharṣi*[3]) is applied to those who knew the old tales. They were sūtas in the most ancient times, though Court brahmans may have possessed such knowledge, for the Rāmāyaṇa makes Daśaratha's priest Vasiṣṭha declare the royal genealogy of Ayodhyā twice,[4] while king Janaka himself sets out his own genealogy.[5]

But in later times, and certainly after the compilation of the Purana and its passing into the hands of Romaharṣaṇa's brahman disciples, the sūtas appear to have gradually lost this particular connexion with these matters, which became in time a speciality of certain brahmans, who thus developed into students and expounders of the Puranas. It is to this class that the description, noticed above, of Purāṇa-jñas, Paurāṇikas, &c., refers when they are brahmans. By devoting themselves especially to the Puranas, they would naturally have tended to diverge from those who studied the Vedas and to form a separate class, for they would very rarely have been able to combine proficiency in both wide fields of literature. The difference between the two classes is noticed, for mention is made of the brahmans who knew the Puranas, as already cited, and brahmans who were wise in the Veda;[6] and Vedic literature itself discloses that the latter class knew little of Puranic tradition, as many an article in the *Vedic Index* shows when compared with information to be gathered from the Puranas. The priestly brahmans would have regarded the Purana-knowing brahmans as having fallen away from the highest brahmanic standard, and on the other hand the latter would naturally have magnified their own office and extolled the Puranas, and have enhanced both by incorporating distinctly brahmanic teaching and practice into the Puranas. Accordingly the Puranas, expressly or impliedly comparing themselves with the Vedas, claim superlative praise for themselves and assert the dignity of the brahmans who recited and expounded them.

There was in fact clear rivalry on the part of the Puranas with

[1] e.g. Vā *99*, 278; and Mat *50*, 88; *271*, 15; with reference to the Pauravas and Aikṣvākus of the Kali age.

[2] *Purāṇa-jñaiḥ śrutarṣibhiḥ*, with reference to the Bhaviṣya, at the close of the dynasties of the Kali age, Mat. *273*, 38.

[3] *Purāṇa-jñāḥ . . . maharṣayaḥ*, Hv *202*, 11445.

[4] Rām i, *70*, 18 f.; ii, *110*, 1 f.: wrongly, see chap. VIII.

[5] Rām i, *71*, 1 f.

[6] MBh xii, *342*, 13023–4. Also Br *225*, 46, 57. Pad iv, *112*, 58.

the Vedas. First as regards antiquity, Vyāsa is said to have arranged the Veda and formed the four Vedas, and the Puranas, putting aside the account of their origin given above, say he divided the one original Purana into the existing eighteen,[1] thus placing themselves in the same chronological rank with the Vedas. Further, the brahmans asserted that the Veda had existed from everlasting, and the Puranas, while acknowledging its primaeval antiquity, claimed for themselves even prior antiquity. Thus five at least declare that at the beginning of things Brahmā remembered the Purana first of all the scriptures before the Vedas issued from his mouths.[2]

Next, as regards their character, the Puranas place themselves on an equality with the Veda, for many of them assert that they are *Veda-sammita*, or *Vedaiḥ sammita*,[3] 'of equal measure with the Veda'; and even a single story is so estimated.[4] The title Veda is sometimes given to them,[5] and so the Vāyu (*1*, 18) calls itself *Purāṇa-Veda*. *Śruti* is applied to their tradition as shown above, and the word *ṛc*[6] and also apparently *sūkta*[7] to their verses. The brahmans extolled the Veda in the highest degree, yet the Puranas exalt themselves even more highly.[8] Consequently they distinguished themselves from *smṛti*.[9] The hymns of the Rigveda were 'seen' by rishis, but all the Puranas except two (the Nāradīya and Vāmana) declare that they were originally delivered by some god,[10] thus claiming a divine authorship, higher than that of rishis; and the Padma even asserts that it is Viṣṇu himself.[11]

[1] Mat *53*, 9–11. Pad v, *1*, 49–51. Kūr i, *52*, 18.

[2] Vā *1*, 60–1. Bḍ i, *1*, 40–1. Mat *3*, 3–4; *53*, 3. Pad v, *1*, 45–7. Śiv v, *1*, 27–8. Cf. Mārk *45*, 20–1: Br *161*, 27–8.

[3] Vā *1*, 11, 194, 202; *4*, 12; *21*, 3. Br *1*, 29; *245*, 4, 21, 27, 39. Viṣ i, *1*, 3: vi, *8*, 12. Pad vi, *1*, 8; *282*, 116. The Bhāg is *brahma-sammita*, Pad vi, *190*, 73. *Veda-sammita* is sometimes toned down to *Veda-sammata*, Vā *103*, 51: or to *śruti-sammata*, Vā *4*, 5; Bḍ i, *3*, 1: or to *Vedaiḥ samita*, MBh i, *62*, 2298, 2329; *95*, 3842. Cf. MBh xii, *341*, 12983; *349*, 13457, 13528.

[4] So the story of Pṛthu Vainya, Br *4*, 26; Hv *4*, 290. Other portions, Br *48*, 3; Pad vi, *223*, 50; *281*, 57.

[5] Cf. Śatapatha Brāhm xiii, *4*, 3, 12–13. Śāṅkhāyana Śr Sūtra xvi, 1. Āśvalāyana Sūtra x, 7. Vā speaks of its *nirukta* (*1*, 203; *103*, 55), and so also Bḍ (i, *1*, 173; iv, *4*, 55) and Pad (v, *2*, 54).

[6] p. 22, note 8, last line but one.

[7] Vā *1*, 19.

[8] Br *245*, 16–40. Pad v, *2*, 49–51. Cf. Viṣ vi, *8*, 3.

[9] Br. *121*, 10; *158*, 32; *175*, 10. Pad vi, *263*, 86, 90.

[10] Vā *1*, 196; *2*, 44; *4*, 12. Bḍ i, *1*, 172; *2*, 47. Mat *1*, 28. Br *1*, 30. Lg i, *2*, 1. Mārk, conclusion, 2–3, 7. Viṣ vi, *8*, 42.

[11] Pad i, *62*, 8.

Thirdly, as regards their teaching and authority, they claim divine sanction, and freely introduce gods as dramatis personae, who give instruction upon all kinds of subjects, thus placing their teaching beyond cavil.[1] Also the strongest censure is passed on those who regarded or treated the recital of the Purana disrespectfully.[2] In late additions the sūta Romaharṣaṇa is called a muni and extolled,[3] and even his son Raumaharṣaṇi is lauded fulsomely, and called *jagad-guru*.[4]

Fourthly, as regards their value and efficacy. The brahmans asserted a supreme position for the Veda, to dispute which was blasphemy, but the Puranas claimed even higher merit for themselves; thus, to give only a few instances, it is said the Purana destroys all sin;[5] it gives every blessing and even final emancipation from existence;[6] it bestows union with Brahmā;[7] it raises one to Viṣṇu:[8] that is, in short, the Puranas gave blessings equal, or rather superior, to anything the Vedas could give.[9] It is said that the Purana should be heard even by brahmans who attained the utmost bounds of sacred knowledge (*brahma-para*),[10] and that even tales in the Purana would make a brahman know the Veda.[11]

Further the brahmans arrogated to themselves the monopoly of revelation and religious ceremonies and ritual. The Puranas, while acknowledging their great privileges, yet inculcated much teaching that virtually superseded brahmanic doctrine in extolling the

[1] e.g. Brahmā speaks of geography, the sun, &c., Br *27-40*; about tīrthas and the māhātmya of Gautamī Gaṅgā (the Godāvarī), *id., 41-177*. Most of the Mat and Var is declared by Viṣṇu himself as the Fish or the Boar. Śiva is often introduced as giving instruction to Pārvatī.

[2] Mat, conclusion, 3-19. Pad iii, *1*, 11.

[3] Viṣ iii, *4*, 10.

[4] Pad vi, *219*, 14-21 (in 21 preferably read *Romaharṣana*).

[5] Vā *103*, 55, 58. Viṣ vi, *8*, 3, 12, 17 &c. Mat *290*, 20; *291*, 29, 32. Var *112*, 63, 75. Br *175*, 89, 90; *245*, 6, 14, 16 &c. Pad i, *62*, 10: ii, *125*, 18 f.: vi, *28*, 56-60; *31*, 64. Even the sins of gods and rishis, Bḍ i, *2*, 47-8.

[6] Br *245*, 32-3. Viṣ vi, *8*, 28-32. Pad i, *62*, 20-23: v, *2*, 52-4. Mat, conclusion, 20. Pad vi, *191*, 26-39 *passim*: *193*, 12 as to the Bhāg.

[7] Vā *103*, 57. Kūr ii, *45*, 133.

[8] Mat *291*, 32. Viṣ vi, *8*, 55. Pad vi, *1*, 17; *191*, 75. Var *112*, 75.

[9] Equal, Lg ii, *55*, 40-1. Superior, Pad iv, *111*, 42: Mārk (my translation), *137*, 14-16, 25-7, 31-2.

[10] Br *245*, 17. Cf. Kūr ii, *45*, 125.

[11] Pad ii, *60*, 28.

superlative efficacy of tīrthas,[1] religious devotion (*yoga*),[2] exercises (*vrata*),[3] and loving faith (*bhakti*),[4] whereby a man can obtain every blessing, remission of every sin and final emancipation from existence.[5] The Padma goes so far as to say, 'enough of vratas, tīrthas, yogas, sacrifices and discourses about knowledge, faith (*bhakti*) alone indeed bestows final emancipation.'[6] Some Puranas do not hesitate to introduce the sacred gāyatrī into a spell,[7] and even to modify and almost parody it.[8]

Lastly as regards the dignity of the brahmans who recited or expounded the Puranas, the Vāyu, Padma and Śiva assert that a brahman was not really wise if he did not know the Purana (p. 1),[9] thus making knowledge of the Purana the crown of all learning; and the laudation is carried farthest in the Padma, which gives directions about reciting the Purana and has much to say about the brahman who knew and expounded the Puranas,[10] proclaiming that—the brahman who declares the Puranas is superior (*viśiṣyate*) to every one; even sin committed by him cannot adhere to him; the Purana destroys the sins of every one else; and if a believer in the Puranas esteems the declarer of them as a guru who gives knowledge of sacred science (*brahma-vidyā*), all his sins disappear.[11] The Matsya imprecates a curse on those who reviled the Purāṇa-jñas.[12] Those who recited the Purana were worthy of signal honour,[13] but various faults disqualified them.[14]

[1] Pilgrimages to tīrthas are extolled everywhere. They are equal to the Vedas, Pad i, *43*, 48; and better than sacrifices, Pad i, *11*, 17.

[2] e.g. Vā *13*. Kūr ii, *2*, 30 f.

[3] e.g. Mat *62* f. Pad vi, *35* f.

[4] Praising Kṛṣṇa is more efficacious than the Veda or anything else, Pad vi, *228*, 39–41. Cf. Viṣ vi, *2*, 39.

[5] Even a specially munificent gift confers greater blessings than the Puranas, Vedas and sacrifices, Mat *83*, 2–3.

[6] Pad vi, *190*, 22. Cf. *ibid.* *256*, 69–70; *257*, 152–3: Br *178*, 186.

[7] Lg ii, *22*, 9; *51*, 18.

[8] Lg ii, *27*, 48, 50, 245, 254, 265; *28*, 61; *18*, 5–26. Pad v, *75*, 97; *76*, 11: vi, *72*, 115, 118–121; *85*, 19; *88*, 33.

[9] Vā also proclaims (*79*, 53) the superiority of the brahman who knew the *itihāsa* as well as the four Vedas.

[10] Pad iv, *109*, 25 f.; *111*, 21 f., 40–9, 63–5. See p. 26 for terms: also VN *9*, 100; Kūr ii, *45*, 120–35.

[11] Pad iv, *110*, 398–402.

[12] Conclusion 11.

[13] Pad iii, *25*, 32–6: iv *109*, 26; *111*, 26–30, 51–8: vi, *29*, 25 f.; *125*, 91–3.

[14] Pad iv, *111*, 59–62.

The Mahābhārata puts forward similar claims for itself; thus it declares it is the chief of all śāstras,[1] it is a Veda[2] and outweighs the four Vedas,[3] it cleanses from sin,[4] it enables a man to attain to Brahmā's abode[5] and Viṣṇu's abode,[6] and it procures final emancipation from existence.[7] These claims are not however quite as thoroughgoing as those that the Puranas assert for themselves, and moreover it seems that the Puranas were first with their claims and the epic followed and copied them (p. 22). The Rāmāyaṇa, being a brahmanical production, is less assertive, and claims but to be equal to the Veda and to free from sin.[8]

CHAPTER III

CONTENTS OF THE EARLIEST PURANAS

It has been explained in the last chapter how the original Purana was compiled. The materials used were *ākhyānas*, *upākhyānas*, *gāthās* and *kalpa-jōktis* (and the equivalent *kalpa-vākya*). Similar materials would appear to have gone to make up the Itihāsa.

The term *kalpa* in a precise sense means a vast cosmic period, but this seems to have been a later application of it, when the scheme of cosmological time was developed. It is not seldom used in a simpler and unspecialized way to mean 'a period of time', 'an age', and this seems to have been its earlier signification, as where it is said, wise men knew the old tales of the old time.[9] In this way *kalpa* is often used loosely;[10] and so also *purā-kalpa*,[11] as where it is declared that *purā-kalpa-vids* knew a particular vrata,[12] and

[1] xviii, *6*, 298.
[2] i, *1*, 261; *62*, 2300. Equal, cf. vii, *52*, 2027; *203*, 9647.
[3] i, *1*, 264–6. Cf. i, *62*, 2314, 2329.
[4] i, *1*, 247; *62*, 2301–2, 2313, 2319–21: xviii, *6*, 219, 310.
[5] i, *62*, 2297. [6] xviii, *6*, 305, 310. [7] xviii, *6*, 298.
[8] vii, *111*, 4–6.
[9] Mat *53*, 63, 73:—

purātanasya kalpasya purāṇāni vidur budhāḥ.

[10] e.g. Mat *57*, 26; *58*, 55; *62*, 36. Pad v, *82*, 45.
[11] e.g. Pad i, *41*, 1: ii, *1*, 11; *28*, 54: v, *23*, 65. Vā *59*, 137, professes to explain it. Cf. also MBh v, *36*, 1352: ix, *48*, 32.
[12] Mat *63*, 1. Pad v, *22*, 105.

proclaim songs sung by king Ambarīṣa.[1] Accordingly *kalpa* must have this general sense when it is used in the above words *kalpa-jōkti* and *kalpa-vākya*.

Purāṇa and *itihāsa*, apart from their application to compilations, are applied to single stories.[2] *Purāṇa* means any 'old tale', or 'ancient lore' generally,[3] and *itihāsa* would seem properly to denote a story of fact in accordance with its derivation *iti ha āsa*, which rather denotes actual traditional history.[4] But the line between fact and fable was hardly definite and gradually became blurred, especially where the historical sense was lacking, and so no clear distinction was made, particularly in brahmanic additions to the Puranas. Hence both words tended to become indefinite. The Vedārthadīpikā calls all the old stories it cites *itihāsas*, and never uses the word *Purāṇa*, I believe, except once, and then of a quotation from 'the Puranas', which agrees with the Mahābhārata.[5] Purana is applied to a single story, whether quasi-historical[6] or mythological[7] or instructive;[8] and so also an itihāsa may be an ordinary tale[9] or quasi-historical,[10] fanciful,[11] mythological[12] or even didactic.[13] In later additions to the Puranas any kind of tale is called an itihāsa, and spurious antiquity was ascribed to

[1] MBh xiv, *31* 876.

[2] See fifth note above. Mat *181*, 5; *247*, 5. MBh i, *175*, 6650. Also the following references.

[3] Mat *53*, 64.

[4] So Yāska uses *aitihāsika* for those who interpreted the Veda with reference to traditional history (*Vedic Index* i, 122. Cf. opening verses in chap. I). It shows that *itihāsa* as traditional history was well understood, and therefore that itihāsas must have been commonly current. *Itihāsas* according to Sāyaṇa are cosmological myths or accounts, such as 'In the beginning this universe was nothing but water', &c.; so SBE xliv, p. 98: but this is very doubtful, because (1) *itihāsa* is, I believe, very rarely found applied to such accounts, (2) the definition of *itihāsa* and the references to it in the Kauṭilīya Arthaśāstra (which will be noticed in chap. IV) distinctly negative it, and (3) so also does Yāska's use of the word *aitihāsika*.

[5] Its notice of Rigv i, *65*. MBh xii, *351*, 13642–3.

[6] MBh i, *122*, 4718: xii, *150*, 5595.

[7] Mat *247*, 5, 8. Pad v, *37*, 110. Cf. MBh xii, *341*, 12983; *349*, 13457, 13528: where spurious antiquity is given.

[8] Mat *181*, 5. Vā *46*, 3.

[9] Pad ii, *47*, 63: iii, *14*, 14 f.

[10] MBh i, *95*, 3840; *104*, 4178. Pad ii, *85*, 15 f.: v, *28*, 47.

[11] Var *53*, 26. Pad iv, *113*, 203/13.

[12] Vā *55*, 2. Pad vi, *19*, 144; *98*, 4; *108*, 1.

[13] Br *240*, 5. Pad v, *59*, 2.

stories, fables, and other matters that are manifestly late by adding the epithet *purātana*.[1] Moreover no strong distinction was made in later times between these terms and ākhyāna, and they are not seldom treated as synonymous.[2]

As collective terms Itihāsa and Purāṇa are often mentioned as distinct,[3] and yet are sometimes treated as much the same; thus the Vāyu calls itself both a Purana and an Itihāsa,[4] and so also the Brahmāṇḍa.[5] The Brahma calls itself a Purana and an Ākhyāna.[6] The Mahābhārata calls itself by all these terms.[7]

The word Purana occurs often in the singular. In various passages it means the Puranas collectively,[8] and in some places it is doubtful whether the singular or plural is intended;[9] but in others[10] it means 'the Purana' and refers apparently to the original Purana, and this seems specially clear where its locative is used in connexion with ancient tenets.[11]

The Purana as so framed was entrusted to the sūta Romaharṣaṇa in virtue of the duties that appertained to sūtas (p. 21), and it is there said that the matters with which sūtas were concerned were displayed in itihāsas and purāṇas, *itihāsa-purāṇeṣu diṣṭā*. It makes no real difference whether we understand these words as meaning that those matters 'were displayed in tales and ancient stories' or as meaning that they 'are displayed in the Itihāsas and Puranas'; for in the former case those tales and ancient stories would have been comprised among the materials used, and the

[1] Mat *72*, 6–10. Pad vi, *77*, 30; *243*, 3: and often. So in the Anugītā, which is a late brahmanical production, e.g. MBh xiv, *20*; *21*; &c.

[2] Vā *54*, 1–3, 115. Br *131*, 2. Pad v, *32*, 8–9: vi, *29*, 1–3; *192*, 16 with *193*, 90–1.

[3] e.g. Mat *69*, 55. Br *161*, 27; *234*, 4. See quotations from Kauṭilya at end of chap. IV.

[4] Vā *103*, 48, 51, 55–8. Cf. *1*, 8.

[5] Bd iv, *4*, 47, 50, 54–8.

[6] Br *245*, 27, 30.

[7] *Itihāsa*, i, *2*, 648; *60*, 2229; &c. *Purāṇa*, i. *1*, 17; *62*, 2298. *Ākhyāna*, i, *1*, 18; *2*, 649–52. *Upākhyāna*, i, *2*, 647.

[8] e.g. Vā *83*, 53. Br *121*, 10; and *173*, 35 in connexion with the Godāvarī, where the original Purana cannot be meant. Also MBh i, *31*, 1438–9; *51*, 2020.

[9] e.g. Vā *50*, 189. Bd ii, *21*, 137. Mat *52*, 11. Br *3*, 50.

[10] Probably MBh i, *4*, 852; *5*, 863.

[11] *Purāṇe niścayaṁ gatam*, Vā *56*, 90; *101*, 21: Bd ii, *28*, 96; iv, *2*, 19: Mat *141*, 81. Similarly Viṣ i, *7*, 6: MBh xii, *208*, 7571. Doubtful MBh xii, *166*, 6205. Perhaps *Purāṇe kīrtita*, Br *5*, 21: Hv *7*, 427.

latter construction would say definitely that they had been incorporated in the Itihāsas and Puranas. It is clear then that the original Purana dealt with ancient traditions about gods, rishis and kings, their genealogies and famous deeds. Itihāsas appear to have remained distinct for some time, and Liṅga i, *26*, 28 mentions the *Śaiva* as one; but afterwards they would seem to have become absorbed into the Puranas.[1]

Genealogies and the deeds of famous kings and rishis constituted two subjects. Traditions about gods and (to some extent) the most ancient rishis and kings would divide themselves into the three subjects of creation, its obvious end and dissolution, and the Manvantaras. The matters then with which the Purana would have dealt were these five subjects, and the truth of the old verse about the five subjects that every Purana should treat of becomes manifest, namely, original creation, dissolution and re-creation, the Manvantaras, ancient genealogies and accounts of persons mentioned in the genealogies.[2] These gave rise to the term *pañca-lakṣaṇa,* as a special epithet of the 'Purana'. This term manifestly could not have been coined after the Puranas substantially took their present composition, comprising great quantities of other matters, especially brahmanic doctrine and ritual, dharma of all kinds, and the merits of tīrthas, which are often expounded with emphatic prominence. It belongs to a time before these matters were incorporated into the Puranas. It is therefore ancient, characterizes the earliest Puranas, and shows what their contents were.

Dharma in all its branches bulks very large in the present Puranas, but is not alluded to nor even implied in any of those five subjects. Hence it was no ingredient of the earliest Puranas, except probably such simple lessons as might be conveyed incidentally in those five subjects.[3] It has been explained how the original Purana was soon developed into four separate versions (p. 23), and thenceforward the Puranic brahmans developed the Puranas. The multifarious

[1] Cf. *Matsya Sāmmada* near the end of chap. IV; and also the use of *itihāsa* in Vedārth *ante*.

[2] Sargaś ca pratisargaś ca vaṁśo manvantarāṇi ca
vaṁśyânucaritaṁ caiva Purāṇam pañca-lakṣaṇam.

Quoted in Bḍ i, *1*, 37–8: Vā *4*, 10–11: Mat *53*, 65: Kūr i, *1*, 12: Śiv v, *1*, 37: Gar i, *215*, 14: Bhav i, *2*, 4–5: Var *2*, 4. Differently expressed in Viṣ iii, *6*, 25: Ag *1*, 14. Wrongly in Bhāg xii, *7*, 8–10. Cf. Viṣ vi, *8*, 2, 13.

[3] Such as are found interspersed in Homer.

other matters now found were thus later additions, such augmentations gradually nullified the ancient fivefold division, and it was then possible that Puranas could be composed which diverged from that character, *pañca-lakṣaṇa*. The Puranas naturally lent themselves to augmentation, and the Puranic brahmans used their opportunities to the full, partly with further genuine traditions, but mostly with additions of brahmanic stories and fables and doctrinal and ritual matter.

The Matsya implies this, for, after describing the eighteen Puranas and the characteristic subjects of a Purana (*53*, 10–59), it adds (66–9) that the five-subject Purana treats also of the māhātmya of Brahmā, Viṣṇu, the sun, Rudra and the earth; and that dharma, wealth, love and final emancipation from existence and what is repugnant thereto are treated of in all the Puranas. The Vāyu, which states the five characteristic subjects, describes the eighteen Puranas briefly (*104*, 2–11), and adds (11–17), that they give instruction about many dharmas belonging to all classes and āśramas, about rivers, sacrifices, austerities and gifts, about yoga, faith, and knowledge, about the cults of Brahmā, Śiva, Viṣṇu, the sun, the śaktis and the Ārhatas[1] and many other matters. Some of these matters, if not most, were certainly not ancient, and very few of them could by any stretch of terms be reckoned within the five characteristic subjects. Hence clearly all these matters were later additions, additions manifestly made by the Puranic brahmans.

The compilation of the original Purana and even of the four versions into which it developed does not mean that all the traditions existing at that time were collected therein, and in fact it would have been impossible to condense them all into the 4,000 verses of which those collections consisted. There must have been much other tradition surviving about ancient times; just as there were traditions about later kings (which were not admitted into the Puranas because they belonged to later times), as indeed Kālidāsa testifies when he alludes to old villagers who were well acquainted with the stories about king Udayana.[2] Such outstanding traditions about ancient times were no doubt taken up and incorporated and so contributed to the augmentation of the Puranas. As specimens of such may probably be reckoned the story about Bhīṣma and

[1] That is, apparently both Jains and Buddhists.
[2] Meghadūta i, 31.

Ugrāyudha,[1] Sagara's campaign in west India,[2] the genealogy of a branch of kings descended from the Yādava Lomapāda,[3] which appear in single passages only. The Mahābhārata also incorporated many such traditions, which are introduced as extraneous vehicles of instruction; such as the stories of Lopāmudrā and Agastya,[4] of Marutta and Saṁvarta,[5] and of Nala.[6]

As regards traditional history there is generally little evidence to show whether particular stories about kings were in the original compilation, yet the character of certain tales suggests that they were there, such as (1) the natural and simple accounts of kings Satyavrata-Triśaṅku[7] and Sagara[8] narrated in the Ayodhyā genealogy, and (2) the frequent narration of and allusions to other tales in a historical setting, such as the legend of Purūravas and his queen Urvaśī,[9] and that of the rishi Cyavana and his princess-wife Sukanyā.[10] For instance, Purūravas and Urvaśī were according to tradition the progenitors of the great Aila race; hence their legend must have existed in the earliest times, and it is noteworthy that Sāyaṇa mentions it as a typical purāṇa.[11] It is found in the present Puranas. Obviously their legend must have existed through all the intervening ages, because, when oral tradition is the only means of perpetuation, things once forgotten are lost for ever. The fact that Purūravas and Urvaśī are mentioned in a hymn of the Rigveda (x, *95*) would not account for the legend that exists, because other persons who are far more prominent in the Veda are unknown to general tradition, as for instance, Vadhryaśva, Divodāsa and Sudās (p. 7). It is true that stories were fabricated in later times about ancient kings and rishis, but such stories betray their character in various ways that will be noticed in chapter V, and stand on a different footing. That hymn by itself is obscure, but

[1] Hv *20*, 1085–1112. [2] Bd iii, *49*. [3] Kūr i, *24*, 6–10.

[4] MBh iii, *96*, 8561 f.: noticed in chap. XIV.

[5] MBh xiv, *5*, 99 f.: discussed in chap. XIII.

[6] MBh iii, *53* to *79*.

[7] Vā *88*, 78–116. Bd iii, *63*, 77–114. Br *7*, 97 to *8*, 23. Hv *12*, 717 to *13*, 753. Lg i, *66*, 3–10. Śiv vii, *60*, 81 to *61*, 19. JRAS, 1913, pp. 888 f.

[8] Vā *88*, 122–43. Bd iii, *63*, 120–41. Br *8*, 29–51. Hv *13*, 760 to *14*, 784. Śiv vii, *61*, 29–43. JRAS, 1919, pp. 353 f.

[9] Vā *91*, 4–52. Bd iii, *66*, 4–22. Br *10*, 4–8. Hv *26*, 1366–70. Mat *24*, 24–34. Viṣ iv, *6*, 20–42. Śatapatha Brāhm xi, 5, 1.

[10] MBh iii, *122*: and chap. XVII. [11] See SBE xliv, p. 98.

was intelligible to those who knew the legend,[1] and therefore implies the existence of the legend when it was composed.[2]

The first three subjects that Puranas should treat of are based on imagination, are wholly fanciful, and do not admit of any practical examination; hence it would be a vain pursuit to investigate them here. The fourth and fifth subjects however, genealogies and tales of ancient kings, profess to be historical tradition and do admit of chronological scrutiny; hence they are well worth considering. It is manifest from the Rigvedic hymns that there was real civilization in India, there were independent kings, and famous exploits were celebrated in song. Independent kings imply separate dynasties. Dynasties had genealogies, hence there were genealogies to be incorporated in the original Purana. The genealogies will be dealt with in chapters VIII and IX. Here may be noticed the fifth subject, and there is plenty of tradition to testify who were the ancient kings renowned for their deeds.

The greatest kings were generally styled *cakravartins*,[3] sovereigns who conquered surrounding kingdoms or brought them under their authority, and established a paramount position over more or less extensive regions around their own kingdoms. There is a list of sixteen celebrated monarchs and their doings, which is called the *Ṣoḍaśa-rājika*, and is given twice.[4] They are these:—

Marutta Āvīkṣita	Māndhātṛ Yauvanāśva
Suhotra Ātithina	Yayāti Nāhuṣa
Bṛhadratha Vīra[5] the Aṅga	Ambarīṣa Nābhāgi
Sivi Auśīnara	Śaśabindu Caitraratha
Bharata Dauṣyanti	Gaya Āmūrtarayasa
Rāma Dāśarathi	Rantideva Sāṅkṛti
Bhagīratha	Sagara Aikṣvāku
Dilīpa Ailavila Khaṭvāṅga	Pṛthu Vainya.

Instead of Sagara the list in the Droṇa-parvan names Rāma Jāma-

[1] So Tennyson's *Dream of Fair Women* is intelligible only to those who know the stories.

[2] The legend is also impliedly referred to in Rigv iv, *2*, 18: see SBE xlvi, 318, 323–4.

[3] Their ideal characteristics are explained in Vā *57*, 68–80; Bḍ ii, *29*, 74–88. Cf. Mat *142*, 63–73.

[4] MBh vii, *55*, 2170 to *70*; xii, *29*, 910–1037: i, *1*, 223–4 (6 verses) speak of 24.

[5] *Vīra* may be an adjective. Probably Bṛhadratha of Magadha.

dagnya; but he does not properly fall into this enumeration because he was not a king. Suhotra Ātithina is Suhotra, the descendant of Vitatha,[1] Bharata's successor, Ātithina being a variant of Vaitathina. All these were eminent kings and all will be found in the genealogies[2] except Pṛthu Vainya, whose lineage stands quite apart from the other genealogies and seems rather mythical.[3] The list does not arrange the kings in any proper order. Māndhātṛ, Sagara, Bhagīratha, Ambarīṣa,[4] Dilīpa (Dilīpa II) and Rāma Dāśarathi belonged to the Ayodhyā dynasty; and Marutta to the Vaiśāla dynasty. Yayāti was of the Aila race; and among his descendants were Bharata, Suhotra, Rantideva and Bṛhadratha in the Paurava line, and Śaśabindu a Yādava and Śivi an Ānava. There were two kings named Gaya Āmūrtarayasa (son of Amūrtarayas), one who reigned at Gayā,[5] and the other on the river Payoṣṇī[6] (the modern Tapti); the former seems to be meant here.

Another list[7] names certain kings who gained the title *samrāj*,[8] 'paramount sovereign', four of the foregoing, Yauvanāśvi (Māndhātṛ),[9]

[1] Extolled as a very prosperous monarch, MBh i, *94*, 3715–9.

[2] The genealogies are discussed in chaps. VII to IX, and the main lines are set out fully in the Table in chap. XII.

[3] His story is given in Vā *1*, 33–36; *62*, 103 f.; and *63*: Bḍ ii, *36*, 103 f.; and *37*: Mat *10*, 3–15: Br *2*, 17–28; *4*, 28 f.: Hv *2*, 74–81; *4*, 283 to *6*, 405: Pad ii, *26* to *37*; *123*, 55 to *125*, 6: v, *8*, 3–34: Kūr i, *14*, 7–21: Ag *18*, 8–18.

[4] There was another Ambarīṣa Nābhāgi, in the very earliest times, see the 'Nābhāgas' in chap. VIII.

[5] MBh iii, *95*, 8518–20, 8528–39: ix, *39*, 2205. He appears to have been a scion of the Kānyakubja dynasty, Bḍ iii, *66*, 32: Vā *91*, 62: Gar i, *139*, 5: Bhāg ix, *15*, 4: Hv *27*, 1425: Br *10*, 23.

[6] MBh iii, *121*, 10293–304. It was this latter apparently who is meant when it is said Māndhātṛ vanquished Gaya, MBh vii, *62*, 2281: xii, *29*, 981.

[7] MBh ii, *14*, 649–50.

[8] He who conquers the whole of Bhārata-varṣa is celebrated as a samrāj; Vā *45*, 86.

[9] Often celebrated. Of him an old verse was sung—'As far as the sun rises and as far as he sets, all that is called Yauvanāśva Māndhātṛ's territory': MBh vii, *62*, 2282–3; xii, *29*, 983: Vā *88*, 68: Bḍ iii, *63*, 69–70: Viṣ iv, *2*, 18: Bhāg ix, *6*, 37. Celebrated in MBh iii, *126*, 10423–68, which describes his birth in an absurd brahmanical fable, noticed in *id.* vii, *62* and xii, *29*, 974–9. *Cakravartin*, *id.* xiii, *14*, 860.

Bhagīratha,[1] Bharata,[2] and Marutta,[3] and a fifth, Kārtavīrya, that is, Arjuna Kārtavīrya of the Haihaya line, who was a very famous monarch and is called both a samrāj and a cakravartin.[4] Other lists name as kings of wide sway,[5] Dilīpa, Nṛga,[6] Nahuṣa, Ambarīṣa and Māndhātṛ: as kings of high renown,[7] Pṛthu Vainya, Ikṣvāku, Yayāti,[8] Ambarīṣa, Śivi Auśīnara,[9] Ṛṣabha Aila, Nṛga, Kuśika, Gādhi,[10] Somaka[11] and Dilīpa: and as kings of great magnificence,[12] Rantideva,[13] Nābhāga (Ambarīṣa), Yauvanāśva (Māndhātṛ), Pṛthu Vainya, Bhagīratha, Yayāti, Nahuṣa and Hariścandra.[14]

A list is given of kings who gained fame by their gifts of cattle,[15] Bhagīratha, Māndhātṛ Yauvanāśva, Bharata, Rāma Dāśarathi, Dilīpa, Purūravas, Uśīnara, Mucukunda,[16] Nṛga, and Somaka, and others of less note. Another list, given twice,[17] names kings who gained great merit by liberality or devotion to brahmans,

[1] After him the Ganges was named Bhāgīrathī. The story is told, MBh iii, *107*, 9918 to *109*, 9965: &c.

[2] Famous in Vedic literature also. A *cakravartin* and *sārvabhauma*, MBh i, *69*, 2814; *74*, 3121: iii, *90*, 8379.

[3] Praised in MBh xii, *20*, 613; Mārk *130* (Translation *129*), 2–18. His story, *ibid.*, and MBh xiv, *4*, 86 f.

[4] Vā *94*, 9, 23. Bd iii, *69*, 9, 23. Br *13*, 166, 174. Hv *33*, 1857, 1865. Mat *43*, 17–18, 26. Pad v, *12*, 120–2. Viṣ iv, *11*, 3. Ag *274*, 5.

[5] MBh xii, *8*, 238.

[6] MBh iii, *88*, 8329–32; *121*, 10291–2: xiii, *2*, 121.

[7] MBh vi, *9*, 314–16.

[8] Extolled for nobleness, MBh iii, *195*, 13256–60; *293*, 16675.

[9] Extolled for piety and truthfulness, MBh iii, *197*, 13319–30; *293*, 16674; xii, *143*, 5461. The fable of the hawk and pigeon is applied to him in MBh iii, *196*, 13274–300; *207*, 13808: xiii, *67*, 3384: xiv, *90*, 2790: but to his father Uśīnara, *130*, 10557 to *131*, 10596: confusedly to Uśīnara Vṛṣadarbha, king of Kāśi, xiii, *32*.

[10] Kuśika and Gādhi were kings of Kānyakubja.

[11] Probably Sahadeva's son, king of North Pañcāla: praised, MBh iii, *125*, 10422. A story about him in *127*, 10471 f.

[12] MBh ii, *52*, 1929–31.

[13] Praised for liberality, MBh iii, *82*, 4096; *207*, 13809; *293*, 16674: xiii, *66*, 3365; *112*, 5544; *150*, 7129: xiv, *90*, 2787.

[14] Praised, MBh ii, *12*, 488–98; xii, *20*, 614. His story is fully discussed, JRAS, 1917, 40 f.

[15] MBh xiii, *76*, 3688–91; *81*, 3806.

[16] Son of Māndhātṛ, Vā *88*, 71–2; Bd iii, *63*, 72; Mat *12*, 35; Hv *12*, 714; Br *7*, 95; &c. Fables are told about him, Br *196*, 18–26: Hv *115*, 6464–89: Viṣ v, *23*, 17–23. Also MBh xii, *74*.

[17] MBh xii, *234*, 8590–8610: xiii, *137*, 6247–71.

namely, Rantideva Sāṅkṛtya, Śivi Auśīnara, Pratardana king of Kāśi, Ambarīṣa, Yuvanāśva,[1] Rāma Dāśarathi, Karandhama's grandson Marutta,[2] Bhagīratha, Devāvṛdha, Janamejaya, Vṛṣādarbhi, Brahmadatta, Mitrasaha,[3] Bhūmanyu, Śatadyumna, Lomapāda,[4] Satyasandha, Nimi of Vidarbha, Manu's son Sudyumna, Sahasrajit and Prasenajit,[5] and others.

Other lists are found,[6] but it is unnecessary to quote more. They contain most of the foregoing names and new names also, but the compilers were no experts, for the names are generally jumbled together without dynastic, genealogical or chronological order. A very few lists do aim at chronological order, and the longest is one that describes the descent of the sword of justice,[7] thus—Manu, Kṣupa, Ikṣvāku, Purūravas, Āyus, Nahuṣa, Yayāti, Pūru, &c.; but the order after Pūru is worthless, thus it places Ailavila (Dilīpa II) before Dhundhumāra, Mucukunda and Yuvanāśva, though he was long posterior to them in the Ayodhyā line. This list is in the Śānti-parvan and is a brahmanical compilation with the usual brahmanical lack of the historical sense, yet it shows who were remembered as righteous rulers even by brahmans.

These lists have been set out, in order that there should be no lack of names of notable kings for comparison. They show that the really famous kings occur repeatedly and were well established in tradition; and that there were many others less celebrated but yet well known. It is very remarkable, as pointed out before (p. 7), how widely these kings differ from those extolled in the Rigveda and Vedic literature, even when the lists are brahmanical. Rigvedic kings are practically non-existent here, and eulogies of kings in all that literature hardly count in the compilation of these lists. This fact shows how entirely apart from general popular

[1] Māndhātṛ's father, who was a great king; so Vā *88*, 65; Bd iii, *63*, 66; Hv *12*, 711; Śiv vii, *60*, 75–6; Br *7*, 92.

[2] That is, Avīkṣita, mentioned above.

[3] Called Kalmāṣapāda, of Ayodhyā. A story about him in chap. XVIII.

[4] Daśaratha's friend, king of Aṅga, in Rām.

[5] Most of these kings will be found in the Table of Genealogies in chap. XII. Consult also the Index.

[6] Very long lists in MBh i, *1*, 223–32: ii, *8*, 319–33: xiii, *115*, 5661–9; *165*, 7674–85. Similar lists occur in brahmanical books, e. g. Maitrāyaṇa-Brāhmaṇa-Upaniṣad i, 4. Short lists in MBh iv, *56*, 1768–9: v, *89*, 3146: vi, *9*, 313–6; &c.

[7] MBh xii, *166*, 6191–201.

thought stood Vedic literature in this matter. The popular scale of values was totally different from that of Vedic brahmans. Hence it is clear how little Vedic brahmans were in touch with public life and interests,[1] and of what small importance Vedic literature is as regards historical matters.

These divergencies and also the fact that the Puranas sometimes contain statements that differ from those in brahmanic literature show that the Puranic stream of tradition flowed independently of the Vedic stream. The former sometimes incorporated brahmanical doctrines and tales, and Vedic literature sometimes borrowed from Puranic and Itihāsic sources.[2] The divergence however is substantial and shows that the Puranic brahmans must have received the different account when they took over the Puranas, and that they preserved it, notwithstanding the disagreements, as being genuine tradition.

Now may be noticed the matters that Āpastamba[3] quotes from Puranas, viz., three doctrines from a Purana, and one from the Bhaviṣyat Purana, as bearing on the contents of the Puranas in his time.

The first passage is translated thus by Bühler[4]—'Now they quote also in a Purâna the following two verses: "The Lord of creatures has declared, that food offered unasked and brought by the giver himself, may be eaten, though (the giver be) a sinner, provided the gift has not been announced beforehand. The manes of the ancestors of that man who spurns such food, do not eat (his oblations) for fifteen years, nor does the fire carry his offerings (to the gods)".' These verses occur in Manu iv, 248-9, as Bühler notes, with some variations. I have not so far found them in any Purana, but they are probably somewhere there.

The second passage is this[5]—A Purana says, 'No guilt[6] attaches to him who smites (or kills)[7] an assailant that intends to injure him; (it is,) wrath indeed touches wrath'. This is in prose, and

[1] This is further discussed in chap. V.

[2] Śatapatha Brāhm xiii, 5, 4. Vedārth *passim*.

[3] Bühler's 2nd edition, Bombay, 1892.

[4] I, 6, 19, 13. SBE ii, 70.

[5] I, 10, 29, 7—Yo hiṁsârtham abhikrāntaṁ hanti manyur eva manyuṁ spṛśati na tasmin doṣa iti Purāṇe. SBE ii, p. 90.

[6] *Doṣa* means 'guilt' rather than 'sin'.

[7] The root *han* means 'to strike even as far as to kill'. 'Smite' is the nearest equivalent.

apparently Āpastamba has not quoted literally but has summarized the dictum of the Purana. His citation is fully supported by the Matsya, which says[1]—'One may indeed unhesitatingly smite (or kill) a guru or a boy or an old man or a brahman very learned in the Vedas, who advances as an *ātatāyin* against one: the smiter (or killer) incurs no guilt whatever in killing an *ātatāyin*; (it is,) wrath meets that wrath'. The agreement in phraseology shows that this is evidently the passage that Āpastamba had in mind. The Padma has a similar passage about the *ātatāyin*, though differently expressed.[2]

Ātatāyin meant originally 'having one's bow drawn (ready for shooting)' and so 'prepared to take another's life'. Then it was applied to cases of murderous assault as in the Matsya and Padma passages, which lay down that it was no offence to kill an *ātatāyin* outright. This was evidently a maxim of popular justice, because Āpastamba cites as his authority, not a law-book, but a Purana. His phraseology shows he was quoting the doctrine as expressed in the Matsya, and Manu afterwards copied the very words of that version (viii, 350–1). *Ātatāyin* was afterwards extended in its scope and applied as a legal term to include other heinous offenders, such as incendiaries, poisoners, robbers, &c., and is so defined in those two Puranas,[3] and similarly in law-books.[4] The word thus came to include one who was actuated by injurious or malign intent,[5] and Āpastamba's expression *hiṁsārtham*, 'in order to injure,' rather suggests that it had acquired its wider meaning before his time.[6]

The third passage[7] is translated thus by Bühler[8]—'Now they quote (the following) two verses from a Purâ*n*a: Those eighty thousand sages who desired offspring passed to the south by Aryaman's road and obtained burial-grounds. Those eighty thousand sages who desired no offspring passed by Aryaman's road to the north and obtained immortality'. I have not found the precise verses

[1] Mat *227*, 115–7. [2] Pad v, *45*, 54–6.

[3] Mat *227*, 117–9. Pad v, *45*, 56–8.

[4] Baudhāyana i, 10, 18, 13. Vasiṣṭha iii, 15–18. Viṣṇu-smṛti v, 189–92. Bṛhāspati ii, 15–16.

[5] A king was of course bound to punish an *ātatāyin*, but an attempt was made to exempt brahmans and nobles, Lg ii, *50*, 9–10. Cf. Bṛhaspati ii, 17.

[6] *Ātatāyin*; MBh iii, *36*, 1420; *41*, 1695: Viṣ vi, *6*, 24.

[7] ii, 9, 23, 3–5. [8] SBE ii, 156–7.

cited by him in any Purana, but the same statements expressed in very similar language are found in the Vāyu, Brahmāṇḍa, Matsya and Viṣṇu, with fuller descriptions.[1] Āpastamba quotes a conciser version.

The passage[2] which cites the Bhaviṣyat Purana runs thus, as translated by Bühler[3]—'"These (sons) who live, fulfilling the rites taught (in the Veda), increase the fame and heavenly bliss of their departed ancestors. In this manner each succeeding (generation increases the fame and heavenly bliss) of the preceding ones. They (the ancestors) live in heaven until the (next) general destruction of created things. (After the destruction of the world, they stay) again in heaven, being the seed (of the new creation)". That has been declared in the Bhavishyatpurâ*n*a'. This is expressed in concise prose, and it is clear that Āpastamba has summarized herein the doctrine of the Bhaviṣyat Purana, and has even severely condensed it. He does not name the ancestors as *pitṛs*, but it is obvious that he has ranked them as Pitṛs, as of course they are.

The present Bhaviṣya appears to be the modern presentation of the ancient Bhaviṣyat. There is nothing in the difference of name. The Matsya says (*53*, 31–2) that the Bhaviṣya specially extols the sun and concerns itself chiefly with 'future' events or events in 'the future';[4] and again, in describing the Sāmba (or Śāmba) Upapurana, it appears to say that the story of Sāmba or Śāmba (the name is written both ways) is the first part of the Bhaviṣyat and constitutes the whole of that Upapurana.[5] The present Bhaviṣya, after a preface (manifestly an addition) expounding dharma, worship of various kinds and other matters, extols and inculcates the majesty of the sun (i, *48* f.), and in connexion therewith tells the story of Kṛṣṇa's son Sāmba.[6] The Varāha (*177*, 34, 51) says the Bhaviṣyat Purana deals with Sāmba. Thus the two names Bhaviṣya and Bhaviṣyat are given to the present Purana,[7]

[1] The chief passages are Vā *50*, 214–22; Bḍ ii, *21*, 164–75; Mat *124*, 102–110; Viṣ ii, *8*, 84, 87–9. Cf. also Vā *8*, 194; *61*, 99–102, 122–3: Bḍ ii, *7*, 180; *35*, 110–3, 146–7.

[2] ii, 9, 24, 3–6.

[3] SBE ii. 158.

[4] This expression is explained in the next chapter.

[5] Mat *53*, 62 where *Bhaviṣyati* must, for the verse describes a work already in existence, be the locative of *Bhaviṣyat*. Cf. Var *177*, 34, 49–51.

[6] In i, *48*, 2, and especially *66* f.

[7] So Macdonell, *Sanskrit Literature*, p. 302.

and there is no difference in name between the ancient Purana and the present one. There is no definite statement what the ancient Bhaviṣyat contained, yet its general purport was expressed in its name, as will be noticed in the next chapter. It is highly improbable that the present Bhaviṣya can be a totally different work from the ancient Bhaviṣyat. It was easier and more natural to tamper with and revise an existing work of acknowledged importance so as to bring it into accordance with later notions than to compose a wholly new work and supersede the earlier authority completely: and it is notorious that the Bhaviṣya [1] has been unblushingly tampered with, as evidenced by its historical account of the Kali age.

But whether the existing Bhaviṣya is the ancient Bhaviṣyat or not is not a question of any consequence in the matter under consideration. It says very little about cosmogony and the ages, and that little is clearly the presentation of later ideas. It is practically worthless as regards all ancient beliefs. To expect to find in it the doctrine that Āpastamba quoted from the Bhaviṣyat is futile, because that became obsolete. If we wish to discover that doctrine in the Puranas, we must look at those which have best preserved the ancient ideas about the Pitṛs, and there we do find it. The fullest account is in the Vāyu [2] and Brahmāṇḍa,[3] which are practically identical. The Harivaṁśa [4] agrees closely therewith, so far as its shorter version goes; and a similar but brief account is given in the Matsya [5] and Padma,[6] which are almost alike. Similar accounts are found elsewhere.[7]

These texts say this.[8] There were various classes of Pitṛs, of different origins, forms, grades and abodes. One broad distinction is into Pitṛs who were divine and Pitṛs who were deceased men.[9]

[1] As presented in the Śrī-Veṅkaṭeśvara edition.

[2] *Passim* in *56*, 13–19, 61–73, 88–92; *71*, 8–78; *72*, 1; *73*, 49–60; *75*, 53.

[3] *Passim* in ii, *28*: iii, *9*, 6–75; *10*, 1, 99–107; *11*, 90.

[4] *Passim* in *16*, 836–77; *17*, 918, 928; *18*, 932–1009.

[5] In *13*, 2–5; *15*, 29, 30; *141*, 12–20, 57–65, 79–81.

[6] In v, *9*, 2–5, 56, 58.

[7] e. g. Var *13*, 16–31.

[8] Where several texts are cited for a statement, they should be collated.

[9] The divine are called *devāḥ pitaraḥ*, Mat *141*, 57; Vā *56*, 61; Bd ii, *28*, 66. Deceased ancestors are called *manuṣyāḥ* (or *mānuṣāḥ*) *pitaraḥ*, Mat *141*, 65; Vā *56*, 73; Bd ii, *28*, 78: or *laukikāḥ pitaraḥ*, Mat *141*,

Also some dwelt in heaven and some in the underworld.[1] The former who dwelt in heaven were as gods,[2] and they and the gods were reciprocally gods and pitṛs.[3] They were the most primeval deities,[4] and were indeed from everlasting,[5] and never cease to exist.[6] But the Pitṛs who were human ancestors (comprising the father, grandfather and great grandfather[7]) attained to and became one with the divine Pitṛs through righteousness[8] and dwelt blissfully in heaven with them.[9] At the end of every thousand yugas they are reborn,[10] they revive the worlds, and from them are produced all the Manus and all progeny at the new creations.[11]

These Puranas thus declare that the *manuṣya pitṛs* attain to the same condition and position as the divine Pitṛs, dwell in heaven and reproduce the world in the next creation—that is, they are the 'seed' which generates fresh life in the next creation.[12] Such is precisely the doctrine which Āpastamba quotes from the Bhaviṣyat. This is corroborated by certain further statements. The Pitṛs are classed with the gods, seven rishis and Manus, and all these are

60; Vā *56*, 64; Bḍ ii, *28*, 69. Mat *141*, 80; Vā *56*, 65–6, 89; and Bḍ ii, *28*, 70–1, 95 define them as father, grandfather and great grandfather.

[1] Vā *71*, 9; Bḍ iii, *9*, 8. Cf. Hv *16*, 847. Mārk *96* and *97*, and Gar i, *89* vary.

[2] Vā *71*, 8: Bḍ iii, *9*, 6: Hv *16*, 837 (and 871). Cf. Vā *71*, 12, 52; *83*, 108: Bḍ iii, *9*, 11, 52: Hv *16*, 851: Mat *13*, 4: Pad v, *9*, 4: Mārk *96*, 13; *97*, 4, 7: Gar i, *89*, 13. 52.

[3] Vā *71*, 34: Bḍ iii, *9*, 35: Hv *17*, 928: Mat *141*, 79. Repeated in Vā *56*, 88; *75*, 53; *83*, 122: Bḍ ii, *28*, 94; iii, *11*, 90. Cf. Var *13*, 18.

[4] Vā *71*, 54 and Bḍ iii, *9*, 54 say *ādi-devāḥ*. Hv *16*, 877 similarly. Cf. Mārk *96*, 39: Gar i, *89*, 39: Mat *15*, 42.

[5] Vā *56*, 92: Bḍ ii, *28*, 98.

[6] Vā *71*, 78: Bḍ iii, *9*, 75. Cf. Bḍ iii, *10*, 105; *20*, 8: Vā *73*, 58 (ending corrupted); *83*, 115: Hv *18*, 1009.

[7] See seventh note above.

[8] Mat *141*, 60, where for *smṛtāḥ* read probably *śritāḥ* (cf. verses 58–9; and first passages in p. 45 note [1]). Similarly Bḍ ii, *28*, 73–4: Vā *56*, 68. Cf. Br *220*, 92.

[9] Mat *141*, 63: Vā *56*, 70–1: Bḍ ii, *28*, 76–7—where *Pitṛmant* is Soma 'the moon', which is so called in Vā *56*, 31; *75*, 56: Bḍ ii, *28*, 33: Mat *141*, 29.

[10] Vā *71*, 60–1: Bḍ iii, *9*, 60–1. Similarly Hv *18*, 937. Mat *13*, 4–5 and Pad v, *9*, 4–5 equivalently. Cf. also Vā *61*, 128–9; *71*, 15: Bḍ iii, *9*, 13.

[11] Mat *15*, 29: Pad v, *9*, 56. Cf. Vā *71*, 57: Bḍ iii, *9*, 57–8.

[12] *Lokānām akṣayârthin*, Vā *83*, 121; Bḍ iii, *20*, 15.

declared to be the *sādhakas* of each new manvantara.[1] Moreover the Pitṛs were a comprehensive body of beings, for the seven chief *ṛṣigaṇas* are also called Pitṛs; [2] and the restoration of humankind at the beginning of a new age is assigned to the seven rishis also,[3] and they are referred to in this function by the words *santaty-artha* and *santānârtha*,[4] and *santāna-kara*,[5] which are synonymous with the word *bījârtha* that Āpastamba uses. The word *bījârtha* itself occurs in similar connexions, namely, in the restoration of population in the Kṛta age after this Kali age. Thus it is applied to Devāpi the Paurava and Maru [6] the Aikṣvāku, who will revive the brahma-kṣatras then; [7] and also to the renewal of the castes then.[8] The word thus has precisely the meaning which Āpastamba gives it, and his application of it to the Pitṛs sums up correctly the function assigned them as shown above.

These Puranas also declare that they repeat the doctrine concerning the Pitṛs, which was expounded in 'a Purana' or more probably in 'the Purana',[9] so that it was the ancient belief. 'The Purana' would obviously mean the original Purana. 'A Purana' might very appropriately mean the Bhaviṣyat, because the Bhaviṣyat would naturally treat of such future matters. From whatever Purana then they quoted this doctrine, they manifestly repeat the ancient belief that would have been expounded in the Bhaviṣyat in Āpastamba's time.

It has been pointed out above, that dharma was no ingredient of the earliest Puranas except probably such simple lessons as might be conveyed incidentally in the five special subjects of those Puranas; and these four doctrines cited by Āpastamba support that view. The third and fourth are not matters of dharma but

[1] Vā *61*, 134, 150–5, 173. Bḍ ii, *35*, 177–82, 201–2.
[2] Vā *65*, 49, 50. Bḍ iii, *1*, 50–51.
[3] Vā *65*, 11, 47–8. Bḍ iii, *1*, 10.
[4] Vā *61*, 158, 161. Bḍ ii, *35*, 185, 189. Mat *273*, 62.
[5] Vā *65*, 48. Bḍ iii, *1*, 47. Mat *145*, 35.
[6] Corrupted to *Mata* in Vā *99*, 437 and Mat *273*, 56. He was a king of Ayodhyā.
[7] Vā *99*, 443: Bḍ iii, *74*, 256: Mat *273*, 61: where the plural is used for the dual, Prakrit-wise. As these Puranas avowedly borrowed their account of the kings of the Kali age from the Bhaviṣya (see next chapter), it seems probable they borrowed this portion also from it, though the present Bhaviṣya has not either. Cf. Viṣ iv, *24*, 46, 48.
[8] Vā *58*, 104–110; Bḍ ii, *31*, 104–111. Less correctly Mat *144*, 94.
[9] Mat *141*, 81 and 16. Vā *56*, 90. Bḍ ii, *28*, 96.

of ancient cosmogony. The second is not dharma properly speaking, for it deals with criminal guilt and not sin, and merely declared a rule of common-sense jurisprudence. The first alone comes within the description of dharma. Only one then of the matters which Āpastamba quotes from Puranas belongs to dharma, and this fact is no proof that dharma was a subject dealt with in the earliest Puranas, because his book was concerned with dharma and he naturally cited only points of dharma.[1] The true inference therefrom would be that the Puranic brahmans had already begun to incorporate some dharma in the Puranas in his time.

CHAPTER IV

THE AGE OF THE ORIGINAL PURANA

THE age of the Puranas may now be considered according to the evidence obtained from themselves and from other sources. In doing this, the discussion must proceed from later known facts to earlier evidence.

The Vāyu Purana existed before A.D. 620, because it is referred to by Bāṇa in his Harṣa-carita,[2] and the writing in a MS. of the Skanda in the Royal Library of Nepal shows that that Purana also existed about that time.[3] Verses praising gifts of land are quoted in various land-grants, that are dated; and some of those are found only in the Padma, Bhaviṣya and Brahma Puranas, and thus indicate that those Puranas were in existence before A.D. 500 and even long before that time.[4] Some of those verses, which occur in grants of the years 475–6 and 482–3, are declared in some grants to have been enunciated by Vyāsa in the Mahābhārata.[5] They do

[1] One might as well argue that, because Maine in *Ancient Law* (chap. v) quotes some verses from the *Odyssey* about certain ancient legal conditions, therefore the *Odyssey* dealt with law.

[2] Chap. III, paragraph 4. Cowell and Thomas, Translation, p. 72. See V. A. Smith, *Early History of India* 3rd ed., pp. 21–22.

[3] *Trans. VIth Oriental Congress*, vol. iii, p. 205. The MS. was sent to Oxford for inspection.

[4] JRAS, 1912, pp. 248–55. Gar may perhaps be added because verses 3*b* and 7 occur in it (ii, *31*, 14 and 4).

[5] JRAS, 1912, 253–4.

not however (as far as I know) occur there, but are found in the Padma and Bhaviṣya, and nowhere else. Such an error, citing the Mahābhārata instead of the Puranas, in a land-grant, which was not a learned treatise, is venial, especially as Vyāsa was believed to be the author of all those works. The mistake shows the pre-eminent position held by the epic then. The important point however is that the grantors assert that a book was the original authority for those verses; not popular lore nor unknown compositions. It follows therefore that either the Padma or the Bhaviṣya or both existed before A.D. 475 and even much earlier, and a similar conclusion, though not so clear, may be drawn as regards the Brahma.

Further the Matsya, Vāyu and Brahmāṇḍa say in their accounts of the dynasties of the Kali age that they borrowed their accounts from the Bhaviṣya;[1] and the internal evidence therein shows that the Bhaviṣya existed in the middle of the third century A.D., the Matsya borrowed before the end of that century, and the Vāyu and Brahmāṇḍa borrowed in the next century.[2] The present Bhaviṣya, as presented in the Śrī-Veṅkaṭeśvara edition, does not contain that account, but another altogether corrupt and false, and the reason is that the Bhaviṣya has been freely tampered with in order to bring its prophecies up to date and the ancient matter utterly vitiated: but those three Puranas show what it contained in the third century, as regards the dynasties of the Kali age.

Next may be considered the mention of the Bhaviṣyat Purana in the Āpastambīya Dharmasūtra (chap. III), and the inferences that may be drawn therefrom.

The 'Purana', as already pointed out, first came into existence as a collection of ancient legendary lore, and this, its original nature, is an essential fact. Āpastamba obviously refers in his citations of Puranas (chap. III) to definite books. Now the Bhaviṣyat Purana plainly professed by its title to treat of 'the future', and its title is a contradiction in terms. The first inference therefore is that such a name could not have been possible until the term Purana had become so thoroughly specialized as to have lost its proper meaning, and had become merely the designation of a particular class of books. It would have required the existence of a number of books called Puranas to produce that change, and manifestly

[1] My *Dynasties of the Kali Age*, pp. vii–viii. JRAS, 1915, pp. 141–2, 517–18. These three Puranas existed before.

[2] *Id.*, pp. xii–xiv, xxiv, xxv. JRAS, 1912, pp. 142–3.

they must have had their own special names to distinguish one from another, and so convert their common title Purana into a mere class designation.[1]

The next inference is that the foregoing change implied long usage—that is, the Puranas began long before Āpastamba's time. His sūtra is estimated by Bühler as not later than the third century B.C., and possibly 150–200 years earlier.[2] His citation of the Bhaviṣyat as an authority shows that it was no new work then, but had acquired an acknowledged position of dignity, which it could not have attained to in less than half a century. Hence the Bhaviṣyat cannot be placed later than the early part of the third century B.C., and even possibly earlier still by the above 150–200 years. At that time the title Purana had completely lost its original meaning, and the question arises, what length of time would have been required to bring about that result. There can be no definite pronouncement on this, but the time cannot have been less than two centuries, considering the conditions of literature in those times, and was probably much longer. Hence Puranas must have existed at least as early as the beginning of the fifth century B.C.; and this lower limit would be shifted 150–200 years earlier if a prior date be given to Āpastamba. It is quite probable therefore that the Matsya existed long prior to him, as indeed his citation of it indicates (p. 44).

The third inference from the name Bhaviṣyat is that before that Purana could have been composed about 'the future' there must have been some general consensus of opinion when 'the future' began. The Bhaviṣyat and Bhaviṣya are referred to here as distinct, the former being the Purana cited by Āpastamba, and the latter that which existed in the third century A.D. as mentioned above, and which, modified by the continual tampering to which it has notoriously been subjected, we have now. When the Bhaviṣyat was composed, whenever that was, obviously everything after that time was 'future', so that the third century B.C. at the latest and all after time fell into 'the future'; and it would have included the two preceding centuries if Āpastamba should be antedated. It is however pretty obvious that 'the future' must have commenced before the Bhaviṣyat was composed, otherwise there

[1] Compare the *Journals* of the Royal Asiatic and other Societies, where the title 'Journal' has completely lost its original meaning.

[2] SBE ii, p. xliii.

would have been little to speak of beyond vague prophecies and teleology, subjects hardly attractive enough of themselves alone to win general interest in a new 'Purana'.[1] Hence 'the future' had probably been reckoned as having begun some time before, so that the author could have commenced with interesting tales of what had taken place before launching out into talk about the real and unknown future. This inference is entirely supported by the statement *ante* that the Bhaviṣyat began with the story of Kṛṣṇa's son Sāmba soon after the Bhārata battle, and by the following further declarations.

There is some definite information concerning, first, what was ranked as 'past', and secondly, what was considered to be 'future'. First, all the epic and Puranic traditions that deal with kings and princes, and less markedly with rishis, stop short soon after the great Bhārata battle. Till that event they are fairly copious, and after that they take in the reign of Yudhiṣṭhira and his brothers, and, in the early and final chapters of the Mahābhārata, speak of their successors Parīkṣit II and Janamejaya III;[2] but there are no traditions about Janamejaya's successors, nor about any of the kings of the great dynasties of Ayodhyā and Magadha after that battle beyond a few curt allusions in the list of the kings of the Kali age.[3] 'The past' therefore was to that extent regarded as ending with the decease of the Pāṇḍavas, or later with Janamejaya III.

As regards 'the future' there are these data. The Vāyu professes to have been narrated in the reign of Asīmakṛṣṇa or Adhisīmakṛṣṇa, the great grandson of that Janamejaya and the sixth in generation from Arjuna, in the Paurava line.[4] The Matsya (*50*, 66) takes the same standpoint. Both definitely declare his successors to be future.[5] Both treat Divākara, king of Ayodhyā, and Senājit, king of Magadha, as reigning contemporaneously with him, and say they were respectively the fifth and seventh in succession from Bṛhadbala and Sahadeva who were killed in the

[1] That was done as in the Kalki Upapurana, but it was a later elaboration and very small in scope.

[2] See Table of Genealogies in chap. XII.

[3] *Dynasties of the Kali Age*, pp. 1 f. Erroneous account in Hv *191* f.

[4] Vā *1*, 12; *99*, 255–8. Bḍ has lost the latter passage in a large lacuna.

[5] Vā *99*, 270. Mat *50*, 77.

great battle. Both declare their successors to be future, and so also does the Vāyu's counterpart, the Brahmāṇḍa.[1] These three Puranas thus start the 'future' kings in those three great dynasties with the sixth or seventh successors of those who took part in that battle; that is, they make 'the future' begin some five or six clear reigns after that battle, or about a century after it, if we put aside the extravagant lengths given to the reigns of Senājit's predecessors in Magadha.[2] This point is more definitely discussed in chapter XV.

The Viṣṇu and Bhāgavata in their accounts speak of Parīkṣit as reigning and his successors as future in the Paurava line,[3] but treat the first kings of Ayodhyā and Magadha after that battle, who were his contemporaries, as future.[4] These two Puranas thus make 'the future' begin some thirty years after the battle as regards Parīkṣit, but immediately after the battle as regards the two other dynasties. The Garuḍa speaks of Janamejaya as reigning in the Paurava line and his successors as future, but apparently treats 'the future' in the two other dynasties as beginning after that battle.[5]

As regards 'the future', then, these statements offer two limits of commencement, an upper, the end of the Bhārata battle, and a lower, about a century later.[6] Everything prior to the former was 'past', everything posterior to the latter was reckoned as definitely 'future', and the interval between them was intermediate, regarded sometimes as 'past' and sometimes as 'future'. The Matsya, Vāyu and Brahmāṇḍa contain the undoubtedly oldest account of the kings of the Kali age and assert the lower limit. The Bhaviṣyat and Bhaviṣya, by including the story of Kṛṣṇa's son Sāmba, took the earlier limit. The Viṣṇu, Garuḍa and Bhāgavata, which were later than the Bhaviṣyat, practically adopted its view. Āpastamba's citation of the Bhaviṣyat is perfectly compatible with either reckoning, for it merely indicates that 'the future' had already begun before the third century B.C.

The reckoning then was this. 'The past' ended and 'the future'

[1] Vā *99*, 282–3, 300. Mat *271*, 5–6, 23. Bd iii, *74*, 113–14 as regards Senājit; its reference to Divākara is lost in the lacuna.

[2] And the 60 years assigned to Parīkṣit II, MBh i, *49*, 1949.

[3] Viṣ iv, *20*, 12–13; *21*, 1. Bhāg ix, *22*, 34–6.

[4] Viṣ iv, *22*, 1; *23*, 1–3. Bhāg ix, *12*, 9; *22*, 46.

[5] Gar i, *140*, 40; *141*, 1, 5, 9.

[6] Further remarks about the Kali age, chap. XV.

began at the close of the Bhārata battle, or at the latest about a century afterwards.[1] The difference is not material for the present purpose. The transition manifestly implies a definite stage in the position of tradition, and indicates that previous tradition must have been collected then and formed into a definite compilation, which closed 'the past'. That would have been the precise consequence of the formation of the original Purana. Tradition says that the original Purana was composed about that time (p. 21).[2] The two therefore agree and the former corroborates the latter. True Puranas multiplied, the Bhaviṣyat was devised, and the Puranic brahmans had ample time to begin incorporating brahmanic matter, before Āpastamba's date.

These conclusions are corroborated by certain statements in the Kauṭilīya Arthaśāstra, which may next be considered. It belongs to the fourth century B.C., about a century earlier than the latest date for Āpastamba.

Kauṭilya says, 'The three Vedas, the Sāman, Ṛc and Yajus, are the threefold (scripture). The Atharva-veda and the Itihāsa-veda are also Vedas'.[3] He calls the Itihāsa a Veda and puts it on the same footing as the Atharva-veda. Clearly therefore the Itihāsa was something as definite and well known as that Veda. He also defines the Itihāsa thus—'Itihāsa means the Purāṇa, Itivṛtta (history), Ākhyāyikā (tale), Udāharaṇā (illustrative story), the Dharmaśāstra and the Arthaśāstra'.[4] All these terms are obviously generic,[5] and Purana here means Puranas. As the Itihāsa was a Veda and definite, its component parts cannot have been indefinite, hence the Puranas were not an indefinite collection of ancient tales but must have been compositions certain and well established in character then. This is corroborated by another passage which says that a minister skilled in the Arthaśāstra should admonish a king, who is led astray, by means of the Itivṛtta and Purāṇa.[6] Here also the terms are generic, and the serious purpose for which the Puranas were to be used shows that they were not mere ancient tales but were definite and instructive compositions.

[1] Estimated at 950 and 840 B.C. respectively, chap. XV.

[2] Vyāsa may have begun it, and Romaharṣaṇa and his disciples would have completed it.

[3] Book i, chap. 3 (p. 7).

[4] Book i, chap. 5 (p. 10).

[5] See JRAS, 1914, p. 1022.

[6] Book v, chap. 6 (p. 255, lines 1, 2)

Kauṭilya enjoins that a prince should spend the afternoon in listening to the Itihāsa;[1] and in order to hear the Puranas the prince would need some one to recite them. Hence among the officials whom a king should retain with salaries are mentioned 'the Paurāṇika, the sūta and the māgadha'.[2] The Paurāṇika here is manifestly one specially conversant with the Puranas; and he is distinguished from the sūta and māgadha. He is also referred to in another passage in a similar setting, apart from them,[3] and separate. Kauṭilya uses the word *Paurāṇika* also to distinguish the Puranic sūta and māgadha from the two castes of mixed origin who were so named, but the former had ceased to exist then (p. 18). Hence the Puranas were old in his time. The three first mentioned, the Paurāṇika, the sūta and the māgadha, were quite different. Of these the latter two mean the mixed castes of sūtas and māgadhas who had succeeded to some at least of the functions of the ancient sūtas and māgadhas;[4] and the Paurāṇika was the person, whether brahman or other, who made the Puranas his speciality. His office proves that the Puranas were well known and established compositions in the fourth century B.C.; and the fact that the original sūta and māgadha were only known then from them shows also that the Puranas went back a considerable time before that century.

It thus appears from Kauṭilya that Puranas, definite works, existed at least as early as the fourth century B.C., possessed an authoritative position, and were not novel works then, but went back a long time previously as the Puranic sūta had completely disappeared.

The Purana was regarded with high respect even by the brahmans who upheld the Vedas specially. Thus the Atharva-veda says[5]—The ṛcs, and the sāmans, the metres, the Purāṇa, together with the Yajus, all gods in the heavens, founded upon heaven, were born of the ucchiṣṭa. The Chāndogya Upaniṣad says[6]—The (hymns of the) Atharvāṅgiras are the bees, the Itihāsa-Purāṇa is the flower: and this simile, as expressed, implies that those hymns

[1] Book i, chap. 5 (p. 10, line 15).
[2] Book v, chap. 3 (p. 245). Cf. MBh xii, *85*, 3203.
[3] Book xiii, chap. 1 (p. 393).
[4] Were they employed for *ākhyāyikās* and *udāharaṇas?*
[5] xi, 7, 24. SBE xlii, 229. Cf MBh viii, *34*, 1498.
[6] iii, 4, 1. SBE i, 39.

drew their sustenance from the Itihāsa and Purana, which must therefore have been ancient like those hymns. Both these passages imply that the Purana was something definite, like the other compositions mentioned, and was not a novel thing then.

Further the Śatapatha Brāhmaṇa calls the Itihāsa-Purāṇa and certain other compositions 'honey-offerings to the gods', and commends their daily study.[1] It also appoints the Itihāsa and Purana for recitation by the priests, calling each a Veda.[2] These passages show that the Itihāsa and Purana were definite compositions. Similarly the Śāṅkhāyana Śrauta Sūtra and Āśvalāyana Sūtra[3] say—On the eighth day he tells the story which begins with *Matsya Sāṁmada* . . . He then says, 'The Itihāsa-veda is the Veda, this is the Veda,' and recites an Itihāsa. On the ninth day he tells the story which begins with *Tārkṣya Vaipaśyata*[4] . . . He then says, 'The Purāṇa-veda is the Veda, this is the Veda,' and recites the Purāṇa.[5]

The story above mentioned that begins *Matsyaḥ Sāṁmadaḥ*[6] appears to be that told in Viṣṇu iv, *2*, 19 f. and Padma vi, *232*, 33 f. about the rishi Saubhari. While practising long austerities he saw a fish named Sammada or Sāmamada joyous with an immense and happy family,[7] and aroused thereby, he married the fifty daughters of Māndhātṛ, king of Ayodhyā, and maintained them in great magnificence and happiness.[8] That is probably what the above brahmanical passage cited. What is there called an itihāsa is found in two Puranas now. I have not found the story about Tārkṣya Vaipaśyata, but it was a story about birds.[9]

[1] xi, 5, 6, 8. SBE xliv, 98. Weber, *Hist. of Indian Lit.*, 93.

[2] xiii, 4, 3, 12–13. SBE xliv, 369.

[3] Śāṅkh xvi, 1. Āśval x, 7, inverting the procedure of the two days; SBE xliv, 369, note 3. Max Müller, *Sanskrit Lit.*, 37, 40.

[4] The Āśval. Sūtra reads *Vaipaścita* (better ?).

[5] The Commentator on the Śāṅkhāyana notes, The Purana uttered by Vāyu should be narrated here. Both Vā and Bḍ were uttered by Vāyu, and were one originally.

[6] Rigv viii, *67* is attributed in the alternative to Matsya Sāmmada; Anukramaṇī and Vedārth.

[7] Śatapatha Brāhm (xiii, *4*, 3, 12) says, King Matsya Sāmmada and his people were water-dwellers. This cannot refer to the Matsya country and people, for their country was anything but watery; so *matsya* must mean 'fish'. Vedārth on Rigv viii, *67* says he was a fish.

[8] This story is further considered in chap. V.

[9] So Śatapatha Brāhm, *loc. cit.*

As pointed out above (p. 54), a collection of tradition must have been made within a century or so after the Bhārata battle, thus closing the 'past' and its traditions, whence all subsequent occurrences belonged to the 'future'. This conclusion is confirmed by a general survey of tradition in the Puranas.

There is much traditional history including fairly copious genealogies down to the time of that battle and the death of Kṛṣṇa and the Pāṇḍavas, and then all the genealogies stop short except those of the three great kingdoms of Hastināpura, Ayodhyā and Magadha, although other old dynasties continued to exist, such as those of Pañcāla, Kāśi, Mithilā, &c.[1] There is a little historical tradition of the century or so that followed the battle, yet only concerning the first five Paurava kings in the first of those three kingdoms, and nothing about the two other kingdoms. After that century or so there is no historical tradition, and the genealogies of those three kingdoms are given in prophetic form, but were manifestly compiled long afterwards out of Prakrit chronicles.[2] Yet there were traditions about those 'future' kings, as, for instance, about the kings in Buddha's time and about king Udayana of Vatsa,[3] and none such are noticed in the Puranas, as far as I am aware. These facts, much traditional history down to the death of the Pāṇḍavas, a very little for a century or so following, and then none whatever in the Puranas, prove that there must have been a closing stage in tradition during that century or so—that is, that the original Purana must have been compiled about that time.

The absolute dearth of traditional history after that stage is quite intelligible, both because the compilation of the Purana had set a seal on tradition, and because the Purana soon passed into the hands of brahmans, who preserved what they had received, but with the brahmanic lack of the historical sense added nothing about later kings—just as the Bhāgavata Purana, which was composed about the ninth century A.D., added nothing to its account of the kings of the Kali age beyond where the Vāyu stopped some four centuries earlier. With the same lack however they have introduced in their own additions to the Puranas notices of brahmans who were later, such as Āsuri, Pañcaśikha, &c.[4] This marked change at that stage betokens the compilation of the original Purana and

[1] My *Dynasties of the Kali Age*, p. 23. See chap. XV.
[2] *Id.* p. 10 and Appendix I.
[3] Meghadūta i, 31.
[4] Discussed in chap. XXVII.

the change in the custody of tradition from the sūtas to the brahmans. It is clear evidence that ancient traditions were collected while they were still well known, and while there was still a class of men whose business it was to preserve them carefully.

The Brāhmaṇas are in accord with this conclusion. The late Śatapatha has far more tradition than the earliest Brāhmaṇas. They were composed while the Purana or Puranas were in their infancy,[1] but it was composed after the Puranas had become established, and by quoting their tradition shows that they existed and that the recluse brahmans who studied the Vedas had at length become aware to some extent of the contents and importance of the Puranas.

CHAPTER V

BRAHMANICAL AND KṢATRIYA TRADITION

So far tradition has been considered in its more general aspect, but a survey of ancient Indian tradition discloses the fact that great differences exist in the character of its multitudinous tales; and we may examine now the main features, according to which traditions may be classified.

The first classification that obviously presents itself is the broad division into the two groups, traditions that are mythological and those that profess to deal with history. Instances of the former are Soma's abduction of Bṛhaspati's wife Tārā and the birth of their son Budha,[2] the birth of Ilā from Manu's sacrifice,[3] and the marriage of Śiva and Pārvatī.[4] With such we have nothing to do here, though myths that explain the origin of the chief races said to have ruled ancient India may suggest clues for exploring the earliest conditions.

Taking then traditions that profess to deal with history, we find that many tales are manifestly and essentially brahmanic, such as

[1] See chap. XXVII.

[2] Vā *90*. Bḍ iii, *65*. Br *9*. Hv *25*. Viṣ iv, *6*, 5–19. Bhāg ix, *14*, 3–14. Ag *273*, 8–11. Mat *23*, 29 to *24*, 3. Gar i, *139*, 1–2.

[3] Vā *85*, 5–9. Bḍ iii, *60*, 4–8. Hv *10*, 615–22. Br *7*, 3–8. Viṣ iv, *1*, 6–8.

[4] Mat *154*. Br *36*. Pad v, *40*. Var *22*. Vā *92*, 29–35. Bḍ iii, *67*, 32–9.

the story of Vasiṣṭha, Viśvāmitra and king Triśaṅku in the Mahābhārata and Rāmāyaṇa,[1] that of Viśvāmitra and king Hariścandra in the Mārkaṇḍeya (*7* and *8*), and that of king Hariścandra, Rohita and Śunaḥśepa in the Aitareya Brāhmaṇa[2] and Śāṅkhāyana Śrauta Sūtra.[3] Others are plainly kṣatriya tales, such as the ballad of king Satyavrata-Triśaṅku, Vasiṣṭha and Viśvāmitra in the Puranas (p. 38), that of king Sagara in the Puranas (p. 38), and that of Bhīṣma and Ugrāyudha in the Harivaṁśa (p. 37). Others again are neither kṣatriya nor brahmanical precisely, but combine features of both those classes and are thus of a mixed or intermediate character, such as the story of Agastya and Lopāmudrā (p. 38), that of king Mitrasaha Kalmāṣapāda,[4] and that of king Janamejaya II Pārīkṣita who hurt Gārgya's son.[5] And there is a fourth class, namely, stories which have obviously been devised in order to explain names.

The contrast between the stories about Triśaṅku, Vasiṣṭha and Viśvāmitra shows clearly that there were two classes of tradition, the brahmanic and the kṣatriya (see p. 6). This is only what might be naturally expected. This distinction in tradition, brahmanic and kṣatriya, is very important and may be paralleled by the difference between legends of saints and tales of chivalry. Brahmanic tradition speaks from the brahmanical standpoint, describes events and expresses feelings as they would appear to brahmans, illustrates brahmanical ideas, maintains and inculcates the dignity, sanctity, supremacy and even superhuman character of brahmans, enunciates brahmanical doctrines and advocates whatever subserved the interests of brahmans;[6] often enforcing the moral by means of marvellous incidents, that not seldom are made up of absurd and utterly impossible details. It often introduces kings, because kings were their chief patrons, yet even so the brahmans' dignity is never forgotten. Kṣatriya tradition, on the other hand, speaks from the kṣatriya standpoint, describes events and expresses feelings as they would appear to kṣatriyas, is concerned chiefly with kings and heroes and their great deeds, and displays the ideas and code of

[1] MBh i, *175*, 6651–91: cf. ix, *41*, 2301–6; *43*: Rām i, *52*, 1 to *55*, 10.
[2] vii, *3*, 1 f. [3] xv, 17–25.
[4] MBh i, *176*, 6696 to *177*, 6791. Viṣ iv, *4*, 19 f. Bhāg ix, *9*, 18–39. VN *9*.
[5] Vā *93*, 21–6.
[6] Pad ii is a good example of brahmanic matter: also BV iv, *24* f.

honour of kṣatriyas. It notices rishis who came into contact with kings, but otherwise is not much concerned with the life and thoughts of rishis. Kṣatriya tales do often indulge in the marvellous, but their marvels are generally mere exaggeration without any didactic purpose; and kṣatriya tradition, even when magnifying the glory of kings, does not disparage brahmans but acknowledges their character and position, though not in the excessive terms often employed in brahmanic tales. Kṣatriya genealogies are of necessity of kṣatriya origin.

The difference between the two kinds of tradition is best brought out where fortunately both the kṣatriya and the brahmanic versions exist. That is found in the stories about Triśaṅku, Vasiṣṭha and Viśvāmitra. The kṣatriya ballad gives a simple and natural account of Triśaṅku's fortunes as affected by those two rishis, while the brahmanical versions are a farrago of absurdities and impossibilities, utterly distorting all the incidents.[1] But it is rare that the two aspects of a story are presented so characteristically, and what is found very often is a story which suggests that it was a kṣatriya version which has been subsequently revised according to brahmanic ideas—that is, a story of the third or intermediate class. The legend of Sunaḥśepa presents different stages of this process.[2] Thus kṣatriya tales sometimes exist without brahmanic counterparts, such as the above story of king Sagara, many brahmanic tales exist without kṣatriya counterparts, and the intermediate class is abundant.

Another marked difference appears between kṣatriya tales on the one hand, and brahmanical tales and tales of an intermediate character on the other hand. In kṣatriya tales there is generally some historical consistency, but the two other classes are generally deficient in the historical sense, often revealing a total lack of it. This lack of the historical sense in ancient Indian literature is a commonplace (p. 2), but it does not hold entirely good as regards kṣatriya tradition. Before the invention of writing, genealogies, ballads and tales are practically the only literature of an historical kind that can exist. Genealogies are essentially chronological; and the old tales, especially those narrated in the course of the best

[1] Discussed in JRAS, 1913, p. 888: 1919, p. 364.

[2] Discussed in JRAS, 1917, p. 44. An absurd instance of brahmanical fancy is the story of Yayāti and his four sons (misnamed), Pad ii, *64* to *84*.

versions of the genealogies, have also an historical character. Royal genealogies certainly do not lack the historical sense, and those kṣatriya tales and ballads are generally consistent in their historical conditions. Since the brahmans did treasure up and hand down the ancient hymns, there is nothing impossible in holding that the sūtas also displayed similar care in preserving traditions committed to their charge, as pointed out in chapter II, until the Purana was compiled, and there were men and brahmans who made old tales and genealogies their special concern.

The lack of the historical sense was a special characteristic of the brahmans. The Vedic texts, notoriously, are not books of historical purpose, nor do they deal with history (p. 2). Before the introduction of writing the brahmans had, like every one else, to rely on tradition when referring to preceding times, and, even after writing was introduced, they discountenanced it so far as their religious books were concerned. There is no want of references to prior events in the Rigveda as well as some to contemporaneous occurrences, and allusions to bygone men and events were necessarily drawn from tradition, such as those to Nahuṣa, Yayāti and others, who were ancient even then. So also the mention of Yadu, Turvaśa (Turvasu), Druhyu, Anu and Pūru is generic, referring to the families and kings descended from them, and not to the progenitors themselves, who had passed away into tradition even then. Similarly as regards Bharata, his descendants are introduced, but he himself was a bygone figure.

The lack of the historical sense, especially among brahmans, while on the one hand it failed to compose genuine history or fabricated incorrect stories and fables, on the other hand has been of valuable service in that it often neglected to revise or harmonize historical tradition. Positively it was a defect, negatively it was often a safeguard, with the result that the Puranic brahmans preserved a large mass of kṣatriya and popular tradition, which was inconsistent with brahmanic stories and tenets, and the bearing of which thereon they did not perceive. Thus not seldom they unconsciously passed on traditions which are a check on brahmanic statements and often refute much of them. When we seek for explanations of the lack, differences of opinion arise. It was not for want of history. There were plenty of historical events in the earliest times (p. 3).

A reason assigned for the lack is that 'the Brahmans, whose task it would naturally have been to record great deeds, had early embraced the doctrine that all action and existence are a positive evil, and could therefore have felt but little inclination to chronicle historical events '.[1] But, as already pointed out, that was not the task of the brahmans but of the sūtas, and what they preserved was incorporated in the Puranas. When the literature of tradition passed into brahmanic custody later, the brahmans were prevented in two ways; first, since the Puranas dealt with ancient tradition, they could not incorporate into them the doings of later kings; and secondly, the above reason applied from the time when the brahmans embraced that doctrine, namely, in and after the age of the Brāhmaṇas and Upaniṣads, when, according to tradition as already explained, Puranas had been compiled.[2] Thenceforward they added no fresh historical events beyond incorporating the account of the dynasties of the Kali age. That doctrine, and its consequence that men should strive to be rid of further existence, was later than the Rigvedic age. The primitive doctrine was different. Asceticism has been practised ardently in India at all times, but its object varied. Under that doctrine it became the means of training the body and mind to a condition which ended virtually in non-existence; but in ancient times the rishis aimed at acquiring superhuman faculties and powers or the reputation of possessing them, and asceticism was the means by which that could be attained. During all that time it was the sūtas who preserved tradition.

There have been, broadly speaking, three classes among brahmans throughout Indian history, namely, (1) the ascetic devotee and teacher, the rishi or muni; (2) the priest and spiritual guide of kings, nobles and people; and (3) the minister of state, royal officer, and those who followed secular employments. The first was the brahman *par excellence*, the saint; the second the priest and preceptor; and the third the semi-secular brahman and sometimes wholly a layman. The first class, devoting itself to an ascetic life, lived apart in secluded hermitages. The second dwelt in cities and towns, ministering to their royal and other patrons, and conversant with what went on around them; they were not ordinarily religious thinkers. The third class were busied chiefly or altogether with

[1] Macdonell, *Sanskrit Literature*, p. 11.
[2] This will be shown further in chap. XXVI.

mundane affairs, and were practically brahmans only by caste;[1] they do not concern us here.

Kings performed sacrifices through their own priests, but invoked the aid of celebrated rishis also on special occasions as various stories show. Both the first and second classes appear to have composed the Rigvedic hymns, but the Brāhmaṇas and Upaniṣads were the product of the meditations and speculations of the first class. These men lived away from the world, immersed in spiritual problems and in close relation to the influences of Nature. Their religious rites, meditations and questionings were deeply and continuously concerned with the divine; the gods were very real to them. Mythology therefore was not an abstract subject, but as real to them as Nature. On the other hand, kings and political life belonged to a sphere with which they had nothing to do and of which they knew little or nothing personally; and political vicissitudes did not affect them. All that they knew of such matters was what penetrated into their seclusion through popular report and tale, mere hearsay, often less real to them than mythology and of far less importance. There was no vivid distinction between history and mythology, and naturally there was a constant tendency to confuse the two, to mythologize history and give mythology an historical garb. We can thus see why there was a total lack of the historical sense among the brahmans who composed the brahmanical literature. It is of course authoritative on the religious matters of which it treats, but one cannot extend its authority to secular matters.

The lack of the historical sense was a fertile source of confusion. It displayed itself in various ways that will be noticed now, and many other illustrations will present themselves in future chapters.[2]

First, it confused different persons of the same name. Preliminary confusion between two different persons, Bali, the Ānava king of the Eastern region, and Bali Vairocana, the demon king, is found

[1] See lists of brahmans to be excluded from śrāddhas, Manu iii, 150f.: MBh xiii, *23*, 1582–93; *90*, 4275–80: Var *190*, 84 f. Such brahmans are often alluded to. *Veda-varjita* cultivators, Pad iv, *110*, 403–4: cultivators, *113*, 204; vi, *181*, 74. *Raṅgopajīvin*, Vā *101*, 164. *Kitavāgraṇī*, Pad vi, *184*, 41. Engaged in vaiśya occupations, MBh xii, *78*, 2917 f.: Pad vi, *177*, 2–3; *238*, 6–7, 15–20. *An-āmnāya-vid*, Pad vi, *171*, 31. Cf. MBh xiii, *33*, 2094–5: Pad v, *44*, 11 f.

[2] e.g. The Maruts and Bharata, chap. XIII. The birth of a Vasiṣṭha and an Agastya from Mitra and Varuṇa, chaps. XVIII and XXII. Janamejaya II and his three sons, chap. IX.

in the story of the former,[1] where three Puranas call him Dānava and Vairocana,[2] in spite of the fact that they give his genealogy as Ānava and make no mention of any Virocana among his ancestors. Further confusion is seen in the allusions to 'king Janaka', for Janaka was the family name of the kings of Videha and various Janakas are distinguished in epic and Puranic tradition,[3] but in brahmanic literature Janaka is regarded as one king.[4] Similarly rishis of the same name were confused: thus the first Viśvāmitra is wrongly called *Bharata-ṛṣabha* in the story of Śunaḥśepa (p. 10); and this term really belonged to one of his descendants long afterwards, probably the Viśvāmitra who was priest to Sudās, i. e. Sudāsa, king of north Pañcāla, who was descended from Bharata.[5] Two other brahmanical books[6] confuse the two Viśvāmitras by reversing the blunder, in styling the descendant 'Gāthi's son', who was the first Viśvāmitra. Again, the Rāmāyaṇa wrongly identifies the Viśvāmitra of Rāma's time with the first Viśvāmitra,[7] and naïvely makes Śatānanda narrate in 'Viśvāmitra's' presence the fable of the first Viśvāmitra's discomfiture by Vasiṣṭha.[8] Similarly, the Vasiṣṭhas, of whom there were many, as will be shown in chapter XVIII, were often confused, until at length they were all regarded as one,[9] who was *cirajīvin*: and so also all the Mārkaṇḍeyas were reckoned as only one,[10] and the Bṛhaspatis are confused.[11]

An excellent instance of this kind of confusion is that of the two Sukas. One Suka had a daughter Kṛtvī or Kīrtti, who married Aṇuha king of South Pañcāla and was mother of king Brahmadatta.[12]

[1] Vā *99*, 26 f. Bḍ iii, *74*, 24–32. Mat *48*, 23 f. Hv *31*, 1682–8. Br *13*, 27–35.

[2] Vā *99*, 65, 66, 72, 97. Bḍ iii, *74*, 66, 68, 74, 99. Mat *48*, 58, 60, 89.

[3] See the notice of this dynasty in chap. VIII.

[4] See *Vedic Index* i, 271.

[5] See JRAS, 1917, p. 64; 1918, p. 236. Also chap. XXI.

[6] Bṛhadd iv, 112. Vedārth on Rigv iii, *53*.

[7] Rām i, *18*, 39–40; *51*, 15. It is brahmanic.

[8] Rām i, *51*, 12 f. See chap. XXI. The Viśvāmitras are confused in MBh xiii, *3*.

[9] MBh i, *174*, 6636–44, where several are confused.

[10] Pad v, *28*, 22, 24. MBh iii, *25*, 952–3. See chap. XVII.

[11] Including descendants. See chap. XVI.

[12] Mat *49*, 56–7. Vā *99*, 179–80. Hv *20*, 1039–44 (calling her also Kīrttimatī), 1065–6; *23*, 1241–2. Viṣ iv, *19*, 12–13. Bhāg ix, *21*, 25 (with confusion about Aṇuha). Gar i, *110*, 13 partially.

The other was Vyāsa's son,[1] far later. It will be shown in chapter XIII that Brahmadatta was a contemporary of the Kaurava king Pratīpa, and that his great great grandson Janamejaya was a contemporary of Pratīpa's great grandson Bhīṣma and of Pṛṣata (Drupada's father). Bhīṣma was of about the same age as Satyavatī, the maiden-mother of Vyāsa,[2] for he was a youth when his father Śantanu married young Satyavatī;[3] hence Vyāsa was younger than Bhīṣma, and his son Śuka was therefore at least a generation later. From Brahmadatta's grandfather Śuka down to Vyāsa's son Śuka there were therefore some six generations. The kṣatriya genealogies and traditions keep the two Śukas distinct, but the brahmanical vaṁśas in their attempt to construct Vyāsa's family identify the two, give Vyāsa's son Śuka a daughter Kīrtimatī, say she was Aṇuha's queen and Brahmadatta's mother, and so make Brahmadatta great grandson of Vyāsa,[4] thus misplacing Aṇuha and Brahmadatta from their true position to one some six generations later. Kṣatriya tradition is right, and the brahmanical lack of the historical sense produces the absurdity that Aṇuha or Brahmadatta would have been king of south Pañcāla at the time of the Bhārata battle when, as the Mahābhārata shows, Drupada was reigning there.

Another instance may be cited from the Śatapatha Brāhmaṇa (xiii, 5, 4, 9 and 21). It says that Bharata seized the sacrificial horse of the Satvants, and adds that his descendants, the Bharatas, were greater than those of any other king. Here it has confused Bharata, the famous Paurava king, with apparently Bharata, the brother of Rāma of Ayodhyā. King Bharata was long prior to the Satvants or Sātvatas, as the synchronisms and the Table of royal genealogies show (chapters XII to XIV), but Rāma and Bharata of Ayodhyā were their contemporaries, and this story is no doubt connected with the conquest of the Śūrasena territory from the Sātvatas and its occupation by Rāma's brother Śatrughna, as will be noticed in chapter XIV. It would have been this Bharata who could have carried off the sacrificial horse, and it was the

[1] MBh i, *1*, 103. Vā *73*, 28–9: &c. See chap. XVIII.

[2] The whole MBh shows this.

[3] MBh i, *100*, 4008–9, 4036–64.

[4] Bd iii, *8*, 92–4. Vā *70*, 84–6 (misreading *Aṇuha* as *Aguha*). Śrīdhara on Viṣ iv, *19*, 12 says the same. Also Kūr i, *19*, 25–7 partially. The vaṁśa in Mat *201*, 30–32 does not introduce this mistake. Consequently Kṛtvī is sometimes called Kīrtimatī, e.g. Hv *20*, 1044.

descendants of the Paurava Bharata, who were the famous Bharatas.

Secondly, the brahmans confused kings, rishis and others with mythological persons of the same names, for names were common to both then as down even to modern times.[1] A few instances of such confusion may be noticed here. Bṛhaspati, the Āṅgirasa rishi, who lived just before Bharata's time,[2] is confused with the divine priest Bṛhaspati.[3] Madhu, the great Yādava king,[4] from whom Kṛṣṇa obtained the patronymic Mādhava, is called a Daitya, a Dānava and an asura,[5] being apparently confused with the demon Madhu whom Viṣṇu killed. Such cases of confusion led to the fabrication of brahmanical fables, and not a few other fables may be suspected to have arisen through similar misunderstanding.

Another instance is that of Tapatī, wife of the Paurava king Saṁvaraṇa. She was daughter of Sūra, Sūrya, or Tapana.[6] These words are treated as meaning 'the sun',[7] and a fable is told how Saṁvaraṇa's priest, a Vasiṣṭha, went to the sun and obtained Tapatī for him.[8] But those words were probably the name of a man, for other names of the sun were used as personal names, such as Prabhākara, Divākara and Bhānu. Sūrya appears to have been a real name, for the Sūryas are spoken of along with the Bhṛgus and Kaṇvas,[9] and the patronymic Saurya is assigned to three rishis, the alleged authors of hymns x, *37*, *158* and *170*. But Tapatī's father being confused with the sun, she became the sun's daughter, and accordingly she is foisted into the myth of the sun and his wives as his daughter along with his sons Manu Vaivasvata, Yama and the Aśvins,[10] confusing historical tradition with mythology and all with an utter disregard of chronological consistency.

Thirdly, the brahmans did not always distinguish between different periods, and so often misplaced persons chronologically

[1] e.g. Śaṅkara, Viṣṇu, Nīlakaṇṭha.

[2] See the synchronisms in chap. XIII.

[3] See chaps XVI and XIX.

[4] Hv *94*, 5164.

[5] Hv *55*, 3061; *91*, 5143, 5157, 5168. Rām vii, *61*, 3, 10, 15.

[6] MBh i, *94*, 3738; *171*, 6530, 6535. Bhāg ix, *22*, 4.

[7] MBh i, *171*, 6521; *172*, 6581–3.

[8] MBh i, *173*, 6596–6610.

[9] Rigv viii, *3*, 16. Cf. i, *117*, 13; *118*, 5. Sūrya was the name of a Dānava also, MBh i, *65*, 2534–5.

[10] e.g. Mat *11*, 9. Viṣ iii, *2*, 4. Pad v, *8*, 44, 74. Var *20*, 8. Mat *11*, 39 then identifies her with some river, probably the Tāpī (modern Tapti).

and brought together as contemporaries persons who were widely separated in time. Such mistakes are innumerable, and only a few of the most glaring can be noticed here.

The brahmanical Sānti-parvan says that Bhīṣma learnt dharma from Bhārgava Cyavana (who belonged to the very earliest age), from Vasiṣṭha and Mārkaṇḍeya (these are only gotra names), and from Rāma (that is, Jāmadagnya, who was long anterior).[1] Similarly, Droṇa is said to have visited Rāma Jāmadagnya.[2] The story of Utaṅka[3] is a farrago of absurdities and chronological errors, plainly brahmanical. So the Bṛhaddevatā (iv, 112) and the Vedārthadīpikā on Rigveda iii, *53* make the first Viśvāmitra (son of Gāthi or Gādhi) contemporary with Śakti Vāsiṣṭha who was far later.[4] This chronological ignorance produces at times the most absurd positions, as where persons are made to describe events long posterior to their time; thus king Dilīpa of Ayodhyā is instructed by his priest 'Vasiṣṭha' about Kaṁsa's tyranny and Kṛṣṇa's birth.[5]

Similarly lists are sometimes given of rishis as present at some gathering, although they belonged to widely different times and could not have been all alive together. The wildest instances of this are the lists of rishis who assembled at the twelve-year sacrifice in Naimiṣa forest;[6] of those who visited Bhīṣma on his death-bed;[7] and of those who attended when Yudhiṣṭhira was installed as king.[8] Kings are sometimes jumbled together.[9] There are many other instances.[10] This lack of the historical sense must always be borne in mind when dealing with brahmanical statements in tradition; thus the order of the kings in Aitareya Brāhmaṇa vii, 5, 34 is wrong, being inverted for the most part.

Fourthly, the historical sense being lacking, the difference between reality and mythology became obliterated. So history was mythologized. The story of Tapatī discussed above illustrates this.

[1] MBh xii, *37*, 1354–6. Cf. vi, *119*, 5534: viii, *2*, 37: xii, *46*, 1570.
[2] MBh i, *130*, 5118–32. Karṇa also, viii, *34*, 1613.
[3] MBh xiv, *53*, 1542 to *58*, 1750.
[4] See among the Vasiṣṭhas, chap. XVIII.
[5] Pad iii, *13*, 8 f.
[6] Pad vi, *219*, 1–12.
[7] MBh xiii, *26*, 1760–6.
[8] MBh ii, *4*, 104–113.
[9] Pad ii, *64*, 41–3.
[10] e.g. Pad i, *39*, 111–14: v, *29*, 13–19: vi, *82*, 4–8. MBh iii, *26*, 985–8: xii, *338*, 12757–60. Rām vii, *1*, 1–6; *19*, 1–6. Hv *268*, 14537–40. Vā *106*, 33–40.

Another instance is an account of Buddhism and Jainism.[1] There was war between the gods and asuras for a divine year, and the gods being worsted besought help of Viṣṇu. He produced Māyāmoha. This being went to the asuras and Daityas at the river Narbadā and beguiled them to forsake the Veda and their own dharma and to blaspheme the Veda, &c. They became Ārhatas. Then the gods renewed the battle and destroyed them. The terms Ārhata, &c., used show that Buddhism and Jainism [2] are meant, and that river is made the place of their origin. The whole story is mythologized, the Buddhists and Jains become asuras and Daityas, and the struggle between brahmanism and them is turned into a war between gods and demons.[3]

Another excellent instance of this is the development of 'Aurva Agni'. There was a Bhārgava rishi named Urva. The traditional history about him and his descendants will be set out in chapter XVII, and here it is sufficient to state the salient points briefly. Ūrva's son was Ṛcīka, his son was Jamadagni, and his son was Rāma; and a descendant was Agni in Sagara's time. All these were therefore Aurvas. Jamadagni means 'devouring fire'—Rāma according to the brahmanical fable destroyed all kṣatriyas off the earth twenty-one times—and Aurva might be treated as meaning 'born from the thigh' (*ūru*), and also 'belonging to the earth' (*urvī*). These names and ideas developed a fable which appears in two forms. According to the first form [4] the Bhārgavas were cruelly treated by the Haihayas, Aurva was born then from his mother's thigh, blinding the Haihayas with his blaze; filled with wrath he determined to destroy the world, but cast the fire of his wrath into the sea, where it became the submarine fire. According to the second form,[5] from Ūrva's thigh was born Aurva Agni, a fuel-less fire, eager to burn up the world, but it was assigned to the submarine region, and this fire is the fire

[1] Viṣ iii, *17*, 8 to *18*, 34. Similarly, Buddhism was for the perdition of the Daityas, Pad vi, *263*, 69–70.

[2] Buddha is called *Jina-suta*, Gar i, *1*, 32.

[3] Rāma Jāmadagnya's war with the Haihayas (chap. XXIV) seems to be the basis of his devāsura war in MBh viii, *34*, 1584–1612, similarly.

[4] MBh i, *178*, 6815 to *180*, 6863: very briefly in xiii, *56*, 2905–9. The whole matter is discussed in JRAS, 1919, pp. 364 f.

[5] Mat *175*, 23–62. Pad v, *38*, 74–112. Hv *46*, 2527–69.

which will destroy the world at the dissolution [1] and is identified with Viṣṇu.[2]

Another instance is the curious Pitṛ-vaṁśa.[3] The seven classes of Pitṛs had each one mind-born daughter (*mānasī kanyā*), namely, Menā, Acchodā (-Satyavatī), Pīvarī, Go, Yaśodā, Virajā and Narmadā. The account (subject to minor variations) stands thus. Menā was wife of Mount Himavant. They had a son Mount Maināka and three daughters, Aparṇā, Ekaparṇā and Ekapāṭalā. Aparṇā became the goddess Umā; Ekaparṇā married the rishi Asita and had a son the rishi Devala; and Ekapāṭalā married Sataśilāka's son, the rishi Jaigīṣavya, and had two sons, Saṅkha and Likhita. Acchodā, the river, transgressing against the Pitṛs, was born as a low-caste maiden (*dāseyī*) from king Vasu of Cedi and a fish who was the apsaras Adrikā; and she became (Kālī) Satyavatī, who was mother of Vyāsa by Parāśara, and of Vicitravīrya and Citrāṅgada [4] by king Śantanu. Pīvarī was wife of Vyāsa's son Śuka, and had five sons and a daughter Kīrtimatī who was Aṇuha's queen and Brahmadatta's mother.[5] Go, called also Ekaśṛṅgā, married the great rishi Śukra and was ancestress of the Bhṛgus. Yaśodā was wife of Viśvamahat, daughter-in-law of Vṛddhaśarman, and mother of Dilīpa II Khaṭvāṅga.[6] Virajā was wife of Nahuṣa and mother of Yayāti.[7] Narmadā, the river, was wife of Purukutsa and mother of Trasadasyu.[8]

[1] Also Mat *2*, 5. See *ibid.* *51*, 29–30: Vā *47*, 76: Bḍ ii, *18*, 79–80, with which cf. Rigv viii, *102*, 4 (*samudra-vāsas*).

[2] Hv *41*, 2149. Vā *97*, 18. Bḍ iii, *72*, 17. Cf. MBh iii, *189*, 12961, 12966–7.

[3] Vā *72*, 1–19; *73*, 1–49. Bḍ iii, *10*, 1–21, 52–98. Hv *18*, 932–99. Br *34*, 41–2, 81–93. Mat *13*, 2–9; *14*, 1 to *15*, 28. Pad v, *9*, 2–56. Also Vā *77*, 32, 74–6. Bḍ iii, *13*, 32, 76–9. Lg i, *6*, 5–9; *70*, 331; *82*, 14–15: ii, *45*, 88.

[4] Mat and Pad (*loc. cit.*) wrongly say they were *kṣetraja* sons. Vicitravīrya's sons, Dhṛtarāṣṭra and Pāṇḍu, were *kṣetraja* by Vyāsa.

[5] This statement is wrong, as shown above.

[6] Three kings of Ayodhyā, see Table of Genealogies in chap. XII. Viśvamahat = Viśvasaha, &c. Vṛddhaśarman = Viśvaśarman, Kṛtaśarman, &c.

[7] Two early kings of the Lunar race, see same Table.

[8] Two kings of Ayodhyā. The genealogies say Purukutsa's wife was Narmadā, without connecting her with the river, Vā *88*, 74: Bḍ iii, *63*, 73 (which has lost 3 lines): Br *7*, 95–6: Hv *12*, 714–5: Śiv vii, *60*, 79: Kūr i, *20*, 27–8: Gar i, *138*, 24. Women in ancient times bore the same names as rivers, see chap. XI. So also Viṣ iv, *3*, 6–12 and Bhāg

Here genuine genealogy is mixed up with mythology, and the whole of this vaṃśa of the Pitṛ-kanyās arose out of a misunderstanding of this word. The genealogies say that Nahuṣa's sons were born of *pitṛ-kanyā* Virajā,[1] connect a *pitṛ-kanyā* with Viśvamahat,[2] and call Kṛtvī a *pitṛ-kanyā*.[3] There can be no doubt that the word meant 'father's daughter', that is 'sister', for union between brother and sister was not unknown, as Rigveda x, *10* about Yama and Yamī shows. Nahuṣa and Viśvamahat married their sisters or half-sisters, and the same may be presumed of Purukutsa and probably of Śukra and Śuka. But the brahmans misunderstood or perverted the word to mean 'daughter of the Pitṛs'[4] (and therefore 'mind-born'), thus mythologizing it, and extended its use. Satyavatī, as a queen and great grandmother of the Pāṇḍavas, was ennobled by the kṣatriyas in the fable making her the offspring of Vasu, king of Cedi;[5] and, as mother of the great Vyāsa, by the brahmans in the additional fable that she was a daughter of the Pitṛs.[6] Menā was purely mythological, but Ekaparṇā and Ekapāṭalā[7] were mistakenly conjoined with Aparṇā-Umā, probably through some similarity in names, much as in the case of Tapatī discussed above.

The converse also occurred: mythology was not only freely brought into tales but was also turned into history. Thus Śiva and Pārvatī are introduced into the account of the long war between the Haihayas and the kings of Kāśi[8] dealt with in chapter XIII; and Indra into the story of Vasiṣṭha, Viśvāmitra and Triśaṅku and that of Hariścandra and Rohita mentioned above.[9] The aitihāsikas also,

ix, *7*, 1–3, but imply her identity with the river. Mat *12*, 36 (where for *Vasudo* read *Trasado*) and Ag *272*, 25 wrongly make her wife of Trasadasyu. Pad v, *8*, 140 goes further wrong, making her wife of (Trasadasyu's son) Sambhūta. The identification of her with the river was a later fancy, as in MBh xv. *20*, 549–50.

[1] Vā *93*, 12. Br *12*, 1. Hv *30*, 1599. Kūr i, *22*, 5. Lg i, *66*, 60–1.

[2] In Vā *88*, 181–2 (*putrikasya*) and Bḍ iii, *63*, 181–2 (*putrikasyāṁ*) read *pitṛ-kanyā*. Lg i, *66*, 31, with Vṛddhaśarman.

[3] Hv *23*, 1242–3.

[4] It is applied to Satyavatī in MBh xii, *351*, 13688 as *pitṛ-kanyakā*, which is rendered in Pratap Ch. Ray's translation, 'a maiden residing in the house of her sire'.

[5] Told in MBh i, *63*, 2371–99. Alluded to, Vā *1*, 40–1.

[6] Alluded to, Vā *1*, 176. [7] They are also names of Umā, Vā *9*, 86.

[8] Vā *92*, 29–61. Bḍ iii, *67*, 32–64. Hv *29*, 1549–82.

[9] But *Indra* in both is probably a perverted misunderstanding of *Devarāj* (Vasiṣṭha), JRAS. 1913, p. 903: 1917, pp. 39, 54, 63.

pushing their method to an extreme, declared that the Aśvins were two kings.[1]

Fifthly, the brahmans freely misapplied historical or other tradition to new places and conditions to subserve religious ends. Thus they transferred the story of Hariścandra, Rohita and Śunaḥśepa[2] and that of Purūravas[3] to the Godāvarī in order to enhance its glory in the Gautamī-māhātmya. They connected Rāma with the R. Lauhitya (Brahmaputra),[4] and Urvaśī with that river[5] and also Mt. Malaya.[6]

Sixthly, the brahmans took some person or incident from historical tradition and freely fabricated edifying religious tales thereon, such as those of kings Hariścandra,[7] Śūrasena[8] and Jayadhvaja.[9]

Each of these classes of tradition may now be considered more in detail.

Kṣatriya tradition comprises genealogies, tales, notices and allusions. The genealogies will be dealt with fully in chapters VII to IX. The tales are of two kinds—those that appear to be historical and those that manifestly are merely laudatory. The former are generally told simply and naturally without excessive exaggeration, and have the appearance of being ancient and genuine, for it is very improbable that they could have been the work of Puranic brahmans, so that they must have belonged to the ancient kṣatriya traditions preserved by the sūtas. They are most trustworthy when narrated simply. The best occur in the genealogies, such as the Puranic stories of Satyavrata-Triśaṅku and Sagara, mentioned above; and others that occur elsewhere are those of Duṣyanta and Śakuntalā,[10] Saṁvaraṇa and Vasiṣṭha,[11] Bhīṣma and Ugrāyudha.[12] They are open to doubt the more they are elaborated and amplified, the most striking example being the detailed account of the early kings of the Vaiśālī dynasty in the Mārkaṇḍeya,[13] wherein occur many anachronisms such as the introduction of Agastya in the earliest times (*115*, 16).

[1] Nirukta xii, 1. [2] Br *104*. [3] Br *101* : *108*; and *175*, 64 (?).
[4] MBh iii, *85*, 8144. [5] *Ibid.* xiii, *25*, 1732.
[6] *Ibid.* xii, *334*, 12597. [7] Mārk *7* to *8*. [8] Br *111*.
[9] Kūr i, *22*, 21–80.
[10] MBh i, *69*, 2816 to *71*, 2913; *73*, 2955 to *74*, 3110.
[11] MBh i, *173* 6617–30. [12] Hv *20*, 1085–1110.
[13] Chapters *113–136* and *109–110*.

The laudatory tales are not generally of historical value, for they are often exaggerated, sometimes absurd or impossible, and frequently violate chronology, such as Rāma Dāśarathi's alleged fight with Rāma Jāmadagnya [1] and that of Bhīṣma with the same,[2] for Rāma Jāmadagnya lived long before them : but sometimes such tales are expressed in less extravagant terms, such as the praise of Arjuna Kārtavīrya [3] and Māndhātṛ,[4] though even these are highly coloured.

All tales however narrated in the genealogies are not kṣatriya tradition, and some are patently brahmanical, such as those of the rishi Saubhari and Māndhātṛ's fifty daughters,[5] of king Vasumanas,[6] and of king Jayadhvaja and his brothers.[7] The first is a pure brahmanic marvel, the second conveys a brahmanic discourse, and the third extols Viṣṇu's supremacy. The contrast between these and true kṣatriya tradition is striking and unmistakable, and such stories inserted in the genealogies are generally found only in the later Puranas.

Notices and allusions occur in the genealogies and elsewhere, and are most trustworthy when introduced naturally, appropriately and simply, such as the mention of Gaurī and her son king Māndhātṛ in the Paurava genealogy,[8] that of Datta Ātreya in connexion with Arjuna Kārtavīrya,[9] and of king Kṛta as disciple of Hiraṇyanābha Kausalya.[10] The Brahmāṇḍa, Vāyu, Brahma, Harivaṁśa and Matsya have the best and most valuable allusions of this kind; others have few, and some have none, such as the Garuḍa and Agni, because they are merely late and concise compilations. Where notices and allusions occur in tales or discourses, their value depends greatly on their context, and they are *per se* the less trustworthy, the more their context is brahmanical, because the brahmans

[1] MBh iii, *99*, 8658–82. Rām i, *74*, 17 to *76*, 24. Pad vi, *269*, 154–179

[2] MBh v, *178*, 7049 to *187*, 7336. Alluded to, i, *67*, 2711–2: v, *116*, 4980; *167*, 5840: vii, *3*, 113: xii, *27*, 806.

[3] Vā *94*, 20 f. Bḍ iii, *69*, 21 f. Mat *43*, 24 f.: &c.

[4] Vā *88*, 67–9. Bḍ iii, *63*, 68–70. MBh vii, *62* : xii, *29*, 974–85.

[5] Viṣ iv, *2*, 19 to *3*, 3. Bhāg ix, *6*, 38–55. Bṛhadd vi, 50–7. Pad vi, *232*, 16, 33–82. Gar i, *138*, 23.

[6] Kūr i, *20*, 31–76. [7] Kūr i, *22*, 21–80.

[8] Bḍ iii, *63*, 66–8. Vā *88*, 64–7. See chap. VI.

[9] Vā *94*, 10. Bḍ iii, *69*, 10. Mat *43*, 15 : &c.

[10] Mat *49*, 75–6. Hv *20*, 1081–2. Vā *99*, 190–1.

lacked the historical sense: thus, for instance in the brahmanical version of the story of Śunaḥśepa the appellation *Bharata-ṛṣabha* given to Viśvāmitra is entirely wrong as mentioned above; and so also the introduction of Agastya into a story about king Nahuṣa,[1] for the Agastyas did not exist then.

Taking next brahmanical tradition and considering those tales only that profess to have a historical basis, three groups may be distinguished:—(1) those that extol rishis and brahmans, (2) those that advocate or describe the merits of tīrthas, and (3) those that commend religious doctrines, rites and observances. Such tales too often indulge in marvels or impossibilities, and it is not always easy to divide the quasi-historical tales from fables that are mythological, for the former have a tendency to treat their subject-matter in a mythological way or to introduce mythology. With this qualification some instances of the three groups may be given.

In the first group may be mentioned the story of the rishi Saubhari's marrying the fifty daughters of Māndhātṛ, king of Ayodhyā,[2] that of Jamadagni's death and Rāma's killing the kṣatriyas off the earth twenty-one times,[3] and the extraordinary tale of Gālava and Yayāti's daughter,[4] to which was fabricated a sequel about Yayāti and his daughter's sons,[5] which is wholly fabulous. Some of such tales appear to have been developed out of incidental statements. Thus the story of Saubhari seems to have grown out of the statement in Rigveda viii, *19*, 36, that Trasadasyu Paurukutsya gave Sobhari fifty maidens. That king was different from Trasadasyu Paurukutsa, grandson of Māndhātṛ, the Kākutstha, king of Ayodhyā, as will be shown in chapter XI, but the two Trasadasyus were confused, so that the Bṛhaddevatā says the maidens were Kākutstha maidens and thus implies that the Trasadasyu of the hymn was the Ayodhyā king, and adds that Sobhari obtained magnificent boons from Indra. The Viṣṇu improved

[1] MBh v, *16*, 521. For the Agastyas, see chap. XXII.

[2] See seventh note above.

[3] MBh iii, *116*, 11089 to *117*, 10210 (there is a mistake in the numbering). No kṣatriya could have put such a story about, manifestly untrue and so discreditable to his class.

[4] MBh v, *113* f.

[5] MBh i, *88*, 3569 to *93*, 3690. Mat *35* to *42*. Cf. MBh iii, *197*, 13301–2.

thereon by definitely making the maidens Māndhātṛ's daughters, by describing those boons as in real existence and by adding many fanciful incidents. The Bhāgavata copied from the Viṣṇu.

Tales about tīrthas (the second group) generally introduce the marvellous or mythology, and it is rare to find any that are rational. So also tales that commend doctrines, rites and observances (the third group) are much the same in their character. Yet a few may be discovered that are rather of an ordinary kind, such as, among the former class, the story of Āpastamba-tīrtha,[1] and that of Bhānu-tīrtha where however the collocation of Madhucchandas with Śaryāti is absurd;[2] and among the latter class, the story of king Suvrata[3] and that of some of Kṛṣṇa's wives who were ravished by bandits after his death.[4]

Brahmanic tales generally are untrustworthy for traditional history, because of the lack of the historical sense; yet sometimes they introduce allusions of an historical kind incidentally, as well as geographical particulars and notices of other matters, and these are useful and sometimes even valuable; but the historical allusions can hardly be trusted of themselves, and should not be relied on unless they are corroborated from elsewhere. The Rāmāyaṇa is highly brahmanical and its stories fanciful and often absurd.

Next comes the intermediate class of stories that show both kṣatriya and brahmanical traits and sentiments combined. These are plainly composite. Since the kṣatriya features are older than the brahmanic as pointed out above, such stories must have been of kṣatriya origin and have been touched up afterwards by the Puranic brahmans. The reverse is not credible from what has been explained about the development of the Puranas. These stories display all grades of modification from tales that are mainly kṣatriya to tales that have become essentially brahmanic. Generally it is possible to trace out the modification only when different versions of the same story exist; but in most cases, while it is fairly evident that modification has taken place, it can only be conjectured what the changes have been.

Kṣatriya stories were often tampered with to subserve brahmanical interests, and different stages of this can be detected. Preliminary

[1] Br *130*. [2] Br *138*. [3] Pad vi, *238*, 6 f.

[4] Mat *70*, 11 f. Pad v, *23*, 74 f.: vi, *279*, 86, 93. MBh xvi, *7*, 222 f. But other statements seemingly differ, Lg i, *69*, 88–90.

tampering is found in the Vāyu version of the story of Satyavrata Triśaṅku;[1] further tampering in the Vāyu account of king Janamejaya III's contest with the brahmans;[2] and still more in the story of king Mitrasaha Kalmāṣapāda, as the various versions show.[3] Where different versions do not exist, we can yet perceive that there has been tampering, as in the story of Agastya and Lopāmudrā.[4] The furthest development occurs where the brahmans took some incident in kṣatriya tradition and enlarged it, till their story loses all resemblance to a kṣatriya tale and becomes a brahmanical fable, as in the above story of Aurva.

It is mainly the brahmanical mistakes and absurdities that have discredited the Puranas. If, however, we put them aside and consider statements and stories that are evidently of kṣatriya origin and have not been over-tampered with by the brahmans, it is remarkable what an amount of consistency they reveal, though unconnected and drawn from different contexts.

The fourth class of stories is connected with names and comprises two kinds, first, statements or anecdotes that provide explanations of names, and secondly, statements or anecdotes that have grown from misunderstanding or misapplication of names.

Of the first kind, some appear to be ancient and may be genuine, such as the explanation of *Pañcāla* from *pañca alam*, which began as a jocose nickname, the 'Five capables', given to the five sons of king Bhṛmyaśva in consequence of a jocular boast of his;[5] of the nickname *Nandanodaradundubhi* of a Yādava king;[6] and possibly of the name *Triśaṅku*.[7] But most of such stories have been coined out of the names themselves, sometimes fanciful, sometimes mistaken, and sometimes absurd. Some no doubt arose from popular etymology, but many were certainly the invention of Puranic brahmans. Some may be fairly old, though silly, as that Ikṣvāku was so named because Manu sneezed,[8] and that Śaśāda got his name

[1] Vā *88*, 78 f.: JRAS, 1913, pp. 889, 894, note [1], 895, note [1].
[2] Vā *99*, 250–5 compared with Mat *50*, 57–64.
[3] See chap. XVIII. [4] MBh iii, *96*, 8553 to *99*, 8644.
[5] Vā *99*, 197–8. Mat *50*, 4. Hv *32*, 1779–80. Br *13*, 95–6. Viṣ iv. *19*, 15. Bhāg ix, *21*, 32–3. JRAS, 1910, p. 48: 1914, p. 284: 1918, p. 238.
[6] Mat *44*, 63. Corrupted, Vā *96*, 117: Bd iii, *71*, 118: Viṣ iv, *14*, 4: Lg i, *69*, 34: Ag *274*, 29. Kūr i, *24*, 49–54 explains it.
[7] Vā *88*, 109. Bd iii, *63*, 108. Br *7*, 19. Hv *13*, 749. Lg i, *66*. 7.
[8] Vā *88*, 9. Br *7*, 44. Viṣ iv, *2*, 3: &c.

because he ate a hare.[1] But many, if not most, are obviously late fabrications, being sometimes fashioned with grotesque ingenuity, such as those explaining the names Māndhātṛ,[2] Videha,[3] Jarāsandha,[4] Gāndinī[5] and Bharadvāja.[6] These are quite on a par with similar explanations in brahmanical books, such as those of Atri,[7] Ayāsya and Aṅgiras,[8] and yūpa.[9]

Of the second kind appear to be the following. Kurukṣetra was so named because king Kuru ploughed it,[10] whereas it really denoted that it was his cultivated territory,[11] east of which lay his tract (apparently less cultivated) called Kurujāṅgala.[12] Sītā received her name, because her father Sīradhvaja[13] found her in a furrow (sītā),[14] whereas it was a natural feminine name expressing the idea of human propagation found in *kṣetra, kṣetraja* and *bīja* (cf. *Ahalyā*); and the mistake led on to the epithet *ayonijā* given her.[15] Arjuna Kārtavīrya had a thousand arms (*bāhu-sahasra*),[16] whereas it seems probable he had the name Sahasrabāhu.[17]

It is clear therefore that the kṣatriya tales found in the Puranas, especially those that are genuinely kṣatriya, belonged to the ancient body of tradition prior to the composition of the Purana. This is

[1] Br *7,* 50. Vā *88,* 12–24. Viṣ iv, *2,* 6: &c.

[2] MBh iii, *126,* 10452–3: xii, *29,* 976–7.

[3] Briefly Vā *89,* 4: Bḍ iii, *64,* 4. Differently, Mat *61,* 32–3. Otherwise Viṣ iv, *5,* 1–5.

[4] Vā *99,* 226. Mat *50,* 31–2. Amplified, MBh ii, *17,* 739.

[5] Vā *96,* 105–8. Bḍ iii, *71,* 106–9. Br *16,* 51. Hv *39,* 2082.

[6] Vā *99,* 140–50. Mat *49,* 17–25. Viṣ iv, *19,* 5–7.

[7] Bṛhad Āraṇyaka Upaniṣad ii, 2, 4.

[8] *Ibid.* i, 3, 8 and 19. Bloomfield, *Atharvaveda,* p. 107.

[9] Aitar. Brāhm. ii, 1, 1.

[10] Vā *99,* 115–6. Mat *50,* 20–1. MBh ix, *54,* 3009 f.

[11] MBh i, *94,* 3739: iii, *129,* 10535. Defined, ix, *54.* Noticed, ix, *39,* 2211–3.

[12] MBh i, *126,* 4901–6: ii, *19,* 793: v, *152,* 5191, 5195: cf. v, *53,* 2127. Rām ii, *68,* 13 (the two lines should be inverted) where Kurujāṅgala is used by an anachronism. Kurukṣetra is also used sometimes by anticipation.

[13] This was a real name. Cf. *Halāyudha, Lāṅgaladhvaja,* MBh v, *3,* 44.

[14] Rām i, *66,* 13–14: ii, *118,* 28–9. Vā *89,* 15–17. Bḍ iii, *64,* 15–18. Pad vi, *269,* 99–103.

[15] Rām i, *66,* 15. Br *154,* 12, 24. Viṣ iv, *4,* 42.

[16] Vā *94,* 11, 15, &c. Mat *43,* 14, 16, &c. Hv *33,* 1851–3. MBh xiii, *152,* 7187, but he had ordinarily only two at home, *ibid.* 7191.

[17] Mat *68,* 10. Ag *4,* 14. This was a name, so also *Sahasrapad,* see Sörensen's Index.

a very important conclusion. The Puranic brahmans took over the kṣatriya traditions; some they preserved without modification; but others they re-shaped more or less according to brahmanic ideas, and these form a considerable portion of the intermediate or combined class mentioned above. Different stages of that process are discernible, as has been noticed.

CHAPTER VI

THE PURANAS AND THEIR GENEALOGICAL TEXTS

THE genealogies of the ancient dynasties are the chief data of an historical kind, and the investigation of traditional history must begin with them. They are given more or less fully by all the Puranas, except the late Varāha, Vāmana, Skanda, Nāradīya and Brahmavaivarta, and the Bhaviṣya which does not deal with the ancient past. Some are found in the Mahābhārata and Rāmāyaṇa. All the accounts are in verse in the śloka metre, except some parts in the Mahābhārata and most of the Viṣṇu. The most important Puranas as regards genealogies are the Vāyu and Brahmāṇḍa, the Brahma and Harivaṁśa, the Matsya (with book V of the Padma) and the Viṣṇu.

The Vāyu and Brahmāṇḍa have the best text of the genealogies. Their accounts agree closely, so that they are really only two versions of the same text. They have a great part of their contents in common, generally almost verbatim, and it appears they were originally one Purana. This is indicated also by the lists given in the Puranas.[1] Nearly all mention the Brahmāṇḍa, putting it last, and omit the Vāyu, though it was one of the best known. The Kūrma[2] also mentions it last and calls it the Vāyavīya Brahmāṇḍa. The Vāyu and Brahmāṇḍa are named separately only in the Vāyu itself and the Garuḍa.[3] These lists are of course late

[1] Mat *53*, 11–58. Viṣ iii, *6*, 22–4. Lg i, *39*, 61–3. Var *112*, 69–72. Pad i, *62*, 2–7: iv, *111*, 90–4: vi, *219*, 25–7; *263*, 77–84. Śiv v, *1*, 38–40. Mārk, p. 659; my translation *137*, 8–11.
[2] Kūr i, *1*, 13–15.
[3] Vā *104*, 2–11 (*Anila*). Gar i, *215*, 15–16 (*Vāyavīya*).

insertions, which could not have been completed till after the latest of these Puranas was composed; yet they show that the two were not regarded as distinct and the differentiation of the one original into two versions with separate names was a later process. Both these Puranas say they were declared by the god Vāyu;[1] thus both were *Vāyu-prokta* and either might be so described; but the use of the name Brahmāṇḍa in the above lists to the general exclusion of the name Vāyu suggests that Brahmāṇḍa was the older and better-known name. Their version may be conveniently called the 'Vāyu version'.

The editions cited are the Ānandāśrama for the Vāyu, and the Veṅkaṭeśvara for the Brahmāṇḍa. Where they differ, the former is generally preferable, because the latter is not a critical edition, and also appears to have been silently emended by the editor, as, for instance, where it reads *iti śrutaḥ* and *viśrutaḥ* instead of *iti śrutiḥ* (p. 19), and probably where it avoids a difficulty by substituting *yogeśvarasya* for *Pauroravasya* (i.e. *Paurūravasya*).[2] But the Vāyu is not invariably better, because sometimes corruptions have passed undetected in it, as where the Viṣṇuvṛddhas have been misplaced,[3] and where it reads Ayāsya's name wrongly.[4] The Brahmāṇḍa has unfortunately one very serious lacuna in its account after iii, *74*, 103, where the latter half of the Ānava genealogy, the whole of that of the Pauravas, and a portion of the Kali age dynasties have been lost, namely, all the matter contained in Vāyu *99*, 102–290. These two appear to be the oldest of the Puranas that we possess now, and are on the whole the most valuable in all matters of traditional history.

The Brahma and Harivaṁśa agree closely in their genealogical account and have practically the same text, subject to small variations. The Brahma is cited from the Ānandāśrama edition. The Harivaṁśa text (Calcutta edition) is better than the Brahma, for the latter has suffered through losses; thus it is manifestly incomplete in the North Pañcāla genealogy, and most copies of it omit the Cedi-Magadha dynasty descended from Kuru (chapter IX). Their version is very similar to the 'Vāyu version', and has the same basis, and appears to be a revision of that version. Sometimes it has omissions, sometimes additions which seem to contain genuine

[1] Vā *1*, 47, 196; *2*, 44. Bd i, *1*, 36.

[2] Bd iii, *66*, 74. Vā *91*, 102. Cf. Hv *27*, 1468; *32*, 1773 and Br *10*, 63. See Kānyakubja dynasty in chap. IX.

[3] Vā *88*, 79. See chap. XXIII. [4] Vā *59*, 101 with Bd ii, *32*, 110.

tradition, sometimes it varies, and sometimes it makes mistakes. It may be called the 'Harivaṁśa version'. It is manifestly later than the 'Vāyu version', and this is best illustrated by the fact that it gives two incompatible origins for the Kānyakubja and Kāśi dynasties, one in each case being necessarily wrong, devised at a later time when erroneous views had obtained currency.

The genealogical record in the Matsya has peculiarities. It may be considered in three parts, (1) its account of the Aikṣvākus, Śāryātas and other sons of Manu, (2) its account of the early Ailas down to Yayāti, and (3) its genealogies of the five Aila races, Yādavas, Pauravas, &c. This third part resembles the 'Vāyu version', and appears to be based on the same original text, and to be not a revision but a distinct version which early became separate. Its variations are additions, omissions, condensations and sometimes corruptions; and on the whole its agreement with the 'Vāyu version' occurs more in the strictly genealogical statements and less in the incidental or collateral matter. The two other parts (1) and (2) differ from the 'Vāyu version', the verses being quite different. The pedigrees are in the main the same, though there are wide divergencies or corruptions in names in the second part and marked disagreements at several stages in the first part. In the first part the account is very concise, without any of the tales and allusions that diversify the 'Vāyu version'. The second part is briefer than the 'Vāyu version', the legends are narrated differently, and some interpolations occur. On the whole the Matsya record is a valuable and in many points independent authority.

The genealogical account in the Padma[1] is in book V, and is practically the same as the Matsya version so far as it goes, the differences being generally small and verbal. It is therefore valuable as a means of checking the Matsya text.

The Viṣṇu account is mainly in prose, with old verses introduced occasionally. It is generally in agreement with the 'Vāyu and Harivaṁśa versions' in the structure of its genealogies, sometimes agreeing rather with the former as in the Aikṣvāku dynasty, and sometimes rather with the latter as in the cases of the Yādavas and Pauravas; but it also has omissions, variations, additions, and 'embellishments' of its own. It leaves out some of the incidents

[1] Ānandāśrama edition.

in those versions, condenses others (as for instance, the famous story of Satyavrata Triśaṅku of Ayodhyā [1]), and adds others again, which are brahmanical fables (as the story of the rishi Saubhari and king Māndhātṛ's daughters) [2] or brahmanized legends (as the story of king Kalmāṣapāda),[3] or tales that seem to have some basis of genuine tradition but have been half mythologized (as the story of Purukutsa and Narmadā).[4] The verses it intersperses are manifestly quotations from older metrical versions, and agree sometimes with the Vāyu and Harivaṁśa versions. It is a late Purana, composed as a single whole upon a consistent plan, and not a collection of materials of various times, as we find in the Vāyu, Brahma and Matsya. From its account of Buddhism and Jainism (p. 68) it appears to have been composed after brahmanism had recovered its supremacy, so that it cannot be earlier than about the fifth century, A.D.[5] and it is brahmanical.

Three other Puranas contain all or nearly all the genealogies, the Garuḍa, Agni [6] and Bhāgavata.[7] Their accounts are all late re-compilations, the Bhāgavata being one of the very latest, about the ninth century A.D. They do not reproduce any of the old verses except rarely, but have re-stated the genealogies in fresh verses, generally in more condensed form. The Garuḍa and Agni give merely bald pedigrees with hardly any incidental allusions. The Garuḍa and Bhāgavata follow the Vāyu tradition as regards the Aikṣvākus, and the Agni the Matsya tradition. As regards the other dynasties, all three follow in a general way the common tradition. The Bhāgavata has used the Viṣṇu in its composition, and so also has the Garuḍa apparently. All three however have peculiarities of their own. The Agni has erred seriously as regards the Kānyakubja and Kāśi dynasties. The Bhāgavata is fuller and contains stories and allusions, which show a marked brahmanical colouring and some corruptions; and it has taken considerable liberties with names. These three Puranas have no authority as regards the genealogies, yet are of use for

[1] iv, *3*, 13–14. [2] iv, *2*, 19 to *3*, 3. P. 73.

[3] iv, *4*, 20–38. [4] iv, *3*, 7–12.

[5] The list of the Puranas in Viṣ iii, *6*, 22–4 could not have been completed until the Bhāgavata and other very late Puranas had come into existence.

[6] Both in Jīvānanda Vidyāsāgar's editions.

[7] The Gaṇapata-Kṛṣṇājī edition.

comparison, and sometimes elucidate the older accounts. The Bhāgavata has a special value, where it restates traditions, found in the older Puranas, that do not harmonize with brahmanical assertions and pretensions and could not have originated with the brahmans; for the fact that it, a thoroughly brahmanical composition, affirms such traditions, is very strong testimony that the traditions were genuine and could not be discarded. It will be often cited therefore in this way.

The Liṅga account is based on the 'Vāyu version', but adapts it to frame its own text. Often it has the same verses, but often also it modifies, curtails, and freely omits, especially incidental and descriptive matter; and it adds occasionally.[1] It also interpolates religious teaching, as where it introduces a long eulogy of Rudra (i, *65*, 46 f.). It however shows traces of the influence of the Matsya version; thus it has the same verses sometimes,[2] and ends the Aikṣvāku genealogy with six kings instead of the Vāyu's twenty-one, just as the Matsya does. The Liṅga is useful for collating with the 'Vāyu version' when the verses agree, and for comparison where they vary; thus, it suggests (i, *65*, 42–3) that the Vāyu's misplaced lines (*88*, 79[b, c]) about the Viṣṇuvṛddhas[3] should probably come after verse 74.

The Kūrma account is a composite production. Now and again it has a few lines like the Vāyu text,[4] and like the Matsya text,[5] in the Aikṣvāku genealogy, but it follows the Matsya rather, where they differ. It is a late composition and shows brahmanical features; thus it omits most of the Vāyu's tales and introduces brahmanical fabrications instead: for instance, it makes Gautama (who was far later) a contemporary of Yuvanāśva I,[6] and tells long fables about king Vasumanas[7] and the Haihaya kings Jayadhvaja and Durjaya.[8]

The Śiva gives only the account of Manu and his offspring (vii, *60*, 1), the Aikṣvākus (ibid., 33) and the Śāryātas (ibid., 20). Its text is similar to that of the 'Harivaṁśa version', but is less accurate and shortens or omits incidental and descriptive matter.

[1] e.g. compare Lg i, *66*, 1 f. with Vā *88*, 77 f.
[2] e.g. Lg i, *66*, 14[b]–20[a] agree with Mat *12*, 39–44.
[3] Bd iii, *63*, 70–80 omit these lines. Cf. Kūr i, *20*, 28.
[4] Thus Kūr i, *21*, 16[a] and 17 agree with Vā *88*, 183[a] and 184.
[5] Kūr i, *21*, 4–8[a] are part of Mat *12*, 39–44.
[6] i, *20*, 13–18.
[7] i, *20*, 32–76.
[8] i, *22*, 22–80; *23*, 6–44.

The Mārkaṇḍeya gives only the account of Manu's offspring (chaps. 111, 112) and the early part of the Vaiśāla dynasty (chaps. 113–36, 109–10), and it narrates the latter at immense length with abundant imaginative description. Its text is its own.

The accounts in the Mahābhārata[1] are peculiar. They are partly in verse and partly in prose, and do not appear to be ancient. They will be noticed in connexion with the genealogies that they treat of.

The Rāmāyaṇa[2] is, as it professes to be, altogether a brahmanical book. Some of its genealogies agree with those in the Puranas, and where it differs from them, as in the Aikṣvāku line, it is manifestly wrong, as will be shown in chapter VIII. The legends it narrates or mentions are generally distorted according to brahmanical notions and through the brahmanical lack of the historical sense.[3]

In examining the genealogies it is of little profit and is likely to be misleading to deal with the accounts in the several Puranas separately. The only trustworthy course is first to collate the texts that generally agree and ascertain as far as possible what original text they indicate, and then construct the genealogy therefrom. By this method individual corruptions and errors can be corrected, losses and omissions remedied, and interpolations and alterations detected with reasonable confidence; and thus a text may be framed which approaches as nearly as is possible to the common original on which all those texts were based. At times divergences occur which are greater than can be so resolved, and we find competing texts, yet they are not on the whole so frequent or serious as to cause material difficulty; and small discrepancies do not really affect the general fabric of the genealogy.

The method here advocated cannot be merely one of pure verbal criticism; some scope must be allowed to discrimination and judgement based on a general study of the Puranic texts. Whether one's individual decisions on the reconstruction of the passages be sound or not must be tested by study devoted to the Puranas; but the principle is sound and provides the only sane way in which these genealogies can be examined. This is the method used here. The texts of the Puranas have been collated throughout, wherever

[1] Calcutta edition. [2] Bombay edition.

[3] e. g. its statement that Yadu was virtually a rākṣasa and his offspring were rākṣasas and yātudhānas (vii, 59, 14, 15, 20) is outrageous.

doubtful points arose; and wherever it is essential to elucidate the discussion, the text that appears to be most probably the nearest approach to the original common text is quoted. It will be often found that, though there may be scope for difference in the selection of particular words in framing the text, yet that does not affect the general sense of the passages, the purport being clear, though the words selected may vary. As an illustration of the advantage of collating the texts may be given the following passage, which shows how important may be what appear to be stray readings.

In the Solar line of Ayodhyā there were three early kings, Prasenajit, his son Yuvanāśva, and his son Māndhātṛ. The Brahmāṇḍa and Vāyu say Gaurī was Yuvanāśva's wife—

atyanta-dhārmikā Gaurī tasya patnī pati-vratā

and call her son Māndhātṛ *Gaurika*.[1] But the Brahma, Harivaṁśa and Śiva say Gaurī was Prasenajit's wife, thus making her Māndhātṛ's grandmother.[2] The question arises, which of these accounts is right? Now there was in the Paurava line an early king whose name is given as Matināra,[3] Antināra[4] and Ratināra,[5] and we may adopt Matināra as the form most often found, though Atināra may be the true original. The Vāyu, Matsya, and Harivaṁśa itself say he had a daughter Gaurī and she was mother of Māndhātṛ;[6] the Harivaṁśa thus contradicting its statement in the former passage. It is clear then that she was wife of Yuvanāśva and not of Prasenajit; and the phrase *atyanta-dhārmikā* in the above line supplies an interesting corroboration of this. This phrase is the general reading in the Brahmāṇḍa and Vāyu, but two copies of the Vāyu read *Atimānātmajā* instead, which is obviously a mistake for *Atinārātmajā* or *Matinārātmajā*, as she was Matināra's daughter; and this rare reading is the right one and confirms the statement in the Paurava genealogy. But it was corrupted and was not understood, and so was altered to the intelligible but commonplace epithet *atyanta-dhārmikā*, which has now almost superseded that true reading. The Brahmāṇḍa and Vāyu therefore have the correct relation, and the three other Purāṇas have altered it. It is

[1] Bd iii, *63*, 66–8. Vā *88*, 64–7 (°*dhārmiko* by mistake).
[2] Br *7*, 90–2. Hv *12*, 709–11. Śiv vii, *60*, 74–6.
[3] MBh i, *94*, 3703; *95*, 3778. Br *13*, 51. Hv *32*, 1715. Ag *277*, 4.
[4] Mat *49*, 7. [5] Vā *99*, 128–9. Viṣ iv, *19*, 2. Gar *140*, 4.
[6] Vā *99*, 130. Mat *49*, 8. Hv *32*, 1716. Bd wanting.

possible to suggest a reason for their tampering with it. It was a very common trait to provide explanations of names, as shown in chapter V, and Māndhātṛ's name is explained in an absurd fable, which says he was born from his father Yuvanāśva's side.[1] That being accepted, it followed that Gaurī was not his mother, and so it was natural to transfer her as wife from Yuvanāśva to Prasenajit.

CHAPTER VII

GENERAL SURVEY OF THE GENEALOGIES

THE general scheme of the genealogies is here first sketched out, and the several dynasties will be dealt with in more detail in the next two chapters, the Solar race in chapter VIII and the Aila or Lunar race in chapter IX.

All the royal lineages are traced back to the mythical Manu Vaivasvata. He is said to have had nine sons,[2] and also a daughter named Ilā or an eldest son Ila who was turned into a woman Ilā.[3] Only four of the sons are important. The chief son Ikṣvāku reigned at Ayodhyā and had two sons Vikukṣi-Śaśāda and Nimi. From the former was descended the great Aikṣvāku dynasty of Ayodhyā, generally known as the Solar race, and the latter founded the dynasty of Videha. Another son Nābhānediṣṭha established the line of kings that reigned in the country known afterwards as the

[1] MBh iii, *126*, 10423–53; vii, *62*, 2274–5; xii, *29*, 974: copied in Viṣ iv, *2*, 13–18. See pp. 40 and 76.

[2] Bḍ iii, *60*, 2–3. Vā *85*, 3–4. Br *7*, 1–2. Hv *10*, 613–14. Lg i, *65*, 17–19. Śiv vii, *60*, 1–2. Kūr i, *20*, 4–6. Ag *272*, 5–7. Cf. also Vā *64*, 29–30; Bḍ ii, *38*, 30–2. These collated suggest this original text:—

> Manor Vaivasvatasyâsan putrā vai nava tat-samāḥ
> Ikṣvākuś caiva Nābhāgo Dhṛṣṭaḥ Śaryātir eva ca
> Nariṣyantas tathā Prāṁśur Nābhāgodiṣṭa eva ca
> Karūṣaś ca Pṛṣadhraś ca navaite Mānavāḥ smṛtāḥ.

Viṣ iv, *1*, 5 and MBh i, *75*, 3140–1 agree generally therewith. The correct form of Nābhāgodiṣṭa is Nābhānediṣṭha, as Viṣ suggests. Gar i, *138*, 2; Mārk *79*, 11–12 and *111*, 4–5; and Bhāg ix, *1*, 11–12 vary. Mat *11*, 40–1 and Pad v, *8*, 75–7 have a different text. MBh i, *1*, 42–7 is a fanciful summary, incorrect.

[3] This is fully dealt with in chap. XXIV.

kingdom of Vaiśālī; a third Śaryāti the dynasty that reigned in Ānarta (Gujarat); and from a fourth Nābhāga were descended the Rathītaras. These are discussed in chapter VIII.

Ilā had a son Purūravas Aila, the progenitor of the great Aila race, who reigned at Pratiṣṭhāna [1] (Allahabad). The early part of the Aila genealogy from him to Yayāti's five sons is given by twelve Puranas and twice by the Mahābhārata, and part is also given by the Rāmāyaṇa.[2]

Purūravas is said to have had six [3] or seven [4] sons, and there is some variation in their names,[5] but only two are important, and nearly all the authorities agree about them, namely, Āyu or Āyus, and Amāvasu. Āyu continued the main line at Pratiṣṭhāna, and from Amāvasu was descended the dynasty of Kānyakubja (Kanauj). Āyu had by Svarbhānu's daughter Prabhā five sons who are all mentioned as important, namely, Nahuṣa, Kṣatravṛddha (or Vṛddhaśarman), Rambha, Raji and Anenas (or synonymously Vipapman).[6] Nahuṣa continued the main line at Pratiṣṭhāna.

[1] Pratiṣṭhāna is Prayāga on the north bank of the Jumna; Vā *91*, 50: Bḍ iii, *66*, 21: Lg i, *66*, 56. Br *10*, 9–10 and Hv *26*, 1371, 1411–2 say it is Prayāga but place it on the north bank of the Ganges. Mat *106*, 30–2 suggests it was on the east side of the Ganges; cf. *111*, 7–9.

[2] MBh i, *75*, 3149–62; *95*, 3760–2: vii, *144*, 6027–30: xiii, *147*, 6831–3. Rām vii, *56*, 25–7 (wrongly calling Purūravas king of Kāśi); *58*, 7–10.

[3] Bḍ iii, *66*, 22–3. Vā *91*, 51–2. Cf. Viṣ iv, *7*, 1: Gar *139*, 2.

[4] Br *10*, 11–12 and Hv *26*, 1372–3 differently. Lg i, *66*, 57–8 (seven sons) and Kūr i, *22*, 1–2 (six sons) are alike but intermediate and corrupt. MBh i, *75*, 3149 (six sons) is somewhat alike. Mat *25*, 33–4; Pad v, *12*, 86–7 and Ag *273*, 15, which have a different text, give eight names, corrupting most of them. Bhāg ix, *15*, 1 is wrong.

[5] Some of the variations are obviously due to misreadings of the names in the old scripts.

[6] Bḍ iii, *67*, 1–2. Vā *92*, 1–2. Br *11*, 1–2. Hv *28*, 1475–6. These agree, except that Br and Hv call Kṣatravṛddha *Vṛddhaśarman*. Lg i, *66*, 59–60 and Kūr i, *22*, 3–4 are similar but name only Nahuṣa. Viṣ iv, *8*, 1, Gar *139*, 7–8 and Bhāg ix, *17*, 1–2 concur in the names. Mat *24*, 34–5, Pad v, *12*, 87–8 and Ag *273*, 16 agree, with different verses. MBh i, *75*, 3150 varies. Svarbhānu was a Dānava king, MBh i, *65*, 2532; *67*, 2648: xii, *227*, 8262–7. Cf. Vā *68*, 8, 22, 24; Bḍ iii, *6*, 8, 23–4; Mat *6*, 20–1, and Viṣ i, *21*, 6, which say Prabhā was his daughter. Svarbhānu was also a name of Rāhu, MBh v, *109*, 3811: vi, *12*, 481–8; *102*, 4619: cf. Vā *52*, 80; *53*, 63–5, 83 (confused). The two must be distinguished, but Viṣ iv, *8*, 1 (read *Rāhor*) confuses them. So also the Dānavas Sūrya and Candramas were different from the sun and moon, MBh i, *65*, 2534–5: Bḍ iii, *6*, 12: Vā *68*, 12.

Kṣatravṛddha founded the dynasty of Kāśi (Benares), for the Brahma and Harivaṁśa, though they call him Vṛddhaśarman at first, give his lineage under his name Kṣatravṛddha.[1] From Raji were descended the Rājeya kṣatriyas, who perished (it is said) in a contest with Indra.[2] Rambha had no sons.[3] From Anenas sprang a line called the Kṣatradharmans, whose names as best ascertainable are these—Anenas, Kṣatradharma, Pratikṣatra, Sañjaya, Jaya, Vijaya, Kṛti (or Jaya), Haryatvata, Sahadeva, Adīna, Jayatsena, Saṅkṛti, and Kṛtadharma (or Kṣatradharma).[4] They seem to have constituted a small dynasty somewhere, but nothing more is said about them: the second of these names became confused with Kṣatravṛddha, and so the Viṣṇu and Garuḍa drop out Anenas and attribute this lineage to Kṣatravṛddha erroneously:[5] and the last name also became confused with Kṣatravṛddha, whose lineage follows this pedigree, in the Brahma (*11*, 31), and was wrongly altered to Kṣatravṛddha.

Nahuṣa had six[6] or seven[7] sons by *pitṛ-kanyā* Virajā, which no doubt means his sister (p. 70). Only two sons are important, Yati and Yayāti. Yati the eldest became a muni and gave up the kingdom,[8] and Yayāti succeeded to it. Yayāti had two wives, Devayānī daughter of the great Bhārgava rishi Uśanas-Śukra,[9] and

[1] Br *11*, 31, beginning with *Kṣatravṛddhasya câparaḥ, vaṁśaḥ* understood. Hv *29*, 1517, beginning with *Kṣatravṛddhasya me śṛṇu.*

[2] Bḍ iii, *67*, 80–104. Vā *92*, 75–99. Br *11*, 3–26. Hv *28*, 1477–1511. Mat *24*, 35–49. Ag *273*, 17–19. Gar i, *138*, 14. Bhāg ix, *17*, 12–16. Pad v, *12*, 88–102.

[3] Br *11*, 27. Hv *29*, 1513. Viṣ iv, *9*, 8. Yet Bhāg ix, *17*, 10–12 provides him with a short lineage wrongly.

[4] Bḍ iii, *68*, 7–11; Vā *93*, 7–11. Br *11*, 27–31 and Hv *29*, 1513–17, both concluding with *Anenasaḥ samākhyātāḥ.* Bhāg ix, *17*, 11–12 wrongly gives Anenas a wholly different line of descendants. Bḍ and Vā preface this genealogy with a passage about king Marutta and Mitrajyotis (verses 1–6) which has no connexion with it and seems misplaced. I do not know what its true connexion is.

[5] Viṣ iv, *9*, 8. Gar i, *139*, 15–17.

[6] Bḍ iii, *68*, 12–13; Vā *93*, 12–13; Br *12*, 1–2; Hv *30*, 1599–1600; Lg i, *66*, 60–62; Kūr i, *22*, 5–6. Viṣ iv, *10*, 1, Gar *139*, 17 and Bhāg ix, *18*, 1 agree; and MBh i, *75*, 3155 partially. But Br, Hv, Lg, and Kūr readings approximate to the Mat and Pad reading.

[7] Mat *24*, 49–50 and Pad v, *12*, 103–4; which vary some of the names corruptly. Ag *273*, 20.

[8] See continuations of passages in second note above.

[9] See chap. XVII.

Śarmiṣṭhā daughter of the Daitya-Dānava-asura king Vṛṣaparvan.[1] The former bore two sons, Yadu and Turvasu, and the latter three, Druhyu, Anu and Pūru.[2] Yayāti divided his territories among them, so that his kingdom developed into five kingdoms, and from his sons were descended the five famous royal lines of the Yadus or Yādavas, the Turvasus, the Druhyus, the Anus or Ānavas and the Pūrus or Pauravas.

Yadu had five[3] or four[4] sons, but only two are important, Sahasrajit (or Sahasrāda) and Kroṣṭu (or Kroṣṭṛ). With them the Yādavas divided into two great branches. Sahasrajit's descendants were named after his grandson Haihaya and were well known as the Haihayas.[5] Kroṣṭu's descendants had no special name, but were known particularly as the Yādavas. The Ānavas after Anu's seventh named successor Mahāmanas divided into two branches under two sons Uśīnara and Titikṣu. The former branch established various kingdoms in the Panjab, and the latter founded a dynasty in East Bihar. The Pauravas gradually developed and established a number of kingdoms in Madhyadeśa. All these lines will be explained fully in chapter IX.

The broad results thus sketched out are exhibited in the annexed genealogical table.

The genealogies profess to give the dynastic lists at length and in correct succession, and say so expressly, *vistareṇānupūrvyā ca*, as regards the Yādava[6] and Paurava[7] lines. But in giving the

[1] Vā *68*, 23–4. Bd iii, *6*, 23, 25. Mat *6*, 20, 22. Viṣ i, *21*, 6.

[2] Bd iii, *68*, 15–16. Vā *93*, 15–17. Br *12*, 4–6. Hv *30*, 1603–4. Lg i, *66*, 64–6. Kūr i, *22*, 7–8. Similarly Ag *273*, 21–3, Viṣ iv, *10*, 1–2 and Bhāg ix, *18*, 29–33; also Gar *139*, 18. Mat *24*, 52–4 and Pad v, *12*, 105–7 say the same in different verses; and MBh i, *75*, 3158–60; *95*, 3760–2. Cf. MBh i, *84*; *85*: Br *146*, 2–7. Turvasu is called Turvaśa in Vedic literature. The sons are said to be four and are wrongly named in late fables in Pad ii, *64*, 11–12; *77*, 105: and *109*, 49–55, where the genealogy is corrupt—an instance of the vitiation of genealogies by late story-makers. The story of Yayāti, Devayānī and Śarmiṣṭhā at great length, Mat *25* to *32*; MBh i, *78* to *83*: differently, Rām vii, *58*; *59*.

[3] Bd iii, *69*, 2. Vā *94*, 2. Br *13*, 153–4. Hv *33*, 1843. Mat *43*, 6–7. Pad v, *12*, 110. Lg i, *68*, 2. Kūr i, *22*, 12–13. Ag *274*, 1 is equivalent but confused.

[4] Viṣ iv, *11*, 3. Gar *139*, 19. Bhāg ix, *23*, 20–1 (corrupt).

[5] So stated expressly in Br *13*, 207; Hv *34*, 1898; Lg i, *68*, 15—which also say they were Yādavas.

[6] Vā *94*, 1. Mat *43*, 5. Hv *32*, 1842. Bd iii, *69*, 1.

[7] Vā *99*, 119. Mat *48*, 103. Br *13*, 2. Hv *31*, 1653.

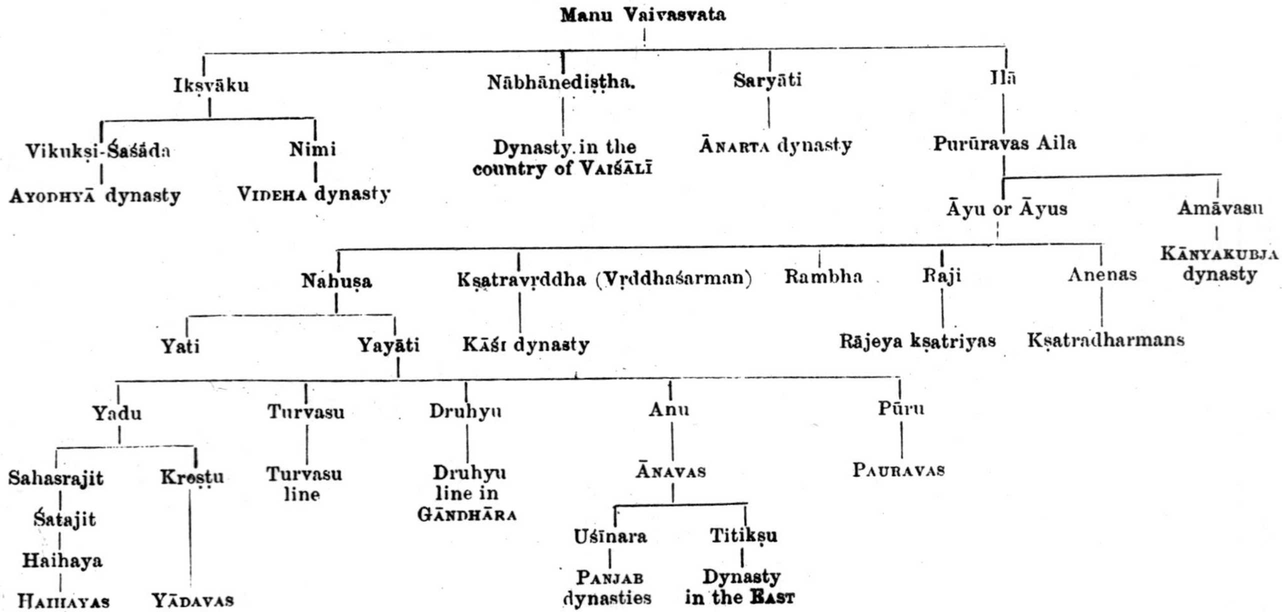

Manu Vaivasvata
Ikṣvāku
Nābhānediṣṭha.
Saryāti
Ilā
Vikukṣi-Śaśāda
Nimi
Dynasty in the country of Vaiśālī
Ānarta dynasty
Purūravas Aila
Ayodhyā dynasty
Videha dynasty
Āyu or Āyus
Amāvasu
Kānyakubja dynasty
Nahuṣa
Kṣatravṛddha (Vṛddhaśarman)
Rambha
Raji
Anenas
Yati
Yayāti
Kāśi dynasty
Rājeya kṣatriyas
Kṣatradharmans
Yadu
Turvasu
Druhyu
Anu
Pūru
Sahasrajit
Kroṣṭu
Turvasu line
Druhyu line in Gāndhāra
Ānavas
Pauravas
Śatajit
Haihaya
Haihayas
Yādavas
Uśīnara
Titikṣu
Panjab dynasties
Dynasty in the East

Aikṣvāku genealogy of Ayodhyā the Puranas do not profess to be complete, and say that only the chief and best-known kings are mentioned.[1] These statements are noteworthy, because the three genealogies profess to cover exactly the same chronological period, all starting from Manu and all ending with the Bhārata battle. Yet, while the Aikṣvāku lists name some 93 kings, the Yādava lists give only about 53 kings, and the Paurava lists only some 45 kings in succession, and prefixing to each of these two the common anterior names Manu, Ilā, Purūravas, Āyu, Nahuṣa and Yayāti, these two lists make their totals 59 and 51 respectively. Moreover, the latter two lists profess to be given at length, while the first does not profess to be exhaustive. The Liṅga throws some light on the meaning of the word *vistareṇa*, in that, after setting out the list of Yādava names as fully as the Vāyu, it adds that it gives the list succinctly, *saṅkṣepeṇa* (i, *68*, 1), which is explained by the fact that its account is more concise. Hence apparently *vistareṇa* does not imply that the list is exhaustive, but that it is the full traditional account. In fact it will be found that gaps occur sometimes in the genealogies, and in one place it is frankly admitted that there is a gap.[2]

The succession of kings in the lists is expressed in four ways, which may be explained by styling the predecessor A and the successor B; namely (1) B was son of A, (2) B was 'of A',[3] no relationship being expressed, (3) B was 'from or after A', the ablative being used or its adverbial form,[4] and (4) B was 'heir' of A.[5] The second and third forms are indistinguishable where the genitive and ablative cases are the same.[6] These different forms may all mean sonship; the last three may include the succession of other relatives, and the third may imply bare succession without particular relationship. None necessarily means immediate sonship[7]

[1] Vā *88*, 213; Bḍ iii, *64*, 213–14; Lg i, *66*, 43. Br *8*, 94; Hv *15*, 831–2 and Mat *12*, 57 somewhat similarly. Viṣ iv, *4*, 49 equivalently. Kūr i, *21*, 60 says truly it gives this genealogy succinctly, *samāsena*.

[2] *Tasyânvavāye mahati*, Mat *49*, 72; Vā *99*, 187.

[3] e.g. Haryaśvasya Nikumbho 'bhūt (Vā *88*, 62).

[4] e.g. Śarūthāt tu Janapīḍas (Vā *99*, 5). Aviddhataḥ Pravīras tu (*ibid.* 121).

[5] e.g. Purukutsasya dāyādas Trasadasyur (Vā *88*, 74).

[6] e.g. Karandhamas Triśānos tu (Vā *99*, 2). Sañjāter atha Raudrāśvas (*ibid.* 123).

[7] Thus Vā *99*, 234 says Devāpi and Śantanu were sons of Pratīpa, but they were really grandsons: see chap. XIII.

or succession[1] for even the first does not always mean it. Absolute precision in genealogical details can hardly be expected and is not indispensable for historical purposes. Kings who were celebrated are well known by name, and the names of others are mainly useful as marking steps in descent, so that it is not material whether insignificant names are perfectly correct. In such cases the name which is best supported is adopted, and the question of names is dealt with in chapter XI.

The fact that the genealogies of some dynasties are fuller than those of others will not be a serious bar chronologically, because synchronisms (which will be discussed in chapters XII to XIV) will fix the positions of the chief kings, and other kings will fall into approximate position accordingly; and thus it will appear where lists are incomplete or gaps occur. Though absolute accuracy is unattainable, yet it may be possible to reach an approximation sufficient for working purposes.

CHAPTER VIII

THE SOLAR RACE

Ayodhyā Dynasty.

THE genealogy of the kings of Ayodhyā, to whom were especially applied the titles, the 'Solar race', the Ikṣvākus, Aikṣvākus or Aikṣvākas, is given by many authorities. Thirteen Puranas give the whole list of kings more or less completely.[2] The Rāmāyaṇa gives the list down to Rāma twice.[3] The Mahābhārata mentions the early part as far as Dṛḍhāśva,[4] and other small portions else-

[1] Thus Ajamīḍha, Ṛkṣa and Saṁvaraṇa in the main Paurava line were not three successive kings; as the table of genealogies in chap. XII shows. Genealogies also were intentionally abbreviated; cf. the Aikṣvāku line in Ag *5*, 3; Gar i, *143*, 2–3.

[2] Bd iii, *63*, 8–214. Vā *88*, 8–213. Br *7*, 44 to *8*, 94. Hv *11*, 660 to *15*, 832. Mat *12*, 25–57. Pad v, *8*, 130–62. Śiv vii, *60*, 33 to *61*, 73. Lg i, *65*, 31 to *66*, 45. Kūr i, *20*, 10 to *21*, 60. Viṣ iv, *2*, 3 to *4*, 49. Ag *272*, 18–39. Gar i, *138*, 17–44. Bhāg ix, *6*. 4 to *12*, 9. Also Saura Upapurana, *30*, 32–73.

[3] Rām i, *70*, 21–44: ii, *110*, 6–35.

[4] MBh iii, *201*, 13515–19; *203*, 13614–22.

where.[1] The Raghuvaṁśa has much of the latter half, from Dilīpa II to Agnivarṇa.[2] All these authorities are on the whole in general agreement, so far as they extend, except the Rāmāyaṇa. Its two lists are practically the same, but differ widely from the others. Most of its names occur in the other lists, but they are arranged in such absolutely different order that its lists cannot be reconciled with the others. There are thus two wholly distinct genealogies, and it is necessary to examine which is more probably right.

The Rāmāyaṇa genealogy is open to great doubt, when considered as a whole or examined in detail. It contains only some 35 kings down to Rāma, whereas the Puranas name some 63 kings in that period, and it will be seen from a comparison of the other dynasties exhibited in the table of genealogies (chapter XII) that its list is manifestly defective in length. It is very improbable that the Rāmāyaṇa alone should be right and all the other authorities wrong; even the late Raghuvaṁśa accepting the latter and rejecting the former.

This conclusion is confirmed when the lists are examined in detail. We may first notice what are undoubted omissions in the Rāmāyaṇa list. It omits Purukutsa and his son Trasadasyu, but they were kings of this line as the Mahābhārata knows.[3] It omits Hariścandra and his son Rohita, yet brahmanical books testify to both.[4] Again it omits Ṛtuparṇa, though he is mentioned in the story of Nala.[5] Also it omits Sudāsa, yet admits his existence by calling Kalmāṣapāda *Saudāsa* in its second list, and contradicts itself by saying Kalmāṣapāda was son of Raghu; and the Mahābhārata declares he was son of Sudāsa.[6] It omits Aśmaka, who according to that epic was Kalmāṣapāda's son.[7] As regards all these kings the Puranas name them and are corroborated by the other authorities mentioned above.

Next as regards the relationships and positions of kings. The

[1] Bāhu to Bhagīratha, MBh iii, *107*, 9912–18: Br *78*, 3–11, 40–7: VN *7* and *8*: Bḍ iii, *47*, 74 to *56*, 32.

[2] Dilīpa II to Atithi in chap. I–XVII; Niṣadha to Sudarśana in XVIII; and Agnivarṇa in XIX.

[3] iii, *98*, 8606–8.

[4] Aitar Brāhm vii, *3*, 1 f. Śāṅkhāy Śr Sūtra xv, 17–25.

[5] MBh iii, *70*, 2766.

[6] MBh xiii, *6*, 326: xiv, *56*, 1656: read with i, *176* to *177*.

[7] MBh i, *177*, 6791.

Rāmāyaṇa places Ambarīṣa three steps above Nābhāga, but he was Nābhāga's son, for Ambarīṣa son of Nābhāga is praised in the epic.[1] It tells, moreover, the well-known story of Hariścandra [2] as a story of Ambarīṣa,[3] and Ambarīṣa may have been another name of Hariścandra ;[4] but if so, it is wrong in making his son Nahuṣa instead of Rohita. The Puranas say there were two Dilīpas, one father of Bhagīratha and the other father or grandfather of Raghu, but the Rāmāyaṇa mentions only one Dilīpa as father of Bhagīratha and great grandfather of Raghu. One Dilīpa was certainly father of Bhagīratha,[5] and the Raghuvaṁśa [6] supports the Puranas that Raghu was son of a Dilīpa, who was necessarily a second Dilīpa. Further the Rāmāyaṇa makes Raghu father of Kalmāṣapāda and places Aja twelve generations below Raghu, while the Puranas make Aja son of Raghu. Now Kalmāṣapāda was son of Sudāsa, even according to the Rāmāyaṇa as shown above, and not son of Raghu, and the Raghuvaṁśa (v, 35–6) corroborates the Puranas that Raghu's son was Aja. Again, the Rāmāyaṇa says Kalmāṣapāda's son was Śaṅkhaṇa, but his son was Aśmaka according to some Puranas [7] or Sarvakarman according to others.[8] The Mahābhārata corroborates the former of these statements in one passage and the latter in another,[9] thus contradicting the Rāmāyaṇa in either case; and the Raghuvaṁśa (xviii, 21–2) confirms the contradiction by saying that Śaṅkhaṇa was son of Vajranābha as the Puranas state.

Further, the Rāmāyaṇa makes Kakutstha son of Bhagīratha and grandson of Dilīpa, but the Puranas say he was son of Śaśāda, and was the third earliest king. The Mahābhārata corroborates them,[10]

[1] MBh iii. *129*, 10514 ; vii, *64*, 2303–18 ; xii, *29*, 993–7. There was another Ambarīṣa, son of Manu's son Nābhāga (see *infra*), but the Ambarīṣa extolled in MBh was apparently the Ayodhyā king.

[2] Aitar Brāhm vii, *3*, 1 f. : Śāṅkhāy Śr Sūtra xv, 17–25 : &c. See JRAS, 1917, 44 f., where the whole story is discussed.

[3] Rām i, *61* and *62*. [4] Lg ii, *5*, 6. [5] MBh iii, *107*, 9916–18.

[6] Raghuv iii, 13–21. Not every archaeological statement in the Raghuv is correct, for it refers to Puṣpapura (i. e. Pāṭalīputra) as existing (vi, 24) in Aja's time; and speaks of the Śūrasena king as a Nīpa (vi, 45–6), whereas the 'Śūrasena' kingdom did not apparently exist then, and its king could hardly have been a Nīpa (see S. Pañcāla).

[7] Vā *88*, 177. Bḍ iii, *63*, 176–7. Viṣ iv, *4*, 38 : &c.

[8] Mat *12*, 46. Br *8*, 82. Hv *15*, 816–17 : &c.

[9] MBh i, *177*, 6787–91 : xii, *49*, 1792–3.

[10] MBh iii, *201*, 13515–16.

and the Raghuvaṁśa supports them in saying (vi, 71–4) that from his time the kings had borne the title Kākutstha and that Dilīpa was his descendant. The Rāmāyaṇa and the Puranas have a group of five kings, Sudarśana, Agnivarṇa, Śīghra, Maru and Prasuśruta, and the Rāmāyaṇa makes them anterior to Rāma, while the Puranas put them long after him. Similarly it places three others, Śaṅkhaṇa, Dhruvasandhi and Susandhi, before Rāma, while the Puranas make them his descendants. As regards these last three and Sudarśana and Agnivarṇa the Raghuvaṁśa [1] corroborates the Puranas that they were long after Rāma, and so also as regards the three others in that it does not notice them, because it closes its account with Agnivarṇa and they succeeded him.

It thus appears that wherever it is possible to check the Rāmāyaṇa and Puranic lists of the Ayodhyā dynasty by other authorities those authorities corroborate the Puranas and contradict the Rāmāyaṇa. Hence the Rāmāyaṇa genealogy must be put aside as erroneous, and the Puranic genealogy accepted. This is not surprising, because the Rāmāyaṇa is a brahmanical poem, and the brahmans notoriously lacked the historical sense.

The Purana lists all agree fairly down to Māndhātṛ, though with much variation in some names; and here the Mahābhārata list also agrees. With Māndhātṛ there is some variation. He had three well-known sons, Purukutsa, Ambarīṣa and Mucukunda.[2] From Ambarīṣa came the Hārita brahmans (chapter XXIII). Mucukunda was a famous king,[3] and of him the fable is told that he went to sleep in a cave and slept on till awakened by Kālayavana, who had pursued Kṛṣṇa into it; then he killed Kāla, and marvelled at the degeneracy of mankind.[4] Purukutsa's son was Trasadasyu [5] who continued the main line. All then fairly agree, subject to some omissions, down to Saudāsa Kalmāṣapāda, but between him and Dilīpa II Khaṭvāṅga [6] two different versions occur, where the names are all different: thus the Brahma, Harivaṁśa, Matsya, Padma, Śiva and Agni generally insert five kings, Sarvakarman, Anaraṇya,

[1] Raghuv xviii and xix.

[2] Mat and Pad add a fourth son.

[3] MBh v, *131*, 4467–9: and pp. 41, 42. Also Hv *115*, 6464: Viṣ v, *23*, 18 f.: Br *196*; *197*: Pad vi, *273*, 51–60.

[4] Hv *115*, 6464–88. Pad vi, *189*, 73; *273*, 51–70. Viṣ v, *23*, 26 to *24*, 5; Br *196*, 16 to *197*, 5.

[5] Mat calls him *Vasuda* (for *Trasada*). Pad errs further.

[6] Br and Hv wrongly call Dilīpa I *Khaṭvāṅga*.

Nighna, Anamitra with a Raghu, and Duliduha; but the seven other Puranas name six, Aśmaka, Mūlaka, Śataratha, Iḍaviḍa (with variations), Vṛddhaśarman and Viśvasaha. It is not material which version we adopt, because their number is practically the same and none were important, but the latter group is supported by the better texts and is preferable.[1] From Dilīpa II Khaṭvāṅga to Daśaratha there is general agreement subject to some divergences; and here the better texts make Dīrghabāhu 'father of Raghu' instead of an epithet of Raghu, though the Raghuvaṁśa omits him. From Daśaratha to Ahīnagu there is general agreement.

After Ahīnagu most of the Puranas give a list of some twenty kings Pāripātra (or Sudhanvan) to Bṛhadbala who was killed by Abhimanyu in the Bhārata battle,[2] agreeing generally in their names, though some of the lists are incomplete towards the end. Thus the Brahma stops at Nala (= Śaṅkhaṇa); the Harivaṁśa at Maru except that it mentions the last king Bṛhadbala; and the Garuḍa at Prasuśruta, where by the loss of some verses closing this dynasty and introducing the Videha line it runs the two together making Prasuśruta father of Udāvasu of that line. But six Puranas, the Matsya, Padma, Liṅga, Kūrma, Śiva and Agni, differ completely, and all except the Siva name, instead of those twenty, six other kings, Sahasrāśva, Candrāvaloka, Tārāpīḍa, Candragiri, Bhānuścandra (with variations) and Śrutāyus. The Śiva names only the first. The Liṅga identifies Śrutāyus with Bṛhadbala, the last in the former list. The former list is certainly preferable for several reasons. The table of royal genealogies (chapter XII) shows that there must have been many more kings than six and quite as many as twenty. The Raghuvaṁśa corroborates it as far as Agnivarṇa. Some of the kings in the long list are named elsewhere, and even in the Matsya which gives the short list; thus, it mentions Hiraṇyanābhin Kausalya as teacher of king Kṛta of Dvimīḍha's line,[3] and Maru as one who with Devāpi the Paurava will restore the kṣatriyas at the end of this Kali age.[4] Further Pāripātra and his successors appear from a comparison of their names to be meant by the Mahābhārata

[1] An explanation of this discrepancy is suggested in chap. XXIV.

[2] MBh vii, *47*, 1864–83.

[3] Mat *49*, 75. Vā *99*, 190. Hv *20*, 1081. Viṣ iv, *19*, 13. This is dealt with in chap. XIV.

[4] Mat *273*, 56, and Vā *99*, 437, where read *Maruḥ* for *Malaḥ*. Vā *32*, 39 (read *Maruḥ*). Bḍ iii, *74*, 250. Viṣ iv, *24*, 45, 48.

story of Parikṣit and his sons.[1] On the other hand there is nothing, as far as I know, to support the short list. The longer list of twenty kings must therefore be accepted.

The Videha Dynasty.

This dynasty was descended from Ikṣvāku's son Nimi (or Nemi)[2] who is called *Videha*,[3] and so was a branch of the Solar race.[4] It is given by five Puranas, and its early part down to Sīradhvaja by the Rāmāyaṇa.[5] All are in substantial agreement down to Sīradhvaja, except that the Garuḍa, as mentioned above, omits the first two kings and makes Udāvasu of this dynasty son of Prasuśruta of Ayodhyā. The Puranas fairly agree about the rest of the genealogy, except that after Śakuni the Viṣṇu, Garuḍa and Bhāgavata insert twelve kings, Añjana to Upagupta, whom the Vāyu and Brahmāṇḍa omit. No doubt these three Puranas are right and the two latter have lost this portion, because the table of genealogies, with the synchronisms, shows that there must have been many more kings than the Vāyu and Brahmāṇḍa have.

Kuśadhvaja was Sīradhvaja's brother and was king of Sāṅkāśyā, as the Puranas generally say and also the Rāmāyaṇa.[6] The Bhāgavata confuses the genealogy here, and gives Kuśadhvaja's successors thus. Its account is supported by the Viṣṇu in a story about Keśidhvaja and Khāṇḍikya,[7] and may be true.

Kuśadhvaja
|
Dharmadhvaja
|
Kṛtadhvaja — **Mitadhvaja**
| |
Keśidhvaja — **Khāṇḍikya**

[1] MBh iii, *192*, 13145–78, 13198. Vyuṣitāśva of this list is different from Vyuṣitāśva of MBh i, *121*, 4686, who was a Paurava.

[2] Vā *88*, 9; *89*, 1, 3. [3] Vā *89*, 4. Bḍ iii, *64*, 4. Viṣ iv, *5*, 12.

[4] Gar i, *139*, 1 says so expressly.

[5] Bḍ iii. *64*, 1–24. Vā *89*, 1–23. Viṣ iv, *5*, 11–14. Gar i, *138*, 44–58. Bhāg ix, *13*. Rām i, *71*, 3–20: but vii, *57*, 18–20 gives a fabulous beginning.

[6] Rām i, *70*, 2–3; *71*, 14–16, 19. Bḍ iii, *64*, 18–19 and Vā *89*. 18 invert two lines and corrupt Sāṅkāśyā; they should read thus:—

bhrātā Kuśadhvajas tasya Sāṅkāśyādhipatir nṛpaḥ
Sīradhvajāt tu jātas tu Bhānumān nāma Maithilaḥ.

[7] Viṣ vi, *6*, 7 to *7*, 104.

From the second king Mithi Janaka (whom the Rāmāyaṇa makes two) it is said the capital Mithilā was named,[1] and hence the kings were called Maithilas.[2] From him, too, the kings were also styled Janaka, and this was the family name, for he was the first king Janaka,[3] and the Janakas are expressly mentioned as a family,[4] and two Puranas conclude with the remark that with Kṛti ends the race of the Janakas.[5] The kings were thus collectively 'Janakas', and many are individually so named, as Sīradhvaja,[6] Dharmadhvaja,[7] Janadeva,[8] Daivarāti,[9] Khāṇḍikya,[10] and also Karāla [11] and Aindradyumni [12] (who are not named in the genealogy).[13] The references to 'Janaka' in the brahmanical books do not therefore necessarily mean one and the same king, but the name is used generically there [14] according to the brahmanical custom and lack of the historical sense, just as various Vasiṣṭhas and Viśvāmitras are mentioned merely as Vasiṣṭha and Viśvāmitra, and are sometimes confused as one Vasiṣṭha and one Viśvāmitra. Moreover, the brahmanical Bhāgavata says of these Maithilas generally that they were skilled in knowledge of the Ātman,[15] so that it is erroneous to assume that only one Janaka is meant in the brahmanical books.

The Vaiśāla Dynasty.

This dynasty was descended from Manu's son Nābhānediṣṭha, and is given by seven Puranas, and also partially by the Rāmāyaṇa and

[1] Bḍ iii, *64*, 6. Vā *89*, 6.

[2] Bḍ iii, *64*, 24. Vā *89*, 23. Viṣ iv, *5*, 14.

[3] Rām i, *71*, 4, *prathamo Janako rājā.*

[4] *Janakānāṁ kule*, Mārk *13*, 11. *Janakānāṁ variṣṭha*, MBh iii, *133*, 10637. *Janakas*, Rām i, *67*, 8; Br *88*, 24. *Janaka-rājāno bahavas*, Br *88*, 22.

[5] Vā *89*, 23; Bḍ iii, *64*, 24—*vaṁśo Janakānām.*

[6] MBh iii, *273*, 15880.

[7] MBh xii, *322*, 11855. Viṣ iv, *24*, 54: vi, *6*, 7. See table in chap. XXVII.

[8] MBh xii, *218*, 7883; *219*, 7930; *321*, 11839–40. See above table.

[9] MBh xii, *312*, 11545–6. [10] Viṣ vi. *5*, 81; *6*, 5, 8.

[11] MBh xii, *304*, 11220; *310*, 11504. Br *240*, 5.

[12] MBh iii, *133*, 10624.

[13] Unnamed 'Janakas', MBh ii, *29*, 1087: xii, *99*, 3664–5; *292*, 10699; *311*, 11518–19; *328*, 12260: xiii, *45*, 2466.

[14] Also Br *88*, 2–3. Cf. 'Pharaoh'. Weber conjectured this, *Hist. of Ind. Lit.*, p. 135.

[15] ix, *13*, 27 (and 20). Cf. Viṣ vi, *6*, 7, 9; *7*, 27 f.

Mahābhārata.[1] None of these works however carries the genealogy beyond Pramati or Sumati, who was the contemporary of Daśaratha, king of Ayodhyā, according to the Rāmāyaṇa.[2] Only four lists are complete, those in the Vāyu, Viṣṇu, Garuḍa and Bhāgavata. The others show various limitations or omissions: thus the Liṅga mentions only the first four kings; the Mahābhārata list is incomplete at the beginning, goes down only to Marutta, and wrongly inserts an Ikṣvāku; the Brahmāṇḍa omits from Prajāni to Avīkṣit, though Marutta was well known as son of Avīkṣit;[3] the Mārkaṇḍeya narrates the doings of these kings at great length but only down to Rājyavardhana; and the Rāmāyaṇa begins the dynasty with Viśāla, wrongly calling him 'son of Ikṣvāku'. Subject to these shortcomings the lists are in substantial agreement.

No nameisgiven to this dynasty or kingdom at first, but king Viśāla is said to have founded Viśālā or Vaiśālī as his capital, and thenceforward the kingdom was that of Vaiśālī, and the kings were styled Vaiśālaka kings.[4] These names may conveniently be extended retrospectively to include the whole dynasty. The first two kings named are Bhalandana and Vatsaprī. Bhalandana is said to have become a vaiśya,[5] and it is declared there were three vaiśya hymn-makers, Bhalandana, Vatsa or Vāsāśva (read *Vatsaprī*?) and Saṅkīla.[6] This Vatsaprī Bhālandana is the reputed author of Rigveda ix, *68*, and probably x, *45* and *46*. Accordingly some Puranas add that these vaiśyas became brahmans.[7]

The Śāryātas.

These were the descendants of Śaryāti, son of Manu, and the list is given briefly by twelve Puranas.[8] There is a fair amount of

[1] Bḍ iii, *61*, 3–18; and *8*, 35–7. Vā *86*, 3–22. Lg i, *66*, 53. Mārk *113* to *136*, and *109* to *110*. Viṣ iv, *1*, 15–19. Gar i, *138*, 5–13. Bhāg ix, *2*, 23–36. Rām i, *47*, 11–17. MBh xiv, *4*, 65–86.

[2] i, *47*, 17, 20. [3] MBh vii, *55*, 2170: xii, *20*, 613; *29*, 910.

[4] Vā *86*, 17, 22. Bḍ iii, *61*, 12, 17. Viṣ iv, *1*, 18–19. Bhāg ix, *2*, 33, 36. Gar i, *138*, 13.

[5] Mārk *113*, 36; *114*, 2; *116*, 3–4. Br *7*, 26. Viṣ iv, *1*, 15. Bhāg ix, *2*, 23.

[6] Bḍ ii, *32*, 121–2. Mat *145*, 116–7.

[7] Br *7*, 42. Hv *11*, 658. Śiv vii, *60*, 30.

[8] Vā *86*, 23–9; *88*, 1–4. Bḍ iii, *61*, 18–24; *63*, 1–4. Br *7*, 27–41. Hv *10*, 642 to *11*, 657. Mat *12*, 21–4. Lg i, *66*, 47–9. Viṣ iv, *1*, 20–34; *2*, 1–2. Pad v, *8*, 126–9. Ag *272*, 11–16. Gar i, *138*, 14. Bhāg ix, *3*, 1–2, 27–36. Śiv vii, *60*, 20–30. Pad vi, *274*, 10 is wrong.

agreement. The dynasty does not play any conspicuous part in tradition, and the genealogy is manifestly curtailed and incomplete. It may be stated thus—Śaryāti, his son Ānarta and daughter Sukanyā (who married the great Bhārgava rishi Cyavana), then Rocamāna, Reva and Raivata Kakudmin. It reigned at Kuśasthalī, the ancient name of Dvārakā (Dvāravatī)[1] in Gujarat, which was named Ānarta after king Ānarta. It did not last long and was destroyed by Puṇyajana Rākṣasas. The remnant of the Śāryātas appear to have afterwards become a tribe among the Haihayas (see next chapter).

Raivata is made the subject of myth in that it is said he visited the Gandharva world and Brahmā's court, stayed there listening to music for long ages, returned to find Kuśasthalī in possession of the Yādavas and then gave his daughter to Balarāma.[2] It seems probable that two Raivatas, who were ages apart, have been confused.

The Nābhāgas.

These were the descendants of Manu's son Nabhāga, and their genealogy is noticed in twelve Purāṇas.[3] All mention Nabhāga or Nābhāga and his son Ambarīṣa,[4] and the Brahmāṇḍa, Vāyu, Viṣṇu, Garuḍa and Bhāgavata add the successors, Virūpa, Pṛṣadaśva and Rathītara. Where this dynasty reigned is wholly uncertain. From Rathītara were descended the Rathītaras who were 'kṣatriyan brahmans' as will be noticed in chapter XXIII.

[1] Mat *69*, 9. Pad v, *23*, 10. Viṣ iv, *1*, 34. Cf. also MBh ii, *13*, 613–4: iii, *20*, 777; *88*, 8348–9: xii, *341*, 12955: xiv, 1535–6. Hv *36*, 1967; *113*, 6265.

[2] See continuation of passages in second note above. The fable sometimes introduces a disquisition on music.

[3] Vā *88*, 5–7. Bḍ iii, *63*, 5–7. Br *7*, 24. Hv *10*, 641. Mat *12*, 20–1. Pad v, *8*, 125–6. Lg i, *66*, 50–1. Śiv vii, *60*, 19–20. Viṣ iv, *2*, 2. Ag *272*, 10–11. Gar i, *138*, 15–16. Bhāg ix, *4*, 1, 13 and *6*, 1–3, with fables intervening. Ag *272*, 17 should probably read *Nābhāga-diṣṭa-putrau*, referring to Nābhānediṣṭha.

[4] This Nābhāga and his son Ambarīṣa must be distinguished from the two similar kings of Ayodhyā, see *ante* and Table of genealogies, chap. XII.

CHAPTER IX

THE AILA OR LUNAR RACE

THIS stock gave rise, as mentioned in chapter VII, to two side branches, the Kānyakubja and Kāśi dynasties, and developed through Yayāti's five sons into five races. The genealogies of all these will now be considered in detail.

The Kānyakubja Dynasty.

Two origins are alleged for the Kānyakubja dynasty. It was descended from Purūravas' son Amāvasu according to seven Puranas,[1] which give the first kings as Amāvasu, Bhīma, Kāñcanaprabha, Suhotra and Jahnu. The genealogy is also given by the Rāmāyaṇa, Agni and twice by the Mahābhārata.[2] The first Mahābhārata account and that in the Rāmāyaṇa leave the origin untouched, but the second account and the Agni derive Jahnu from the Paurava line, making him son of Ajamīḍha; and the Brahma and Harivaṁśa [3] inconsistently give both versions. From Jahnu to Kuśa all the lists agree,[4] there is variation as regards Kuśa's sons, and from Gādhi to Viśvāmitra and the end all agree generally.

The derivation from Ajamīḍha is certainly wrong. He was the seventh successor of Bharata. Viśvāmitra was the descendant of Jahnu by some eight steps, and must, if Jahnu was son of Ajamīḍha, have been some fifteen generations below Bharata; but it is well known that Bharata was son of king Duṣyanta and Śakuntalā [5] who was daughter of a Viśvāmitra;[6] so that Viśvāmitra was an ancestor of Bharata. Viśvāmitra cannot have been both an ancestor and

[1] Bd iii, *66*, 22–68, 75: Vā *91*, 51–96, 103: Br *10*, 13–60, 68: and Hv *27*, 1413–31, 1457, 1473: which all agree. Viṣ iv, *7*, 2–17, Gar i, *139*, 2–7 and Bhāg ix, *15*, 3 to *16*, 36 (which calls Amāvasu *Vijaya*) concur with them.

[2] Rām i, *32*, 1 to *34*, 6. Ag *277*, 16–18. MBh xii, *49*, 1717–20, 1745; and xiii, *4*, 201–5, 246 (with i, *94*, 3722–3).

[3] Second version, Br *13*, 82–92; Hv *32*, 1756–76.

[4] Vedārth, Introduction to Rigv iii, says Kuśika's father (Gāthin's grandfather) was Iṣīratha; this name does not occur in the genealogies. There is room for its insertion, see Table of genealogies, chap. XII.

[5] MBh i, *2*, 371; *74*, 2988, 3103–6; *95*, 3782: vii, *68*, 2387: xii, *29*, 938: xiv, *3*, 50: and Paurava genealogies.

[6] MBh i, *72* (in fabulous form), 2945; *95*, 3782.

a descendant of Bharata. The story of Śakuntalā is one of the best alleged tales in ancient tradition, so that Viśvāmitra was certainly prior to Bharata and therefore to Ajamīḍha, and the versions which make his ancestor Jahnu son of Ajamīḍha are certainly wrong. Moreover it will be seen from the discussion of Jahnu, Viśvāmitra and their contemporaries in chapter XIII, that they belonged to the age of the early Aikṣvāku, Haihaya and Paurava kings, long anterior to Bharata and Ajamīḍha. The error appears also from the condition, that it makes this kingdom arise at the same time as N. and S. Pañcāla, though they comprised all its territory.

The error probably arose out of Rigveda iii, *53*, 12, which, referring to king Sudās, says 'this prayer of Viśvāmitra safeguards the Bhārata folk'; and Aitareya Brāhmaṇa vii, *3*, 5 and Śāṅkhāyana Śrauta Sūtra xv, 25, where Viśvāmitra is called *Bharata-ṛṣabha*, 'leader of the Bharatas'. Sudās, or Sudāsa as he is called in the genealogy, was a king of the North Pañcāla dynasty, which was descended from Ajamīḍha and Bharata.[1] He and his dynasty were therefore Bharatas or Bhāratas, for the name Pañcāla (p. 75) had not come into approved use then.[2] One of Viśvāmitra's descendants, called by his gotra name merely Viśvāmitra, was his priest, as the hymn shows, and therefore the religious guardian and leader of these Bharatas or Bhāratas. Afterwards misunderstanding began. That Viśvāmitra might, not inappropriately, be styled a *Bharata-ṛṣabha*, the term used in the Brāhmaṇa and Sūtra. These books however, through the brahmanical lack of the historical sense, confused him with his ancestor, the first Viśvāmitra, and applied this term to the first Viśvāmitra. It thus became wholly erroneous as mentioned above, and the Bharatas did not come into existence till after his time. Further, this term might be taken to imply that he was himself a Bhārata, and, as the brahmans were not learned in kṣatriya genealogies, or perhaps considered the above allusions as authoritative, it was so understood, with the result that Viśvāmitra was held to be a descendant of Bharata.[3] Consequently it was necessary to introduce him and his well-known ancestor Jahnu into the Paurava genealogy somewhere after Bharata; and, as Ajamīḍha had three sons who ruled the separate kingdoms of Hastināpura and

[1] See Table of Royal Genealogies, chap. XII.
[2] JRAS, 1914, p. 284: 1918, pp. 238–9.
[3] So Sāyaṇa on Rigv iii, *53*, 24.

North and South Pañcāla, it was easy to assign Jahnu of the Kānyakubja kingdom [1] as another son to him, especially as Jahnu and Ajamīḍha had near ancestors named Suhotra. Connected with this mistake is the alteration which the Brahma and Harivaṁśa make in the ancestral name *Paurorava* (i.e. *Paurūrava*) applied rightly to Viśvāmitra in the Vāyu, namely, changing it to *Paurava*.[2]

Kāśi Dynasty.

Two origins are alleged for the Kāśi (Benares) dynasty also. It was descended from Āyu's son Kṣatravṛddha according to seven Puranas,[3] which give the first four kings as Kṣatravṛddha, Sunahotra (or Suhotra), Kāśa (or Kāśya) and Dīrghatapas. But the Brahma and Harivaṁśa give another account also, identifying Sunahotra or Suhotra with Suhotra of the Paurava line, whom they place as son of Vitatha (really son of Bṛhatkṣatra and great-grandson of Vitatha), and so, deriving this dynasty from Suhotra Paurava, give the early kings thus—Vitatha, Suhotra, Kāśika and Dīrghatapas. They thus inconsistently give both origins for the dynasty. The Agni follows this version, though confusedly and faultily.[4] Both versions agree on the whole in their lists of the kings, except that the second has various omissions. The list is not a long one and reaches down only to king Bharga, but at what stage in the chronology he is to be placed is wholly uncertain. The kings in the Pāṇḍavas' time were Subāhu and Abhibhū.[5]

The former version is clearly right and the latter is wrong, because Divodāsa and Pratardana of this dynasty, as will be seen from the discussion about the synchronisms in chapter XIII, were contemporaries of the Haihaya kings and lived anterior to Vitatha and Suhotra of the Paurava line. The origin of the error here is not so easily conjecturable as of that in the Kānyakubja genealogy, yet it appears to have arisen from confusing Kṣatravṛddha and his successor Sunahotra or Suhotra here with Bṛhatkṣatra and his successor Suhotra of the Paurava dynasty.

[1] Oblivious of territorial confusion, as mentioned above.

[2] He was a descendant of Purūravas but not of Pūru, Vā *91*, 102. Br *10*, 63 and Hv *27*, 1468; *32*, 1773 wrongly; and Bḍ substitutes *yogeśvara* (iii, *66*, 74).

[3] Bḍ iii, *67*, 1–79. Vā *92*, 1–75 (text corrupt). Br *11*, 32–61. Hv *29*, 1518–98. Viṣ iv, *8*, 1–9. Gar i, *139*, 8–14. Bhāg ix, *17*, 2–10.

[4] Br *13*, 63–79. Hv *32*, 1733–54. Ag *277*, 9–14.

[5] MBh ii, *29*, 1080: and vii, *95*, 3528; viii, *6*, 173. Cf. v, *197*, 7650.

The Haihayas.

The genealogy of the Haihaya branch of the Yādavas is given by twelve Puranas.[1] They all agree generally, except that there are differences and some uncertainty in the account of Tālajaṅgha's offspring, and there the best texts collated say this—Tālajaṅgha had many sons, called the Tālajaṅghas, of whom the eldest was king Vītihotra: the Haihayas comprised five families, the Vītihotras, Śāryātas,[2] Bhojas, Avantis and Tuṇḍikeras, who were all Tālajaṅghas:[3] Vītihotra's son was king Ananta, and his son was Durjaya Amitrakarśana. The Brahma and Harivaṁśa give, instead of the last two lines, six other lines,[4] but these seem doubtful inasmuch as they assign to this branch persons and families who apparently belonged to the other branch.

The Yādavas.

The genealogy of the other branch descended from Yadu's son Kroṣṭu and known as the Yādavas proper may be conveniently noticed in two parts, the first from Kroṣṭu to Sātvata and the second the remainder.

The first part is given by twelve Puranas.[5] They all agree generally, though with considerable variations in some of the names, down to Parāvṛt's sons. Then they leave the further descent of the senior line from his eldest son, and follow the line of his younger son Jyāmagha, who (or whose son Vidarbha) carved out the kingdom of Vidarbha. This line soon divided into three sub-lines, the senior of which apparently continued there for a time, while the second descended from Kaiśika (who is often miscalled

[1] Bḍ iii, *69*, 3–55. Vā *94*, 3–54. Br *13*, 154–207. Hv *33*, 1844–98. Mat *43*, 7–49. Pad v, *12*, 110–49. Lg i, *68*, 3–20. Kūr i, *22*, 13–21; *23*, 1–4, 45. Viṣ iv, *11*, 3–7. Ag *274*, 1–11. Gar i, *139*, 19–24. Bhāg ix, *23*, 21–30.

[2] So Mat, which appears to be right; all the other authorities corrupt the name. They were the remnant of the Śāryātas (*ante*). This appears to be the explanation of the incorrect statement in MBh xiii, *30*, 1945–6, that Haihaya and Tālajaṅgha were descended from Śaryāti.

[3] This seems to be the meaning, for the Vītihotras were certainly Tālajaṅghas.

[4] Lg has five of them and Kūr three.

[5] Bḍ iii, *70*, 14–48. Vā *95*, 14–47. Br *15*, 1–30. Hv *37*, 1969–99. Mat *44*, 14–47. Pad v, *13*, 1–30. Lg i. *68*, 21–49. Kūr i, *24*, 1–32. Viṣ iv, *12*. Ag *274*, 12–23. Gar i, *139*, 25–35. Bhāg ix, *23*, 30 to *24*, 6. Partially, MBh xiii, *147*, 6833–4; Hv *117*, 6588–92.

Kauśika) established itself in Cedi, and the third from Lomapāda reigned elsewhere. All the authorities agree in the main about these developments, and the Kūrma (i, *24*, 6–10) gives Lomapāda's sub-line for thirteen descents. The genealogies then follow the senior line of Vidarbha from Kratha, whom the Brahma and Harivaṁśa call Bhīma,[1] and all are in general agreement down to Devakṣatra, though with variations in some of the names. Then occur differences down to Sātvata, and the texts collated suggest the names set out in the Table of genealogies in chapter XII.

Lomapāda's sub-line is given thus—Lomapāda, Babhru, Āhṛti,[2] Śveta, Viśvasaha, Kauśika, Sumanta, Anala, Śveni, Dyutimant, Vapuṣmant, Bṛhanmedhas, Śrīdeva, and Vītaratha. Where they reigned is not stated.

The second part begins with Sātvata's sons, Bhajamāna, Devāvṛdha, Andhaka and Vṛṣṇi,[3] and comprises the various families that developed from them. It is given by the same twelve Puranas, but the accounts are not all clear, for several reasons. Some of the pedigrees have become confused in some Puranas through mistakes in names, partly at least due to misreadings of old scripts; as where the Brahmāṇḍa and Vāyu misread *Andhakāt* as *Satyakāt* in giving Andhaka's descendants; and the Brahma and Harivaṁśa misread *Vṛṣṇer* as *Kroṣṭor* in giving Vṛṣṇi's descendants, and then seemingly regard him as Yadu's son Kroṣṭu, so mentioning some of the lines of descent twice. Moreover some passages seem to have become misarranged, and lines have sometimes been lost. Some uncertainty was caused by the fact that there were several persons with the same names in these families, and thus it seems that Vṛṣṇi's eldest son by one wife was Sumitra known also as Anamitra, and his youngest son by another wife was Anamitra too; while Vṛṣṇi was a favourite name. The difficulties can only be cleared up by

[1] The same descendants are given to both.

[2] Much variation in these two names.

[3] The best texts, Bḍ iii, *71*, 1–2; Vā *96*, 1–2; Br *15*, 30–31; Hv *38*, 1999–2000; Mat *44*, 47–8; Pad v, *13*, 31–2; and Lg i, *69*, 1–2; collated give this reading:—

> Sātvatāt sattva-sampannān Kausalyā suṣuve sutān
> bhajinam Bhajamānaṁ tu divyaṁ Devāvṛdhaṁ nṛpam
> Andhakaṁ ca mahā-Bhojaṁ Vṛṣṇiṁ ca Yadu-nandanam
> teṣāṁ hi sargāś catvāraḥ—

Viṣ, Ag, and Bhāg multiply them by treating their epithets as separate names. Kūr is defective.

collating the various passages in those Puranas, which are based on the same original metrical text more or less accurately.[1] That being done, the results are shown in the pedigrees set out *infra*.

There is no difficulty about Bhajamāna, for only his sons are mentioned, and the texts, though partially corrupt, yet when collated make the account clear.[2]

Nor is there any difficulty about Devāvṛdha, because only his son Babhru is named, and the texts[3] collated say his lineage were the Bhojas of Mārttikāvata as stated in the concluding half verse.[4]

The real difficulties occur with regard to Andhaka's and Vṛṣṇi's descendants, and these are elucidated in detail.

Andhaka had four sons, but only two are important, Kukura and Bhajamāna. From Kukura were descended the Kukuras,[5] and Bhajamāna's descendants were specially styled the Andhakas.[6] The genealogy of both as elucidated by collating the texts is given in the table opposite.

Vṛṣṇi's progeny present the most difficulty, because he had at least four sons, two with the same name, and from them were descended various families, and because the accounts are not always compact.

[1] Viṣ iv, *13*, 1 f. Ag *274*, 24 f. Gar i, *139*, 36 f., and Bhāg ix, *24*, 6 f. have recast the account and show much confusion, especially the last three, but are useful for comparison.

[2] Bd iii, *71*, 3–6ᵃ. Vā *96*, 3–6ᵃ. Br *15*, 32–4. Hv *38*, 2001–3. Mat *44*, 49–50. Pad v, *13*, 33–35ᵃ. Lg i, *69*, 3 and Kūr i, *24*, 37 are incomplete. Cf. Viṣ iv, *13*, 2 : Ag *274*, 25ᵃ : Gar i, *139*, 37 : Bhāg ix, *24*, 7ᵇ–8.

[3] Bd iii, *71*, 6ᵇ–18ᵃ. Vā *96*, 6ᵇ–17ᵃ. Br *15*, 35–45ᵃ. Hv *38*, 2004–14ᵃ. Mat *44*, 51–60. Pad v, *13*, 35ᵇ–45ᵃ. Lg i, *69*, 4–9. Kūr i, *24*, 35–6, 38ᵃ. Cf. Viṣ iv, *13*, 3–6; Ag *274*, 25ᵇ–27ᵃ; Gar i, *139*, 38ᵃ; Bhāg ix, *24*, 9–11.

[4] It should run thus, but Mat, Pad and Kūr corrupt it and Lg varies it :—

tasyânvavāyaḥ sumahān Bhojā ye Mārttikāvatāḥ.

[5] Bd iii, *71*, 116–35ᵃ and Vā *96*, 115–34, which misread the first word *Andhakāt* as *Satyakāt*. Br *15*, 45ᵇ–62. Hv *38*, 2014ᵇ–31. Mat *44*, 61–76. Pad v, *13*, 45ᵇ–62. Lg i, *69*, 32–42. Kūr i, *24*, 46ᵇ–65 has only the first five lines and then varies. The opening words should be *Andhakāt Kāśya-duhitā*. Cf. Viṣ iv, *14*, 3–5; Ag *274*, 27ᵇ–33; Gar i, *139*, 43ᵇ–48ᵃ; Bhāg ix, *24*, 19–25.

[6] Bd iii, *71*, 136ᵇ–44. Vā *96*, 135–42. Br *16*, 1–8. Hv *39*, 2032–9. Mat *44*, 77–85. Pad v, *13*, 63–72ᵃ. Kūr i, *24*, 66–7 is different. Lg nil. There is much variation in the unimportant names. Kūr wrongly makes Kṛṣṇa's father Vasudeva grandson of Kṛtavarman. Cf. Viṣ iv, *14*, 6–7; Ag *274*, 34–38ᵃ; Gar i, *139*, 48ᵇ–50; Bhāg ix, *24*, 26–27ᵃ.

The Yādavas—The Sātvatas.

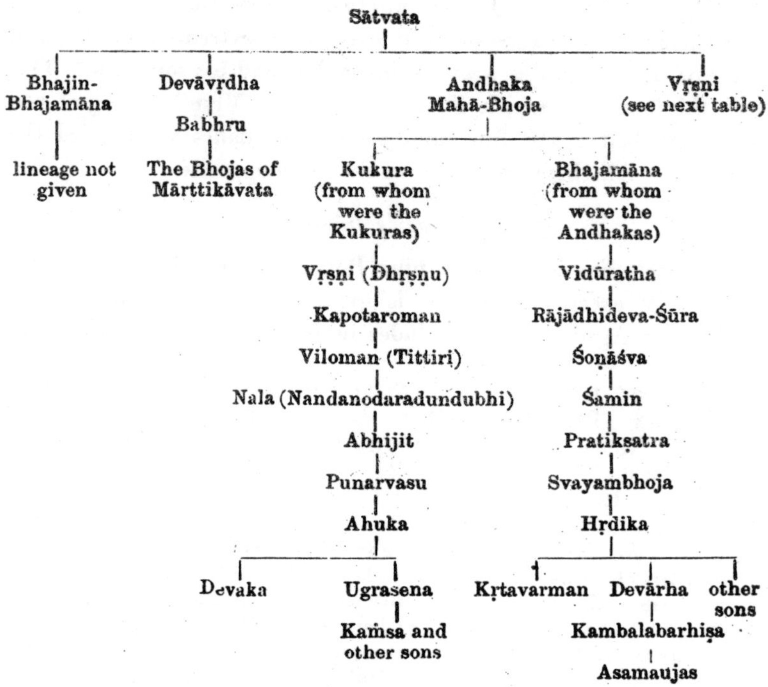

Moreover the Brahma, Harivaṁśa and Padma misread his name as Kroṣṭu or Kroṣṭṛ, and appear to confuse him with his ancestor, Yadu's son Kroṣṭu or Kroṣṭṛ, and that this is a mistake is shown by their reading Vṛṣṇi correctly in the first line about the family of the Śainyas.[1] There were three lines of descent of the Vṛṣṇis from Vṛṣṇi's three sons Anamitra, Yudhājit and Devamīḍhuṣa;[2] and Anamitra there means the eldest son (by Gāndhārī), who was also called Sumitra. But there was also a fourth line from his youngest son Anamitra (by Mādrī) as will appear, whose descendants were called Śainyas. Vṛṣṇi's lineage, so far as it can be made out from a collation of the important texts, is shown in the next table, and a comparison of its length with that of the Kukuras and Andhakas shows that it must omit several generations.

Vṛṣṇi's offspring begin with that of the eldest son (by Gāndhārī) Sumitra, called Anamitra by the Brahma and Harivaṁśa, down

[1] See sixth note *infra*.

[2] Br *14*, 2, 35. Hv *35*, 1907, 1945.

to Sátrājit,[1] and Satrājit's children are mentioned separately.[2] Yudhājit's descendants divided into two families, those of Śvaphalka and Citraka.[3] Devamīḍhuṣa's line is given extremely briefly, and some of the authorities wrongly invert him and his son Sūra.[4] This was the family in which Kṛṣṇa was born.[5] Vṛṣṇi's youngest son Anamitra had a son Śini, and their descendants were called the Śainyas.[6] All these are shown in the table opposite.

Turvasu's lineage.

Turvasu's line is given by nine Puranas,[7] and all are in general agreement, except that there is great variation in some of the names, the Agni wrongly includes in it the Gāndhāras who were

[1] Bd iii, *71*, 18^{b}–21. Vā *96*, 17^{b}–20. Br *16*, 9–11. Hv *39*, 2040–2. Mat *45*, 1–3. Pad v, *13*, 72^{b}–75^{a}. Lg i, *69*, 10–12. Also Br *14*, 1–2 and Hv *35*, 1906–7, which give only the first two lines. Kūr i, *24*, 38^{b}–39 is different. Cf. Viṣ iv, *13*, 7–8; Ag *274*, 38^{b}–40; Gar i, *139*, 39; Bhāg ix, *24*, 12–13^{a}.

[2] Bd iii, *71*, 54–7. Vā *96*, 53–5. Br *16*, 45^{b}–49^{a}. Hv *39*, 2076^{b}–80^{a}. Mat *45*, 19–21. Pad v, *13*, 93^{b}–6. Lg and Kūr nil.

[3] Bd iii, *71*, 102–115. Vā *96*, 101–114. Br *14*, 3–13 (inaccurate); *16*, 49^{b}–59. Hv *35*, 1908–21 (inaccurate); *39*, 2080^{b}–89. Mat *45*, 25–33 and Pad v, *13*, 98–105^{a} (without Citraka's line). Lg i, *69*, 18–31. Kūr i, *24*, 42–46^{a} partially agrees. There are considerable variations in the verses, especially in Mat and Pad where some lines are obviously corrupt. Cf. Viṣ iv, *14*, 2; Ag *274*, 46–7^{a}; Gar i, *139*, 41–3^{a}; Bhāg ix, *24*, 14^{b}–18.

[4] Bd iii, *71*, 145–60^{a}. Vā *96*, 143–59^{a}. Br *14*, 14–24^{a}, 25^{b} f. Hv *35*, 1922–34^{a}, 1935^{b} f. Mat *46*, 1–10, 23–4. Pad v, *13*, 108^{b}–117. These collated show that Devamīḍhuṣa was the father (or ancestor) and Śūra the son (or descendant). So MBh says Śūra was son of Devamīḍha (vii, *144*, 6030–1) and father of Vasudeva (*ibid.*: also i, *67*, 2764; *111*, 4382). MBh xiii, *147*, 6834–5 says Śūra was son (descendant) of Citraratha, referring to his distant ancestor. Kūr i, *24*, 67–70 confusedly joins this line on to Hṛdika in the Andhaka line. Cf. Viṣ iv, *14*, 8–12; Ag *274*, 47^{b}–8; Gar i, *139*, 50^{b}–55; Bhāg ix, *24*, 27^{b}–44.

[5] Vasudeva's and Kṛṣṇa's families, Bd iii, *71*, 160^{b} f.: Vā *96*, 159^{b} f.: Br *14*, 36 f.: Hv *36*: Mat *46*, 11–22: Pad v, *13*, 123^{b} f.: Lg i, *69*, 43 f.: Kūr i, *24*, 68 f. Cf. Viṣ iv, *15*, 11 f.; Ag *274*, 49 f.; Gar i, *139*, 56 f.; Bhāg ix, *24*, 45 f.

[6] Bd iii, *71*, 100–1. Vā *96*, 99–100. Mat *45*, 22–4. Pad v, *13*, 97. Hv *35*, 1934^{b}–5^{a} (condensed). Lg i, *69*, 15^{b}–17. Kūr i, *24*, 40–1. Br *14*, 24^{b}–5^{a}. Cf. Viṣ iv, *14*, 1; Ag *274*, 45^{b}–46^{a}; Gar i, *139*, 38^{b}, 39^{b}, 40; Bhāg ix, *24*, 13^{b}–14.

[7] Bd iii, *74*, 1–6. Vā *99*, 1–6. Br *13*, 141–8. Hv *32*, 1829–36. Mat *48*, 1–5. Viṣ iv, *16*. Ag *276*, 1–3. Gar i, *139*, 63–4. Bhāg ix, *23*, 16–18. Turvasu is called Turvaśa in Vedic literature.

The Yādavas (Sātvatas) continued—The Vṛṣṇis.

Gāndhārī = Vṛṣṇi = Mādrī

- (by Gāndhārī) Sumitra or Anamitra I
  - Nighna
    - Prasena
    - Satrājit
      - Bhaṅgakāra
        - Sabhākṣa
- (by Mādrī)
  - Yudhājit
    - Pṛśni
      - Śvaphalka
        - Akrūra
          - Devavant and Upadeva
      - Citraka
        - Pṛthu &c.
  - Devamīḍhuṣa
    - Śūra
      - Vasudeva
        - Balarāma
        - Kṛṣṇa
      - other sons
  - Anamitra II
    - Śini (whose descendants were the Śainyas)
      - Satyaka
        - Yuyudhāna
          - Asaṅga
            - Yugandhara
  - Śini ?

Druhyus, and the Viṣṇu, Garuḍa and Bhāgavata omit the last part. Marutta the great king of this dynasty (whom the Matsya incorrectly calls Bharata) had no son and adopted Duṣyanta the Paurava, and thus this line is said to have merged into the Paurava line, as the Brahmāṇḍa, Vāyu, Brahma and Harivaṁśa declare. Yet it is added that from this line or from Duṣyanta there was a branch which founded the kingdoms of Pāṇḍya, Cola, Kerala, &c. in the south.[1] The line stands thus, greatly abbreviated—Turvasu, Vahni, Garbha, Gobhānu, Trisānu, Karandhama, Marutta, Duṣyanta, Śarūtha (or Varūtha), Aṇḍīra; and Pāṇḍya, Kerala, Cola and Kulya (or Kola).

Druhyu's lineage.

Druhyu's line is given by nine Puranas,[2] and all are in general agreement, except that the Brahma and Harivaṁśa wrongly divide it into two, assigning to him the successors down to Gāndhāra, and Dharma and the remainder to Anu. This mistake of theirs is the cause or result of their erroneously making the Ānavas a branch growing out of the Paurava line, as will be explained in noticing the Ānava genealogy. The line stands thus—Druhyu with two sons Babhru and Setu, then Setu's descendants, Aṅgāra-setu,[3] Gāndhāra, Dharma, Dhṛta,[3] Durdama,[3] Pracetas, to whom the Brahma and Harivaṁśa add Sucetas. Four Puranas add that Pracetas' offspring spread out into the mleccha countries to the north beyond India and founded kingdoms there.[4]

The Ānavas.

The genealogy of Anu's descendants, the Ānavas, is given by nine Puranas.[5] All agree substantially, except that the Brahma and Harivaṁśa wrongly make Anu's lineage descend from Kakṣeyu,

[1] Cf. Pad vi, *250*, 1–2. This is not improbable. Turvasu princes may have carved out such kingdoms.

[2] Bḍ iii, *74*, 7–12. Vā *99*, 7–12. Br *13*, 148–53. Hv *32*, 1837–41. Mat *48*, 6–9. Viṣ iv, *17*. Gar i, *139*, 64–5. Ag *276*, 4–5ª. Bhāg ix, *23*, 14–16.

[3] These names have variations. The name Aṅgāra is supported by MBh xii, *29*, 981; cf. also *id.* iii, *126*, 10465.

[4] Bḍ, Vā, and Mat (*loc. cit.*) thus:—

Pracetasaḥ putra-śataṁ rājānaḥ sarva eva te
mleccha-rāṣṭrâdhipāḥ sarve hy udīcīṁ diśam āśritāḥ.

Viṣ more fully. Bhāg briefly. See JRAS, 1919, p. 361.

[5] Bḍ iii, *74*, 12 f. Vā *99*, 12 f. Br *13*, 14 f. Hv *31*, 1669 f. Mat *48*, 10 f. Viṣ iv, *18*, 1. Ag *276*, 5 f. Gar i, *139*, 65 f. Bhāg ix, *23*, 1 f.

one of the sons of Raudrāśva of the Paurava line, and wrongly assign to Anu part of Druhyu's progeny,[1] as mentioned above. The seventh king after Anu, Mahāmanas, had two sons, Uśīnara and Titikṣu, and under them the Ānavas divided into two great branches; Uśīnara and his descendants occupied the Panjab, and Titikṣu founded a new kingdom in the east, viz., in East Behar.

Uśīnara's posterity is given by the same nine Puranas,[2] the fullest account being in the Brahmāṇḍa, Vāyu, Brahma and Harivaṁśa. It stands thus, with the kingdoms that his descendants founded:—

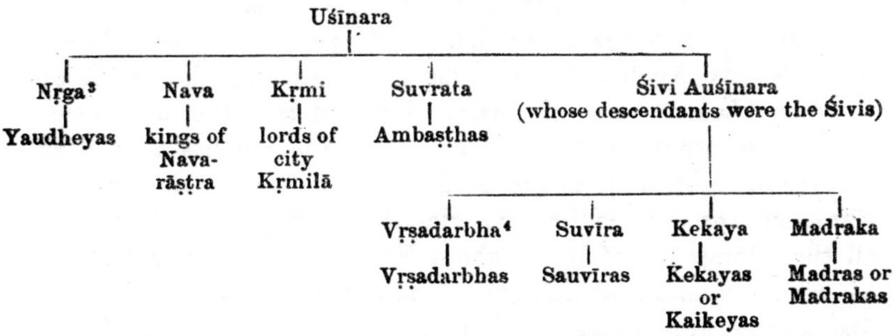

Titikṣu's lineage is given by the same nine Puranas.[5] All agree substantially, except that the Brahmāṇḍa has lost all after Dharmaratha in a great lacuna, the Vāyu omits from Satyaratha to Campa, the Viṣṇu, Garuḍa and Bhāgavata omit Jayadratha's descendants, and the Brahma and Agni omit Vijaya and his line. The best accounts are in the Matsya and Harivaṁśa. This 'Kingdom in the East' was divided among Bali's five sons into five kingdoms, Aṅga, Vaṅga, Kaliṅga, Puṇḍra and Suhma. He was quite distinct from Bali son of Virocana, the Daitya (p. 64). This genealogy with the Aṅga line is given in the Table in chapter XII.

[1] Br *13*, 152–3. Hv *32*, 1840–1.

[2] Passages in continuation of those in second note above.

[3] Probably referred to in MBh ix, *55*, 3029–31.

[4] Miscalled *Bṛhadgarbha*, MBh iii, *197*, 13321. See xiii, *93*, 4420, 4424.

[5] Bd iii, *74*, 24–103. Vā *99*, 24–119. Br *13*, 27–49. Hv *31*, 1681–1710. Mat *48*, 21–108. Viṣ iv, *18*, 1–7. Ag *276*, 10–16. Gar i, *139*, 68–74. Bhāg ix, *23*, 4–14. Cf. MBh xiii, *42*, 2351 (Citraratha).

The Pauravas.

The genealogy of Pūru's descendants, the Pauravas, is found in eight Puranas and also twice in the Mahābhārata, and may be conveniently considered in three portions, only the more important features and differences being noticed; the first, from Pūru to Ajamīḍha, the second from Ajamīdha to Kuru, and the third from Kuru to the Pāṇḍavas. The Brahmāṇḍa has lost all the Pauravas in a large lacuna.

In the first portion all the Puranas [1] agree more or less down to Matināra; but the two Mahābhārata accounts [2] differ, the first having many names as in the Puranas but being manifestly confused; [3] and the second omitting Raudrāśva and Ṛceyu, but inserting a group of ten kings Sārvabhauma, Jayatsena, Avācīna, Ariha, Mahābhauma, Ayutanāyin, Akrodhana, Devātithi, Ariha and Ṛkṣa between Ahaṁyāti and Matināra. None of the other authorities know of this group in this position, and all the Puranas place it as a group of eight kings in the third portion between Vidūratha and Bhīmasena, except the Brahma, Harivaṁśa and Agni which omit all these kings except Ṛkṣa (who is Ṛkṣa II). The Mahābhārata has certainly misplaced this group, and for several reasons. Its own first account agrees with the Puranas in knowing nothing of this group here. The account says that two of these kings married princesses of Aṅga, one a princess of Kaliṅga, and two married princesses of Vidarbha, but those kingdoms were not founded till long after Matināra's time, as will appear from the synchronisms in chapter XIII and Table of genealogies in chapter XII. That table and the synchronisms also show that it is impossible these ten kings could find room at this stage; and further that, if they could be inserted here, there would be an unaccountable gap in the third portion. The group must therefore be removed from here and put where the Puranas place it, in the third portion, and where it is thoroughly in position.

[1] Vā *99*, 119–166. Br *13*, 2–8, 50–63, 80–1. Hv *31*, 1653–68; *32*, 1714–32, 1754–5; with *20*, 1053–5. Mat *49*, 1–43. Viṣ iv, *19*, 1–10. Ag *277*, 1–9, 15. Gar i, *140*, 1–8. Bhāg ix, *20*, 1–39; *21*, 1, 20–1.

[2] MBh (first) i, *94*, 3695–3720; (second) i, *95*, 3764–89.

[3] It says Pūru's son Pravīra married a Śaurasena princess (3696), and his son Manasyu married a Sauvīra princess (3697), but Śūrasena and Suvīra did not come into existence till later; see chap. XIV and Anavas *ante*.

From Taṁsu to Duṣyanta there is great uncertainty. The chief texts, the Vāyu, Matsya, Brahma and Harivaṁśa, have a certain seeming agreement, yet really supply no intelligible pedigree, as will appear if we try to construct one from their statements. All that seems clear is that there was a remarkable woman Ilinā and that her grandson was Duṣyanta.[1] The Mahābhārata accounts turn her into a king Ilina. Queens were sometimes turned into kings mistakenly,[2] but I am not aware of any instance of the reverse; so that these accounts appear to be incorrect, and the genealogical verse quoted is not found in these Puranas. The other Puranas which are later have connected up a pedigree, but differ incompatibly and omit Ilinā altogether. The truth is, there is a serious gap in the genealogy here, as will appear from the discussion of the synchronisms in chapter XIII.

From Duṣyanta to Hastin (or Bṛhat[3]), who founded or named Hastināpura, the lists fairly agree. Hastin had two sons Ajamīḍha and Dvimīḍha. Ajamīḍha continued the main Paurava line at Hastināpura, and Dvimīḍha founded a separate dynasty, which is not specially named and may be called the Dvimīḍha line, and which will be noticed *infra*. This portion is shown in the following table.

The second portion from Ajamīḍha to Kuru is given by the same eight Puranas[4] and the two Mahābhārata accounts.[5] Ajamīḍha had three sons, and they originated separate dynasties. The eldest line from Ṛkṣa I continued the main line at Hastināpura, and here the lists agree down to Kuru, inserting only Saṁvaraṇa between them; but it will appear from the synchronisms and the Table of genealogies in chapters XIV and XII that there must have been more generations, and that not a few names have been lost here, probably both before and after Ṛkṣa. The two other sons, Nīla

[1] Cf. also Vā *68*, 23, 24; Bd iii, *6*, 23, 25.

[2] As Mat *12*, 37, Pad v, *8*, 142 and Ag *272*, 26 do with Satyavrata Triśaṅku's queen Satyarathā; as Gar i, *138*, 22 does with Māndhātṛ's queen Bindumatī; and as Mat *50*, 6 does with Vadhryaśva's mother Indrasenā.

[3] So Br, Ag, and Hv; but Hv *20*, 1053–4 names Hastin.

[4] Vā *99*, 211–17. Br *13*, 102–7. Hv *32*, 1795–1800. Mat *50*, 17–21. Viṣ iv, *19*, 18. Ag *277*, 25–6. Gar i, *140*, 24–5. Bhāg ix, *22*, 3–4.

[5] MBh (first) i, *94*, 3721–2, 3724–39; (second) i, *95*, 3790–1.

Pauravas

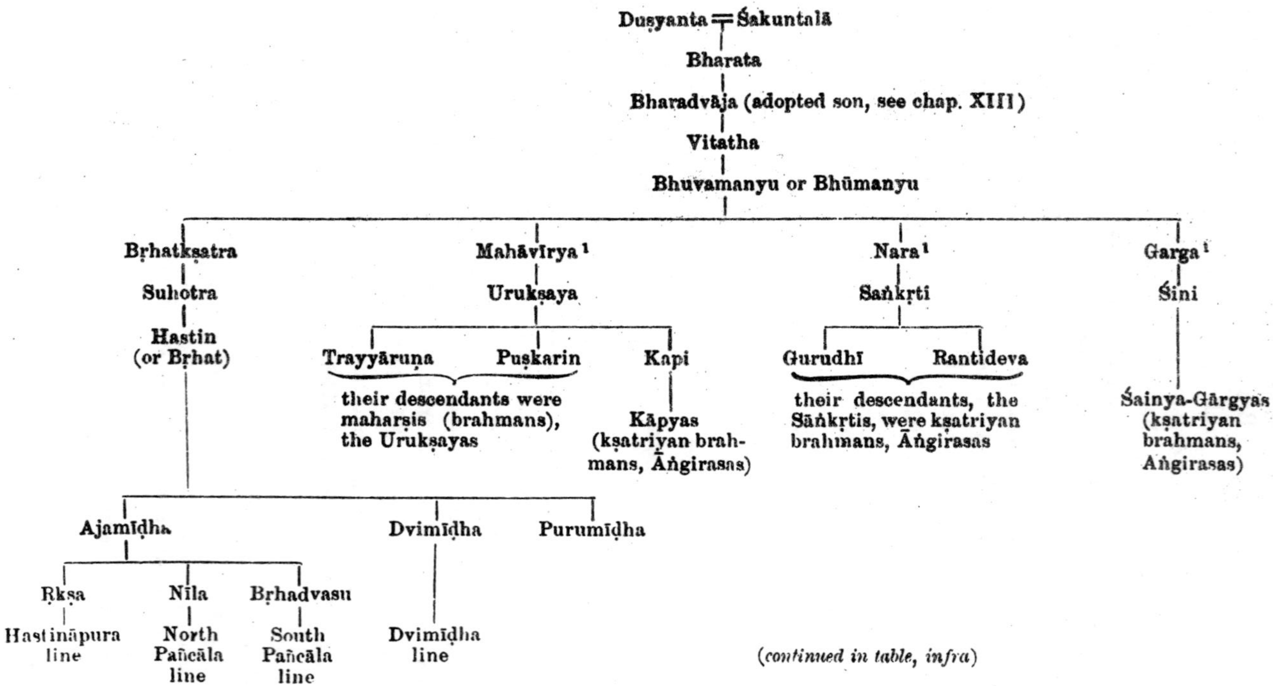

(*continued in table, infra*)

[1] These families are explained in chap. XXIII.

and Bṛhadvasu,[1] founded the dynasties of North and South Pañcāla respectively, which will be noticed separately. The Mahābhārata does not say anything about the origin of these two dynasties, except that its first account baldly declares that Ajamīḍha had two sons Duṣyanta and Parameṣṭhin, and from them came all the Pañcālas, which except in the names agrees with the Purāṇas. South Pañcāla was approximately the portion of Pañcāla south of the Ganges as far as the R. Carmaṇvatī (Chambal), and its capitals were Kāmpilya[2] and Mākandī. North Pañcāla was the portion north of the Ganges, with its capital at Ahicchattrā,[3] whence it was called the Ahichattra country.[4]

Bharata's descendants were called the Bharatas or Bhāratas;[5] so all these dynasties, the main line at Hastināpura[6] and those of the Dvimīḍhas and of North[7] and South Pañcāla, were Bhāratas.

The third portion from Kuru to the Pāṇḍavas is given by the same authorities.[8] There are some discrepancies among Kuru's immediate descendants, but the text suggested by collating the chief accounts[9] clears them up. It shows that Kuru had three

[1] So Vā. Mat *Bṛhadanu*. Hv, Viṣ, Gar, and Bhāg *Bṛhadiṣu*.

[2] MBh v, *193*, 7500: xii, *139*, 5137.

[3] Called also Chattravatī, MBh i, *166*, 6348.

[4] MBh i, *138*, 5507–16.

[5] MBh i, *2*, 371; *62*, 2320–1; *74*, 3123: iv, *28*, 912: xiii, *76*, 3690. Vā *99*, 134. Mat *24*, 71; *49* 11. Br *13*, 57. Hv *32*, 1723, &c. So also Śatapatha Brāhm (p. 65).

[6] So habitually in the MBh. Sörensen (p. 123) treats *Bhārata* in iii, *106*, 8847 as applying to Sagara, but it really refers to Janamejaya, to whom the MBh professes to have been recited.

[7] Thus Dhṛṣṭadyumna, who belonged to this line, is called *Bharatarṣabha*, MBh vi, *50*, 2066.

[8] Vā *99*, 217–18, 229–49. Br *13*, 108–23. Hv *32*, 1801–2, 1813–28. Mat *50*, 23, 34–56. Viṣ iv, *19*, 19; *20*. Ag *277*, 27, 31–40. Gar i, *140*, 25, 30–40. Bhāg ix, *22*, 4, 9–33. MBh (first) i, *94*, 3740–51; (second) i, *95*, 3792–3835. His ancestor Yayāti is called, by anticipation or through lack of the historical sense, 'augmentor of the Kuru race,' MBh i, *86*, 3541–2; and so also Saṁvaraṇa, MBh i, *171*, 6527; *172*, 6562; *173*, 6611.

[9] Kuros tu dayitāḥ putrāḥ Sudhanvā Jahnur eva ca
Parikṣito mahātejāḥ pravaraś cārimardanaḥ
* * *
Parikṣitasya dāyādo babhūva Janamejayaḥ
Janamejayasya putrās tu traya eva mahārathāḥ
ŚrutasenÔgrasenau ca Bhīmasenaś ca nāmataḥ
Jahnus tv ajanayat putraṁ Surathaṁ nāma bhūmipam
Surathasya tu dāyādo vīro rājā Vidūrathaḥ—&c.

sons, Parikṣit I[1] the eldest, Jahnu and Sudhanvan. The account deals first with Sudhanvan's descendants, an offshoot, in which was Vasu who conquered and founded anew the kingdoms of Cedi and Magadha: its genealogy is noticed separately *infra*. The account then returns to the main line, to Parikṣit I's lineage. His son was Janamejaya II, and his sons were Śrutasena, Ugrasena and Bhīmasena. Then the account drops them, passes to Jahnu, and gives his descendants who became the main Paurava line.[2] Śrutasena, Ugrasena and Bhīmasena are not described as kings, and the fact that their line stops and the account passes to Jahnu's son Suratha as king shows that Janamejaya's branch lost the sovereignty, which then vested in Suratha. The cause of this is explained by a story told earlier in the genealogy. Janamejaya II injured the rishi Gārgya's son and was cursed by Gārgya; he was abandoned by his people, and was in great affliction; he sought help from the rishi Indrota Daivāpa Śaunaka, who purified him with a horse-sacrifice.[3] He did not however recover the sovereignty, and so his three sons passed into oblivion.[4]

The Mahābhārata's two genealogies of the main line are different and mutually inconsistent, though if the group of kings, Sārvabhauma to Ṛkṣa II, be brought from the first portion into its proper place here, the second genealogy approximates to the Purana

[1] Written indifferently as Parīkṣit and Parīkṣita.

[2] Viṣ, Gar and Ag agree with this *résumé*, except that Viṣ and Gar (unless its reading be amended) make Janamejaya's three sons his brothers. Bhāg says Parikṣit I had no offspring. Ag follows Hv with one or two more mistakes. MBh i, *3*, 661–2 and Bhāg ix, *22*, 35 confuse this Janamejaya II with the later Parikṣit's son Janamejaya III, who reigned after the Bhārata battle; and then make the same mistake as Viṣ and Gar. Var *193*, 1–5 also confuses them. The Parikṣit who got Vāmadeva's horses was a different person, a king of Ayodhyā (MBh iii, *192*, 13145, 13179 f.), and probably the same as Pāripātra of that line.

[3] Vā *93*, 21–6. Bḍ iii, *68*, 20–6. Hv *30*, 1608–13. Br *12*, 9–15. Lg i, *66*, 71–7, Also MBh xii, *150* to *152*, which amplifies and brahmanizes it.

[4] This explains the allusions in the Śatapatha Brāhm (xiii, 5, 4, 1) and Śāṅkhāyana Śr Sūtra (xvi, 9, 7) to Janamejaya Pārikṣita and his three sons (not brothers), the Pārikṣitīyas, and also the question in the Bṛhadāraṇyaka Upaniṣad (iii, 3), 'Whither have the Pārikṣitas gone?' if their extinction be implied: but the answer 'Thither where aśvamedha sacrificers go' suggests the opposite, because such sacrifices procured great blessings, as is declared in this story in MBh xii, *152*, 5674. See Weber, *Hist. of Indian Lit.*, pp. 125–6, 135–6, 186: and *Vedic Index*, i, p. 520.

account. The Brahma, Harivaṁśa and Agni omit them all except Ṛkṣa II.

The Dvimīḍhas.

The Dvimīḍha dynasty is given by six Puranas.[1] It is derived correctly by the Vāyu, Viṣṇu, Garuḍa and Bhāgavata, but is wrongly attributed to Ajamīḍha by the Matsya and Harivaṁśa; and the Viṣṇu by the loss of words, that closed the South Pañcāla dynasty with Bhallāṭa's son Janamejaya and opened this, says Dvimīḍha was Bhallāṭa's son and thus tacks it on to that line. This is clearly wrong, because it thus makes Ugrāyudha of this dynasty the tenth descendant from Bhallāṭa, but he killed Bhallāṭa's son Janamejaya, and both of them were contemporaries of Bhīṣma, as will be explained in chapter XIII.[2] As regards the kings the lists agree generally (the Vāyu and Matsya having the best texts), with however some mistakes. Thus the Viṣṇu, Garuḍa and Bhāgavata omit four kings, Sudharman to Rukmaratha; and the Bhāgavata, misunderstanding the relation of teacher and disciple between Hiraṇyanābha of Kosala and king Kṛta,[3] wrongly introduces the former here as Kṛta's father, and also wrongly assigns the last five kings as Nīpa's descendants in the South Pañcāla line. The Vāyu, Matsya and Harivaṁśa declare that in Sārvabhauma's lineage was Mahant Paurava, thus indicating a gap between them. This line is set out in the Table of Genealogies in chapter XII.

North Pañcāla.

This dynasty, which reigned in the portion of Pañcāla north of the Ganges, is given by eight Puranas.[4] All are in substantial agreement (except that the Brahma is incomplete) down to Divodāsa's son Mitrayu. Then divergencies occur as regards Mitrayu's son and Sṛñjaya and Cyavana-Pañcajana, and the Brahma, Harivaṁśa and Agni call Sudāsa *Somadatta*. After that all agree. This

[1] Vā *99*, 184–93. Mat *49*, 70–9. Hv *20*, 1075–85. Viṣ iv, *19*, 13–15. Gar i, *140*, 14–16. Bhāg ix, *21*, 27–30.

[2] Mat in a brahmanical fable says wrongly that Ugrāyudha, and so this dynasty, belonged to the Solar race (*49*, 61).

[3] So Vā, Hv and Mat. Also Bd ii, *35*, 38–40, 49: Vā *61*, 33, 35, 44; and Viṣ iii, *6*, 4, 7.

[4] Vā *99*, 194–211 and Mat *50*, 1–16, which have the best text. Hv *32*, 1777–94. Br *13*, 93–101. Viṣ iv, *19*, 15–18. Ag *277*, 18–25. Gar i, *140*, 17–24. Bhāg ix, *21*, 30 to *22*, 3.

North Pañcāla Dynasty

Ajamīḍha
|
Nīla
|
Suśānti
|
Purujānu or Purujāti
|
Ṛkṣa
|
Bhṛmyaśva
(who had five sons called the Pañcālas)

- Mudgala [1]
  - Brahmiṣṭha = Indrasenā
    - Vadhryaśva = Menakā
      - Divodāsa (Atithigva)
        - Mitrayu
        - Maitreya Soma [2]
        - (whose successor was, apparently his son,)
        - Sṛñjaya
        - Cyavana-Pañcajana (Pijavana)
        - Sudāsa (Sudās)-Somadatta
        - Sahadeva (Suplan)
        - Somaka-Ajamīḍha
        - Jantu
        - (whose distant descendant was)
        - Pṛṣata
        - Drupada
      - Ahalyā = Śaradvant (Āṅgirasa)
        - Śatānanda
        - ⋮
        - Satyadhṛti
          - Kṛpa
          - Kṛpī
- Sṛñjaya
- Bṛhadiṣu a king
- Yavīnara
- Kāmpilya or Kapila, or Kṛmilāśva

[1] From Mudgala were descended the Maudgalyas ; see chap. XXIII.

[2] From him were the Maitreyas, brahmans.

is a very noteworthy dynasty, because many of its kings play an important part in the Rigveda. Pañcajana appears to be a mistake for the Vedic Pijavana, and Sudāsa is the Vedic Sudās.[1] It stands with its incidental information as in the preceding table.

Bhṛmyaśva's territory was apparently subdivided among his five sons as petty rājās. The eldest branch soon rose to prominence under Vadhryaśva, Divodāsa, and Sudās. It decayed after Sudās' death and was subdued by Saṁvaraṇa of the main Hastināpura line.[2] It then became insignificant, and so there is a large gap after Jantu until Pṛṣata revived the dynasty in Bhīṣma's time. Droṇa with the aid of the Hastināpura princes conquered Pṛṣata's son Drupada, retained North Pañcāla for himself, and transferred him to South Pañcāla,[3] so that this family reigned over South Pañcāla in the period treated of in the Mahābhārata. From Sṛñjaya of the main branch here were descended the Sṛñjayas and from Somaka the Somakas, both of which families attended Drupada[4] who was a Somaka.[5] This dynasty is also noteworthy because it became brahmanic, as will be explained in chapter XXIII.

South Pañcāla.

This dynasty, which reigned south of the Ganges and was descended from Ajamīḍha as mentioned above, is given by six Puranas.[6] All these are in general agreement down to Nīpa except that there is much variation in the names of the first five kings. From Nīpa were descended the Nīpas. Then all agree substantially, except that the Matsya wrongly derives Nīpas chief son Samara and Samara's successors from a younger son of Senajit by a misreading of *Kāvyāc ca* for *Kāmpilye*; the Bhāgavata omits most of these successors, and the Garuḍa the last three kings. The Viṣṇu omits the last king Jamamejaya and wrongly tacks the Dvimīḍha line on to this (see above).

[1] This dynasty is considered in chap. X, and fully in JRAS, 1918, pp. 229 f.

[2] See synchronisms in chap. XIV.

[3] MBh i, *138*, 5444–5513; *166*, 6341–54.

[4] Sṛñjayas, MBh i, *138*, 5476: vi, *16*, 631: &c. Somakas, i, *185*, 6975; *193*, 7174: vi, *75*, 3288: &c. Both, vi, *89*, 3889; *90*, 3952.

[5] Called *Saumaki*, MBh i, *131*, 5192.

[6] Vā *99*, 167, 170–182. Mat *49*, 47–59. Hv *20*, 1055–73. Viṣ iv, *19*, 11–13. Gar i, *140*, 10–13. Bhāg ix, *21*, 22–26.

Cedi, Magadha, &c.

The dynasties in these countries were descended from Kuru's son Sudhanvan (*ante*), and the genealogy is found in seven Puranas.[1] His fourth successor, Vasu, conquered the kingdom of Cedi,[2] which belonged to the Yādavas (*ante*), and obtained the title Caidyoparicara, 'the overcomer of the Caidyas'.[3] He also subdued and annexed the adjoining countries as far as Magadha. He had five sons, Bṛhadratha, Pratyagraha, Kuśa or Kuśāmba called Maṇivāhana, Yadu (or Lalittha), and a fifth Māvella, Māthailya or Māruta. He divided his territories and established them in separate kingdoms. They were the Vāsava kings, and occupied countries and towns named after themselves.[4] Cedi and Magadha were two of those kingdoms, two others from their position must have been Kauśāmbī and Karūṣa,[5] but the fifth is not clear.

The eldest son Bṛhadratha took Magadha and founded the famous Bārhadratha dynasty there.[6] Kuśa or Kuśāmba obviously had Kauśāmbī, Pratyagraha may have taken Cedi, and Yadu Karūṣa. It seems probable the fifth kingdom[7] was Matsya. The Matsyas existed before (probably as a Yādava tribe), because they were opponents of Sudās;[8] and Vasu may have conquered this country also, which adjoined Cedi on the north-west. There is no account given anywhere about the Matsya dynasty, except that fable[9]

[1] Vā *99*, 217–28. Mat *50*, 23–34. Hv *32*, 1801–13. Viṣ iv, *19*, 19. Ag *277*, 27–31. Gar i, *140*, 25–30. Bhāg ix, *22*, 4–9. Also one MS. of Br, see Br *13*, 109, note.

[2] MBh i, *63*, 2334–5, 2342. Vā *93*, 26–7. Bḍ iii, *68*, 27. Hv *30*, 1614–15. Br *12*, 15–16.

[3] This title was afterwards misunderstood as *Caidya Uparicara*, and *uparicara* was taken to mean 'moving on high', and so fable said he could soar through the air. So *upari-cara*, MBh i, *63*, 2367 : Viṣ iv, *19*, 19 : Gar i, *140*, 26 : &c. *Ūrdhva-cārin*, Vā *57*, 110 : Mat *143*, 25–6 : Bḍ ii, *30*, 31 : &c. *Antarikṣa-ga*, Vā *99*, 220 : Mat *50*, 26 : Hv *32*, 1804 : cf. MBh xii, *339*, 12834. He was also called *rājoparicara*, MBh xii, *338*, 12754 : *339*, 12838.

[4] MBh i, *63*, 2360–5 ; and genealogies above. Rām i, *32*, 1–11 is wrong, a jumble of several dynasties.

[5] Pad vi, *274*, 16–17 says Dantavakra (king of Karūṣa) was of Caidya lineage.

[6] Also Hv *117*, 6598.

[7] Māvellakas are mentioned, MBh vii, *91*, 3255 : viii, *5*, 138.

[8] Rigv vii, *18*, 6. See the positions of Sudāsa and Vasu in the Table of Genealogies in chap. XII.

[9] MBh i, *63*, 2371–98 : impossible even chronologically as regards Kālī.

made Vasu the parent, through a fish, of two children, the fisher-maiden Kālī (p. 69) and a son named Matsya, who became a king. The genealogies in the Viṣṇu and Bhāgavata insert Matsya among Vasu's sons, and those in the other Puranas add Kālī and Matsya to the above five. Thus tradition suggests that one of Vasu's sons was king of Matsya, and except to account for this there was no reason for introducing him into that fable: possibly then the fifth son should be Matsya, and his kingdom Matsya.

After Vasu the genealogies give only the Magadha dynasty. All are in general agreement, subject to variations in names, except that the Brahma ends with Bṛhadratha's grandson Ṛṣabha, and the Viṣṇu and Bhāgavata by abbreviation make Jarāsandha Bṛhadratha's son. As regards the collateral dynasties we know only the kings who reigned in the Pāṇḍavas' time, namely, Damaghoṣa, his son Śiśupāla Sunītha, and his son Dhṛṣṭaketu, kings of Cedi;[1] Vṛddhaśarman and his son Dantavakra, kings of Karūṣa;[2] Virāṭa, king of Matsya.[3]

CHAPTER X

GENERAL CREDIBILITY OF THE GENEALOGIES

THE question naturally arises whether credence can be attached to the foregoing royal genealogies. Kingdoms and dynasties existed, as we know even from the Vedic literature, and their genealogies must have existed and would have been preserved as long as the dynasties endured. It is incredible that the students of ancient traditional lore, who existed continuously as pointed out in chapter II, discarded or lost those famous genealogies and preserved spurious substitutes. This does not mean that spurious genealogies were never fabricated, for some were devised as will be noticed; but fictitious pedigrees presuppose genuine pedigrees, and it is absurd

[1] MBh i, *187*, 7028–9: ii, *44*, 1575–96: v, *79*, 2857: &c. Vā *96*, 157–8. Mat *46*, 6. Hv *35*, 1930; *117*, 6599–6601. Br *14*, 20. Bd iii, *71*, 158–9. Viṣ iv, *14*, 11.

[2] Vā *96*, 255. Bd iii, *71*, 156. Hv *35*, 1931–2. Br *14*, 21–2. MBh ii, *13*, 575, 577. Viṣ iv, *14*, 11.

[3] MBh iv, *5*, 245–7; *7*, 225; *68*, 2164.

to suppose that fiction completely ousted truth: so that, if any one maintains that these genealogies are worthless, the burden rests on him to produce, not mere doubts and suppositions, but substantial grounds and reasons for his assertion. Common sense thus shows that these genealogies cannot be fictitious, and the foregoing question is narrowed down to this, whether they can be accepted as substantially trustworthy. Their credibility can be tested in various ways.

First, by contemporary corroboration, and here we have a signal instance in the large agreement between the genealogy of the North Pañcāla kings and the incidental references to many of them in the Rigveda.[1]

Mudgala (called Bhārmyaśva by the Anukramaṇī) is mentioned in hymn x, *102*, 5, 9; Indrasenā[2] in verse 2, and Vadhryaśva may be hinted at by the words *vadhriṇā yujā* in verse 12. Vadhryaśva is named in x, *69*, 1 f., and in vi, *61*, 1, which says Divodāsa was his son. Sṛñjaya is mentioned in iv, *15*, 4. Cyavana is probably meant in x, *69*, 5, 6,[3] and his other name Pañcajana is no doubt a misreading of Pijavana. His son Sudāsa is named as Sudās Paijavana in vii, *18*, 22, 23, and verse 25 says Sudās was son (i.e. descendant) of Divodāsa. Aitareya Brāhmaṇa vii, 34 says Sahadeva was descended from Sṛñjaya, and hymn iv, *15*, 7–10 says Somaka was his son. Further, iii, *53*, 9, 11, 12, 24 and vi, *16*, 19 show that Divodāsa and Sudās were descendants of Bharata. In all these particulars the hymns agree with the genealogy, and they are too numerous and too closely interrelated to permit of any doubt that these Vedic kings were the North Pañcāla kings.

Further, references to Vadhryaśva's fire in x, *69*, 2, 4, 9, 10 show that he and its reputed author, his descendant, Sumitra, exercised priestly functions; and so also as regards Divodāsa and his fire in viii, *103*, 2. Hymn i, *130*, 7, 10 proves that some of the descendants of Divodāsa *the warrior* were rishis and brahmans; and x, *133* is attributed to Sudās. These allusions confirm the statements in the genealogy that Mudgala's descendants were 'kṣatriyan brahmans', as will be discussed in chapter XXIII.

This is the only dynasty to which connected references occur in the Rigveda and that can be tested thereby. Those references

[1] Fully discussed in JRAS, 1918, pp. 229 f.

[2] Also MBh iii, *113*, 10093.

[3] *Cyavano . . . apratiratho* of the genealogy = *śūra iva dhṛṣṇuś Cyavanaḥ* of the hymn.

entirely corroborate the genealogy; and the statements in the latter show that it could not have been framed therefrom but was independent. Its genuineness, accuracy and independence prove that it must have been contemporaneous with the dynasty and as old as the hymns themselves. This conclusion affords a very strong presumption that the other genealogies are also genuine and true; the want of evidence regarding them is wholly on the side of the Vedic literature, and its silence proves nothing adverse.

Secondly, the genealogies are corroborated by the testimony of other works in their support. Of this we have a cogent instance in the Raghuvaṁśa and the Ayodhyā genealogy. The Puranas give one version of that genealogy and the Rāmāyaṇa another and absolutely incompatible version as already pointed out (chap. VIII), and those Puranas and the Rāmāyaṇa were in existence when Kālidāsa composed the Raghuvaṁśa; yet he followed the Puranic version in the portion of the genealogy that he gives which is common to both. Putting aside Dilīpa, because the comparison from him is uncertain, since the Rāmāyaṇa names only one Dilīpa while the Puranas mention two, and starting from Raghu about whom there is no doubt, he gives four kings, Raghu, Aja, Daśaratha and Rāma as in the Puranas, instead of the Rāmāyaṇa version of 14 or 15 kings; so that he virtually declares the Puranas are right and the Rāmāyaṇa wrong. His work also testifies that the Puranic version is no late composition, but was so well established as authoritative in his time that even the Rāmāyaṇa could not invalidate it; and proves that, as his entire list from Dilīpa II down to Agnivarṇa agrees substantially with the list in the Vāyu, Brahmāṇḍa, Brahma, Harivaṁśa and Viṣṇu, the Puranic list was the same substantially in his time as we have it now. If then the Puranic genealogy of Ayodhyā was held to be right then, in spite of the Rāmāyaṇa, that is strong evidence that it is ancient and trustworthy. It is reasonable to conclude that equal care has been bestowed on the other dynasties, and there is a strong presumption that they had been equally well preserved during the preceding centuries, that is, that they are the original genealogies and therefore genuine.

Thirdly, the existence of spurious genealogies testifies in favour of these genealogies. They are of two kinds, first, the wrong derivation of true genealogies, and secondly, wholly spurious pedigrees. Of the former kind several have been noticed in chapter IX, and the plainest instance is the derivation of the Kānyakubja dynasty from Ajamīḍha of the Paurava line, which has been demonstrated there to be wrong. Of wholly spurious genealogies there are two kinds, first the brahman vaṁśas, which will be dealt with afterwards (chapters XVI f.) and are obviously late attempts to construct vaṁśas out of the information that was available; and secondly, imaginary genealogies, such as those connected with Dakṣa and creation, and that of the various kinds of Fires.[1] The difference between the royal genealogies and such genealogies is most striking, revealing the distinction between what is genuine and what is a fake.

An excellent instance of a spurious genealogy is the account of the Yādavas in the Harivaṁśa (*94*, 5138 f.). It says Madhu, a king who reigned from Madhuvana on the river Jumna to Surāṣṭra and Ānarta (Gujarat), was descended from Yadu and Yayāti (5164). His daughter married Haryaśva, a scion of the Aikṣvāku race, and their son was Yadu, and from this Yadu were descended the Yādavas (5180, 5191). It thus makes Madhu both a Yādava and also grandfather of Yadu the ancestor of the Yādavas. It says the Yadu race thus issued from the Ikṣvāku race (5239), although it acknowledges that Madhu was already a Yādava, and introduces the further absurdity that this Yadu was like his ancestor Pūru (5176). Lastly, it styles Madhu a Daitya (5143) and a Dānava (5157),[2] although it acknowledges he was of the Lunar race (5165). The whole story is a mass of absurd confusion; and the confusion is carried on into the accounts of this Yadu's five sons (*95*, 5205 f.), except the short passage (5242–8) which appears to contain genuine tradition because it is corroborated elsewhere (see chapter XIV).

Fourthly, by the treatment of defects and mistakes. These were inevitable in the handing down of tradition, but there was a real endeavour to ascertain and preserve the genealogies correctly, because, as shown in chapter II, there were men who made a special study of ancient genealogies, and certain terms used, such as *vaṁśavittama* and *icchanti*, indicate that tradition was carefully examined and the best adopted. It was afterwards, when the brahmans obtained the custody of the Puranas, that questionable influences came into play.

[1] MBh iii, *218* to *220*. Vā *29*, 1 f. Mat *51*, 2 f. Viṣ i, *10*, 14–17. &c.

[2] Hv *55*, 3060–3110, which tells part of the same story, also calls Madhu a Dānava (3061), and his 'son' Lavaṇa a Dānava (3063) and a Daitya (3086).

Still it was difficult to make material changes which would not be inconsistent with statements elsewhere, and as they lacked the historical sense they could hardly accomplish that, and so their errors can be detected. Many instances of defects and mistakes have been noticed in the preceding chapters, and only two need be cited here as illustrations. As regards defects, there is the gap in the Paurava pedigree between Taṁsu and Duṣyanta: the text in the oldest and best Puranas remains confused, and it is the later compositions that attempt to reconstruct the descent. As regards mistakes, the fact that the Rigveda, Aitareya Brāhmaṇa and Śāṅkhāyana Śrauta Sūtra connect 'Viśvāmitra' with the Bharatas in no way disturbed the best Puranas in their derivation of the Kānyakubja dynasty from Āyu's son Amāvasu; and the derivation of it from Bharata's descendant Ajamīḍha was manifestly known to be doubtful, because the Brahma and Harivaṁśa, though they give it, give also the true version, and none of the other Puranas adopted it except the late Agni: so that mistaken post-Vedic interpretation was powerless to overthrow the kṣatriya tradition, and even the late brahmanical Bhāgavata was unmoved by it.

Fifthly, by a comparison of these with brahman genealogies. The brahmans, and the Puranic brahmans as much as other brahmans, had a natural and obvious incentive to preserve and, if necessary, to fabricate brahman genealogies. The brahmans have constituted a priestly power unique in history; they aggrandized themselves in every way and their pretensions have been notorious; yet, as pointed out (chapter XVI), they have produced no real brahman genealogy. If then they did not construct their own genealogies, it is absurd to suppose they fabricated elaborate kṣatriya genealogies; and the only reasonable conclusion is that these genealogies are ancient and genuine kṣatriya tradition which was incorporated in the Purana. The internal evidence corroborates this, for these genealogies in the earliest Puranas are, on the whole, manifestly kṣatriya literature, as, for instance, the stories of Triśaṅku and Sagara, so often alluded to, show.

Sixthly, the genealogies declare that from time to time members of royal families became brahmans as the Kāṇvas (chapter XIX), or became kṣatriyan brahmans, many of whom developed into true brahman gotras, as will be explained in chapter XXIII. Such statements cannot have originated with the brahmans, because it was not to the interest of any brahman gotra to allege such a beginning, and it is incredible that they, deeply interested as they were in exalting their own status, would have asserted that any brahman gotra sprang from kṣatriyas, except the Viśvāmitras, whose kṣatriya ancestry was notorious; and in fact their Vedic literature says nothing about such matters. These statements were too damaging to exclusive brahmanic pretensions. The brahmans then did not put them into the genealogies. The statements came from kṣatriya sources, and were notices which occurred naturally in the course of the royal genealogies. The Puranic brahmans found these notices therein and preserved them, although Vedic brahmans ignored such facts. The statements therefore were genuine ancient tradition and were known to be true beyond gainsaying; so the Viṣṇu, a late brahmanic Purana, acknowledges them freely, and even the Bhāgavata, later still and more avowedly brahmanic, though it ignores some of them, yet admits the most important cases. The statements must have originated with the incidents they describe, and therefore the genealogies which contain them were equally ancient and contemporaneous, and these considerations show that all was preserved with care.

Seventhly, the genealogies give an account, how the Aryans dominated North India and the north-west of the Dekhan, and it is the only account to be found in the whole of Sanskrit literature of that great ethnological fact. They do not allude to that conquest except in very general terms,[1] yet those terms show they did know of it. They give no actual account of that, but the genealogies when co-ordinated show how the 'Aila' race extended its rule over precisely the very regions over which the Aryans established themselves. This subject will be fully dealt with hereafter (chapter XXV). This outcome was not the object of the genealogies, and they were not constructed to establish it; hence the fact that they do tacitly disclose how a great ethnological change took place is strong evidence that they are genuine and true.

Against the statements of the Puranas and Mahābhārata about matters of traditional history, arguments from Vedic literature are adduced of two kinds—arguments from statements and allusions, and arguments *ex silentio*. Both these have been discussed already

[1] As where it is said, the five races descended from Yayāti, namely, the Yādavas, Turvasus, Anavas, Druhyus and Pauravas, overspread the entire earth. Vā *93*, 103; *99*, 462. Bd iii, *68*, 105–6. Hv *30*, 1619–20. Lg i, *67*, 26. Kūr i, *22*, 11. Br *12*, 20–1.

in pages 10–12. Only a few remarks need be added here. As regards statements in that literature, *contemporary* references to historical matters are trustworthy, and they do not clash with kṣatriya historical tradition in the Puranas as far as I am aware; but references to prior traditional history have no such authority, though they may be of use. Arguments regarding historical matters drawn from the silence of that literature are particularly worthless. Thus it is a mistake to assert that, because the Rigveda makes no mention of the Aila (or Lunar) race, there was no such race.[1] One might argue with more force that, because the banyan, the most characteristic tree of India, is not mentioned in the Rigveda,[2] there were none in India when the hymns were composed.

These considerations show that the genealogies have strong claims to acceptance. This does not mean that they are complete and altogether accurate, because no human testimony is free from defects and errors; and it has been shown in the preceding pages, and more will appear in the following pages, that there are defects, gaps and errors in them, especially when taken singly, but many of these blemishes can be corrected by collating the various texts, and others can be remedied by statements found elsewhere. Nevertheless, it is quite clear that they are genuine accounts and are substantially trustworthy. They give us history as handed down in tradition by men whose business it was to preserve the past; and they are far superior to historical statements in the Vedic literature, composed by brahmans who lacked the historical sense and were little concerned with mundane affairs.

[1] JRAS, 1914, p. 735. [2] Macdonell, *Sansk. Lit.*, pp. 146–7.

CHAPTER XI

CONSIDERATION OF NAMES

When the genealogies are examined, differences are found in that a name or even several names appear in one or more lists while wanting in others. These variations are often unsubstantial, and may be due to faults sometimes in the MSS and sometimes in the structure of the genealogy itself. The former faults arise through copyists' mistakes or defects in the MSS. Omissions may include one or two kings, as will appear on comparing the common text of the Vāyu and Matsya in the North Pañcāla dynasty,[1] or a group of kings, as will appear from the common text of the Brahmāṇḍa and Vāyu in the Vaiśāla dynasty.[2] A case where a passage is in the process of disappearing occurs in the Brahma when compared with its counterpart in the Harivaṁśa in the North Pañcāla dynasty.[3] Large omissions would be due to loss of pages in the ancient MSS; and the clearest example of this is the great lacuna in the Brahmāṇḍa (p. 78).

Variations in the structure of a genealogy may be due to one or other of six causes, and in illustrating them it will be convenient to choose mainly from the Ayodhyā line. First, a name may be left out by mere omission, probably accidental; thus the Bhāgavata and Kūrma omit Ambarīṣa, and the Harivaṁśa omits Hiraṇyanābha, both well-known kings. Secondly, little-known kings are omitted; thus the Matsya, Padma, Liṅga and Kūrma insert after Dṛḍhāśva a king Pramoda, whom the other Puranas omit, and they and the Agni and Garuḍa omit Prasenajit, father of Yuvanāśva I, whom all the others mention. There is no good reason to think that either Pramoda or Prasenajit has been invented, and the omission is no doubt due to their unimportance. Thirdly, names have been displaced; and thus the Matsya, Padma and Agni misplace Dilīpa II, Dīrghabāhu, Raghu and Aja as Raghu, Dilīpa, Aja and Dīrghabāhu. Fourthly, a name has been converted into an epithet; thus most Puranas make Dīrghabāhu and Raghu father and son, and the Matsya, Padma and Agni treat them as separate, but the

[1] Vā *99*, 208–9. Mat *50*, 15. [2] Bd iii. *61*, 4–5. Vā *86*, 4–9.
[3] Br *13*, 97 and note thereto. Hv *32*, 1781–90.

Brahma, Harivaṁśa and Śiva treat Dīrghabāhu as an epithet of Raghu, the Raghuvaṁśa omits him accordingly, and the Garuḍa mentions him, omitting Raghu. Here the weight of authority is in favour of Dīrghabāhu as a separate king and not as an epithet of Raghu.[1] Fifthly, an epithet may conversely be turned into a king; thus the Viṣṇu, Agni and Bhāgavata coin new sons for Sātvata the Yādava out of the epithets applied to his genuine sons (chapter IX); and the epithet Kausalya belonging to Hiraṇyanābha as king of Kosala becomes a separate king Kauśalya, his son, in the Raghuvaṁśa (xviii, 27). Lastly, there may be a pure blunder, as where the Matsya, Padma and Agni turn Satyavrata Triśaṅku's wife Satyarathā into a son Satyaratha, and where the Garuḍa changes Māndhātṛ's wife Bindumatī into a son Bindumahya.

Differences occur also in names, but they are often superficial, and a few are noticed here out of the many that may be cited. Names are curtailed. Sometimes the final component is omitted, thus Kāñcanaprabha of the Kānyakubja dynasty becomes merely Kāñcana in the Viṣṇu and Garuḍa; Rohitāśva of the Ayodhyā line is generally called Rohita; and Bhīma Pāṇḍava's full name was Bhīmasena.[2] In other cases the first component is omitted, thus Devātithi of the Pauravas becomes Atithi in the Garuḍa; and the Bhāgavata calls Prasenajit of Ayodhyā Senajit.[3] Similarly the prefix *su* not seldom disappears in the later Puranas, and so Suśruta of Videha becomes Śruta in the Bhāgavata, which abounds in such modifications and also attempted emendations. Again names may be altered by misreadings, as Vasumata *alias* Sumati of Ayodhyā by an easy misreading of *v* as *c* or *vice versa*.[4] Further, names are changed by metathesis, thus Durdama of the Haihayas appears as Durmada in the Vāyu and Brahmāṇḍa, and the rishi Indrapramati appears as Indrapratima.[5]

Another cause of variation, which is only superficial, is the use of synonyms. Thus Anenas, son of Āyu, appears as Vipāpman; Kṣemadhanvan of Ayodhyā as Sudhanvan in the Agni; Kalmāṣa-

[1] Dīrghabāhu was a name; so one of Dhṛtarāṣṭra's sons, MBh i, *67*, 2740: vi, *97*, 4349: vii, *164*, 7337.

[2] MBh i, *67*, 2746; *124*, 4854. So in tales, as Sindhu for Sindhu-dvīpa, Br. *169*, 4, 19.

[3] So in tales, as Kuṇḍala for Maṇikuṇḍala, Br *170*, 4, 52.

[4] Vāyu *88*, 76, *jajñe Vasumato nṛpaḥ*, and Brahmāṇḍa iii, *63*, 75, *jajñe ca Sumatir nṛpaḥ*.

[5] Bd ii, *32*, 115: iii, *8*, 96–7. Vā *59*, 105; *70*, 88. Mat *145*, 110.

pāda of Ayodhyā as Kalmāṣāṅghri;[1] and Hiraṇyavarman, king of Daśārṇa, appears as Hemavarman and Kāñcanavarman.[2]

Real differences also occur in names, and many of these are easily explainable as misreadings of old scripts. A few out of many such cases may be given here, and the probable mutation is suggested, but in some instances it might have taken place reversely.

Thus misreadings of *dh* and *v* (or *b*) are not uncommon. Vyuṣitāśva of Ayodhyā is Dhyuṣitāśva in the Vāyu; Suvarman of Dvimīḍha's line in the Vāyu is Sudharman in the Matsya and Harivaṁśa; and in the Videha line Pratīndhaka of the Rāmāyaṇa is Pratinvaka in the Vāyu and Pratimbaka in the Brahmāṇḍa; and the Bhāgavata by a double misreading transforms Tridhanvan of Ayodhyā into Tribandhana. Similarly Ārādhi of the Paurava line in the Vāyu is Ārāvin in the Viṣṇu; and by a further easy misreading of *r* as *v* in the later script Ārādhi becomes Āvādhīta in the Garuḍa, and by a second easy mistake between *v* and *c* Ārāvin appears as Avācīna in the Mahābhārata (i, *95*, 3771). Some of these changes seem to be due to a desire to emend a name so as to make it intelligible.

Among easy misreadings of other letters, the following may be cited. By reading *tr* as *v* Trasadasyu of Ayodhyā (shortened probably to *Trasada*) was altered to Vasuda in the Matsya. By confusing *ṛ*, *kṛ*, *kra* and *ku* in later mediaeval script, Ṛta of Videha in the Vāyu and Viṣṇu is Kṛta in some copies of the Vāyu and Kratu in the Brahmāṇḍa; Kṛteyu of the Pauravas in the Vāyu is Ṛteyu in the Viṣṇu and Garuḍa; and Ṛtujit of Videha in the Viṣṇu became, by a further easy mistake between *tu* and *la* in later script, Kulajit in the Garuḍa. By confusion between *dh* and *gh* in the later script, we find in the Druhyu line Dharma is Gharma in the Agni and Garuḍa; and Dhṛta is Ghṛta in the Matsya, Harivaṁśa and Agni, while Ghṛta by a further easy misreading is Dyūta in the Brahma. Again *t* and *j* are sometimes easily mistaken in the later script, so in the Videha line Devarāta and Kīrtirāta are Devarāja and Kīrtirāja in some copies of the Vāyu. *P* and *y* were easily confused, so in the Paurava line Sampāti = Saṁyāti of the Mahābhārata and Agni; and Ahampāti of the Viṣṇu and Bhāgavata = Ahaṁyāti of the Mahābhārata (i, *95*, 3766–8). So also

[1] Ag *272*, 31–2. Bhāg ix, *9*, 18.
[2] MBh v. *190*, 7419; *193*, 7493, 7506, 7511 and 7518.

th and *py*, and thus in the Turvasu line Sarūtha of the Vāyu = Sarūpya of the Brahmāṇḍa. Again *s* and *bh* were sometimes rather alike, so in the Ayodhyā line Sindhudvīpa = Bhindhudvīpa of the Viṣṇu, and Prasuśruta = Prabhusuta of the Brahmāṇḍa. In the mediaeval script *gu* and *śva* might be mistaken, and so Ahīnagu of Ayodhyā becomes Ahīnāśva in the Agni. Similarly Śaṅkhaṇa of Ayodhyā (probably by metathesis, Khaśana) appears as Khagaṇa in the Bhāgavata and Gaṇa in the Garuḍa.

The cohesion of a euphonic *r*, or the treating of an initial *r* as belonging to the preceding word may explain in the Paurava line the forms Rahampāti of the Harivaṁśa and Ahampāti of the Viṣṇu and Bhāgavata; also of Rantināra in the Vāyu and Antināra in the Matsya, while Antināra and the form generally found, Maṭināra, may perhaps be due to mistake between *ma* and *a*.

Sometimes the connecting link between variant names is found readily in the Prakrit form. Ancient names do occur in both Sanskrit and Prakrit shape, for the famous Kānyakubja king appears as Gāthi and Gāthin in the brahmanical literature [1] and as Gādhi in the Epics and Puranas. The examination of names in this light is an interesting study. The most cogent illustration of connexion through Prakrit is the name of the famous Paurava king, who is called Duṣyanta (with a common variation Duṣmanta) [2] in the Mahābhārata and Puranas, but Duṣṣanta and Duḥṣanta in brahmanic tradition because his son Bharata is styled Dauṣṣanti and Dauḥṣanti in the Aitareya and Śatapatha Brāhmaṇas respectively.[3] These forms can be reconciled through a Prakrit form Duṣṣanta or Dussanta, of which they are different Sanskrit equivalents, the form Duṣyanta being probably right and the brahmanic one mistaken. Similarly we have Nabhāka in Vedic literature and Nabhāga in the Puranic genealogies; and the Bhārgava rishi Apnavāna's name was 'emended' to Ātmavant (see chapter XVII). Other variant names which can be explained through Prakrit forms are the following in the Videha dynasty: Bṛhaduktha (Brahmāṇḍa and Viṣṇu) and Bṛhaduttha (Vāyu),

[1] For names cited from Vedic literature, see *Vedic Index*.

[2] Hv *32*. 1721–4. Vā *99*, 133–4. Viṣ iv, *19*, 2.

[3] *Vedic Index*, i, 382. Also Vedārth on Rigv vi, *52*, in its verses 12 and 14. Aitar Brāhm viii, 23. Śatapatha Brāhm xiii, 5, 4, 11–14, where the patronymic *Saudyumni* given to Bharata is probably a brahmanical mistake for *Dauṣyanti*, which it also calls him.

which, by an easy misreading of *dra* for *du*, appears as Bṛhadratha in the Rāmāyaṇa: Śakuni (Vāyu and Brahmāṇḍa), through *Sakuni*, *sa Kuni*, appears as Kuni (Viṣṇu), and by an easy mistake of *l* for *n* as Kuli (Garuḍa): and Svāgata (Vāyu and Brahmāṇḍa) appears as Sāśvata in the Viṣṇu, where the two forms may perhaps be connected through a possible Prakrit form read as *Sāgata* or *Sāśata* (*g* and *ś* being mistaken).

Other divergencies of this kind might be noticed, and will occur to any one who examines the variant names. All such variations are not material, however, because the distinguished kings are well known and the names of the less known kings are not important except as supplying links in the chain of a genealogy; and as long as the descents are labelled, it is not material whether the labels are perfectly accurate.

We may now consider sameness of name of different persons. It was quite common. Abundant examples might be given.[1] A few of the more important are cited here, and others will be found on consulting Macdonell and Keith's *Vedic Index*, Sörensen's *Index to the Mahābhārata*, and the Dictionaries. Forgetfulness of the fact that the same names reappeared in India as in other countries has led to the strangest conjectures and identifications.

Sameness of name was well known among kings and princes, for it is expressly declared that there were a hundred Prativindhyas, Nāgas, Haihayas, Dhṛtarāṣṭras, Brahmadattas, Paulas, Śvetas, Kāśis and Kuśas, eighty Janamejayas, a thousand Śaśabindus and two hundred Bhīṣmas and Bhīmas:[2] also that there were two Nalas, one king of Ayodhyā and the other the hero of the 'Story of Nala'.[3] So there were two famous Arjunas, Kārtavīrya and Pāṇḍava, and a third in Rigveda i, *222*, 5. The genealogical lists in chapter XII show that other names were not uncommon, such as Divodāsa, Sṛñjaya and Sahadeva; and the number of duplicates is very large. Further, it is expressly stated that in the main Paurava line were two Ṛkṣas, two Parikṣits, three Bhīmasenas and two Janamejayas;[4] and all these appear in that genealogy, if

[1] It is noticed in MBh i, *65*, 2535.

[2] Bd iii, *74*, 267–9. Vā *32*, 49–52; *99*, 453–5. MBh ii, *8*, 333–6. Mat *273*, 71–3.

[3] Vā *88*, 174–5. Bd iii, *63*, 173–4. Br *8*, 80, 89. Hv *15*, 815, 830–1. Lg i, *66*, 24–5. Pad v, *8*, 160–1 blunders over them. There were others besides, see Table of Genealogies in chap. XII.

[4] Br *13*, 112–13. Hv *32*, 1817–18.

we include Bhīmasena Pāṇḍava. Similarly brahmans had the same names, thus there were two Śaktis, four brahman Rāmas, Jāmadagnya and three others,[1] three named Suśravas,[1] two Śukas (pp. 64–5), &c. Also kings and brahmans often had the same names.[2] There were two royal Rāmas, one the famous king of Ayodhyā and the other Balarāma, besides four brahman Rāmas mentioned above: four Kṛṣṇas at least, the king, Dvaipāyana-Vyāsa, Devakīputra and Hārīta: five Babhrus, a son of the Yādava Lomapāda, a king in the Druhyu line, the Yādava Devāvṛdha's son, and two brahmans: and three Cyavanas, the Bhārgava rishi and two kings, one of N. Pañcāla and the other a descendant of Kuru.

Moreover kings, princes, and brahmans had the same names as gods and mythological beings and heavenly bodies. There was a Varuṇa among the Vasiṣṭhas[3] and among the Bhārgavas.[4] Agni was the name of an Aurva rishi (p. 68) and of a maharṣi.[5] Called Bharata were (1) the famous Paurava king, (2) Rāma's brother, and (3) a mythical king after whom (it is said) India was called Bhāratavarṣa.[6] Aruṇa was the dawn, and two brahmans were so named. Śukra was the name of (1) the ancient Bhārgava rishi, (2) the planet Venus,[7] and (3) Jābāla. Named Bali was an Ānava king and also the Daitya king Vairocana (p. 63). Rishis and others were named after deities; and heavenly bodies were called after rishis and others, such as the seven stars of the Great Bear and the star Canopus.

Further, kings and brahmans sometimes had the same names as peoples and places. Thus there were a people called *Aśmaka*,[8] yet it was also the name of a king of Ayodhya[9] and of a brahman.[10] *Aṅga* was the name of a country and people (East Bihar), and of

[1] See *Vedic Index*.

[2] For the kings here mentioned, where other ref rences are not given, consult the Table of Genealogies in chap. XII, and for the brahmans, *Vedic Index*.

[3] See chap XVIII.

[4] Anukramaṇī and Vedārth on Rigv ix, *65*. Aitareya Brāhm iii, 34, 1.

[5] Aitareya Brāhm vii, 5, 34.

[6] Vā *33*, 51–2. Bd ii, *14*, 60–2. Lg i, *47*, 20, 24. Viṣ ii, *1*, 28, 32.

[7] See chap. XVI: both called Uśanas also.

[8] MBh vii, *37*, 1605–8; *85*, 3049; viii, *8*, 237. Hv *119*, 6724. Apparently in the Dekhan.

[9] See genealogy, and MBh i, *122*, 4737; *177*, 6791.

[10] MBh xii, *47*, 1592.

the king after whom it was said to have been called, and also of the reputed author (Aurava) of Rigveda x, *138*. *Aja*, king of Ayodhyā, had the same name as a people. *Puṣkara* was the name of (1) a son of Rāma's brother Bharata, (2) Nala's brother in the 'Story of Nala', (3) a town, the modern Pokhar, (4) one of the mythical continents, and (5) many other persons. *Kuru*, the Paurava king, had the same name as the people, the northern Kurus who dwelt beyond the Himalayas. Such similarity in name must not confuse what is wholly different. Thus king Kuru had nothing to do with the northern Kurus, and to connect him with them merely because of their common name is on a par with saying that Aṅga Aurava mentioned above was an Aṅga; or that Aśmaka king of Ayodhyā was an Aśmaka; or that the brahman Kirāta was one of the rude Kirāta folk.

There are no passages, as far as I know, that lend colour to any connexion between king Kuru's descendants (the Kurus) and the northern Kurus, except perhaps two: one says that in the time of Dhṛtarāṣṭra's and Pāṇḍu's youth the southern Kurus rivalled the northern Kurus;[1] and the other says that, when the victorious Pāṇḍavas re-entered Hastināpura, flags waving in the wind displayed in a way (*iva*) the southern and northern Kurus.[2] The people of Hastināpura were not Kurus, but the name Kuru of the royal family was extended to their people and country according to a common Indian usage.[3] Both passages occur in rhapsodies on the extraordinary happiness of the Kaurava kingdom at those times, and the similarity of name suggested the comparison of the Kurus (Kauravas) with the northern Kurus, a simple folk whose condition is portrayed as one of continual ideal bliss.[4] The comparisons are merely happy poetic similes, and do not indicate racial identity.[5] The adjective 'northern' was added to distinguish the Himalayan folk.

Kings and brahmans also bore the names[6] of animals, as Ṛkṣa,

[1] MBh i, *109*, 4346. [2] MBh xiv, *70*, 2053.

[3] So Gāndhāra; and Pañcāla (p. 75). Cf. our 'Rhodesia' and 'Rhodesian'.

[4] Mat *105*, 20; *113*, 69–77. Pad i, *4*, 2–11. Vā *45*, 11 f. MBh i, *122*, 4719–23: vi, *7*, 254–66: xiii, *102*, 4867–8. Rām iv, *43*, 39–53. Lg i, *52*, 19–23: &c.

[5] Further study has led me to cancel the remarks that I made in my Translation of the Mārkaṇḍeya, p. 345.

[6] For most of the following names, see *Vedic Index*; also Sörensen's *Index to the MBh*, and Table of Genealogies in chap. XII.

Ṛṣabha, Kuruṅga, and Vatsa; of birds, Śakuni, Haṁsa, Śuka, and Ulūka; of trees and plants, as Aśvattha, Plakṣa, Nala, and Muñja; of inanimate objects, as Śaṅkha, Dṛti, Aśman [1] and Droṇa; and even of ceremonies, as Aśvamedha: also of parts of the body, as Bāhu, Karṇa, Cakṣus; and of abstract ideas, as Śakti and Manyu.

Further, not only was sameness of name common, but names of father and son sometimes recur; thus in the Paurava line there were two Parīkṣits with sons called Janamejaya. There is nothing improbable in such duplication, and it is less than has occurred in dynasties in other countries. Other instances are these. Śrutarvan Ārkṣa is praised in the Rigveda, and another is mentioned later as a contemporary of Kṛṣṇa.[2] There were two kings called Gaya son of Amūrtarayas (p. 40). There were two kings Karaṇdhamas, one in the Vaiśāla dynasty and the other in Turvasu's lineage.[3] The former had a son Avīkṣit and a grandson, the famous Marutta; the latter had a son Marutta. They are sometimes confused.[4] One Pratardana, son of Divodāsa, was king of Kāśi and is one of the reputed authors of Rigveda x, *179*; while Pratardana Daivodāsi, the reputed author of ix, *96*, appears to have been a descendant of Divodāsa, king of North Pañcāla.

Purukutsa and his son Trasadasyu were kings of Ayodhyā. The Rigveda (iv, *42*, 8, 9) mentions a king Trasadasyu, son of Purukutsa, who is a different and later person. The former Purukutsa was son of Māndhātṛ, as the Aikṣvāku genealogies show; the latter is called *Daurgaha* and *Gairikṣita*,[5] 'son or descendant of Durgaha and Girikṣit'. The former Trasadasyu was prior to Bharata as the synchronisms in chapter XIII show; the latter Trasadasyu was contemporary with Aśvamedha Bhārata [6] and is praised by Sobhari Kāṇva; [7] Aśvamedha was a descendant of Bharata, and the Kāṇvas sprang from Bharata's descendant Ajamīḍha as will be shown in chapter XIX; hence the latter Trasadasyu was far later than the former. There were thus two Purukutsas with sons named Trasadasyu. Those of

[1] MBh xii, *28*, 834–5. [2] Rigv viii, *74*, 4, 13. Hv *119*, 6725.

[3] Distinguished in Vā *99*, 2: Bd iii, *74*, 2: Br *13*, 143: Hv *32*, 1831.

[4] So Br *13*, 144–5 and Hv *32*, 1832–3, by interpolating two lines stating that the latter Marutta gave his daughter to the rishi Saṁvarta, whereas it was the former who did so. MBh xii, *234*, 8602 makes the same mistake, but xiii, *137*, 6260 corrects it. See chap. XIII.

[5] See *Vedic Index*, i, 231, 327.

[6] Rigv v, *27*. These synchronisms are fully discussed in chap. XIV.

[7] Rigv viii, *19*, 2, 36.

Ayodhyā were well known, as even the Śatapatha Brāhmaṇa shows.[1] Those in the Rigveda were apparently Pūru kings[2] and probably belonged to some minor dynasty descended from Bharata; and are unknown to kṣatriya fame. There was no Ikṣvāku line of Pūru princes.

Similar remarks apply to queens and women as the following examples show.[3] Sameness of name was common; thus, three queens in the Paurava dynasty are said to have had the name Sunandā;[4] there were two Indrasenās,[5] two Satyavatīs (Ṛcīka's wife and Śantanu's queen), and many Mālinīs. Women had the names of animals and birds, as two Gos (Śukra's wife and Yati's wife),[6] and Haṁsī; of plants or flowers, as Mālatī,[7] Padminī and Kamalā; of inanimate objects, as Akṣamālā, Araṇi and Sītā; and also of abstract ideas, as Maryādā and Sannati.[8]

Further, women had the same names as rivers, and this fact is proved by the injunction that a brahman should not marry a maiden having such a name.[9] Thus the queen of king Purukutsa, son of Māndhātṛ, of Ayodhyā was named Narmadā;[10] Yauvanāśva's (Māndhātṛ's) granddaughter Kāverī was wife of Jahnu, king of Kānyakubja;[11] Sarasvatī was queen of the Paurava king Matināra or Rantināra;[12] and Kālindī (= Yamunā) was the name of the wife of Asita (= Bāhu) king of Ayodhyā,[13] and also of a wife of Kṛṣṇa.[14] There were three queens named Dṛṣadvatī, (1) wife of a

[1] xiii, 5, 4, 5; which yet seems to confuse them.

[2] *Vedic Index*, i, 327.

[3] If no references are given here, the names will be found in Sörensen's *Index to the MBh*, and in the Dictionary.

[4] MBh i, *95*, 3769, 3785, 3797.

[5] Vadhryaśva's mother. The other, MBh iii, *57*, 2237.

[6] P. 69: and Vā *93*, 14; Hv *30*, 1601: &c. Also Brahmadatta's queen according to Bhāg ix. *21*, 25.

[7] Mat *208*, 10.

[8] Mat *20*, 26. Hv *23*, 1261.

[9] Manu iii, 9. Ag *243*, 4. Pad vi, *223*, 45.

[10] Vā *88*, 74. Bḍ iii, *63*, 73. Br *7*, 95–6. Hv *12*, 714–15. Lg i, *65*, 41–2. Kūr i, *20*, 27–8. Śiv vii, *60*, 79. Mat *12*, 36 and Pad v, *8*, 140, where for *Narmadā-patiḥ* read °*pateḥ*.

[11] Vā *91*, 58–60. Bḍ iii, *66*, 28–30. Hv *27*, 1421–3; *32*, 1761–2. Br *10*, 19–20; *13*, 87.

[12] Vā *99*, 129. MBh i, *95*, 3779–80 (identifying her with the river). Mat *49*, 7 calls her *Manasvinī*.

[13] So Rām i, *70*, 33: ii, *110*, 20.

[14] Hv *118*, 6701. Vā *96*, 234; &c.

king of Ayodhyā,[1] (2) Viśvāmitra's queen,[2] and (3) wife of Divodāsa, king of Kāśi.[3] Urvaśī was wife of Purūravas,[4] and Urvaśī was also the original name of the Ganges.[5] This sameness of name led to the identification of these women with the rivers, with sometimes a story to explain it—all obviously fanciful interpolations due to the desire to explain names (p. 75). So Narmadā is identified with the river (p. 69); and Kāverī because of Yuvanāśva's curse was turned into the river, which may mean either the large river in the south or the southern tributary of the Narbadā.[6] The former is improbable because it is more than a thousand miles distant; and the latter is no doubt meant, because the princess Kāverī was daughter or niece of queen Narmadā. Similarly, the remark that Yuvanāśva cursed his wife Gaurī and she became the river Bāhudā[7] is probably to be explained in a like way, though the connexion is wanting in the names as they stand.

Again, women had the same names as stars or constellations; thus there were two Rohiṇīs (one wife of Vasudeva,[8] and the other wife of Kṛṣṇa[9]), several Revatīs (Balarāma's wife and others), a Citrā,[10] and Rādhā; hence Arundhatī,[11] wife of a Vasiṣṭha,[12] may not perhaps be mythical. Moreover, women had the same names as mythological persons, such as apsarases; thus Vadhryaśva's queen in the North Pañcāla dynasty was Menakā,[13] the queen of Tṛṇabindu of the Vaiśāla dynasty was Alambuṣā,[14] and the Paurava Raudrāśva's queen was Ghṛtācī.[15] The last two are called apsarases,

[1] Vā *88*, 64; Bḍ iii, *63*, 65; Hv *12*, 709; Br *7*, 90; all of which appear to identify her with the river. Śiv vii, *60*, 73–4.

[2] Vā *91*, 103. Br *10*, 67. Hv *27*, 1473; *32*, 1775. Bḍ iii, *66*, 75.

[3] Vā *92*, 64. Bḍ iii, *67*, 67. Br *11*, 49. Hv *29*, 1586.

[4] MBh i, *75*, 3149. Vā *91*, 4. Mat *24*, 32: &c.

[5] MBh vii, *60*, 2254: xii, *29*, 961.

[6] Mat *189*, 2 f. Pad i, *16*, 2 f. Kūr ii, *39*, 40–1. JRAS, 1910, p. 868.

[7] Vā *88*, 66. Bḍ iii, *63*, 67. Br *7*, 91. Hv *12*, 710. Śiv vii, *60*, 75.

[8] Vā *96*, 160–1. Br *14*, 36: &c. [9] Vā *96*, 233. Hv *118*, 6701: &c.

[10] Name of Subhadrā, Hv *36*, 1952.

[11] The star Alcor in the Great Bear is called Arundhatī.

[12] MBh i, *199*, 7352. Vā *70*, 83. Mat *201*, 30.

[13] Vā *99*, 200. Hv *32*, 1783. Mat *50*, 7.

[14] Gar i, *138*, 11. Viṣ iv. *1*, 18 and Bhāg ix, *2*, 31, which identify her with the apsaras. Rām i, *47*, 12 inaccurately.

[15] Vā *99*, 123. Hv *31*, 1658. Mat *49*, 4. Bhāg ix, *20*, 5. Another Ghṛtācī (MBh i, *5*, 871: xiii, *30*, 2004) and the wife of a Vasiṣṭha (chap. XVIII); neither was an apsaras.

but Vadhryaśva's queen was certainly not an apsaras, and the sameness of name no doubt suggested that Ghṛtācī and Alambuṣā were apsarases.[1]

Such similarities were nothing uncommon. Manu iii, 9 gives the plainest proof that such names did really occur, for he says a brahman should not marry a maiden who bore the name of a constellation, tree or river, of a low caste, of a mountain, of a bird, snake or slave, or of anything terrifying. Women then had such names, and so also had men; and the instances cited show that the range of names was wider than what Manu prohibits. In such conditions there was every chance of mistaking the application of names, confounding different persons of the same name,[2] confusing persons with things, devising fanciful explanations and fabricating mythology. Some illustrations of these tendencies have been given above, as the identifications of queens with rivers; and others occur, as where Vyāsa's wife Araṇi is turned into the piece of wood used for kindling fire, and so their son Śuka was born therefrom.[3]

It is quite permissible therefore to suspect similar fancies in other cases. For instance, Bhīṣma is often called *Gāṅgeya*,[4] *Jāhnavī's* son[5] and *Bhāgīrathī's* son,[6] and a fable is narrated that he was begotten by king Santanu of the river Ganges.[7] It is not euhemerism to suggest that his mother had the name Gaṅgā[8] or the patronymic Jāhnavī[9] or Bhāgīrathī,[10] that tradition forgot her, and that fancy then confused her with and finally superseded her by the river. Again, it is said that king Gādhi of Kānyakubja was an incarnation of Indra, and the story suggests that the truth was he had also the name Indra or one of its synonyms such as Purandara.[11]

[1] Bharata's mother Śakuntalā is absurdly called an apsaras, Śatapatha Brāhmaṇa, xiii, 5, 4, 13.

[2] So Nahuṣa in Rigv i, *122* is different from Nahuṣa, father of Yayāti, as will be shown in connexion with Pajriya Kakṣīvant in chap. XIX.

[3] So MBh xii, *326*, 12192–6, which is brahmanical.

[4] MBh i, *99*, 3965: iv, *64*, 2078: v, *186*, 7307: &c.

[5] MBh v, *177*, 7015: vi, *122*, 5746.

[6] MBh xiii, *139*, 6294: xiv, *2*, 24.

[7] MBh i, *97*, 3889 to *100*, 4006: xii, *37*, 1351.

[8] This was a feminine name, see the Dictionary.

[9] MBh xiii, *84*, 3942.

[10] MBh v, *186*, 7317. A woman's name, Br *136*, 3.

[11] MBh xii, *49*, 1718–20 Vā *91*, 63–5. Bd iii, *66*, 33–5. Br *10*, 24–7; *13*, 90–1, Hv *27*, 1426–9; *32*, 1764–5. Vedārth, introduction to Rigv iii.

The same was alleged of king Vikukṣi of Ayodhyā, because probably he had also the name Devarāj.[1] Otherwise there appears to be no reason why those two kings should have received that distinction. Further examples will be found in the following pages and especially among the Vasiṣṭhas in chapter XVIII.

These examples and those in chapter V show how the misunderstanding of names and the desire to explain them led to the fabrication of fanciful tales and mythology. Indeed a great deal of the mythology is no doubt the work of brahmans who lacked the historical sense and mistook facts, and it is not euhemerism to look in that direction for the origin of silly stories and mythology connected with persons.

On the other hand, names may not be explained as eponymous or personifications without more ado (p. 13). Thus countries are said sometimes to have been named after kings, such as Gāndhāra,[2] Ānarta,[3] and Sauvīra;[4] and similarly towns, such as Śrāvastī,[5] Hastināpura[6] and Vaiśālī[7] from the kings who founded them. To assert that such kings are merely eponymous is to disregard the evidence supplied by many countries and all times. One might equally assert that Alexander, Seleucus and Constantine were merely eponymous heroes of Alexandria, Seleucia and Constantinople; or that Columbus, Tasman and Rhodes were mythical persons invented to account for Columbia, Tasmania and Rhodesia. It has been a universal practice to name countries, towns, mountains and rivers, especially in newly developed regions, after discoverers, conquerors, founders and celebrated men, and the same method must have been adopted by the Aryans who conquered North India and founded new kingdoms and towns there.

[1] Mat *12*, 26.
[2] Vā *99*, 9. Hv *32*, 1839. Mat *48*, 7, Bḍ iii, *74*, 9. Br, *13*, 150–1.
[3] Mat *12*, 22. Vā *86*, 24. Hv *10*, 644: &c.
[4] Vā *99*, 23–4. Mat *48*, 19–20. Hv *31*, 1680–1.
[5] Vā *88*, 27. Mat *12*, 30. Hv *11*, 670: &c.
[6] MBh i, *95*, 3787. Mat *49*, 42. Vā *99*, 165: &c.
[7] Vā *86*, 17. Bḍ iii, *61*, 12. Viṣ iv, *1*, 18.

CHAPTER XII

SYNCHRONISMS AND TABLE OF ROYAL GENEALOGIES

THE genealogies regarded singly help to elucidate difficulties, as in distinguishing between different kings and rishis of the same names, and how necessary this is will appear from the articles on Divodāsa, Vasiṣṭha, Viśvāmitra, Bharadvāja, &c., in the *Vedic Index*, where the information drawn solely from Vedic literature with its lack of the historical sense leaves many points in perplexity, because different persons of the same name cannot be distinguished therefrom.

Thus, in the first place, the genealogies show there were at least two kings named Divodāsa, one a king of Kāśi, and the other a king of N. Pañcāla, but the *Vedic Index* combines them in its article 'Divodāsa'. Similarly, there were two Sudāsas, one a king of Ayodhyā whose son was Kalmāṣapāda, and the other a king of N. Pañcāla, the Sudās of the Rigveda; but they have been confused in the stories about the murder of the rishi Śakti (chapter XVIII). Secondly, as regards families. The attempt to elucidate the Bharatas or Bhāratas in the *Vedic Index* is attended with perplexity, but the whole of the difficulties disappear when we learn from the genealogies that Bharata, the great Paurava king, had a numerous progeny, and that his descendants divided into many branches, some of which were kṣatriyas and others became brahmans (chapter XXIII). Thirdly, as regards different individuals of rishi families, who are often mentioned merely by their simple gotra name, as Bhṛgu, Vasiṣṭha, Viśvāmitra, &c. The Vedic literature often does not distinguish them, but the genealogies show that when a Vasiṣṭha is mentioned in connexion with Hariścandra, Sagara, Kalmāṣapāda, and Daśaratha of Ayodhyā, a different person is meant in each case.

The genealogies considered singly, however, are of little chronological value, because we have no data for providing a definite historical setting for individual kings, and because, though they aim at fullness, yet admittedly they do not record the name of every king (chapter IX), so that their length or brevity does not fix the chronological durations of the dynasties. A clear illustration of this appears on comparing the Ayodhyā and Vaiśāla lines, for both start from Manu, and Daśaratha of the former was contemporary with Pramati of the latter according to the Rāmāyaṇa, yet the lists of the latter line contain only about half as many names as the lists of the former to that point. But the genealogies would become of relative historical value if they can be connected together so as to supplement one another and form a combined and consistent scheme, in which each checks and elucidates the others, so that all settle into an arrangement relatively harmonious. The genealogies are, for the most part, separate and independent, each pursuing its own course without concerning itself with others, yet co-ordinate allusions do occur incidentally sometimes. If points of contact can be discovered either in them or elsewhere, which bring kings in two or more lines into connexion, they help towards the construction of a combined genealogical scheme; and since such points generally occur incidentally, co-ordination not being the intention of the genealogists, the co-ordination gains a definite probability of being real and true. The more numerous such points, the more abundant become the means of constructing and testing the combined framework and the greater the probability of historical trustworthiness. That is, we must seek for synchronisms.

In dealing with synchronisms certain cautions must be borne in mind. First must be noted the lax use of personal names as gotra names instead of patronymics. Kṣatriya tradition generally distinguished between personal names and patronymics, and the same care is often found in the Brāhmaṇas and Upaniṣads, as where Janamejaya is styled *Pārikṣita*, Sahadeva *Sārñjaya*, and Somaka *Sāhadevya*;[1] but sometimes, especially in the Veda, the personal name is used instead of the patronymic, and thus Vasiṣṭha,[2] Viśvāmitra,[3] Jamadagni,[4] Kaṇva,[5] &c., are used in the plural collectively for Vāsiṣṭhas, Vaiśvāmitras, Jāmadagnyas, Kāṇvas, &c.; and similarly Yadus, Turvaśas, Druhyus, Anus and Pūrus are spoken of.[6]

This practice, combined with the brahmans' lack of the historical sense, tended to blur historical differences and led to the confusion

[1] Aitar Brāhm vii, 5, 8.
[2] Rigv vii, *7*, 7; *12*, 3.
[3] Rigv iii, *1*, 21; *18*, 4.
[4] Rigv iii, *53*, 16.
[5] Rigv i, *44*, 8; *46*, 9; *47*, 10.
[6] Rigv i, *108*, 8.

of persons having the same name or patronymic, so that, to cite the most striking instances, all the Vasiṣṭhas became jumbled into one Vasiṣṭha and all the Viśvāmitras into one Viśvāmitra. Hence the mention of a person by the simple name is no sure criterion that the original person of that name is intended, but often means a descendant. This must be especially observed when brahmans are mentioned only by their gotra names. Thus among the Bhārgavas Uśanas-Śukra,[1] Cyavana,[2] his descendant Ṛcīka,[3] his grandson Rāma Jāmadagnya,[4] and another late rishi[5] are all called Bhṛgu simply. The only safe way of distinguishing brahmans in references of an historical kind is to discriminate them according to the kings with whom they were associated, for the royal genealogies afford the only chronological criteria. Otherwise the confusion is inextricable, as may be seen in the perplexities attending the Vasiṣṭhas, Bharadvājas, Viśvāmitras, &c., in the *Vedic Index*.

Secondly, the use of a patronymic does not always denote that the person to whom it is applied was the son of the bearer of the simple name, but often means a descendant. This is patent as regards tribal or family names, such as Yādava, Paurava, Bhārata and Kaurava; and is also clear in less comprehensive names, as when Rāma is called Rāghava after his great grandfather Raghu,[6] and Kṛṣṇa is styled Dāśārha, Mādhava, Sātvata, Vārṣṇeya and Śauri after various ancestors,[7] as well as Vāsudeva after his father. This use of patronymics seems to be more frequent in kṣatriya than in brahmanic traditions; thus Ṛcīka (p. 68) and the later rishi Agni of Sagara's time[8] are both called Aurva after their common ancestor Ūrva. Moreover, a man had various patronymics from different ancestors, and the choice in poetry was often governed by the metre; and perhaps this may explain Kakṣīvant's patronymic *Auśija* in Rigveda i, *18*, 1, instead of *Dairghatamasa* or *Aucathya*.[9]

Thirdly, sameness of name does not always imply identity of person, and this is abundantly clear from what has been pointed out in the last chapter. Whether identity can be reasonably inferred must depend on other considerations, especially any data of a

[1] Vā *97*, 140. [2] MBh xiii, *51*, 2685.
[3] Vā *91*, 93. Pd iii, *66* 57. Pad vi, *268*, 13.
[4] MBh vii, *70*, 2435. [5] MBh xiii, *30*, 1983–96.
[6] MBh iii, *277*, 16030.
[7] MBh i, *221*, 7987–9, 8012; *222*, 8078; *223*, 8083–4.
[8] Vā *88*, 157 with Mat *12*, 40. See chap. XVII.
[9] See chap. XIX.

chronological kind. Thus, when it is said that Māndhātṛ of Ayodhyā married Śaśabindu's daughter Caitrarathī Bindumatī,[1] it may be safely inferred from the position and circumstances of both that Śaśabindu was the famous Yādava king, son of Citraratha. But when the Mahābhārata says that Ahaṁyāti of the Lunar race married Kṛtavīrya's daughter,[2] it is clear that it cannot mean Kṛtavīrya the Haihaya king, for the two kings were widely apart in time.

Synchronistic references occur in three ways: first, those that are definite and have every appearance of being genuine and that when tested with other allusions are harmonious; secondly, those that may be true but are too vague to be of any use; and thirdly, those that are spurious and untrue. The latter two classes may be briefly considered before we proceed to genuine synchronisms.

Of the second class are notices of rishis and kings by their gotra names merely, as where Janaka, king of Videha, is introduced in various philosophical discussions, for Janaka was the royal family name and many Janakas are mentioned (chapter VIII); or where personal names are used as gotra names, such as the references to Bharadvājas at different times.

The third class of references requires rather more notice, because they are sometimes precise and circumstantial, but examination shows their falsity. It comprises three kinds of allusions: first, those that are purely laudatory and introduce persons on special occasions in defiance of chronology merely to enhance the dignity of the hero or the occasion; secondly, those that have grown or been developed out of some allusion but are mistaken; and thirdly, those that are wholly spurious.

Of the first of these kinds is the introduction of famous rishis, as noticed at page 67; and as where it is said the Ātreya rishi Durvāsas visited the Pāṇḍavas in their exile,[3] though his real period was far anterior and he is introduced into the story of Śakuntalā, their distant ancestress. It is generally rishis who appear on such occasions in defiance of chronology, and rarely that kings so appear. The second kind comprises all sorts of notices, from brief allusions to long stories. As such may be cited these—Māndhātṛ

[1] Vā *88*, 70. Bd iii, *63*, 70–1: &c. See chap. XIII.

[2] MBh i, *95*, 3768. No patronymic given. Its list is not reliable (chap. IX), and certainly goes wrong at that point.

[3] MBh iii, *261*. 15499.

conquered the Aṅga Bṛhadratha,[1] who was long posterior: and Bhagīratha was a contemporary of Jahnu, king of Kānyakubja.[2] It is in brahmanical stories that such spurious synchronisms are generally found, and they are often mere expedients for hanging some precept or doctrine upon, as that Suhotra, the Paurava king, encountered Śivi Auśīnara to learn deference to superior virtue[3]; or for the purpose of exalting the dignity of brahmans, as that Agastya vanquished Nahuṣa.[4] Similarly are erroneously connected Madhucchandas Vaiśvāmitra as priest to Śaryāti,[5] Cyavana as cursing the Haihaya king Kṛtavīrya,[6] and many others.[7]

The story of Gālava's doings[8] is an excellent instance of the third kind of spurious synchronisms. In order to earn the special fee required by his teacher Viśvāmitra he obtained from king Yayāti Nāhuṣa[9] his daughter Mādhavī and offered her in turn to king Haryaśva of Ayodhyā, king Divodāsa of Kāśi, king Uśīnara of Bhojanagara, and Viśvāmitra himself, each for a fourth part of the fee, and they begot of her one son each, Vasumanas, Pratardana, Śivi and Aṣṭaka respectively. Then he returned her to her father. This story makes all those kings and Viśvāmitra contemporary, and three facts show its absurdity. First, Uśīnara was a descendant of Anu, Yayāti's son, by some generations; secondly, this the first Viśvāmitra was a distant descendant in the Kānyakubja line, which sprang out of the Aila race just before Yayāti's time; and thirdly, Gālava was Viśvāmitra's own son![10]—a fact of which the story is ignorant.[11] The appended table of genealogies will display these errors clearly. Haryaśva and Uśīnara probably were contemporaries, but Viśvāmitra was later and Divodāsa (Pratardana's father) later still, as will be shown by the genuine synchronisms in the next chapter; and Yayāti was far earlier. The story makes kings Vasumanas, Pratardana, Śivi and Aṣṭaka brothers and contemporaries, and this

[1] MBh xii, *29*, 981, where some names as Aṅgāra are right but other names have been inserted wrongly or are corrupted.

[2] Bd iii, *56*, 44–8, a late story.

[3] MBh iii, *194*, 13249–55.

[4] MBh v, *16*, 521–37.

[5] Br *138*, 2–3.

[6] Mat *68*, 7–9.

[7] e.g. MBh xii, *49*, 1790–9; *99*, 3664 f.

[8] MBh v, *105*, 3732 to *106*; *113* to *118*.

[9] It wrongly calls Yayāti king of all the Kāśis, *id.* *114*, 3918. Kāśi was a separate kingdom, and the story itself assigns Divodāsa to it.

[10] MBh xiii, *4*, 251. Vā *88*, 87–90; *91*, 100. Bd iii. *63*, 86–9; *66*, 72. Br *7*, 106–9; *10*, 59. Hv *12*, 726–9; *27*, 1462; *32*, 1769.

[11] So MBh xiii, *18*, 1349, unless different Gālavas and Viśvāmitras are confused.

statement appears elsewhere also,[1] especially in a further fable [2] that Yayāti was cast out from heaven for pride and fell at Naimiṣa forest, where those four kings were assembled, and they were made known to him as his daughter's sons. The story is manifestly a brahmanical fabrication, and may have been developed from the fact that the three verses of which Rigveda x, *179* consists are attributed one each to Śivi, Pratardana and Vasumanas (who is called son of Ruśadaśva or Rohidaśva, which are almost synonymous with Haryaśva), in order to explain how the single verses composed by these three kings became combined into one hymn.[3] But how Aṣṭaka is joined with them is uncertain.

We may now investigate what are genuine synchronisms, and these will be dealt with in the next two chapters. It will be convenient, however, for ease of reference to set out the combined scheme of genealogies of all the important dynasties, as established by genuine synchronisms, and this is displayed in the following table. The dynasties have been arranged in the table according to geographical position, as far as is feasible, those that reigned in the west on the left side, those in the east on the right, and the others in the middle. The names of kings whose positions are fixed by synchronisms or otherwise are printed in italics, and the famous kings are indicated by an asterisk. As already explained, the lists are not equally full, and the deficiencies appear very plainly from the table; hence, where there are no synchronisms and the lists are defective, the names that occur are spaced out, but this arrangement is only tentative and the position of such a name merely indicates the best possible approximation. Among the last kings of Videha, Kṛtakṣaṇa is mentioned,[4] and kings later than the battle are set out in the list in chapter XXVII. Smaller or shorter dynasties, which have not been brought into this list, are given in chapters VIII and IX, such as the Śāryātas, Nābhāgas and various branches of the Yādavas.

[1] MBh iii, *197*, 13301–2. Mat *35*, 5.
[2] MBh i, *88* to *93*: v, *119*, 4041 to *122*, 4097. Mat *37* to *42*.
[3] Possibly also each king's mother was named Mādhavī.
[4] MBh ii, *4*, 122.

TABLE OF ROYAL

	YĀDAVAS	HAIHAYAS	DRUHYUS	TURVASUS	KĀNYA-KUBJA	PAURAVAS
1	Manu	... ...	Manu	Manu	Manu	Manu
2	Ilā	... ...	Ilā	Ilā	Ilā	Ilā
3	Purūravas*	... ...	Purūravas*	Purūravas*	Purūravas*	Purūravas*
4	Āyu*	... ...	Āyu*	Āyu*	Amāvasu	Āyu*
5	Nahuṣa*	... ...	Nahuṣa*	Nahuṣa*	... ...	Nahuṣa*
6	*Yayāti**	... ...	*Yayāti**	*Yayāti**	... ...	*Yayāti**
7	Yadu	... ...	Druhyu	Turvasu	... ...	Pūru*
8	Kroṣṭu	Sahasrajit	... ...	... ...	... ...	Janame-jaya I
9	... ...	... ...	... ...	... ...	Bhīma	Pracinvant
10	... ...	... ...	... ...	... ...	... ...	Pravīra
11	Vṛjinīvant	Śatajit	... ...	... ...	... ...	Manasyu
12	... ...	... ...	Babhru	... ...	... ...	Abhayada
13	... ...	... ...	... ...	... ...	... ...	Sudhanvan-Dhundhu
14	Svāhi	Haihaya	... ...	Vahni	Kāñcana-prabha	Bahugava
15	... ...	... ...	... ...	... ...	... ...	Saṁyāti
16	... ...	... ...	... ...	... ...	... ...	Ahaṁyāti
17	Ruśadgu	Dharma-netra	Setu	... ...	... ...	Raudrāśva
18	... ...	... ...	... ...	... ...	... ...	Ṛceyu
19	*Citraratha*	Kunti	... ...	... ...	Suhotra	*Matināra*
20	*Śaśabindu**	... ...	... ...	... ...	... ...	Taṁsu
21	Pṛthuśra-vas	Sāhañja	*Aṅgāra*	Garbha	... ...	... ...
22	Antara	... ...	... ...	... ...	... ...	... ...
23	... ...	Mahiṣmant	Gāndhāra	... ...	*Jahnu**	... ...
24	Suyajña	... ...	... ...	... ...	Sunaha	... ...
25	... ...	*Bhadra-śreṇya**	... ...	... ...	Ajaka	... ...
26	Uśanas	... ...	Dharma	... ...	Balākāśva	... ...
27	... ...	*Durdama*	... ...	... ...	... ...	... ...
28	Śineyu	Kanaka	... ...	Gobhānu	Kuśa	... ...
29	... ...	... ...	Dhṛta	... ...	Kuśāśva-*Kuśika*	... ...
30	Marutta	Kṛtavīrya	... ...	... ...	*Gādhi**	... ...
31	... ...	*Arjuna**	... ...	... ...	... ...	... ...
32	Kambala-barhis	... ...	Durdama	... ...	*Viśvāmitra**	... ...
33	... ...	Jayadhvaja	... ...	... ...	... ...	... ...

GENEALOGIES

Kāśi	Ānavas, NW.	Ānavas, E.	Ayodhyā	Videha	Vaiśālī	
Manu	Manu	... ...	Manu	... ...	Manu	1
Ilā	Ilā	... ...	Ikṣvāku*	... ...	Nābhānediṣṭha	2
Purūravas*	Purūravas*	... ...	Vikukṣi-Śaśāda	Nimi	... ...	3
Āyu*	Āyu*	... ...	*Kakutstha*	... ...	... ...	4
Nahuṣa*	Nahuṣa*	... ...	Anenas	Mithi Janaka	... ...	5
Kṣatravṛddha	*Yayāti**	... ...	Pṛthu	... ...	Bhalandana	6
... ...	Anu	... ...	Viṣṭarāśva	... ...	... ...	7
... ...	... ...	... ...	Ārdra	Udāvasu	Vatsaprī	8
Sunahotra	... ...	... ...	Yuvanāśva I	... ...	... ...	9
... ...	Sabhānara	... ...	Śrāvasta	...	... ...	10
... ...	... ...	... ...	Bṛhadaśva	Nandivardhana	... ...	11
Kāśa	... ...	... ...	Kuvalāśva	... ...	Prāṁśu	12
... ...	Kālānala	... ...	Dṛḍhāśva	... ...	... ...	13
... ...	... ...	... ...	Pramoda	Suketu	... ...	14
Dīrghatapas	... ...	... ...	Haryaśva I	... ...	... ...	15
... ...	Sṛñjaya	... ...	Nikumbha	... ...	Prajāni	16
Dhanva	... ...	... ...	Saṁhatāśva	Devarāta	... ...	17
... ...	... ...	... ...	Akṛśāśva	... ...	... ...	18
Dhanvantari	Purañjaya	... ...	*Prasenajit*	... ...	... ...	19
... ...	... ...	... ...	*Yuvanāśva II*	Bṛhaduktha	Khanitra	20
Ketumant I	... ...	... ...	*Māndhātṛ**	... ...	... ...	21
... ...	Mahāśāla	... ...	*Purukutsa**	... ...	... ...	22
Bhīmaratha	... ...	... ...	*Trasadasyu*	Mahāvīrya	... ...	23
... ...	Mahāmanas	... ...	Sambhūta	... ...	Kṣupa	24
Divodāsa I	... ...	... ...	Anaraṇya	... ...	... ...	25
Aṣṭāratha	Uśīnara*	Titikṣu	Trasadaśva	Dhṛtimant	... ...	26
... ...	Śivi*	... ...	Haryaśva II	... ...	... ...	27
... ...	... ...	... ...	Vasumata (or Vasumanas)	... ...	Viṁśa	28
... ...	*Kekaya*	... ...	Tridhanvan	Sudhṛti	... ...	29
... ...	... ...	Ruśadratha	*Trayyāruṇa*	... ...	... ...	30
... ...	... ...	... ...	... ...	...	...	31
... ...	... ...	... ...	*Satyavrata-Triśaṅku**	Dhṛṣṭaketu	Viviṁśa	32
...	... ...	... ...	*Hariścandra**	... ...	...	

	Yādavas	Haihayas	Druhyus	Turvasus	Kānyakubja	Pauravas
34	Rukmaka-vaca	*Tālajaṅgha*	... ...	Triśānu	Aṣṭaka	... ...
35	... ...	... ...	Pracetas	... ...	... ...	... ...
36	Parāvṛt	*Vītihotra*	... ...	... ...	Lauhi	... ...
37	... ...	... ...	... ...	... ...	... ...	... ...
38	Jyāmagha*	Ananta	Sucetas	... ...	... ...	... ...
39	... ...	Durjaya	... ...	... ...	... ...	... ...
40	*Vidarbha*	Supratīka	... ...	*Karandhama*		... ...
		Cedi				
41	Kratha-Bhīma	Kaiśika	... ...	*Marutta*	... ...	... ...
42	Kunti	Cidi	... ...	... ...	... ...	... ...
43	Dhṛṣṭa	... ...	... ...	(*Duṣyanta*)	... ...	*Duṣyanta**
44	Nirvṛti	... ...	... ...	... ...	... ...	*Bharata**
45	Vidūratha	... ...			... ...	... ...
46	Daśārha	... ...	... ...	... ...	... ...	(Bharad-vāja)
47	Vyoman	... ...	... ...	... ...	... ...	Vitatha
48	Jīmūta	... ...	... ...	... ...	... ...	Bhuvaman-yu
49	Vikṛti	... ...	... ...	... ...	... ...	Bṛhatkṣa-tra
50	*Bhīmaratha*	*Vīrabāhu*	... ...	... ...	... ...	Suhotra
51	Rathavara	*Subāhu*	Dvimīḍhas	N. Pañcāla	S. Pañcāla	Hastin
52	... ...	... ...				
53	Daśaratha	... ...	Dvimīḍha	... ...	... ...	Ajamīḍha*
54	Ekādaśa-ratha	... ...	... ...	... ...	... ...	... ...
55	Śakuni	... ...	Yavīnara	Nīla	Bṛhadvasu	... ...
56	Karambha	... ...	... ...	Suśānti	Bṛhadiṣu	... ...
57	... ...	... ...	Dhṛtimant	Purujānu	Bṛhaddha-nus	... ...
58	Devarāta	... ...	... ...	Ṛkṣa	Bṛhatkar-man	... ...
59	Devakṣatra	... ...	Satyadhṛti	Bhṛmyaśva	Jayadratha	... ...
60	Devana	... ...	Dṛḍhanemi	Mudgala	Viśvajit	... ...
61	Madhu*	... ...	... ...	(Brahmiṣ-ṭha)	... ...	... ...
62	Puruvaśa	... ...	Suvarman	Vadhryaś-va*	Senajit	... ...
63	Purudvant		Sārvabhau-ma	Divodāsa*	Rucirāśva	Ṛkṣa I
64	Jantu (Aṁśu)	... ...	... ...	Mitrayu	Pṛthuṣeṇa	... ...
65	Satvant	... ...	Mahant-Paurava	Maitreya Soma	Pāra I	... ...

Kāśi	Ānavas, NW.	Ānavas, E.	Ayodhyā	Videha	Vaiśālī	
... ...	... ...	Hema	*Rohita*	... ...	... ...	34
... ...	... ...	... ...	Harita, Cañcu	Haryaśva	Khanīnetra	35
... ...	... ...	... ...	Vijaya	... ...	... ...	36
... ...	... ...	... ...	Ruruka	... ...	... ...	37
Haryaśva	... ...	Sutapas	Vṛka	Maru	*Karandhama*	38
Sudeva	... ...	... ...	*Bāhu (Asita)*	... ...	*Avīkṣit*	39
Divodāsa II	... ...	... ...	... ...	... ...	*Marutta**	40
*Pratardana**	... ...	*Bali**	*Sagara**	Pratīndhaka	Nariṣyanta	41
Vatsa	... ...	... ...	Asamañjas	... ...	Dama	42
*Alarka**	... ...	*Aṅga*	*Aṁśumant*	... ...	... ...	43
... ...	... ...	... ...	Dilīpa I	Kīrtiratha	Rāṣṭravardhana	44
Sannati	... ...	... ...	Bhagīratha*	... ...	Sudhṛti	45
Sunītha	... ...	... ...	Śruta	... ...	Nara	46
... ...	... ...	Dadhivāhana	Nābhāga	Devamīḍha	Kevala	47
Kṣema	... ...	... ...	Ambarīṣa*	... ...	Bandhumant	48
... ...	... ...	... ...	Sindhudvīpa	... ...	Vegavant	49
Ketumant II	... ...	... ...	Ayutāyus	Vibudha	Budha	50
... ...	... ...	Diviratha	Ṛtuparṇa	... ...	... ...	51
Suketu	... ...	... ...	Sarvakāma	... ...	*Tṛṇabindu**	52
... ...	... ...	... ...	Sudāsa	Mahādhṛti	Viśravas	53
Dharmaketu	... ...	Dharmaratha	Mitrasaha-Kalmāṣapāda*	... ...	Viśāla	54
... ...	... ...	... ...	Aśmaka	... ...	Hemacandra	55
Satyaketu	... ...	... ...	Mūlaka	Kīrtirāta	Sucandra	56
... ...	... ...	Citraratha	Śataratha	... ...	Dhūmrāśva	57
Vibhu	... ...	... ...	Aiḍaviḍa-Vṛddhaśarman	... ...	Sṛñjaya	58
... ...	... ...	... ...	Viśvasaha I	Mahāroman	Sahadeva	59
Suvibhu	... ...	Satyaratha	Dilīpa II-Khaṭvāṅga*	... ...	Kṛśāśva	60
... ...	... ...	...	Dīrghabāhu	Svarṇaroman	... ...	61
Sukumāra	... ...	... ...	Raghu*	... ...	Somadatta	62
... ...	... ...	... ...	Aja	Hrasvaroman	Janamejaya	63
Dhṛṣṭaketu	... ...	*Lomapāda**	*Daśaratha**	*Sīradhvaja*	*Pramati*	64
... ...	... ...	... ...	*Rāma**	Bhānumant	... ...	65

	YĀDAVAS	YĀDAVAS	DVIMĪḌHAS	N. PAÑCĀLA	S. PAÑCĀ	PAURAVAS
66	*Bhīma Sātvata*	... ...	... ...	*Sṛñjaya*	Nīpa	... ...
67	*Andhaka*	Vṛṣṇi	... ...	Cyavana*	... ...	... ...
68	... ...	... ...	... ...	*Sudāsa**	... ...	... ...
69	Kukura	... ...	... ...	Sahadeva	... ...	*Saṁvaraṇa*
70	... ...	... ...	... ...	*Somaka*	... ...	... ...
71	... ...	... ...	... ...	Jantu	... ...	*Kuru**
72	... ...	... ...	... ...	... ...	... ...	
73	Vṛṣṇi	... ...	... ...	... ...	... ...	Parikṣit I
74	... ...	... ...	... ...	... ...	... ...	Janame-jaya II
75	... ...	... ...	... ...	... ...	... ...	(Bhīmasena, &c.)
76	... ...	Devamī-ḍhuṣa	Rukma-ratha	... ...	Samara	Vidūratha
77	Kapota-roman	... ...	... ...	... ...	... ...	Sārva-bhauma
78	... ...	... ...	Supārśva	... ...	Pāra II	Jayatsena
79	... ...	... ...	Sumati	... ...	... ...	Arādhin
80	Viloman	... ...	... ...	... ...	Pṛthu	Mahā-bhauma
81	... ...	... ...	Sannati-mant	... ...	... ...	Ayutāyus
82	... ...	... ...	Sanati-	... ...	Sukṛti	Akrodhana
83	Nala	... ...	... ...	... ...	... ...	Devātithi
84	... ...	... ...	*Kṛta*	... ...	Vibhrāja	Ṛkṣa II
85	... ...	... ...	... ...	... ...	... ...	Bhīmasena
86	Abhijit	... ...	... ...	... ...	Aṇuha	Dilīpa
87	... ...	... ...	... ...	... ...	*Brahma-datta**	*Pratīpa**
88	... ...	... ...	... ...	... ...	Viṣvaksena	... ...
89	Punarvasu	Śūra	... ...	... ...	Udaksena	(Ṛṣṭiṣeṇa)
90	... ...	...	Ugrāyudha	... ...	Bhallāṭa	*Śantanu**
91	... ...	...	Kṣemya	*Pṛṣata*	*Janamejaya*	(*Bhīṣma*)
92	*Ugrasena*	*Vasudeva*	Suvīra		... ...	*Vicitravīrya*
93	*Kaṁsa**	... ...	Nṛpañjaya	*Droṇa*	*Drupada**	*Dhṛtarāṣṭra**
94	... ...	*Kṛṣṇa**	Bahuratha	*Aśvatthāman*	*Dhṛṣṭadyum-na*	*Pāṇḍavas**
95	... ...	*Sāmba*	... ...	... ...	*Dhṛṣṭaketu*	*Abhimanyu*

[*Here occurred the*

KĀŚI	ĀNAVAS, NW.	ĀNAVAS, E.	AYODHYĀ	VIDEHA	VAIŚĀLĪ	
Veṇuhotra	... ...	Caturaṅga	... ...	Pradyumna-Śatadyumna	... ...	66
... ...	... ...	... ...	*Kuśa*	Muni	... ...	67
Bharga	... ...	... ...	Atithi	Ūrjavaha	... ...	68
		Pṛthulākṣa	Niṣadha	Sanadvāja	... ...	69
... ...	... ...	... ...	Nala	Śakuni	... ...	70
PAURAVAS	PAURAVAS	Campa	Nabhas	Añjana	... ...	71
		... ...	Puṇḍarīka	Ṛtujit	... ...	72
Jahnu	Sudhanvan	Haryaṅga	Kṣemadhanvan	Ariṣṭanemi	... ...	73
... ...	Suhotra		Devānīka	Śrutāyus	... ...	74
Suratha	Cyavana	Bhadraratha	Ahīnagu	Supārśva	... ...	75
	Kṛta	... ...	Pāripātra	Sañjaya	... ...	76
MAGADHA	CEDI	... ...	Dala, Bala	Kṣemāri	... ...	77
... ...	Vasu Caidya*	Bṛhatkarman	Uktha	Anenas	... ...	78
Bṛhadratha	Pratyagraha ?	... ...	Vajranābha	Mīnaratha	... ...	79
Kuśāgra	... ...	... ...	Śaṅkhana	Satyaratha	... ...	80
... ...	... ...	Bṛhadratha	Vyuṣitāśva	Upaguru	... ...	81
Ṛṣabha	... ...	... ...	Viśvasaha II	Upagupta	... ...	82
Puṣpavant	... ...	Bṛhadbhānu	*Hiraṇyanābha*	Svāgata	... ...	83
... ...	... ...	... ...	Puṣya	Suvarcas	... ...	84
Satyahita	... ...	Bṛhanmanas	Dhruvasandhi	Śruta	... ...	85
Sudhanvan	... ...	... ..	Sudarśana	Suśruta	... ...	86
... ...	... ...	Jayadratha	Agnivarṇa	Jaya	... ...	87
Ūrja	... ...	... ...	Śīghra	Vijaya	... ...	88
... ...	... ...	Dṛḍharatha	Maru	Ṛta	... ...	89
Sambhava	... ...	... ...	Prasuśruta	Sunaya	... ...	90
... ...	... ...	... ...	Susandhi	Vītahavya	... ...	91
Jarāsandha	*Damaghoṣa*	Viśvajit	Amarṣa and Sahasvant	Dhṛti	... ...	92
... ...	... ...	... ...	Viśrutavant	Bahulāśva	... ...	93
Sahadeva	*Śiśupāla**	*Karṇa**	*Bṛhadbala*	*Kṛtakṣaṇa*	... ...	94
Somādhi	*Dhṛṣṭaketu*	*Vṛṣasena*	Bṛhatkṣaya	... ...	... ...	95

Bhārata battle.]

CHAPTER XIII

MAJOR SYNCHRONISMS ESTABLISHED

IN endeavouring to establish synchronisms, first may be noticed those kings and rishis about whom there are copious or very clear statements.

There is a very early group of synchronous kings. The Aikṣvāku genealogy of Ayodhyā states plainly that Prasenajit's son Yuvanāśva married Gaurī and their son was Māndhātṛ. The Paurava genealogy says Matināra's daughter Gaurī was mother of Māndhātṛ. Here there can be no doubt, for the statements are separate and explicit (chapter VI). Prasenajit therefore was contemporary with Matināra, Yuvanāśva was one generation below and Māndhātṛ two generations. Further, the Ayodhyā genealogy says that Māndhātṛ married Śaśabindu's daughter Bindumatī Caitrarathī, who was the eldest of many brothers;[1] and the Yādava genealogy names Śaśabindu, son of Citraratha, as a famous king who had very many sons.[2] Here also there can be no doubt; hence Māndhātṛ was one generation below Śaśabindu. Next Jahnu of Kānyakubja married the granddaughter of Yauvanāśva,[3] that is, Māndhātṛ; hence he was two generations below Māndhātṛ.[4] From all these we have a clear set of synchronisms thus—

Paurava	*Aikṣvāku*	*Yādava*	*Kānyakubja*
Matināra	Prasenajit	Citraratha	
Gaurī	Yuvanāśva II	Śaśabindu	
	Māndhātṛ	Bindumatī	
	Purukutsa		
	Trasadasyu		Jahnu

[1] Vā *88*, 70–1. Hv *12*, 712–13. Br *7*, 92–4. Bḍ iii, *63*, 70–1. Viṣ iv, *2*, 19. Bhāg ix, *6*, 38. Śiv vii, *60*, 76–7. Gar i, *138*, 22, corrupt.

[2] Vā *95*, 18–20. Hv *37*, 1971–3. Bḍ iii, *70*, 19–20, Mat *44*, 18–20 Br *15*, 4. Viṣ iv, *12*, 1–2. Pad v, *13*, 3–5. Ag *274*, 13–14. Bhāg ix *23*, 31–3. Also MBh vii, *65*, 2321–4.

[3] Vā *91*, 58–9. Bḍ iii, *66*, 28–9. Hv *27*, 1421–3; *32*, 1761–2. Br *10*, 19–20; *13*, 87.

[4] A wrong synchronism of Jahnu, Bḍ iii, *56*, 44–8.

The next group of synchronisms is that in which Viśvāmitra and his nephew Jamadagni are the central figures. King Kṛtavīrya of the Haihayas had the Bhārgavas as his priests and enriched them. His successors tried to recover the wealth, but the Bhārgavas resisted. The Haihayas maltreated them, and the Bhārgavas fled to other countries for safety.[1] Gādhi or Gāthi was then king of Kānyakubja and had a daughter Satyavatī. The Bhārgava rishi Ṛcīka Aurva, son of Ūrva, married her and had a son Jamadagni, and about the same time Gādhi had a son[2] Viśvaratha.[3] Viśvaratha, after succeeding to the kingdom,[4] relinquished it, placed his family in a hermitage near Ayodhyā[5] and gave himself up to austerities for twelve years, after which he became a brahman with the name Viśvāmitra. He returned and succoured prince Satyavrata Triśaṅku[6] of Ayodhyā who had befriended his family, and restored him to the throne, overcoming the opposition of the then Vasiṣṭha,[7] whose personal name was Devarāj.[8] Jamadagni married Kāmalī Reṇukā, daughter of Reṇu, a minor king belonging to the Ikṣvāku race, and their son was Rāma Jāmadagnya.[9] Triśaṅku was succeeded by his son Hariścandra, who had a son Rohita, and Viśvāmitra and Jamadagni attended as priests at the sacrifice at which Śunaḥśepa was substituted for Rohita.[10] Kṛtavīrya was succeeded by his son Arjuna Kārtavīrya, who was a great king (p. 41). After a long reign he had dissension with Jamadagni, his sons killed

[1] MBh i, *178*, 6802 to *179*, 6827. See chap. XVII for Ūrva.

[2] MBh iii, *115*, 11044–67 : v, *118*, 4005–7 : xii, *49*, 1721–46 : xiii, *4*, 205–47. Vā *91*, 66–87. Bḍ iii, *66*, 36–58. Hv *27*, 1430–51 ; *32*, 1765–7. Br *10*, 28–49. Viṣ iv, *7*, 5–16. Bhāg ix, *15*, 5–11.

[3] Vā *91*, 92–3. Bḍ iii, *66*, 63–5. Hv *27*, 1456–9. Br *10*, 53–6.

[4] MBh ix, *41*, 2299, 2300. Rām i, *51*, 20. Bṛhadd iv, 95.

[5] He was connected with the Ayodhyā dynasty through marriage; see infra.

[6] Called Mataṅga, MBh i, *71*, 2925.

[7] Vā *88*, 78–116. Bḍ iii, *63*, 77–114. Br *7*, 97 to *8*, 23. Hv *12*, 717 to *13*, 753. Śiv vii, *60*, 81 to *61*, 19. Lg i, *66*, 3–10. Viṣ iv, *3*, 13–14. Bhāg ix, *7*, 5–6. All fully discussed, JRAS, 1913, pp. 888–900. See chap. XVIII.

[8] MBh xiii, *137*, 6257 : cf. xii, *234*, 8601. JRAS, 1913, pp. 896, 903 : 1917, pp. 39, 54, 63.

[9] MBh iii, *116*, 11072–4 : v, *116*, 3972 : xii, *49*, 1746–7. Vā *91*, 89–91. Bḍ iii, *66*, 60–3. Hv *27*, 1453–5. Br *10*, 50–3.

[10] Aitar Brāhm vii, *3*, 1 f. Śāṅkhāyana Śr Sūtra xv, 17–25. Bhāg ix, *7*, 7–25. Br *104*. MBh xiii, *3*, 186–7. Rām i, *61*, *62*. All discussed, JRAS, 1917, pp. 40, 44 f.

Jamadagni, and Rāma killed him.[1] Here then we have these synchronisms :—

Haihaya	*Bhārgava*	*Kānyakubja*	*Aikṣvāku*
Kṛtavīrya	Ūrva	Gādhi	Trayyāruṇa
Arjuna	Ṛcīka	Satyavatī	
	Jamadagni	Viśvāmitra	Triśaṅku
			Hariścandra
	Rāma[2]		Rohita

This group is connected with the preceding group by both the Ayodhyā and Kānyakubja genealogies, and also by the collateral statement that Kuśika, Gādhi's father, married Paurukutsī, a 'descendant of Purukutsa', and she was Gādhi's mother.[3] Jahnu was a contemporary of Purukutsa's son Trasadasyu (*ante*), and Viśvāmitra of Triśaṅku. The genealogies give seven descents from Jahnu to Viśvāmitra, and eight descents from Trasadasyu to Triśaṅku. They thus tally, and Paurukutsī was Purukutsa's descendant in about the sixth degree.

[1] MBh i, *104*, 4172 : iii, *115*, 11035 ; *116*, 11089–98 ; *117*, 10202–3 : vii, *70*, 2429 : xii, *49*, 1761–8. Vā *94*, 38, 47. Bd iii, *69*, 38, 48. Hv *34*, 1890. Viṣ iv, *11*, 7. Mat *43*, 44. Br *13*, 196–7 ; *213*, 114. Cf. Lg i, *68*, 10 : Kūr i, *22*, 20 : Hv *42*, 2314. Cf. MBh viii, *5*, 144 : xii, *362*, 13879–80 : xiv, *29*, 824–31.

[2] It should be noted that a curious statement occurs in the Ayodhyā genealogy in six Puranas, which speak of Rāma at a much later time, in the reign of king Mūlaka (chap. VIII). Vā *88*, 178–9 and Bd iii, *63*, 178–9 say Mūlaka was in fear of Rāma and lived protected by a guard of women (*nārī-kavaca*). Lg i, *66*, 29, Kūr i, *21*, 14, Viṣ iv, *4*, 38 and Bhāg ix, *9*, 40 say much the same. This must be connected with the statement in MBh xii, *49*, 1770–8, which says that a thousand years after Rāma had destroyed all the kṣatriyas, a fresh generation of them, including Pratardana and others, had grown up, and he destroyed them all again and again till twenty-one times ; and with the further statement (*ibid.* 1792–3) that then Sarvakarman, who is placed as king of Ayodhyā at the same time as Mūlaka (chap. VIII), was brought up in secret. All this MBh account is brahmanic and mostly fable ; hence these two statements are of no chronological value, and the statement about Mūlaka would seem to be a reflex of the fable, incorporated in the Ayodhyā genealogy, while the secret bringing up would explain the phrase *nārī-kavaca.* This matter is further noticed in chap. XXV. A similar fanciful mistake, MBh v, *146*, 4978–81.

[3] Vā *91*, 63–6 ; Bd iii, *66*, 33–6 ; Br *10*, 24–8 ; and Hv *27*, 1426–30 have the fullest text. Collated they suggest this reading :—

Gādhir nāmâbhavat putraḥ Kauśikaḥ Pākaśāsanaḥ
Paurukutsy abhavad bhāryā Gādhis tasyām ajāyata.

There is an extensive series of events which connect the Haihaya dynasty with those of Kāśi and Ayodhyā. The Haihaya dynasty rose to power under king Bhadraśreṇya, apparently in South Malwa, and extended its sway eastwards. His fourth successor, the great Arjuna Kārtavīrya mentioned above, reigned at Māhiṣmatī (the modern Mandhata in the R. Narbada[1]), carried, it is said, his arms over the whole earth and came into conflict with Āpava Vasiṣṭha,[2] so that he overran all Madhyadeśa. Afterwards the Tālajaṅghas and other Haihayas, attended by hordes from beyond the north-west, attacked Ayodhyā and drove the king Bāhu from the throne. Bāhu begot a son Sagara, and Sagara defeated all those enemies, regained his kingdom and destroyed the Haihaya power.[3] Arjuna's contemporaries have been mentioned above, namely, Triśaṅku and Hariścandra of Ayodhyā. The genealogies give six more Haihaya kings, and Sagara was eighth in descent from Hariścandra. Thus the genealogies tally with the story of Sagara.

There are further synchronisms of certain Kāśi kings with Bhadraśreṇya and the Tālajaṅghas, which arise out of a story told in the Kāśi genealogy.[4] It runs thus. Divodāsa, son of Bhīmaratha, was king of Kāśi and (in consequence of a curse, it is alleged) abandoned his capital Vārāṇasī, and established himself in another city on the river Gomatī in the extreme east of his territory. Bhadraśreṇya, the Haihaya king, seized the kingdom,[5] and a Rākṣasa named Kṣemaka occupied the city. Divodāsa recovered the kingdom from Bhadraśreṇya's sons, but afterwards Bhadraśreṇya's son Durdama re-established himself in it. Divodāsa was succeeded by his brother Aṣṭāratha. Pratardana was the son of Divodāsa, and he recovered

[1] JRAS, 1910, pp. 441–6, 867–9. Also Pad vi, *115*, 3–4; *179*, 2.

[2] Vā *94*, 39–45; *95*, 1–13. Bḍ iii, *69*, 39–44; *70*, 1–14. Mat *43*, 41–3. Hv *33*, 1881–6. Br *13*, 189–94. MBh xii, *49*, 1753–8, which says Āpava's hermitage was near the Himalayas.

[3] Vā *88*, 121–43. Bḍ iii, *63*, 119–41. Br *8*, 28–51. Hv *13*, 760 to *14*, 784. Śiv vii, *61*, 22–43. Viṣ iv, *3*, 15–21. Also Bḍ iii, *47*, 74 to *48*, 46, which appears to contain genuine tradition. MBh iii, *106*, 8832. JRAS, 1919, pp. 354–8. Rām i, *70*, 28–37; ii, *110*, 15–24; these call Bāhu *Asita*. Also Pad vi, *21*, 11–34.

[4] Vā *92*, 23–8, 61–8 and Bḍ iii, *67*, 26–31, 64–72, which are the best. Br *11*, 40–54. Hv *29*, 1541–8, 1582–91. Parts of it in Br *13*, 66–75; Hv *32*, 1736–49.

[5] Called king of Benares, Vā *94*, 6; Bḍ iii, *69*, 6; Mat *43*, 11; Hv *33*, 1848; Pad v, *12*, 114.

the kingdom and put an end to the strife with the Haihayas. His grandson Alarka killed the Rākṣasa Kṣemaka and regained the city. All these events occupied a thousand years, that is, a very long time.

This story is supplemented by a further fragment of kṣatriya tradition.[1] The piece of genealogy prefixed to the latter is confused, but shows this much, that the tradition relates to the Haihayas after the time of Tālajaṅgha and in particular to the descendants of king Vītahavya among them.[2] Haryaśva king of the Kāśis fought with the Vītahavya-Haihayas at the confluence of the Ganges and Jumna. They killed him and returned to the city of the Vatsyas.[3] His son was Sudeva and they defeated him. His son was Divodāsa, and he retreated and built a city, called Vārāṇasī also, at the confluence of the Ganges and Gomatī. They attacked, defeated and drove him from his city. He took refuge with his purohita Bharadvāja. His son Pratardana attacked and destroyed the Vaitahavyas, and the Vītahavya king found refuge with a Bhṛgu rishi, who saved him by declaring and making him a brahman.[4] This is confirmed from brahmanic books, which say Bharadvāja was Divodāsa's purohita and gave Pratardana the kingdom.[5]

Putting the two stories together, it is clear that the former gives the beginning and the end of the long contest between the Haihayas and Kāśis; that the latter narrates the latter part of it; that in the Kāśi dynasty there were two Divodāsas, one who was son of Bhīmaratha at the beginning and the other who was son of Sudeva at the end; that between them reigned at least three kings, Aṣṭāratha, Haryaśva and Sudeva; that the former story prima facie, but not necessarily, confuses the two Divodāsas;[6] and that Pratardana[7] was son of Divodāsa II. It is also plain that

[1] MBh xiii, *30*, 1949–96. [2] *Ibid.* 1946–53, 1958, 1965.

[3] Used here by anticipation.

[4] MBh xiii, *30*, 1984, 1995 f. Pratardana's conquest, xii, *96*, 3576.

[5] Pañcaviṁśa Brāhm xv, 3, 7. Kāṭhaka Saṁhitā xxi, 10. *Vedic Index* ii, 98. These refer to this Divodāsa and not the Rigvedic Divodāsa of N. Pañcāla. Also MBh xiii, *34*, 2126. It is doubtful which Divodāsa is meant in xii, *96*, 3577. The allusion in xii, *99*, 3664 seems spurious.

[6] This is what the brahmanical fable of Gālava does (MBh v, *116*, 3960–77), calling Divodāsa son of Bhīmasena and father of Pratardana: see chap. XII.

[7] MBh xii, *234*, 8594, and xiii, *137*, 6294 say, Pratardana king of Kāśi.

Vītahavya of the second story [1] = Vītihotra of the genealogies (chapter IX), both being Haihaya kings subsequent to Tālajaṅgha. The whole account thus becomes quite intelligible, the only uncertain point being, which Divodāsa built the second capital; he was probably Divodāsa I, but this point is not material here.

The first story makes Divodāsa I contemporary with Bhadraśreṇya and Durdama. The second makes Haryaśva contemporary with Vītahavya's sons, so that he falls after Vītihotra of the genealogies. The intermediate kings have been lost, as would be natural in the confusion of the dispossession.[2] Hence Haryaśva's great grandson Pratardana would fall just after Supratīka, the last Vītihotra-Haihaya king named in the genealogies, and this would be his natural position as the destroyer of the Vītahavya or Vītihotra family. Pratardana did not subdue all the Haihayas. It was Sagara who did that, hence Pratardana cannot be placed after Sagara. Sagara evidently completed what Pratardana began, hence he must be placed alongside Pratardana. These traditions then establish the following synchronisms, and these stories and the genealogies are in harmony :—

Kāśi	*Haihayas*	*Ayodhyā*
Divodāsa I	Bhadraśreṇya	
Aṣṭāratha	Durdama	
	Kanaka	
	Kṛtavīrya	
	Arjuna Kārtavīrya	
(blank)		Triśaṅku
	Jayadhvaja	Hariścandra
	Tālajaṅgha	Rohita
		Harita and Cañcu
	Vītihotra (Vītahavya)	Vijaya aud Ruruka
Haryaśva	Ananta	Vṛka
Sudeva	Durjaya	Bāhu (Asita)
Divodāsa II	Supratīka	
Pratardana		Sagara

These results lead on to further synchronisms in and after Sagara's time. The Haihayas, as mentioned, overran Madhyadeśa,

[1] MBh xiii, *30*, 1950–1.

[2] Similar blanks caused by the overthrow of a dynasty or its sinking into insignificance will be found between Taṁsu and Duṣyanta, and between Somaka and Pṛṣata in the N. Pañcāla dynasty (chap. IX).

so that the Paurava kingdom in the Ganges-Jumna doab was overthrown; and this conclusion is corroborated by the fact that the hordes from the north-west, who aided them in the conquest of Ayodhyā, could not have reached it without passing over the Paurava territory and also the Kānyakubja kingdom, which disappeared from this time, for its genealogy ceases with Viśvāmitra's grandson Lauhi. Sagara's destruction of the Haihaya power would naturally have carried him to the Narbadā and their capital there, Māhiṣmatī. South of that was the kingdom of Vidarbha, and there are notices which show that it had just come into existence then. An account of Sagara's expedition there says the Vidarbha king made peace with him by giving him his daughter Keśinī in marriage,[1] and the genealogies say clearly that Sagara had two wives, and the best of them name one as Keśinī daughter of Vidarbha himself,[2] who gave his name to the country. Vidarbha therefore was a generation earlier than Sagara.

This synchronism may be combined with another. There were two kings named Marutta, one son of Avīkṣit and grandson of Karandhama of the Vaiśāla dynasty (p. 39), and the other, son of Karandhama of Turvasu's lineage; and they must be carefully distinguished. The latter had no son and adopted Duṣyanta the Paurava.[3] Duṣyanta afterwards recovered the Paurava kingdom, revived the dynasty, and so is styled its vaṁśa-kara.[4] The adoption could only have taken place before he gained that position, and this corroborates the conclusion that that kingdom was in abeyance, so that Duṣyanta, as the heir in exile, might naturally accept such adoption. He could only have restored the Paurava dynasty after the Haihaya power had been destroyed by Sagara and Sagara's empire had ended, so that he would be one or two generations later than this Marutta, and two later than Sagara. We have then these synchronisms :—

[1] Bḍ iii, *49*, 1–3; *51*, 31, 37.

[2] Vā *88*, 155; Bḍ iii, *63*, 154; Br *8*, 63; and Hv *15*, 797. Rām i, *38*, 3. Also Viṣ iv, *4*, 1; Gar i, *138*, 29; Bhāg ix, *8*, 15; VN *8*, 64; and MBh iii, *106*, 8833, 8843. Mat *12*, 39, 42 and Pad v, *8*, 144, 147 give different names, one being Prabhā, a Yādava princess (Vidarbha was a Yādava): similarly Lg i, *66*, 15; Kūr i, *21*, 4; and Ag *272*, 28.

[3] Vā *99*, 3–4 and Bḍ iii, *74*, 3–4; both corrupting Duṣyanta's name. Mat *48*, 2–3 (where read *Pauravaś câpi*); also Br *13*, 144–6; Hv *32*, 1832–4; and Viṣ iv, *16*, 2.

[4] MBh i, *68*, 2801. Bhāg ix, *23*, 17–18.

Vidarbha	*Aikṣvāku*	*Paurava*	*Turvasus*
Vidarbha			Karandhama
	Sagara		Marutta
	Asamañjas		
	Aṁśumant	Duṣyanta	(Duṣyanta)

There are more synchronisms belonging to the same period, in which the Āṅgirasa rishis Bṛhaspati, Dīrghatamas and Bharadvāja are the central figures.

First is a story about Bṛhaspati and Saṁvarta, which contains pieces of tradition, though largely marred by later extravagances.[1] Aṅgiras[2] was priest to king Karandhama of the Vaiśāla dynasty. Karandhama's son was Avīkṣit, and his son the famous Marutta Āvīkṣita.[3] Aṅgiras had two sons, Bṛhaspati and Saṁvarta, who were thus Marutta's hereditary priests[4] and lived in his kingdom of Vaiśālī. They were at perpetual strife. Bṛhaspati declined to be Marutta's priest, declaring that he was Indra's priest,[5] so Marutta chose Saṁvarta and by his aid performed magnificent sacrifices.[6] This Marutta gave his daughter to Aṅgiras Saṁvarta (chapter XI).

Another story runs thus.[7] There were two rishis, Bṛhaspati[8] and his elder brother, who is called Ucathya in the Vedārthadīpikā and Bṛhaddevatā, Utathya in the Mahābhārata, Uśija in the Brahmāṇḍa and Matsya, and Aśija or Asija (but sometimes Uśija) in

[1] MBh xiv, *4*, 85 to *7*, 179 (for *putram* in line 99 of Calcutta edition read *pūrvam*); *8*, 214–17: &c. Vā *86*, 9–11. Bd iii, *61*, 5–7. Bhāg ix, *2*, 26–8.

[2] This is merely a gotra name. Bṛhadd v, 102 identifies him with the primaeval mythical Aṅgiras. See chaps. XVI, XIX.

[3] MBh xiii, *137*, 6260. Mārk *122*, 7 to *133*, 5 contains a long story about them. Śatapatha Brāhm xiii, 5, 4, 6 calls this Marutta the Āyogava king.

[4] MBh xiv, *4*, 85; *6*, 124, 126, 133; *7*, 155.

[5] So also MBh i, *170*, 6464. He seems to be confused, at least partially, with the mythical divine priest Bṛhaspati.

[6] Also MBh iii, *129*, 10528–9: vii, *55*, 2170–3: xii, *29*, 910–13. Mārk *130* (*129*), 11–18. Aitareya Brāhm viii, *4*, 21 says he consecrated Marutta. Rām vii, *18* has a brahmanical fable: so also MBh xiv, *64*; *65*.

[7] MBh i, *104*, 4179–92: xii, *343*, 13177–82. Bd iii, *74*, 36–46. Bhāg ix, *20*, 36–8. Twice narrated in Vā *99*, 36–46, 141–50 and Mat *48*, 32–42; *49*, 17–26. Bṛhadd iv, 11–15. Vedārth on Rigv vi, *52*. These versions have differences, and have received later touches, especially where the incidents are made to supply explanation of names.

[8] Vā confuses him with the mythical divine priest, Bṛhaspati.

the Vāyu. Utathya is a very common variant for Ucathya,[1] and Aśija a mistake for Uśija. There are therefore two distinct names, Ucathya and Uśija, and it will be shown further on that Ucathya is the correct name of this rishi. He had a wife Mamatā, and their son was Dīrghatamas, who was born blind. Bṛhaspati is said to have consorted with her, and his son was Bharadvāja. That there was a rishi Dīrghatamas Aucathya Māmateya, 'son of Ucathya and Mamatā', who was blind, is proved by the Rigveda;[2] and that there was also a rishi Bharadvāja Bārhaspatya, 'son of Bṛhaspati', is asserted by the Sarvānukramaṇī in ascribing many hymns in book VI to him.[3]

This story continues with Dīrghatamas.[4] He lived in his paternal cousin's hermitage, whom the Puranas apparently call Śaradvant, but indulged in gross immorality or misbehaved towards the wife of the younger Autathya[5] (Aucathya). Hence he was expelled and set adrift in the Ganges. He was carried downstream to the Eastern Ānava kingdom and was there welcomed by king Bali. This incident finds support in the Rigveda (i, *158*, 3, 5), where he speaks of having been delivered from bodily hurt and from danger in the rivers; and it is not improbable, because these Āṅgirasa rishis were living, as mentioned above, in the kingdom of Vaiśālī, so that he might easily have been put on a raft in the Ganges there and have drifted some seventy miles down to the Monghyr and Bhāgalpur country, which was the Ānava realm, and was soon afterwards called the Aṅga kingdom. There Dīrghatamas married the queen's śūdra nurse and had Kakṣīvant and other sons;[6] and at Bali's desire begot of the queen Sudeṣṇā five sons, Aṅga, Vaṅga, Kaliṅga, Puṇḍra and Suhma, who were called the Bāleya kṣatra and also Bāleya brahmans. This is strange yet not

[1] He was an Āṅgirasa, MBh xii, *90*, 3362: xiii, *154*, 7240, &c.

[2] Rigv i, *147*, 3; *152*, 6; *158*, 1, 4, 6. Hymns i, 140–64 are ascribed to him. Also Bṛhadd iii, 146.

[3] Also Bṛhadd v, 102. Vā *64*, 26. Bḍ ii, *38*, 27. MBh xiii, *30*, 1963.

[4] Vā *99*, 26–34, 47–97. Bḍ iii, *74*, 25–34, 47–100. Mat *48*, 23–9, 43–89. The last part in Hv *31*, 1684–90; Br *13*, 29–31; Viṣ iv, *18*, 1; Bhāg ix, *23*, 5. MBh i, *104*, 4193–221, with variations: xii, *343*, 13177–84. Bṛhadd iv, 21–5, where the sequel shows the word *jīrṇa* is a manifest mistake. Similarly Vedārth on Rigv i, *116*.

[5] Mat says *Gautama*, but this seems a misreading, as the sequel shows. Vā *65*, 101 and Bḍ iii, *1*, 106 say Śaradvant was Utathya's son.

[6] So also MBh ii, *20*, 802, which calls her Auśīnarī.

improbable, for brahmans did render such services.[1] Afterwards he gained his sight,[2] and assumed the name Gotama or Gautama.[3]

Next, there is a story about the famous Paurava king, Duṣyanta's son Bharata, and Bharadvāja.[4] Bharata had three wives and sons by them; they killed their sons because he was disappointed in them, and he was thus bereft of heirs. In order to obtain a son he performed many sacrifices and lastly made an offering to the Maruts; they gave him[5] Bṛhaspati's son Bharadvāja as an adopted son. Bharadvāja thus became a kṣatriya; he did not succeed Bharata, but begot a son named Vitatha; Bharata then died. Bharadvāja afterwards consecrated Vitatha as the successor, and then either died or departed to the forest.[6] This is a very remarkable

[1] Thus, it is said, a Vasiṣṭha begot Aśmaka of king Kalmāṣapāda's queen; MBh i, *122*, 4736–7; *177*, 6787–91: Vā *88*, 177: Bḍ iii, *63*, 177: Lg i, *66*, 27–8: Kūr i, *21*, 12–13: Bhāg ix, *9*, 38–9. Vyāsa begot Dhṛtarāṣṭra and Pāṇḍu. See also MBh i, *64*, 2460–4; *104*, 4176–8. Brahmans with their ascetic habits escaped the enervating influences of courts.

[2] He may not have been blind, but purblind, very shortsighted, and his sight may have improved in old age, as happens in such cases.

[3] Vā *99*, 92. Bḍ iii, *74*, 94. Mat *48*, 83–4. Bṛhadd iv, 15.

[4] Vā *99*, 137–40; Mat *49*, 14–15; Hv *32*, 1726–7; Br *13*, 58. Ag *277*, 7–8. Also MBh i, *94*, 3710–12, which differs slightly. Fairly fully, Vedārth on Rigv vi, *52*.

[5] For an explanation of this see *infra*.

[6] The fullest and best account is given by Mat *49*, 27–34 and Vā *99*, 152–8, which are closely alike. Also Hv *32*, 1727–31 and Br *13*, 59–61 (the former being fuller) which are based on the same original text. The texts collated suggest the following version:

tasmin kāle tu Bharato bahubhiḥ kratubhir vibhuḥ
kāmya-naimittikair yajñair ayajat putra-lipsayā
yadā sa yajamāno vai putraṁ nâsādayat prabhuḥ
yajñaṁ tato Marut-somam putrârthe punar āharat
tena te Marutas tasya Marut-somena toṣitāḥ
upaninyur Bharadvājam putrârtham Bharatāya vai
dāyādo 'ṅgirasaḥ sūnor aurasas tu Bṛhaspateḥ
saṅkrāmito Bharadvājo Marudbhir Bharatam prati
Bharatas tu Bharadvājam putram prāpya vibhur bravīt
prajāyāṁ saṁbhṛtāyāṁ vai kṛtârtho 'haṁ tvayā vibho
pūrvaṁ tu vitathe tasya kṛte vai putra-janmani
tatas tu Vitatho nāma Bharadvājāt suto 'bhavat
tasmād divyo Bharadvājo brāhmaṇyāt kṣatriyo 'bhavat
dvyāmuṣyāyaṇa-nāmā sa smṛto dvi-pitaras tu vai
tato 'tha Vitathe jāte Bharataḥ sa divaṁ yayau
Bharadvājo divaṁ yāto hy abhiṣicya sutam ṛṣiḥ

Note the Prakritism in the last words, for *sutaṁ ṛṣi*, anusvāra giving the long syllable required. Br and Hv correct the irregularity by reading—

Vitathaṁ câbhiṣicyâtha Bharadvājo vanaṁ yayau.

story and deserves careful consideration, because it throws much light on the traditional accounts of Bharata's successors, the Bharatas or Bhāratas.

It is emphasized by the statement in the Vāyu that Bharadvāja by the adoption became a kṣatriya and had two fathers, and so was called *dvyāmuṣyāyaṇa*.[1] The Matsya varies this statement, but still says that from Bharadvāja were descended brahmans and kṣatriyas who were known as *dvyāmuṣyāyaṇa-kaulīnas*,[2] which also appears to be true.[3] Of these two versions the Vāyu's is manifestly the earlier, for the statement that a distinguished brahman became a kṣatriya's son could never have come from a brahmanic source, and that in the Matsya is also plainly a softening down of it, as the retention of the word *dvyāmuṣyāyaṇa* shows, which otherwise was uncalled for.[4] Neither version could have been composed by the brahmans after the Purana passed into their hands as described in chapter II. The Vāyu's statement is manifestly ancient kṣatriya tradition, which they found in the Purana and could not discard as false, but which was unpalatable and was therefore modified in the Matsya, and also in some copies of the Vāyu.[5]

According to the brahman vaṁśas there were two Āṅgirasa rishis, Ucathya and Uśija,[6] and that the names are distinct is proved by the fact that Aucathya[7] occurs in Rigveda i, *158*, 1, 4, and Auśija in i, *18*, 1 and x, *99*, 11. The former means Dīrghatamas by implication and he is so called in the Anukramaṇī as author of hymns i, *140–64*. He is made son of Ucathya in the foregoing story by the Mahābhārata, Bṛhaddevatā and Vedārthadīpikā, but son of Uśija in the Purana version and called Auśija in the

[1] Lines 13 and 14 are the Vā reading, except that it has *dvimukhyāyana* incorrectly. The adjective *dvi-pitaraḥ* is noteworthy as not good Sanskrit. Cf. Mat *196*, 52.

[2] Tasmād api Bharadvājād brāhmaṇāḥ kṣatriyā bhuvi
dvyāmuṣyāyaṇa-kaulīnāḥ smṛtās te dvi-vidhena ca.

[3] But see Vedārth on Rigv vi, *52*.

[4] Other brahmans begot kṣatriya sons without any such complication, as mentioned above.

[5] Thus some Vāyu MSS. read:—
tasmād divo Bharadvājā brāhmaṇāḥ kṣatriyā viśaḥ
dvyāmuṣyāyaṇa-nāmānaḥ smṛtā dvi-pitaras tu vai.

[6] Vā *59*, 90, 93; *65*, 100. Pd ii, *32*, 99; iii, *1*, 105–6. Mat *196*, 4 (read *Uśijaṁ*), 11.

[7] *Vedic Index* has accidentally omitted this name, but mentions it in i, 366.

vaṁśas.[1] Presumably therefore both Ucathya and Uśija were his ancestors, and this is further corroborated. Auśija in the first passage above is Kakṣīvant, and in the second Ṛjiśvan. Kakṣīvant is called 'born of Uśij' by the Anukramaṇī and Vedārthadīpikā on Rigveda i, *116*, and therefore Auśija[2] in the latter, relying on the words *Kakṣīvantaṁ ya Auśijaḥ* in i, *18*, 1. This would be a metronymic, if the śūdra woman whom Dīrghatamas married was named Uśij.[3] This may be true, yet seems rather to be a guess to explain the appellation, for it is unnecessary inasmuch as Kakṣīvant, being Dīrghatamas's son, had the patronymic Auśija already.[4] Moreover, that derivation is not really a satisfactory explanation, for Ṛjiśvan was also Auśija as mentioned above, and it cannot hold good for him, because (1) he is called *Vaidathina*, 'son (or descendant) of Vidathin', in Rigveda iv. *16*, 13, and Vidathin was the name of a Bharadvāja,[5] and (2) it is said he was son of 'Bharadvāja'.[6] Thus Ṛjiśvan was descended from Vidathin Bharadvāja,[7] and not from Dīrghatamas and that śūdra woman, and his appellation Auśija cannot be a metronymic, but is really a patronymic. It proves that his father or ancestor Vidathin Bharadvāja was descended from Uśija, and that there was an ancestor Uśija. 'Uśij' seems to have been invented to explain Auśija[8] through the lack of the historical sense. Uśija then was ancestor of both Dīrghatamas and Bharadvāja, and Dīrghatamas's father was Ucathya. Uśija therefore must have been ancestor of their fathers,[9] Ucathya

[1] Vā *65*, 102 and Bḍ iii, *1*, 106, where read *athAuśijo* probably. Anuvākānukramaṇī 21 appears to be confused. In Mat *48*, 83 for *Asito* read *Auśijo*.

[2] Also Pañcaviṁśa Brāhm xiv, 11, 16–17. Bṛhadd iii, 125.

[3] So Bṛhadd iv, 24–5: Śatapatha Brāhm ii, 3, 4, 35: and Vedārth on Rigv i, *116*. Anukramaṇī implies it.

[4] In MBh xiii, *150*, 7108 read *Auśijaḥ*. [5] So Bṛhadd v, 102.

[6] So Vedārth on Rigv vi, *52*, which assigns to 'Bharadvāja' four other 'sons', Suhotra, Śunahotra, Nara and Garga, all five being 'grandsons' of both Bṛhaspati and Bharata; and this Bharadvāja was Vidathin (see p. 163). It has however abbreviated the genealogy, for they were not sons but descendants, see Table of Pauravas (chap. IX) and chap. XXIII.

[7] The mention of Vaidathina as apparently distinct from Ṛjiśvan in Rigv v, *29*, 11, does not invalidate this, for the preceding note shows there were other Vaidathinas.

[8] So Vedarth account rather suggests.

[9] Auśija Dīrghaśravas named with Kakṣīvant in Rigv i, *112*, 11 may well have been one of this family who became a merchant.

and Bṛhaspati, who were thus not sons but descendants of Aṅgiras.[1] Ucathya and Bṛhaspati may have been brothers as stated above and Saṁvarta may have been their youngest brother;[2] and Uśija may well have been their father.[3] The Puranas in the above story seem to have confused Uśija with his son or descendant Ucathya.

Vitatha was clearly Bharadvāja's son, as the Brahma and Harivaṁśa say explicitly in line 12, which is their reading. The Vāyu[4] and Matsya[5] readings of this line make out that Bharadvāja was known as Vitatha, but line 15, which both of them and also the Brahma and Harivaṁśa have, stultifies that, for necessarily Bharadvāja was born before the adoption, and line 16, which the Matsya has and the Brahma and Harivaṁśa[6] give more clearly, shows that Vitatha and Bharadvāja were different persons. The confusion of the two will be explained farther on. Consequently the reading of the Brahma and Harivaṁśa in line 12 is right, and those of the Vāyu and Matsya require only the simple emendation of *Bharadvājaḥ* to *Bharadvājāt* or *Bhāradvājaḥ* and would then agree. The fact that Bharata's successors in the Paurava line were really of brahmanic origin is of the highest importance, and helps to elucidate many peculiar features in their history.

The Aitareya Brāhmaṇa says Dīrghatamas consecrated Bharata with the mahābhiṣeka.[7] He could not have done that until he had established his reputation, that is, not until he was old; and he certainly lived to a great age.[8] He would therefore be two (or even possibly three) generations senior to Bharata. Hence the first Bharadvāja, who was his equal in age, could not have been taken as soon as born to Bharata as a son, as alleged.[9] That both these rishis were some two generations older than Bharata is corroborated by the facts shown above that Bharadvāja was purohita to Divodāsa, king of Kāśi, and, if a young man then, would have been contemporary with Pratardana, who was contemporary with Sagara and one or two generations prior to Duṣyanta—that is, two or three

[1] Bṛhadd v, 102–3 has abbreviated the genealogy.

[2] So Vedārth on Rigv vi, 52.

[3] The brahman vaṁśas are manifestly uncertain about their precise relationships, see chap. XIX.

[4] Tataḥ sa Vitatho nāma Bharadvājas tathâbhavat.

[5] Tatas tu Vitatho nāma Bharadvājo nṛpo 'bhavat.

[6] Vitathaṁ câbhiṣicyâtha Bharadvājo vanaṁ yayau.

[7] viii, 23 and 21. Bhāgavata ix, *20*, 25 says Māmateya, i.e. Dīrghatamas, was his priest.

[8] Rigv i, *158*, 6.

[9] Vā *99*, 151 f. Mat *49*, 26 f.

prior to Bharata. The aged Dīrghatamas, and Bharadvāja also,[1] may thus have lived till the beginning of Bharata's reign. Though that, the first, Bharadvāja could not have been given in adoption to Bharata, yet his grandson (or perhaps great grandson) may have been so given, and this was no doubt the Bharadvāja named Vidathin above, because the fact that the Vāyu, Brahmāṇḍa and Bhāgavata confuse the adopted Bharadvāja with his son Vitatha strongly suggests that it was Vidathin who was adopted. These Puranas have confused the two Bharadvājas as they have apparently confused the names Vidathin and Vitatha.[2]

The introduction of the Maruts into this story illustrates how mythology apparently grew out of a misunderstanding of names. Bṛhaspati lived in the kingdom of Marutta, as mentioned above, and was a preceptor among the Maruttas. The Bṛhaddevatā (v, 102–3), misunderstanding this name through the brahmanic lack of the historical sense, says he was a preceptor among the Maruts. His son Bharadvāja was born there, among the Maruttas, and so also would have been his grandson (or great grandson) Vidathin Bharadvāja. When king Bharata lost his sons, Dīrghatamas, if his priest then (or one of his family, if he was then dead), might naturally have suggested that his own relative, the young Bharadvāja, might be adopted. So the youth was brought from the Maruttas and given in adoption to the king; and this act, by the same misunderstanding, was mythologized into the statement that the Maruts gave Bharadvāja to Bharata.[3]

From all these traditions then we get these synchronisms:—

Pauravas		*Āṅgirasas*		*Vaiśālas*	*E. Anavas*
		(Aṅgiras)		Karandhama	
		Uśija		Avīkṣit	
	Ucathya	Bṛhaspati	Saṁvarta	Marutta	Bali
	Dīrghatamas	Bharadvāja			
Duṣyanta	Kakṣīvant				Aṅga, &c.
Bharata					
Vidathin-Bharadvāja		Vidathin-Bharadvāja			
Vitatha					

[1] A 'Bharadvāja' knew most and lived longest, Aitareya Āraṇyaka i, 2, 8. SBE i, 169.

[2] The derivation of *Vitatha* in lines 11–12 above may be an afterthought.

[3] Similar and further confusion appears in Śatapatha Brāhm xiii, 5, 4, 6, which says the Maruts were Marutta Āvikṣita's guardsmen, Agni his chamberlain, and the Viśve Devās his counsellors: SBE, xliv, p. 397.

Putting together these results and those established earlier and arrived at independently, we have these synchronisms :—

Kāśi	*Ayodhyā*	*Pauravas*	*Āṅgirasas*	
Divodāsa II			Ucathya	Bṛhaspati
Pratardana	Sagara		Dīrghatamas	Bharadvāja
Vatsa	Asamañjas			
Alarka	Aṁśumant	Duṣyanta	Kakṣīvant	
		Bharata		
				Vidathin

It thus appears that Bṛhaspati's son Bharadvāja was a younger contemporary of Divodāsa II of Kāśi. This entirely agrees with what has been mentioned incidentally above, that Bharadvāja was Divodāsa's purohita, a statement found both in the epic and in brahmanical books—thus confirming the two sets of synchronisms. Bṛhaspati and Bharadvāja belonged to the country of Vaiśālī, which was contiguous to the kingdom of Kāśi, and so Bharadvāja could quite naturally have become purohita in the latter; indeed the preceding remarks about all these Āṅgirasas show that they steadily migrated westwards.

Another synchronism is that well known connecting Daśaratha, king of Ayodhyā (Rāma's father), Sīradhvaja Janaka, king of Videha (Sītā's father), Daśaratha-Lomapāda,[1] king of Aṅga, the rishi Ṛṣyaśṛṅga, and Pramati (or Sumati [2]), king of Vaiśālī. This is declared in the Rāmāyaṇa and is alluded to elsewhere.[3] That epic makes an Aśvapati, king of Kaikeya, also contemporary;[4] and this may be true, though it is not supported elsewhere.[5]

There are kṣatriya accounts of Brahmadatta and Bhīṣma, which lead to important synchronisms.

Those about Brahmadatta say this.[6] Aṇuha of the Nīpa family, who was king of S. Pañcāla and reigned at Kāmpilya, married Kṛtvī, daughter of Śuka,[7] and their son was Brahmadatta, called

[1] He gave his daughter Śāntā to Ṛṣyaśṛṅga, Rām i, *9*, 19 ; *10*, 32–3 : Vā *99*, 103 : Br *13*, 40 : Hv *31*, 1696–7 : Maṭ *48*, 94–5.

[2] So Rām i, *47*, 17. Viṣ iv, *1*, 18. Bhāg ix, *2*, 36.

[3] e.g. MBh iii, *110*, 10008–9 ; *273*, 15880 ; Bhāg ix, *23*, 7–8.

[4] Rām ii, *1*, 2 ; *9*, 22.

[5] If so, there was another of the same name, far later ; *Vedic Index*, i, p. 44, and chap. XXVII.

[6] Hv *20*, 1039–52, 1065–6 ; *23*, 1241–63 ; *24*, 1302–4. Mat *20*, 21–6 ; *21*, 11–16, 29–31. Pad v, *10*, 67–71, 98–102, 115–17. MBh xii, *344*, 13261–5. (Pad vi, *131*, 93 speaks of a Brahmadatta of the Solar race in a fable, and Buddhist Jātakas of a Brahmadatta, king of Kāśi.)

[7] Not Vyāsa's son Śuka, see p. 138.

Pitṛvartin. He was a contemporary and friend of Bhīṣma's grandfather (really great grandfather, as will appear), Pratīpa, the Kaurava king. Brahmadatta married Sannati,[1] daughter of a Devala.[2] A Jaigīṣavya[3] is said to have taught Brahmadatta, who by his instruction made a yoga-tantra.[4] His sons were Śaṅkha and Likhita (p. 69)[5] and his disciples are named.[6] Brahmadatta gave wealth to Śaṅkha.[7]

Pratīpa's successor according to the genealogies was Śantanu,[8] called Śāntanu generally in the Mahābhārata and Puranas, and said to have been his son; but this is an instance of the omission of unimportant names, for both brahmanic and ordinary traditions assert that Śantanu had an elder brother Devāpi,[9] who was well known and is often alluded to.[10] This Devāpi is mentioned in Rigveda x, *98* and is there called Ārṣṭiṣeṇa,[11] 'son of Ṛṣṭiṣeṇa'. It is clear therefore that Devāpi and Śantanu were not sons of Pratīpa but grandsons, Ṛṣṭiṣeṇa being father of Devāpi if not of Śantanu also, and that, as Devāpi declined the throne and Śantanu succeeded

[1] Bhāg ix, *21*, 25 calls her *Go*.

[2] So Mat and Hv; and the latter (*23*, 1261) calls him Devala Asita, that is, Devala, son of Asita, see the Kāśyapas, chap. XX (Padma v, *10*, 71 calls him Sudeva); but this seems a mistake.

[3] This is a patronymic: others are mentioned, e.g. Lg i, *92*, 52–3; Pad vi, *250*, 279. A Jaigīṣavya and Asita Devala in a brahmanical fable, MBh ix, *51*; xii, *229*, 8431–2.

[4] Bhāg ix, *21*, 25–6; but this is a late statement.

[5] Mentioned, MBh xii, *23*, 668–9: Var *197*, 18.

[6] Kūr i, *48*, 18–20.

[7] MBh xii, *234*, 8603: xiii, *137*, 6261 (but 6263 is a brahmanical anachronism).

[8] So called in Vā *99*, 234, 237; Mat *50*, 39, 42; Bhāg ix, *22*, 12–13.

[9] So the genealogies. Also Nirukta ii, 10: Bṛhadd vii, 155 to viii, 9; MBh i, *94*, 3750–1; *95*, 3797–8: v, *148*, 5056–66.

[10] Vā *32*, 39–42; *99*, 437, 439: Bḍ iii, *74*, 250, 252: Mat *273*, 56, 58: Viṣ iv, *24*, 45, 48: Bhāg iv, *22*, 12, 17–18: all of which say he still lives and will restore the Paurava race in the new Kṛta age.

[11] The references to Ārṣṭiṣeṇa in *Vedic Index* i, 378 require modification. No Ārṣṭiṣeṇa is named in MBh i, *94*, 3750–1. Ārṣṭiṣeṇa and Devāpi in MBh ix, *40*, 2281–2, and *41*, 2285–94 are manifestly different persons as those passages show, Devāpi being this prince; but that Ārṣṭiṣeṇa is there said to have lived in the Kṛta age (far earlier) and is no doubt the ancient prince Ārṣṭiṣeṇa who became a brahman, as stated in Vā *92*, 5–6; Bḍ iii, *67*, 6; and also Hv *29*, 1520; Br *11*, 34. That Ārṣṭiṣeṇa and Devāpi Ārṣṭiṣeṇa must therefore be distinguished. Ārṣṭiṣeṇa in Bḍ ii, *32*, 105 and Vā *59*, 97 (*Adviṣeṇa*) would as a mantra-reciter be probably Devāpi. Arṣṭiṣeṇa in Vā *91*, 116 and Bḍ iii, *66*, 87 might be either.

Pratīpa, Ṛṣṭiṣeṇa had probably died early and so is omitted in the genealogies.[1] Bhīṣma therefore as Śantanu's son was great grandson of Pratīpa.[2]

The story goes thus. Ugrāyudha, the Paurava king of Dvimīḍha's line, killed Pṛṣata's grandfather[3] (king of N. Pañcāla), and Pṛṣata took refuge at Kāmpilya in S. Pañcāla.[4] Ugrāyudha then killed Brahmadatta's great great grandson Janamejaya Durbuddhi,[5] the last Nīpa king of S. Pañcāla.[6] He next menaced the Kaurava kingdom after Śantanu's death, but Bhīṣma killed him and restored Pṛṣata to his kingdom of Ahicchattra (N. Pañcāla).

The foregoing data yield these synchronisms:—

Dvimīḍhas	*Kauravas*	*N. Pañcāla*	*S. Pañcāla*
	Pratīpa		Brahmadatta
			Viṣvaksena
	(Ṛṣṭiṣeṇa)		Udaksena
Ugrāyudha	Śantanu		Bhallāṭa
	Bhīṣma	Pṛṣata	Janamejaya

There are many synchronisms in the story of the Pāṇḍavas in the Mahābhārata,[7] comprising the Pauravas from Śantanu to Arjuna's son Abhimanyu, grandson Parikṣit II and great grandson Janamejaya III; Vasudeva, Kṛṣṇa and all his relations; Damaghoṣa, king of Cedi, his son Śiśupāla-Sunītha and grandson

[1] So also if *Aulāna* in verse 11 is Śantanu's patronymic (as suggested in *Vedic Index* i, 129, 378, and possibly rightly), for then Ṛṣṭiṣeṇa and Ulāna (?) would have been Pratīpa's sons and have both died in his lifetime; thus Devāpi and Śantanu would have been first cousins, and practically brothers, their fathers being dead and omitted.

[2] About Śantanu's time may be placed Duṣṭarītu Paumsāyana, since he was a contemporary of Balhika Prātipīya (Śatapatha Brāhm xii, 9, 3, 1–3 and 13). He was king of the Sṛñjayas (*Vedic Index* ii, 371), i. e. of N. Pañcāla, and would fall in the gap between Jantu and Pṛṣata. Bālhika or Vāhlīka, Prātipeya or Prātipīya son (descendant) of this Pratīpa, is often mentioned in the MBh; e. g. i, *95*, 3797: v, *22*, 693: vii, *157*, 6932–4: xi, *22*, 621.

[3] Hv *20*, 1083, which calls the latter *Nīpa*; but it may perhaps have confused him with the kings of S. Pañcāla, who were the Nīpas.

[4] Hv *20*, 1111–12.

[5] He is probably Janamejaya of the Nīpas who destroyed all his relatives and friends, MBh v, *73*, 2727–9.

[6] Hv *20*, 1066–72, 1085–1112. So also the genealogies of the two dynasties. Mat *49*, 59–68 confuses the story, and wrongly says Ugrāyudha was of the Solar race. Also MBh xii, *27*, 808.

[7] Full references in Sörensen's *Index*.

Dhṛṣṭaketu; Vṛddhaśarman and his son Dantavakra, kings of Karūṣa;[1] Ugrasena and Kaṁsa, kings of Mathurā; Jarāsandha and his son Sahadeva, kings of Magadha; Drupada, king of S. Pañcāla, his son Dhṛṣṭadyumna and grandson Dhṛṣṭaketu; Bṛhadbala, king of Ayodhyā; Karṇa and his son Vṛṣasena, kings of Aṅga; and many others. These are exhibited so far as they come into the table above.

Lastly, some time after the battle, there is the synchronism of the Paurava (Kuru) king Adhisīmakṛṣṇa, the Ayodhyā king Divākara and the Magadha king Senājit,[2] who will be noticed in chapter XV.

CHAPTER XIV

MINOR SYNCHRONISMS ESTABLISHED

NEXT may be considered a number of minor synchronisms, which connect only a few persons or relate to a brief space of time.

The earliest of these is that Yayāti's eldest brother Yati married Go, daughter of Kakutstha[3] or (better) Kākutstha.[4] He thus married Kakutstha's daughter or granddaughter, and Kakutstha can be none other than the early king of Ayodhyā, after whom various descendants were styled Kākutstha. Yayāti therefore should be placed one, or preferably two generations below Kakutstha.

There is a synchronism connecting the Ayodhyā and Druhyu dynasties. The Druhyus occupied the Panjab, and Māndhātṛ of Ayodhyā had a long war with the Druhyu king Aruddha[5] or Aṅgāra[6] and killed him.[7] The latter's successor was Gāndhāra, who gave his name to the Gāndhāra country.[8]

[1] For the marriage connexions between these four groups, see Vā *96*, 148–59, Bd iii, *71*, 150–60, Mat *46*, 3–9, Viṣ iv, *14*, 10–13: less clearly, Br *14*, 19–23, Hv *35*, 1827–33. Kuntī's story is in MBh i, *111* f.

[2] Vā *99*, 270, 282, 300. Mat *50*, 77; *271*, 5, 23. Bd iii, *74*, 113.

[3] Br *12*, 3, and Hv *30*, 1601. [4] Vā *93*, 14 and Bd iii, *68*, 13.

[5] So Vā *99*, 7–8. Bd iii, *74*, 7–8. Supported by Gar *139*, 64; Viṣ iv, *17*, 2; Bhāg ix, *23*, 15; and Mat *48*, 6.

[6] So Hv *32*, 1837–8. Br *13*, 149–50. Also MBh xii, *29*, 981–2; but in vii, *62*, 2281–2, seemingly as *Sudhanvan*.

[7] Referred to in MBh iii, *126*, 10465, where he is called 'king of Gāndhāra' by anticipation.

[8] Vā *99*, 9. Bd iii, *74*, 9. Hv *32*, 1839. Br *13*, 150–1. Mat *48*, 7.

Next are some synchronisms connected with Lopāmudrā. She was daughter of a king of Vidarbha,[1] and married Agastya.[2] The king is called *Vaidarbha*, 'son (or descendant) of Vidarbha'; and is named Nimi twice.[3] No king of this name occurs in the Vidarbha genealogy (chapter XII, Table), but he was obviously a son or near descendant of Vidarbha, and *Nimi* is probably a misreading of *Bhīma*,[4] another name of Vidarbha's son Kratha, or perhaps the name of another son. By Lopāmudrā's favour Alarka, king of Kāśi, grandson of Pratardana, had, it is said, a very long and prosperous reign.[5] Agastya and she were thus contemporary with Alarka, and were two or three generations below Vidarbha and Pratardana. These synchronisms harmonize with those deduced about those kings in chapter XIII.

The story about Lopāmudrā and Agastya goes on to make three kings, Śrutarvan, Bradhnaśva and Trasadasyu Paurukutsa their contemporaries,[6] but it gives no particulars about the first two and wrongly says Trasadasyu was of the Ikṣvāku race, for Trasadasyu the Aikṣvāku was far earlier than Sagara, who was a younger contemporary of Vidarbha as shown above. The synchronisms (*infra*) show that the later Trasadasyu Paurukutsya (p. 133), who was a Bhārata, was a contemporary of Ṛkṣa and a younger contemporary of Divodāsa's father Vadhryaśva. A king Śrutarvan Ārkṣa, 'son of Ṛkṣa,' is mentioned,[7] and the two Ṛkṣas are probably the same.[8] Hence the Bhārata Trasadasyu, Vadhryaśva and Śrutarvan were practically contemporaries, and Böhtlingk and Roth's conjecture that Bradhnaśva is an error for Vadhryaśva seems right. A synchronism then inferred from the Rigveda has been

[1] MBh iii, *96*, 8561–3, prefaced by a brahmanical fable.

[2] MBh iii, *97*, 8570–6: iv, *21*. 654–5: v, *116*, 3971, where she is called Vaidarbhī. Rigv i, *179*. Rām v, *24*, 11.

[3] MBh xiii, *137*, 6255: xii, *234*, 8600, where *Vaidarbha* is corrupted to *Vaideha*.

[4] Helped no doubt by the above corruption, Nimi being the first king of Videha. Vidarbha and Videha were liable to be confused; so Pad iv, *112*, 50.

[5] Vā *92*, 67. Bḍ iii, *67*, 71. Br *11*, 53; *13*, 74. Hv *29*, 1590; *32*, 1748.

[6] MBh iii, *98*, 8595–8608.

[7] Rigv viii, *74*, 4, 13. Śrutarvan alone, x, *49*, 5.

[8] Śrutarvan would then be a Paurava king in the blank between Ṛkṣa and Saṁvaraṇa; chap. XII, Table.

wrongly attached to Agastya and Lopāmudrā,[1] who were considerably earlier as shown, and the two Trasadasyus have been confused. This is a spurious synchronism, a brahmanical addition to glorify Agastya, and reveals the lack of the historical sense.

Sagara was a younger contemporary of Vidarbha as shown above. It is stated in the story of Nala that Bhīma, king of Vidarbha, and Vīrabāhu, king of Cedi, were contemporaries,[2] and the latter's son Subāhu and Ṛtuparṇa, king of Ayodhyā, were contemporaries.[3] This agrees entirely with the genealogies, for they make Bhīmaratha (of which Bhīma there is the shortened form) tenth successor of Vidarbha and Ṛtuparṇa tenth successor of Sagara, the latter being a younger contemporary of the former.

Another group of synchronisms may be collected from the Rigveda, though falling mostly outside the purview of the genealogies. Divodāsa Atithigva was king of North Pañcāla.[4] His son Indrota, Ṛkṣa's son, and Aśvamedha's son Pūtakratu were contemporaries.[5] Pūtakratu's son was Dasyave-Vṛka,[6] a prince who was also a rishi.[7] Aśvamedha was contemporary with Trasadasyu Paurukutsya, who was apparently a Pūru king,[8] so Trasadasyu was son of Purukutsa;[9] and Purukutsa was son of Girikṣit and grandson of Durgaha.[10] Trasadasyu had a son Tṛkṣi.[11] Sobhari Kāṇva was contemporary with Trasadasyu.[12] Contemporary with Divodāsa was Prastoka,[13] who was a Sārñjaya,[14] that is, a descendant (not son) of Sṛñjaya, the brother of Mudgala, who were Bhāratas; contemporary with Prastoka was Abhyāvartin Cāyamāna;[15] and Aśvamedha was a descendant of Bharata.[16] These two princes also probably belonged to the petty kingdoms descended from Mudgala's brothers. The Ṛkṣa mentioned above was probably the king of Hastināpura, who

[1] There was of course an Agastya living then.

[2] MBh iii, *53*, 2076; *69*, 2706–8.

[3] MBh iii, *64*, 2531; *65*, 2576; *66*, 2627–8: *70*, 2766. See Vā *88*, 174; Bḍ iii, *63*, 173; Br *8*, 80; Hv *15*, 815.

[4] See the dynasty in chap. IX.

[5] Rigv viii, *68*, 15, 16, 18.

[6] *Id.* viii, *56*, 2.

[7] *Id.* viii, *51*, 2. *Vedic Index* i, 346.

[8] Rigv v, *27*, 3, 4. *Vedic Index* i, 327.

[9] Rigv iv, *42*, 9; viii, *19*, 36.

[10] *Id.* iv, *42*, 8. *Vedic Index* i, 327. Or *vice versa*.

[11] Rigv viii, *22*, 7.

[12] *Id.* viii, *19*, 2, 32, 36.

[13] *Id.* vi, *47*, 22, 25.

[14] Anukramaṇī and Vedārth. Bṛhadd v, 124.

[15] Vedārth on Rigv vi, *75*. Bṛhadd v, 124.

[16] So Anukramaṇī on Rigv v, *27*; and also Vedārth, which wrongly renders *Bhārata* as 'son of Bharata'.

is called in the genealogies son of Ajamīḍha and father of Saṁvaraṇa, but the table of genealogies shows that there were many generations, and that son means descendant and father means ancestor. From these data we get these synchronisms :—

Pauravas			*N. Pañcāla*		*Kāṇvas*
	Bhāratas		*Mudgalas*	*Sṛñjayas*	
		Durgaha			
		Girikṣit			
		Purukutsa	Vadhryaśva		
Ṛkṣa	Aśvamedha	Trasadasyu	Divodāsa	Prastoka	Sobhari
	Pūtakratu	Tṛkṣi	Indrota		
	Dasyave-Vṛka				

There is a story that connects the Yādavas and Rāma of Ayodhyā. It is prefaced by a spurious genealogy noticed in chapter X, but the material passage [1] appears to contain genuine tradition because it is corroborated elsewhere and explains the name of the country Śūrasena. It gives these descendants of the great Yādava king Madhu,[2] namely, Mādhava, his son Satvata, his son Bhīma and his son Andhaka, and these tally with the genealogical version Satvant, Sātvata, and Andhaka. It says Bhīma Sātvata was contemporary with Rāma ; Rāma's brother Śatrughna killed the Yādava Lavaṇa, cut down the forest Madhuvana and built the city Mathurā there ; when Rāma and his brothers died, Bhīma recovered the city ; and Andhaka reigned there contemporary with Rāma's son Kuśa at Ayodhyā. The genealogies say that Śatrughna killed the Mādhava Lavaṇa, went to Madhuvana, built Mathurā and reigned there with his two sons Subāhu and Śūrasena.[3] Here then we have Satvant and Bhīma contemporary with Rāma, and Andhaka with Kuśa.

Another version [4] amplifies what the genealogies say with some mistaken embellishments, as that Lavaṇa was son, instead of descendant, of Madhu, and that Madhuvana was in Ayodhyā territory, whereas South Pañcāla separated them. The Rāmāyaṇa

[1] Hv *95*, 5242–8.

[2] In all the stories cited here Madhu is wrongly called a Dānava and a Daitya, see p. 66 ; and so also Lavaṇa. Cf. Br *213*, 137.

[3] Vā *88*, 185–6. Bd iii, *63*, 186–7. Rām vii, *62*, 6 and Viṣ iv, *4*, 46, wrongly calling Lavaṇa a Rākṣasa ; and so also Bhāg ix, *11*, 14. Śatrughna's killing Lavaṇa also in Ag *11*, 6–7 ; Raghuv xv, 2–30 ; Pad vi, *271*, 9 ; Var *178*, 1.

[4] Hv *55*, 3060–96.

gives a third version, similar but largely amplified and brahmanized with various mistakes.[1] Mathurā was the capital of the Śūrasena country; the country appears to have obtained its name from Śatrughna's son Śūrasena,[2] and Andhaka's descendants reigned there down to Ugrasena and Kaṁsa; so the second version says.

Andhaka's brother Bhajamāna married two daughters of Sṛñjaya.[3] Nothing is said to identify this Sṛñjaya, but the reference suggests he was well known, and the best known Sṛñjaya was the king of N. Pañcāla. The genealogical table framed according to the synchronisms established shows that Sṛñjaya of N. Pañcāla must have reigned about this time, and as Andhaka's and Bhajamāna's father Bhīma Sātvata reigned at Mathurā as just shown, a marriage alliance between the two neighbouring dynasties would be quite natural. There can be little doubt then in identifying these two Sṛñjayas. Combining then all these particulars we have these synchronisms :—

N. Pañcāla	*Yādavas*	*Ayodhyā*	
	Satvant	Rāma	Śatrughna
Sṛñjaya	Bhīma Sātvata		Śūrasena
	Bhajamāna, Andhaka	Kuśa[4]	

This is corroborated by another allusion. In two lists of royal munificence to brahmans it is said king Śatadyumna gave a splendid furnished house to the brahman Maudgalya,[5] descendant of king Mudgala, of N. Pañcāla (chapter IX). King Mudgala therefore was earlier than Śatadyumna. The only Śatadyumna mentioned was a king of Videha, Sīradhvaja's second successor. Sīradhvaja was Rāma's father-in-law (*ante*), so Śatadyumna would have been Rāma's younger contemporary and therefore (according to the

[1] Rām vii, *64* to *70*, calling Lavaṇa a Rākṣasa and wrongly connecting him with Rāma's early ancestor Māndhātṛ.

[2] So also Rām vii, *70*, 6–9 may imply. Lg i, *68*, 19 suggests a different explanation, that it was named after an earlier Śūrasena, a son of the Haihaya Arjuna Kārtavīrya; but no other authority supports that, and the Haihaya territory appears to have lain farther south, as mentioned *ante*.

[3] Vā *96*, 3. Bd iii, *71*, 3. Br *15*, 32. Hv *38*, 2001, Mat *44*, 49. Pad v, *13*, 33.

[4] Kuśa and his brother Lava were born late in Rāma's life.

[5] MBh xiii, *137*, 6265 (Maudgalya): xii, *234*, 8606 (Mudgala; using the single name for the patronymic).

synchronisms just set out) a contemporary of Sṛñjaya of N. Pañcāla. Sṛñjaya was Mudgala's fourth or fifth successor, and the Maudgalya brahmans would have been established three or four generations in Śatadyumna's time—thus entirely harmonizing with the above allusion.

There is a synchronism between Divodāsa's and Ṛkṣa's descendants. Divodāsa's fifth successor Sudās (Sudāsa, chapter IX) defeated his foes on the Jumna and again defeated Pūru and others in battle on the river Paruṣṇī (modern Ravi);[1] hence he must have driven Pūru out of the Paurava kingdom of Hastināpura first to the Jumna and then as far west as the Ravi. Tradition says that the Paurava Saṁvaraṇa was driven out of Hastināpura by a Pañcāla king and took refuge many years near the river Sindhu, but afterwards with a Vasiṣṭha's aid recovered his kingdom and established a lordship over all kṣatriya princes,[2] which means he subdued Pañcāla. The genealogies say Sudāsa's kingdom declined after his death,[3] and the Rigveda shows that Somaka was less opulent than Sudās.[4] Moreover a Vasiṣṭha was Sudās's priest,[5] but there are no hymns by any Vasiṣṭha in honour of his successors. There was also a long gap between Jantu and Pṛṣata, during which N. Pañcala was dominated by Hastināpura. It is clear then that Sudās drove Saṁvaraṇa out, and that Saṁvaraṇa and his son Kuru conquered Sahadeva or more probably Somaka.[6] Hence Saṁvaraṇa was a younger contemporary of Sudās and Kuru of Somaka.

Kavaṣa lived in Sudās's reign and was drowned apparently at Sudās's battle with the ten kings; he was old (*vṛddha*) then and famous (*śruta*).[7] He was no doubt Kavaṣa Ailūṣa,[8] the reputed author of hymn x, *33*, because that is in praise of king Kuruśravaṇa Trāsadasyava, and that king, as a near descendant of Trasadasyu who was a contemporary of Divodāsa (*ante*), would have lived about the time of Divodāsa's fourth and fifth successors Cyavana and

[1] Rigv vii, *18* and *33*; and *19*. *Vedic Index* ii, 186; i, 499.

[2] MBh i, *94*, 3725–39.

[3] Vā *99*, 209. Mat *50*, 15. Hv *32*, 1792. Br *13*, 100.

[4] Rigv iv, *15*, 7, 8 compared with vii, *18*, 22, 23.

[5] Rigv vii, *18* and *33*. Aitar Brāhm vii, 5, 34; viii, 4, 21.

[6] Because it is said Somaka sacrificed on the Jumna, MBh iii, *125*, 10420–2; and that could only have been before Saṁvaraṇa's reconquest. All this is fully discussed in JRAS, 1918, pp. 233–8, 246–8.

[7] Rigv vii, *18*, 12. *Vedic Index* i, p. 143.

[8] A śūdra rishi, son of Ilūṣa and a slave-girl, Aitar Brāhm ii, 3, 19.

Sudās. The two Kavaṣas thus lived at the same time and were no doubt the same rishi. He was thus contemporary with Saṁvaraṇa. Further, Tura Kāvaṣeya consecrated Janamejaya Pārikṣita and was his purohita.[1] Tura was by his patronymic a descendant of Kavaṣa, and Janamejaya was Janamejaya II, son of Parikṣit I who was Saṁvaraṇa's grandson. They would thus have been contemporary. Kavaṣa appears to have been on Saṁvaraṇa's side, and his near descendant Tura consecrated Saṁvaraṇa's great grandson Janamejaya.

King Kṛta or Kṛti of the Dvimīḍha line was, as all the passages which mention him say,[2] the disciple of Hiraṇyanābha or Hiraṇyanābhi Kausalya, and made twenty-four saṁhitās of sāmans; they were the 'eastern sāmans', and the chanters of them were called Kārtas or Kārtis after him. Hiraṇyanābha was a king of Kosala,[3] but his position is confused in three passages, which place him five generations after Vyāsa[4]; and that is wrong, because it would make him one of the 'future' kings after the Bhārata battle (chapter III), but he was not one of them[5] and the genealogies fix his position clearly as No. 83 in the Ayodhyā dynasty;[6] and because it is incredible that, after the brahmans had established the Vedic schools, two kings could have been such authorities on the sāmans. Kṛta was one step below Hiraṇyanābha.

Hiraṇyanābha as Kṛta's teacher was learned in the sāmans, and they constructed the 'eastern sāmans'. They lived before Vyāsa, but when Sukarman Jaimini taught Pauṣyañji the Sāmaveda, Pauṣyañji taught his disciples 500 (*sic*) saṁhitās of sāmans, and they were known as the 'northern sāman chanters'. Then notice had to be taken of the older 'eastern sāman chanters', and they had to be brought into the Vedic schools, so Hiraṇyanābha was

[1] Aitar Brāhm vii, 5, 34; viii, 4, 21, *Vedic Index* i, p. 314. Bhāg ix, *22*, 35–7 confuses this Janamejaya with the later Janamejaya III Pārikṣita (chap. IX) and misplaces Kāvaṣeya with the latter.

[2] Genealogies, Mat *49*, 75–6: Hv *20*, 1080–2: Vā *99*, 189–91 (which reads *Kauthuma* wrongly): Viṣ iv, *19*, 13: Bhāg ix, *21*, 28–9 (6 saṁhitās). Also Vā *61*, 44–8 and Bd ii, *35*, 49–55 (which name his twenty-four disciples and misread *Kārta* as *Krānta*); Viṣ iii, *6*, 7.

[3] Chapter XII, Table. *Vedic Index* ii, 506.

[4] Vā *61*, 27–8, 33. Bd ii, *35*, 31–2, 39–40. Viṣ iii, *6*, 1–4. Discussed in chap. XXVII.

[5] My *Dynasties of the Kali Age*, pp. 9, 10.

[6] A descendant was probably Para Āṭṇāra Hairaṇyanābha, Śatapatha Brāhm xiii, 5, 4, 4: *Vedic Index*, i, 491; ii, 506.

assigned as a second disciple to Sukarman,[1] and is said to have constructed 500 saṁhitās also.[2] This erroneous harmonizing was added to the Ayodhyā genealogy, and it is there stated[3] that Hiraṇyanābha was the disciple of Jaimini's grandson (Brahmāṇḍa says, Pauṣyañji) in the eastern sāmans, learnt 500 saṁhitās from him and also taught a Yājñavalkya yoga.

Next may be noticed various data which do not yield synchronisms proper, yet help to indicate the position of kings and rishis. They consist generally of brief allusions. Not every such allusion is worthy of consideration, but where the same fact is referred to in various passages, the consensus becomes important. Some of them are marital notices and the Paurava genealogy in the Mahābhārata (i, *95*, 3764 ff.) goes so far as to name the wife of every king in it, but it is not wholly trustworthy, as shown in chapter IX, and it is highly improbable that every queen's name could be remembered. Caution must also be shown in dealing with personal names, especially of rishis, and patronymics, as pointed out above. Thus Duṣyanta the Paurava married Śakuntalā, daughter of Viśvāmitra, as abundant passages declare;[4] but the position of the first and great Viśvāmitra has been defined above by copious tradition as earlier than Duṣyanta's period; hence she was not his daughter, but the daughter of a Viśvāmitra who was one of his near descendants. The genealogies of Ayodhyā say Satyavrata Triśaṅku married a Kaikeya princess,[5] and this statement may be accepted because his story has been handed down in a kṣatriya ballad (p. 59). Hence the Kaikeya dynasty had come into existence before his time; and therefore according to the genealogies all the other Panjab kingdoms also, the Śivis, Madras, Sauvīras, &c. (chapter IX). Hence it is possible that his son Hariścandra's queen was a Śaivya princess, as the Mārkaṇḍeya says (*7*, 35; &c.), though its story is a fable. Jyāmagha the Yādava, who was later, married a Śaivya princess.[6]

[1] Not difficult with the lack of the historical sense. The misplacement is similar to that of Brahmadatta, p. 65.

[2] See fourth note above.

[3] Vā *88*, 207–8. Bḍ iii, *63*, 207–8. Viṣ iv, *4*, 48 and Bhāg ix, *12*, 3–4 somewhat similarly.

[4] e. g. MBh i, *72*, 2941 to *73*, 2972. Bhāg ix, *20*, 8–22.

[5] Vā *88*, 117. Bḍ iii, *63*, 115. Br *8*, 24. Hv *13*, 754. Śiv vii, *61*, 20. Lg i, *66*, 10.

[6] Vā *95*, 32. Bḍ iii, *70*, 33. Br *15*, 16. Hv *37*, 1984. Lg i, *68*, 37. Mat *44*, 32 reads *Caitrā*.

CHAPTER XV

THE FOUR AGES, CHRONOLOGY AND DATE OF THE BHĀRATA BATTLE

TIME that is treated as historical in tradition is divided into four ages (*yuga*), the Kṛta (or Dharma or Satya), Tretā, Dvāpara and Kali (or Tiṣya), and this reckoning appears to have an historical basis, though later speculations elaborated it into an amazing yet precise scheme of cosmogony. That scheme does not render this reckoning of four ages unworthy of attention, because the genealogies refer to them sometimes, and it appears that they did correspond to certain periods.

It is noteworthy that this theory of the four ages did not apply to the whole world. It is declared repeatedly that these ages prevailed in India (*Bhārata varṣa*),[1] and the descriptions of the other continents (*varṣa*) say nothing about the ages occurring there,[2] and portray conditions incompatible therewith. The four ages therefore concerned India only, and it is declared that they prevailed only in India.[3] The position of these ages in the seventy-one four-age periods which made up a manvantara[4] in the cosmological scheme was therefore a later elaboration. The early idea was that the four ages were a peculiarity of India alone, hence obviously the explanation of them must be sought for in the conditions of ancient India.

It is a commonplace of history that great wars, conquests or political changes put an end to one age and usher in a new age, or mark the transition from one to the other; and so the Mohammedans and the British introduced new ages into India. It is natural therefore to surmise that similar changes occurred and were so regarded in ancient India, and indications of this are found in

[1] MBh vi, *10*, 387. Vā *24*, 1 : *45*, 137 ; *57*, 22. Bḍ ii, *16*, 68–9 ; *29*, 23. Mat *142*, 17. Br *27*, 64. Pad i, *7*, 3.

[2] The ages do not obtain in Plakṣadvīpa ; Vā *49*, 22 ; Bḍ ii, *19*, 24.

[3] So Br *19*, 20. Viṣ ii, *3*, 19. Lg i, *52*, 32.

[4] Vā *45*, 69 and Mat *114*, 1 suggest that even the theory of the fourteen Manus applied only to India. Vā *45*, 67 and Mat *113*, 78 have *Bhārata yuga*.

tradition.[1] The end of the Dvāpara age was admittedly marked by the Bhārata battle, for it is declared that the battle occurred in the interval (*sandhyā*) between the Dvāpara and Kali ages;[2] but this was afterwards modified,[3] and the beginning of the Kali age was fixed at the passing away of the great heroes of that battle, Kṛṣṇa and the Pāṇḍavas, in order apparently to obviate the repugnant idea that the deified Kṛṣṇa lived into the Kali age, according to the express statement that that age began immediately he died.[4] The broad fact however is clear, that the Dvāpara age closed with that battle, and that the Kali age began with the changes in the political condition of N. India that ensued.

Tradition speaks also of an earlier time of great destruction and misery, when the kṣatriyas were well-nigh exterminated and North India was plunged into grievous calamities,[5] and brahmanic fable attributes that to Rāma Jāmadagnya, though kṣatriya tradition shows it really occurred in consequence of the devastating raids of the Haihayas, from whom Sagara delivered the land and restored peace (chapter XXIV). That time may naturally have marked the transition from one age to another. There is no later similar period of calamity that suggests itself as a change of age, but tradition treats Rāma's destruction of Rāvaṇa and the Rākṣasas of the Dekhan and Ceylon as an epoch of signal vengeance upon evil foes.[6] The table of genealogies in chapter XII comprises all the kings from the beginning of the Kṛta to the end of the Dvāpara age, and shows that Sagara's destruction of the Haihayas and Rāma's reign divide the whole period into three parts of not very unequal length, which might well constitute three ages. This arrangement produces a scheme of four ages which is sensible, though exactitude cannot of course be expected.

[1] This is developed otherwise, MBh v, *131*, 4473–8: xii, *69*, 2693–5.

[2] MBh i, *2*, 282. But sometimes it is said the Kali age had already begun before the battle; e.g. MBh vi, *66*, 3012: ix, *61*, 3364; and in the curious tale of the sleeping Mucukunda, Hv *115*, 6483; Viṣ v, *24*, 5; Br *197*, 5.

[3] e.g. Kūr i, *27*, 8.

[4] Mat *273*, 49–50. Vā *99*, 428–9. Bd iii, *74*, 241. Viṣ iv, *24*, 35, 36, 40: v, *38*, 8. Bhāg xii, *2*, 29, 30, 33. Br *212*, 8. See p. 53. Mr. Jayaswal treats this as a chronological basis, *Journal*, B. and O. Research Socy. iii, pp. 254 f.

[5] MBh xii, *49*, 1775–89: also iii, *117*, 10201–5.

[6] Hv *42*, 2327. Br *213*, 126. Gar i, *215*, 8–9.

This division accords with what tradition says about the transition from one age to another. Kṛṣṇa lived at the time of the Bhārata battle and the close of the Dvāpara age.[1] Rāma Dāśarathi lived in the interval between the Tretā and Dvāpara ages.[2] To Rāma Jāmadagnya is assigned the same position, and the references say he lived in the Tretā age,[3] and smote the kṣatriyas in the interval between the Tretā and Dvāpara ages.[4] But this was Rāma Dāśarathi's position, and that particularization is clearly wrong, for Rāma Jāmadagnya was avowedly prior as shown by the synchronisms in chapter XIII, and the allegation that he destroyed all kṣatriyas off the earth twenty-one times (really the long-continued Haihaya devastations) is wholly incompatible with the story of Rāma Dāśarathi. It is obvious that Rāma Jāmadagnya belonged to the interval between the Kṛta and Tretā ages, when in fact the Haihayas had their dominion, and the references should be to the Kṛta age and that interval. The Kṛta age then ended with the destruction of the Haihayas; the Tretā began approximately with Sagara and ended with Rāma Dāśarathi's destruction of the Rākṣasas; and the Dvāpara began with his reinstatement at Ayodhyā and ended with the Bhārata battle: so that, taking the numbers in the table of genealogies, the division is approximately thus, the Kṛta Nos. 1–40, the Tretā Nos. 41–65, and the Dvāpara Nos. 66–95.

These considerations show how the belief arose that Viṣṇu became incarnate when conditions on earth had become evil, in order to destroy wickedness and re-establish righteousness,[5] for his three chief alleged historical incarnations were, the earliest Rāma Jāmadagnya, the second Rāma Dāśarathi, and the last Kṛṣṇa. Such statements are brahmanical, and historical consistency cannot be expected in all.[6] The misstatement of Rāma Jāmadagnya's position arose probably from the notion that the Kṛta age was one of unblemished righteousness.

There are allusions to the ages sometimes in the genealogies, and

[1] MBh xii, *341*, 12953–4: cf. vi, *66*, 3012.

[2] MBh xii, *341*, 12949.

[3] MBh xii, *341*, 12948.

[4] MBh i, *2*, 272; yet *64*, 2480 absurdly makes the Kṛta (read Tretā) age begin after Rāma's devastation (2459). Hv *106*, 5869. Gar i, *215*, 7 is nearly right.

[5] Vā *96*, 232; *97*, 64–6; *98*, 69, 98. Bd iii, *73*, 70, 97. Mat *47*, 235, 247. Br *180*, 26–7; *181*, 2–3.

[6] So it seems to be said the Pāṇḍavas lived in the interval between the Tretā and Dvāpara ages, MBh iii, *121*, 10310; *125*, 10409.

these (when without the elaboration of the ages which will be noticed) appear to be sometimes right, and tend to show that there was in kṣatriya tradition some memory of the chronological position of certain important events. Thus king Bāhu of Ayodhyā lived in the Dharma (Kṛta) age,[1] which agrees with the position, No. 39, determined for him. Karandhama of the Vaiśāla dynasty reigned at the beginning of the Tretā age,[2] and his twelfth successor Tṛṇabindu reigned at the third mouth of that age,[3] which appears to mean the beginning of the third quarter of it: and the positions, Nos. 38 and 52, determined for them practically agree with the approximate limits assigned to that age above. But most such allusions occur in stories and discourses, often brahmanic, and are sometimes right but more often wrong.[4] There is an inclination to assign events to the Tretā age,[5] and the expression *Tretā-yuga*[6] means at times little or nothing more than 'once upon a time'. Such statements are generally worthless for chronological purposes.

It is unnecessary here to pursue this matter into the later fully developed theory of the yugas and manvantaras, wherein 71 four-age periods (*catur-yuga*) made up a manvantara. It was a fanciful brahmanical elaboration; and one feature in it is that the present time is the Kali age in the 28th four-age period of the Vaivasvata manvantara, so the events of traditional history were sometimes distributed among those 28 periods.[7] Thus a pretentious passage declares[8]—Datta Ātreya as Viṣṇu's fourth incarnation and Mārkaṇḍeya lived in the 10th Tretā age (i.e. in the Tretā age of the 10th four-age period); Māndhātṛ as his fifth incarnation[9] and Utathya lived in the 15th Tretā; Rāma Jāmadagnya as his sixth and Viśvāmitra lived in the 19th Tretā; Daśaratha's son Rāma as his seventh and Vasiṣṭha

[1] Bḍ iii, *63*, 121. Vā *88*, 123. Hv *13*, 761, Br *8*, 30. Śiv vii, *61*, 23.

[2] Vā *86*, 7. Or his son, MBh xiv, *4*, 80.

[3] Bḍ iii, *8*, 36–7; *61*, 10–11. Vā *70*, 31; *86*, 15.

[4] e.g. Vā *30*, 76: Bḍ ii, *13*, 83: Mārk *7*, 1: MBh xiii, *14*, 701–2; *150*, 7128.

[5] e.g. Vā *8*, 201; *9*, 46; *30*, 76; *57*, 39, 43; *91*, 48.

[6] e.g. Br *34*, 48: Vā *67*, 43.

[7] A short explanation will be found in Hastings's *Dict. of Religion and Ethics*, s.v. 'Puranas'.

[8] Vā *98*, 88–97. Bḍ iii, *73*, 87–97. Mat *47*, 242–6.

[9] Interpolated in Vā *88*, 69. Not in Bḍ.

lived in the 24th age[1]; Vyāsa as his eighth with Jātūkarṇya, and Kṛṣṇa as his ninth with Brahma-Gārgya lived in the 28th Dvāpara.[2] Such assignments sometimes observe some chronological consistency, often they are erratic, and in any case, being brahmanical notions lacking the historical sense, they are unreliable.

Date of the Bhārata battle.

As the Bhārata battle marked the end of the Dvāpara age and is a great landmark, it is well to reach some estimate of its probable date.[3]

Candragupta began to reign in or about 322 B.C. He was preceded by the nine Nandas,[4] Mahāpadma and his eight sons, who are said to have enjoyed the earth one hundred years. To Mahāpadma are assigned 88 years and to his sons 12 years. The best reading says, not that he reigned 88 years, but that he would be (that is, lived) 88 years; and a hundred years for the joint lives of him and his sons accord with an ordinary genealogical estimate, and are not unreasonable, as his life was long. It is improbable in the circumstances of that time that he could have gained the throne of Magadha until he was grown up, or, say, 20 years old at least.[5] The reigns of the nine Nandas would then be reduced to 80 years, and we may reckon that they began approximately at (322 + 80) 402 B.C.

The next question to consider is the time between Mahāpadma's inauguration and the Bhārata battle. For this three sets of data are alleged. First, there reigned in Magadha during that time 22 Bārhadrathas, 5 Pradyotas and 10 Śiśunāgas, and the total of all their reigns is (940 + 138 + 330) 1408 years, while the totals of the durations of the dynasties vary from (1000 + 138 + 360) 1498 to (723 + 52 + 163) 938 years according as we take all the highest or all the lowest figures.[6] Secondly, it is said that the period from Mahāpadma's inauguration back to Parikṣit's birth, which occurred

[1] So also Bd iii, *8*, 54: Vā *70*, 48: Br *213*, 124. Yet inconsistently, Rāvaṇa lived in the Tretā in the second period, Br *176*, 15–16: and both are placed in the 27th period, Pad v, *14*, 67–8.

[2] In the 27th, Pad v, *23*, 7–9.

[3] In the following discussion I refer for convenience to my *Dynasties of the Kali Age*, as DKA.

[4] DKA, pp. 25–6, 69–70.

[5] A variation in this estimate makes no material difference.

[6] DKA, pp. 13–22, 67–9.

soon after the battle,[1] was 1050 (or 1015) years.[2] These figures are so discrepant that it is clear no reliable tradition has survived in them. It cannot be said that any one of them is more trustworthy than the others. No calculation can be based on all of them combined, and to make computations from one or other of them is purely random work.[3] Besides they are all demonstrably wrong. From the Bhārata battle to Mahāpadma there were 30 Paurava kings (for Yudhiṣṭhira must be reckoned in) and 29 Aikṣvākus (excluding Siddhārtha, i. e. Buddha, who did not reign), beside the 37 Māgadha kings; hence on a reckoning of the kings as 30, the foregoing figures, 1408, &c., give average reigns of 47, 50, 31 and 35 years respectively, which are all impossible when tested by real historical averages as will be shown. Those figures therefore cannot be relied on. The third set of data is that Mahāpadma exterminated all kṣatriyas, and that until then there reigned contemporaneously for the same length of time 24 Aikṣvākus, 27 Pañcālas, 24 Kāśis, 28 Haihayas, 32 Kaliṅgas, 25 Aśmakas, 36 Kurus, 28 Maithilas, 23 Śūrasenas and 20 Vītihotras.[4] Here we have safer ground, for the (names and so) number of kings in a dynasty was a much simpler matter and more easily remembered than figures of the lengths of reigns and dynasties; and this information about ten contemporary dynasties eliminates peculiarities and extravagances about single dynasties and enables us to make prudent calculations by means of averages of all ten. The investigation will proceed on these lines.

It would have taken Mahāpadma some time to conquer all those kingdoms, the nearer earlier and the more distant later; and it will not be far out if we strike a mean, say, of 20 years after his accession for their destruction,[5] and so fix the year (402–20) 382 B.C. for their mean termination. That list of contemporary kings can be tested as regards its period and the number of kings. The dynastic account gives the Paurava, Aikṣvāku and Bārhadratha kings from the time of the battle, but the prophetic portion of it starts from the

[1] MBh xiv, *66* to *70*. [2] DKA, pp. 58, 74.

[3] Mr. Jayaswal in *Journal, B. and O. Research Socy.* i, pp. 67 f.: iii, pp. 246 f.: iv, pp. 26–35. The astronomical statements obviously cannot have scientific precision, and can only have been formed by estimate at the close. Very probably regnal years have been unduly swelled by reckoning for a king his *yuvarāja* period as well as his reign proper.

[4] DKA, pp. 23–4, 69.

[5] This estimate may be varied without material diffe-

point of time when the Paurava king Adhisīmakṛṣṇa, the Aikṣvāku Divākara and the Bārhadratha Senājit were reigning contemporaneously, for it is clearly stated in the Paurava list that the future kings were 25, Adhisīmakṛṣṇa and his 24 successors, and in the Bārhadratha list that they were 16, Senājit and his 15 successors; the predecessors in both cases not being so reckoned. Hence in these three dynasties that point of time is the real initial point throughout and the extermination by Mahāpadma is the final point.

The number of kings can be tested as regards the Aikṣvākus and the Kurus who were the Pauravas. The Aikṣvāku list names 25 future kings from Divākara (omitting Siddhārtha), and the list of contemporary kings says 24 Aikṣvākus, so that the two agree practically. The Paurava-Kuru list names 25 future kings, and the contemporary list says 36; but another well-attested reading in the latter says 26,[1] and it was pointed out[2] that, because of the ease with which *tr* and *v* might be confused, 'in many cases either [20 or 30] may be read as other data may indicate, irrespective of the weight of the MSS.' This reading 26 is no doubt the true reading, because it accords better with the other numbers in the contemporary list and agrees practically with the 25 in the former list. The practical agreement in these two dynasties, the only cases we can test, indicates that the contemporary list is also reckoned from the same initial point as the three detailed dynasties.

According to the contemporary list then there reigned between those initial and final points, 24 Aikṣvākus, 27 Pañcālas, 24 Kāśis, 28 Haihayas, 32 Kaliṅgas, 25 Aśmakas, 26 Kurus (Pauravas), 28 Maithilas, 23 Śūrasenas and 20 Vītihotras,[3] that is 257 kings in ten kingdoms, or a mean of 26 kings. For these 26 then we must allow reigns of medium length, and the question is, at how many years should a medium length be reckoned? The longest average of reigns occurred among the 20 Vītihotras, the shortest among the 32 Kaliṅgas. Thus 20 long reigns = 32 short reigns = 26 medium reigns, whence we obtain the proportion—longest average : shortest average : medium average : : 26 : 16¼ : 20. I have examined 14 series of from 20 to 30 kings in various eastern

[1] DKA, p. 24, note 16. [2] *Id*, p. xxiii, § 39.

[3] It is said the Vītihotras had passed away before the Pradyotas began, DKA, pp. 18, 68. If so, they should be omitted; yet the reckoning here would not be materially modified.

and western countries; the longest average just exceeded 24 years in one case, the shortest was about 12, and the average of all was 19; but the average was higher in western countries and lower in eastern countries. Hence as a medium average for these contemporary eastern dynasties we must take something less than 19, and 18 years will be a fair and even liberal estimate. The duration of these ten contemporary kingdoms then would be 26 × 18, that is, 468 years, and their period would be from 850 to 382 B.C. when Mahāpadma exterminated them.

In this calculation the Magadha kings have not been included, since they are omitted from the contemporary list, and the date 850 B.C. may now be tested with reference to them. From Senājit (850) till Mahāpadma overthrew the Śiśunāgas (402) reigned 16 Bārhadrathas, 5 Pradyotas and 10 Śiśunāgas; that is, 448 years are allowed for 31 reigns—an average of 14½ years. This lower average is quite probable because of the violence that overthrew those dynasties, and it is about the average I have found in eastern dynasties. The above estimate therefore of 18 years for a medium peaceful reign appears just, and the date 850 B.C. is highly probable.

This year 850 would be the approximate mean date of the beginnings of the reigns of Adhisīmakṛṣṇa, Divākara and Senājit; and therefore the standpoint during their reigns, dividing the 'past' from the 'future' in the prophetic account,[1] would be a few years later, say, about 840 B.C.

To get the time of the Bhārata battle, we must add the kings who preceded those three kings, namely, 5 Pauravas (for Yudhiṣṭhira's reign must be included), 4 Aikṣvākus and 6 Bārhadrathas, that is, a mean of 5, and here for so short a period the medium reign probably was longer, say 20 years.[2] Hence we must add (5 × 20) 100 years, and the date of the battle may be fixed approximately as (850 + 100) 950 B.C.[3] This reckoning has avoided special figures

[1] See Vā *1*, 12–15; *99*, 258–9, 282, 300; Mat *1*, 4–5; *50*, 66–7; *271*, 5, 23: and p. 52.

[2] The 60 years assigned to Parikṣit II cannot be relied on (p. 53).

[3] Mr. Jayaswal fixes the battle in 1424 B.C., and other Indian writers favour similar early dates, all working on the above chronological statements in the Puranas (which are discrepant) without checking their figures by comparison with reliable data from dynasties elsewhere. Such a comparison shows that their calculations produce results contrary to general experience: thus his date makes the medium average of 31 reigns from the battle to Mahāpadma about 33 years, an incredible length.

or unique statements, except in the one case of the Nandas where no other course is available; and has proceeded upon general averages (1) of the number of kings belonging to 11 contemporaneous dynasties and (2) of the lengths of reigns computed from the reliable data of 14 historical dynasties in other countries; thus it has eliminated all peculiar features and is a reasonable general approximation.[1]

If we should seek to make an estimate of the ages before the battle, it would be prudent to take a smaller length for the average reign, because only one line, that of Ayodhyā, is practically complete, while there are gaps in the other dynasties, so that there is little scope for taking medium averages of all the dynasties and eliminating peculiarities. The lowest average mentioned above, 12 years, therefore would be a sounder estimate. Since however it is said that insignificant kings have been omitted from the genealogies (p. 89), it may be contended that the average should be increased to compensate for lost kings, say, 13 or 13½ years per step in the table in chapter XII; but the uncertainty and peculiarity in such details require caution, and it would be more prudent to adhere to 12 years as the average. To contend for immense antiquity for the earliest ages is discredited by the historical sense; and to push back the antiquity of those ages to vast figures is to weaken *pro tanto* the trustworthiness of tradition about them when everything depended on memory alone.[2]

Another consequence of such dating is to prolong also the ages before the battle; and to put back the antiquity of any event is to weaken the trustworthiness of tradition about it.

[1] With a possible error of being too liberal. For further calculations see end of chap. XXIV.

[2] Indian writers are prone to do this; e.g. Abinas Chandra Das in his *Rigvedic India*.

CHAPTER XVI

BRAHMAN FAMILIES AND CHRONOLOGICAL TABLE OF RISHIS

VAṀŚAS, or so-called genealogies, of the chief brahman families are given in some of the Puranas,[1] and shorter notices or portions are found in others[2] and in the Mahābhārata.[3] These all belong to the present Vaivasvata manvantara. Besides them somewhat similar genealogies assigned to the Svāyambhuva manvantara are mentioned in some Puranas,[4] and are mainly mythical, though they introduce the names of some rishis well known in the present age. Professedly however they do not belong to the present age and may be put aside.

These brahman genealogies present a remarkable contrast with those of the royal dynasties. It is the difference between a genuine genealogy and one subsequently compiled; between a genealogy that grew contemporaneously with the prolongation of the dynasty, and a genealogy that was pieced together by some compiler out of such materials as he could collect and understand in after times. The bulk of the royal genealogies consists of persons who are named nowhere else; and it would be impossible to construct them out of the notices of kings which occur elsewhere. The brahman vaṁśas are defective in all their features. They do not set out continuous descent except occasionally for a very few steps. They are often manifestly incomplete where they give such descents, because they may assign only a few steps to periods in which the royal genealogies place many kings, as will be seen in the pedigree from Śakti to Vyāsa among the Vasiṣṭhas. Where they do set out copious names, the names form merely a list without any genealogical connexion.

[1] Bḍ iii, *1* and *8*. Vā *65* and *70*. Mat *195* to *202*.

[2] Bḍ ii, *32* and *33*. Vā *59*. Lg i, *63*, 49–55, 68–92. Kūr i, *19*. See p. 69.

[3] MBh i, *5* to *9*.

[4] Bḍ ii, *11*. Vā *10*, 29 f.; *28*; *31*, 16–18. Viṣ i, *10*, 2–14. Lg i, *5*, 24–6, 38–49; *70*, 270 f. Kūr i, *13*. Mārk *52*.

There is little truly genealogical matter in these vaṁśas which cannot be found in various passages elsewhere. They mix up gods and mythological persons with real rishis, as will be seen.

So far as tradition indicates, the ancient rishis kept practically no genealogies. Brahmanical books contain lists of the rishis through whom certain teaching was handed down (p. 4), but no lists of natural descents. Spiritual pedigrees exist, natural pedigrees are wanting. It was one of the duties of the sūtas (p. 15) to preserve the genealogies of rishis as well as of kings, and presumably they observed it as far as they were able, but the task must have been well-nigh impossible, inasmuch as the rishis generally dwelt in secluded hermitages, many of their descendants were of no note, their relations and families were not matters of public interest and report, and their gotras multiplied unmanageably. Rishi genealogies could never have been as copious as the dynastic genealogies; certainly, if they ever were so, they were not transmitted so sedulously, for they do not exist now.

The brahman families claimed descent from mythical rishis, of whom there were eight, Bhṛgu, Aṅgiras, Marīci (whose son was Kaśyapa), Atri, Vasiṣṭha, Pulastya, Pulaha and Kratu. They are called mind-born sons of Brahmā,[1] but fable devised another origin for them with fanciful etymologies of their names.[2] It appears in various places with variations, but the general explanation is this. Brahmā offered a sacrifice and Bhṛgu came into existence from it, next Aṅgiras, and then the others, and Kavi is also named sometimes as the same as Bhṛgu and sometimes as distinct. Śiva, who had the form of Varuṇa, took Bhṛgu as his son, hence Bhṛgu and the Bhārgavas were famed as Vāruṇa; Agni took Aṅgiras, hence Aṅgiras was known as Āgneya; and one account says Brahmā took Kavi, who was therefore known as Brāhma, but adds that Śiva as Varuṇa took him, so that Kavi was also Vāruṇa. The account says Bhṛgu begot seven sons, Aṅgiras eight and Kavi eight; the sons named were not sons but descendants in various degrees.

[1] e.g. Vā *9*, 68–9; but differently, 99–104. The number of the mind-born sons varies. Brahmā the Pitāmaha created them, so they were called *paitāmaharṣis*, Mat *171*, 28.

[2] Vā *65*, 21, 35–48. Bḍ iii, *1*, 20, 35–47. Mat *195*, 5–11. MBh xiii, *85*, 4121–5, 4145–54, 4163. Bṛhadd v, 97–101, quoted by Vedārth as introduction to Rigv v. Alluded to, Vā *1*, 128; *30*, 76: Bḍ ii, *13*, 83–4. Cf. MBh i, *5*, 869–70; *66*, 2605.

Of the eight rishi progenitors, however, the last three, Pulastya, Pulaha and Kratu, produced no true brahman families, as will be explained,[1] and only from the five others did genuine brahman families claim descent. But it was known that these five families were not all of equal antiquity, because it is said, 'Four original families (*mūla-gotra*) came into existence, Aṅgiras, Kaśyapa, Vasiṣṭha and Bhṛgu; through action (*karmataḥ*) other families were produced'[2]—omitting Atri. Tradition supports the later origin of the Ātreyas, and indicates that the Kāśyapas also began later (see chapter XX), so that the only families whose existence is carried back in tradition to the earliest antiquity are the Bhārgavas and Vasiṣṭhas, and perhaps the Āṅgirasas. Still the general allegation came to be that the ancestors of all the families were the mythical primaeval rishis. In the following chapters all these families will be discussed, so far as they purport to have an historical connexion; and here the ground may be cleared by noticing briefly the mythological allegations about certain primaeval rishis in these families. It is said that Pulastya's offspring were Rākṣasas, Vānaras, Kinnaras and Yakṣas;[3] that Pulaha's offspring were Kimpuruṣas, Piśācas, goblins, lions, tigers and other animals;[4] and that Kratu had no wife or child, and remained celibate, according to most accounts,[5] but according to other accounts the Vālakhilyas were his offspring[6]

The most noticeable allegations are made regarding 'Bṛhaspati' son of 'Aṅgiras'. It seems from an examination of the statements that three primary Bṛhaspatis must be distinguished. First, the Bṛhaspati who had a wife Tārā; Soma seduced her and had a son Budha by her.[7] Here Bṛhaspati means the planet,[8] and this

[1] Seven *ṛṣi-gaṇas* are named after them all except Kratu, Vā *65*, 49–50; Bḍ iii, *1*, 49–51.

[2] MBh xii, *298*, 10877–8; a brahmanical admission.

[3] MBh i, *66*, 2751. Rākṣasas, Rām iii, *32*, 23.

[4] MBh i, *66*, 2572. Vā *69*, 204 f., 325 f.; *70*, 64–5; *73*, 25, 44. Bḍ iii, *8*, 70–2. Kūr i, *19*, 15–16. Lg i, *63*, 66–7 (for *Pulastyasya* read *Pulahasya*).

[5] Vā *70*, 66. Bḍ iii, *8*, 72–3. Lg i, *63*, 68. Kūr i, *19*, 16.

[6] Pad vi, *218*, 64. MBh i, *66*, 2573 (where *Pataṅga-sahacāriṇaḥ* = *Vālakhilyāḥ*). Mārk *52*, 24–5. Ag *20*, 14.

[7] Vā *90*, 28–43. Bḍ iii, *65*, 29–44. Br *9*, 19–32. Hv *25*, 1340–55. Mat *23*, 29 to *24*, 7. Pad v, *12*, 33–58. Viṣ iv, *6*, 7–19. Bhāg ix, *14*, 4–14. Cf. MBh v, *108*, 3972.

[8] Heavenly bodies were named after rishis, as is clearly shown by *Vasiṣṭha*, the name of a real rishi and also of the star ζ in the Great Bear.

story appears to be an astronomical myth about Jupiter, the Moon, Mercury, &c. Secondly, the Bṛhaspati who is called the priest or guru or ācārya of the gods in their war with the asuras (Daityas and Dānavas), whose powerful priest was the Bhārgava Uśanas-Śukra.[1] Both these rishis are assigned a chronological position in that that war is placed in Yayāti's reign and Yayāti married Śukra's daughter Devayānī (p. 86).[2] Thirdly, the historical rishi Bṛhaspati who has been discussed above (chapter XIII). It may be added, fourthly, that the descendants of this last are often undistinguished from him as 'Bṛhaspatis'.

The third Bṛhaspati was an Āṅgirasa, the first of course was not, and it is not clear whether the second was such or not. But they are constantly confused, especially in the later stories, as regards both their functions and the epithet 'Aṅgiras'.[3] So the first, the planet,[4] is called in the story of Tārā and in some Puranas the guru of the gods[5] and an Aṅgiras.[6] The first and second are further confused and identified in astronomical accounts, and so the planet is styled the *ācārya* of the gods and also *Aṅgiras*,[7] where *Aṅgiras* seems to be borrowed, if not from the second, yet certainly from the third Bṛhaspati; for it seems probable that the second was not an Aṅgiras in the sense of Aṅgiras as a gotra, but may have got that appellation through confusion with the third, since no Āṅgirasas appear definitely until far later in Karandhama's reign (chapter XIII). Further, attributes of the second are erroneously

[1] MBh i, *76*, 3185 f.: vii, *63*, 2295: xii, *29*, 990. Mat *25*, 6 f.; *249*, 4 f. Cf. MBh ix, *37*, 2102: Pad vi, *8*, 44–6, 50; *146*, 6–10; &c.

[2] Bṛhaspati is introduced in the fable about Nahuṣa, MBh v, *10*, 360 f.; *14*, 480. It seems to me from some consideration of the *devâsura* wars, that the stories of the conflicts between the devas and asuras are based, partly, on religious struggles in the earliest times: cf. p. 68.

[3] Vide Sörensen's *Index* as regards the MBh.

[4] The epithet *bṛhattejas* is often applied to 'Bṛhaspati'. Apparently it properly belonged to the planet (Mat *128*, 48: Vā *53*, 81: Bḍ ii, *24*, 89: Lg i, *61*, 18), and was afterwards transferred to the other Bṛhaspatis in the confusion; e.g. to the third Bṛhaspati (MBh i, *104*, 4180), to 'Bṛhaspati' father of Śaṁyu (Vā *71*, 48–9).

[5] Mat *23*, 30. Pad v, *12*, 34. Viṣ iv, *6*, 7. Bhāg ix, *14*, 5. Cf. Hv *25*, 1342.

[6] See seventh note above, except Mat and Pad.

[7] Vā *53*, 81, 107. Bḍ ii, *24*, 89, 132. Mat *128*, 48. Lg i, *61*, 18. Cf. MBh i, *66*, 2606.

applied to the third, as where the latter is called the priest of the gods.[1]

Among the Bhārgavas Bhṛgu and Kavi are purely mythical, but as regards Uśanas-Śukra, who is called their son, it must be noted that Uśanas and Śukra were names of the planet Venus also, and the two must be distinguished. The rishi always appears as the great priest of the Daityas and Dānavas (chapter XVII) and as the antagonist of the second Bṛhaspati with the same chronological position. But he and the planet were confused and identified,[2] and so the latter is styled in astronomical accounts *Bhārgava*, the 'sacrificing priest of the asuras' and 'divine'.[3] Further, since the first and second Bṛhaspatis were confused, the antagonism led to this rishi's being foisted as Bṛhaspati's adversary into the story of Tārā in late Puranas.[4]

The mythical rishi Atri was made one with the mythical Atri, who is called a primaeval prajāpati[5] and father of Soma,[6] the moon. Then he is confused with the Atri who was the father (or progenitor) of Datta and Durvāsas (who will be noticed in chapter XIX), and so Soma is made the brother of those two rishis.[7] Prabhākara, the earliest Ātreya mentioned, is connected in a fable with the sun,[8] and the fable has no doubt been evolved out of his name and Svastyātreya the name of his descendants, and is explained as referring to an eclipse of the sun.[9]

Kaśyapa son of Marīci is alleged to be the progenitor of the Kāśyapa brahmans, but there is no mention of any rishi called Kaśyapa until Rāma Jāmadagnya's time, as will be shown in chapter XX, and Marīci's son Kaśyapa is made a prajāpati,[10] or is

[1] MBh i, *104*, 4180: xiv, *5*, 108 to *6*, 125.

[2] MBh i, *66*, 2606–7; and genealogy, next chapter.

[3] Vā *53*, 80, 106; Bḍ ii, *24*, 89, 131; and Lg i, *61*, 17 (all *deva*). But Mat *128*, 47, 63 (*Daitya*).

[4] Viṣ iv, *6*, 8, 10. Bhāg ix, *14*, 6.

[5] Hv *5*, 292. MBh xiii, *65*, 3289.

[6] Vā *90*, 1–11, 46–7. Bḍ iii, *65*, 1–11. Mat *198*, 1. Hv *25*, 1311. Br *9*, 1.

[7] Br *144*, 2–4. Pad vi, *218*, 60–1. Mārk *17*, 5–10; *52*, 21–2. Kūr i, *13*, 7–8. Ag *20*, 12. Genealogy in chap. XX.

[8] Genealogy in chap. XX. Vedārth, introduction to Rigv v. MBh xiii, *156*, 7292–7302.

[9] Bṛhadd v, 12. MBh i, *123*, 4807 and Hv *261*, 14148 say Atri was stirred up when the sun was destroyed. Śatapatha Brāhm v, 3, 2, 2.

[10] Kūr i, *19*, 16. Pad v, *37*, 77: vi, *218*, 59–60. Mat *6*, 1 f.

identified with the Kaśyapa who in accounts of the creation is made the progenitor of all beings, and is called the father of the gods and asuras.[1] Thus the first account given that professes to be a vaṁśa of the Kāśyapas[2] diverges off into the creation. It declares that in this lineage the world had its origin, thus: Marīci begot a son, the prajāpati Ariṣṭanemi, who afterwards became Kaśyapa[3] and married Dakṣa's daughters, whence came the origin of all beings. It is also said Nārada was Brahmā's son but, because of Dakṣa's curse, became the son of Kaśyapa or of Kaśyapa's son:[4] and further that Kaśyapa begot Nārada, Parvata and Arundhatī, whom Nārada gave as wife to 'Vasiṣṭha'.[5] It is all myth.

Besides the foregoing brahman families other brahman families and gotras arose, which claimed no primaeval antiquity. They were of three classes. First, the Viśvāmitras, who were descended from Viśvāmitra, king of Kānyakubja, who became a brahman and established an independent family. Secondly, sub-families founded by kṣatriya princes, some of which became brahmans forthwith, such as the Kāṇvas and Vītahavyas (chapters XIX and XVII), while others became first kṣatriyan brahmans, as will be explained in chapter XXIII, were incorporated into pure brahmanic families and then became entirely brahmans. These two classes took their rise at definite chronological stages. The third class comprised brahman families, such as the Agastyas (chapter XXII), which appeared, but the origin of which is uncertain.

In considering notices of rishis, it is very necessary to remember the cautions explained in chapter XII. It will be convenient here to give a table showing the chronological position of the ancient rishis, as they are ascertained in the preceding and following chapters, and it is arranged according to the scale in the table of royal genealogies in chapter XII, that is, the numbers correspond in both tables, and the two read together show what kings and rishis were contemporaries. This table will elucidate the discussions

[1] MBh i, *65*, 2519; *66*, 2598: xiii, *12*, 556–7.

[2] Bḍ iii, *1*, 113 f. Vā *65*, 109 f., which seems corrupt. Cf. Kūr i, *20*, 1–4.

[3] MBh xii, *208*, 7574 says that Marīci begot Kaśyapa, who was known by both the names Kaśyapa and Ariṣṭanemi. MBh iii, *184*, 12660, 12665 call an 'Ariṣṭanemi' *Tārkṣya*.

[4] Vā *65*, 135–42. Bḍ iii, *2*, 12–18.

[5] Vā *70*, 79–80. Bḍ iii, *8*, 86–7. Lg i, *63*, 78–80. Kūr i, *19*, 20.

in the following chapters. The Matsya (*195* to *202*) gives copious lists of rishis and gotras in the brahman families, and it will be found that gotras of the same name sometimes existed in two families.[1] This renders it at times hardly certain to which family a rishi mentioned by his gotra name should be assigned, yet generally one gotra was far more distinguished than the other, so that it is reasonable to place such a rishi in the family in which the gotra was distinguished. Where a rishi is mentioned only by his gotra name without any personal name, the former is placed within inverted commas; and where a rishi can be assigned only tentatively to a particular position, his name is marked thus (?). Rishis and teachers after the Bhārata battle are dealt with in chapter XXVII.

[1] Thus, *Paulastya* besides being a family was also a Bhārgava gotra (Mat *195*, 30). *Kutsa* was both Āṅgirasa and Bhārgava (*id. 195*, 22; *196*, 37). There were *Kāṇvas* among the Vasiṣṭhas, as well as *Kāṇvāyanas* (*Kāṇvas*) among the Āṅgirasas (*id. 196*, 21; *200*, 9).

CHRONOLOGICAL TABLE OF RISHIS

	Bhārgavas	Āṅgirasas	Vasiṣṭhas	Other Families
1	... ...	... ...	'Vasiṣṭha'	... ...
2	Cyavana	... ...	'Vasiṣṭha'	... ...
3	... ...	... ...	'Vasiṣṭha'	... ...
4	... ...	... ...	... ...	... ...
5	Uśanas-Śukra	(Bṛha ati)	... ...	... ...
6	Śaṇḍa and Marka. Apnavāna	... ...	... ...	... ...
7–17	... ...	... ...	... ...	... ...
18	... ...	... ...	... ...	Prabhākara-Ātreya
19–29	... ...	... ...	... ...	... ...
30	Ūrva	... ...	Varuṇa	... ...
31	Ṛcīka-Aurva	... ...	Āpava-Vāruṇi	Datta-Ātreya. Durvāsas-Ātreya (?)
32	Jamadagni, Ajīgarta	... ...	Devarāj	(Viśvaratha-) Viśvāmitra
33	... ...	... ...	... ...	Madhucchandas, Ṛṣabha, Reṇu, Aṣṭaka, Kati (or Kata?) and Gālava, Viśvāmitras
34	{Rāma, Śunaḥśepa}	... ...	... ...	Śunaḥśepa-Devarāta-Viśvāmitra
35	... ...	... ...	... ...	... ...
36	... ...	... ...	... ...	... ...
37	... ...	... ...	... ...	... ...
38	... ...	Atharvan	... ...	... ...
39	... ...	Uśija	... ...	'Kaśyapa'
40	Agni-Aurva, Vītahavya	Ucathya, Bṛhaspati, Saṁvarta	Atharva-nidhi I-Āpava	... ...
41	... ...	Dīrghatamas, Bharadvāja, Śaradvant I	... ...	... ...
42	... ...	... ...	... ...	'Viśvāmitra' (Śakuntalā's father), Kaṇva-Kāśyapa, Agastya (and Lopāmudrā)
43	... ...	Kakṣīvant I	... ...	... ...
44	... ...	Śaṁyu	... ...	... ...
45	... ...	... ...	... ...	... ...
46	... ...	Vidathin-Bharadvāja (adopted by Bharata)	... ...	... ...
47	... ...	... ...	... ...	... ...
48	... ...	... ...	... ...	... ...
49	... ...	Garga, Nara	... ...	... ...
50	... ...	Urukṣaya, Saṅkṛti	... ...	... ...
51	... ...	Ṛjiśvan (?)	... ...	... ...
52	... ...	Kapi	... ...	... ...
53	... ...	... ...	... ...	... ...
54	... ...	'Bharadvāja' (with Ajamīḍha)	Śreṣṭhabhāj	... ...

	BHĀRGAVAS	ĀNGIRASAS	VASIṢṬHAS	OTHER FAMILIES
55	... ...	Kaṇva	... ...	... ...
56	... ...	Medhātithi-Kāṇva	... ...	... ...
57	... ...	... ...	... ...	... ...
58	... ...	... ...	... ...	... ...
59	... ...	... ...	... ...	... ...
60	... ...	... ...	Atharva-nidhi II	Śāṇḍilya-Kāśyapa
61	... ...	Maudgalya	... ...	... ...
62	(Vadhryaśva)	... ...	... ...	... ...
63	(Divodāsa)	Pāyu, Śaradvant II. Sobhari-Kāṇva	... ...	Vibhāṇḍaka-Kāśyapa, Arcanānas-Ātreya
64	(Mitrayu), Parucchepa-Daivodāsi	... ...	'Vasiṣṭha' (with Daśaratha)	Ṛṣyaśṛṅga-Kāśyapa, Rebha-Kāśyapa, Śyāvāśva-Ātreya
65	Maitreya, Pratardana-Daivodāsi, Pracetas	Kakṣīvant II-Pajriya	... ...	Andhīgu-Ātreya
66	Anānata-Pārucchepi, Vālmīki	... ...	... ...	... ...
67	Sumitra-Vādhryaśva	... ...	'Vasiṣṭha' (with Sudās)	... ...
68	... ...	... ...	Śakti, Śatayātu	'Viśvāmitra' (with Sudās), Nidhruva-Kāśyapa
69	... ...	Vāmadeva	Parāśara-Śāktya, Suvarcas	... ...
70	... ...	Bṛhaduktha	... ...	... ...
71	Devāpi-Śaunaka	... ...	... ...	... ...
72	... ...	... ...	... ...	... ...
73	Indrota-Śaunaka	.. ...	... ..	Vaibhāṇḍaki-Kāśyapa
74	... ...	... ...	... ...	... ...
75-85	... ...	... ...	... ...	... ...
86	... ...	... ...	... ...	'Jaigīṣavya'
87	... ...	... ...	... ...	Śaṅkha and Likhita, Kaṇḍarīka, Bābhravya-Pāñcāla
88	... ...	... ...	... ...	... ...
89	... ...	... ...	(Sagara)	... ...
90	... ...	... ...	Parāśara-Sāgara	... ...
91	... ...	'Bharadvāja'	'Jātūkarṇya'	Asita-Kāśyapa, Visvaksena (-Jātūkarṇya ?)
92	... ...	... ...	Kṛṣṇa-Dvaipāyana-Vyāsa	Agniveśa ?
93	... ...	Kṛpa, Droṇa	Śuka	Asita-Devala, Dhaumya and Yāja, all Kāśyapas
94	Vaiśampāyana	Aśvatthāman, Paila	Bhūriśravas, &c.	Lomaśa, 'Jaimini', Sumantu

CHAPTER XVII

THE BHĀRGAVAS

THE Bhārgavas claimed descent from the primaeval rishi Bhṛgu, and they are also called Bhṛgus indiscriminately ; thus Cyavana is called Bhṛgu [1] and Bhṛgu's son ; [2] his descendant Ṛcīka is equally called Bhṛgu [3] and Bhṛgu's son ; [4] and Ṛcīka's grandson Rāma Jāmadagnya is also called Bhṛgu [5] and Bhṛgu's son.[6] This general use of the name Bhṛgu produces great confusion, if it is taken to denote one and the same rishi, but when applied to a rishi it means simply a Bhṛgu, a Bhārgava.

The vaṁśa of the Bhārgavas is set out in Vāyu *65*, 72–96, Brahmāṇḍa iii, *1*, 73–100 and Matsya *195*, 11–46. The first two give the best genealogical account; the third is fullest as regards names and gotras. Brief accounts are also found in the Mahābhārata.[7] The Vāyu and Brahmāṇḍa texts collated are treated here as the genealogy. It shows that real tradition has been mixed up with mythology, Uśanas-Śukra is identified with the planet Venus, and among Bhṛgu's offspring are included gods and semi-divine personages. The Matsya account says Bhṛgu married Puloman's daughter Divyā, and had by her the twelve Bhṛgu gods,[8] Cyavana and Apnavāna ; Apnavāna's son was Aurva and his son was Jamadagni. The best Mahābhārata account [9] says Bhṛgu had two sons, Śukra-Kavi-Graha [10] who was guru of the Daityas and gods (*sura*), and Cyavana ; Cyavana married Manu's daughter Āruṣī and had a son Aurva ; Aurva's son was Ṛcīka, who had a hundred sons, the eldest of whom was Jamadagni ; and Jamadagni had four sons of

[1] MBh xiii, *51*, 2685.

[2] *Id.* iii, *122*, 10316.

[3] Vā *65*, 93 ; *91*, 93. Bd iii, *66*. 57.

[4] MBh xiii, *56*, 2910. Vā *91*, 67–8, 71 : &c.

[5] MBh vii, *70*, 2435.

[6] See Sörensen's *Index*, Rāma [1].

[7] i, *5* to *9*; *66*, 2605–13 : and xiii, *85*, 4145–6 gives a curt and inaccurate summary.

[8] Alluded to, Vā *64*, 4 ; Bd ii, *38*, 4.

[9] i, *66*, 2605–13.

[10] Confusing him with the planet.

whom Rāma was the youngest. The other Mahābhārata passages will be considered separately.

The foregoing versions give the earliest Bhṛgus as Uśanas-Śukra and Cyavana, as brothers. Both are often spoken of as Bhārgavas.[1] The former is sometimes called Kavi,[2] sometimes made distinct from Kavi,[3] and more often made Kavi's son,[4] often Kāvya [5] and sometimes best of the Kavis,[6] so that tradition places Kavi above him. Moreover it will be seen that he is placed later than Cyavana by tradition, because Cyavana is connected with Manu's son Śaryāti [7] and Śukra with Yayāti, who was later. Hence the two most ancient Bhārgavas were Cyavana, who is called Cyavāna in Vedic literature, and Uśanas-Śukra.

Cyavana, it is often said, married Sukanyā, daughter of Manu's son, king Śaryāti,[8] and sacrificed for him.[9] He is also connected with Manu's other son Pṛṣadhra.[10] His position is therefore clearly fixed, though late, and especially brahmanic, tales wrongly introduce him as existing at other periods;[11] and he is made the subject of fable even in the Rigveda.[12]

Uśanas-Śukra, for he had both names,[13] is generally connected with the Daityas, Dānavas and asuras, who meant originally tribes

[1] For Cyavana, see *ante*. For Uśanas-Śukra, MBh i, *81*, 3387 : xii, *291*, 10665: xiii, *98*, 4687–8 : &c. Mat *249*, 4 f. Br *73*, 31, 34.

[2] MBh i, *76*, 3196. Pad vi, *8*, 46.

[3] MBh i, *66*, 2606 : xiii, *85*, 4150.

[4] MBh i, *66*, 2606 : *76*, 3204 ; Vedārth on Rigv viii, *84*.

[5] MBh i, *85*, 3527 : xii, *291*, 10660 : xiii, *98*, 4741. Mat *25*, 9. Pad vi, *8*, 47. See *Kāvya*, *Vedic Index* i, p. 153.

[6] *Kavi-vara*, the genealogy. *Kavīndra*, MBh xiii, *98*, 4690.

[7] The connexion of Cyavana with Nahuṣa in MBh xiii, *51* is a manifest late brahmanical fable.

[8] MBh iii, *121*, 10313 ; *122*, 10320–44 ; *124*, 10371 f. : iv, *21*, 650–1 : v, *116*, 3970. Vā *86*, 23. Bḍ iii, *61*, 19. Pad iv, *14*, 49 f. Rām v, *24*, 11. Āruṣī (*ante*) may mean Aurva's mother.

[9] MBh xiv, *9*, 249. Cf. Aitareya Brāhm viii, *4*, 21.

[10] Vā *86*, 1–2. Bḍ iii, *61*, 1–2. (Bhāg ix, *2*, 3–15.)

[11] As with king Kuśika of Kānyakubja, MBh xiii, *52* to *56* : in the Rāmāyaṇa story of Sagara's birth (i, *70*, 31–2 : ii, *110*, 20): in Rāma's reign, Pad iv, *14*, 26 : Rām vii, *60*.

[12] As that the Aśvins restored him to youth, *Vedic Index* i, 264 ; MBh iii, *123* : Bhāg ix, *3*, 2–17. The fable shows he was far more ancient than the hymns.

[13] MBh i, *65*, 2544 : *76*, 3204 ; *85*, 3527 : xii, *291*, 10662, 10687–90 ; *291*, 10760. Mat *25*, 25.

hostile to the Aryans, being called their *guru*,[1] *ācārya*,[2] *upādhyāya*,[3] *purohita*,[4] and *yājaka*.[5] His intimate connexion with them is often alluded to.[6] In later notices his position was improved and he became *guru* or *ācārya* of the gods (*deva*) as well as of the Daityas,[7] and then more positively of the gods and asuras[8]—an impossible status. So he is called divine,[9] but never, as far as I know, unequivocally teacher or priest of the gods alone. The change was manifestly in this direction, for it is incredible that it could have been the reverse way, since the Daityas and Dānavas were metamorphosed into demons by later fancy; hence in the passages where he is called priest of the *suras*, 'gods,' also, the word *sura* has probably superseded *asura* sometimes. Why the change took place is not clear, but improvement may have been felt to be required after that metamorphosis and after the Bhārgavas became famous brahmans; and it is worthy of note that fables say Śiva took Kavi as his son (chapter XVI), and Umā prevented Śiva from slaying Uśanas, whence Uśanas became her son.[10]

His original position comes out clearly from stories of the war between the *devas* (gods) and *asuras*.[11] He was on the asuras' side and restored the slain asuras to life by means of a potent spell called *mṛta-sañjīvanī*,[12] which he had obtained from Śiva[13] and which the devas did not know.[14] The devas' priest Bṛhaspati could

[1] MBh i, *66*, 2607; *81*, 3367. Mat *30*, 9. Br *95*, 26–8; *146*, 24–5. Pad vi, *4*, 10.

[2] Vā *62*, 80; *97*, 94 f.: *98*, 27. Bḍ ii, *36*, 94: iii, *72*, 95 f. Kūr i, *19*, 17. Pad vi, *4*, 14.

[3] MBh i, *65*, 2544: cf. *78*, 3310. [4] Mat *25*, 9. MBh i, *76*, 3188.

[5] Vā *53*, 80. Bḍ ii, *24*, 89. Lg i, *61*, 17. Hv *221*, 12200.

[6] With Vṛtra, MBh xii, *280*, 10004, 10012. With Bali, Br *73*, 24, 31, 36; MBh xiii, *98*, 4687. Taught Prahlāda, MBh xii, *139*, 5203. Against the gods, Pad vi, *211*, 20; Viṣ i, *17*, 48; MBh xii, *291*, 10660–5, with a fable to explain it.

[7] MBh i, *66*, 2607.

[8] Line 7 of the genealogy. Viṣ i, *12*, 97. Hv *2*, 66.

[9] See chap. XVI, but *Daitya* in Mat. MBh xii, *291*, 10660. He is made father of Devī, wife of Varuṇa, MBh i, *66*, 2616.

[10] MBh xii, *291*, 10693. Bḍ iii, *10*, 17–18. Vā *72*, 15–16. Br *34*, 90–1. Lg ii, *13*, 6.

[11] MBh i, *76*, 3187 to *78*, 3281. Mat *25*, 6 to *27*, 3; *47*, 59–234. Bḍ iii, *72*, 92 to *73*, 69. Vā *97*, 91 to *98*, 68. Śukra among the asuras. Bṛhaspati among the devas, MBh xv, *28*, 753.

[12] Also Br *95*, 26, 30.

[13] Also Lg i, *35*, 16–17, 25: Pad vi, *146*, 3. [14] Also Br *95*, 26.

not restore the slain devas to life, until (according to one version[1]) his son Kaca succeeded by stratagem in learning the spell from Śukra. Then the devas got it and vanquished Śukra and the asuras.[2]

The genealogy says Śukra's wife was the *pitṛ-kanyā* Go,[3] and they had four sons, Tvaṣṭṛ, Varūtrin, Śaṇḍa (or Ṣaṇḍa) and Marka.[4] Tvaṣṭṛ introduces, and passes off into, mythology, with his alleged two sons, Triśiras-Viśvarūpa and Viśvakarman. Varūtrin had three sons (named), who were priests of the Daityas,[5] hostile to Indra, and so perished. Śaṇḍa and Marka were priests of the asuras according to Vedic literature,[6] and are mentioned in the Puranas[7] in connexion with a great war between the devas and the Daityas and Dānavas. It is said that at the devas' entreaty they abandoned the Daityas and Dānavas and helped the devas, who then were victorious; and it appears to be said that Śukra then cursed them.[8] Śukra had a daughter Devayānī by (the genealogy says) Jayantī;[9] and she married king Yayāti (p. 86). Tradition then leaves Uśanas-Śukra's lineage in this position, that it sank as the Daityas fell and disappeared in one way or another, and certainly no brahman family (as far as I am aware) claimed descent from him, unless possibly the Mārkaṇḍeyas were descended from Marka (see *infra*).

It must be noticed that Cyavana's family and Uśanas-Śukra's family appear to have occupied different regions. Cyavana is always connected with the west of India, the country around the Gulf of Cambay,[10] in or near Śaryāti's territory Ānarta (Gujarat) as shown by the story of his marrying Sukanyā, and by the

[1] MBh i, *76*. Mat *25*. [2] Also Ag *240*, 1.

[3] Probably his sister, see pp. 69–70.

[4] MBh i, *65*, 2544–5 names them differently, and says they were *asura-yājakas*.

[5] The Vā reading *brahmiṣṭhā sura-yājakāḥ* is clearly wrong and should be *brahmiṣṭhâsura-yājakāḥ* for *brahmiṣṭhāḥ asura-yājakāḥ* by double sandhi as is not uncommon in the Puranas. Cf. Viṣ i, *17*, 48, where Bhārgavas were purohitas to the Daitya king Hiraṇyakaśipu.

[6] Both called *asura-rakṣas*, Śatapatha Brāhm iv, 2, 1, 4–6.

[7] They do not occur in the MBh. Ṣaṇḍha in Pad v, *19*, 272.

[8] Vā *97*, 72, 86; *98*, 63–7. Bd iii, *72*, 72, 87; *73*, 63–8. Mat *47*, 54, 229–33.

[9] So also Vā 97, 149–54; *98*, 20: Bd iii, *72*, 150–6; *73*, 19: Mat *47*, 114–21, 186. These say Jayantī was Indra's daughter.

[10] Later passages connect 'Cyavana' with other places, as noticed above; and MBh iii, *89*, 8365.

statement that he performed austerities near the Vaidūrya Mts (the west portion of the Satpura range) and the R. Narmadā.[1] Uśanas-Śukra is connected rather with the central region of N. India, for Yayāti king of Pratiṣṭhāna (Allahabad) met his daughter Devayānī near his own territory and married her;[2] and Kapālamocana on the Sarasvatī is called his tīrtha.[3] Cyavana's descendants remained connected with west India,[4] and when the Haihayas dominated that region and the Śāryāta kingdom perished (p. 98), they became associated with the Haihayas. It is they who produced the great Bhārgava family, that has now to be considered.

Two sons are given to Cyavana and Sukanyā, Apnavāna and Dadhīca. Apnavāna is mentioned in the Rigveda,[5] and his name is corrupted in the Puranas to Āpnuvāna,[6] Āpravāna,[7] Ātmavāna[8] and Ātmavant.[9] The Matsya account wrongly makes Cyavana and Apnavāna brothers, because Apnavāna's wife Ruci has the patronymic Nāhuṣī, which means no doubt that she was daughter of the Aila king Nahuṣa, so that he would have been a younger contemporary of Nahuṣa and therefore a descendant rather than brother of Cyavana. Dadhīca is hopelessly enveloped in fable.[10] A son Sārasvata is assigned to him, of whom a fable is narrated.[11] Another account gives another son, Pramati, to Cyavana,[12] but the connexion has been greatly contracted as will be explained.

The genealogy says Apnavāna's son was Ūrva, but it has contracted the pedigree, because, as the following account shows, Ūrva was later and therefore was a descendant.[13]

A notice of these Bhārgavas is given in two accounts. One says[14]—The Bhṛgus or Bhārgavas were priests to king Kṛtavīrya

[1] MBh iii, *122*, 10316 with *121*, 10310–13; *124*, 10374–7. Pad iv, *14*, 12–26, 46–53; *16*, 3, connecting him with the R. Payoṣṇī (Tapti). Cf. also MBh iii, *102*, 8740.

[2] Also Br *146*, 2–4: Mat *27*, 12–15; *30*, 4–5.

[3] MBh ix, *40*, 2249–51, 2262.

[4] MBh iii, *118*, 10223 and context. Brahmanical fables about Cyavana, MBh xiii, *50* to *56*.

[5] See *Vedic Index*. Not in MBh.

[6] Mat *195*, 15, 17, 29, 32, 35.

[7] In the Bd genealogy.

[8] In the Vā genealogy.

[9] Vā *59*, 96. Bd ii, *32*, 104. Mat *145*, 98. Pad vi, *82*, 4.

[10] Fables, MBh ix, *52*, 2929–60: xii, *344*, 13211–12.

[11] MBh ix, *52*, 2931–49, 2960–77.

[12] MBh i, *5*, 870–1; *8*, 939.

[13] So MBh xiii, *4*, 207 calls Ūrva's son Ṛcīka 'son of Cyavana'.

[14] MBh i, *178*, 6802–15.

(of the Haihayas) and he bestowed great wealth on them. After his death the princes of his family demanded it back, but the Bhārgavas refused to give it up. They used violence to the Bhārgavas, and the Bhārgavas fled to other countries for safety. One of the Bhārgava wives gave birth to a son then who was called Aurva (p. 68). The other account says,[1] in prophetic form—The kṣatriyas fell out with the Bhārgavas and slew them, and Bhārgava Ūrva[2] was born then. His son was Ṛcīka. Both accounts[3] say that the son born then cherished great wrath against the adversaries but stayed it awhile. That was natural. The Bhārgavas were filled with anger against the Haihayas, yet could not contend successfully against them. They could look for revenge only through force of arms, and further notices show that they turned their thoughts to arms and sought alliance with kṣatriyas in marriage. Ṛcīka was a famous rishi.[4]

Thus Ṛcīka Aurva became skilled in archery.[5] He sought in marriage Satyavatī daughter of Gādhi or Gāthin, king of Kānyakubja. Gādhi did not relish his suit and tried to evade it by demanding a gift of a thousand peculiarly coloured horses, it is said, but Ṛcīka supplied them and gained her.[6] The genealogy says Ṛcīka had many sons, of whom Jamadagni was the eldest.[7] None of the others are named, but perhaps Ajīgarta was one, for his son Śunaḥśepa was a Bhārgava and was adopted by Viśvāmitra.[8] Jamadagni was trained to archery and arms,[9] and allied himself with the royal hou e of Ayodhyā, for he married Reṇukā daughter

[1] MBh xiii, *56*, 2905–7.

[2] Ūrva is also mentioned, Hv *46*, 2527; Pad v, *38*, 74.

[3] MBh i, *178*, 6815 to *180*, 6855: xiii, *56*, 2908–10.

[4] MBh iii, *115*, 11046, 11055: xii, *49*, 1721, 1731. Vā *91*, 66–8. Bd iii, *66*, 37–8. Br *10*, 29–30. Hv *27*, 1431–2. Viṣ iv, *7*, 5–6. Rām i, *61*, 16–17.

[5] MBh xiii, *56*, 2910. Cf. Rām i, *75*, 21–2. MBh xii, *234*, 8607 and xiii, *137*, 6267 say Dyutimant king of Śālva gave his kingdom to Ṛcīka.

[6] MBh iii, *115*, 11044–54: v, *118*, 4005–7: xii, *49*, 1721–2: xiii, *4*, 205–19; *56*, 2913–14. Rām i, *34*, 7. Also in Kānyakubja genealogies, p. 99.

[7] So also MBh i, *66*, 2611–13: iii, *115*, 11067: xii, *49*, 1744.

[8] See JRAS, 1917, pp. 58–61. Bd iii, *66*, 63–7. Vā *91*, 92–6. Br *10*, 64–6. Hv *27*, 1470–2; *32*, 1774. Br *10*, 53–4 and Hv *27*, 1456–7 wrongly make Śunaḥśepa son of Ṛcīka and younger brother of Jamadagni; and so alluded to in MBh xii, *294*, 10759. Viṣ iv, *7*, 17. Bhāg ix, *16*, 30, 32.

[9] MBh iii, *115*, 11069–70: xiii, *56*, 2910–12. Cf. Rām i, *75*, 22–3.

of Reṇu, a junior rājā of that line;[1] but he was a peaceful rishi and left martial exploits alone.[2]

Jamadagni had four[3] or five[4] sons, of whom Rāma was the youngest and greatest.[5] Rāma is always described as a great warrior, skilled in all weapons,[6] especially in archery.[7] Though a brahman, he is generally spoken of as virtually a kṣatriya,[8] combining the two characters, *brahma-kṣatra.*[9] The battle-axe is mentioned as his special weapon,[10] whence he is sometimes called Paraśu-Rāma[11] in later writings, to distinguish him from Rāma of Ayodhyā, who is then called Rāmacandra.[12]

These Aurvas lived in Madhyadeśa where they had fled and married,[13] and the Haihaya king Arjuna Kārtavīrya is said in his conquests there to have molested Jamadagni. There was hostility, and Arjuna's sons killed Jamadagni. Rāma in revenge killed Arjuna and also, it is said, many Haihayas (p. 151). The Haihayas pursued their devastating raids through N. India, until Sagara annihilated their power (p. 156). The brahmans confused all these occurrences in the fable that Rāma destroyed all kṣatriyas off the

[1] MBh iii, *99*, 8658; *116*, 11072–3: v, *116*, 3972. See Kānyakubja genealogies, p. 99. Alluded to, Pad vi, *268*, 8, 73–4; *269*, 158. That was about the time of Satyavrata Triśaṅku's exile; see p. 59 and JRAS, 1913, pp. 885–900. Fable, MBh xiii, *95*; *96*.

[2] MBh iii, *116*, 11071: xii, *49*, 1744: xiii, *56*, 2912.

[3] MBh i, *66*, 2612.

[4] MBh iii, *116*, 11074, 11080, where their names are given in a fable of Rāma's killing his mother.

[5] Bḍ iii, *21* to *47*, 62, a long brahmanical fable about him.

[6] MBh i, *66*, 2613: iii, *116*, 11088: vii, *70*, 2427. Ag *4*, 13.

[7] Vā *91*, 91. Bḍ iii, *66*, 62–3. Br *10*, 52–3. Hv *27*, 1455.

[8] Hence perhaps he does not appear in the *Vedic Index*.

[9] So genealogy: also Vā *65*, 94: Bḍ iii, *1*, 98. *Brāhmaṇaṁ kṣatra-dharmāṇam*, MBh xiii, *56*, 2914. Why Jamadagni's uncle, the kṣatriya Viśvāmitra, became a brahman, and Jamadagni's son Rāma became virtually a terrible kṣatriya, was explained by a fable about two *carus* given to Jamadagni's and Viśvāmitra's mothers; MBh iii, *115*, 11055–67: xii, *49*, 1722–44: xiii, *4*, 220–46: and the Kānyakubja genealogies (p. 99): noticed, MBh xiii, *56*, 2914–17.

[10] MBh i, *104*, 4172: vii, *70*, 2434: xii, *49*, 1748–9: xiii, *14*, 864. Hv *42*, 2316; *96*, 5302–4. Br *213*, 116. Ag *4*, 17.

[11] Bḍ iii, *37*, 15. Viṣ iv, 7, 16; *11*, 7. Vedārth on Rigv i, *65*.

[12] Pad iv, *17*, 14, 65: vi, *143*, 4; *281*, 25.

[13] Jamadagni lived on the Ganges' bank, Pad vi, *268*, 21. Bḍ iii, *26*, 42–3; *45*, 1–5 say on the R. Narmadā, a late brahmanical tale probably.

earth twenty-one times.[1] Consequently he is often styled the exterminator of the kṣatriyas.[2] But tradition, while apparently accepting that fable, redressed the honour of the kṣatriyas by two anachronistic fables, that Rāma challenged Rāma of Ayodhyā to fight and was defeated, and that he had a long contest with Bhīṣma also and was worsted (p. 72).

It is fabled that Rāma, after exterminating the kṣatriyas, sacrificed at Rāma-tīrtha with Kaśyapa as his upādhyāya and gave him the earth (or a golden altar) as his fee: whereupon Kaśyapa banished him to the southern ocean, and the ocean made the Śūrpāraka country (near Bombay) for Rāma, and Rāma dwelt there.[3] Other stories say Rāma retired then to Mt. Mahendra,[4] which is generally identified with the Mahendra range in Orissa: and he is fabled to have lived on there till long ages later.[5] He is also fictitiously introduced into tales about later princes (e. g. pp. 67, 72).

The next Bhārgava rishi mentioned is the Aurva who succoured Sagara of Ayodhyā[6] and whose name was Agni.[7] He is the last Aurva alluded to.

About the same time lived king Vītahavya (or Vītihotra, p. 155), whom a Bhṛgu rishi saved from Pratardana of Kāśi by impliedly asserting that he was a brahman, and who consequently became

[1] MBh i, *61*, 2459–64; *104*, 4172–6: iii, *115*, 11033–8; *116*, 11089 to *117*, 10204: xii, *48*, 1706; *49*, 1750–78; *362*, 13879: xiii, *14*, 866: xiv, *29*, 817–34. Pad vi, *268*, 23–76. Br *213*, 114–18. Ag *4*, 12–19; Hv *42*, 2317. Cf. MBh i, *66*, 2613; *167*, 6382; *188*, 7047. Explained in chap. XXIV.

[2] e. g. MBh i, *66*, 2613: vii, *70*, 2429–39: xii, *49*, 1747, 1768–78.

[3] MBh iii, *85*, 8185 (cf. *88*, 8337): vii, *70*, 2440–7: ix, *50*, 2835–8: xii, *49*, 1778–82: *234*, 8600: xiii, *62*, 3136. Cf. Br *213*, 119; Hv *42*, 2318–20; Pad vi, *268*, 77. MBh iii, *117*, 10204–10, which says the tīrtha is in Samantapañcaka, on the R. Sarasvatī (ix, *38*, 2163; *45*, 2501: Mat *7*, 3) in Kurukṣetra (MBh i, *1*, 12–13: ix, *54*, 3008). Cf. MBh xiii, *14*, 865–6; *84*, 3960–2; *137*, 6256: xiv, *29*, 824–34: differently xiii, *85*, 4183; *86*, 4220.

[4] MBh iii, *99*, 8681–2; *85*, 8158; *117*, 10209: v, *187*, 7338: vii, *70*, 2447: xii, *2*, 59. Ag *4*, 19–20. Br *213*, 122. Hv *42*, 2322. Pad i, *39*, 14. Bḍ iii, *47*, 39–62.

[5] MBh i, *130*, 5118–20: iii, *99*, 8681–12; *117*, 10211–13: v, *176*, 6054: xii, *2*, 59 to *3*, 107. Hv *42*, 2321–2. See p. 152, note [2].

[6] Rām wrongly calls him Cyavana, see *ante*. P. 153.

[7] Mat *12*, 40. Pad v, *8*, 144. Lg i, *66*, 15. Kūr i, *21*, 5. VN *7*, 60; *8*, 8, 9. JRAS, 1919, pp. 364–5.

a brahman.[1] His descendants are set out for fifteen generations. His son was Gṛtsamada, whose eleventh descendant was Pramati, whose son was Ruru, whose son was Śunaka, from whom came the Śaunakas.[2] It is not said which family he was adopted into, but it was the Bhārgavas, because the last portion of that genealogy, with all the preceding ancestry omitted, is given in an account which makes Pramati to be son of Cyavana,[3] and because Vītihavya, Gṛtsamada and the Śaunakas are named in the Bhārgava vaṁśa.[4] It is however said elsewhere that a Śunaka and the Śaunakas were descended from a Gṛtsamada, a son of Sunahotra, son of Kṣatravṛddha, who founded the Kāśi dynasty [5] (p. 86). Both these stories make a Gṛtsamada ancestor of the Śaunakas. On the other hand, it is said there was a Gṛtsamada, who was son of Śunahotra by birth, was (or became) an Āṅgirasa, and afterwards became a Bhārgava of the Śaunaka gotra.[6] It is said in the first story that Vītahavya's son Gṛtsamada is mentioned in the Rigveda,[7] but this is inconsistent, because the above comment on the Rigveda means that the Śaunakas were a Bhārgava gotra before this Gṛtsamada's time, and he became virtually a descendant of Śunaka by the adoption into the Śaunakas. It appears that there were two Gṛtsamadas and two Śunakas, and therefore two Śaunaka gotras; and the others will be found among the kṣatriyan brahmans in chapter XXIII; hence there were numberless 'Śaunakas'.

The only Śaunaka of importance with a personal name was Indrota, who is called Daivāpa in Vedic literature, that is, son of Devāpi Śaunaka. The story about him has been narrated above (p. 114) and fixes his time as that of Janamejaya II Pārikṣita. A Śaunaka was the chief of the rishis at the great sacrifice in Naimiṣa forest, to whom it is said the Mahābhārata [8] was recited, and also the Matsya and other Puranas,[9] in the reign of Adhisīmakṛṣṇa (p. 52).

[1] MBh xiii, *30,* 1983–96.

[2] *Ibid.* 1997–2006.

[3] MBh i, *5,* 870–3; *8,* 939–40. Hence Pramati is wrongly introduced at the earliest time in Mārk *114,* 29 f.

[4] Mat *195,* 18, 36, 39, 44–5. 'Śaunaka' is often mentioned, e.g. MBh i, *1,* 2; Mat *1,* 5; Pad v, *1,* 11.

[5] Vā *92,* 2–4. Bd iii, *67,* 2–4. Br *11,* 31–3. Hv *29,* 1517–19.

[6] Anukramaṇī, introduction to Rigv ii, and Vedārth *id.* and on ix, *86.*

[7] MBh xiii, *30,* 1997–9.

[8] MBh i, *1,* 2.

[9] Mat *1,* 5. Hv *1,* 11.

Another Bhārgava was Vālmīki of the Rāmāyaṇa,[1] called Prācetasa.[2] Other Bhārgavas are named in Janamejaya III's time.[3]

The genealogy also says that many outsiders among other rishis were known as Bhārgavas,[4] and such were the following who are named by the Matsya, Maudgalāyana, Sāṅkṛtya, Gārgyāyaṇa and Gārgīya, Kapi, Maitreya, Vadhryaśva and Divodāsa.[5] All these were 'kṣatriyan brahmans' (chapter XXIII). The Matsya account says in conclusion, 'These noble men who have been mentioned, born in the Bhṛgu vaṁśa, were founders of royal gotras.'

The genealogy says there were seven *pakṣas* or groups among the Bhārgavas, named Vatsa, Bida, Ārṣṭiṣeṇa, Yaska, Vainya or Pathya, Śaunaka and Mitreyu,[6] and the Matsya list mentions them all [7] except Vainya or Pathya, but Pathya is obviously a mistake for Pṛthya, and Vainya and Pṛthya are the same, viz. those who claimed descent from Pṛthu son of Vena, for Vainya Pṛthu is included in a list of eighteen Bhārgava hymn-makers,[8] and appears as Venya Pṛthī in Ṛigveda x, *148*, 5. That list names Bida,[9] Ārṣṭiṣeṇa and Śaunaka also and fourteen others.

Among the Bhārgavas were also the Mārkaṇḍeyas,[10] and Mārkaṇḍa is mentioned as a gotra-founder among the Bhārgavas,[11] but there is no mention of them in the genealogy. Mārkaṇḍeya is a patronymic from Mārkaṇḍa,[12] and these are sometimes treated as equivalent terms.[13] 'Mārkaṇḍeya' is a vague and elusive

[1] A late Vālmīki perhaps composed the Rāmāyaṇa, and then was identified with the Vālmīki of Rāma's time.

[2] Rām vii, *93*, 16, 18 ; *94*, 25. Mat *12*, 51. Pad v, *8*, 155. MBh xii, *57*, 2086.

[3] MBh i, *53*, 2045, 2049 : xiii, *40*, 2262, 2268, 2300.

[4] Ṛṣy-antareṣu vai bāhyā bahavo Bhārgavāḥ smṛtāḥ. The words *vai bāhyāḥ* might be also read as *vaivāhyāḥ*, and the meaning would also be true but jejune. So the Mat account notices certain gotras as *paras-param avaivāhya* (*195*, 32, 36, 40, 42, 45).

[5] Mat *195*, 22–3, 33, 38, 40, 42.

[6] Vā corrupts the names.

[7] Mat *195*, 17, 18, 30, 34–6, 40.

[8] Vā *59*, 96–7. Bḍ ii, *32*, 104–6. Mat *145*, 98–100. These reckon him as two persons.

[9] Mentioned, Bḍ ii, *33*, 15.

[10] Called Bhārgava, MBh iii, *183*, 12617 ; *188*, 12902 ; *190*, 13010 : &c. Born in Bhṛgu's line, Var *15*, 4. Pad v, *28* professes to give the origin of Mārkaṇḍeya.

[11] Mat *195*, 20.

[12] Mentioned, Pad v, *28*, 61 ; *29*, 19. Not in *Vedic Index*.

[13] Mat *103*, 13–15. Pad i, *40*, 15, 27–34.

figure, often mentioned as a distinguished rishi and introduced at various times and with reference to various places.[1] There was of course a family of Mārkaṇḍeyas, yet 'Mārkaṇḍeya' is regarded sometimes as only one rishi who was long-lived.[2] He appears always without any personal name or definite connexion. Though a Bhārgava, 'Mārkaṇḍeya' always stands rather apart, and there is no real explanation, as far as I know, how the Mārkaṇḍeyas arose. Mārkaṇḍeya is said to have been a son of a rishi Mṛkaṇḍa or Mṛkaṇḍu,[3] but they are placed in the Svāyambhuva manvantara,[4] which is irrelevant here. It seems probable that Mārkaṇḍa is to be connected with Marka,[5] son of Uśanas-Śukra. All Śukra's descendants by holding to non-Aryan tribes disappeared, except Śaṇḍa and Marka as mentioned above; and if so, the descendants of Marka would have obtained a permanent position among the Aryans, and may have been the Mārkaṇḍeyas.

CHAPTER XVIII

THE VASIṢṬHAS

THE Vasiṣṭha family was connected with the kings of Ayodhyā from the earliest times and the Vasiṣṭhas were their hereditary priests.[6] Thus a Vasiṣṭha is mentioned in connexion with Ikṣvāku and his son Vikukṣi-Śaśāda,[7] and with Ikṣvāku's son Nimi the first king of Videha; but these particular allusions may be mythical and the fable about Nimi and Vasiṣṭha will be noticed *infra*. Many Vasiṣṭhas can be distinguished in tradition, but they have been sadly confused in brahmanic stories through the habit of

[1] e. g. MBh iii, *84*, 8058–9; *88*, 8329–30; *183*, 12597–8.

[2] MBh iii, *183*, 12598–9: Pad v, *28*, 22, 24; vi, *236*, 3, 92: which say he is immortal. Cf. MBh iii, *25*, 952–3.

[3] Pad v, *28*, 3 f.; vi, *236*, 1–2, 18. Ag *20*, 10. Mentioned, Vā *41*, 44; Pad vi, *263*, 27.

[4] Vā *28*, 5. Bḍ ii, *11*, 7. Viṣ i, *10*, 4. Mārk *52*, 16.

[5] *Marka* + the rare affix *aṇḍa*; Whitney's Grammar, § 1201. The affix has been found in an inscription, *Indian Antiquary*, 1910, p. 212. *Mṛkaṇḍa* is a name invented.

[6] Bḍ iii, *48*, 29. Viṣ iv, *3*, 18. Pad vi, *219*, 44; *237*, 1. MBh i, *174*, 6642.

[7] Vā *88*, 14, 19, 21. Bḍ iii, *63*, 15, 20, 22.

referring to them only by their gotra name Vasiṣṭha. It is rare to find any Vasiṣṭha mentioned by his personal name until we reach Śakti, and the confusion may be illustrated in two ways. First, the epithet of the primaeval mythical Vasiṣṭha, 'Brahmā's son', is applied to the fifth [1] of the Vasiṣṭhas distinguished here, and also to the fourth and seventh confused; [2] and similarly Arundhatī [3] is the name of the wife of the mythical Vasiṣṭha and also of the fourth Vasiṣṭha,[4] of the fifth,[5] and of the seventh.[6] Secondly the confusion went so far that it was declared that one Vasiṣṭha had been priest to many generations of Aikṣvākus,[7] and finally that there was only one great Vasiṣṭha who had lived through all the ages.[8]

Consequently the framing of the Vasiṣṭha genealogy became perplexing and difficult; still a vaṁśa was constructed. The Vāyu, Brahmāṇḍa and Liṅga [9] give a common version with minor variations. The Kūrma gives a short and different version, which hardly merits notice. The Matsya has a full list of the rishis and gotras without any pedigree except the piece from 'Vasiṣṭha' to Dvaipāyana (Vyāsa).[10] Collating the first three texts, the version appended seems most probable,[11] omitting the first nine lines which refer to

[1] Raghuv i, 64, 93. Pad vi, *199*, 32 ; *219*, 38. [2] Lg i; *64*, 8, 37.

[3] MBh i, *233*, 8456–7. Others which are vague, MBh i, *199*, 7352 : iii, *113*, 10092 : &c. Mat *187*, 45. Rām v, *24*, 10.

[4] Lg. i, *64*, 5, 14, 16, &c.

[5] Raghuv i, 56–7 ; ii, 71. Pad vi, *198*, 25.

[6] Mat *201*, 30 ; and genealogy following. MBh i, *174*, 6638 f. is confused.

[7] Bd iii, *48*, 35.

[8] MBh i, *174*, 6638–45. Cf. *sanātana*, xiii, *78*, 3733.

[9] Vā *70*, 79–90. Bd iii, *8*, 86–100. Lg i, *63*, 78–92.

[10] Kūr i, *19*, 20–7. Mat *200* and *201*.

[11] Arundhatyāṁ Vasiṣṭhas tu Śaktim utpādayat sutam *
Sāgaraṁ † janayac Chakter Adṛśyantī Parāśaram
Kālī Parāśarāj jajñe Kṛṣṇaṁ Dvaipāyanaṁ prabhum
Dvaipāyanād Araṇyāṁ vai Śuko jajñe guṇânvitaḥ
utpadyante ca Pīvaryāṁ ṣaḍ ime Śuka-sūnavaḥ
Bhūriśravāḥ Prabhuḥ Śambhuḥ Kṛṣṇo Gaurāś ca pañcamaḥ
kanyā Kīrtimatī caiva yoga-mātā dhṛta-vratā
jananī Brahmadattasya patnī sā tv Aṇuhasya ca
Śvetāḥ Kṛṣṇāś ca Gaurāś ca Śyāmā Dhūmrāḥ sa-mūlikāḥ

* So also Kūr i, *19*; 23. Lg *sutam utpādayac chatam*.

† So Vā. Bd *Svāgajaṁ*. Lg *jyāyaso*.

the mythical Vasiṣṭha. The genealogy consists of three distinct sections, lines 1–11, 12–16 and 17–18, which seemingly start from one and the same Vasiṣṭha but really give separate disconnected pedigrees as will appear. It is not accurate, but may supplement information derived from elsewhere; and the only safe course is to distinguish the several Vasiṣṭhas in connexion with the kings with whom they were associated, and if possible to fix the distinction by names or by appellations that are applied to them and that may be personal names or may reasonably be utilized as such.

The earliest Vasiṣṭha who has a definite position was the famous priest of Ayodhyā in the reigns of Trayyāruṇa, Satyavrata-Triśaṅku and Hariścandra, whose story has been alluded to (p. 151), and may be narrated here.[1]

Satyavrata was banished by his father Trayyāruṇa and was kept in exile by Vasiṣṭha, who held the kingdom on Trayyāruṇa's departure. Then occurred a famine for twelve years. At that time Viśvaratha was king of Kānyakubja, but relinquished his kingdom, gave himself up to austerities,[2] became a brahman and took the name Viśvāmitra. He championed Satyavrata's cause, and overcoming Vasiṣṭha's opposition restored him to the throne. Satyavrata appointed Viśvāmitra the royal priest. Vasiṣṭha, thus

Ūṣmādā Dārikāś * caiva Nīlāś caiva Parāśarāḥ
Parāśarāṇām aṣṭau te pakṣāḥ proktā mahātmanām
ata ūrdhvaṁ nibodhadhvam Indrapramati-sambhavam
Vasiṣṭhasya Kapiñjalyāṁ Ghṛtācyām udapadyata
Kuṇīti † yaḥ samākhyāta Indrapramatir ucyate
Pṛthoḥ sutāyāṁ sambhūtaḥ putras tasyâbhavad Vasuḥ
Upamanyuḥ sutas tasya yasyême hy Aupamanyavaḥ
Mitrāvaruṇayoś caiva Kuṇḍino ye ‡ pariśrutāḥ
ekârṣeyās tathā cânye Vasiṣṭhā nāma viśrutāḥ
ete pakṣā Vasiṣṭhānāṁ smṛtā ekādaśaiva tu.

* Some Vā, *Ūṣmapā Dārakāś*. Lg *Nīlo Bādarikaś*. The correct reading may be *Ūṣmā Bādarikāś*?

† Some Vā *Kuśīti*. There was a Kuśīti much later, see chap. XXVII. A Kuṇi mentioned, Hv *268*, 14538.

‡ Bḍ *Kuṇḍineyāḥ*. Lg *Kauṇḍinyā ye*.

[1] For the references, see p. 151 note [2]. Brahmanic versions (fables), MBh i, *175*: ix, *41*, 2296–2314: but differently, v, *105*, 3720–31; Rām i, *51*, 16 to *60*, 34. Fully discussed, JRAS, 1913, pp. 888–900: 1917, pp. 37–40.

[2] The references in p. 151, note [2] say 'in low lands near the sea', *sāgarânūpe*; but MBh ix, *40*, 2273–9, 2283; *41*, 2307, 2313 say at Ruṣaṅgu's tīrtha on the R. Sarasvatī. The two might agree, if the sea then encroached on the Rajputana desert; see note in chap. XXV.

deprived of the kingdom and the priesthood, bore deadly enmity against Viśvāmitra, and sought revenge by denying his brahmanhood. Vasiṣṭha's personal name was Devarāj.

The story goes on thus.[1] On Satyavrata's death his son Hariścandra was placed on the throne by Viśvāmitra, and Viśvāmitra offered the rājasūya sacrifice for him. But Vasiṣṭha's hatred and opposition led to Viśvāmitra's being obliged to depart, and he went to Puṣkara and gave himself up to austerities there.[2] Vasiṣṭha thus regained the priesthood. Hariścandra then begot a son Rohita, whom he had vowed to sacrifice to Varuṇa, but put off fulfilment for some twenty-two years, and then Rohita saved himself by buying the rishi Ajīgarta's son Śunaḥśepa as a victim in his own stead. Śunaḥśepa was a Bhārgava and appears to have been Viśvāmitra's grand-nephew, and, when the sacrifice was due, Viśvāmitra took part in it (his brahmanhood being now acknowledged), it was turned into a formal rite, and Śunaḥśepa was set free. Śunaḥśepa, having lost his position in his own family by the sale, was adopted by Viśvāmitra as his son with the name Devarāta.[3]

About the same time, according to tradition and the same synchronisms, lived Āpava Vasiṣṭha, whose hermitage near the Himalayas Arjuna Kārtavīrya burnt and who cursed him.[4] Āpava appears to be a patronymic, for he is called 'son of Varuṇa', Vāruṇi,[5] and *āpu* is supposed to be equivalent to *Varuṇa.*

The next great Vasiṣṭha was priest of Ayodhyā in the time of Hariścandra's eighth successor, Bāhu, whose position has been established above (p. 155). Bāhu was driven from his throne by the Haihaya-Tālajaṅghas aided by Śakas, Kāmbojas, Yavanas, Pāradas and Pahlavas from the north-west, but Vasiṣṭha maintained his position. Afterwards Bāhu's son Sagara conquered all those

[1] Aitar Brāhm vii, *3*, 1 f. Śāṅkhāyana Śr Sūtra xv, 17–25. Vedārth on Rigv i, *24*. Br *104*, Bhāg ix, *7*, 7–27. MBh xiii, *3*, 186–7. Brahmanic version (fable), Rām i, *61*, 5 to *62*, 27. Fully discussed in JRAS, 1917, pp. 40–67.

[2] It is this period of austerities probably that has been so magnified in the brahmanic versions.

[3] Also Viṣ iv, *7*, 17: Bhāg ix, *16*, 30–2. P. 198.

[4] Vā *94*, 39–47; *95*, 10–13. Bd iii, *69*, 39–47; *70*, 9–14. Mat *43*, 41; *44*, 12–14. Br *13*, 189–94. Hv *33*, 1884–8. MBh xii, *49*, 1753–8. Mat *68*, 9, erroneously calls him Cyavana. MBh i, *99*, 3924–5 wrongly places the hermitage near Mt. Meru.

[5] Vā *94*, 42–3. Bd iii, *69*, 42–4. MBh i, *99*, 3924–6.

foes, regained the kingdom and determined to exterminate those tribes, which had meanwhile settled down in his territories, but Vasiṣṭha interposed and made him spare them.[1] This Vasiṣṭha is called Āpava[2] and Atharvanidhi,[3] and these may be taken as a name to distinguish him, Atharvanidhi I Āpava, from Atharvanidhi II who will be mentioned soon. He is confused with Devarāj Vasiṣṭha in brahmanical tales, and thus his connexion with the Śakas and other tribes led to the absurd detail in the fables about the contest between Vasiṣṭha and Viśvāmitra, that Vasiṣṭha's cow created all those and other tribes to fight against Viśvāmitra.[4]

The fourth noted Vasiṣṭha was priest to Mitrasaha Kalmāṣapāda Saudāsa, king of Ayodhyā; the fifth was priest to Dilīpa II Khaṭvāṅga; the sixth was priest to Daśaratha and his son Rāma; and the seventh was priest to Paijavana Sudās (Sudāsa), king of N. Pañcāla (p. 116). The fifth is sometimes introduced as having instructed Dilīpa,[5] and they are the dramatis personae in the first three cantos of the Raghuvaṁśa,[6] where (i, 59) the epithet Atharvanidhi is given him. This may be taken as a name for him, and he may therefore be known as Atharvanidhi II, to distinguish him from the third Vasiṣṭha. The sixth holds a prominent position in the Rāmāyaṇa, but no special personal epithet seems to be applied to him.

The common name Vasiṣṭha, and the similarity in the names of their royal patrons, led to the fourth and the seventh Vasiṣṭhas being somewhat confused. A Vasiṣṭha had a son Śakti,[7] who had a son Parāśara, as the genealogy says; he was one of these two Vasiṣṭhas, and, as some of the stories confuse them, it is necessary to discuss and distinguish them.

As regards the fourth Vasiṣṭha the simplest story is this.[8] The

[1] All fully discussed in JRAS, 1919, pp. 353–63.

[2] Bd iii, *49*, 43.

[3] VN *8*, 63. JRAS, 1919, pp. 362–3.

[4] Rām i, *54*, 18 to *55*, 3. MBh i, *175*, 6683–6: ix, *41*, 2304–5: xiii, *78*, 3732–3. JRAS, 1919, p. 364.

[5] e. g. Pad vi, *220*, 1–2.

[6] The story is also told in Pad vi, *197*, 98 to *199*, 65. One has copied from the other apparently.

[7] MBh xii, *351*, 13642; and Vedārth on Rigv i, *65*, which quotes the former's verse as from 'Puranas'. Śakti is often called Śaktri in the Epic and Puranas.

[8] Viṣ iv, *4*, 20–38. Bhāg ix, *9*, 18–39. Also Rām vii, *65*. VN *9*, 3–151 similarly as far as the killing of the brahman.

king Kalmāṣapāda Saudāsa beguiled by a Rākṣasa, offered Vasiṣṭha human flesh as food and was cursed by him. He then became a Rākṣasa and cannibal,[1] and killed and devoured a brahman, but after twelve years regained his sanity. At his desire Vasiṣṭha begot a son Aśmaka of the queen Madayantī.[2]

As regards Sudās and his priest Vasiṣṭha the simplest story is in two parts. One[3] is that, at a great sacrifice by Sudās, Viśvāmitra was overcome by Śakti, but the Jāmadagnyas gave him speech and succoured the Kuśikas. The other[4] is that Śakti went to the forest, the king's servants who were under Viśvāmitra's bidding cast him into a forest fire, and Vasiṣṭha on learning of Śakti's fate restrained his grief.[5]

Next come the stories that introduce confusion. The Bṛhaddevatā says Vasiṣṭha Vāruṇi's hundred sons were slain by the Saudāsas, or by Sudāsa who in consequence of a curse had been transformed into a Rakṣas.[6] The Liṅga says that a Rākṣasa instigated by Viśvāmitra possessed king Kalmāṣapāda Saudāsa and in consequence of Śakti's curse devoured Śakti and all Vasiṣṭha's hundred sons; and Śakti's widow Adṛśyantī bore Parāśara afterwards.[7] The Mahābhārata amplifies the tale greatly.[8] Kalmāṣapāda had a dispute with Śakti and struck him and was cursed by him. Viśvāmitra, who coveted Vasiṣṭha's position, caused a Rākṣasa to possess the king, and the king then offered human flesh as food to an indigent brahman and was cursed by him. The king became a Rākṣasa,[9] a cannibal[10] maniac, and killed Śakti and all Vasiṣṭha's hundred sons.[11] Vasiṣṭha without seeking revenge tried to destroy himself, but in vain, and Śakti's widow Adṛśyantī then bore Parāśara. After twelve years Vasiṣṭha cured the king and they were reconciled. Vasiṣṭha then begot Aśmaka of the queen

[1] Alluded to, MBh xiii, *6*, 326: xiv, *56*, 1656.
[2] Wife of Saudāsa, Rām v, *24*, 12.
[3] Bṛhadd iv, 112–15. Vedārth on Rigv iii, *53*.
[4] Anukramaṇī and Vedārth on Rigv vii, *32*.
[5] I know of no allusions to these two stories in the Puranas.
[6] Bṛhadd vi, 28 (Saudāsas), 33–4 (Sudāsa), on Rigv vii, *104*.
[7] Lg i, *63*, 83; *64*, 2–47.
[8] MBh i, *176* and *177*; *182*, 6891–6912. Alluded to, *id.* xiii, *78*, 3732–5: Vā *1*, 175–7; *2*, 10–11: Bḍ i, *2*, 10–11.
[9] Alluded to, Pad vi, *132*, 11–12.
[10] Alluded to, MBh iii, *207*, 13817–18.
[11] Attributed to Viśvāmitra, MBh xiii, *3*, 183: i, *174*, 6640–1.

Madayantī.[1] Manu says 'Vasiṣṭha swore an oath to Paijavana', and the commentators explain (turning the story round) that before king Sudās Viśvāmitra accused Vasiṣṭha of being a Rakṣas or Yātudhāna and eating his (the king's) hundred sons, and Vasiṣṭha took an oath denying the charge.[2]

This last story may be mistaken, but it is unnecessary to examine the differences in all these stories, because the material question here concerns Vasiṣṭha's son Śakti, whether he was killed by Kalmāṣapāda Saudāsa, or by Sudās (or his people, the Saudāsas), for both cannot be true and the two kings were apart in time (pp. 147–8).

There is one certain fact, Parāśara, Śatayātu and 'Vasiṣṭha' were contemporaries of Sudās Paijavana.[3] That Parāśara was Śakti's son is well attested;[4] and also that Śakti was killed;[5] and it is said his widow Adṛśyantī bore Parāśara after his death,[6] a statement that appears true, and otherwise there is no reason why it should have been made in the above stories, and it finds some support from the above Rigvedic passage which omits Śakti. Śatayātu then could not be Śakti and was probably another son of Vasiṣṭha.[7] Thus Śakti lived in the time of Sudās of N. Pañcāla and not in that of Kalmāṣapāda Saudāsa of Ayodhyā; hence he has been wrongly introduced into the story of the latter king. It seems then most probable, that Kalmāṣapāda in his madness killed the sons of his priest 'Vasiṣṭha', and that Śakti alone, the son of Sudās's priest 'Vasiṣṭha', was killed in Sudās's reign. The Bṛhaddevatā has kept the two occurrences distinct in the passages cited above, but otherwise they have been confused, and the Mahābhārata and Liṅga, which know nothing of Sudās, have combined both

[1] Alluded to, MBh i, *122*, 4736–7: xii, *234*, 8604: xiii, *137*, 6262. Also Vā *88*, 177; Bd iii, *63*, 177; Kūr i, *21*, 12–13.

[2] Manu viii, 110. Cited Nārada i, 243.

[3] Rigv vii, *18*, 21–22. 'Vasiṣṭha' is connected with him and consecrated him; Aitar Brāhm vii, 5, 34; viii, 4, 21.

[4] Anukramaṇī and Vedārth on Rigv i, *65*. MBh i, *181*, 6885 (*Śāktra*), 6866 (*Śāktreya*): xii, *351*, 13642: &c.

[5] See references above.

[6] MBh and Lg accounts above. Implied in Vā *1*, 175 (read *Adṛśyantyām*); cf. *id*. *2*, 12. She is named, MBh v, *116*, 3970.

[7] So Geldner suggested: *Vedic Index* ii, 352.

occurrences into one story and transferred the whole of it to Kalmāṣapāda Saudāsa.[1]

We may endeavour to distinguish these two Vasiṣṭhas further as regards their personal names. Kalmāṣapāda's Vasiṣṭha is called *brahma-kośa*,[2] and twice *śreṣṭha-bhāj*.[3] Either word might be an epithet or name. The former word appears to be an epithet, 'treasury of sacred lore,' because it is joined with other epithets,[4] and is applied to other rishis also.[5] *Śreṣṭhabhāj* is rare, and as an adjective, 'sharing in or possessing the best,'[6] has no obvious fitness in its context, where it would be quite appropriate as a name; and it is not given to any other rishi as far as I am aware. It may, then, be reasonably taken as a name, and Kalmāṣapāda's Vasiṣṭha may be distinguished as Śreṣṭhabhāj.

Sudās's Vasiṣṭha is not alluded to in Puranic tradition, but is mentioned in three stories in the epic, if he was the Vasiṣṭha who is connected with Saṁvaraṇa in them, namely, how Saṁvaraṇa was driven out of his kingdom of Hastināpura by a Pañcāla king (who was Sudās) and after obtaining 'Vasiṣṭha's' aid recovered his kingdom;[7] how afterwards 'Vasiṣṭha' obtained Tapatī as wife for Saṁvaraṇa; and how afterwards again 'Vasiṣṭha' governed the kingdom during twelve years of drought when Saṁvaraṇa was absent.[8] No special epithet is applied to Vasiṣṭha in the latter two stories,[9] but in the first he is called Suvarcas.[10] This was a name, not uncommon,[11] hence it may reasonably be taken here also as a name, and Saṁvaraṇa's Vasiṣṭha at that time may be distin-

1 So also Vā *1*, 175. Also MBh xii, *49*, 1792–3 (which is brahmanical), wrongly making Parāśara preserve (Kalmāṣapāda-) Saudāsa's son Sarvakarman (see p. 152) in Rāma Jāmadagnya's time, all three persons being widely apart in time.

2 MBh xiii, *78*, 3733, 3735.

3 MBh i, *177*, 6760, 6788.

4 *Siddha*, *sanātana*, and *gavām upaniṣad-vidvān*.

5 To Atri, Vā *64*, 27; Bd ii, *38*, 28. Cf. Vā *28*, 5; Bd ii, *11*, 6.

6 So in MBh xii, *343*, 13163, *pratibuddhas tu śreṣṭha-bhāk*. Sörensen does not give it. *Śreṣṭha-bhāgin* as an adjective, Vā *60*, 37; Bd ii, *34*, 40.

7 MBh i, *94*, 3725–37. P. 172. JRAS, 1918, pp. 245–8.

8 MBh i, *173*, 6618–30. P. 66. JRAS, 1917, pp. 38–9.

9 In MBh i, *173*, 6596, Calcutta edition, for *amitraghnaṁ* read *amitraghnas* as in the Bombay edition.

10 MBh i, *94*, 3733.

11 A king, MBh xiv, *4*, 72. A prince, i, *117*, 4549. A rishi, Mārk *99*, 11. See dictionary also.

guished as Vasiṣṭha Suvarcas. But Sudās's Vasiṣṭha was an old man in Sudās's reign, because his grandson Parāśara was old enough to take part in the hymn (vii, *18*). He might be the Vasiṣṭha in the first story, but can hardly have been the Vasiṣṭha of the second and third stories.

It seems more probable, however, that the same Vasiṣṭha is meant in the three stories, and in that case Saṁvaraṇa's Vasiṣṭha would not be the same as Sudās's Vasiṣṭha, but rather a son. If so, there is no name to be assigned to Sudās's Vasiṣṭha, and Saṁvaraṇa's Vasiṣṭha would have the name Suvarcas,[1] and would be the ninth 'Vasiṣṭha' of note, reckoning Śakti as the eighth. Till this time the Vasiṣṭhas had been almost exclusively connected with Ayodhyā or Videha,[2] and Sudās's Vasiṣṭha is the first who was definitely priest to an Aila king.[3] It may be suggested that the conquest of Śūrasena and Mathurā by Rāma's brother Śatrughna (p. 170), a little earlier than Sudās's reign, may have led some of the Vasiṣṭhas into other kingdoms. Afterwards the Vasiṣṭhas spread elsewhere, and various places were connected with 'Vasiṣṭha'.[4]

In these three rishis, 'Vasiṣṭha,' his son Śakti and his son Parāśara, occurs the first genuine pedigree[5] in the genealogy (lines 1, 2), the first part of the first section. It goes on to say that Parāśara was father of Kṛṣṇa Dvaipāyana, that is, Vyāsa, by Kālī. Now Vyāsa was certainly son of a Parāśara and Kālī, as will be noticed, but he was born in king Śantanu's reign and she became Santanu's queen. There was a long interval with many kings between Sudās (Sudāsa) of N. Pañcāla and Śantanu (p. 148), and it is impossible that Śakti's son Parāśara of Sudās's time[6] could have been Vyāsa's father. Vyāsa then was son of a Parāśara but not of Parāśara Śāktya. Hence there must have been two Parāśaras. This is not improbable (p. 130), and certain particulars support this conclusion.

[1] Probably priest to Saṁvaraṇa's son Kuru. MBh ix, *39*, 2211–13.

[2] They belonged to the 'east', so MBh v, *107*, 3773.

[3] Rantideva Sāṅkṛtya, who was earlier (p. 39), is said to have done honour to a 'Vasiṣṭha', MBh xiii, *137*, 6250: xii, *234*, 8591. In brahmanical fables 'Vasiṣṭha' is connected with king Nahuṣa the Aila erroneously, Pad ii, *108*; also as priest with Purūravas, Br *151*, 8, 10.

[4] e.g. MBh i, *215*, 7813–14: iii, *82*, 4097–8.

[5] Mat *201*, 30–31. Kūr i, *19*, 23.

[6] This Parāśara is said to have destroyed Rākṣasas, MBh i, *181*, 6866–85; Lg i, *64*, 107; Viṣ i, *1*, 4–34.

First, Parāśara (line 2) is called *Sāgara* or *Svāgaja*, and these two words are an instance of the importance of readings that appear unmeaning (p. 83). The Liṅga's reading *jyāyaso* throws no light on them, for it is obviously an 'emendation' to suit the alteration it has made in the preceding line, declaring that Śakti was the eldest of the hundred sons according to its confusion of the stories noticed above. *Svāgaja* suggests *svāgraja*, but the possible readings *svāgrajaṁ*, *svāgrajo* and *svāgrajāt* are untenable, if we consider the force of *sva*, the fact that Śakti had only one son Parāśara who was born after his death, and the consequent meaning of the sentence. *Sāgaram* or *Svāgajam* must therefore be an accusative agreeing with *Parāśaram*. Śakti's son was Parāśara Śāktya, hence the passage suggests that there was a Parāśara called *Sāgara* or *Svāgaja*, and that it has blended the two.

Secondly, the Anukramaṇī, in its mention of Parāśara as part author of hymn ix, *97*, seems conscious of a difference. It says that 'Vasiṣṭha' saw the first three verses, that the nine 'Vasiṣṭhas', Indrapramati, Vṛṣagaṇa, Manyu, Upamanyu, Vyāghrapad, Śakti, Karṇaśrut, Mṛlīka and Vasukra, each saw three more verses separately, and that Parāśara composed 14 and 'Kutsa' the rest. It thus knew that Śakti was a Vasiṣṭha, and also that he had a son Parāśara, for it attributes hymns i, *65* to *73* to Parāśara Śāktya, and so knew that Parāśara was a Vasiṣṭha. If then this Parāśara of ix, *97* was Śakti's son, it might naturally have called him Vasiṣṭha or Śāktya, yet it does not do so and leaves his name without particularization. This suggests that there might be a Parāśara other than Śāktya.[1] The Vedārthadīpikā on the same hymn tends to confirm this doubt, for it specifies 'Vasiṣṭha' as Maitrāvaruṇi, calls the nine others 'sons of Vasiṣṭha', yet makes no reference to Parāśara, who as author of 14 verses was more important than any of them, thus suggesting that it was not clear who this Parāśara was. Those nine Vasiṣṭhas were not all sons of one Vasiṣṭha, for Upamanyu was Indrapramati's grandson, as will appear, and the Vedārthadīpikā says they composed their verses all quite independently. The hymn therefore was not composed

[1] Rigv v, *29* is attributed to Gaurivīti Śāktya, but x, *73* and *74* simply to Gaurivīti by the Anukramaṇī, and it will appear among the Sāṅkṛtyas in chap. XXIII that there were probably two Gaurivītis: but the Vedārth ascribes the two latter hymns also to Śāktya.

at one time, but grew in the course of time, so that Parāśara's later 14 verses may well have been added by a second Parāśara.

There are reasonable grounds then, chronological and textual, for holding that there were two Parāśaras, and there is no improbability in this, for there were other Parāśaras later still; see chapter XXVII. The same names reappeared, as is proved by the fact that one of Kṛṣṇa Vyāsa's grandsons also was called Kṛṣṇa as the genealogy (lines 2–6) and other authorities that will be noticed say. To this later Parāśara,[1] who lived in Śantanu's time, we may fairly attach the epithet Sāgara or Svāgaja. Svāgaja is not grammatically a properly formed patronymic, but Sāgara is; hence we may prefer the latter and distinguish him as *Sāgara*, 'son of Sagara'.[2] The genealogy would then have blended the two Parāśaras,[3] just as it will now be shown to have confused two Śukas, yet its preservation of these two epithets has saved some trace of the distinction.

Next comes the second part of the first section. Kṛṣṇa Dvaipāyana Vyāsa[4] was the son of this later Parāśara by the fisher-maiden Kālī, who was called Satyavatī[5] and became king Śantanu's queen.[6] Vyāsa's wife was Araṇī, and their son was Śuka,[7] called Kārṣṇi,[8] Vaiyāsaki[9] and Āraṇeya.[10] Śuka's wife was Pīvarī, who appears to have been his half-sister, for the expression *pitṛ-kanyā* in her case could not mean 'daughter of the Pitṛs' (p. 69). They had five sons, and also, it is said, a daughter Kīrtimatī, and, if so, the genealogy is certainly wrong in making her Aṇuha's queen and Brahmadatta's mother, by confusing two Śukas as shown

[1] Pārāśarya Sārika (MBh ii, *4*, 108) was probably his descendant.

[2] Sagara was a real name, that of the famous king of Ayodhyā. A more curious case, Samudra father of Aśva, Śatapatha Brāhm xiii, 2, 2. 14.

[3] So also MBh i, *60*, 2209: xii, *351*, 13642–3: xiii, *24*, 1677. Viṣ iii, *3*, 18, 21; *4*, 2; vi, *2*, 6, 9, 10.

[4] He is called a Vasiṣṭha, Vā *1*, 10.

[5] MBh i, *60*, 2208–9; *63*, 2396 f.: &c. Pp. 69–70. Viṣ vi, *2*, 10.

[6] MBh i, *95*, 3801–2; *100*, 4011 to *101*, 4067: &c.

[7] MBh i, *1*, 103; *63*, 2418: xii, *231*, 8485: &c. *Id.* xii, *326*, 12187–97 in a brahmanical fable makes Śuka the son of Vyāsa through the *araṇī*. Lg i, *63*, 85 gives them a second son Upamanyu apparently erroneously, see *infra*.

[8] MBh xii, *327*, 12258; *328*, 12264.

[9] MBh xii, *231*, 8485. Bd ii, *33*, 14.

[10] MBh xii, *326*, 12207; *329*, 12339, 12342: &c.

above (p. 64). The five sons were Bhūriśravas,[1] Prabhu (or Pṛthu), Śambhu, Kṛṣṇa and Gaura.

The Matsya says that Parāśara's descendants composed six pravaras, sub-families, named Gaura, Nīla, Kṛṣṇa, Śveta, Śyāma and Dhūmra;[2] but the genealogy says they formed eight pakṣas, 'groups,' namely, six bearing those six names and two others, which the readings leave doubtful but of which one seems probably Bādarika.

The second section of the genealogy (lines 12–16) says that 'Vasiṣṭha' had by his wife Kapiñjalī Ghṛtācī a famous son Indrapramati,[3] well known as Kuṇin or Kuṇīti.[4] He married Pṛthu's daughter and had a son Vasu,[5] and Vasu had a son Upamanyu,[6] the progenitor of the Upamanyus or Aupamanyavas. Indrapramati was a well-known rishi,[7] and there were more than one rishi named Upamanyu, as will appear. These two and Śakti and six other Vasiṣṭhas, as mentioned above, each composed three verses of Rigveda ix, *97*, all independently, so that Upamanyu's contribution must have been some time after Indrapramati's, if the order of the rishis is chronological; and Indrapramati later than Maitrāvaruṇi Vasiṣṭha, if the opening verses were composed by the latter.[8]

The third section of the genealogy (lines 17–18) says that from Mitra and Varuṇa sprang the Vasiṣṭhas who were called Kuṇḍins, Kuṇḍineyas or Kauṇḍinyas.[9] This deals with the Vasiṣṭha who was called Maitrāvaruṇa[10] or Maitrāvaruṇi.[11] This name is

[1] Mentioned, Bḍ ii, *33*, 14.

[2] Mat *201*, 33–8, which gives the gotras in each sub-family.

[3] Also Vā *60*, 25, 27. Mat *200*, 13. There was a later Indrapramati, see chap. XXVII.

[4] Or *Kuśīti*; see the genealogy. Also a later Kuśīti, chap. XXVII.

[5] He may be Vasumant, who was famous, Vā *64*, 27: Bḍ ii, *38*, 29.

[6] Upamanyu occurs in Rigv i, *102*, 9.

[7] Mat *145*, 109–11; Vā *59*, 105–6; Bḍ ii, *32*, 115–16:

> Vasiṣṭhaś caiva Śaktiś ca tṛtīyaś ca Parāśaraḥ
> caturtha Indrapramatiḥ pañcamas tu Bharadvasuḥ
> ṣaṣṭhas tu Maitrāvaruṇaḥ * Kuṇḍinaḥ saptamas tathā
> ity ete sapta vijñeyā Vāsiṣṭhā brahma-vādinaḥ.

Where * Mat reads *Mitrāvaruṇaḥ*.

[8] So Vedārth on the hymn.

[9] A Kauṇḍinya, MBh ii, *4*, 111.

[10] Rigv vii, *33*, 11. Third note above.

[11] MBh i, *178*, 6801: ix, *43*, 2386: xii, *304*, 11222. Br *240*, 7. Bṛhadd v, 160. Vedārth on Rigv i, *166*, introduction to vii, and on ix, *97*.

acknowledged to be a patronymic and is taken to mean 'son of Mitra and Varuṇa', and is explained by a fable, that from them both, after they saw the apsaras Urvaśī, Vasiṣṭha was born in a jar and so was son of both, and Agastya also was so begotten and born at the same time.[1] The fable appears in Rigveda vii, *33*, but the statements there are hardly consistent or have blended different fancies, for verse 13 says both were so born in a jar together,[2] while verse 12 says that Vasiṣṭha was born of Urvaśī the apsaras.

The fable was obviously devised to explain the name Maitrāvaruṇa, and the hymn has combined that with another fable that 'Vasiṣṭha' (and not Agastya[3]) was born of Urvaśī in order to explain the metronymic *Aurvaśa* which was the name of a 'Vasiṣṭha'.[4] This view is supported by another fact, that a reason why 'Vasiṣṭha' was born from Mitra and Varuṇa was necessary and was supplied by another fable, often linked with the former. Nimi, the first king of Videha, and 'Vasiṣṭha' had a quarrel and cursed each other to become bodiless (*vi-deha*); [5] both then went to Brahmā and he assigned Nimi to the eyes of creatures, whence they wink (*nimeṣa*), and said Vasiṣṭha should be son of Mitra and Varuṇa with the name Vasiṣṭha.[6] This fable has manifestly been fabricated or modified to explain the name *Videha* and supply a reason for the birth from Mitra and Varuṇa.

The fable is impossible. *Maitrāvaruṇa* is a proper patronymic from *Mitrāvaruṇa*. The earliest rishis sometimes bore the names

[1] Sarvānukramaṇī and Vedārth on Rigv i, *166*. Nirukta v, 13. Mat *61*, 26–31, 36, 50; *201*, 23–9. Pad v, *22*, 29–34, 37–40. Viṣ iv, *5*, 6, Cf. MBh xiii, *158*, 7372. Differently, Rām vii, *56*, 12–23; *57*, 1–9. Vasiṣṭha's lawbook says this Vasiṣṭha was Śatayātu (xxx, 11; SBE xiv, p. 140)—chronologically impossible, see *ante*.

[2] Bṛhadd v, 149–56 develops this story with details and adds a third outcome of this production, namely, 'Matsya'.

[3] No Agastya is called *Aurvaśa*, as far as I know. *Aurvaśeya* is said to be a name of 'Agastya' by lexicographers.

[4] Bṛhadd ii, 37, 44, 156: iii, 56. Under *id.* ii, 37 Prof. Macdonell says hymns vii, *101* and *102* are ascribed to him.

[5] Mat *61*, 32–6; *201*, 1–17. Pad v, *22*, 34–7. Viṣ iv, *5*, 1–5. Vā *89*, 4. Bd iii, *64*, 4. Bhāg ix, *13*, 1–6. Rām vii, *55* to *56*, 11; *57*, 9–16.

[6] Mat *201*, 17–22 and Pad v, *22*, 37–40, where the signification of the name seems to be that offered by Bṛhadd v, 156, 'from the root *vas*, expressive of pre-eminence'. Bhāg ix, *13*, 6–11.

of gods (p. 131), and if they chose the double name of these two gods who are so often united, it would appear as Mitrāvaruṇa,[1] which does actually occur as the name of a Vasiṣṭha.[2]

The genealogy makes this Vasiṣṭha Maitrāvaruṇa ancestor only of the Kuṇḍins, or Kuṇḍinas as the name is more often given. This family obviously took its name from its ancestor, just like the Viśvāmitras, Kaṇvas and others. Hence he was Kuṇḍin, or Kuṇḍina, Maitrāvaruṇa, son of Mitrāvaruṇa. Kuṇḍina is named as a Vasiṣṭha twice and mentioned along with Mitrāvaruṇa,[3] and both (p. 214) were Vasiṣṭhas who were *brahma-vādins*. Kuṇḍina would naturally be connected with *kuṇḍin*, 'having a pitcher,' and Maitrāvaruṇa was taken to mean 'son of Mitra and Varuṇa'; thus these two names reveal at once how the above fables were fabricated by way of folk etymology.

The fable about Vasiṣṭha and Agastya is very ancient, because it was current when hymn vii, *33* was composed in or soon after the reign of Sudās, whom it praises and whose chronological position has been fixed (p. 172); and it required time for its development. So far as it concerns Agastya it will be further noticed in chapter XXII. The Vasiṣṭhas were a well known family then, as verses 2–9 show; hence it obviously refers to some progenitor, and therefore Maitrāvaruṇa was a Vasiṣṭha far earlier than Sudās's priest Vasiṣṭha. Vasiṣṭha Maitrāvaruṇi is said to have composed the first three verses of hymn ix, *97* and hymns vii, *1* and *3* to *17*,[4] and even all the hymns in the seventh maṇḍala,[5] but vii, *33* can be his

[1] The long medial *ā* might be a relic of the dual formation *Mitrā-varuṇau*, as in the plural compound *Mitrā-Varuṇa-Dakṣāṁśa-*, &c. (Bṛhadd iv, 82), or the lengthening of the medial vowel, as in *viśvānara*, *Viśvāmitra*, *gūrtāvasu* (see Macdonell's *Vedic Grammar*, p. 10, 4 d). If the meaning were really 'relating to (descended from) Mitra and Varuṇa', *Maitrāvāruṇa* might perhaps be expected, as *Maitrābārhaspatya* shows.

[2] See twelfth note *ante*, where Mat reading *Mitrāvaruṇa* is probably correct rather than Vā and Bd reading *Maitrā°*, for the latter might easily be an 'emendation' of the former, whereas the reverse is highly improbable. Mitrāvaruṇa is mentioned again, Mat *200*, 16, and is probably the true name. The Vedārth may support this perhaps, for it attributes hymn viii, *67* in the alternative to Mānya (i.e. an Agastya), *Mitrāvaruṇa-putra*, which means naturally 'son of Mitrāvaruṇa'; whereas 'son of Mitra and Varuṇa' should rather be *Mitra-Varuṇa-putra* in its Sanskrit.

[3] Mat *200*, 15, 16.

[4] Bṛhadd v, 160.

[5] Vedārth on i, *166*, and introduction to vii.

only if Maitrāvaruṇi means a descendant of Maitrāvaruṇa, for Maitrāvaruṇa, as shown, lived far earlier. The epic applies Maitrāvaruṇi to the fourth Vasiṣṭha, who was Kalmāṣapāda's priest,[1] and this is quite possibly right; but the Bṛhaddevatā calls him Vāruṇi (vi, 33–4), perhaps for short. All that seems clear is that Maitrāvaruṇa was Kuṇḍina and was long prior to Sudās's Vasiṣṭha, and that Mitrāvaruṇa Vasiṣṭha was earlier still.[2]

The patronymic Vāruṇi is also applied to a Vasiṣṭha who sang the fable about king Nāhuṣa (Yayāti?) and the Sarasvatī,[3] and to Āpava Vasiṣṭha (*ante*). A Vasiṣṭha unspecified is said to have had a father Varuṇa.[4]

Other Vasiṣṭhas are alluded to: thus, one was purohita of Mucukunda,[5] as would be natural, since this Mucukunda was no doubt the son of Māndhātṛ of Ayodhyā (p. 93); and another, as mentioned above, received honour from king Rantideva, who was about contemporary with king Hastin (pp. 112, 146).

The Jātūkarṇyas were a Vasiṣṭha gotra.[6] This name is a patronymic, and so there were several of the name. Jātūkarṇa or a Jātūkarṇya is said to have taught Vyāsa the Veda[7] and the Purana,[8] and is described as Vyāsa's predecessor as regards the Veda.[9] There were other Jātūkarṇyas later.[10]

[1] MBh i, *178*, 6801.

[2] Some passages even make Maitrāvaruṇi Vasiṣṭha the purohita of Manu's sons, Mat *12*, 4–5: Pad v, *8*, 109–10. This may have some connexion with the above fable and with the fable that Manu's daughter Ilā was produced by Mitra and Varuṇa at Manu's sacrifice; Vā *85*, 6, 9, 13; Bd iii, *60*, 5, 8, 12; Hv *10*, 615–22; Br *7*, 3–8; Viṣ iv, *1*, 6–8.

[3] Bṛhadd vi, 20–4.

[4] *Id.* vi, 11–15.

[5] MBh xii, *74*, 2811–14.

[6] Mat *200*, 19. Vā *1*, 9–10. Bhāg ix, *2*, 21 says Jātūkarṇya famed as Kānīna was Agniveśya, and derives him from Nariṣyanta, Manu's son (chap. XXIV): if so, he would be a different person in a different gotra.

[7] Vā *1*, 44. Hv *42*, 2364. Vedic literature says Vyāsa was a disciple of Viṣvaksena, *Vedic Index*, ii, 339. The two may be the same.

[8] Bd i, *1*, 11.

[9] In the fanciful lists of the successive Vyāsas in the 28 Dvāparas of this manvantara, Vā *23*, 115–219: Bd ii, *35*, 116–25: Viṣ iii, *3*, 11–19: Lg i, *7*, 12–18; *24*, 12–127: Kūr i, *52*, 1–8.

[10] See *Vedic Index*.

CHAPTER XIX

THE ĀṄGIRASAS AND KĀṆVAS

THE mythical founder Aṅgiras has been noticed in chapter XVI, and also the divine priest Bṛhaspati. A vaṁśa of the Āṅgirasas is given by the Brahmāṇḍa and Vāyu, and the Matsya gives a long list of the rishis and gotras.[1] Genealogical statements are found elsewhere but are few and brief. 'Aṅgiras,' like the names of the other primaeval rishis, is applied indiscriminately to Āṅgirasa rishis; thus Utathya is so called,[2] and also Droṇa or his father Bharadvāja.[3] The names Bṛhaspati[4] and Bharadvāja[5] were also freely used instead of patronymics, as will appear, and are often quite vague.

The accounts in the Brahmāṇḍa and Vāyu collated suggest the probable text; but they are not a genuine genealogy, for they mix up mythological persons as the Āṅgirasa deities and Ṛbhus with historical persons and have confused the relationships of the rishis. We must therefore consider the various Āṅgirasa rishis according to the information available elsewhere. A remarkable point is that the genealogy gives the first Aṅgiras the name Atharvan and makes Atharvan Aṅgiras the progenitor of all the Āṅgirasas,[6] so that 'Atharvan' and 'Aṅgiras' become equivalent, and they may all be designated Atharvāṅgiras.

The earliest rishi who is called an Aṅgiras is the priest Bṛhaspati who supported the gods (*devas*)[7] in their war against the Daityas, Dānavas and asuras, who were aided by the priest Uśanas-Śukra

[1] Bd iii, *1*, 101–13. Vā *65*, 97–108. Mat *196*.

[2] MBh xii, *90*, 3362.

[3] MBh v, *150*, 5114.

[4] e.g. Vā *59*, 131.

[5] e.g. Vā *59*, 131. In fables, Br *121*; *133*.

[6] Atharvāṅgiras = Aṅgiras, MBh v, *17*, 548–51, which says Aṅgiras has the name Atharvāṅgiras in the Atharvaveda and connects him with that. Muṇḍaka Upaniṣad i, *1*, 1–2 mythologizes; SBE xv, 27.

[7] Referred to in MBh i, *76*, 3188: xii, *37*, 1353; *152*, 5667; *338*, 12752: probably in vi, *50*, 2073. For the divine priest, see chap. XVI; and the devâsura wars, p. 187, note 2.

(chapter XVII). That story gives him a chronological position, but it seems doubtful if he really was an Aṅgiras, for he is not, I believe, ever derived from Atharvan Aṅgiras. Fable in one form says he had a son Kaca (p. 196). References to 'Bṛhaspati' occur in connexion with other persons, which show the lack of the historical sense and are vague, and being worthless for the present purpose are not cited here.[1]

The earliest time at which Āṅgirasas are alleged to have existed was in the reign of Māndhātṛ king of Ayodhyā, for he himself, his sons, grandsons and his descendants the Viṣṇuvṛddhas and Hārītas are said to have joined the Āṅgirasas (chapter XXIII), but no Āṅgirasas are named about that time.

The earliest time at which a real Āṅgirasa rishi is alleged to have existed was in the reign of Hariścandra of Ayodhyā, when Ajīgarta sold his son Śunaḥśepa as a sacrificial victim instead of Rohita, and Ayāsya officiated as a priest at the ceremony (chapter XVIII). In the brahmanical books Ajīgarta is called an Āṅgirasa, but they have made mistakes (pp. 10, 100) and introduce extravagant mythology into the story; and they are no doubt wrong in making Ajīgarta an Āṅgirasa, because better authority says his son Śunaḥśepa was a Bhārgava (chapter XVII). Ayāsya was an Āṅgirasa rishi,[2] but no reliance can be placed on those books when they say he was present, in view of those mistakes and because the Brahma substitutes (though probably wrongly) Vāmadeva for him. There is nothing to show to what time Ayāsya should be assigned. He was the reputed author of hymns.[3]

The traditions which give the earliest genuine historical setting to the Āṅgirasas connect them with the kings who reigned in the portion of North Bihar of which Vaiśālī became the capital afterwards (p. 97). They come into notice there first with king Karandhama, his son Avīkṣit and his son the famous Marutta Āvīkṣita, being their hereditary priests. Their chronological position and connexions have been explained above (pp. 157 f.),

[1] e.g. MBh vii, *94*, 3476.

[2] So the genealogy. *Vedic Index.* Bḍ ii, *32*, 110. Vā *59*, 101 (*Āyāpya*). Mat *196*, 4 (*Ajasya*). Not in Sörensen's *Index to the MBh*, but for *Payasyaḥ* in xiii, *85*, 4147 read *Ayāsyaḥ*.

[3] Rigv ix, *44* to *46*: x, *67* and *68*.

namely, of Uśija, his three sons [1] Ucathya [2] (or Utathya), Bṛhaspati [3] and Saṁvarta,[4] Ucathya's son Dīrghatamas by his wife Mamatā, and Bṛhaspati's son Bharadvāja [5] and descendant (probably great grandson) Vidathin Bharadvāja. These rishis thus began in the country of Vaiśālī, and moved westwards in time. Bharadvāja moved to Kāśi, and became purohita to king Divodāsa II of Kāśi.[6] Vidathin Bharadvāja was adopted by king Bharata as his son (p. 159), and the Bhāradvājas remained connected with the Paurava dynasty.

Dīrghatamas was set adrift in the Ganges and carried down to the country called Aṅga afterwards. He lived there and married a śūdra woman,[7] to whom the name Uśij appears to be wrongly attributed (p. 161). She is called Auśīnarī.[8] By her he had Kakṣīvant and other sons. He gained his sight and assumed the name Gautama or Gotama.[9] He and his śūdra-born sons went to Girivraja in the country known afterwards as Magadha,[10] and after long austerities they attained brahmanhood there. Kakṣīvant begot many sons who were called the Kuṣmāṇḍa [11] Gautamas, and he must be distinguished from a later Kakṣīvant (*infra*). Towards the end of his life Dīrghatamas consecrated king Bharata. These particulars have been discussed above (pp. 158, 162).

[1] 'Aṅgiras' is called father of the three, and confused with the primaeval rishi, MBh i, *66*, 2569.

[2] He is wrongly made to instruct Māndhātṛ Yauvanāśva in a brahmanical story, MBh xii, *90*, 3362. An absurd fable is told about him, saying his wife was Soma's daughter Bhadrā, xiii, *154*, 7240–63. Called Aṅgiras in both.

[3] 'Bṛhaspati' is wrongly made to instruct Vasumanas, king of Kosala, in a brahmanical story, MBh xii, *68*, 2536–41. He is called Aṅgiras, *ibid*. 2595.

[4] He was an Āṅgirasa, MBh xiv, *10*, 281; younger brother of Bṛhaspati xii, *29*, 913.

[5] So also Vā *64*, 26: Bd ii, *38*, 27.

[6] MBh xiii, *30*, 1963, See pp. 154 and 164.

[7] MBh i, *104*, 4193–4, 4205, say he had a wife Pradveṣī and sons Gautama, &c., before he was set adrift.

[8] MBh ii, *20*, 802.

[9] So, apparently, Bṛhadd iii, 125; MBh xii, *343*, 13184. But sometimes *Gautama* is treated as an earlier patronymic, being given to him and his younger brother, Mat *48*, 53, 84. This name (*go-tama*) has no doubt some connexion with the allegation of his immoral imitation of cattle, Vā *99*, 47–61, 88–92; Bd iii, *74*, 47–61, 90–4; Mat *48*, 43–56, 79–84.

[10] MBh ii, *20*, 798–805 says the sons were born there.

[11] Or *Kṛṣṇāṅga*, as some copies of Vā read.

A paternal cousin of Dīrghatamas is called Śaradvant,[1] but nothing more is said of him. The Śaradvant mentioned in the genealogy may be he or a later Śaradvant, *infra*.

Bharadvāja Bārhaspatya Vidathin, who was adopted by Bharata (p. 163), is said to have had five sons, Suhotra, Śunahotra, Nara, Garga and Ṛjiśvan, who were Bhāradvājas and could claim optionally to be grandsons of Bṛhaspati or of Bharata.[2] The option involved that they could be either brahmans or kṣatriyas, and the mention of it implies that they exercised it, as will appear in chapter XXIII. The Vedārthadīpikā also says they belonged to the Bārhaspatya gotra of Śaṁyu (who is elsewhere declared to have been son of a Bṛhaspati,[3] and was therefore prior to these five persons), and they expanded[4] the family of the Bhāradvājas; but its genealogy is contracted and incorrect, for they were not brothers, and they were not sons but descendants of Vidathin Bharadvāja.[5] Ṛjiśvan was a son or descendant of Vidathin, for he is called *Vaidathina*;[6] and he is also called son of 'Bharadvāja' and son's son of 'Bṛhaspati' or of Bharata,[7] where the word 'son' obviously does not mean immediate sonship. Accordingly, since he and the other four mentioned were born in the Paurava line and yet he was of Śaṁyu's gotra, Śaṁyu son of 'Bṛhaspati'[8] must be placed before Vidathin and after the Bṛhaspati mentioned above; and Ṛjiśvan with or soon after Garga and Nara's son Saṅkṛti (pp. 112, 191).

A later Bharadvāja was connected with the Paurava king Ajamīḍha.[9] Next may be mentioned Pāyu, who was a Bhāradvāja.

[1] Vā *99*, 48, 57–62. Bḍ iii, *74*, 48, 58–62.

[2] Anukramaṇī and Vedārth on Rigv vi, 52. The latter's account hardly agrees with the itihāsa it quotes, for it explains the option by asserting the five sons had two mothers, while the itihāsa says they were all sons of one wife (verse 14) and explains that option by the adoption (verses 12–15).

[3] Vā *71*, 37–8, 48–9. Bḍ iii, *9*, 38, 49; *20*, 17. Śatapatha Brāhm i, 9, 1, 26.

[4] Read *nirvṛtty-artham* in Vedārth *loc. cit.*?

[5] See p. 112, and also chap. XXIII.

[6] Rigv iv, *16*, 13: v, *29*, 14. Ṛjiśvan Auśija in x, *99*, 11 may be the same, because Bharadvāja was descended from Uśija (p. 161).

[7] Vedārth on Rigv ix, *98*.

[8] Vā *71*, 48–9; *83*, 13–14, 129. Bḍ iii, *9*, 49–50: *19*, 12–13 with *20*, 23. Cf. MBh iii, *218*, 14131.

[9] Vā *99*, 168–9. Mat *49*, 45–6.

He was a contemporary of Prastoka Sārñjaya, Abhyāvartin Cāyamāna, and Divodāsa king of N. Pañcāla.[1]

Vāmadeva was a well-known Āṅgirasa rishi, as the genealogy says.[2] Hymns ascribed to him show he was a Gautama[3] and refer to Dīrghatamas.[4] In one hymn 'Vāmadeva' shows he was later than Ṛjiśvan Vaidathina,[5] and others ascribed to him indicate he was later than Divodāsa Atithigva and Trasadasyu[6] who were contemporaries (p. 170), and was a contemporary of Somaka Sāhadevya.[7] Elsewhere 'Vāmadeva' is connected with kings Śala and Dala,[8] who appear to be the kings of Ayodhyā, No. 77 (p. 149), later still. These indications suggest that the first Vāmadeva lived in the time of Somaka. Descendants of his would appear later, and among them Bṛhaduktha is called his son and was a well-known rishi.[9] 'Vāmadeva' consecrated Durmukha Pāñcāla.[10] Other references to 'Vāmadeva' are quite vague.[11]

The next noted Āṅgirasa was Śaradvant, son of a Gautama,[12] who married Ahalyā,[13] sister of king Divodāsa of N. Pañcāla (p. 116); and his descendants are given in the N. Pañcāla genealogy,[14] but the pedigree is very greatly abbreviated, only three generations being mentioned from Divodāsa's time to that

[1] Anukramaṇī and Vedārth on Rigv vi, *75*. Bṛhadd v, 124–8, 138–9. P. 170.

[2] Also Vā *59*, 90, 101 : Bd ii, *32*, 110 : Mat *145*, 104 ; *196*, 4, 35–6.

[3] Rigv iv, *4*, 11 ; *32*, 9, 12. Bṛhadd iv, 126–7. *Vedic Index* ii, 286.

[4] Rigv iv, *4*, 13. Also Auśija, *21*, 6–7.

[5] *Id.* iv, *16*, 13, 18.

[6] *Id.* iv, *26*, 3 ; *38*, 1.

[7] *Id.* iv, *15*, 7–10. Vedārth on Rigv iv, 15.

[8] MBh iii, *192*, 13180 f. MBh xii, *92* to *94* about Vasumanas are indeterminate and brahmanical.

[9] Vā *59*, 93, 102. Bd ii, *32*, 101, 111. Mat *145*, 95, 105 ; *196*, 35–6. *Vedic Index* ii, 71. Anukramaṇī and Vedārth on Rigv x, *54* to *56*.

[10] Aitareya Brāhm viii, 23.

[11] e.g. Manu x, 106 : Pad vi, *281*, 6, 11.

[12] MBh i, *130*, 5072 : v, *165*, 5768.

[13] It is of her that Rām tells the story of Indra's seduction of Ahalyā (i, *48*, 14 f.) in that her son was Śatānanda (*id.* *51*, 1–6). It is told again with fanciful additions (*id.* vii, *30*, 21–35). Often alluded to, MBh v, *11*, 373 : xii, *344*, 13205 : xiii, *41*, 2328 ; *153*, 7218 : Lg i, *29*, 27 : with variations. Also *Vedic Index* : Br *122*, 49 : Pad v, *51*. The story is attached in a fable to Medhātithi Gautama and his son Cirakārin. MBh xii, *267*, 9482–9552.

[14] Vā *99*, 201–5. Mat *50*, 8–12. Hv *32*, 1784–8. Viṣ iv, *19*, 16–18. Ag *277*, 22–3. Wrongly in Bhāg ix, *21*, 34–6. MBh i, *130*, 5072–89, omitting Śatānanda and Satyadhṛti.

of Śantanu, namely Śatānanda, Satyadhṛti and the twins Kṛpa and Kṛpī, whom Śantanu succoured.[1] All these were Gautamas[2] and therefore descendants of Ucathya.[3] There is nothing to fix the times of Śatānanda and Satyadhṛti.

Another Kakṣīvant was the author of Rigveda i, *116* and *117*, where he calls himself Pajriya Kakṣīvant. These hymns and also *118* to *126* are attributed to Kakṣīvant Dairghatamasa Auśija, but this rishi cannot be the former Kakṣīvant (*ante*), because (1) Dīrghatamas and his son Kakṣīvant lived in the time of Duṣyanta and Bharata (p. 163), (2) this Pajriya Kakṣīvant speaks of Divodāsa[4] (who appears to be the king of N. Pañcāla) but not of Pijavana nor Sudās, whence it seems he lived between them, (3) there was a long interval of many kings between Bharata and his descendant Divodāsa (p. 146), and (4) the description and treatment of this young rishi in the story of him and king Svanaya Bhāvayavya[5] does not accord with the base birth of the earlier Kakṣīvant. The two Kakṣīvants therefore were different persons. This rishi belonged to the family of the Pajras,[6] of whom there is no mention before Dīrghatamas. Moreover, it will be shown in the following section that the Kaṇvas did not come into existence till after Ajamīḍha, so that the reference in hymn *117*, 8 to Kaṇva and that in i, *18* (attributed to Medhātithi Kāṇva) to 'Kakṣīvant who is Auṣija' as a contemporary, both show that Pajriya Kakṣīvant could not be the earlier Kakṣīvant, but was a later descendant, for Pajra was an Auśija.[7] Thus there were two Kakṣīvants, both Auśijas, the first son of Dīrghatamas in Bharata's time and the second son (or descendant) of Pajra (and also probably a descendant of Dīrghatamas) soon after Divodāsa. The Anukramaṇī and Vedārthadīpikā have confused them. This fixes the time of king Svanaya as between Divodāsa and Sudās.[8]

[1] Also MBh i, *63*, 2435–6: v, *165*, 5767–8.

[2] So Kṛpī, MBh i, *130*, 5114–15; and Kṛpa, *137*, 5433.

[3] Vā reading *Ṛtathyā* in the genealogy should be *Autathyā* (=*Aucathyā*). Mat *ākhyātā* and Hv *ete te* have 'emended' the patronymic they did not understand (cf. pp. 82–3). This Śaradvant apparently is called *Autathya Gautama*, Vā *64*, 26: Bd ii, *38*, 28.

[4] Rigv i, *116*, 18.

[5] Bṛhadd iii, 141–50.

[6] Rigv i, *126*, 2, 4, 5.

[7] Rigv i, *122*, 4, 7, 8. Hence Nahuṣa there is different from Nahuṣa father of Yayāti.

[8] He belonged probably to one of the petty Pañcāla dynasties descended from Bhṛmyaśva (p. 117).

Kṛpa brings us down to the reign of Śantanu of Hastināpura. A Bharadvāja had his hermitage at Gaṅgādvāra [1] and was of Aṅgiras' lineage.[2] Pṛṣata was then king of N. Pañcāla and was his friend. Pṛṣata's son Drupada and Bharadvāja's son Droṇa were playmates,[3] but Drupada on becoming king despised Droṇa. Droṇa was a great archer and warrior and taught Dhṛtarāṣṭra's sons and the Pāṇḍavas all the art of war.[4] With the Pāṇḍavas' aid he conquered Drupada (p. 116), and apparently became himself king of N. Pañcāla. He married Kṛpī, and their son was Aśvatthāman.[5] This Bharadvāja is said to have taught Agniveśa the art of the āgneya weapon, and Agniveśa taught it to Droṇa.[6]

Other Bṛhaspatis and Bharadvājas are mentioned, but with want of personal distinction.[7] One Bṛhaspati gave his daughter Romaśā to king Svanaya Bhāvayavya:[8] another is said to have been the preceptor of king Vasu of Cedi:[9] and another the preceptor of Vyāsa's son Śuka.[10] One Bharadvāja taught Śatruñjaya king of the Sauvīras:[11] another with his son Yavakrī is connected with Raibhya and his sons Arvāvasu and Parāvasu.[12] Many other Āṅgirasas, authors of Vedic hymns and others, are mentioned, some of whom were of more or less note, such as Hiraṇyastūpa, Kutsa, Gotama Rāhūgaṇa [13] and Āpastamba;[14] but there is no sufficient evidence to fix their positions. A Caṇḍa Kauśika, called son of Kakṣīvant Gautama, is made contemporary with Bṛhadratha and Jarāsandha, kings of Magadha, by contracting the genealogy.[15]

[1] The story is in MBh i, *130*, 5102–12; *166*, 6328–35.
[2] So his son Droṇa, MBh i, *130*, 5122; *132*, 5280.
[3] The fable of Droṇa's birth is noticed under the *Agastyas*, chap. XXII.
[4] MBh i, *67*, 2705–6; *132*; *166*, 6344–7.
[5] MBh i, *130*, 5114–15. Viṣ iv, *19*, 18.
[6] MBh i, *130*, 5107–8; *139*, 5524–5.
[7] 'Bṛhaspati' wrongly with Māndhātṛ, MBh xiii, *76*, 3668. A Bharadvāja, Manu x, 107.
[8] Rigv i, *126*, 6–7 Bṛhadd iii, *155* to iv, 3. His position has just been fixed, *ante*.
[9] MBh xii, *338*, 12753–6.
[10] *Id*. *326*, 12209–10.
[11] *Id*. *140*, 5249–50.
[12] *Id*. iii, *135*, 10703–4: see chap. XXI.
[13] Rigv i, *77* and *78*. The story in Śatapatha Brāhm i, 4, 10–19 (SBE xii, 104–6) is a brahmanical fable.
[14] MBh iii, *297*, 16875: xiii, *66*, 3320. To be distinguished from the Āpastambi gotra among the Bhārgavas, Mat *195*, 33.
[15] MBh ii, *16*, 688 to *17*, 740.

A Paila, son of Vasu, is mentioned with the Pāṇḍavas.[1] For later Āṅgirasas, see chapter XXVII.

The genealogy says there were 15 parties (*pakṣa*) among the Āṅgirasas, but 16 or 17 names are given, namely, Ayāsya, Utathya (Ucathya), Vāmadeva, Auśija, Bhāradvāja, Sāṅkṛti, Garga, Kaṇva, Rathītara, Mudgala, Viṣṇuvṛddha, Harita, Kapi, Rūkṣa (read Urukṣaya), Bharadvāja, Ārṣabha and Kitu. Matsya *196* names all these as gotras except the last two. Of these parties, however, the nine, Sāṅkṛtis to Urukṣayas, were not Āṅgirasas by origin, but sprang from kṣatriyas and were incorporated among the Āṅgirasas. The Kaṇvas became brahmans straightway, as will be now explained, but all the rest of these became kṣatriyan brahmans, as will be explained in chapter XXIII, and ultimately wholly brahmans. Most of these names are also mentioned as those of celebrated Āṅgirasa hymn-makers.[2]

Kāṇvas or Kāṇvāyanas.

Among the Āṅgirasas were the Kāṇvas,[3] and they were an offshoot from the Paurava line, as all the authorities agree, but two distinct points are assigned for their branching off in two different accounts. Both accounts say, Kaṇva had a son Medhātithi, and from Medhātithi were descended the Kāṇvāyanas who were brahmans. One account says, Kaṇva was son of Apratiratha (or Pratiratha), one of the sons of king Matināra (or Rantināra, p. 144): but the other makes Kaṇva son of Ajamīḍha, a king who was Martināra's successor by some 32 generations. This difference involves a great discrepancy as to the time when Kaṇva lived. Both origins can hardly be true, for it is difficult to believe that Kāṇvas started from 'Medhātithi son of Kaṇva' twice over many generations apart, that is, the double origin of a single brahman family from two persons ages apart. A gotra called Kāṇvas is named among the Vasiṣṭhas,[4] but, even assuming that that unique mention is correct, that gotra appears unknown otherwise; and the above two accounts undoubtedly refer to one and the same family of Kāṇvas.

The earlier origin is given by the Vāyu, Harivaṁśa, Viṣṇu and

[1] *Id. 32*, 1239. He may be connected with Vyāsa's disciple Paila, p. 21.

[2] Vā *59*, 98–102. Bd ii, *32*, 107–12. Mat *145*, 101–6.

[3] Vā *99*, 199. Mat *50*, 5. Hv *32*, 1782. [4] Mat *200*, 9.

Bhāgavata.[1] The Agni mentions Pratiratha, Kaṇva and Medhātithi, and the Garuḍa makes Medhātithi son of Pratiratha,[2] but neither say anything about Kāṇvāyanas, and so do not assert that the Kāṇvāyanas began at this point.

The later origin from Ajamīḍha is given by the Vāyu, Matsya, Viṣṇu and Garuḍa,[3] which are all in agreement, while the Bhāgavata[4] derives from him the Priyamedhas instead, who also were Āṅgirasas.[5]

The Harivaṁśa, Brahma and Agni make Jahnu son of Ajamīḍha and Keśinī, and so substitute the Kānyakubja dynasty for the Kāṇvāyanas, and this is clearly wrong (pp. 99 f.). Their false substitution here shows that they have ousted some other line of descendants, and the only other line at this point mentioned anywhere is the Kāṇvāyana family, hence the inference is that it originated here. The Bhāgavata moreover in giving Praskaṇva the earlier origin is clearly wrong, because Praskaṇva Kāṇva was not earlier than Sudās of N. Pañcāla,[6] and therefore was long posterior to the time it assigns him. Of the four Puranas therefore which assert the earlier origin, the Bhāgavata is wrong, the

[1] Vā *99*, 130–1, misreading *Kaṇṭha* and *Kāṇṭhāyana* here as also elsewhere (e. g. verses 199, 344, 346):—

dhuryo 'pratirathasyâpi Kaṇvas tasyâbhavat sutaḥ
Medhātithiḥ sutas tasya yasmāt Kāṇvāyanā dvijāḥ.

Dhurya appears to be an adjective, but even if a name does not affect this question. Viṣ iv, *19*, 2 agrees closely. Hv *32*, 1718 says—

putraḥ Pratirathasyâsīt Kaṇvaḥ samabhavan nṛpaḥ
Medhātithiḥ sutas tasya yasmāt Kaṇvo 'bhavad dvijaḥ.

Bhāg ix, *20*, 6–7 :—

Kaṇvo 'pratirathâtmajaḥ
tasya Medhātithis tasmāt Praskaṇvâdyā dvijātayaḥ

which is equivalent, for Praskaṇva was a Kāṇva.

[2] Ag *277*, 5. Gar *140*, 4.

[3] Mat *49*, 46–7 and Vā *99*, 169–70 (which here also misreads *Kaṇṭha* and *Kaṇṭhāyana*):—

Ajamīḍhasya Keśinyāṁ Kaṇvaḥ samabhavat kila
Medhātithiḥ sutas tasya tasmāt Kāṇvāyanā dvijāḥ.

Similarly Viṣ iv, *19*, 10 and Gar *140*, 9.

[4] Bhāg ix, *21*, 21 :—

Ajamīḍhasya vaṁśyāḥ syuḥ Priyamedhâdayo dvijāḥ.

[5] Anukramaṇī on Rigv viii, *2*.

[6] Rigv i, *47*, 2, 5, 6 (attributed to him): *45*, 3–5, which show he was later than Priyamedha.

Harivaṁśa highly suspect because of its untrue substitution of the Kānyakubja dynasty at the later point, and the Vāyu and Viṣṇu give both accounts and therefore stultify themselves. The weight of authority then is in favour of the later origin.

Next, there appears to be nothing to show that the Kāṇvas existed before Ajamīḍha. A Kaṇva is mentioned in Duṣyanta's time. He adopted Śakuntalā, and Duṣyanta met her in his hermitage and married her, but this Kaṇva is expressly called a Kāśyapa (see next chapter), and so could not be a member of the Kāṇvas, who were Āṅgirasas. Kaṇva was his personal name. There is no other mention of any Kaṇva before Ajamīḍha. On the other hand there were many Kāṇvas after him, as the Rigveda shows. By the group of synchronisms at page 163, Sobhari Kāṇva's position has been fixed, and (accepting the Anukramaṇī's ascriptions of authorship) there are the following indications: Pragātha Kāṇva was contemporary with Durgaha's grandsons,[1] and so the positions of his father Ghora, brother Kaṇva and three sons are fixed; Pṛṣadhra Kāṇva was contemporary with Dasyave-vṛka;[2] and Praskaṇva has been noticed above. Through Kakṣīvant Pajriya (*ante*) can be placed Devātithi Kāṇva,[3] Vatsa Kāṇva,[4] Sadhvaṁśa Kāṇva (who was later than Trasadasyu)[5] and Medhātithi Kāṇva[6]—all later than Ajamīḍha.

It is clear that the Kāṇvas sprang from Ajamīḍha[7] and not from Matināra's son Apratiratha, and this accords with the fact that both just before and after Ajamīḍha the Paurava line threw off branches which became brahmans, as will be explained in chapter XXIII. The erroneous earlier origin may perhaps be explained by the Harivaṁśa text. It says Apratiratha's son was Kaṇva, a king, and quite possibly there was a junior king Kaṇva then, and afterwards the second line—

Medhātithiḥ sutas tasya yasmāt Kāṇvāyanā dvijāḥ

which is found generally in both accounts and belongs properly to the second, was mistakenly added to the first, especially when Jahnu was foisted in as a son of Ajamīḍha and ousted the Kāṇvāyanas from their proper place. The Kāṇvas thus belonged to the

[1] Rigv viii, *65*, 12. Bṛhadd vi, 35–9.
[2] Rigv viii, *56*, 1, 2. [3] *Id.* viii, *4*, 17. [4] *Id.* viii, *6*, 47.
[5] *Id.* viii. *8*, 4, 7, 8, &c. [6] *Id.* i, *18*, 1. Medhātithi II?
[7] 'Ajamīḍha' is named among the Āṅgirasas, Mat *196*, 47.

period of the N. Pañcāla dynasty (pp. 146, 148), and various Kāṇva rishis are named in connexion with Rigvedic hymns. The position of one, Sobhari, has been fixed as mentioned. Others were earlier and later, as noticed above, and the positions of others can be perceived in a general way through allusions to kings, to themselves and to other persons, but can hardly be particularized.[1]

CHAPTER XX

THE ĀTREYAS

The mythical rishi Atri has been noticed above (chapter XVI), and the name is also loosely applied to various Ātreyas, as will be noticed. The genealogy of the Ātreyas is given in Brahmāṇḍa iii, *8*, 73–86, Vāyu *70*, 67–78 and Liṅga i, *63*, 68–78; and also partially in connexion with the Paurava dynasty in Brahma *13*, 5–14 and Harivaṁśa *31*, 1658, 1661–8. All these passages are closely alike and collated suggest the original text. The Matsya (*197*) gives a list of Ātreya rishis and gotras. The genealogy is very brief in its range,[2] confuses Prabhākara with the primaeval mythical Atri in making him father of Soma, and explains the names Prabhākara and Svastyātreya by a brahmanical fable evidently fabricated out of them. So far as it is genealogical it agrees with tradition elsewhere.

Prabhākara, who is called Atri or Ātreya,[3] is the earliest of this family to whom an historical position is given, namely, that he married the ten daughters of Bhadrāśva or Raudrāśva and Ghṛtācī. Bhadrāśva, as he is called in two Puranas,[4] or Raudrāśva, as he is generally called,[5] was an early Paurava king; the Vāyu, Matsya and Bhāgavata name his queen as Ghṛtācī;[6] and the Vāyu, Brahma

[1] MBh, see Sörensen, where Kaṇva Kāśyapa (*ante*) must be distinguished. In fables, Br *85*; *148*.

[2] Kūr i, *19*, 18–19 shortens and confuses the account.

[3] So also Vā *99*, 127. See chap. XVI.

[4] Mat *49*, 4. Ag *277*, 3.

[5] MBh i, *94*, 3698. Vā *99*, 123–7. Viṣ iv, *19*, 1. Gar i, *140*, 2. Bhāg ix, *20*, 3. Br *13*, 4. Hv *31*, 1658.

[6] Generally confused with the apsaras, see p. 135.

and Harivaṁśa add, their ten daughters married the Ātreya Prabhākara. Prabhākara's position is therefore defined. The genealogy says he had ten sons, called the Svastyātreyas,[1] and from him the best Ātreya gotras were descended. Chief among his Svastyātreya descendants (not sons) were two famous rishis Datta and Durvāsas.[2]

Datta Ātreya, or Dattātreya as he is generally called,[3] is always connected in tradition with the great Haihaya king Arjuna Kārtavīrya, who propitiated him and was favoured by him.[4] He was therefore, from this position, a descendant (not son) of Prabhākara. In late or brahmanical stories however he is wrongly introduced at other times.[5] He is said to have been placid, beneficent and unblemished,[6] and is regarded as the fourth incarnation of Viṣṇu;[7] yet he is sometimes described as addicted to sensual pleasures and spirituous liquor.[8] It is said he had a son Nimi, who was the first to institute the śrāddha.[9]

Durvāsas Ātreya is called Datta's brother,[10] but his position is not definite, because he is not certainly connected with any king, and he appears often in tales, introduced at all stages of traditional history, especially in brahmanical stories.[11] He is nearly always presented as a very irascible and furious rishi,[12] and his character

[1] A Svastyātreya, Bṛhadd iii, 56; Hv *168*, 9571. One is the reputed author of Rigv v, *50* and *51*. A Svasti, Bṛhadd i, 128; &c.

[2] Mārk *17*, 6–16 mythologizes their birth and characters.

[3] e. g. Br *213*, 106, 110. Mārk *17*, 7. MBh xiii, *153*, 7224.

[4] MBh iii, *115*, 11036: xii, *49*, 1750–1: xiii, *152*, 7189; *153*, 7224; *157*, 7351. Vā *94*, 10–11. Bḍ iii, *69*, 10–11. Br *13*, 161. Hv *33*, 1852–3; *42*, 2309. Mārk *18* and *19*. Mat *43*, 15. Pad v, *12*, 118. Viṣ iv, *11*, 3. Bhāg ix, *15*, 17; *23*, 24. Ag *274*, 5.

[5] e. g. earlier with the Aila king Āyu, Pad ii, *103*, 101–135. Later with Alarka, Mārk *16*, 12; *37*, 26; &c.: Br *180*, 31–2: Gar i, *218*.

[6] Genealogy, line 22. Mārk *17*, 6, 13, 18.

[7] Vā *98*, 89. Bḍ iii, *73*, 88. Mārk *17*, 7. Genealogy. Br *213*, 106–13. Hv *42*, 2305–12.

[8] Mārk *17*, 20–5; *18*, 23, 28–31. Pad ii, *103*, 106–9, 114.

[9] MBh xiii, *91*, 4328–46. But xiv, *92*, 2887 attributes it to Jamadagni. Both lived about the same time.

[10] Both sons of Atri, Br *117*, 2: Ag *20*, 12. See chap. XVI.

[11] e. g. with the ancient Ambarīṣa (pp. 39 f.), Bhāg ix, *4*, 35 f. With an ancient king Śvetaki, MBh i, *223*, 8098, 8132–41. With Rāma Dāśarathi, Pad vi, *271*, 44. With Bhīṣma, MBh xiii, *26*, 1763. With Kuntī, MBh i, *67*, 2768; *111*, 4385. With the Pāṇḍavas, MBh iii, *85*, 8265. With Kṛṣṇa, Hv *298* to *303*. In myth, Ag *3*, 1–2.

[12] Mārk *17*, 9–16. Viṣ i *9*, 4, 6. MBh iii, *259*, 15415 f.

is well taken off in a story about Kṛṣṇa.[1] Curses imprecated by him serve at times to explain pitiable misfortunes and hardly-merited sufferings.[2] He is called an incarnation of Śiva.[3] No gotras appear to have claimed descent from him.

The genealogy says that among gotras descended from Datta four were widely renowned, named after their founders, Śyāvāśva, Mudgala (or Pratvasa), Balāraka (or Vāgbhūtaka or Vavalgu) and Gaviṣṭhira. The Matsya mentions as gotra names, Śyāvāśva and Gaviṣṭhira (*197*, 5, 7, 8), but not the second and third. I have found nothing to elucidate Mudgala. Six Ātreyas were hymn-makers,[4] Atri, Arcanānas, Śyāvāśva, Gaviṣṭhira, Balgūtaka (or Avihotra, or Karṇaka), and Pūrvātithi. The fifth is plainly the same as the third gotra, but it is difficult to fix the correct name.

Arcanānas was an Ātreya and Śyāvāśva was his son. Both are mentioned in the Rigveda. Many hymns are attributed to Śyāvāśva[5] and one to his son Andhīgu.[6] Arcanānas and Śyāvāśva sacrificed for king Rathavīti Dārbhya, and Śyāvāśva married his daughter. Contemporaries then were Taranta and Purumīḍha, both of whom are said to have been sons of Vidadaśva.[7] In two of those hymns Śyāvāśva mentions Trasadasyu,[8] who would be the Trasadasyu mentioned in other hymns and whose position has been fixed above (p. 163). This fixes the position of Arcanānas and Śyāvāśva as soon after his time.

Other Ātreyas are mentioned, such as the 'Atri' (one or several), who received wealth from Tryaruṇa, Trasadasyu and Aśvamedha, and also from king Rauśama,[9] and whose position (but not name or names) is fixed accordingly (p. 163): also a Babhru, who was priest to Ṛṇaṁcaya.[10]

[1] MBh xiii, *159*, 7414 f.
[2] As in the play of Śakuntalā, Act iv, introduction.
[3] MBh i, *223*, 8132. Mārk *17*, 9–11. Viṣ i, *9*, 2.
[4] Vā *59*, 104; Bḍ ii, *32*, 113–14; Mat *145*, 107–9; collated.
[5] Rigv v, *52* to *61*, *81*, *82*: viii, *35* to *38* and ix, *32* simply to Śyāvāśva.
[6] *Id.* ix, *101*.
[7] Rigv v, *61* and Vedārth thereon. Bṛhadd v, 50–81. *Vedic Index* i, 36: ii, 400. SBE xxxii, 359.
[8] Rigv viii, *36*, 7; *37*, 7.
[9] Bṛhadd v, 13, 31.
[10] *Id.* v, 13, 33–4.

The Kāśyapas.

The accounts of the mythical Kaśyapas have been noticed in chapter XVI. Two so-called vaṁśas of the Kāśyapas are found, one of which is wholly mythical and has been noticed there. The other deals with historical members of the Kāśyapa brahman family and is given by four Puranas.[1] Their versions are based on a common original, and are closely alike, but the Kūrma has introduced some variations, which do not however materially alter the purport. The Vāyu, Brahmāṇḍa and Liṅga collated suggest the original reading. The Matsya (*199*) gives a long list of rishis and gotras.

The genealogy says that Kaśyapa had two sons Vatsāra and Asita. Vatsāra begot Nidhruva and Raibhya. Nidhruva married Sumedhas, daughter of Cyavana and Sukanyā, and was the progenitor of the Kuṇḍapāyins. Raibhya was progenitor of the Raibhyas. Asita married Ekaparṇā and their son was Devala, best of the Śāṇḍilyas.[2] But this genealogy is hopelessly wrong, as will appear from a chronological survey of Kāśyapa rishis who are mentioned.

Vatsāra (or Vatsara, as it appears sometimes) is not mentioned in the *Vedic Index*.[3] Kaśyapa, he, Naidhruva, Raibhya, Asita and Devala were the six Kāśyapa brahmavādins,[4] and he is one of the seven rishis now said to be stationed in the sky.[5] His alleged son Nidhruva's wife cannot have been the daughter of Cyavana and Sukanyā, for they belonged to the very earliest age, and the reading *Sukanyāyāṁ* should probably be *tu kanyā yā*, meaning that his wife was daughter of a Cyavana, who may have been the king of N. Pañcāla, as will appear in the next paragraph. A Naidhruvi is once mentioned in Vedic literature, and a Kuṇḍapāyin also.[6] A Nidhruvi is the reputed author of Rigveda ix, *63*. Raibhya[7] (or Rebhya), the name of the other son assigned to Vatsāra, is a

[1] Vā *70*, 24–9. Bḍ iii, *8*, 28–33. Lg i, *63*, 49–55. Kūr i, *19*, 1–7.

[2] The last line of the genealogy seems unintelligible.

[3] Can he be Avatsāra of Rigv v, *44*, 10? An Avatsāra was son of Prasravaṇa, Aitar Brāhm ii, 3, 24.

[4] Vā *59*, 103. Bḍ ii, *32*, 112–13. Mat *145*, 106–7. This suggests his identification with Avatsāra.

[5] Vā *64*, 28. Bḍ ii, *38*, 29.

[6] *Vedic Index*, s.v.

[7] He must be distinguished from a Raibhya among the Viśvāmitras (chap. XXI). A Raibhya and his son Kukṣi, MBh xii, *350*, 13588–9.

patronymic, and should no doubt be Rebha; and if so, he may be the Rebha Kāśyapa who is the reputed author of Rigveda viii, *97*,[1] and perhaps also the Rebha who is called a rishi[2] and mentioned several times in the hymns.[3] Nothing can be fixed about his time, except that he was prior to Kakṣīvant Pajriya, who mentions him.[4] This synchronism shows that the Cyavana mentioned above cannot be the primaeval rishi and is more probably the N. Pañcāla king (p. 148). The other persons named in the genealogy will be noticed in turn.

The earliest time at which a Kaśyapa is mentioned is that of Rāma Jāmadagnya, who, according to brahmanic fable, offered a great sacrifice with Kaśyapa as his upādhyāya (p. 200).

The next Kāśyapa is Kaṇva Kāśyapa, in whose hermitage Śakuntalā dwelt.[5] She married the Paurava king Duṣyanta and was mother of the famous king Bharata.[6] 'Kaṇva' is said to have been the chief priest at Bharata's sacrifices,[7] and Bharata gave him gifts;[8] and he is no doubt this Kaṇva (or perhaps his son). The Kāṇva family had not come into existence then as shown in the last chapter.

The next Kāśyapa was the progenitor of the Śāṇḍilyas.[9] His position is not known, but they existed in the time of Dilīpa II Khaṭvāṅga, king of Ayodhyā, because an old verse says that a Śāṇḍilya sacrificed for him;[10] and they would be even earlier, if the statement is reliable, that Bhūmanyu, probably the Paurava king, gave food to a Śāṇḍilya.[11] These allusions show that the genealogy is wrong if it means, as it seems to mean, that the Śāṇḍilyas sprang from Asita or Devala, who were far later.

The next Kāśyapa was Vibhāṇḍaka, who had his hermitage on the R. Kauśikī (the modern Kosi in N. Bihar). His son was

[1] Hymns ix, *99* and *100* are attributed to his two sons.

[2] Rigv i, *117*, 4.

[3] *Vedic Index* ii, 226.

[4] Rigv i, *116*, 7, 24; *117*, 4, 6.

[5] MBh i, *70*, 2870, 2874, 2893–4; *73*, 2975. The play of Śakuntalā, verses 18, 26, &c.

[6] MBh i, *73*, 2972; *74*, 3105–6, 3117–18: xiv, *3*, 50. Also the play. Bhāg ix, *20*, 8–22. Śatapatha Brāhm xiii, 5, 4, 13.

[7] MBh i, *74*, 3122.

[8] MBh vii, *68*, 2387: xii, *29*, 942.

[9] Named in the Mat list, *199*, 18. But a Śāṇḍili is named among the Vasiṣṭhas also, Mat *200*, 5.

[10] Vā *73*, 41–2. Bd iii, *10*, 90–1. Hv *18*, 991–3.

[11] MBh xiii, *137*, 6266.

the rishi Ṛṣyaśṛṅga, whom Lomapāda, king of Aṅga, in whose territory they lived, inveigled to his capital to bring rain after a long drought, and to whom he gave his daughter Śāntā in marriage.[1] Ṛṣyaśṛṅga was afterwards invited to the court of Daśaratha, king of Ayodhyā, and performed a sacrifice that the king might have a son.[2] A descendant Vaibhāṇḍaki, whose name was apparently Pūrṇabhadra, is connected with Lomapāda's fourth successor Haryaṅga.[3]

Next would probably come Nidhruva and Rebha as noticed above.

The next famous Kāśyapa was the rishi Asita.[4] His wife was Ekaparṇā (p. 69), and their son was Devala.[5] This portion is given in the genealogy. Devala is often called Asita Devala,[6] and sometimes even simply Asita;[7] hence it is not always clear which is meant, and he must be distinguished from other Devalas.[8] The genealogy says that Devala, and therefore Asita presumably, were Śāṇḍilyas, thus indicating that it is imperfect, and that they must have had an ancestor Śaṇḍila, who lived much earlier, as pointed out above. Asita is made contemporary with Bhīṣma, for he had asked for Satyavatī in marriage;[9] Devala with the Pāṇḍavas,[10] and Devala's younger brother (cousin?) Dhaumya

[1] MBh iii, *110*, 9989 to *113*, 10093: xii, *234*, 8609: xiii, *137*, 6269. Rām i, *9* and *10*. Cf. Viṣ iv, *18*, 3. It is said Lomapāda had a son through Ṛṣyaśṛṅga's favour, Vā *99*, 104; Mat *48*, 95–6; Br *13*, 41; Hv *31*, 1697–8.

[2] Rām i, *11*, 19 f. But not so in MBh iii, *273*, 15877–9.

[3] Hv *31*, 1700–1. Br *13*, 44. Mat *48*, 98–9 (Vibhāṇḍaka).

[4] Mat *199*, 19. Lg i, *63*, 51. Bṛhadd ii, 157. Probably MBh xii, *47*, 1594. Anukram and Vedārth on Rigv ix, *5* and *24*. Asita Dhānva of the asuras (*Vedic Index* i, 399) would be different. There were several Asitas, see Sörensen.

[5] Lg i, *63*, 53–4. MBh xii, *1*, 4: xiii, *139*, 6298: &c. So implied in MBh ix, *51* and perhaps ii, *52*, 1917. But one brahmanical book inverts the relation and calls Asita *Daivala* wrongly, *Vedic Index* i, 380.

[6] MBh ii, *4*, 105; *11*, 441; *12*, 510; *58*, 2038: &c.

[7] MBh xii, *229*, 8431–6; *276*, 9874–7.

[8] A son of Viśvāmitra, Hv *27*, 1462; Br *10*, 60. The father of Brahmadatta's queen Sannati, Mat *20*, 26; Hv *24*, 1274–8, 1297–8: but Hv *23*, 1261–2 identifies him with Asita Devala wrongly. A son of Pratyūṣa (mythical?), MBh i, *66*, 2590; Vā *66*, 26; Bḍ iii, *3*, 27; Br *3*, 41; Hv *3*, 159; &c.

[9] MBh i, *100*, 4045. With Yudhiṣṭhira, ii, *76*, 2574.

[10] MBh ii, *53*, 1917: iii, *85*, 8263: xii, *1*, 3–5.

became their purohita.[1] Both Asita and Devala were celebrated brahma-vādins, as mentioned above;[2] and other statements are made about them in brahmanical accounts.[3]

Various other Kāśyapas are mentioned, such as Yāja, who became king Drupada's sacrifice;[4] but they are generally indefinite or unimportant.

The genealogy says there were three groups among the Kāśyapas, the Śāṇḍilyas, Naidhruvas and Raibhyas.

CHAPTER XXI

THE VIŚVĀMITRAS

THE family of the Viśvāmitras was founded by the great Viśvāmitra, and the story about him has been narrated above (p. 205). His brahmanhood was disputed by the great Devarāj Vasiṣṭha, and he succeeded in establishing it, with the result that he held a position independent of all other brahmans, and so founded an independent brahman family, the only separate brahman family founded by a kṣatriya.[5] His position has been fixed above (p. 152). The various Viśvāmitras who will be noticed are however often confused, and sometimes regarded as one and the same person,[6] with the result that no allusions occur which can well suggest names to distinguish them. An account of Viśvāmitra and his sons is given by four Puranas[7] and the texts should be collated. Lists

[1] MBh i, *183*, 6914, 6918–19; &c.: xv, *23*, 632. P. C. Roy's translation of xiv, *64*, 1903 makes Agniveśya his (Yudhiṣṭhira's) priest, and says Āgniveśya was another name of Dhaumya: but *purohita* and *Āgniveśya* are distinct, and the rendering should be 'his priest' (i.e. Dhaumya) 'and Āgniveśya'.

[2] Rigv ix, *5* to *24* are ascribed to one or other of them.

[3] e.g. Asita declared *pṛthivī-gīta* ślokas to Dharmadhvajin Janaka, Viṣ iv, *24*, 54. Devala in Pad vi, *197*, 27 f.

[4] MBh i, *167*, 6362 f.: ii, *78*, 2662.

[5] MBh xiii, *3*, 185; *4*, 247–8.

[6] e.g. MBh i, *71*, 2921–8.

[7] Hv *27*, 1460–3; *32*, 1767–9. Br *10*, 57–60; *13*, note to verse 91. These are closely alike. Vā *91*, 96–7 and Bḍ iii, *66*, 68–9 are alike but give only two lines. But all these sons may not have been sons of the first Viśvāmitra.

of the gotras are also given by various authorities and will be noticed.

Viśvāmitra had many sons, chief among them being Madhucchandas, Kati (or Kata?) Ṛṣabha, Reṇu, Aṣṭaka[1] and Gālava.[2] He also adopted the Bhārgava Śunaḥśepa with the name Devarāta and made him the chief of all his sons.[3] Aṣṭaka appears to have succeeded Viśvāmitra in the kingdom of Kānyakubja (p. 146), but all the rest were entirely brahmans. Accounts concur (though differing in details) that Viśvāmitra's sons did not all accept Devarāta's headship; and it is said that Viśvāmitra cursed those who repudiated it to become dog-eaters or mlecchas,[4] such as Andhras, Puṇḍras and Śabaras.[5] The Rāmāyaṇa says absurdly that he cursed all his sons, because they refused to offer themselves as victims in Śunaḥśepa's stead, to be dog-eaters dwelling like the Vasiṣṭhas among the lowest castes.[6] This is certainly wrong, for Madhucchandas and others were not degraded. There are allusions at times to degraded Viśvāmitras,[7] but it is difficult to say what that means,[8] and it is distinctly stated that all his sons were munis who declared sacred lore.[9]

The Bhāgavata says[10]—Madhucchandas was the middle son. The elder sons resented Devarāta's position, but Madhucchandas and the younger sons accepted it; so Viśvāmitra blessed them and Devarāta as 'Kuśikas', and they constituted the Kauśika gotra, while the elder sons were separate and known as 'Viśvāmitras'.

[1] Vedārth on Rigv ix, *70* and x, *104*. But possibly sons of different Viśvāmitras have been mixed up. The 13 chief Kuśikas are named, Pd ii, *32*, 117–19; Mat *145*, 111–14.

[2] In story of Satyavrata Triśaṅku, p. 38. MBh xiii, *4*, 251. In various stories, Mārk *20*, 42 to *21*, 4; VN *21*, 33. Cf. p. 142, and second note above.

[3] P. 206. Rām i, *57*, 3–4 gives him four sons with names all wrong. Bṛhadd iv, 95 and Bhāg ix, *16*, 29 say 101.

[4] MBh xiii, *3*, 188.

[5] Aitareya Brāhm vii, 18. Śāṅkhāyana Śr Sūtra xv, 26.

[6] Rām i, *62*, 9–17.

[7] As Rākṣasas, Vā *69*, 195; *70*, 53, 56: Bd iii, *8*, 59, 62.

[8] It may have been developed out of the story that a Viśvāmitra, compelled by hunger, once ate dog's flesh from a caṇḍāla's hand; Br *93*, 5–24; Manu x, 108; MBh xii, *141*, 5344–5417. But more probably it means that some of Viśvāmitra's descendants became priests to non-Aryan tribes and so degenerated to the level of their clients. It is said he created yātudhānas, MBh xiii, *3*, 4. See Paulastyas, note, next chapter.

[9] MBh xiii, *4*, 248, 259.

[10] Bhāg ix, *16*, 29, 33–7.

But tradition hardly seems to acknowledge this distinction, for the Viśvāmitras generally seem to have been known as Kuśikas and Kauśikas, after Viśvāmitra's grandfather king Kuśika (p. 144).

The next Viśvāmitra was the father of Śakuntalā, Duṣyanta's queen and Bharata's mother (*ante*). Nothing particular is said about him and he is generally confused with the first Viśvāmitra,[1] though there was a considerable interval between them (pp. 144, 146). His position is therefore fixed. A Viśvāmitra is next mentioned in the story of Kalmāṣapāda Saudāsa, king of Ayodhyā, but he appears to have been mistakenly introduced into it through confusing this Saudāsa with Sudāsa (p. 208). A later Viśvāmitra is introduced in the Rāmāyaṇa, as obtaining Rāma's help to destroy the demon Tārakā, and as narrating various wonderful legends to Rāma.[2] There were of course Viśvāmitras at that time, but his appearance there is doubtful and seems intended to glorify Rāma.[3] Moreover, he is there wrongly identified with the first Viśvāmitra,[4] and the brahmanic fable of the contest between that Viśvāmitra and Vasiṣṭha is narrated as concerning him.[5]

An important Viśvāmitra was the rishi who was connected with Sudās (Sudāsa) king of N. Pañcāla (p. 148), and was a rival of the seventh Vasiṣṭha noticed in chapter XVIII. Both these rishis were priests to Sudās, as the Rigveda shows,[6] and one appears to have ousted the other; and the point for consideration here is which was first Sudās's priest, and which afterwards. It is said that Vasiṣṭha consecrated Sudās as king,[7] and this if accepted would settle the question. Tradition says that this Vasiṣṭha's son Śakti was killed by Sudās's servants through Viśvāmitra's instigation (p. 208); and there are two facts, first, that there is no hymn by any Vasiṣṭha in praise of Sudās's son Sahadeva or grandson Somaka; and secondly, hymn iii, *33*, attributed to Viśvāmitra, describes the Bharatas as crossing the rivers Śutudrī (Sutlej) and Vipāś (Beas), and appears to refer to Sudās and his Bharatas, because no Viśvāmitra is said to have been priest to the other Bhārata line, the Pauravas of Hastinā-

[1] As in MBh i, *71*, 2923–8, where he and other Viśvāmitras are confused.

[2] Rām i, *18*, 39 f. Viṣ iv, *4*, 41–2 copies.

[3] The Rāmopākhyāna (MBh iii, *276*) says nothing about it.

[4] Rām i, *18*, 39–40.

[5] *Id.* i, *51*, 19 f.

[6] Viśvāmitra; iii, *53*, 9, 11, 12. Vasiṣṭha; vii, *18*, 4, 22, 23.

[7] Aitareya Brāhm viii, 4, 21.

pura; that is, it appears to refer to Sudās's campaign against Saṁvaraṇa westwards into the Panjab. These considerations corroborate the point that Sudās's first priest was Vasiṣṭha, that Vasiṣṭha's son Śakti was killed through Viśvāmitra's instigation, and that ultimately Vasiṣṭha departed to Saṁvaraṇa and Viśvāmitra became Sudās's priest.[1] Manu's story (p. 209) may help to explain how Viśvāmitra ousted Vasiṣṭha.

'Viśvāmitra' is said to have had a son Raibhya,[2] who had two sons Arvāvasu and Parāvasu.[3] They are connected in stories with 'Bharadvāja' and his son Yavakrī, and a king Bṛhaddyumna,[4] and with Vasu king of Cedi and a Raibhya Dhanus;[5] and Parāvasu with Rāma Jāmadagnya;[6] but these allegations are inconsistent brahmanical fables.[7] The river Kauśikī (Kosi in N. Behar) was said to have been specially connected with 'Viśvāmitra', and named after his patronymic Kauśika.[8] Other references to 'Viśvāmitra' occur,[9] but are uncertain, especially as the different Viśvāmitras and Kauśikas were confused.

Viśvāmitra's descendants formed many gotras, and more lists are given of them than in any other brahman family. Four Puranas contain lists, which are all different versions of one and the same original list.[10] The Matsya (*198*) gives a longer list, which agrees with those lists in ten names only. The epic also gives a long list of rishis in this family, and only some fifteen names practically agree with those in the former lists.[11] The gotra names generally found in these lists are—Babhru, Devarāta, Gālava, Hiraṇyākṣa, Jābāla, Karīśi, Kuśika or Kauśika, Lohita, Madhucchandas, Pāṇini, Saindhavāyana, Śālaṅkāyana, Suśruta, Tārakāyaṇa, Yājñavalkya.[12]

[1] See p. 172, and JRAS, 1918, pp. 233–8, 246–8. *Vedic Index* ii, 89 inverts this.

[2] MBh xii, *49*, 1771. A Raibhya also among the Kāśyapas (*ante*).

[3] MBh iii, *135*, 10704; *138*, 10792: xii, *49*, 1771–2.

[4] MBh iii, *135* to *138*.

[5] MBh xii, *338*, 12754–8.

[6] MBh xii, *49*, 1772–5.

[7] See tables, pp. 144 f., 191 f.

[8] MBh i, *71*, 2924: iii, *84*, 8109–10; *110*, 9987–90.

[9] e. g. Kauśika, MBh ii, *20*, 807; v, *116*, 3972. Gālava's son Śṛṅgavant, ix, *53*, 2992–5.

[10] Vā *91*, 97–102. Bd iii, *66*, 69–74. Hv *27*, 1463–9; *32*, 1770–3. Br *10*, 61–3; *13*, note to verse 91. See p. 101.

[11] MBh xiii, *4*, 248–59.

[12] There was a Yājñavalkya gotra among the Vasiṣṭhas also, Mat *200*, 6.

CHAPTER XXII

AGASTYAS, PAULASTYAS, PAULAHAS, AND KRATUS

Agastyas.

THERE is no genealogy of the Agastyas, and the Matsya alone (*202*) gives a list of gotras, which it calls their vaṁśa. 'Agastya' appears in various stories at various times from the earliest age down to the Pāṇḍavas' time,[1] and there is great indefiniteness about the Agastyas.

Fable, which has been noticed in connexion with Vasiṣṭha Maitrāvaruṇa (chapter XVIII), gives 'Agastya' an origin with 'Vasiṣṭha' in making them both born in a water-jar, sons of the two gods Mitra and Varuṇa, 'Agastya' being thus 'Vasiṣṭha's' younger brother.[2] Hence 'Agastya' had the patronymic Maitrāvaruṇi,[3] and the names Kumbhayoni,[4] Kumbhajanman [5] and other synonyms.[6] Maitrāvaruṇi really meant 'son (or descendant) of Mitrāvaruṇa', but was taken to mean 'son of Mitra and Varuṇa'[7] (as explained in chapter XVIII), and so the common patronymic of 'Vasiṣṭha' and 'Agastya' led to the fable that they were begotten together; and it is noteworthy that no reason is given why 'Agastya' was so born, such as is given for 'Vasiṣṭha'.

Kumbhayoni may have been a real name, for queer names were not uncommon, as witness Tṛṇabindu, Śunaḥśepa and many others, and it can be matched with Urjayoni, the name of a son of Viśvāmitra.[8] If so, it would naturally have led to the allegation that he was born in a jar, just as Vasiṣṭha's name Kuṇḍina

[1] e.g. with king Nahuṣa, MBh v, *16*, 520–1: xiii, *99* f. (fable). With Rāma Jāmadagnya, MBh xiii, *84*, 3967–9. With Bhīṣma, *id. 26*, 1761. All fables.

[2] Also Mat *61*, 19: Pad v, *22*. 20–1; *33*, 121.

[3] MBh iii, *103*, 8776: xii, *344*, 13216: xiii, *99*, 4771: &c. Vedārth on Rigv i, *166*. Shortened to *Vāruṇi*, MBh iii, *103*, 8774–5; *105*, 8805–7.

[4] Mat *61*, 50. Pad v, *22*, 56. MBh iii, *98*, 8595–6: xii, *344*, 13216.

[5] Raghuv xii, 31.

[6] Cf. Bd iii, *35*, 42, 53.

[7] MBh xii, *208*, 7595: xiii, *150*, 7113: *165*, 7666.

[8] MBh xiii, *4*, 258.

did (*ante*); but it seems more likely to have been coined out of the fable, thus—'Vasiṣṭha' and 'Agastya' were both Maitrāvaruṇa, interpreted as 'son of Mitra and Varuṇa'. 'Vasiṣṭha' was Kuṇḍina, interpreted to mean 'connected with a jar', therefore Agastya must also have been their son born at the same time and in the same way, and so was *Kumbha-yoni*. This is illustrated by Droṇa, whose name gave rise to a precisely similar explanation,[1] whence he also is styled Kumbhayoni[2] and Kumbhasambhava.[3] Hence the name would seem to have been devised out of the fable, and it may be noted that 'Vasiṣṭha' is never called Kumbhayoni, because he had the name Kuṇḍina; and the fable was also utilized to explain Mānya, the patronymic of an Agastya.

As noticed above, the stories in which 'Agastya' is introduced at various times are generally brahmanic stories, unsupported otherwise, and worthless chronologically. The only Agastya, to whom a genuine historical position is assigned, is the rishi who married Lopāmudrā, and whose place has been fixed above (p. 168). He is sometimes called Kumbhayoni and Maitrāvaruṇa.[4] Their son was, it is said, Dṛḍhasyu, who was called Idhmavāha also.[5] Dṛḍhasyu's name is variously given as Dṛḍhāsya, Dṛḍhāyus and Dṛḍhadyumna; and Idhmavāha as Vidhmavāha and Indrabāhu.[6] They were however different persons,[7] because the former is no doubt Dṛḍhacyuta,[8] the reputed author of Rigveda ix, *25*; and Idhmavāha was his son, for as the reputed author of ix, *26* he is called Dārḍhacyuta. 'Agastya' and these two are said to have been the most famous Agastis.[9]

The Veda throws very little light on the Agastyas because it mentions them only by their family name Agastya. 'Agastya' is said to be the author of hymns i, *165* to *191*, but this is only the family name and no doubt includes several Agastyas, for, while to the Agastya who married Lopāmudrā would belong hymn *179*, the author of hymn *185* apparently calls himself Sumedhas (verse 10), and the Sumedhases were a gotra among the Agastyas.[10] Āgastyas

[1] MBh i, *63*, 2434–5; *130*, 5102–6; *137*, 5433; *166*, 6328–32.
[2] MBh vii, *157*, 6947; *185*, 8364, 8367.
[3] MBh vii, *157*, 6956; *193*, 8823.
[4] Mat *61*, 50, 53.
[5] MBh iii, *99*, 8640–2.
[6] Mat *145*, 114; *202*, 8, 11.
[7] So treated in Mat *loc. cit.*; Bd ii, *32*, 119–20.
[8] He seems to be referred to in Vedārth on Rigv ix, *5*.
[9] Mat *145*, 114–15.
[10] Mat *202*, 2.

are alluded to sometimes,[1] but very few are mentioned by name besides those noticed above.[2] One was Māna, for the author of hymn *189* calls himself Māna's son; the Mānas are mentioned and the patronymic Mānya occurs.[3] Māndārya is probably another patronymic pointing to a Mandāra, and Māna and Mandāra were in the same line of descent because the author of hymns *165* and *166* calls himself Māndārya Mānya,[4] and it is said that Mānya was Maitrāvaruṇi, son (or descendant) of Mitrāvaruṇa.[5]

There is nothing to show when or how the Agastyas arose. The fable noticed above connects 'Agastya' with 'Vasiṣṭha', but that seems merely a fabrication from the fact that a Vasiṣṭha and an Agastya both had the same patronymic *Maitrāvaruṇa*. Tradition generally connects 'Agastya' with the southern region[6] and even with Ceylon.[7] Thus 'Agastya' met Lopāmudrā at the great tīrtha on the river Sindhu,[8] that is the Sindh, a southern tributary of the Jumna. 'Agastya' is called 'lord of the southern region',[9] and is sometimes said to dwell on Mt. Malaya[10] at the extreme south. Canopus, the brightest star in the southern hemisphere, bears his name. Fables also connect 'Agastya' with the south, such as his altering the height of the Vindhya Mts.,[11] the story of Ilvala and Vātāpi,[12] and others.[13] He had a hermitage apparently near Mt. Vaidūrya[14] (the western part of the Satpura range), another called Saubhadra on the southern ocean,[15] and another among the Pāṇḍyas.[16] But the Agastyas spread elsewhere, and so mention is made of 'Agastya' in connexion with the Jumna, Prayāga and other places,[17] and Gayā appropriated some of the fame of Agastya and Lopāmudrā.[18]

[1] MBh iii, *26*, 971: xii, *344*, 13216 (Calc. edition).
[2] One Śarmin, MBh xiii, *68*, 3400. [3] Rigv i, *177*, 5; *184*, 4, 5.
[4] As Kakṣīvant is styled Dairghatamasa and Auśija (p. 161).
[5] Anukramaṇī and Vedārth on Rigv viii, *67*.
[6] Rām iii, *11*, 78–84; Br *84*, 8; *118*, 6, 8. Raghuv iv, *44*.
[7] Mat *61*, 51 (Laṅkā). [8] MBh iii, *130*, 10541.
[9] Br *118*, 2; *158*, 11: Hv *117*, 6591. 'Conqueror,' Rām vi, *117*, 14.
[10] Mat *61*, 37. Pad v, *22*, 40. Vā *48*, 20–3. Rām iv, *41*, 15–16.
[11] MBh iii, *104*. Br *118*, 2–8.
[12] MBh iii, *96*, 8543–52; *99*, 8615–32; *206*: xii, *141*, 5389. Rām iii, *11*, 55 f.
[13] Pad v, *19*, 160 f.; *22*, 40 f. Many in MBh.
[14] MBh iii, *88*, 8344. [15] MBh i, *216*, 7839–46; *217*, 7877.
[16] MBh iii, *88*, 8339: probably *118*, 10217.
[17] MBh iii, *87*, 8314–17; *96*, 8540; *99*, 8645–6; *161*, 11794: &c.
[18] Vā *108*, 53–6; *111*, 53.

The Paulastyas.

An account which professes to give an historical explanation of Pulastya's offspring is found in five Puranas.[1] It derives them from the royal line of Vaiśālī. 'Nariṣyanta, son of Marutta, had a son Dama (p. 147). His (eighth) successor was Tṛṇabindu, who was king at the third mouth of the Tretā age (p. 178). Tṛṇabindu's daughter was Ilavilā and he gave her to Pulastya. Their son was the rishi Viśravas Ailavila.[2] Viśravas had four wives, a Bṛhaspati's[3] daughter Devavarṇinī, Mālyavant's daughters Puṣpotkaṭā and Vākā, and Mālin's daughter Kaikasī. Viśravas's son by Devavarṇinī was Kubera Vaiśravaṇa,[4] and Kubera had four sons Nalakūbara, Rāvaṇa,[5] Kumbhakarṇa, and Vibhīṣaṇa and a daughter Śūrpanakhā. Kaikasī bore Daśagrīva and other sons; Puṣpotkaṭā bore Khara and other sons; and Vākā various sons. Pulastya's offspring (putting aside Kubera) were Rākṣasas, and the Matsya says (*202*, 12–13) that Pulastya, seeing that, adopted Agastya's son (who is not named)[6] and so the Paulastyas were Āgastyas.

The account continues. These Āgastyas were thus classed along with the great body of Rākṣasas, and they together with another group called Vaiśvāmitras or Kauśikas were reckoned Paulastya Rākṣasas.[7] How the Vaiśvāmitras or Kauśikas came to be treated as such is not explained (but see chapter XXI, note). The Paulastyas thus comprised three groups, Pulastya's own descendants, the Āgastyas and the Vaiśvāmitras or Kauśikas; and Kubera was king of all the Yakṣas and of the Āgastyas and Vaiśvāmitras, who

[1] Vā *70*, 29–56. Bd iii, *8*, 34–62. Lg i, *63*, 55–66. Kūr i, *19*, 7–15. Pad vi, *269*, 15–19 and Bhāg ix, *2*, 31–2, partially. Cf. MBh iii, *273*, 15881 to *274*, 15896: differently, Rām vii, *2* to *5* and *9*; see iii, *22*.

[2] He dwelt on R. Narmadā, MBh iii, *89*, 8357–8. This, if true, would make the Paulastyas begin there, in the NW. Dekhan.

[3] He is called *ācārya* of the gods, being identified with the semi-mythical Bṛhaspati (chap. XVI).

[4] Called *Ailavila*, MBh v, *138*, 4717–8: ix, *48*, 2753.

[5] As regards Rāvaṇa's relations, see also Rām iii, *48*, 2–5; *50*, 9; *68*, 16: iv, *58*, 19: v, *23*, 6–8: vi, *19*, 10; *35*, 6.

[6] Mārk *52*, 22–3 says Pulastya's son was Dattoli, who was known as Agastya in the Svāyambhuva manvantara. Cf. Ag *20*, 13.

[7] It is perfectly clear that *Rākṣasa* here does not mean demon, but uncivilized non-Aryan tribes.

were Paulastya Rākṣasas, cruel brahma-rākṣasas,[1] who studied the Veda and performed austerities and religious exercises.[2] There were four other groups who were reckoned Rākṣasas, three of which were active in the day time, but the Paulastyas, Āgastyas, Kauśikas and Nairṛtas were active at night.[3] Wise Āgastya brahma-rākṣasas are said to attend on Kauberaka (Kubera?) on Hiraṇyaśṛṅga.[4]

It is noteworthy that all the Paulastyas (except Kubera, who was reckoned a god) belonged to S. India and Ceylon, and that Pulastya is made a contemporary of Tṛṇabindu, whose position has been fixed (p. 178), so that Pulastya was not a primaeval rishi, and a definite time is assigned for the origin of the Paulastyas.[5] As already shown, Viśvāmitra and Agastya existed before that time, so Vaiśvāmitras and Āgastyas could have been incorporated among the Paulastyas. At the same time it must be noted that some passages connect these Paulastya Rākṣasas with the Himalayan region also,[6] and Kubera with Ceylon[7] as well as with that region.[8]

[1] This appears to be an epithet of the Āgastyas and Vaiśvāmitras, and to mean Rākṣasas who had been or were descended from brahmans, or brahmans who had allied themselves with Rākṣasas. Cf. also Vā *69*, 195–6; Bd iii, *7*, 162–3. Rām i, *8*, 17 and *12*, 18 speak of 'wise brahma-rākṣasas'.

[2] This is noteworthy with reference to chap. XXI, note. Paulastya yātudhānas are mentioned, MBh vii, *156*, 16372. Their Veda might be the Atharvaveda.

[3] These words seem to mean, from the preceding description, that these degraded brahmans performed their religious rites at night.

[4] Vā *47*, 60–1, Bd ii, *18*, 63–4.

[5] This does not harmonize with the story that, when Arjuna Kārtavīrya captured 'Rāvaṇa' and imprisoned him at Māhiṣmatī, Pulastya appealed for leniency, and Arjuna then released 'Rāvaṇa'; for Arjuna was much earlier than Tṛṇabindu: Vā *94*, 35–6; Bd iii, *69*, 35–7; Hv *33*, 1876–8; Br *13*, 184–7; Mat *43*, 37–9; Pad v, *12*, 136–8. Fancifully elaborated, Rām vii, *31* to *33*. *Rāvaṇa* is probably not a personal name, but a Sanskritized form of the Tamil word *iṟeivaṉ* or *iṟaivaṉ*, 'God, king, sovereign, lord' (JRAS, 1914, p. 285); and if so, Arjuna may have captured a Dravidian *rāvaṇa* or king, and Pulastya may have been introduced afterwards (Viṣ iv, *11*, 6 says nothing about Pulastya), when the Rāvaṇas were confused.

[6] e.g. MBh iii, *274*, 15901: v, *110*, 3830. Rām iii, *32*, 14–16. Pad vi, *269*, 20–1.

[7] e.g. Rām vii, *3*, 22–33. MBh iii, *274*, 15920–1.

[8] e.g. MBh v, *110*, 3830–1, 3840: xiii, *19*, 1412 f.; *110*, 4860.

Paulahas.

Pulaha's fabulous progeny has been noticed (chapter XVI), but the Matsya says (*202*, 10–11) that Pulaha had three sons (who are not named [1]) and, not being pleased with them, adopted Agastya's son Dṛḍhāsya (that is, Dṛḍhacyuta, *ante*), and so the Paulahas were Āgastyas. The Padma says (vi, *218*, 62–3) that he begot a son Dambholi, who had been Agastya formerly.[2] No further particulars are given of the Paulahas.

Kratus.

Kratu has been noticed (chapter XVI), and the Matsya says (*202*, 8–9) that he adopted 'Agastya's' son Idhmavāha (*ante*), and the Kratus therefore were Āgastyas.

CHAPTER XXIII

KṢATRIYAN BRAHMANS

A PECULIAR combination of the kṣatriya and brahman, of the prince and priest, has now to be noticed, in that branches of royal families became brahmans at times and yet retained their kṣatriya status, and were described as *kṣatropetā dvijātayaḥ*, which may be rendered 'kṣatriyan brahmans'. This happened in several families and can be best studied among the junior branches of the Pauravas after Bharata's time.

Much has been written about early contests between brahmans and kṣatriyas, and Muir has noticed most of them,[3] but the subject may be discriminated more properly thus. Contests were of three kinds, first, where a king slighted, quarrelled with, injured or killed a brahman; secondly, where he, as a kṣatriya, arrogated the right to perform religious ceremonies himself and so disputed or infringed brahmanic privileges; and thirdly, where a kṣatriya sought to become a brahman. The vast majority of contests mentioned were of the first kind. Very few of the second kind are recorded, and they arose only in later times when the brahmans had established

[1] Mārk *52*, 23–4 calls them Kardama, Aṛvavīra and Sahiṣṇu. Cf. Ag *20*, 13.

[2] Compare eleventh note above. [3] *Sanskrit Texts* i, pp. 58–174.

their right to perform sacrifices, such as king Janamejaya III's dispute,[1] for it seems that in early times kings themselves sacrificed. These two kinds were the analogues of disputes and contests in Europe between the temporal and spiritual powers. The third is the only kind that concerns us here, and of this kind there is really none, as far as I am aware, except the great contest between Vasiṣṭha and Viśvāmitra. That has been described above (p. 205) and was a personal quarrel, not a general denial of a kṣatriya's right to become a brahman, and Vasiṣṭha's denial of Viśvāmitra's brahmanhood was simply a means of revenge.[2] The brahmans in later times distorted the story into ridiculous fables, which extolled their pretensions.

There was no general denial of a kṣatriya's right in those early times to become a brahman.[3] There are abundant instances of kings' becoming rishis, *rājarṣis*, without any difficulty, and that was tantamount to becoming brahmans. The earliest is that of Nahuṣa's son Yati, who relinquished the kingdom to his brother Yayāti and became a brahman muni.[4] Others prior to Viśvāmitra were Māndhātṛ, Kāśya and Gṛtsamada, and after his time there were numerous instances, as will be shown.[5]

The term *kṣatropetā dvijātayaḥ* was used comprehensively sometimes, as shown in a passage which enumerates many of them.[6] There it includes three classes: kṣatriyas who relinquished their own status and became brahmans, such as Viśvāmitra; others of lower rank who became brahmans, such as Kakṣīvant (p. 220); and kṣatriyas who became brahmans and still retained their kṣatriya status, that is, 'kṣatriyan brahmans', and it is this class to which the term more properly and mainly applies. They developed in both the Solar and Lunar lines, rarely and only in the earliest times in the former, oftener and at various periods in the latter. They were real brahmans with the kṣatriya status superadded.[7] There

[1] Mat *50*, 57–65. Vā *99*, 250–6.

[2] JRAS, 1913, p. 900; 1917, pp. 41–44.

[3] Impliedly acknowledged in allusions, e.g. MBh i, *137*, 5432.

[4] Bḍ iii, *68*, 14. Br *12*, 3. Hv *30*, 1602. Vā *93*, 14. Lg i, *66*, 63. MBh i, *75*, 3156. Mat *24*, 51 and Pad v, *12*, 104 say he became a Vaikhānasa yogin. Cf. Ag *273*, 21. P. 167.

[5] A Janaka became a brahman through a Yājñavalkya's boon, so Śatapatha Brāhm xi, 6, 2, 10.

[6] Vā *91*, 115–18. Bḍ iii, *66*, 86–9.

[7] Parallels occurred in later times, as in the Kāṇvāyana dynasty (Mat *272*, 32–7. Vā *99*, 343–7. Bḍ iii, *74*, 156–160. Viṣ iv, *24*, 12. Bhāg xii, *1*, 19–21), and in the Marāṭha Peshwas.

is no suggestion that there was any difficulty in the assumption of brahmanhood in such cases, and hymns composed by such persons were admitted into the Rigveda. Princes who became rishis in the earliest times are often described as having qualified themselves by long austerities, but, apart from the general statement about austerities in the passage cited above, there is no indication that these 'kṣatriyan brahmans' underwent any such initiation, and it seems they merely assumed brahmanhood. In the Lunar line those after Bharata's time could claim brahman ancestry, because they were descended from the Bharadvāja, whom Bharata adopted as son and who continued his lineage (p. 159 f.), so that they could regard themselves as kṣatriyas or brahmans or both combined.[1]

There were two differences between these kṣatriyan brahmans and Viśvāmitra. First, he relinquished his kṣatriyahood and kingdom to become a brahman: they relinquished nothing and assumed brahmanhood. The combination however was not stable, and the members gravitated to one or the other status; thus the eldest princes, who succeeded to the throne, became mainly kṣatriya, and their successors gradually dropped their brahmanic character, while among the junior scions the latter predominated and they developed into pure brahmans. The other difference was that Viśvāmitra established a separate brahman family as noticed above, but these kṣatriyan brahmans were admitted into, and their descendants formed gotras in, one or other of the great brahman families, especially the Āṅgirasas and Bhārgavas.

There is no good reason to distrust the tradition about these kṣatriyan brahmans, as has been shown above (p. 124). Even the Bhāgavata, avowedly a brahmanic Purana, acknowledges the origin of the Urukṣayas, Kapis, Gārgyas, Priyamedhas and Maudgalyas from the Paurava dynasty,[2] as will be shown. That brahmans sprang from this dynasty is alluded to in other passages.[3]

The sub-families of kṣatriyan brahmans may now be considered individually according as they sprang first from the Solar and secondly from the Lunar race.

[1] See Vedārthadīp on Rigv vi *52*. [2] Bhāg ix, *21*, 19–21, 33.

[3] Mat *50*, 88; Vā *99*, 278; Viṣ iv, *21*, 4:—*brahma-kṣatrasya yo yonir vaṁśaḥ*; which is true, whether we take it as 'brahmans and kṣatriyas', or as 'those who combined the brahman and kṣatriya status'. Even Bhāg ix, *22*, 44 similarly, and ix, *20*, 1 says of this dynasty:—

yatra rājarṣayo vaṁśyā brahma-vaṁśyāś ca jajñire.

Kṣatriyan brahmans in the Solar race.

Viṣṇuvṛddhas and Hārītas.

The chief development in the Sôlar race occurred among the descendants of king Māndhātṛ (p. 93), who was reckoned a kṣatriyan brahman,[1] and their genealogy stands thus according to four Puranas[2]:—

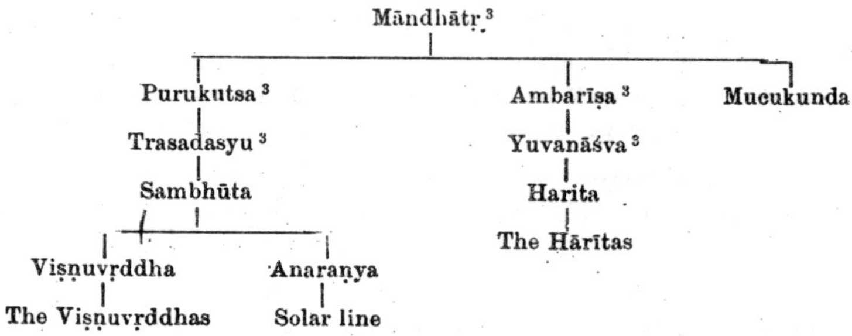

The texts say the Viṣṇuvṛddhas and Hārītas were kṣatriyan brahmans[4] and joined the Āṅgirasas; accordingly both are mentioned in the vaṁśa of the Āṅgirasas.[5] Nothing more appears to be said about them.[6]

Rathītaras.

Descended from Manu's son Nābhāga was Rathītara (p. 98). His sons, born kṣatriyas, became Āṅgirasas, and the Rathītara gotras were kṣatriyan brahmans.[7] Accordingly they are named

[1] He and Purukutsa, Vā *91*. 115–16: Bḍ iii, *66*, 86–7.

[2] Lg i, *65*, 39–43. Kūr i, *20*, 25–8. Vā *88*, 71–5 and 79 *b* and *c* (see p. 81). Bḍ iii, *63*, 72–3 (incomplete). Almost similarly, Viṣ iv, *2*, 19; *3*, 5, 12: Bhāg ix, *6*, 34–8; *7*, 1–4. Cf. Gar i, *138*, 22–3.

[3] All these were hymn-makers among the Āṅgirasas, Vā *59*, 99, 102: Bḍ ii, *32*, 108, 112: Mat *145*, 102, 106. Nābhāka Kāṇva imitated Mandhātṛ's manner of praise, Rigv viii, *40*, 12; and x, *134* is attributed to Mandhātṛ. The Kāṇvas were Āṅgirasas, chap. XIX.

[4] Cf. Vā *91*, 117: Bḍ iii, *66*, 88.

[5] Vā *65*, 107. Bḍ iii, *1*, 111. Mat *196*, 33, 39, where read probably *Viṣṇuvṛddha* for *Viṣṇusiddhi*.

[6] Two Hārītas, *Vedic Index* i, 184: Pad vi, *220*, 43.

[7] Vā *88*, 5–7; Bḍ iii, *63*, 5–7 and Viṣ iv, *2*, 2 say:—

ete kṣatra-prasūtā vai punaś cÂṅgirasaḥ smṛtāḥ
Rathītarāṇām pravarāḥ kṣatropetā dvijātayaḥ

Bhāg ix, *6*, 1–3 quotes this verse incorrectly and makes the Rathītaras sons of Rathītara's wife and Aṅgiras; and the commentator on Viṣ repeats the misconception. Cf. Vā *91*, 117: Bḍ iii, *66*, 88.

among the Āṅgirasas.[1] It has been shown that the Āṅgirasas hardly appeared as a full brahman family until the time of Karandhama, the Vaiśāla king (pp. 157 f.); but when the Rathītaras were incorporated among them is uncertain; and it is possible that the Rathītara line of ancestry has been greatly abbreviated. They are rarely referred to.

Kṣatriyan brahmans in the Lunar race.

Śaunakas and Ārṣṭiṣeṇas.

The first instance occurred in the Kāśi dynasty. Sunahotra, one of the earliest kings, had three sons, Kāśa, Śala and Gṛtsamada. Gṛtsamada's son was Śunaka, and from him were descended the Śaunakas, who comprised all four castes. Śala's son was Ārṣṭiṣeṇa. The Śaunakas and Ārṣṭiṣeṇas were kṣatriyan brahmans.[2] 'Son' here means probably 'descendant', but even so, this statement implies a very early time for these two gotras. It is not said that they were admitted into any of the great brahman families. This Ārṣṭiṣeṇa is the rishi mentioned above (p. 165, note [11]). There was a Śaunaka among the Bhārgavas (p. 201) who was different, and these Śaunakas would seem to be the gotra named among the Ātreyas.[3] Nothing more, however, definite is said about these two sub-families.

Bhāratas.

It has been pointed out (p. 159) that king Bharata adopted the Āṅgirasa rishi Bharadvāja as his son, and Bharadvāja begot Vitatha who continued the Paurava dynasty, and consequently that the Bhāratas could assert either kṣatriya paternity or brahman paternity or both combined.[4] Some of the junior branches did avail themselves of this option, and their development into kṣatriyan brahmans and brahmans occurred at three stages.

The first arose among Vitatha's near successors. The portion of the genealogy which explains this is found in four Puranas.[5] The

[1] Mat *196*, 38.

[2] Vā *92*, 3–6. Bd iii, *67*, 3–6. Br *11*, 32–4. Hv *29*, 1518–20. Bhāg ix, *17*, 2–3 somewhat similarly.

[3] Mat *197*, 2, where perhaps read *ŚaunakĀrṣṭiṣeṇau.*

[4] Anukramaṇī and Vedārth on Rigv vi, *52*. P. 221.

[5] Mat *49*, 35–41. Vā *99*, 158–64. Viṣ iv, *19*, 9–10. Bhāg ix, *21*, 1–2, 19–20.

oldest and best versions are in the Matsya and Vāyu, which are derived from a common original, and show variations chiefly due to corruptions. The Viṣṇu in prose agrees closely with them, and the Bhāgavata repeats the account fairly clearly. The other accounts either say nothing, or speak briefly and incorrectly, in no case noticing the brahmanic developments.

By collating the Matsya and Vāyu (the former being the better), and using the Viṣṇu and Bhāgavata for comparison, a version that seems fairly trustworthy can be obtained and is given below.[1] The genealogical tree obtained therefrom is given on p. 112. It is definitely stated that from the three younger sons of Bhuvamanyu sprang four brahman sub-families, from Mahāvīrya the Urukṣayas and Kāpyas, from Nara[2] the Sāṅkṛtis, and from Garga[3] the Gargas or Gārgyas, that the Urukṣayas became brahmans, and that the Gargas, Sāṅkṛtis and Kāpyas were kṣatriyan brahmans. Even the brahmanical Bhāgavata says plainly that Gārgya from a kṣatriya became a brahman. These sub-families will now be considered separately.

Sāṅkṛtis or Sāṅkṛtyas.

The Sāṅkṛtis were kṣatriyan brahmans and joined the Āṅgirasas, and they are named as a gotra among the Āṅgirasas,[4] and Saṅkṛti

Dāyādo Vitathasyâsīd Bhuvamanyur mahāyaśāḥ
mahābhūtopamāḥ putrāś catvāro Bhuvamanyavaḥ
Bṛhatkṣatro Mahāvīryo Naro Gargaś ca vīryavān
Narasya Saṅkṛtiḥ putras tasya putrau mahaujasau
Gurudhī Rantidevaś ca Sāṅkṛtyau tāv ubhau smṛtau
Gargasya caiva dāyādaḥ Śinir vidvān ajāyata
smṛtāḥ Śainyās tato Gārgāḥ kṣatropetā dvijātayaḥ
Mahāvīrya-sutaś * câpi dhīmān āsīd Urukṣayaḥ
tasya bhāryā Viśālā tu suṣuve putraka-trayam
Trayyāruṇam Puṣkariṇaṁ Kapiṁ caiva mahāyaśāḥ †
Urukṣayāḥ smṛtā hy ete sarve brāhmaṇatāṁ gatāḥ
Kāpyānāṁ tu varā hy ete trayaḥ proktā maharṣayaḥ ‡
Gargāḥ Saṅkṛtayaḥ Kāpyāḥ kṣatropetā dvijātayaḥ
saṁśritÂṅgirasam § pakṣam—

* Mat *Āhārya-tanayaś.* † Accusative plural = Prakrit *mahāyaśā.*
‡ A line seems to have dropped out as they are not named.
§ That is, *saṁśritāḥ Āṅgirasam* by double sandhi.

[2] Rigv vi, *35* and *36* are attributed to Nara.
[3] Rigv vi, *47* is attributed to Garga.
[4] Mat *196*, 30, 32. Cf. Vā *91*, 115; Bd iii, *66*, 86. But a rishi Sāṅkṛti Ātreya is mentioned, MBh xii, *234*, 8596.

is named as a hymn-maker among them.[1] Of the two Sāṅkṛtis mentioned Rantideva was a famous king (pp. 39–42) renowned for liberality and hospitality.[2] His kingdom was on the R. Carmaṇvatī (Chambal), for that river was connected with him;[3] it embodied his fame, and his capital was Daśapura.[4] With him the kṣatriya status predominated, but his kingdom disappeared, and his descendants would seem to have become brahmans.

The other Sāṅkṛti's name is given as *Guruvīrya* (Vāyu), *Gurudhī* (Matsya), *Guru* (Bhāgavata) and *Ruciradhī* (Viṣṇu), He is no doubt the same rishi who is named among the Āṅgirasas as Guruvīta[5] and Gauravīti,[6] and the correct name is Gaurivīti. Rigveda v, *29* is attributed by the Anukramaṇī to Gaurivīti Śāktya and x, *73* and *74* to Gaurivīti simply, but the Vedārthadīpikā says nothing about the former and ascribes the latter to Gaurivīti Śāktya. If Śāktya refers to Vasiṣṭha's son Śakti (pp. 207 f.), then Gaurivīti Śāktya was a Vāsiṣṭha and later than this time.[7] But nothing clear can be decided, because there was also a Śakti among the Āṅgirasas.[8]

Gargas or Gārgyas.

The Gārgyas were a well-known family and were reckoned among the Āṅgirasas, and so also their sub-family of the Śainyas.[9] Garga and Śini are named as hymn-makers among the Āṅgirasas.[10] Various Gargas[11] or Gārgyas are mentioned in tradition; thus, taking them in order, a Gārgya cursed Janamejaya II Pārikṣita for injuring his son (p. 114); another was Vasudeva's purohita, and

[1] Bḍ ii, *32*, 107. Mat *145*, 101. Vā *59*, 98.

[2] MBh iii, *82*, 4096; *293*, 16674: vii, *67*, 2361–74: xii, *29*, 1017–1021; *234*, 8591: xiii, *66*, 3351, 3365; *137*, 6250. Bhāg ix, *21*, 2 f.

[3] MBh vii, *67*, 2360: xii, *29*, 1016. Pad i, *24*, 3.

[4] Meghadūta i, 46–8.

[5] Mat *145*, 102. The corresponding name in Vā *59*, 99 and Bḍ ii, *32*, 108 is *Purukutsa*.

[6] Mat *196*, 32. Also a *Guru*, *ibid.* 45.

[7] He is made contemporary with Ṛṣabha Yājñatura, king of the Śviknas (Śatapatha Brāhm xii, 8, 3, 7; xiii, 5, 4, 15), and though Ṛṣabha's position is unknown, Pratīdarśa Śvaikna was a contemporary of Suplan-Sahadeva, king of N. Pañcāla (*id.* ii, 4, 4, 3–4), p. 148.

[8] Mat *196*, 25.

[9] Mat *196*, 23, 24 (where for *Saitya* read *Śainya*), 48.

[10] Bḍ ii, *32*, 107. Vā *59*, 98. Mat *145*, 101.

[11] A Gārgya, 'son of Viśvāmitra', is mentioned, MBh xiii, *4*, 254.

was father of Kālayavana,[1] who fought against Kṛṣṇa and was killed. Also Vṛddha Garga [2] and Kuṇi Garga [3] are mentioned; and others.[4]

Urukṣayas and Kāpyas.

Mahāvīrya in the genealogy is called Āhārya in the Matsya version in line 8. The importance of stray readings has been pointed out (p. 83) and *Āhārya* is supported by another statement which says he was a hymn-maker among the Āṅgirasaṣ.[5] Āhārya would seem therefore to be the better form,[6] but the variation suggests that the name may be corrupt. Rigveda x, *118* is ascribed to Urukṣaya Āmahīyava, 'son of Amahīyu', and it seems quite probable that Amahīyu may be the true name here,[7] for Mahāvīrya and Āhārya might be easy corruptions of it.[8]

Urukṣaya and Kapi would seem to be named as hymn-makers among the Āṅgirasas.[9] The genealogy speaks of the Kāpyas as distinct from the Urukṣayas, for it says the Urukṣayas all became brahmans (line 11) and the Kāpyas were kṣatriyan brahmans (line 13).[10] Hence it suggests that the descendants of Urukṣaya's two elder sons formed the Urukṣayas, and those of Kapi a distinct gotra. All joined the Āṅgirasas, and so in the Āṅgirasa vaṁśa is named Urukṣaya,[11] though not Kapi unless Kapibhū stands for it.[12]

[1] Br *14*, 48–56. Hv *110*, 6163–6; *111*, 6243–5; *115*, 6428 f. Pad vi, *273*, 2.

[2] MBh ix, *38*, 2132: xiii, *125*, 5996. Mat *229*, 2.

[3] MBh ix, *53*, 2981.

[4] *Vedic Index.* A folk-tale of 'Garga's' seven disciples and their transmigrations is connected with king Brahmadatta, Mat *19*, 12 to *21*; Pad v, *10*, 46 f.; &c. It appears in other connexions, e.g. Hv *19*, 1013 f.; &c. Alluded to, MBh xii, *344*, 13264–5; Ag *117*, 54–5; &c.

[5] Vā *59*, 100. Bd ii, *32*, 109. Mat *145*, 103 (*'svahāryaś*).

[6] The reading in line 3 then would be *tathÂhāryo.*

[7] If so, the Amahīyu to whom ix, *61* is ascribed is certainly a different and later rishi, for the hymn alludes to Divodāsa.

[8] So also in the passage cited in third note above.

[9] Comparing the passages cited in fourth note above, the probable reading of the second pāda would seem to be *Rukṣayaḥ Kapir eva ca*, where the initial *u* might have combined with, or been dropped after, the preceding *ca*, for such irregularities do occur in the Puranas.

[10] Also Vā *91*, 115: Bḍ iii, *66*, 86.

[11] Mat *196*, 29.

[12] *Ibid.* 48–9.

Maudgalyas and Maitreyas.

The next group of kṣatriyan brahmans arose out of the N. Pañcāla dynasty, which was Bhārata, and is set out above (p. 116).[1] Mudgala's eldest son became a brahman. His descendants, the Mudgalas or Maudgalyas, were kṣatriyan brahmans and joined the Āṅgirasas.[2] His grandson Vadhryaśva and Vadhryaśva's son Divodāsa both exercised priestly functions as the Rigveda shows,[3] and appear to have joined the Bhārgavas, for both of them are named in the Bhārgava vaṁśa.[4] Divodāsa's successor was king Mitrayu who was a brahman, and his son was Maitreya, from whom came the Maitreyas, who were kṣatriyan brahmans and joined the Bhārgavas,[5] and accordingly they were named in the Bhārgava vaṁśa.[6] Neither the Maudgalyas nor the Maitreyas produced any rishi of note. A Maudgalya has been mentioned (p. 171), and three others are alluded to.[7] The Viṣṇu Purana professes to have been declared by Parāśara to a Maitreya. Other Maitreyas are noticed in the *Vedic Index*.[8]

Vādhryaśvas and Daivodāsas.

Here may be noticed some of the descendants of Vadhryaśva and Divodāsa. Parucchepa Daivodāsi, the reputed author of Rigveda i, *127* to *139* would seem to have been alive with Divodāsa (*130*, 7) and would therefore have been his son or grandson; and his son or descendant was Anānata, the reputed author of ix, *111*. Pratardana Daivodāsi, the reputed author of ix, *96*, would seem to have been a near descendant of Divodāsa. Sumitra Vādhryaśva, the author of x, *69* and *70*, was a contemporary of king Cyavana Pijavana (p. 120). All these were probably Bhārgavas, as were Vadhryaśva and Divodāsa.

[1] Fully discussed in JRAS, 1918, pp. 230–1, 239–43.

[2] Vā *99*, 198–201. Mat *50*, 5–7. Hv *32*, 1781–4. Br *13*, 97.

[3] Rigv x, *69*, 2, 4, 9, 10 : viii, *103*, 2.

[4] Mat *195*, 42. Divodāsa in Mat *145*, 100; Vā *59*, 87; Bḍ ii, *32*, 106.

[5] Vā *99*, 206–7. Mat *50*, 13–14. Hv *32*, 1789–90. Br *13*, 97 (note).

[6] Mat *195*, 40. See also p. 202.

[7] (1) Pad vi, *68*, 5; *111*, 21–33, which says the Mudgalas were ***viśikha***, 'devoid of the top-knot'. (2) Br *136*, 1. (3) MBh iii, *259* to *260*.

[8] Also MBh iii, *10*, 352, 363 : xiii, *120*, 5794–5.

Other rishis.

Lastly may be noticed Devāpi Ārṣṭiṣeṇa,[1] the author of hymn x, *98*, whose story is often told.[2] He was apparently the eldest grandson of king Pratīpa, and Śantanu a younger grandson (p. 165). He was an excellent prince[3] but had a skin disease,[4] and so was excluded from the throne by the opposition of the people which was led by the brahmans,[5] or he declined it in Śantanu's favour.[6] So Śantanu became king. Devāpi departed to the forest in his youth[7] and became a muni, a teacher of the gods.[8] But a twelve-year drought occurred, which was attributed to the supersession, so Śantanu offered him the kingdom;[9] but he declined it, became Śantanu's purohita instead,[10] and composed Rigveda x, *98*.[11]

[1] To be distinguished from another Ārṣṭiṣeṇa, p. 165.

[2] Vā *99*, 234, 236. Mat *50*, 39–41. Br *13*, 117. Hv *32*, 1822. Viṣ iv, *20*, 4–9. Bhāg ix, *22*, 12, 14–17. Other references in p. 165, note [9].

[3] MBh v, *148*, 5054–66.

[4] MBh v, Bṛhadd; leprosy, so Mat.

[5] Mat, MBh v.

[6] Bṛhadd, Bhāg.

[7] MBh i and v, Vā, Mat, Viṣ, Bhāg.

[8] Vā, Br, Hv.

[9] Nirukta, Bṛhadd, Viṣ, Bhāg.

[10] Nirukta, Bṛhadd.

[11] Or, according to Viṣ and Bhāg, Śantanu's ministers (or brahmans) sent teachers who maliciously perverted Devāpi from the Vedas, and he was therefore excluded as a heretic—an amazing story, incompatible with the hymn, with Vā *99*, 236, Br *13*, 117, Hv *32*, 1822, and with the future destined for him, p. 165, note [10].

CHAPTER XXIV

ANCIENT HISTORY FROM TRADITION

ALL the genealogical data have now been considered, synchronisms co-ordinating them have been established, and the resulting chronological scheme has been set out in the tables at pages 144–9 and 191–2. That is a skeleton, and an attempt may now be made to add thereto all the other particulars to be gathered from tradition, and to sketch in outline the course of history which all that information suggests. This is now offered here, based on what tradition actually says. It is impossible to avoid repeating a good deal of what has been narrated above in various connexions, but that has been reduced as much as possible, and this sketch should be read with the genealogical exposition in chapters VII to IX and with the discussions of synchronisms in chapters XII to XIV and elsewhere. The authorities for every statement are cited in the notes or by reference to preceding pages, and no statement is made without authority. In considering this outline we must put aside views formed from brahmanical literature, for to construct history from theological works and especially works with a strong priestly bias and lacking the historical sense is inadmissible (pp. 10, 14, 61). There is nothing in this account inconsistent with the Rigveda, as far as I am aware, if we do not read preconceived ideas into the Veda.

Tradition naturally begins with myth, and the myth that seeks to explain the earliest conditions in India derives all the dynasties that reigned there (not the populace) from a primaeval king Manu Vaivasvata, son of Vivasvant (the sun), as briefly noticed above (p. 84). It is narrated in three forms, of which the second and third have more in common than the first. According to the first,[1] Manu had ten sons of whom the eldest was Ila, and Ila while on conquest entered Śiva's grove Śaravana and became changed into a woman, Ilā, because Umā had laid a curse that any male creature which entered it should become female. Ilā consorted with Budha, son

[1] Mat *11*, 40 to *12*, 19. Pad v, *8*, 75–124. Amplified into a brahmanical romance and connected with the Godāvarī, Br *108*. King Ila mentioned, Pad ii, *64*, 41.

of Soma (p. 58), and Ila (*sic*) had by him a son Purūravas Aila. Then through Śiva's favour Ilā became a Kimpuruṣa named Sudyumna, a man one month and a woman another month. According to the second form,[1] Manu had nine sons and offered a sacrifice to Mitra and Varuṇa to obtain a son, but a daughter Ilā was born therefrom. She met Budha and bore Purūravas. Then she became a man named Sudyumna but through the same curse[2] was turned into a woman. Finally, through Śiva's favour she regained manhood as Sudyumna. The third form[3] agrees generally in this version, but places the transformation into manhood and back again into womanhood before she met Budha. Other books condense or combine these versions.[4]

Purūravas was thus fabled to be the son of Ilā or Ila by Budha,[5] and was well known as Aila.[6] Sudyumna had three sons,[7] two of whom were Utkala and Gaya, and the third is named Haritāśva[8] or Vinatāśva[9] or shortly Vinata.[10]

Manu had nine other sons (p. 84), and divided the earth, that is, India, into ten portions.[11] The distribution among the sons is not stated and some were excluded as Pṛṣadhra. Some Puranas imply that Sudyumna had a portion,[12] but others say he obtained none

[1] Vā *85*. Bḍ iii, *60*. Br *7*, 1–23. Hv *10*, 613–40. Śiv vii, *60*, 2–19. The last three omit the final transformation into womanhood and back into manhood. Cf. Śatapatha Brāhm i, 8, 1.

[2] Vā *85*, 27 and Bḍ iii, *60*, 27 call the forest Umāvana.

[3] Viṣ iv, *1*, 5–11. Mārk *111* Bhāg, fully, ix, *1*, 11–40.

[4] Lg i, *65*, 17–31 combines the first and second forms. Kūr i, *20*, 4–10 combines all three. Ag *272*, 5–10 and Gar i, *138*, 2–3 condense the story. Rām vii, *87* to *90* follows the first form but confusedly; and says Ila was king of Bālhi (*87*, 3; *90*, 18) or Bālhīka (*87*, 7). MBh says (i, *75*, 3140–4; *95*, 3760) Manu's daughter was Ilā and her son was Purūravas, she being both his mother and his father. Cf. Br *226*, 34.

[5] Also Mat *24*, 9–10. Viṣ iv, *6*, 20. Vā *90*, 45; *91*, 1. Bḍ iii, *65*, 45; *66*, 1. Br *9*, 33; *10*, 1. Hv *25*, 1357; *26*, 1363. Gar i, *139*, 2.

[6] Rigv x, *95*, 7, 18: and passages cited above.

[7] Vā *85*, 18–19. Bḍ iii, *60*, 17–19. Br *7*, 17–19. Hv *10*, 631–2. Śiv vii, *60*, 14–15. Lg i, *65*, 26–7. Ag *272*, 8–9. Mat *12*, 16–18. Pad v, *8*, 121–3.

[8] So Mat and Pad.

[9] So the others in second note above.

[10] So Viṣ iv, *1*, 12: Kūr i, *20*, 9: and Gar i, *138*, 3. Mārk *111*, 15–16 and Bhāg ix, *1*, 41 vary.

[11] Vā *85*, 20–1. Bḍ iii, *60*, 20–1. Br *7*, 20–1. Hv *10*, 633–5. Śiv vii, *60*, 16. Cf. Baudhāyana ii, 2, 3, 2.

[12] Mat *12*, 18–19 and Pad v, *8*, 123–4.

because he had been a woman.[1] Nevertheless the authorities generally declare, first, that he received the town Pratiṣṭhāna[2] and gave it to Purūravas[3]; and secondly, that his three sons had territories of their own,[4] thus Utkala had the Utkala country,[5] Vinatāśva had a western country,[6] and Gaya had the city Gayā and the eastern region; but according to two Puranas,[7] Gaya had only the city Gayā, and Haritāśva had the eastern region together with the Kurus, that is, the Northern Kurus. These three principalities may be designated here collectively the 'Saudyumnas', a name which is sometimes given to them.[8]

The nine sons assigned to Manu[9] were Ikṣvāku, Nābhāga[10] (or Nṛga[11]), Dhṛṣṭa, Śaryāti, Nariṣyanta, Prāṁśu,[12] Nābhānediṣṭha,[13] Karūṣa and Pṛṣadhra.

From Karūṣa were descended the numerous kṣatriya clans of the Kārūṣas, who were determined fighters.[14] They occupied the

[1] So those in second note above (except Śiv); Viṣ iv, *1*, 12; and Lg i, *65*, 29.

[2] The later Prayāga (Allahabad): see p. 85.

[3] Vā *85*, 21–3; Bd iii, *60*, 21–2; Br *7*, 21–3; Hv *10*, 635–6; Śiv vii, *60*, 17–19; and Lg i, *65*, 29–31; collated. Viṣ iv *1*, 12–13, Ag *272*, 9–10, and Bhāg ix, *1*, 42 equivalently. Mārk *111*, 17–18 varies.

[4] The passages cited in ninth note above suggest this text:—

> Utkalasyôtkalaṁ rāṣṭraṁ Vinatāśvasya paścimaṃ
> dik pūrvā tasya rājarṣer Gayasya tu Gayā purī.

Bhāg ix, *1*, 41, is late and wrong.

[5] The country west of Bengal and south of Gayā.

[6] Not particularized, and never alluded to afterwards.

[7] Mat *12*, 18 and Pad v, *8*, 123.

[8] e.g. Vā *99*, 266.

[9] P. 84. MBh i, *75*, 3142–3 says he had 50 other sons, who perished through mutual dissension.

[10] More probably *Nabhāga*. Cf. *Nabhāka* in Rigv viii, *40*, 5.

[11] So Bd and Viṣ. Lg calls him *Nābhāga* and also *Nṛga* (i, *66*, 45). Bhāg makes two sons of these names.

[12] *Kuśanābha* in Mat and Pad. Śiv and Mārk differ.

[13] This name has been greatly corrupted (through the influence of the name Nābhāga), thus, *Nābhāgodiṣṭa*, *Nābhāgāriṣṭa*, &c., and then split up into two, *Nābhāga* and *Diṣṭa*, *Ariṣṭa* or *Riṣṭa*. It is the *Nābhānediṣṭha* (as Viṣ reading *Nābhāganediṣṭa*, iv, *1*, 5, 15, shows) which occurs in Rigveda x, *61*, 18, a hymn attributed to him.

[14] Vā *86*, 2–3. Bd iii, *61*, 2–3. Br *7*, 25, 42. Hv *11*, 658. Mat *12*, 24. Pad v, *8*, 129. Śiv vii, *60*, 31. Ag *272*, 17. Mārk *113*, 1. Lg i, *66*, 51. Viṣ iv, *1*, 14. Gar i, *138*, 4. Bhāg ix, *2*, 16, which says they protected N. India, i. e. from attacks from the south.

Karūṣa country, the region round the modern Rewa and eastwards to the R. Sone.[1] From Dhṛṣṭa[2] came a number of clans called Dhārṣṭakas, who were reckoned kṣatriyas.[3] Nothing further is said about them except that the Śiva says they occupied the Balhīka country,[4] which may mean Balkh, but was more probably the Vāhlīka country in the Panjab.[5] About Nariṣyanta's offspring there is much confusion. Some Puranas say they were the Śakas.[6] If so, they lay outside India. The late Bhāgavata gives a list of his descendants, and says they developed into the Āgniveśyāyana brahmans;[7] but this, if true, more probably refers to Nariṣyanta, king of the Vaiśāla dynasty.[8] Pṛṣadhra, it is said, became a śūdra, because he killed his guru's cow and was cursed[9]: and two Puranas say the guru was Cyavana.[10] Nābhāga[11] and his son Ambarīṣa (p. 98) probably reigned on the R. Jumna,[12] but their line played no part in traditional history. Nābhānediṣṭha's line reigned in the country of Vaiśālī (p. 96);[13] and Śaryāti, who

[1] Mārk, my translation, p. 341.

[2] Hv, Lg and Śiv, *Dhṛṣṇu*. Mat *12*, 20–1; Pad v, *8*, 125–6; and Lg i, *66*, 46 give him three sons.

[3] Vā *88*, 4–5. Bḍ iii, *63*, 4–5. Br *7*, 25. Hv *10*, 642. Viṣ iv, *2*, 2. Ag *272*, 11. But Gar i, *138*, 15 says these kṣatriyas became 'vaiśyas', and Bhāg ix, *2*, 17 'chiefly brahmans'.

[4] Śiv vii, *60*, 20—Vārṣṇeyo (*read* Dhārṣṇeyā) Ballhīkaṁ kṣetram āvasan.

[5] Mārk, my translation, p. 311.

[6] Br *7*, 24; Hv *10*, 641; Ag *272*, 10; and Śiv vii, *60*, 19, say—*Nariṣyataḥ Śakāḥ putrāḥ*. Mat *12*, 20 and Pad v, *8*, 125 give him instead a son *Śuka*; and Lg i, *66*, 49 a son *Jitātman*.

[7] ix, *2*, 19–22—ending with Agniveśya who was the great rishi Jātukarṇya famed as Kānīna; and from him sprang the Āgniveśyāyana family of brahmans. But see p. 217.

[8] Br *7*, 27 is misplaced and refers to Nariṣyanta and Dama of the Vaiśāla dynasty; cf. Vā *86*, 12: Bḍ iii, *61*, 8: and p. 147.

[9] Br *7*, 43. Hv *11*, 659. Lg i, *66*, 52. Śiv vii, *60*, 32. Mat *12*, 25. Ag *272*, 18. Viṣ iv, *1*, 13. Gar i, *138*, 4. Pad v, *8*, 130. Bhāg ix, *2*, 3–14 amplifies the story with inventions.

[10] Vā *86*, 1–2. Bḍ iii, *61*, 1–2.

[11] Nṛga is sometimes substituted for Nābhāga (*ante*), and Bhāg ix, *2*, 17–18 provides Nṛga with descendants, but that genealogy seems to have been fashioned partly by mistakenly inverting the ancestry of king Nṛga and his grandfather Oghavant in MBh xiii, *2*, 120–3. Lg i, *66*, 45 is absurd. See eighth note below.

[12] MBh iii, *129*, 10514. It would have soon disappeared under the early Aila conquests.

[13] Vaiśālī is Basār, JRAS, 1902, pp. 267 f.

is called Śaryāta in brahmanical books,[1] founded the dynasty of Ānarta (p. 97).

Ikṣvāku, the eldest and chief son, obtained Madhyadeśa,[2] and was the progenitor of the Solar race or dynasty,[3] with its capital at Ayodhyā. There are two versions of the development of his descendants. One found in six Puranas[4] says—Ikṣvāku had a hundred sons,[5] chief of whom were the eldest Vikukṣi, and Nimi and Daṇḍa (or Daṇḍaka): of those sons fifty, chief of whom was Śakuni, were kings in Uttarāpatha (N. India) and forty-eight others, chief of whom was Vaśāti, were rulers in Dakṣiṇāpatha (the Dekhan).[6] Vikukṣi (also named Śaśāda) succeeded Ikṣvāku and reigned at Ayodhyā, and his successor was Kakutstha (p. 93). The other version is given by four Puranas[7] and runs thus:—Ikṣvāku had a hundred sons of whom the eldest was Vikukṣi[8] (and, as the Padma says, two others were Nimi and Daṇḍaka). Vikukṣi had fifteen sons who were kings north of Meru, and the 114 others[9] were kings south of Meru. The eldest (of Vikukṣi's sons) was Kakutstha. The Bhāgavata (ix, *6*, 4–5) gives a third version, but it is too late to be worthy of notice. The other Puranas give no such information.

From Ikṣvāku's son Nimi (or Nemi) sprang the dynasty that reigned in Videha.[10] He dwelt in a town famed as Jayanta (of which however nothing more seems to be known) and the capital

[1] See *Vedic Index*, ii, 364, 375.

[2] Br *7*, 20. Hv *10*, 634. Śiv vii, *60*, 17. Lg i, *65*, 28. Cf. Bḍ iii, *60*, 20; Vā *85*, 21.

[3] Mat *12*, 15. Pad v, *8*, 120. Other accounts imply it.

[4] Vā *88*, 8–11, 20, 24; Bḍ iii, *63*, 8–11, 21, 25; Br *7*, 45–8, 51; Hv *11*, 661–4, 667; and Śiv vii, *60*, 33–5, 37; collated. Viṣ iv, *2*, 3, 6 agrees.

[5] So also MBh xiii, *2*, 88.

[6] Among them would be his tenth son Daśāśva, who reigned at Māhiṣmatī on the R. Narbadā and whose descendants are mentioned, according to MBh xiii, *2*, 88–172. King Nṛga, who is mentioned, *ibid.* 120–3, and who appears to be the same as Nṛga who reigned on the R. Payoṣṇī (Tapti: MBh iii, *88*, 8329–32; *120*, 10290; *121*, 10291), was probably of a different family. See *infra*.

[7] Mat *12*, 26–8; Pad v, *8*, 130–3; more briefly Lg i, *65*, 31–2, and Kūr i, *20*, 10–11; collated.

[8] These Puranas do not mention Śaśāda as his name.

[9] That is, apparently, the rest of Ikṣvāku's and Vikukṣi's sons.

[10] See pp. 84, 95–6, 215.

was also Mithilā, which is said to have been named after his son Mithi.[1]

Some of the Puranas, as just mentioned, assign to Ikṣvāku a third son called Daṇḍa or Daṇḍaka, and it is said that after him was named the great Daṇḍaka forest[2] which more or less covered the Dekhan. This seems to be an eponym to account for the name of the forest, because it clashes with the other statements about the many kings that occupied the Dekhan. However that may be, the noteworthy point is that the original sovereignty in that region was attributed to the same stock or race which was dominant in Ayodhyā and Videha.[3]

The kingdoms mentioned continued as they have been described, with the exception of the Aila dynasty at Pratiṣṭhāna. That quickly developed. Northward its expansion was limited by the kingdom of Ayodhyā and southward by the warlike Kārūṣas, hence its extension began north-westward and eastward along the Ganges. Purūravas was succeeded by Āyu at Pratiṣṭhāna, and another son Amāvasu founded another kingdom, the capital of which was then or afterwards Kānyakubja (Kanauj).[4] Āyu was succeeded by Nahuṣa,[5] and another son Kṣatravṛddha established himself at Kāśi (Benares).[6] Nahuṣa was a famous king.[7] His son and successor Yayāti was a renowned conqueror,[8] extended his kingdom widely, and was reckoned a samrāj.[9] He appears to have conquered not only all Madhyadeśa west of the Ayodhyā and Kānyakubja kingdoms, and north-west as far as the R. Sarasvatī,[10] but also the

[1] Vā *89*, 1–2, 6. Bḍ iii, *64*. 1–2, 6.

[2] Pad v, *34*, 5, 14–59. Rām vii, *81*, 18–19. The Daṇḍakas are mentioned, MBh ii, *30*, 1169: their kingdom, xiii, *153*, 7223.

[3] So even Bhāg says (ix, *1*, 2–3)—Satyavrata, king of Draviḍa, became Vivasvant's son Manu, and his sons were Ikṣvāku and others, kings.

[4] First mentioned as the capital in Gādhi's time, MBh v, *118*, 4005.

[5] Fables about them in MBh, and Pad ii, *103*, 101 to *117*. Nahuṣa and Yayāti, Rām ii, *5*, 10: iii, *66*, 7.

[6] Kāśi capital, Vā *92*, 6, 18, 21; Bḍ iii, *67*, 7, 20, 23. Vārāṇasī, Vā *92*, 23–68; Bḍ iii, *67*, 26–72.

[7] He had a large kingdom, MBh i, *75*, 3151–4.

[8] Vā *93*, 90. Bḍ iii, *68*, 19, 92. Mat *24*, 55–6. Lg i, *67*, 13. Br *12*, 4, 18. Hv *30*, 1602, 1616. MBh xii, *29*, 987. Yayāti Nāhuṣa is often mentioned.

[9] MBh i, *75*, 3156. Also *sārvabhauma*, *129*, 10516.

[10] Rigv vii, *95*, 2. MBh ix, *42*, 2349–52. Cf. Bṛhadd vi, 20–4. Nābhāga's line (*ante*) thus disappeared early.

country west, south, and south-east of his territory of Pratiṣṭhāna.[1] He had five sons, Yadu, Turvasu, Druhyu, Anu and Pūru (p. 87). After a long reign[2] he divided his territories among them.[3] Pūru the youngest is said to have been the most dutiful[4] and Yayāti installed him as his successor[5] in the ancestral sovereignty in the middle region, that is, in the southern half of the Ganges-Jumna doab with the capital Pratiṣṭhāna, and gave the elder sons the out-lying territories.[6] The texts collated show that Yadu got the south-west, Turvasu the south-east, Druhyu the west and Anu the north.[7] These directions are taken with reference to the ancestral kingdom that Pūru obtained; hence Yadu's realm lay in the country watered by the rivers Chambal (Carmaṇvatī), Betwa (Vetravatī) and Ken (Śuktimatī); Druhyu's kingdom in the country west of the Jumna and north of the Chambal; Anu's realm comprised the northern portion of the Ganges-Jumna plain; and Turvasu's kingdom the territory around Rewa, the Kārūṣas, who occupied it (*ante*) having been subdued, for nothing more is said

[1] MBh v, *113*, 3905 rightly makes Pratiṣṭhāna his capital, but *114*, 3918 is wrong, see p. 142.

[2] He is fabled to have had extra life, because Pūru gave him his own youth in exchange for his old age for a time; Vā *93*, 28–75; Bḍ iii, *68*, 29–76; Br *12*, 22–48; Hv *30*, 1621–47. Mat *32* to *34*: MBh i, *75*, 3161–80; *83* to *85*; Viṣ iv, *10*, 3–8; Bṛ *146*; Rām vii, *58*; *59*. The old age is made the result of Uśanas-Śukra's curse in Mat, MBh, Rām and Viṣ.

[3] Vā *93*, 90. Bḍ iii, *68*, 92. Br *12*, 18. Hv *30*, 1617. Lg i, *67*, 13 (incorrectly). So MBh vii, *63*, 2296 speaking of the four sons other than Pūru: xii, *29*, 990.

[4] See second note above.

[5] MBh i, *75*, 3181; *85*, 3531; v, *148*, 5051: vii, *63*, 2301.

[6] MBh i, *87*, 3555: iii, *129*, 10515–16: xii, *29*, 991. Mat *36*, 5, 12.

[7] Vā *93*, 88–90. Bḍ iii, *68*, 90–2. Kūr i, *22*, 9–11. Lg i, *67*, 11–12. These suggest the following text:—

> Abhiṣicya tataḥ Pūruṁ sva-rājye sutam ātmanaḥ
> diśi dakṣiṇa-pūrvasyāṁ Turvasuṁ tu nyaveśayat
> dakṣiṇâparato rājā Yaduṁ jyeṣṭhaṁ nyaveśayat
> pratīcyām uttarasyāṁ ca Druhyuṁ cÂnuṁ ca tāv ubhau.

Viṣ iv, *10*, 16–18 is similar, but corrupts *dakṣiṇâparato* to *dakṣiṇāpathato*. Hv *30*, 1617–19 is similar, but misplaces Yadu in *pūrvôttarasyāṁ*, which is impossible because there lay the Ayodhyā kingdom. Br *12*, 19–20 is somewhat alike, but misplaces Yadu in *pūrvasyām*, which is impossible because Kāśi lay there. The late Bhāg (ix, *19*, 22–3) follows the Viṣṇu's mistake, reading for *dakṣiṇāpathato* its equivalent *dakṣiṇato*, and interchanges Turvasu and Druhyu.

about Karūṣa until Vasu king of Cedi conquered it long afterwards (p. 118).[1]

At this time then the Aila race had dominated the whole of mid North India with the exception of the Ayodhyā kingdom, and had developed into seven kingdoms, those of Yayāti's five sons and the two earlier of Kānyakubja and Kāśi. It had subjugated Madhyadeśa and made it emphatically Aila. The other kingdoms mentioned above continued, except that the Kārūṣas, and apparently the Nābhāgas, had been subdued. The Saudyumna stock remained unaffected. The Ayodhyā realm prospered,[2] and one of its early kings named Śrāvasta is said to have founded the city Śrāvastī.[3] The chief development occurred among Yadu's descendants, who increased and divided at once into two great branches, the Haihayas and Yādavas (p. 87). Subsequent occurrences show that the Yādava branch occupied the northern portion of Yadu's territory and the Haihayas the southern part.

There is some suggestion that the southern part of the Rajputana desert was still a very shallow sea[4] in those times, for in the story of the rishi Utaṅka Srāvasta's second successor Kuvalāśva is said to have killed a Rākṣasa, Daitya or asura, Dhundhu (whence he got the name Dhundhumāra), near a sand-filled sea called Ujjālaka in the desert plains, which mean that desert.[5] Again, Viśvāmitra performed austerities and attained brahmanhood at Ruṣaṅgu's tīrtha on the R. Sarasvatī, in low lands near the sea (p. 205, note [2]). The Sarasvatī would have flowed into that sea. Further, there

[1] MBh v, *148*, 5046–52 says—Yadu was disobedient and dwelt in Nāgasāhvaya, so Yayāti cursed him and removed him to Gāndhāra: but this is wrong, because the Yādavas never were in Gāndhāra, and Nāgasāhvaya, i.e. Hastināpura, did not exist till built long afterwards, probably by Hastin. MBh i, *85*, 3533, Mat *34*, 30 (and Pad v, *12*, 109 partially), give instead a wholly different account, thus:—

Yados tu Yādavā jātās Turvasor Yavanāḥ smṛtāḥ
Druhyoḥ sutās tu vai Bhojā Anos tu mleccha-jātayaḥ

which seems unintelligible compared with all other tradition, and is probably late and certainly very doubtful.

[2] The statement in MBh i, *95*, 3765 that Pūru's second successor Prācinvant conquered the east is coined out of his name wrongly.

[3] So the genealogies, especially in Vā and Bd. Śrāvastī is identified with Saheṭh Maheṭh, JRAS, 1909, pp. 1066 f.

[4] *Imp. Gaz. of India* (1907), i, p. 38.

[5] Vā *88*, 28–60. Bd iii, *63*, 31–62. Br *7*, 54–86. Hv *11*, 676–703. Viṣ iv, *2*, 13. MBh iii, *200*, 13489 to *203*, 13625. Bhāg ix, *6*, 21–3. The story, though in fabulous form, is worthy of note.

is no mention (as far as I know) of any crossing the southern part of the desert even long afterwards.[1] If the sea did extend then over the southern part of that desert, that will throw some light on subsequent developments, and explain the fact that the southern part of the Indus region appears to have lain outside all early historical tradition.

The Yādava branch first developed a great kingdom under its king Śaśabindu, who was a famous cakravartin,[2] which means he extended his sway over neighbouring countries. The neighbouring countries were the Paurava realm on his east and the Druhyu territory on his north. He appears to have conquered the Pauravas, because there is a great gap in the Paurava genealogy from this point till Duṣyanta restored the dynasty long afterwards,[3] which means that the dynasty underwent an eclipse. He also probably pressed on the Druhyus and forced them more into the Panjab, as will appear. He had many sons, who were known as the Śaśabindu or Śāśabindava princes;[4] hence it would seem that his territories were divided among them into many small principalities, for none of his successors were of great note.

The kingdom of Ayodhyā then rose to very great eminence under Yuvanāśva II[5] and especially his son Māndhātṛ.[6] The latter married Śaśabindu's daughter Bindumatī (p. 150). He was a very famous king, a cakravartin and a samrāj, and extended his sway very widely[7] (pp. 39, 40). He must have overrun the Kānyakubja

[1] The pilgrims' itinerary (MBh iii, *82*, 4097–5032) was from Arbuda (Mount Abu) south to Prabhāsa (Somnath), then north to the junction of the Sarasvatī with the sea, south to Dvāravatī (Dwārkā), then to the mouth of the Indus (which must have been partly by sea), and north up the Indus. There is absolutely nothing in historical tradition (which goes back far beyond the Rigveda) to support the conditions conjectured by Abinas Ch. Das in his *Rigvedic India* (map at p. 90), and the whole of tradition negatives them as this and the next two chapters show.

[2] See p. 39. Also Vā *95*, 19. Bḍ iii, *70*, 19. Mat *44*, 18. Pad v, *13*, 3. Viṣ iv, *12*, 1. Ag *274*, 13. Bhāg ix, *23*, 32.

[3] See pp. 144, 146, 156–7.

[4] See passages following those cited in second note above. Also MBh vii, *65*, 2322–4 : xii, *29*, 999 : Lg i, *68*, 26 : Gar i, *139*, 26.

[5] Wrongly called Saudyumni in an absurd fable, MBh iii, *126*, 10432–5.

[6] Called *Mandhātṛ* in Rigveda. See the genealogies.

[7] MBh iii, *126*, 10462. Kings are mentioned as conquered by him, MBh vii, *62*, 2281–2 : xii, *29*, 981–2 : but the names are uncertain. Gaya might be the king on the Payoṣṇī (p. 40), and Nṛga (if correct) the king in p. 257 note [6]. For another later Nṛga, p. 109.

kingdom and the prostrate Paurava realm,[1] because, pushing beyond them westwards, he had a long contest with and conquered the Druhyu king, who appears to have been then on the confines of the Panjab;[2] so that the next Druhyu king Gāndhāra retired to the north-west and gave his name to the Gāndhāra country (p. 167). These indications suggest that he also pressed on the Ānavas, who lay almost between him and the Druhyus. There is no allusion that he assailed the Yādavas, nor probability, because the Śāśabindavas were his brothers-in-law. He appears to have been a great sacrificer and a hymn-maker.[3]

Māndhātṛ had three sons, Purukutsa, Ambarīṣa and Mucukunda.[4] Tradition suggests that Māndhātṛ or his sons carried their arms south to the river Narmadā.[5] Purukutsa's wife was named Narmadā;[6] and a fable says that the Nāgas induced him through the river's mediation to destroy the Mauneya Gandharvas, who had despoiled them.[7] Moreover Mucukunda, who was a famous king (p. 93), appears to be the Mucukunda whom the Harivaṁśa describes in an erroneous setting. He built and fortified a town on the rocky bank of that river, at the foot of both the Vindhya and Ṛkṣa (Satpura) ranges, that is, at a place where the two ranges approach the river. It was Māhiṣmatī,[8] the modern Māndhātā on an island in the river.[9] He also built a spacious town named Purikā on the

[1] For he sacrificed on the R. Jumna (MBh iii, *125*, 10421), which was in Paurava or Ānava territory.

[2] He sacrificed in the country afterwards called Kurukṣetra (*id. 126*, 10467), which was Druhyu or Ānava land then.

[3] Chap. XXIII. Agni was Mandhātṛ's chiefest Dasyu-slayer, Rigv viii, *39*, 8. The Aśvins are said to have succoured him among the *kṣetrapatyas*, no doubt referring to his conquests; *id.* i, *112*, 13.

[4] See chap. XXIII. The fable about his fifty daughters and the rishi Saubhari is discussed, p. 73.

[5] Purukutsa at the Narmadā, Viṣ i, *2*, 9; vi, *8*, 44.

[6] Page 69, and genealogies.

[7] Viṣ iv, *3*, 6–12 (bis); and so identified, p. 69.

[8] Hv *95*, 5218–28, the genealogy of which is wrong, as explained, see pp. 122, 170. His city Māhiṣmatī existed long before the time of Mādhava and Sattvata, who are made contemporaries of Mucukunda in this story (verses 5205–6, 5240–2). It was the capital also of Arjuna Kārtavīrya (see *infra*).

[9] The passages that show this are—Hv *33*, 1870. Br *13*, 176–8. Vā *94*, 28 and Bd iii, *69*, 28 (in both which for *hema* read *phena*). Raghuv vi, 43. Pad v, *12*, 130–2. Mat *43*, 29–31. Discussed in JRAS, 1910, pp. 444–7, 867–9.

south bank near the Ṛkṣa range. They were his capitals. His kingdom did not survive long, as will appear.

The supremacy of Ayodhyā soon waned, and the Kānyakubja kingdom rose into local prominence under its king Jahnu;[1] and shortly afterwards, and perhaps in consequence of the disturbances caused by Māndhātṛ's conquests, three great movements occurred among the Haihayas, Ānavas and Druhyus.

The Haihayas prospered in their region of South Malwa, and one of their kings Sāhañja is said to have founded a city called Sāhañjanī,[2] and his son Mahiṣmant also the town Māhiṣmatī[3] mentioned above. Their successor Bhadraśreṇya[4] carried his arms eastward, conquered the kingdom of Kāśi, took possession of Benares and reigned there, which means that he traversed the prostrate Paurava kingdom. The Kāśi king Divodāsa I recovered his territory and capital from Bhadraśreṇya's sons, sparing one young son Durdama, but abandoned it afterwards[5] and built a new capital on the R. Gomatī at the eastern border of his land. The Rākṣasa Kṣemaka then took possession of Benares, and Durdama reconquered the kingdom. This occupation by Rākṣasas suggests that the country had been so devastated by war that rude tribes from the forests around occupied it; and in consonance with this it is said a conflict took place between Anaraṇya king of Ayodhyā, who reigned about this time, and a Rāvaṇa,[6] who would be a king from the Dekhan.[7] The Haihayas held the Kāśi territory and seem to have been mainly engaged in raiding N. India.

[1] After him the Ganges which flowed through his territory was named Jāhnavī. But a fable is told to explain it, Vā *91*, 54–8: Bḍ iii, *66*, 25–8: Br *10*, 15–19; *13*, 83–6: Hv *27*, 1417–21; *32*, 1757–61: Viṣ iv, *7*, 2–3: Bhāg ix, *15*, 3: MBh xiii, *4*, 202. Bḍ iii, *56*, 44–8 an anachronism.

[2] Only Br *13*, 156 and Hv *33*, 1845–6 say so. His name is given differently by Mat, Vā, &c.

[3] Only Hv *33*, 1847 says this; and, if this is true, he probably captured the place from Mucukunda's successors, and gave it his own name. Pad vi, *115*, 4 says it was founded by Mahiṣa.

[4] All this account is discussed, p. 153.

[5] This is explained as the consequence of a curse by Nikumbha in a fable about Śiva and Pārvatī in connexion with Benares: Vā *92*, 24–61: Bḍ iii, *67*, 27–64 and Hv *29*, 1542–82, 15491. Br *11*, 41–3, 54 and Hv *32*, 1737–9 relate the curse briefly.

[6] Rāvaṇa killed him, so Bḍ iii, *63*, 74; Lg i, *65*, 44; Rām vi, *60*, 8–10 and vii, *19* (amplified), both identifying him with the later Rāvaṇa killed by Rāma. Reversely, Vā *88*, 75.

[7] Other Rāvaṇas will be mentioned. Bhāg ix, *6*, 33 errs.

The movements among the Ānavas and Druhyus seem to have been connected. The Ānavas (p. 108) rose to power about this time under two able kings, Mahāśāla and Mahāmanas, and the latter appears to have encroached on the east of the Panjab, because he is styled a cakravartin and lord of the seven dvīpas.[1] Under his two sons, Uśīnara and Titikṣu, the Ānavas divided into two branches. One branch headed by Uśīnara[2] established separate kingdoms on the eastern border of the Panjab (p. 109), namely, those of the Yaudheyas, Ambaṣṭhas, Navarāṣṭra and the city Kṛmilā; and his famous son Śivi Auśīnara (pp. 39–41) originated the Śivis[3] in Śivapura and, extending his conquests westwards, founded through his four sons the kingdoms of the Vṛṣadarbhas, Madras (or Madrakas), Kekayas (or Kaikeyas) and Suvīras (or Sauvīras), thus occupying the whole of the Panjab except the north-west corner. The Druhyus ruled in the Panjab at that time (*ante*), so that Śivi and his sons must have driven them back into that corner, which became known as Gāndhāra after the Druhyu king Gāndhāra. There the Druhyus maintained their position permanently, and it is said that five generations afterwards they began to multiply and in time founded many principalities in the mleccha countries in the northern region beyond India.[4] They would have formed the dominant kṣatriya class there and have also carried their religion there.

The other branch of the Ānavas under Titikṣu moved eastward and, passing beyond Videha and the Vaiśālī country, descended into East Bihar among the ruder Saudyumna stock. There they founded a kingdom, which was called the kingdom in the east (p. 109), and which afterwards developed into Aṅga and four other kingdoms as will be explained.

About this time lived Kuśa, king of Kānyakubja, and his younger son Amūrtarayas[5] (or Amūrtarayas' son Gaya) is said to have carved

[1] Vā *99*, 16–17. Bd iii, *74*, 15–16. Mat *48*, 14. If, as seems probable, *dvīpa* here means 'doab', he might well have been lord of the northern portions of the seven doabs from the R. Gomatī north-westwards.

[2] Well known, MBh xiii, *67*, 3689.

[3] Called Śivas in Rigv vii, *18*, *7*.

[4] See p. 108, notes [2] and [4]. The mention of a 'hundred sons' means here 'near descendants' as it does elsewhere.

[5] Vā *91*, 62. Bd iii, *66*, 32. Viṣ iv, *7*, 3. Gar i, *139*, 5. Hv *27*, 1425 and Br *10*, 23 call him *Mūrtimant*. Mat *49*, 8 wrongly makes him son of the Paurava king Antināra (= Matināra).

out for himself a kingdom from another portion of the Saudyumna stock in the country known afterwards as Magadha:[1] and this was quite possible, for the only intervening territory was Kāśi, which had been ravaged by the Haihayas. Gaya reigned in the Gayā district and was a king of note (pp. 39, 40). Nothing more is said of this dynasty, except that it was overthrown afterwards.[2] The genealogies give Amūrtarayas a younger brother Vasu;[3] and it is said Vasu founded a kingdom at Girivraja,[4] but this is very doubtful, for he seems to be confused with Vasu Caidya who conquered Magadha afterwards (p. 118).

It was about this time apparently that the Sāryāta kingdom in Gujarat came to an end.[5] The capital Kuśasthalī was captured by Puṇyajana Rākṣasas, and the Śāryātas fled inland to other countries where they developed into bands of noble kṣatriyas; and Śāryātas are mentioned as forming one of the five groups of the Haihaya-Tālajaṅghas (p. 102). The Harivaṁśa adds that ultimately they became merged with hill tribes,[6] which would seem to mean that, after Sagara destroyed the Haihaya power, they became so merged.

The principal brahmans who dwelt in the lower region of the Narbadā were the Bhārgavas. They were ill-treated by the successors of the Haihaya king Kṛtavīrya and fled into Madhyadeśa. About that time or a little earlier was born the famous rishi Ṛcīka Aurva, who was chief among them.[7] Kṛtavīrya's son Arjuna[8] then propitiated Datta the Ātreya and was favoured by him (p. 229). He was a great monarch and conqueror (p. 41), and continuing

[1] Rām i, *32*, 7 says in Dharmāraṇya; which was a wood near Gayā, MBh iii, *84*, 8063–4; *87*, 8304–8: xiii, *25*, 1744; *165*, 7655. The Rām genealogy, however, is full of errors, p. 118.

[2] By Rākṣasas Rām i, *24*, 25–31. But long afterwards the queen of Dilīpa II of Ayodhyā is said to have been a Māgadha princess; Pad vi, *198*, 2–4: Raghuv i, 31, 57.

[3] First four passages, third note above.

[4] Rām i, *32*, 2–3, 7–10, where Vaidarbhī is an anachronism.

[5] Vā *88*, 1–4. Bd iii, *63*, 1–4. Br *7*, 37–41. Hv *11*, 653–7. Śiv vii, *60*, 28–30. Viṣ iv, *2*, 1–2. Bhāg ix, *3*, 36.

[6] So probably also Br reading, corruptly.

[7] These events are fully noticed, pp. 68, 151, 197–9.

[8] For his doings, see the Haihaya genealogies (p. 102). He is highly extolled there (p. 41) and in MBh xii, *49*, 1759: xiii, *152*, 7188–9: Mārk *19*, 21–31. But he is sometimes described as a bad king, especially in stories of his conflict with Rāma Jāmadagnya, e.g. MBh iii, *115*, 11038–42: xii, *49*, 1755–8: xiv, *29*, 818 f: Pad vi, *268*, 34 f.

the successes mentioned above, raised the Haihaya power to preeminence during a long reign. He captured Māhiṣmatī from the Karkoṭaka Nāgas [1] and made it his fortress-capital. He extended his conquests from the mouth of the Narbadā [2] as far as the Himalayas (p. 206). He defeated a Rāvaṇa, who is called king of Laṅka (in Ceylon) and had apparently come northward on conquest, and imprisoned him in Māhiṣmatī but released him afterwards.[3] The Bhārgavas were incensed against the Haihayas and sought to strengthen their position by alliances with kṣatriyas and the use of arms.[4] Thus Ṛcīka Aurva married Satyavatī, daughter of Gādhi, king of Kānyakubja. Their son was Jamadagni, and Gādhi's son Viśvaratha became the brahman Viśvāmitra, and was succeeded by his son Aṣṭaka.[5] Jamadagni married a princess of Ayodhyā.

At that time the kingdom of Ayodhyā passed through a crisis. King Trayyāruṇa banished his only son Satyavrata Triśaṅku and handed the realm over to his priest Devarāj Vasiṣṭha, but after twelve years Viśvāmitra restored Satyavrata to the throne, overcoming Vasiṣṭha. Satyavrata was succeeded by his son Hariścandra; Rohita succeeded him and is said to have built a fortress-town Rohitapura.[6]

Arjuna had many sons.[7] Chief among them was Jayadhvaja who reigned in Avanti; and others were Śūra and Śūrasena,[8] who may have had territories of their own.[9] Jayadhvaja's son was Tālajaṅgha, and he had many sons, chief of whom was Vītihotra. At the end of his long reign Arjuna came into collision with Jamadagni and his son Rāma. The genealogical accounts do not explain how that happened, except as the result of Āpava's curse

[1] The Karkoṭakas were in the Dekhan, MBh viii, *44*, 2066. Karkoṭaka was a Nāga chief, iii, *66*, 2611: viii, *34*, 1483: Hv *168*, 9502: cf. Pad vi, *242*, 2. They may have conquered Māhiṣmatī, see *ante*.

[2] This region was Anūpa; cf. MBh iii, *116*, 11089; *117*, 10209.

[3] See p. 242. Noticed, Raghuv vi, 38–40.

[4] All this fully discussed, pp. 151, 197–9, 205–6.

[5] So Kānyakubja genealogies, p. 146. Acknowledged in the brahmanical fable of Gālava and its sequel (p. 73): MBh iii, *197*, 13301–2; v, *118*, 4019, 4024: Mat *37*, 6.

[6] Hv *13*, 756.

[7] For these particulars see the genealogies, p. 102.

[8] They are named in Bd. iii, *45*, 1; *46*, 21, 23.

[9] See p. 171. There is no clear mention of the Śūrasenas about this time except in Bd iii, *49*, 5–6, but that seems to be an anachronism, for it speaks of their capital Madhurā (Mathurā) also, which was not founded till afterwards, as will be narrated.

(p. 206). The simplest stories say that Arjuna or his sons raided Jamadagni's hermitage, ill-treated him and carried off his calf; Rāma in revenge killed Arjuna; Arjuna's sons killed Jamadagni; and Rāma declared war against them and slew many of them and of the Haihayas.[1] These stories are largely brahmanical,[2] and there is no kṣatriya version,[3] yet some incidental allusions suggest that Rāma and the Bhārgavas were supported by the princes of Ayodhyā and Kānyakubja, who were allied to them by marriage[4] and who would naturally have opposed the dangerous raids of the Haihayas. Such a combination would explain how Rāma vanquished the Haihayas. Hostilities then ceased for a time.[5] The Haihayas received a set-back,[6] because it was not till later that they overcame Kānyakubja and Ayodhyā.

The Haihayas grew in power, and comprised five leading groups, the Vītihotras,[7] Śāryātas,[8] Bhojas,[9] Avantis and Tuṇḍikeras, all of whom were Tālajaṅghas (p. 102). Their dominion stretched from the Gulf of Cambay to the Ganges-Jumna doab and thence to Benares.[10] They continued their raids and there is no suggestion that they founded new kingdoms in the countries they overran. The Kānyakubja kingdom soon fell, for the dynasty ends with Aṣṭaka's son Lauhi. The kingdom of Ayodhyā was open to assault, and the Haihayas attacked it with the co-operation of Śakas,

[1] MBh iii, *115*, 11035; *116*, 11089 to *117*, 10203: vii, *70*, 2429–33: xii, *49*, 1760–70: xiii, *34*, 2126. See pp. 151, 199.

[2] Wholly brahmanical fables are Bḍ iii, *21*, 5 to *47*, 61, which make it all turn on Jamadagni's wonderful cow; and Pad vi, *268*, which says she was the celestial cow Surabhi!

[3] Bḍ iii, *47*, 64–87 contains the nearest approach to a kṣatriya account, and is noteworthy. It says nothing about the destruction of all kṣatriyas.

[4] This would account for the remark in *id.* 74, that many years afterwards the Tālajaṅgha 'remembering the former hostility' attacked Ayodhyā and drove out Sagara's father. Pad vi, *268*, 73–4 and *269*, 158, though brahmanical, admit that Rāma acknowledged his kinship with the Ayodhyā princes and did not destroy them.

[5] MBh xii, *49*, 1769–76.

[6] Bḍ iii, *47*, 67–73, apparently exaggerating, says that Tālajaṅgha and the Haihaya princes then took refuge a long time at the Himalayas, and regained their kingdom only when Rāma turned from war to austerities.

[7] Or Vītahotras or Vītahavyas, p. 155.

[8] See pp. 97, 98, 102, &c.

[9] This is the first appearance of this family, except the doubtful statement about Druhyu's offspring, *ante*.

[10] MBh xiii, *30*, 1946, 1950–4.

Yavanas, Kāmbojas, Pāradas and Pahlavas from the north-west,[1] and this fact shows that all the kingdoms between the north-west and Ayodhyā must have been overthrown. In fact, the long-continued Haihaya devastations left North India a tempting prey to the hardy races of that frontier. Bāhu[2] king of Ayodhyā was driven from his throne, took refuge in the forest and died near the hermitage of Aurva Bhārgava, whose personal name was Agni.[3] His queen gave birth to a son Sagara there and Aurva educated him.

The Haihaya conquests had thus reached to the kingdoms of Vaiśālī and Videha. The Vaiśālī realm was then under the rule of Karandhama, his son Avīkṣit and his son Marutta, three noted kings (pp. 147, 157). It is said that Karandhama was besieged by a confederacy of kings and at length defeated them; that Avīkṣit had a great conflict with the king of Vidiśā (Besnagar) and others and was captured, but Karandhama and his allies beat them and rescued him; and that Marutta had a contest with Nāgas.[4] There can be little doubt that those enemies were the Haihayas, for Vidiśā was in the Haihaya region, and that they were beaten off. There is no indication that the Haihayas conquered the Vaiśāla kings, and Marutta was a famous king and cakravartin.[5] The Haihaya conquests eastwards must have been stopped by some kingdom, and tradition suggests that it was these Vaiśāla kings who did that.[6]

About the time of Karandhama was Parāvṛt, king of the Yādava

[1] Narrated in the kṣatriya ballad in Vā *88*, 122–43; Bḍ iii, *63*, 120–41; Br *8*, 29–51; Hv *13*, 760 to *14*, 784; and Śiv vii, *61*, 23–43. Also in Viṣ iv, *3*, 15–21: Pad vi, *21*, 12–34: VN *7*, 7 to *8*, 63: Bḍ iii, *47*, 74 to *48*, 49: Bhāg ix, *8*, 2–7 (late): Rām i, *70*, 28–37 and ii, *110*, 15–24 (partially). Discussed in JRAS, 1910, pp. 9–10; 1914, pp. 279–81; 1919, pp. 354–61.

[2] Called *Asita* in Rām.

[3] Mat *12*, 40. Pad v, *8*, 144. Lg i, *66*, 15. Synonyms, *Vahni*, Kūr i, *21*, 5. *Tejonidhi*, VN *7*, 60; *8*, 8, 9.

[4] Mārk *121* to *131*, a long account with fanciful details, yet not brahmanical. It makes Avīkṣit's conflict grow out of a svayaṁvara at Vidiśā.

[5] See pp. 39–41. MBh xii, *29*, 981, which says that Māndhātṛ conquered Marutta, cannot mean this Marutta, for Māndhātṛ was long prior. The corresponding passage, *id.* vii, *62*, 2281–2 does not name Marutta.

[6] But MBh iii, *129*, 10528–9 perhaps goes too far in its enthusiasm in saying that Marutta sacrificed on the Jumna near Kurukṣetra.

branch. It is said[1] he placed his two youngest sons in Videha. This is improbable, for the Haihayas dominated all Madhyadeśa, and Videha is no doubt a mistake for Vidiśā.[2] His son Jyāmagha was expelled by his two elder brothers and sought his fortune southward in the hilly upper region of the Narbadā, at Mekalā,[3] Mṛttikāvatī[4] and in the Ṛkṣa hills (Satpura range), which country was wild and inhabited by Nāgas and other rude tribes. He established himself on the R. Śuktimatī (the Ken), in the hills near its source. There he led a predatory life. He or his son Vidarbha moved south and carved out a kingdom on the Tapti, and there Vidarbha reigned, the country being called Vidarbha (Berar), and the capital Vidarbhā and Kuṇḍina.[5]

When Ayodhyā was conquered, the foreign tribes settled down in the country. They were kṣatriyas, had the ministrations of brahmans and observed brahmanic rites.[6] Hence the then Vasiṣṭha, Atharvanidhi I Āpava (p. 207), maintained his position as the great priest of Ayodhyā among them. So the kingdom remained for more than twenty years till Sagara attained manhood.

Meanwhile the Kāśi kings had been carrying on a long struggle from the eastern portion of their territory, which adjoined the Vaiśālī kingdom, against the Haihayas, and at length Pratardana, son of Divodāsa II, defeated the Vītahavyas (or Vītihotras, who were the chief Tālajaṅgha-Haihayas) and recovered his territory, though not Vārāṇasī itself, which was still occupied by Rākṣasas (pp. 153–5). He or his son Vatsa[7] carried the victory farther,

[1] All these occurrences in Vā *95*, 27–36 : Bḍ iii, *70*, 28–37 : Br *15*, 11–21 : Hv *37*, 1979–88 : Mat *44*, 28–37 : Pad v, *13*, 11–20 : Lg i, *68*, 32–9.

[2] So one MS of Br. reads.

[3] Mekala hills, north-west of Chhattīsgaṛh : Mārk, my translation, p. 341.

[4] South of Vatsabhūmi, MBh iii, *253*, 15245.

[5] *Vidarbhā*, MBh iii, *71*, 2772 : Hv *117*, 6588, 6606. *Kuṇḍina*, MBh v, *157*, 5363 : Hv *104*, 5804 ; *106*, 5855 ; *118*, 6662, 6693. Also *Kuṇḍinagara*, Hv *108*, 6003. They were the same, MBh iii, *73*, 2852–3 : Hv *117*, 6588–91. A later capital *Bhojakaṭa* was founded by Rukmin in Kṛṣṇa's time, MBh v, *157*, 5361–4 : Hv *118*, 6690–3.

[6] Implied in the first five passages in fifth note above ; and particularly in Bḍ iii, *48*, 29–47. JRAS, 1919, pp. 358–61.

[7] *Id.* Hence Pratardana was called Śatrujit, and Vatsa's other names were Ṛtadhvaja and Kuvalayāśva ; Viṣ iv, *8*, 5–7 ; Gar i, *139*, 10–11. A fanciful tale about them, Mārk *20* to *26*. Bhāg ix, *17*, 6 confuses these names.

and annexed the country around Kauśāmbī, which was thence named the Vatsa country.[1]

Sagara had by this time reached manhood. He defeated the Tālajaṅgha-Haihayas and regained Ayodhyā.[2] He extended his campaign and subdued all the other enemies in N. India. He crushed the Haihayas in their own territories, and annihilated their dominion, and nothing more is said about them till long afterwards. He determined to destroy the foreign tribes, but at their entreaties Vasiṣṭha interposed; so Sagara spared their lives but reduced them to great religious and social degradation. Then he invaded Vidarbha and made peace by marrying the king's daughter (p. 156), and was received with honour by the Śūrasena Yādavas, who were his mother's brethren. He was a famous monarch (p. 39).

Vatsa's son Alarka followed up Pratardana's successes by driving the Rākṣasas out of Vārāṇasī, and re-establishing it as the Kāśi capital, during a long and prosperous reign.[3]

All these events may be summed up thus. Arjuna Kārtavīrya and the Haihayas maltreated the Bhārgavas and killed Jamadagni. Rāma and the Bhārgavas (with probably the help of Kānyakubja and Ayodhyā) killed Arjuna and punished the Haihayas, who were then checked in their career of conquests.[4] There the enmity between them ended.[5] After Rāma's time the Haihayas recovered their power and extended their conquests into N. India, making continual raids, overthrowing kingdoms, founding none, and devastating the countries, which were then overrun by tribes from the north-west also. The kṣatriyas must have perished by thousands. The Haihayas overwhelmed Kānyakubja and Ayodhyā, but were arrested by the Vaiśālī kings, and afterwards Sagara destroyed all those

[1] Vā *92*, 65, 73. Bd iii, *67*, 69, 78 (where for *vaṁśau* read *Vatsyo*). Br *11*, 50, 60; *13*, 68, 78. Hv *29*, 1587, 1597; *32*, 1741, 1753. Vatsa in MBh xiii, *30*, 1946 is used by anticipation, meaning the country, and not a person as Sörensen (see Haihaya[1], p. 316) takes it; and so also Vatsya in *id.* 1951.

[2] These events are described in the passages in fourteenth note above, and especially in Bd iii, *48* to *49*, 10, which seems generally to have preserved something like genuine kṣatriya tradition. Noticed in MBh iii, *106*, 8831–3.

[3] See passages following those in p. 153, note [4]; also p. 168. Mārk *27* to *44* has a long brahmanical and incorrect account of him.

[4] Cf. MBh v, *155*, 5281–6.

[5] So a Bhṛgu rishi afterwards saved the Vītahavya king from Pratardana's vengeance by turning him into a brahman, p. 200.

enemies, rescued India from those evils and re-established peace.[1] The carnage and ruin must have continued nearly a century, and the deplorable condition to which North India was reduced[2] may be imagined by that caused by the Marāṭhas and the Persian and Afghan invasions in the eighteenth century, for the Haihayas occupied the same region as the Marāṭhas and the two periods are strictly comparable and remarkably alike.

All these events were turned by the brahmans into the fable that Rāma destroyed all kṣatriyas off the earth twenty-one times, slaughtering each generation as it grew up.[3] It seems to have arisen thus. The slaughter began with Rāma's killing the Haihayas, and their career was checked a while. The brahmans knew that the carnage began again and continued long, though through their lack of the historical sense they did not understand that it occurred after Rāma's time, first, through the Haihayas, and lastly through Sagara: but it was easy, since the Bhārgavas were no longer at enmity with the Haihayas, to imagine that Rāma was still at work and to attribute the Haihaya devastations to him; and finally it was quite simple to credit Sagara's final destruction of all the enemies to Rāma, who was an Aurva (pp. 198–9), because it was alleged that Sagara destroyed them with Rāma's magical fire-weapon, which Bhārgava Aurva who educated him gave him,[4] and that the great Tālajaṅgha kṣatriya host was destroyed by Aurva single-handed.[5]

Sagara had a long reign.[6] He discarded his eldest son Asa-

[1] Peace described, though not in his name, MBh i, *64*, 2467–80.

[2] Fancifully described in MBh xii, *49*, 1784–6.

[3] See p. 200, note [1]. It is sometimes alleged that the kṣatriyas were renewed by the kṣatriya ladies and brahmans, MBh i, *64*, 2459–64; *104*, 4176–8: xiv, *29*, 833.

[4] See first seven passages in p. 268, note [1].

[5] MBh xii, *153*, 7223, which suggests confusion of the two Aurvas. Similarly Pratardana's defeat of the Vaitahavyas is attributed to his priest Bharadvāja (p. 154), MBh xiii, *34*, 2126; which also says the Bhṛgus conquered the Tālajaṅghas.

[6] Myth says Sagara had 60,000 sons by one of his wives (p. 19), while his other wife had only one son Asamañjas. They followed Sagara's sacrificial horse to the S.E. ocean, where it disappeared in the earth. They dug down in the ocean to the lower region, and all except four were burnt up by Kapila (who was Viṣṇu). By Kapila's favour the ocean (*samudra*) restored the horse to Sagara and became Sagara's son (*sāgara*). Vā *88*, 144–63. MBh iii, *106*, 8831 to *107*, 9912. Hv *14*, 785 to *15*, 806. Rām i, *38* to *41*. &c.

mañjas for cruelty to the citizens, and was succeeded by Asamañjas's son Aṁśumant.[1]

When Sagara established his empire over North India, the only noticeable kingdoms that survived were the Videha, Vaiśālī and Ānava kingdoms in the east, Kāśi in Madhyadeśa, Turvasu's line in the hilly country of Rewa, the new kingdom of Vidarbha, and apparently the Yādava branch on the R. Chambal. After his death, the overthrown dynasties appear to have generally recovered themselves, and the Yādavas of Vidarbha seem to have extended their authority northward over the Haihaya territory. Vidarbha had three sons, one Bhīma Kratha succeeded him; Cidi, the son of another son Kaiśika, founded the dynasty of Caidya kings in Cedi,[2] the country lying along the south of the Jumna;[3] and the third Lomapāda founded a separate kingdom, the position of which is not defined (p. 103). Kaiśikas however still dwelt in Vidarbha with the Krathas.[4] The Ānava kingdom in the east, the nucleus of which was Aṅga, became divided up into five kingdoms, said to have been named after king Bali's sons (p. 158), Aṅga, Vaṅga, Kaliṅga, Puṇḍra and Suhma.[5] The capital of Aṅga was Mālinī, and its name was changed afterwards to Campā or Campāvatī (Bhāgalpur) after king Campa.[6]

The Paurava claimant then was Duṣyanta, for the Paurava realm had been overthrown since Māndhātṛ's time, and Duṣyanta had been adopted as heir by Marutta of Turvasu's line, but after Sagara's death he re-established the Paurava dynasty (pp. 108, 156). His son by Śakuntalā was the famous and pious Bharata.[7] Their

[1] Vā *88*, 167–9. Bd iii, *51*, 51–69; *55*, 22; *63*, 164–5. MBh iii, *107*, 8884–95. Rām i, *38*, 20–3: ii, *36*, 16, 19–26; *110*, 26. VN *8*, 71, 121. Br *8*, 73; *78*, 40–3. Hv *15*, 807–8. His four sons were *vaṁśa-karas*, that is apparently, established minor dynasties, Vā *88*, 148–9: Bd iii, *63*, 146–7.

[2] See passages following those cited in p. 269, note [1]. Also Hv *117*, 6588–9. Cedi in the story of Nala, MBh iii, *65*, 2578, &c.

[3] JASB, vol. lxiv (1895), Part I, no. 3.

[4] e.g. Hv *117*, 6588–91.

[5] See p. 158, note [4]. *Vaṅga*, central Bengal. *Puṇḍra*, NW Bengal. *Suhma*, Hooghly and Midnapur. *Kaliṅga*, the Orissa coast (except north part of Balasore) and Ganjam.

[6] MBh xii, *5*, 134: xiii, *42*, 2359. Vā *99*, 105–6. Mat *48*, 97. Br *13*, 43. Hv *31*, 1699, Viṣ iv, *18*, 4. It was on the Bhāgīrathī, MBh iii, *84*, 8141; and in Sūta-viṣaya, *id. 307*, 17151. Bhāg ix, *8*, 1 is wrong.

[7] Pp. 39–41, 232. Called also *Sarvadamana*, MBh i, *74*, 2995; vii, *68*, 2383.

territory however appears to have been shifted to the northern portion of the Ganges-Jumna doab, for Pratiṣṭhāna is no longer mentioned and its district was included in the Vatsa realm. Some passages make Hastināpura [1] the capital of Duṣyanta and Bharata,[2] and say Bharata's territory stretched from the R. Sarasvatī to the Ganges,[3] and that is no doubt right, because he was a great monarch with a wide sway (pp. 39–41); but their fifth successor Hastin is distinctly stated to have founded that city.[4] If those passages are right, Hastin may have enlarged it and given it his name. Bharata's successors were the Bharatas or Bhāratas (p. 113), and how his line was continued has been explained above (pp. 159–61).

Such seems to have remained the condition of India for some time. Ayodhyā rose to prominence again under Aṁśumant's second successor Bhagīratha,[5] and Bhagīratha's third successor Ambarīṣa Nābhāgi [6] (pp. 39–41). The Yādavas appear to have been divided up into a number of small kingdoms,[7] and at the western end of the Satpura hills was the small principality of Niṣadha, the king of which about this time was Nala.[8] Bharata's fifth successor Hastin made Hastināpura his capital (see above), and soon after Hastin's time Tṛṇabindu's second successor Viśāla built Viśālā or Vaiśālī [9] as the capital of the kingdom which has been hitherto called the kingdom of Vaiśālī in anticipation.

[1] It had many synonyms based on the fact that *hastin* means 'elephant', e.g. Gajasāhvaya, Vāraṇāhvaya, Nāgasāhvaya.

[2] Duṣyanta's, MBh i, *74*, 3000. Bharata's, *id. 94*, 3736.

[3] MBh vii, *68*, 2384 : xii, *29*, 939.

[4] MBh i, *95*, 3787. Vā *99*, 165. Mat *49*, 42. Viṣ iv, *19*, 10. Bhāg ix, *21*, 20.

[5] After him the Ganges was called Bhāgīrathī, because he is fabled to have brought it down (from heaven): sequels to passages in twelfth note above; also Bḍ iii, *56*, 32–53 ; Br *78*, 55–77 ; Pad vi, *22*, 7–18 ; *267*, 52–4 ; Vā *47*, 24–40. The fable was developed by tacking it on to the story of Sagara's burnt sons (said note); MBh iii, *107*, 9903 to *109*, 9965 ; &c.

[6] Extolled, Vā *88*, 171–2 : Bḍ iii, *63*, 171–2 : Lg i, *66*, 21–2.

[7] e.g. Vidiśā (Besnagar). Pad ii, *21*, 4–13 and vi, *29*, 18 profess to name certain of its kings.

[8] P. 169. His story, MBh iii, *53* to *79*. For its position, Mārk, my translation, p. 343. Nala is alluded to elsewhere, Mat *12*, 56 : Hv *15*, 815, 830–1 : Br *8*, 80, 93 : Vā *88*, 174–5 : Bḍ iii, *63*, 173–4 : Pad v, *8*, 160–1 (wrongly) : Lg i, *66*, 24–5 : Viṣ iv, *4*, 18.

[9] Vā *86*, 15–17. Bḍ iii, *61*, 12. Viṣ iv, *1*, 18. Rām i, *47*, 12. Bhāg ix, *2*, 33.

Hastin had two sons, Ajamīḍha and Dvimīḍha, and under them the Paurava dynasty expanded and formed fresh kingdoms. A cousin of Hastin, Rantideva Sāṅkṛti, a famous king, who was also a Paurava, had a kingdom with capital Daśapura, that encroached into the Yādava territory and lay on the R. Chambal.[1] Dvimīḍha founded the dynasty of the Dvimīḍhas (pp. 111, 115) in a new realm which was apparently the modern district of Bareilly.[2] Ajamīḍha's realm was divided on his death among his three sons, the main kingdom with the capital Hastināpura, and the two others in the Krivi country (named Pañcāla afterwards[3]) which had evidently been conquered, namely, a northern called Ahicchattra, of which the capital was then or soon afterwards Ahicchattrā and Chattravatī, and a southern, of which the capitals were afterwards Kāmpilya and Mākandī (p. 113). These three dynasties were Pauravas, Bhāratas and Ājamīḍhas. Paurava was always applied to the main branch at Hastināpura. Ājamīḍha was never generally used, but in so far as it was used was also applied to that branch.[4] The use of Bhārata will be noticed.

About this time Kalmāṣapāda reigned at Ayodhyā, and the kingdom seems to have gone through trouble immediately afterwards, because the genealogies then give two lines of kings (pp. 93–4), which suggest that there was a division with two rival lines reigning for some six or seven kings, until Dilīpa II Khaṭvāṅga re-established the single monarchy. It seems possible to connect this split with Kalmāṣapāda's conduct to Vasiṣṭha described above (pp. 208–9), for it can hardly be doubted that the brahmans of Ayodhyā would have been inflamed and have sought revenge. This would explain the statements that Sarvakarman in one line was brought up in secret, and that Mūlaka in the other fled to the

[1] See pp. 39–42, 112, 249.

[2] The indications are these. It must have been part of or adjacent to the Paurava territory of Hastināpura. It did not comprise Pañcāla, which remained to Ajamīḍha as will appear. One of its later kings Kṛta was a disciple of Hiraṇyanābha king of Kosala (p. 173), whence presumably they were neighbours. A later king Ugrāyudha killed Pṛṣata's grandfather in N. Pañcāla and then overthrew S. Pañcāla (p. 166), whence presumably N. Pañcāla intervened between him and S. Pañcāla.

[3] Śatapatha Brāhm xiii, 5, 4, 7. *Vedic Index* i, p. 198. Krivi has nothing to do with *Kuru*, for king Kuru was considerably later.

[4] e.g. MBh i, *94*, 3737 : ii, *44*, 1601 : iii, *5*, 249 : &c.

forest for safety. There would have been a contest similar to that of Rāma Jāmadagnya's time described above, and the two contests would through the lack of the historical sense have been confused in brahmanic stories as shown (p. 152).

The main line at Hastināpura was undistinguished and played no noteworthy part at first, for the names of all its kings except Ṛkṣa have been forgotten till Saṁvaraṇa's time (pp. 146, 148). The northern of the two other kingdoms first rose to eminence. One of its early kings, Bhṛmyaśva,[1] had five sons, to whom was given the nickname *Pañcāla* (p. 75),[2] and it seems they all received principalities because of that explanation and because one of the younger sons is called a king (p. 116). His territory then, which was not large, would have been divided into five small districts, and Mudgala and the other sons would have been quite petty rājās.[3] Mudgala's son and descendants became brahmans, the Maudgalyas (p. 251), but his grandson Vadhryaśva raised the kingdom, and Vadhryaśva's son Divodāsa augmented it (p. 120). They and their successors are the kings who play a prominent part in the Rigveda, and the other kings, who are named with them there, were probably the petty rājās in the lineage of Mudgala's brothers. All these kings of N. Pañcāla were kṣatriyan brahmans (chapter XXIII).

About Mudgala's time Ayodhyā rose to prominence under a famous king Dilīpa II Khaṭvāṅga[4] and his immediate descendants Raghu, Aja and Daśaratha, and by this time the country had acquired the name Kosala.[5] Videha was flourishing, and there was a kingdom at Sāṅkāśyā, where Sīradhvaja Janaka killed its king and installed his brother Kuśadhvaja.[6] The Yādavas seem to have been divided into small kingdoms, but about this time the noted king Madhu must have consolidated them, if his territory extended from Gujarat to the Jumna as alleged,[7] and the Paurava kingdom which belonged

[1] Nirukta ix, 23–4.

[2] So also Ag *277*, 20: Gar i, *140*, 19.

[3] Mudgala's petty status would help to explain the hymn attributed to him, Rigv x, *102*, with the Vedārth annotation. *Vedic Index* ii, p. 166. JRAS, 1910, p. 1328: 1918, p. 235.

[4] Pp. 39–41, 207.

[5] So in Rām; and Rāma's mother was Kausalyā. Rām ii, *49*, 8–12 makes remarks about its south-western boundary.

[6] So Rām i, *70*, 2–3 (which says it was on the R. Ikṣumatī): *71*, 16–20.

[7] Hv *94*, 5157–73. See p. 170.

to Rantideva (*ante*) had succumbed. His descendants were the Madhus or Mādhavas.[1]

In Daśaratha's time then the Yādavas had a powerful kingdom, the Pauravas had at least four states in the Ganges-Jumna plain, with North Pañcāla particularly prominent, and among the Pauravas there had been a great development of brahmanism as explained in chapter XXIII. It is remarkable then in the Rāmāyaṇa, that Kosala's friendliest relations were with the eastern kingdoms of Videha, Aṅga and Magadha (*sic*), the Panjab kingdoms of Kekaya, Sindhu and Sauvīra, the western kingdom of Surāṣṭra (*sic*),[2] and the Dākṣiṇātya kings, for these are specially named among the invitations sent out for Daśaratha's sacrifice; and no mention is made of any of the kings of the middle region of North India except Kāśi.[3] This remark holds good for the Rāmāyaṇa generally. Prayāga is described as in a great forest, opposite Śṛṅgaverapura the capital of a Niṣāda kingdom on the north side of the Ganges[4]—which is very improbable as the Vatsa kingdom comprised that region.

The story of Daśaratha's son Rāma[5] brings South India into view definitely for the first time. The Yādavas had established themselves in the north-west portion of the Dekhan, and all the rest of the Dekhan lay outside the scope of traditional history except in the above notices of the two Rāvaṇas, and was largely occupied by the great Daṇḍaka forest. Yet the religion of North India had penetrated that region, for the story often speaks of munis there whom the Rākṣasas maltreated. There was a large colony of people who are called Rākṣasas in the lower Godāvarī

[1] Br *15*, 27. Hv *37*, 1994–5. Lg i, *68*, 47.

[2] Surāṣṭra extended to Prabhāsa, MBh iii, *88*, 8344–6. Cf. xiv, *83*, 2477–8, though it is confused.

[3] Rām i, *13*, 21–9; though Hastināpura and Pañcāla are mentioned elsewhere, ii, *68*, 13. Matsyas are mentioned (ii, *10*. 37) and Vīra-matsyas (ii, *71*, 5).

[4] *Id.* ii, *50*, 33 to *52*, 11: *54*, 1–8.

[5] The Rāmāyaṇa is strongly brahmanical, full of traditions and statements rendered largely fabulous, and its statements must be received with caution (e.g. pp. 91 f). Rāmopākhyāna, MBh iii, *272* to *291*. Shortly in Hv *42*, 2324–58: Pad vi, *269*: Kūr i, *21*, 17–53: Br *123*: Gar i, *142*, 10–18; *143*. Noticed, Mat *12*, 50–1: Pad v, *8*, 155: &c. Pad narrates what it calls the *Purātana Rāmāyaṇa* (iv, *112*) in rather colloquial style, and also the story (v, *35*).

valley called Janasthāna,[1] and it appertained to a flourishing kingdom of Rākṣasas in Ceylon with their capital Laṅkā, which is described as situated on a hill in or jutting out into the southern ocean.[2] These so-called Rākṣasas were not uncivilized, for Laṅkā is described in the most glowing terms,[3] and allowing for poetical exaggeration both therein and also to the contrary in personal descriptions,[4] it is obvious that their civilization was as high as that of North India.[5] These Rākṣasas were evidently a sea-going people, as the connexion of their colony in Janasthāna with Laṅkā indicates. Their king was 'Rāvaṇa', called also Daśagrīva (and synonymously Daśaśīrsa, Daśānana &c.). Rāvaṇa, a name given also to the two earlier kings above mentioned, was probably the royal title, the Tamil *iṟaivaṉ*, 'king' (p. 242); and Daśagrīva or one of its synonymous forms was probably his personal Dravidian name Sanskritized, which accordingly gave rise to the fable that he had ten heads. The story of Rāma appears now largely as fable, but it is fairly clear that the fabulous in it is a perversion of simpler occurrences distorted gradually in accordance with later brahmanical ideas about Rākṣasas and the marvellous, especially in the Rāmāyaṇa.

Through the intrigue of his step-mother Rāma was banished, with his wife Sītā and brother Lakṣmaṇa, from Ayodhyā to spend fourteen years in the Daṇḍaka forest.[6] He travelled south to Prayāga, then south-west to the region of Bhopal, then south across the Narbada, and then to a district where he dwelt ten years. That was probably the Chhattisgaṛh district, because that was called

[1] MBh iii, *276*, 15986: vii, *59*, 2226. Rām ii, *116*, 11: iii, *18*, 25.

[2] Rām iii, *47*, 29; *57*, 4: iv, *58*, 20, 24: v, *2*, 19; *4*, 24–5; *65*, 10–11: vi, *3*, 21–2; *113*, 54. MBh iii, *277*, 16035; *281*, 16252. The hill is called Trikūṭa, Rām vi, *2*, 11; *39*, 17–19; *40*, 2–3; *125*, 3: but cf. v, *1*, 200–2; *2*, 1. Tradition says it was south-east of Trincomali, and has been swallowed up by the sea, Winslow's *Tamil Dict.* s. v. *Ilaṅkai*. The name Laṅkā was also extended to mean Ceylon.

[3] Rām v, *4* f. Rāvaṇa and his brothers knew the Veda and were religious! MBh iii, *274*, 15901.

[4] e.g., as regards Śūrpaṇakhā, Rām iii, *17*, 9f, a ridiculous travesty since she was a princess. Rāvaṇa sometimes has two arms and is otherwise beautiful, Hopkins, *Epic Mythology*, 42. The Rākṣasas had beauty, *id.* 39: MBh iii, *113*, 10070–1; *274*, 15894, 15897.

[5] Rāvaṇa and his fellow Rākṣasas are said to have been descended from the royal family of Vaiśālī, see Paulastyas, chap. XXII.

[6] For the geography, JRAS, 1894, pp. 231 f.

Dakṣiṇa Kosala, and in it was a hill called Rāmagiri. His long stay there would have connected it with his home, Kosala; hence probably arose its name.[1] Afterwards he went south to the middle Godāvarī, where he came into conflict with the Rākṣasa colony of Janasthāna. It is said he avenged on the Rākṣasas their ill-treatment of munis. Rāvaṇa carried Sītā off to Laṅkā.[2] Rāma went south-west to Pampā lake and there met Sugrīva (with his counsellor Hanumant) who had been expelled by his brother Bālin, king of Kiṣkindhā.[3] They went south there, and Rāma killed Bālin and placed Sugrīva on the throne. These persons and the people of Kiṣkindhā are called monkeys, but they were a Dravidian tribe and were apparently akin to the Rākṣasas of Laṅkā, for Rāvaṇa and Sugrīva are spoken of as 'like brothers'.[4] With their aid Rāma proceeded south to what was afterwards Pāṇḍya, crossed over to Ceylon by Adam's Bridge, killed Rāvaṇa and recovered Sītā. Thus the only civilized communities in S. India mentioned at that time were in Janasthāna and at Kiṣkindhā. No others are alluded to, not even the Pāṇḍyas, through whose country Rāma passed. Hence Pāṇḍya had not then come into existence, nor therefore Cola or Kerala[5] (p. 108).

Rāma succeeded to the throne of Ayodhyā and was its last famous sovereign. His brothers obtained kingdoms elsewhere. Bharata's mother was a Kaikeya princess and he obtained that kingdom apparently.[6] His two sons Takṣa and Puṣkara are said to have conquered Gāndhāra and reigned there in Takṣaśilā and Puṣkarāvatī respectively.[7] Lakṣmaṇa had two sons, Aṅgada and Candraketu, and to them are assigned two countries near the Himalayas, with the capitals Aṅgadīyā and Candracakrā respectively, both in

[1] Also later, the people of Eastern Kosala (i.e. Kosala) through fear of Jarāsandha migrated to the south, no doubt to this district, MBh ii, *13*, 591–2; cf. *30*, 1117. JRAS, 1908, p. 323. See eleventh note *infra*.

[2] It is said, through the air; but probably by sea.

[3] Its description, Rām vi, *28*, 30–2; but cf. iv, *33*, 1–5.

[4] Rām v, *51*, 2–3: vi, *20*, 10.

[5] They are mentioned only in the later geographical chapter, iv, *41*, 12, 19. Cola and Kerala are introduced erroneously into the story of Sagara, Br *8*, 50, Hv *14*, 782; see JRAS, 1919, p. 358. Raghuv vi, 60 has therefore an anachronism.

[6] But Raghuv xv, 87 says he got the Sindhu country.

[7] Vā *88*, 189–90. Bd iii, *63*, 190–1. Viṣ iv, *4*, 47. Pad v, *35*, 23–4. Pad vi, *271*, 10, Ag *11*, 7–8, and Raghuv xv, 88–9 miscall Gāndhāra *Gandharva*.

Kārapatha-deśa.[1] Śatrughna (marching probably round by Prayāga, for no mention is made of the Pañcālas,) attacked the Sātvata-Yādavas on the west of the Jumna, killed Mādhava Lavaṇa and built the capital Mathurā in the country thenceforward called Śūrasena, and his two sons Subāhu and Śūrasena reigned there (pp. 170–1).[2] Rāma[3] had two sons Kuśa and Lava.[4] Kuśa succeeded him and is said to have founded a town Kuśasthalī on the Vindhya hills.[5] Lava obtained the northern portion of Kosala with the city Śrāvastī. Those collateral kingdoms seem to have disappeared soon. Bhīma Sātvata expelled Śatrughna's sons from Mathurā, and he and his descendants reigned there (p. 170). The two states in Gāndhāra receive no further notice and were probably absorbed among the Druhyus. Nothing more is said about the principalities of Lakṣmaṇa's sons nor about Lava's kingdom. Henceforth Ayodhyā plays no prominent part in traditional history, and the chief actors are the Pauravas and Yādavas.

The large Yādava kingdom appears to have been divided among Sātvata's four sons, Bhajamāna, Devāvṛdha, Andhaka and Vṛṣṇi.[6] Bhajamāna's kingdom is not specified, and his descendants attained no distinction. Devāvṛdha is connected with the R. Parṇāśā (the modern Banas in West Malwa), and he, his son Babhru and his descendants reigned at Mārttikāvata, which was apparently in the Śālva country[7] around Mt. Abu. Andhaka reigned at Mathurā,

[1] Vā *88*, 187–8. Bd iii, *63*, 188–9. Viṣ iv, *4*, 47. Raghuv xv, 90. Pad v, *35*, 24 : vi, *271*, 11–12 places them mistakenly in Madra.

[2] Raghuv xv, 36 says he put his two sons Śatrughātin and Subāhu in Mathurā and Vidiśā.

[3] The later story of Rāma after his return to Ayodhyā is told in Pad iv, *1* to *68* ; Rām vii. Shortly, Pad vi, *270*, *271*. Fancifully, Pad iv, *113*.

[4] It is said they sang a poem composed by Vālmīki praising Rāma's exploits before Rāma ; and so *kuśīlava* came to mean a 'minstrel' (Mat *227*, 119. MBh xiii, *90*, 4280). This is not improbable, cf. the words, *euhemerist*, *burke*, *boycott*, *bowdler*. What they sang could not have been the present Rāmāyaṇa, which is a brahmanical production of much later date : see p. 202, note [1].

[5] Not Kuśasthalī in Gujarat, but presumably on the eastern spurs of the Vindhya range near Dakṣiṇa Kosala. Pad vi, *271*, 54–5 is mistaken and confuses the two Kuśasthalīs.

[6] For all these particulars, see pp. 103 f.

[7] MBh iii, *20*, 791 : cf. xvi, *7*, 245. It must be distinguished from Mṛttikāvatī mentioned above. Mārttikāvata existed before, e.g. according to the story of Rāma Jāmadagnya, MBh iii, *116*, 11076 : vii, *70*, 2436.

the chief Yādava capital, as mentioned above. He had two sons, Kukura and Bhajamāna. Kukura and his descendants, the Kukuras, formed the main dynasty there down to Kaṁsa, while this Bhajamāna's descendants, who were specially known as the Andhakas, formed a princely line somewhere there, and Kṛtavarman was their king in the Pāṇḍavas' time.[1] Vṛṣṇi reigned probably at Dvārakā in Gujarat, because his descendant Akrūra reigned there.[2] Besides these there were Vidarbha, and other Yādava kingdoms in Avanti,[3] Daśārṇa[4], &c., and probably a small Haihaya kingdom at Māhiṣmatī.[5] The Bhojas were a family among the Haihayas (p. 102), and yet the name Bhoja is used widely of many Yādavas. Andhaka was the 'great Bhoja', and Devāvṛdha's descendants were Bhojas (p. 105). Ugrasena and his son Kaṁsa were Bhojas,[6] and so was Kṛtavarman.[7] So also Bhīṣmaka and his son Rukmin of Vidarbha.[8] In fact the Bhojas were widespread,[9] and it would almost seem as if the name belonged to the Yādavas generally, except perhaps the Vṛṣṇis in Gujarat.[10]

About this time there reigned in North Pañcāla Sṛñjaya, his son Cyavana-Pijavana and his son Sudāsa-Somadatta, the Vedic Sudās (p. 120). Cyavana was a great warrior, and Sudās extended his territory.[11] They raised the dynasty to its height. They seem to have conquered both the Dvimīḍha dynasty and South Pañcāla, for there is admittedly a gap in the former genealogy (p. 115) which appears to occur at this time, and the reference to king Nīpa and his sons in the latter implies the same apparently at this time, just as a similar remark about Somaka afterwards[12] certainly

Its adjective *Mārttikāvatika*, *id.* vii, *48*, 1892; and °*vataka*, *id.* iii, 14, 629; *116*, 11076.

[1] MBh xi, *11*, 309; and Sörensen's *Index*.

[2] Vā *96*, 60. Bḍ iii, *71*, 62. Br *17*, 5. Hv *40*, 2095. Viṣ iv, *13*, 35–70; *14*, 2.

[3] Mat *44*, 66, 70. Pad v, *13*, 56. Bḍ iii, *71*, 128. Hv *38*, 2023. Br *15*, 54.

[4] MBh v, *190*, 7417 f. Hv *91*, 4967.

[5] MBh ii, *30*, 1124: v, *165*, 5751.

[6] Hv *55*, 3102–4; *113*, 6263, 6380. MBh vii, *11*, 388–9.

[7] MBh v, *56*, 2252; *164*, 5737: &c.

[8] MBh v, *157*, 5350–1, 5366. Hv *92*, 5016; *99*, 5496.

[9] MBh ii, 13, 570. [10] It is never applied, I believe, to Kṛṣṇa.

[11] Rigv vii, *20*, 2. P. 120.

[12] Compare Vā *99*, 175–6, 209–10: Mat *49*, 52–3; *50*, 15–16: Hv *20*, 1060–2; *32*, 1793: Br *13*, 99–101: Viṣ iv, *19*, 11, 18. *Vaṁśakara* is applied to the king who restored a dynasty; so Duṣyanta (p. 156), and Saṁvaraṇa, MBh i, *94*, 3724; *95*, 3790.

covers a long gap. Sudās drove the Paurava king Saṁvaraṇa of Hastināpura out, defeating him on the Jumna. His conquests stirred up a confederacy of the neighbouring kings to resist him—Pūru (Saṁvaraṇa), the Yādva (the Yādava king of Mathurā), the Śivas (Śivis, who were Ānavas, p. 109), Druhyus (of Gāndhāra, *ante*), Matsyas (west of Śūrasena), Turvaśa (the Turvasu prince, apparently in Rewa) and other smaller states.[1] Sudās defeated them in a great battle near the R. Paruṣṇī (Ravi), and Pūru, Saṁvaraṇa, took refuge in a fortress near the R. Sindhu (Indus) many years. Sudās was succeeded by his son Sahadeva and grandson Somaka, and the kingdom declined.[2] Saṁvaraṇa recovered his kingdom of Hastināpura with 'Vasiṣṭha's' aid (p. 210) probably from Somaka,[3] and so conquered North Pañcāla. His son Kuru raised the Paurava realm to eminence and extended his sway beyond Prayāga, which means that he subdued South Pañcāla which intervened. He gave his name to Kurukṣetra and to Kurujāṅgala, which adjoined it on the east and in which Hastināpura lay (p. 76).[4] His successors were called the Kurus or Kauravas, a name that was extended also to the people.[5]

Kuru's grandson Janamejaya II lost the throne, which then passed to a younger branch (p. 114), and the kingdom appears to have declined. North Pañcāla had sunk into insignificance, but the Dvimīḍha dynasty revived, and also South Pañcāla under the Nīpas in their capital Kāmpilya. Soon afterwards Vasu, a descendant of Kuru, conquered the Yādava kingdom of Cedi and established himself there, whence he was known as Caidya-uparicara (p. 118). His capital was Śuktimatī on the R. Śuktimatī (the Ken).[6] He extended his conquests eastwards as far as Magadha and apparently north-west also over Matsya which existed before as just mentioned; hence he was reckoned a samrāj and cakravartin.[7] He divided his territories among his five sons, consisting of Magadha, Cedi,

[1] MBh i, *94*, 3725–39. Rigv vii, *18*; *19*, 3, 6, 8. JRAS, 1910, pp. 49–50: 1918, pp. 246–8. *Vedic Index* ii, 186.

[2] Sudās perished through ill conduct, Manu vii, 41.

[3] Somaka is said to have put his only son Jantu to death in order to obtain more sons; MBh iii, *127*, 10471 to *128*, 10497. Noticed briefly in the genealogies.

[4] MBh i, *109*, 4337, 4360: *199*, 7355.

[5] So the genealogies. These Kurus have nothing to do with the Uttara Kurus, p. 132.

[6] MBh i, *63*, 2367: iii, *22*, 898: xiv, *83*, 2467.

[7] MBh i, *63*, 2362. Hv *154*, 8815.

Kauśāmbī, Karūṣa and apparently Matsya. His eldest son Bṛhadratha took Magadha, with Girivraja as his capital,[1] and founded the famous Bārhadratha dynasty there; and with it Magadha for the first time took a prominent place in traditional history.

Later, the Kauravas again became eminent under Pratīpa[2] and his successor Śantanu, who superseded his elder brother or cousin Devāpi (p. 252); and South Pañcāla under Brahmadatta (p. 164). Ugrāyudha of the Dvimīḍhas conquered North Pañcāla and destroyed the dynasty in South Pañcāla. He then attacked the Kauravas after Śantanu's death, but Bhīṣma killed him, and Pṛṣata, the heir to North Pañcāla, who had taken refuge in Kāmpilya, recovered his ancestral kingdom (p. 166). S. Pañcāla with its dynasty destroyed would seem to have been under the sway of the Kauravas.

Jarāsandha, king of Magadha, then rose to the highest power,[3] and extended his supremacy around,[4] and as far as Mathurā, where Kaṁsa, the Yādava king, who had married two of his daughters, acknowledged him as overlord. Kaṁsa relying on his favour tyrannized over his own subjects, and Kṛṣṇa killed him. This roused Jarāsandha's wrath against Kṛṣṇa and the Bhojas of Mathurā. For a time they resisted him,[5] but feeling their position there insecure migrated in a body to Gujarat and established themselves in Dvārakā,[6] where Kṛṣṇa ultimately obtained the leadership.[7]

Śantanu's grandsons were Dhṛtarāṣṭra and Pāṇḍu. Dhṛtarāṣṭra had many sons Duryodhana, &c., who as the elder branch were called the Kauravas. Pāṇḍu had five sons, Yudhiṣṭhira, Bhīma, Arjuna, Nakula and Sahadeva, who were known as the Pāṇḍavas. Pāṇḍu died early, and there was intense jealousy between the cousins.

[1] MBh ii, *13*, 626–7; *20*, 798–800, 810; which he built, Hv *117*, 6598. Rājagṛha was also the capital, i, *113*, 4451; *204*, 7476 : iii, *84*, 8082 : xiv, *82*, 2436–7, 2444—apparently the same.

[2] Famous, MBh v, *148*, 5053.

[3] These events are described in MBh ii, *13*, 571–632; *18*, 761–7 : Hv *87* to *93*; *99*; *100*; *117*, 6579 f: Br *195*, 1–12.

[4] Over Karṇa king of Aṅga, MBh xii, *5*, 134. Over Cedi, Hv *117*, 6602–3. Over Aṅgas, Vaṅgas, Kaliṅgas and Puṇḍras, *ibid.* 6607.

[5] A long account of the war, Hv *87* to *94*, 5138; *99*; *100*; *110*.

[6] Kṛṣṇa's story, Br *180* to *212* : Hv *57* to *190* : Viṣ v : Bhāg : Pad vi, *272* to *279*. Briefly, MBh v, *47*, 1881–92.

[7] His later war with kings, Hv *282* to *293*; *295* to *320*.

Pṛṣata was succeeded by his son Drupada in North Pañcāla, but Droṇa, whom Drupada treated with disdain, conquered him with the aid of the young Pāṇḍavas and Kauravas. Droṇa got both North and South Pañcāla, and keeping North Pañcāla for himself gave Drupada South Pañcāla. With Drupada in that transfer went the Sṛñjayas and Somakas, for they accompanied him at the Bhārata battle.[1]

The young Pāṇḍavas then contended with Duryodhana and the other sons of Dhṛtarāṣṭra for their share of the Kaurava territory and received the small principality of Indraprastha (Delhi). Being ambitious they had to reckon with Jarāsandha, and Bhīma and Arjuna with Kṛṣṇa's help killed him, their common enemy.[2] They were banished for fourteen years, as the penalty of losing at dice, and at the end of that time re-claimed their principality, but Duryodhana refused all terms, and they appealed to arms. They were aided by the Matsyas, Cedis, Kārūṣas, Kāśis, South Pāñcālas, Western Māgadhas and the Western Yādavas from Gujarat and Surāṣṭra; and on Duryodhana's side were all the Panjab nations, and all the other kingdoms of Northern India and the north of the Dekhan. The contest began rather as an armed demonstration,[3] but soon developed into deadly earnest, and ended in the victory of the Pāṇḍavas, with the slaughter of nearly all the kings and princes who took part in it.[4] It was the famous Bhārata battle. Yudhiṣṭhira became king of the Kurus[5] and reigned at Hastināpura.

Much stress has been laid on the fact, that the Brāhmaṇas and Sūtras make no reference to the Pāṇḍavas and the Bhārata battle,[6] as throwing doubt on the alleged events, but the explanation is simple. That battle was a purely political contest, had no religious significance, and (though described at great length in the epic) was a brief struggle between the Pāṇḍavas and Dhārtarāṣṭras. All that it decided was which of them should hold the Kuru realm. Hence it did not concern the recluse brahmans who composed the religious

[1] MBh i, *131*, 5134–45. Hv *20*, 1113–15. P. 116.

[2] MBh ii, *19* to *23*, 930. Pad vi, *279*, 1–12.

[3] The feats attributed to Bhīṣma, who was a very old man, show that the early fighting is greatly exaggerated.

[4] All discussed in JRAS, 1908, pp. 309 f.

[5] MBh xiv, *89*, 2679: xv, *37*, 1012: xvii, *1*, 8: &c.

[6] Weber, *Hist. of Ind. Lit.*, p. 136. Not in *Vedic Index*.

literature, and naturally they did not mention it. Moreover, the name Pāṇḍava was a transient one. The sons of Dhṛtarāṣṭra and of Pāṇḍu were cousins, all Kurus or Kauravas, and the patronymic Pāṇḍava was needed as distinctive only during their struggle, for the Pāṇḍavas when they conquered succeeded as Kurus to the Kuru realm, their cousins were all killed, and the name Pāṇḍava had no longer any *raison d'être*. Consequently it appears far less often in the last seven books than in the earlier books of the epic, and naturally finds no place in the religious literature which was composed after the kingdom was settled in Yudhiṣṭhira's successors.[1] This matter is a signal illustration of the difference between kṣatriya and brahmanic thought (p. 59), and of the futility of expecting purely secular history in the priestly books. Politically and for kṣatriyas that contest and its results were a very great event; religiously and for brahmans (especially recluse brahmans) it had no importance whatever.

Dhṛtarāṣṭra after some years longer retired to the forest[2] and was consumed in a conflagration.[3] The accounts of what happened subsequently, so far as tradition discloses events, are chiefly in the early and closing chapters of the Mahābhārata[4] and the prophetic sketches of 'future kings' in the Puranas.[5] Some years after the battle[6] the Yādavas of Gujarat were ruined by fratricidal strife and Kṛṣṇa died. Under Arjuna's leadership they abandoned Dvārakā (on which the sea encroached) and Gujarat and retreated northwards, but were attacked and broken up by the rude Ābhīras of Rajputana. Arjuna established Hārdikya's son at Mārttikāvata, Yuyudhāna's grandson on the R. Sarasvatī, and bringing the bulk of the people to Indraprastha (Delhi) placed Vajra, the surviving Vṛṣṇi prince, as king over them.[7] Yudhiṣṭhira and his brothers then abdicated and placed Arjuna's grandson Parikṣit II on the throne.[8]

[1] See chap. XXVI and XXVII.

[2] MBh xv, *1*, 6; *3*, 71 say 15 years—an exaggeration?

[3] MBh xv, *37* f.

[4] The accounts there appear grossly distorted as manifestly brahmanic fable, but no doubt embody real facts.

[5] My *Dynasties of the Kali age*, pp. 65–69.

[6] MBh xvi, *1*, 1, 13 say 36 years—an exaggeration?

[7] MBh xvi, *7*, 185–253: xvii, *1*, 8, 9. Br *210* to *212*. Viṣ v, *37*; *38*. Pad vi, *279*, 56 f. Ag *15*.

[8] MBh xvii *1*. Br *212*, 91–5.

The great slaughter of kṣatriyas in the battle must have seriously weakened the stability of the kingdoms, especially in the north-west, which was faced by hostile frontier tribes. Consequently it is not surprising that the accounts indicate disorganization. Nāgas established themselves at Takṣaśilā and assailed Hastināpura—which indicates that the Panjab kingdoms that played so prominent a part in the battle had fallen, and certainly little more is heard of them.[1] The Nāgas killed Parikṣit II, but his son Janamejaya III defeated them and peace was made. Still they held the north-west, the principalities on the Sarasvatī and at Indraprastha disappeared, and Hastināpura remained the outpost of the Hindu kingdoms of North India.[2]

So affairs remained for a time, but Janamejaya's fourth successor abandoned Hastināpura and made Kauśāmbī his capital, because (it is said) Hastināpura was carried away by the Ganges. The explanation is inadequate, because, if that were the whole truth, he could have chosen some other town near by as a new capital, and there was no necessity to move more than 300 miles south across South Pañcāla to Kauśāmbī. Manifestly he was obliged to abandon all the northern part of the Ganges-Jumna doab, and there can be no doubt that he was driven south by pressure from the Panjab. This retreat mixed up the Kurus of Hastināpura with the South Pañcālas, and led to the combination of the Kurus and Pañcālas (including the Sṛñjayas), that is, the blended Kuru-Pañcālas,[3] a fusion which may be reckoned, according to the dates estimated in p. 182 (for this king was Adhisīmakṛṣṇa's son), at about 820 B.C. The Kaurava-Pauravas thus reigned at Kauśāmbī which was in the Vatsa country, and one of the latest kings was Udayana, who was a king of note.[4]

No further changes are alluded to for a long time. A list is given of the noteworthy kingdoms that continued to exist (p. 180), viz. states in the eastern part of North India, Ayodhyā, Kāśi, the

[1] So the Brāhmaṇas, which began soon after this time (chap. XXVII), have very little to say about them. This explains *Vedic Index* ii, 430, s. v. Sindhu, which notices the change.

[2] MBh i, *43*, 1786 to *44*, 1807; *50*, 2007 to *58*, 2175: xviii, *5*, 178 f. See p. 114. A brahmanical account, Hv *191*, *192*, *195*, *196*.

[3] JRAS, 1920, p. 99. Weber, *Hist. of Ind. Lit.*, p. 135, note, and *Vedic Index* i, p. 165 differ as to whether they constituted one single kingdom.

[4] My *Dynasties of the Kali age*, pp. 7, 66.

Maithilas (of Videha), Bārhadrathas (of Magadha, which probably included Aṅga), and Kaliṅga; the middle states of the Vītihotras, Haihayas and Aśmakas; and those that bounded these along their west side, North Pañcāla, the Kurus (the combined Kuru-Pañcālas), Śūrasena and Avanti. The omission from the list of all the countries further west and north-west is significant, and suggests that great changes had occurred there. This is corroborated by allusions to the Panjab nations in the Mahābhārata, which show a steady deterioration in brahmanic estimation from the time of the battle when their princes ranked equally with those of Madhyadeśa, until at length those nations are pronounced to be wicked and mlecchas [1] and are unsparingly reprobated.[2]

The first change recorded occurred in Magadha, where the Bārhadrathas were supplanted by the Pradyotas, and these afterwards by the Śiśunāgas. Next, it is said, Mahāpadma Nanda destroyed all those kingdoms and brought all their territories under his sole sway.[3]

Here this attempted outline may close, for the Śiśunāgas and the subsequent history are dealt with in V. A. Smith's *Early History of India*, but something may be added with regard to the chronology down to Candragupta.

The calculations made in pages 179–82 yielded these approximate dates as regards Magadha—Senājit began to reign about 850 B.C.; he and his 15 successors, and the 5 Pradyotas and the 10 Śiśunāgas reigned altogether 448 years (the average reign being thus about 14½ years); Mahāpadma then began in 402; he and his eight sons reigned 80 years; and Candragupta ascended the throne in 322 B.C. According to that average the 5 Pradyotas with 72 years would have begun in 619 B.C., and the 10 Śiśunāgas with 145 years in 547 B.C.; but the synchronisms of Buddha, Bimbisāra and Ajātaśatru (the fifth and sixth Śiśunāgas)[4] show that Ajātaśatru had come to the throne before Buddha's death about 487 B.C., and that the beginning of the Śiśunāgas should be placed earlier than 547 though not necessarily as early as 602 B.C. The above average makes the combined duration of the Pradyotas and Siśunāgas (72 + 145) 217 years; and it is noteworthy that the

[1] MBh vii, *93*, 3379–80: xii, *207*, 7560–1.
[2] MBh viii, *40*, 1836–58; *44*, 2028 to *45*, 2110. JRAS, 1919, p. 360.
[3] My *Dynasties af the Kali age*, pp. 18–25, 68–9.
[4] Discussed, Smith's *Early Hist. of India*, pp. 31–3, 44–8.

Matsya gives the Pradyotas 52 years and can be read as assigning the Śiśunāgas 163 years, that is, 215 years altogether. This remarkable agreement suggests that the only modification needed in the above calculations is to transfer 20 years from the Pradyotas to the Śiśunāgas, whereby the chronology may be arranged thus :—

Accession of Senājit Bārhadratha	B.C. 850.
He and 15 Bārhadratha kings (average, 14½ years)	231 years.
Beginning of the Pradyotas	B.C. 619.
5 Pradyotas (average, 10½ years)	52 years.
Beginning of the Śiśunāgas	B.C. 567.
10 Śiśunāgas (average, 16½ years)	165 years.
Accession of Mahāpadma Nanda	B.C. 402.
He and his eight sons	80 years.
Accession of Candragupta	B.C. 322

These figures will I think be found to fit in with all the chronological particulars[1]; yet, if any further adjustment is needed, we might quite fairly shorten the Bārhadratha period by a few years (½ year per reign), and date the beginning of the Pradyotas about 627 B.C. and that of the Śiśunāgas about 575 B.C., or both even 5 years earlier.

CHAPTER XXV

INFERENCES SUGGESTED BY TRADITIONAL HISTORY

WHAT the foregoing account based on tradition suggests may now be considered as regards the origins of the dynasties, Aryan and non-Aryan peoples and tribes, the Aryan occupation of India and how the Aryans entered India. Here also one must put away all preconceived ideas and see what tradition indicates.

The whole of the myth regarding origins has been set out (pp. 253 f). In it there is no connexion between Manu's nine sons and Purūravas Aila and Sudyumna except through Ilā with

[1] We are not bound to fix Bimbisāra's reign at 28 years precisely, nor Ajātaśatru's at 27, as tradition alleges.

her fabulous changes of form. It seems probable that three different myths have been blended together in an attempt to unify the origins of three different dominant races, said to have been derived from Manu, Purūravas and Sudyumna, and apparently constituting three separate stocks.

Tradition thus alleged that at the earliest time all the kings and chiefs throughout India, with two exceptions, belonged to one common stock descended from Manu; and it says so doubly, because it declares, first, with regard to his sons that he divided the earth (that is, India) among them, and secondly, with regard to the offspring of his son Ikṣvāku that they were kings throughout the whole of India [1] according to both the versions given (p. 257). It also says that of that common stock four kingdoms were pre-eminent, namely, the Aikṣvākus at Ayodhyā, the Janakas in Videha, another (afterwards called the Vaiśālakas) in the country immediately north of Patna, and the Śāryātas at Kuśasthalī in Ānarta; with apparently three less prominent, the Kārūṣas in the country around Rewa, a kingdom at Māhiṣmatī on the R. Narbada, and another on the R. Payoṣṇī (p. 257, note [6]); with perhaps an eighth, the Dhārṣṭakas in the Panjab (p. 256), and possibly a ninth, Nābhāga's line, on the Jumna (p. 256). Those two exceptions were first, Purūravas Aila at Pratiṣṭhāna, and secondly, the Saudyumnas, who occupied the town Gayā, the country eastward of a line drawn roughly from Gayā to Cuttack, and the region north of the Ganges eastward of Videha and the Vaiśālaka kingdom.

According to tradition then Purūravas Aila and his lineage at Pratiṣṭhāna formed one stock, the chieftains of Gayā and eastern India formed a second stock, and all the kings and chiefs of the rest of India belonged to a third stock with their principal dominion in Oudh and North Bihar. The first is the well-known *Aila* or *Aiḍa* [2] race, often called the 'Lunar race' because myth derived it from Soma, 'the moon'. The second may be distinguished as the *Saudyumna* race,[3] as already mentioned (p. 255), but it never played any noteworthy part. The third has no definite common name in tradition, yet being derived from the sons of Manu, son of

[1] Rām iv, *18*, 6 has probably a reminiscence of this, where Rāma says to Bālin at Kiṣkindhā, 'This earth belongs to the Ikṣvākus'.

[2] Aiḍa Purūravas, Vā *2*, 20; *56*, 1, 5, 8; Bḍ i, *2*, 20; ii, *28*, 1, 9.

[3] Saudyumnas distinct from Ailas and Aikṣvākus, Vā *99*, 266.

Vivasvant, 'the sun,' it might be designated the *Mānava* and 'Solar' race. The term Mānava is used sometimes to denote particularly Manu's immediate descendants,[1] and so is applied in the myth to Sudyumna.[2] It is also extended to distant descendants more as a racial term than as a patronymic,[3] and is used as a definite racial term in distinction from Aila.[4] But Mānava commonly meant simply 'man', and became hardly characteristic. The title 'Solar' is generally restricted to the Aikṣvāku[5] dynasty of Ayodhyā, and so cannot well be applied to the whole stock. A general term is however needed, and this stock may be described and distinguished by the name *Mānva*,[6] which is equivalent to *Mānava*, but not being found in Sanskrit is a neutral term.

According to these traditions royal power first developed mainly in the Gangetic plain, in the towns Ayodhyā, Mithilā, Pratiṣṭhāna and Gayā, with an off-lying branch at Kuśasthalī on the western sea-coast, and apparently two others on the rivers Narbadā and Tapti. The Mānva city Ayodhyā is made the most ancient,[7] and these allegations imply that civilization was as far advanced (or perhaps more so) among the Mānvas as among the Ailas, when the latter entered India.

These traditions deal only with the ruling classes, the kings, chiefs and kṣatriyas, and not with brahmans nor the people generally. It is nowhere declared (as far as I am aware) that

[1] Applied to Karūṣa, Bhāg ix, *2*, 16. To Śaryāta, Aitareya Brāhm viii, 21. To Sukanyā, Pad iv, *15*, 1–2: v. *8*, 106. To Manu's sons, p. 84, note [2]; Mat *12*, 1, 8. Manu lord of the Mānavas, Rām i, *5*, 6; *6*, 20.

[2] Vā *85*, 16, 24. Bd iii, *60*, 15, 22.

[3] To Marutta of the Vaiśālī kingdom, MBh xiii, *137*, 6260. Also Pathyā Mānavī, in references, p. 218, note [1]. Cf. *vaṁśo Mānavānām*, MBh i, *75*, 3138–40; also ii, *20*, 803. Certain rishis are called *Mānava* rishis, MBh xiii, *150*, 7107–9.

[4] Vā *61*, 86 and Bd ii, *35*, 96, which say:—

Mānave caiva ye vaṁśe Aila-vaṁśe ca ye nṛpāḥ.

The Ikṣvāku race and Aila race are clearly distinguished as different, MBh ii, *13*, 568–9: Vā *32*, 47–8; *99*, 266, 431–2, 438–9, 450–1: Bd iii, *74*, 244–5, 263–4: Mat *50*, 74; *273*, 52–3, 57–8, 65, 68–9.

[5] Pad vi, *274*, 10–11 wrongly extends *Ikṣvāku* to Śaryāti's line.

[6] After the analogy of *Yādva* from *Yadu*, and *Mādhva* from *Madhu*.

[7] Founded by Manu, Rām i, *5*, 6: ii, *71*, 18. He reigned there, *id.* i, *6*, 20. So also Vikukṣi, Br *7*, 46: Hv *11*, 662.

brahmans, vaiśyas and śūdras generally were Manu's offspring.[1] The brahmans expressly claimed other origin (chap. XVI). Nothing is said about the real origin of the vaiśyas, śūdras and populace generally. The brahmanical figment that the four castes were produced from different parts of Brahmā's body in no wise asserts any common origin. There are, however, abundant indications that India contained many folk of rude culture or aboriginal stock, such as Niṣādas,[2] Dāsas and Pulindas. Powerful races of hostile character are often mentioned, such as Dānavas, Daityas, Rākṣasas, Nāgas and Dasyus. Some of these were partially civilized, while others were rude and savage and were sometimes cannibals. Those races were reduced to subjection and their barbarous practices were repressed; and, as they came under the influence of Aryan civilization, those names became opprobrious, until at length they ceased to possess any ethnological force and turned into purely evil appellations, just like the word *asura*, and all became synonymous with the meaning 'demon'.[3] This process has gone on continuously;[4] thus, Piśāca was originally the name of a tribe[5] and ultimately turned to mean an impish goblin. The following are instances.

These names, Dānava, Daitya, &c., denoted peoples originally.[6] Thus king Yayāti married Śarmiṣṭhā, daughter of Vṛṣaparvan (p. 87) who was king of the Dānavas and a Daitya.[7] The Śālvas were a people of note, who occupied the country around Mt. Ābu,[8] and they are called Dānavas and Daiteyas.[9] Bhīma killed the Rākṣasa chief Hiḍimba, and had by his sister Hiḍimbā a son

[1] Even MBh i, *75*, 3138–9 does not imply that, which says—From Manu was the race of the Mānavas; the Mānavas were brahmans, kṣatriyas and others; brahmans were then united with kṣatriyas.

[2] The Niṣādas were fabled to have sprung from Pṛthu, son of Vena. For references, see p. 16, note [6].

[3] e.g. Asuras (Mat *25*, 8, 39), Dānavas (*id.* 17, 30, 39), Daityas (*id.* *26*, 17) and Rākṣasas (*id.* *25*, 37). Vā *68*, 14. Bḍ iii, *6*, 14.

[4] At the present day the caṇḍālas in some parts of Bengal repudiate that appellation and call themselves *namaśūdra*.

[5] ZDMG, lxvi, 49. JRAS, 1912, 711. Pad v, *74*, 12.

[6] See MBh xii, *228*, 8359–413.

[7] MBh i, *80*, 3337–8; *82*, 3410; *83*, 3455. Mat *30*, 10; *31*, 14. Yet he is called an asura, MBh i, *81*, 3369; Mat *30*, 11: and his daughter also, Vā *93*, 16; Mat *27*, 8; *31*, 3: Hv *30*, 1603; &c.

[8] MBh iv, *1*, 12; *30*, 972: v, *174*, 5977–9.

[9] MBh iii, *14*, 633–4; *17*, 695, 710; *22*, 885–6. Ag *275*, 22.

Ghaṭotkaca,[1] who was king of the Rākṣasas[2] and took part and was killed in the Bhārata battle.[3] Bhagadatta, king of Prāgjyotiṣa (north-east Bengal),[4] took part in that battle with a contingent of Cīnas,[5] and his kingdom is called mleccha,[6] and it and his city belonged to Dānavas, Daityas and Dasyus.[7] In all these cases these names obviously refer to human beings. Similarly the Rākṣasas in the story of Rāma were the inhabitants of Ceylon and the Godāvarī valley (p. 277).[8]

As these peoples were generally enemies, these names turned to mean alien and hated, hostile or savage, men.[9] So Kṛṣṇa's son Aniruddha married the daughter of Bāṇa, who is called king of the Daityas.[10] These names next became terms of hatred, opprobrium and abuse. Thus the adherents of Kaṁsa, king of the Yādavas at Mathurā, are called Dānavas;[11] and Madhu, the great king of the Yādavas, Kṛṣṇa's ancestor, from whom he obtained the patronymic Mādhava, is styled a Daitya and king of the Dānavas, although his descent from Yayāti and Yadu is acknowledged (p. 66). This abusive use led to the attribution of evil characteristics to such people, who were then described as demonic beings, and so these terms approximated to *asura* in meaning.[12] Thus Madhu's descendant, Lavaṇa Mādhava, is called Dānava, Rākṣasa and asura (p. 170); Jarāsandha, the great king of Magadha, who was a Bhārata, is stigmatized as an asura;[13] and the Buddhists and Jains are treated as asuras and Daityas.[14]

[1] MBh i, *152* to *155*. [2] MBh vi, *82*, 3559; *84*, 3663.

[3] MBh v, *161*, 5591: vii, *180*, 8171–2.

[4] JASB, lxvi, Part I, p. 104.

[5] MBh v, *18*, 584: cf. ii, *25*, 1002.

[6] With Yavanas, MBh ii, *50*, 1834.

[7] MBh v, *47*, 1889: xii, *341*, 12956–7. Hv *121*, 6791–6; *122*, 6885–8. Yet he is called an asura, MBh vii, *29*, 1290; and his kingdom, v, *47*, 1887.

[8] Rāvaṇa called an asura, Pad vi, *143*, 3.

[9] The passages cited in the preceding notes will illustrate this. Various classes of Rākṣasas are named, Vā *69*, 164 f.: Bd iii, *7*, 132 f.

[10] Hv *175* to *177*; *190*. Pad vi, *277*, 3–4, 17; and even 'lord of the *bhūtas*', *ibid.* 25/11.

[11] MBh xii, *341*, 12954.

[12] So the Chinese called Europeans 'foreign devils', and Chinese Christians 'secondary foreign devils'.

[13] MBh xii, *341*, 12960–1.

[14] P. 68. Br *160* seems to give similar expression to the contest between brahmanism and Dravidian religion in the south.

Finally, in the latest stories and versions of stories all these names and *asura* became virtually synonymous and meant 'demons';[1] and are so used, as in the story of Kuvalayāśva,[2] and in the fables of devâsura wars.[3] These changes in the application of these terms give some help towards discriminating tales and allusions as old or as late, while we remember, however, that older stories underwent modifications later, as pointed out (p. 74).

By far the greater part of ancient historical tradition deals with the doings of the Aila stock, its growth and expansion. Quite different were the fortunes of the Mānva stock. It occupied the greatest part of India originally, but steadily lost ground before the Ailas. At two epochs it is said to have risen in the Ayodhyā realm to paramount dominion, first, in Māndhātṛ's conquests, and again when Sagara overthrew the Haihayas and foreign tribes, but the supremacy was short-lived, and the Ailas renewed their progress. After Sagara's time the three Mānva kingdoms of Ayodhyā, Videha and Vaiśālī played almost entirely a conservative part, influencing little the political development of India, which thenceforward was worked out by the two Aila branches, the Pauravas and Yādavas. The expansion of these two and the other branches has been explained in the last chapter. We may now take stock of the racial and political changes that had taken place, down to the time of the Bhārata battle.

Of the Mānva kingdoms, that existed originally, three remained, those of Ayodhyā, Videha and Vaiśālī; and all the Dekhan except the NW. part remained unchanged, though it is said that the ruling families in Pāṇḍya, Cola and Kerala were offshoots from the Turvasu branch of the Ailas (p. 108).

The Saudyumnas had been almost overwhelmed by the Ānavas and Pauravas, and were restricted to the Utkalas and other clans which occupied the hilly tracts from Gayā to Orissa. All North and East Bengal was held by the Prāgjyotiṣa kingdom, which is nowhere connected with any of these races and would seem to have been founded by an invasion of Mongolians from the north-east, though tradition is silent about this outlying development. The configuration of the five Ānava kingdoms in the east, the Aṅgas,

[1] See also Mat *245*, 1–34: Rām ii, *9*, 11–13; *44*, 11.
[2] Mārk *20*, 42 to *21*, 89.
[3] e.g. Mat *129* to *140*; *179*: Lg i, *71*; *94*: Pad v, *38* to *41*.

Vaṅgas, Puṇḍras, Suhmas and Kaliṅgas, which held all the sea-coast from Ganjam to the Ganges delta, and formed a long compact curved wedge with its base on the sea-coast and its point above Bhāgalpur, suggests that there had also been an invasion from the sea, that penetrated up the Ganges valley, leaving the hilly tracts on its west and east alone;[1] and this conjecture, if reasonable, would mean that the invaders had driven the Saudyumna stock into those hilly tracts, and that that had taken place before those five kingdoms were formed. But there is no trace in tradition of any such invasion of this distant region.

All the rest of North India and the north-west part of the Dekhan had been dominated by the Aila stock and was held thus:—

The Pauravas ruled the whole of the Ganges and Jumna plain from the Siwalik hills to Magadha, except Śūrasena (which was Yādava) and Kāśi, namely, the kingdoms of Hastināpura, Pañcāla, Cedi, Vatsa, Karūṣa and Magadha (in all of which the ruling families were Bhāratas), and possibly Matsya. Kāśi was an Aila kingdom of earlier foundation (p. 258).

The Yādavas held all the country between the Rajputana desert and a line drawn roughly from Bombay to SE. Berar and then north to the Jumna, excluding petty chieftainships in the hills and probably Matsya.

The Ānavas held (1) all the Panjab (except the NW. corner), comprising the kingdoms of Sindhu, Sauvīra, Kaikeya, Madra, Vāhlīka, Śivi and Ambaṣṭha; and (2) all East Bihar, Bengal proper (except the north and east) and Orissa, comprising the kingdoms of Aṅga, Vaṅga, Puṇḍra, Suhma and Kaliṅga.

The Druhyus held the Gāndhāra kingdom and the NW. frontier, and are said to have spread out beyond that and established kingdoms in the mleccha countries outside in early times.

The Turvasu line had disappeared, except that the Pāṇḍya, Cola and Kerala dynasties claimed descent from it.

These results are exhibited in the annexed table and map.[2] They do not mean that the Aila stock constituted the bulk of the population, but that it had conquered those lands and was the dominant body in them. It supplied the kṣatriya class, which would have influenced the bulk of the people profoundly, so that the higher

[1] JRAS, 1908, p. 851.

[2] Published in JRAS, 1914, p. 290: now revised.

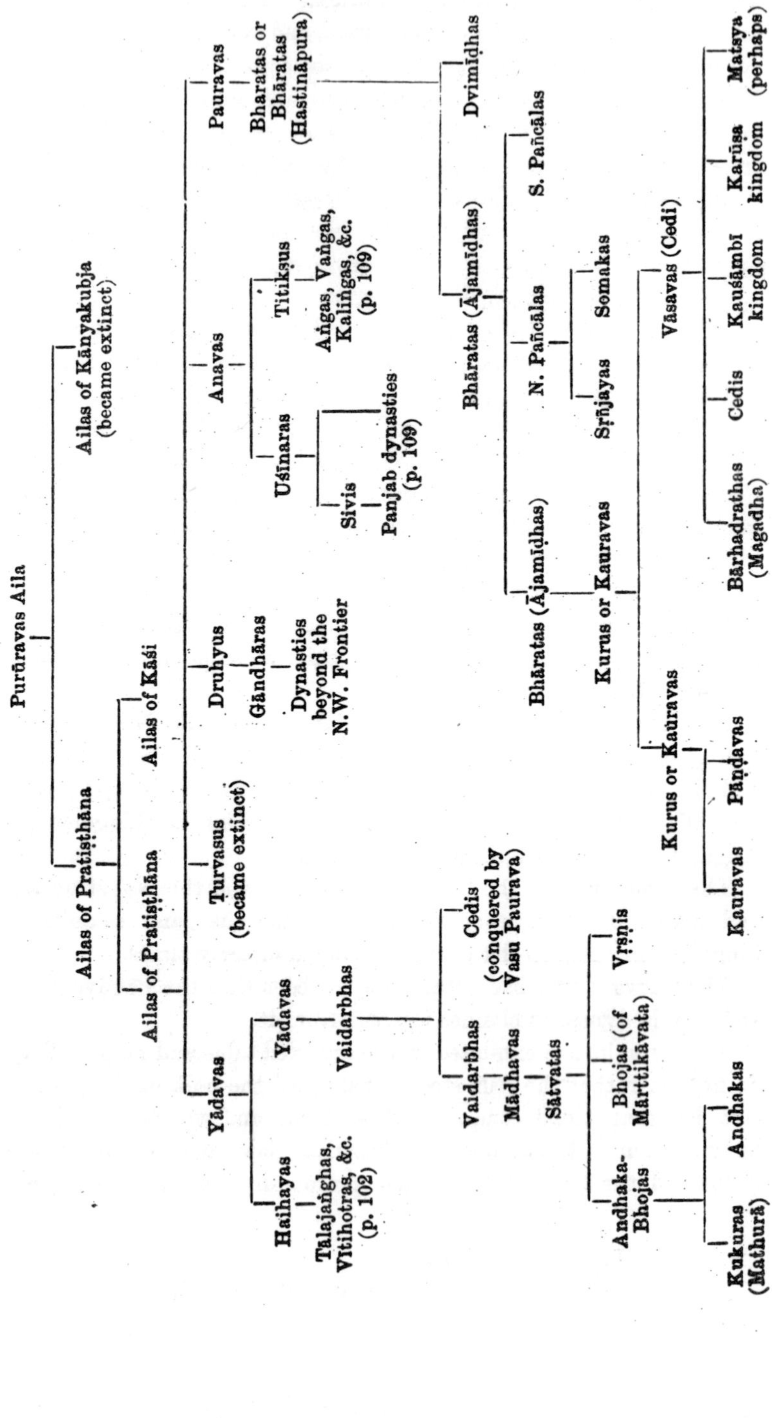
Purūravas Aila
Ailas of Pratiṣṭhāna
Ailas of Kānyakubja (became extinct)
Ailas of Pratiṣṭhāna
Ailas of Kāśi
Yādavas
Turvasus (became extinct)
Druhyus
Anavas
Pauravas
Haihayas
Yādavas
Gāndhāras
Uśīnaras
Titikṣus
Bharatas or Bhāratas (Hastināpura)
Tālajaṅghas, Vītihotras, &c. (p. 102)
Vaidarbhas
Dynasties beyond the N.W. Frontier
Sivis
Panjab dynasties (p. 109)
Aṅgas, Vaṅgas, Kaliṅgas, &c. (p. 109)
Vaidarbhas
Cedis (conquered by Vasu Paurava)
Bhāratas (Ājamīḍhas)
Bhāratas (Ājamīḍhas)
Dvimīḍhas
Mādhavas
N. Pañcālas
S. Pañcālas
Sātvatas
Kurus or Kauravas
Sṛñjayas
Somakas
Andhaka-Bhojas
Bhojas (of Mārttikāvata)
Vṛṣṇis
Kurus or Kauravas
Vāsavas (Cedi)
Kukuras (Mathurā)
Andhakas
Kauravas
Pāṇḍavas
Bārhadrathas (Magadha)
Cedis
Kauśāmbī kingdom
Karūṣa kingdom
Matsya (perhaps)

classes were no doubt largely leavened with Aila blood, though the lower grades would have remained racially the same, namely, the various groups of pre-existing folk.

The broad result stands out clear that the Aila stock, which began in a small principality at Allahabad, had dominated the whole of North India and down to Vidarbha, with the exception of the three Mānva kingdoms of Ayodhyā, Videha and Vaiśālī; and these had been influenced by the Ailas. So it is said, the earth was dominated by the five races (*vaṁśa*) descended from Yayāti.[1] This result agrees exactly with the Aryan occupation of India, so that what we call the Aryan race is what Indian tradition calls the Aila race, and so Aila = Aryan. The Saudyumna stock would no doubt be the Muṇḍā race and its branch the Mōn-Khmēr folk in the east;[2] and in the intervening region it would have been subjugated by the Ānava occupation, and also by a prior invasion of Bengal by new-comers from the sea if the above surmise of such an invasion be true. The Mānva stock, which held all the rest of India including the above three kingdoms, seems naturally to declare itself Dravidian.[3] These conclusions are not put forward anywhere in the genealogies or Puranas. True, it is said that the earth was dominated by the five races[4] descended from Yayāti, but the ethnical significance of this statement is nowhere noticed, and no precedence is accorded to those

[1] P. 124. Cf. Mat *24*, 20–1: Pad v, *12*, 72.

[2] Grierson, *Linguistic Survey of India*, iv, pp. 8, 21.

[3] The fact that many of the names of the early kings of the Mānva stock have a Sanskrit appearance does not necessarily militate against this, because they would have naturally been Sanskritized in the course of time. Daityas, Dānavas and Rākṣasas also have Sanskritic names. Later kings no doubt adopted Aryan names.

[4] The term 'the five peoples' often used in Rigv and other Vedic literature has received three explanations; (1) the five tribes descended from Yayāti; (2) the five families of the Pañcālas; and (3) all people: *Vedic Index* i, p. 466. This last is possible, for in the present day 'five' is used to convey general comprehensiveness, thus *pāñc jan* often means 'everybody'. It is hardly necessary that the term should have the same meaning everywhere, and it may be suggested that all three are possible. It may have the first meaning in Rigv i, *7*, 9; vi, *14*, 4; *46*, 7; ix, *65*, 23 and x, *45*, 6, for these hymns are attributed to rishis who lived before the Pañcālas existed. It may have the second meaning in iii, *53*, 16 and iv, *38*, 10; and possibly in viii, *9*, 2; *32*, 22 and x, *60*, 4; but not probably in i, *176*, 3 or ix, *92*, 3. As regards other passages in Rigv there appear to be no chronological indications.

Aila families, for in the genealogical accounts the post of honour in being described first is always given to the Solar or Mānva race. The unintentional way in which these conclusions present themselves from those accounts lends strong support to their truth, and those who maintain other views about the Aryan occupation of India must explain how such accounts arose, possessing no ethnical bias and yet enshrining real ethnical facts.

Moreover, these conclusions are entirely supported by the evidence of language, as set out by Sir G. Grierson.[1]

According to tradition in chapter XXIV the Ailas or Aryans began at Allahabad, conquered and spread out north-west, west and south, and had by Yayāti's time occupied precisely the region famed as Madhyadeśa. They possessed that Mid-land definitely and made it their own thoroughly, so that it was 'their true pure home', as Sir G. Grierson describes it linguistically.[2] They expanded afterwards into the Panjab and East Afghanistan, into West India and the north-west Dekhan, into East and South Bihar and into Bengal—precisely as he finds the Aryans did linguistically in those very regions, which he calls the 'Outer Band'.[3] Also it has been pointed out that the Ayodhyā realm was non-Aila, was not subdued by the Ailas and was only influenced by them. This agrees exactly with his linguistic inference, that in Oudh 'there is a mixture [of language] of the same nature, although here the Midland language has not established itself so firmly as it has in the west and south'.[4]

Thus the political account as tradition reveals it accords precisely with Sir G. Grierson's linguistic exposition, and explains the linguistic facts simply and fully. Current opinion, in order to explain those facts, postulates not only an invasion of Aryans from the north-west, but even a double invasion, and the theory is that 'the inhabitants of the Midland represent the latest stage of Indo-Aryan immigration', and that the latest invaders entered 'into the heart of the country already occupied by the first immigrants, forcing the latter outwards in three directions, to the east, to the south and to the west'.[5] This theory is improbable in itself, and certainly implies a severe and bitter struggle between the second and the first immigrants, of which one would expect to find some echo in tradition, for it concerned the very heart of India, yet

[1] *Imp. Gaz. of India* (1907), i, pp. 349 f. [2] *Id.* p. 357.
[3] *Id.* p. 358. [4] *Id.* p. 359. [5] *Id.* p. 358.

there is absolutely none. It is wholly unnecessary according to tradition.

Moreover, as will be shown in the next chapter, the bulk of the Rigveda was composed in the great development of brahmanism that arose under the successors of king Bharata who reigned in the upper Ganges-Jumna doab and plain. The language of the Rigveda, as Sir G. Grierson holds, represents the archaic dialect of the upper doab, and that was the region in which the Aryan speech was the purest and whence it spread outwards.[1] The two agree.

Lastly, there was some connexion between Sudyumna and the Uttara Kurus and Kimpuruṣas,[2] and that accords with the connexion which Sir G. Grierson notices between the Muṇḍā language and the 'Pronominalized Himalayan languages'.[3] In every respect therefore the evidence of language accords with the Puranic accounts, and is strong testimony to the value of tradition.

These conclusions raise the question, what does tradition say about the origin of the Ailas or Aryans? It makes the Aila power begin at Allahabad, and yet distinctly suggests that they came from outside India. The legends and fables about the progenitor Purūravas Aila all connect him with the middle Himalayan region.[4] He was closely associated with the Gandharvas. His wife Urvaśī was a Gandharvī, as well as called an apsaras.[5] The places he frequented were the river Mandākinī, Alakā, the Caitraratha and Nandana forests, the mountains Gandhamādana and Meru, and the land of the Uttara Kurus—regions to which the Gandharvas were assigned.[6] From the Gandharvas he obtained sacrificial fire; his sons were known in the Gandharva world;[7] and he ultimately became united with the Gandharvas.[8] Further, the fables about

[1] *Imp. Gaz. of India* (1907), p. 357.

[2] P. 255. Mat *12*, 16–19. Pad v, *8*, 121–4. Lg i, *65*, 22.

[3] *Imp. Gaz. of India*, i, pp. 386–7. JRAS, 1907, p. 188.

[4] Except one fable in Mat *115* to *120* about him as king of Madra in a former birth.

[5] Vā *91*, 9, 25. Bḍ iii, *66*, 9. Hv *26*, 1374.

[6] Mat *114*, 82. MBh v, 110, 3830–1 : vi, *6*, 212. Vā *39* to *41*. For the geography, see Mat *113*; *114*, 59 f; *121*; Vā *35*; *41*; *47*.

[7] They all married Gandharva maidens, Kūr i, *23*, 46 : but not Ayu.

[8] Vā *91*, 5–8, 40–8, 51. Bḍ iii, *66*, 5–8, 19, 22. Hv *26*, 1367–70, 1402–10. Br *10*, 5–8, 11. Ag *273*, 14. Lg i, *66*, 57. MBh i, *75*, 3148. Mat *24*, 19. Pad v, *12*, 70–1. Śatapatha Brāhm xi, 5, 1, 13–17. Viṣ iv, *6*, 38 f. Cf. Vā *1*, 189. Similarly Yayāti, MBh i, *75*, 3172; *85*, 3508; *119*, 4637 : v, *110*, 3831.

his birth (pp. 253–4) point to that region, and two accounts connect his alleged parent Ila with the northern country Ilāvṛta, which they say was named after him.[1]

Now these tales are mythical,[2] and tradition becomes mythical when it reaches back to origins, yet such mythical tales can hardly have sprung from pure imagination, and must have been developed from some germ of reality. They certainly suggest that Purūravas's origin was in that north region; and this agrees with and explains the fact that that region, the countries in and beyond the middle of the Himalayas, has always been the sacred land of the Indians. Indian tradition knows nothing of any Aila or Aryan invasion of India from Afghanistan, nor of any gradual advance from thence eastwards. On the other hand it distinctly asserts that there was an Aila outflow of the Druhyus through the north-west into the countries beyond, where they founded various kingdoms and so introduced their own Indian religion among those nations.[3]

The north-west frontier never had any ancient sacred memories, and was never regarded with reverence. All ancient Indian belief and veneration were directed to the mid-Himalayan region, the only original sacred outside land;[4] and it was thither that rishis and kings turned their steps in devotion, never to the north-west. The list of rivers in Rigveda x, *75* is in regular order from the east to the north-west[5]—not the order of entrance from the north-west, but the reverse. If the Aryans entered India from the north-west, and had advanced eastward through the Panjab only as far as the Sarasvatī or Jumna when the Rigvedic hymns were composed, it is very surprising that the hymn arranges the rivers, not according to their progress, but reversely from the Ganges which they had hardly reached.[6] This agrees better with the course of the Aila expansion and its outflow beyond the north-west.[7] It was, however, a route for any one travelling from the Ganges to the north-west,

[1] Mat *12*, 14. Pad v, *8*, 119.
[2] Other mythical details; MBh i, *75*, 3144: Vā *2*, 15: Bḍ i, *2*, 15.
[3] P. 264. JRAS, 1919, pp. 358–61.
[4] See the eulogy of the Northern region, MBh v, *110*: vi, *12*.
[5] So Sir M. A. Stein, JRAS, 1917, p. 91.
[6] Macdonell, *Sansk. Lit.* pp. 143, 145.
[7] Perhaps the arguments used to prove the advance of the Aryans from Afghanistan into the Panjab might simply be reversed.

as the author of the hymn perhaps did.[1] Again, Sudās's battle with the ten kings had (as shown in the last chapter) nothing to do with the progress of the Aryans from the north-west into India, for he was an Aila king of North Pañcāla, and the Ailas (or Aryans) had entered and dominated North India long before his time. It was part of his conquests westward into the Panjab (p. 2). Further remarks that go to corroborate these conclusions will be found in the next chapter.

The notices of rivers in the Rigveda are no certain guide as to all that the Aryans knew of the geography of India then, for, while the Sindhu and Sarasvatī are mentioned often, no other rivers in N. India are alluded to more than once, twice or thrice.[2] The Sindhu no doubt attracted attention because of its immense size, and the Sarasvatī because of its sanctity,[3] which was largely due to its being in the territory of the Bhārata kings of Hastināpura, among whom (and not in the Panjab [4]) the development of Rigvedic brahmanism took place, as will be explained in the next chapter.[5] The Rigveda knows of the Sarayu, and there is no good reason for doubting that that is the river of Oudh. Its silence about the Vindhya Mts. and other geographical features proves no ignorance, when one considers its silence about the banyan (p. 125), about salt,[6] and about the Pāriyātra hills (the Aravalli range), which the Aryans had actually reached according to the current view.

Tradition or myth thus directly indicates that the Ailas (or Aryans) entered India from the mid-Himalayan region, and its attitude towards the NW. frontier lends no support to any invasion from that quarter.[7] These are very noteworthy facts. Myth suggests

[1] He, Sindhukṣit Praiyamedha, would have been a descendant of Ajamīḍha (p. 226), the Bhārata (p. 146), who reigned on the Ganges.

[2] See *Vedic Index*, names of rivers.

[3] See remarks about it in next chapter.

[4] *Vedic Index*, ii, p. 295, s.v. Vitastā, note [2].

[5] If the southern part of the Rajputana desert was a very shallow sea in early times (p. 260), the Sarasvatī flowed into it (*Vedic Index* ii, 436). A small rise in the level of that area would have turned the sea into desert and affected the river.

[6] Macdonell, *Sansk. Lit.* p. 150.

[7] The only passages which may lend support to the theory of a north-western invasion are the two in the Rām, which make Ila king of Bālhi or Bālhīka (p. 254, note [4]), if these words mean Balkh; but they might mean the Vāhlīka country in the Panjab (Mārk, my translation, p. 311), and the Rām is quite untrustworthy in its traditions when uncorroborated elsewhere (pp. 82, 93).

the country Ilāvṛta in the north as the region from which they came. Purūravas's name Aila occurs in the Rigveda and appears to be more ancient than the fable of Manu's daughter Ilā,[1] which seems to have been devised in order to explain that name, for such explanatory tales were common (p. 75). The suggested connexion between *Ila* and *Ilāvṛta* may be ancient and may merit credence.[2] In this regard it may be noted that Sudyumna, the male form of Ilā, is said to have been a Kimpuruṣa and ultimately departed to Ilāvṛta. The Kimpuruṣas were placed in that same north region;[3] so that myth connects the Saudyumna stock with that land, and in some Puranas with the Northern Kurus (p. 297). If then the Ailas did not enter India from the north-west, we must, in considering tradition and the conclusions it suggests, put away all ideas drawn from that hypothesis.

Further light is thrown on this matter by a treaty between a Hittite king and a king of Mitanni found at Boghazkeui. It mentions, as noticed by Professor Jacobi,[4] certain gods who can be none other than Mitra, Varuṇa, Indra and the Nāsatyas (Aśvins). These are Indian Aryan gods,[5] and he has shown that they could not belong to the period prior (according to the current theory) to the separation of the Indian and Iranian branches. The date of the treaty has been fixed reliably now about 1400 B.C., and therefore the folk of Mitanni who worshipped these gods had arrived there earlier, probably late in the sixteenth century. These facts prove (1) that there was an outflow of people from India before the fifteenth century B.C.; (2) that they brought Aryan gods from India; (3) that therefore Aryans and their gods existed in India before the sixteenth century; and (4) that the Aryans had entered India earlier still. These facts and conclusions are hardly reconcilable with the current theory about the entrance of the Aryans into NW. India and the composition of the hymns of the Rigveda.[6]

[1] See Professor Keith, JRAS, 1913, pp. 412 f.

[2] Cf. the formation of *Ilāvṛta* with *Brahmāvarta* and *Āryāvarta*.

[3] e.g. Vā *46*, 4–18; Lg i, *52*, 33–43: Mat *121*, 71.

[4] JRAS, 1909, p. 723. The published text is in *Keilschrifttexte aus Boghazköi*, vol. i, No. 1, Rev. 55–6. I have to thank Professor Langdon for information on this matter.

[5] The names of the gods and kings are discussed seriatim in *Amer. Journal of Sem. Lang.* vol. 33, p. 261. The names of the gods might not be significant singly, but the four combined give cumulative evidence of Indian origin that cannot be explained away.

[6] Professor Jacobi's remarks, *loc. cit.*; Professor Keith, JRAS, 1914, p. 737 f.

But these facts and conclusions are in full agreement with what tradition says about the outspread of the Druhyus beyond the north-west of India (p. 264), for that is assigned to about the time No. 40 in the genealogical table (p. 146), namely, some 55 steps earlier than the Bhārata battle of 950 B.C. (p. 182); and if we allow 12 years per step (p. 183), that outflow would have begun 950 + 660, that is, about 1600 B.C., and would have spread gradually to allow of the appearance of Indian gods in the treaty of 1400 B.C. Tradition shows that the Ailas or Aryans had entered North India earlier still, and had dominated the greater part of it by the time of that outflow. Their entry, calculated on the 92 steps from Purūravas to the Bhārata battle, according to the same scale, would be placed 950 + 1104, that is, about 2050 B.C. Indian tradition and the facts of that treaty are thus in complete harmony, and the former furnishes a simple and sufficient explanation of the latter. This is testimony to the value of Indian tradition, and goes to show that the genealogies are substantial and may supply a scale for approximate chronological computation. Those migrants kept the names of their gods correctly, but the kings naturally modified their own names as they and their language became more separated from India.

Further, if we accept the current theory, the above conclusions from the treaty would require that the assumed Indo-Iranian period should be placed much earlier than the sixteenth century B.C.—a result that would render the theory hardly tenable. The above tradition suggests that there may have been no such period, and that the Iranians may have been an offshoot from India, for the outspread from India can not only account for the existence of gods with Indian names and kings with Iranian-like names in the treaty, but may also have led to the genesis of the Iranians. The linguistic and religious differences of Iran may be explained quite as well in this way as by the current theory.[1]

Vedic literature says, I believe, nothing about the entrance of the Aryans from the north-west into India. If one starts with that view, arguments for it may no doubt be discovered in the Rigveda; but if one puts aside all preconceived ideas and examines the hymns in the light of historical tradition, nothing will, I think, be found in

[1] *Imp. Gaz. of India* (1907), i, pp. 352 f. It may be noticed that Druhyu's descendants are said to have been *Bhojas* (p. 260, note [1]), and sun-worshipping priests were called *Bhojakas* (Bhaviṣya i, *117*).

them really incompatible with traditional history, and a great deal is elucidated thereby. Moreover, tradition explains why the sacred land of the Aryans was the region north of the mid-Himalayas—a fact which the prevalent view does not account for; and the connexion of Persia with India does not prove that the Aryans entered India from that direction, for it may find a quite possible explanation reversely in the outflow of Druhyus as just shown.

The current theory, that the Aryans invaded India through the north-west after separating from the Iranians, and entered in two streams, must face and account for the following facts and considerations: (1) Indian tradition knows nothing whatever of that. (2) The north-west and the Panjab were not regarded as an ancient home, nor with veneration or special esteem. (3) Tradition has preserved copious and definite accounts giving an entirely different description of the earliest Ailas (Aryans) and their beginnings in India. (4) The mid-Himalayan region was the sacred land, and those accounts reveal why. (5) They elucidate the Aila domination of India so that it agrees with the Aryan occupation, geographically and linguistically, altogether accurately yet quite unostentatiously. (6) Tradition makes the brahmans originally a non-Aryan institution, ascribes the earliest of the Rigvedic hymns to non-Aryan kings and rishis, and makes the earliest connexion of the Vedas to be with the eastern region and not with the Panjab, as will appear in the next chapter. (7) All this copious tradition was falsely fabricated, and the truth has been absolutely lost, if the current theory is right; is this probable? (8) If all this tradition is false, why, how, and in whose interests was it all fabricated? (9) If it is false, how comes it that the fifth point above is right? (10) Indian tradition suggests a reverse origin for the Iranians, which is linguistically tenable, which harmonizes with the Boghaz-keui treaty, and which can account for their language and religion.

CHAPTER XXVI

THE ANCIENT BRAHMANS AND THE VEDAS

SOMETHING may be discovered from historical tradition about the condition of the earliest brahmans and about the composition of the Rigveda and the other Vedas. Here we must premise that it is futile to expect to learn the truth about these matters from the priestly literature, because that was composed after the brahmans had put forward their pretensions about themselves and the Veda. Naturally they would set out therein their own version of what they then held (and what they wished others to believe) about these matters, and would say nothing that would stultify the same, as they actually did with regard to Viśvāmitra (pp. 60, 244). Facts or traditions that proved awkward for their developed pretensions would not be admitted, as has been pointed out with regard to Vyāsa (p. 10) and the kṣatriyan brahmans (p. 124). There was nothing strange in such conduct. It was simply what priesthood has not seldom done,[1] and the brahmans formed a priestly caste supreme in position and education, pride and influence. The views here put forward were not reached through any preconceived speculation, but evolved themselves gradually out of all the preceding investigation, and are all based on definite statements which are cited. They are all drawn from traditions, which could not have been fabricated in late times, as will appear, but are ancient, and of which the brahmans have been the custodians for more than two thousand years. They are a signal illustration of the fact, that the Puranic and Epic brahmans preserved ancient traditions, quite unconscious that those traditions often belied the brahmanic pretensions which were developed later (p. 61).

The accounts given in chapters XVII to XXII show what tradition discloses about ancient rishis and brahmans, with an attempt to fix their chronological position, the results of which are exhibited in pages 191–2. Those accounts bring out the following particulars touching the earliest positions of the great brahman families,

[1] The present Bhaviṣya (p. 46) is a striking instance of what religious unscrupulousness is not ashamed to perpetrate.

and these particulars stand, even apart from that chronological scheme.

The Vasiṣṭhas were connected originally and for long with Ayodhyā, and slightly with the junior kingdom of Videha. The Bhārgavas consisted of two branches, one derived from Cyavana and the other from Uśanas-Śukra. Cyavana was connected with Śaryāti and the country of Ānarta, and his descendants afterwards with the Haihayas who occupied the neighbouring region of the Narbada, when apparently the Śāryāta kingdom had fallen. Uśanas was the priest of the Daityas and Dānavas (or asuras) in mid North India, and his descendants disappeared. The earliest Āṅgirasas alleged (unless we reckon Bṛhaspati, the priest of the devas against Uśanas) were connected with Māndhātṛ king of Ayodhyā; the earliest Āṅgirasa rishi named was connected with Hariścandra king of Ayodhyā; and the earliest definite Aṅgiras was priest to the Vaiśālī dynasty, and so also were his near descendants. The earliest Ātreya, Prabhākara, was not connected as priest with any dynasty, though he married the daughters of the Paurava king Raudrāśva; and the first well-known Ātreya, Datta, became attached to the Haihaya king, after the Haihayas had broken with Cyavana's descendants. The first mention of any Kāśyapa brahman occurs with Rāma Jāmadagnya the Bhārgava in Madhyadeśa. These were the five famous families that were brahmans from their beginning. The Agastyas arose later and their origin is uncertain, yet tradition connects them with the Dekhan. The other brahman families and gotras that sprang from kṣatriya stocks do not concern us here.

It thus appears that of the true brahman families the earliest began with the Mānvas, as the Vasiṣṭhas at Ayodhyā and Cyavana's branch of the Bhārgavas in Ānarta; or began with Daityas and Dānavas,[1] as Uśanas-Śukra's branch of the Bhārgavas. Those that arose later began either with the Mānvas, as the Āṅgirasas in the Ayodhyā and Vaiśālī kingdoms; or with the outermost Aila race in the west, as the Ātreyas with the Haihayas; or later in Madhyadeśa, as the Kāśyapas with the Bhārgava Rāma Jāmadagnya; or in the Dekhan, as the Agastyas probably. Not a single brahman was connected as priest with any of the early Aila kings; merely three intermarriages are alleged, namely, Apnavāna's with Nahuṣa's daughter Ruci (p. 197), Yayāti's with Uśanas's daughter

[1] Dānava rishis are mentioned, MBh iii, *169*, 12101.

Devayānī (p. 86) and Prabhākara's mentioned above. Thus the earliest brahmans were priests to the Mānvas or to the Daityas and Dānavas, but never to the early Ailas. Bṛhaspati, the so-called Āṅgirasa priest of the devas, makes no exception, for he is not connected as priest with any Aila. No brahman then was priest to an Aila, that is Aryan, king in the very earliest times (except in a few late brahmanical fables). 'Mānava brahmans'[1] and 'Mānava rishis'[2] are alluded to, but never I believe 'Aila brahmans or rishis'.

This conclusion is not likely to have been the result of fabrication, and the negative argument is corroborated by the direct fact that tradition speaks of the earliest Aila kings actually opposing brahmans, but never says that any of the earliest Mānvas did so. Two occasions are alleged when early Māṇva kings had disagreements with brahmans, namely, very early between Nimi and 'Vasiṣṭha' (p. 215), and much later between Marutta and Bṛhaspati (p. 157), and both arose, not through antagonism, but through injured friendship, because those brahmans failed to sacrifice as those kings desired. Quite different was the attitude of the earliest Aila kings. They are praised in general terms sometimes in fables; thus Purūravas is extolled,[3] Nahuṣa and Yayāti made large gifts of cattle,[4] and Yayāti helped the devas against the Daityas and Dānavas;[5] but when spoken of in connexion with brahmans they are severely censured. So it is said that Purūravas made war on vipras and robbed them of their jewels, he was deaf to advice, and intoxicated with power perished through the curse of the maharṣis.[6] Also he coveted the golden sacrificial floor of the rishis of Naimiṣa forest and was killed by them.[7] His son Āyu was chosen by the rishis and behaved righteously;[8] and it may be noted that he

[1] MBh i, *75*, 3140. [2] *Id.* xiii, *150*, 7107.

[3] Vā *91*, 1–4. Bd iii, *66*, 1–4. Mat *24*, 10–15, 20. Pad v, *12*, 62–6, 71. Br *10*, 1–4. Hv *26*, 1363–6.

[4] MBh xiii, *81*, 3806. Nahuṣa praised in a fable, *id. 51*.

[5] MBh vii, *63*, 2295: xii, *29*, 990: but it is not referred to in the account of the devâsura war that occurred early in his time before his marriage (Mat *25*, 6 f; *27*, 3 f: MBh i, *76*, 3185 f; *78*, 3281 f), and it is discredited in that he married the daughters of the Daitya priest Uśanas and the Dānava king Vṛṣaparvan (pp. 86–7).

[6] MBh i, *75*, 3145–7. Cf. Mat *24*, 18: Pad v, *12*, 70.

[7] Vā *2*, 14–23; confusedly *1*, 188–92. Bd i, *2*, 14–23; confusedly *1*, 162–7. Śiv v, *2*, 93–4.

[8] Vā *1*, 191–2; *2*, 23–4. Bd i, *1*, 166–7 corrupt; *2*, 23–4.

married the daughter of Svarbhānu, who was a Dānava and asura.[1] But his son Nahuṣa, who made no such alliance and married his own sister (p. 86), became intoxicated with pride,[2] made the rishis pay tribute and oppressed them grievously.[3] Nothing of the kind is said about Yayāti, and he married Uśanas-Śukra's daughter Devayānī and the Dānava king Vṛṣaparvan's daughter,[4] yet he was cursed by Uśanas on Devayānī's complaint.[5]

There can be no doubt that herein we have ancient tradition. The close connexion constantly asserted between Uśanas-Śukra and the Daityas and Dānavas[6] could not have been the product of later times, when the Bhārgavas were a renowned family and those people were regarded as demonic. So also as regards the early Ailas, because from them were descended the Yādavas and Pauravas, from the Yādavas sprang Kṛṣṇa, and from the Pauravas the famous Bhāratas. To praise Uśanas-Śukra[7] and these early Ailas[8] would be the natural inclination of after times; but to depict the latter as inimical to brahmans would be repugnant, hence the allusions that present them as such are specially noteworthy.

Brahmanism then originally was not an Aila or Aryan institution. The earliest brahmans were connected with the non-Aryan peoples, and were established among them when the Ailas entered. This is corroborated by the close connexion that existed between them and the Daityas, Dānavas and asuras. It has just been pointed out as regards Uśanas-Śukra. The Dānava Śambara is

[1] P. 85. Vā *1,* 188; *68,* 8, 22, 24. Bḍ iii, *6,* 23–4.

[2] MBh iii, *99.* Rebuked by rishis, xii, *263,* 9388–90.

[3] MBh i, *75,* 3153. Cf. Pad v, *17,* 179; *19,* 141. Developed into a long brahmanical fable, MBh v, *10* to *17,* which calls him *abrahmaṇya* (*14,* 469) and a hater of brahmans (*17,* 556), and glorifies Agastya (an anachronism) who turned him into a snake for his impiety. Told briefly, MBh xii, *344,* 13214–6: xiii, *99,* 4753 to *100,* 4806. Alluded to, MBh iii, *103,* 8777: Lg i, *29,* 28. Freed therefrom by Yudhiṣṭhira, MBh iii, *178,* 12386 to *181,* 12533: xiii, *100,* 4800–3—a necessary supplementary fable.

[4] Pp. 86–7. Also Vā *68,* 23–4: Bḍ iii, *6,* 23, 25.

[5] MBh i, *83,* 3446 f. Mat *32,* 23 f. Vā *93,* 29. Viṣ iv, *10,* 3–5.

[6] Pp. 194–5. Accounts are given of the Daityas, Vā *67,* 57 f; Bḍ iii, *5,* 3 f; Mat *6,* 7 f; Viṣ i, *21,* 1–3, 13, 14; Pad v, *6,* 40–8: and of the Dānavas, Vā *68,* 1 f; Bḍ iii, *6,* 1 f; Mat *6,* 16 f; Viṣ i, *21,* 4–13; Pad v, *6,* 49–61.

[7] e.g. MBh xii, *281,* 10025–9. Hv *20,* 1159–78.

[8] e.g. Purūravas, Mat *13,* 62: Br *101.* Yayāti, Pad ii, *74*; *75.*

represented as devoted to brahmans.[1] It is said that the Bhārgavas were purohitas to Hiraṇyakaśipu,[2] the original Daitya monarch,[3] and that 'Vasiṣṭha' was his hotṛ.[4] Further, it is often declared that Indra incurred the sin of brahmanicide by killing Vṛtra[5] and Namuci,[6] so that those two famous Dānavas were brahmans.[7] The ideas, that brahmans were priests to demons, that demons themselves were brahmans, and that the chief of the gods incurred the most heinous sin by killing demons, were so grotesque, if not blasphemous, to orthodox brahmanism, that they could never have been imagined in later times, and are not, I believe, to be found in brahmanical literature. Indeed in the Rigveda Indra is often praised for slaying Vṛtra and other demons,[8] so that these ideas must be more ancient still. In the Rigveda Uśanas (who is a figure of the distant past) was rehabilitated,[9] and Indra's sin of killing brahmans had become his great glory of destroying demons;[10] so change had taken place before that, and tradition has preserved ideas more primitive than the hymns that speak of these matters.

There is nothing in the names of the great brahman families inconsistent with this conclusion. *Kaśyapa* may be non-Aryan, for it invites comparison with *kaśipu* in the name of the Daitya monarch *Hiraṇyakaśipu*. *Aṅgiras* and *Atri* might be non-Aryan quite as well as Aryan. The only names that ostensibly are Sanskrit are *Bhṛgu* and *Vasiṣṭha*, and yet strangely enough they are those that are most definitely connected with non-Aryans, for the Vasiṣṭhas were originally priests to the Mānvas of Ayodhyā, and the two earliest Bhṛgus were associated, Cyavana with the Mānvas of Ānarta, and Uśanas-Śukra with the Daityas and Dānavas. The Sanskritic look of their names then does not prove Aryan origin;

[1] MBh xiii, *36*. [2] Viṣ i, *17*, 48.

[3] MBh iii, *102*, 8758; *271*, 15834–5. Mat *161*, 2. Pad v, *42*, 2, 87. Hv *42*, 2238–9; *231*, 12610.

[4] MBh xii, *344*, 13209–10 impliedly.

[5] MBh v, *12*, 411–13: xii, *283*, 10153–200. Rām vii, *85*, 19; *86*, 2. Cf. Br *122*, 48–9. It is said, Vṛtra's offspring were Rākṣasas and yet were *brahmavid* and *dhārmika*, Vā *68*, 34–6: Bḍ iii, *6*, 35–7.

[6] MBh ix, *44*, 2430–44.

[7] Praised as righteous, Pad vi, *263*, 19–21.

[8] Macdonell, *Vedic Mythology*, pp. 58 f. [9] *Id.*, p. 147.

[10] So also in fables of Indra's killing Vṛtra, as Mat *172* to *178*; Pad v, *37* and *38*; Hv *43* to *49*.

and similarly many Daityas, Dānavas and Rākṣasas have names equally Sanskritic in appearance. Non-Aryan names appear to have been Sanskritized or translated into Sanskrit equivalents; indeed both processes prevailed.[1]

What the very early brahmans were is evidenced by what is said about their doings. They are sometimes connected with sacrifices, especially in late tales and late versions of older stories,[2] but what is constantly associated with them is *tapas*, 'austerities'.[3] That was their chief pursuit and main exercise, and its efficacy was in their belief to acquire superhuman powers which would enable them to dominate the natural and supernatural worlds: hence it is often alleged that by *tapas* they (and other men also[4]) gained from the gods the boons they wanted, or that the gods were terrified and endeavoured to break their *tapas*. It was in that age what sacrifice became afterwards.[5] Their reputation rested on their claim to possess 'occult' faculties and powers and the popular belief that they possessed them. Thus it appears that the original brahmans were not so much priests as 'adepts' in matters supernatural, 'masters' of magico-religious force, wizards, medicine-men.[6] Their reputation gave them very high rank, equal to that of their princes. They do not appear to have constituted a caste then. It is said brahmans were united (*saṅgata*) with kṣatriyas originally,[7] and as

[1] e.g. see JRAS, 1913, pp. 396 f.

[2] Cf., for instance, in p. 254 the accounts of Manu's sacrifice in Vā &c. (note [1]) with those in Viṣ &c. (note [3]) which introduce a priest.

[3] *Tapas* was first and *dharma* afterwards, MBh xiii, *98*, 4692. Brahmans became perfect by *tapas*, *id*. *36*, 2177: and so also kṣatriyas and others, Vā *91*, 115–18; Bḍ iii, *66*, 86–9. *Tapas* excelled sacrifice, Vā *57*, 121–5; *91*, 114: Bḍ ii, *30*, 39–43: Mat *143*, 37–41. *Tapas* modified through Buddhism (?), Vā *11*, 9.

[4] The Dānavas were noted for *tapas*; see their character in Vā *68*, 1–3 and Bḍ iii, *6*, 1–3, where the Vā text appears preferable. The Daityas were drinkers of soma, but not the Dānavas, so Bḍ iii, *6*, 14: differently in Vā *68*, 14; but from the context Bḍ reading seems preferable and Vā corrupt.

[5] Macdonell, *Sansk. Lit.*, pp. 182–3.

[6] J. Kennedy expressed a somewhat similar view (JRAS, 1920, p. 40), after I reached this conclusion. Pad vi, *230*, 20 says, 'Of yore in the Kṛta age brahmans were *tapasvins*, a non-brahman was never a *tapasvin*'. Magical powers were ascribed to the earliest rishis and magical wiles to the Daityas and Dānavas. Cf. Hastings' *Encyclopaedia of Religion and Ethics*, v, 1–2.

[7] MBh i, *75*, 3139.

shown (p. 244) there was no difficulty in early times in kṣatriyas' becoming brahmans. Thus it is intelligible that intermarriages took place between the brahmans and the early Aila royal family.[1]

While tradition thus clearly indicates that brahmanism was alien to the earliest Ailas, it yet offers very little suggestion as to what their religious practices were. It is said that Purūravas obtained sacrificial fire from the Gandharvas, learnt the way of making fire from aśvattha firesticks and sacrificed therewith, and that out of that fire he himself constituted three separate fires.[2] He and his successors therefore performed sacrifices of some kind, and appear to have sacrificed for themselves, for nothing is said of any priests in connexion with them, except that in a few late brahmanical tales or additions brahmans are made their priests. Thus, the Ṣoḍaśa-rājika says[3] that Yayāti offered multitudes of various sacrifices and lavished wealth on the brahmans, but its description shows by its sacrificial anachronisms that it has been elaborated by late brahmanic hands, and in fact it greatly overdoes its eulogy of the kings for brahmanism.

Marriage connexions tended to bring brahmans and the early Aila kings together and remove their antagonism, and Yayāti's eldest brother Yati became a muni (p. 86). Further, the victorious expansion of the Ailas over the non-Aryans seriously affected the position and prestige of the brahmans and discredited their magical pretensions, so that those who adhered to the non-Aryans shared in their downfall and disappeared, as happened with Uśanas-Śukra's descendants (p. 196). Hence regard for their own future would have inclined them towards the Ailas. That necessitated some assimilation of their religious beliefs and practices with those of the Ailas, and caused a gradual change from magic to religious worship, from medicine-man to priest proper.

Approximation first appeared among the outermost Yādavas in the west, for Cyavana's descendants (Bhārgavas) became priests to the Haihayas (pp. 197, 265), and, when they broke with the Haihayas, the Ātreyas succeeded to their position (pp. 198, 229).

[1] Bhāg ix, *18*, 5 with the ideas of a late age wonders at Yayāti's marriage with Śukra's daughter (p. 86) as *pratiloma*.

[2] Vā *91*, 40–8. Bḍ iii, *66*, 19 (incomplete). Hv *26*, 1402–10. A corresponding brahmanical fable, Hv *213*, 11859–63. The three fires are not specified.

[3] P. 39. MBh vii, *63* : xii, *29*, 987–9.

The Kāśyapas arose in Madhyadeśa after the Haihaya devastations (p. 232). During all that period the Paurava kingdom in Madhyadeśa was in abeyance, and there is no mention of any brahmans with the northern branch of the Yādavas (p. 261), or the Ānavas or the Druhyus. Later on, the Āṅgirasas, who appeared in the non-Aila kingdom of Vaiśālī, moved west to the Aila realm of Kāśi (p. 220) and then to the newly revived Paurava kingdom in the Ganges-Jumna doab in Bharata's time, where they flourished greatly and admitted into their ranks the kṣatriyan brahmans who developed soon afterwards among his descendants (pp. 247 f). Kaṇva Kāśyapa was there in Duṣyanta's time (p. 232). In fact, in the Ganges-Jumna doab, the region specially occupied by the Ailas, it was not until Duṣyanta's and Bharata's period that any brahman became connected with them as priest (p. 232).

Those brahmans who associated with the Ailas thus became established and multiplied into the great brahman families, and the others disappeared or took lower rank,[1] except the Vasiṣṭhas who maintained their high position in the powerful Mānva kingdom of Ayodhyā. The Aila kings appear to have been their own sacrificers, and the brahmans on becoming established among them assimilated Aila religious ideas and rites and became priests, and Aila princes also became brahman-priests. Brahmanism thus gradually changed its character and became the well-known system, priestly and not magical,[2] which took its great development among the Bhāratas as displayed especially in the Rigvedic hymns of the times of Vadhryaśva, Divodāsa and their successors.[3] It owed a great deal to Bharata and his descendants. He was a powerful and pious monarch, he adopted the brahman Bharadvāja as his son, and not only were his successors (p. 159) friendly to brahmans, but many of them also became brahmans (chapter XXIII). The infusion of royal scions into the ranks of the brahmans must have enhanced brahmanhood greatly and also no doubt modified it, and therefrom

[1] As happened afterwards apparently with Vaiśvāmitras, pp. 235, note [8]; 242, note [1]. There is some substance in MBh xiii, *152*, 7200–2. They no doubt degenerated into low-class priests, such as are found in S. India.

[2] The magical character however never wholly left it, and gradually turned its new rites into the elaborate and practically magical sacrifices of the Brāhmaṇas.

[3] Pp. 120, 251. Cf. Macdonell, *Sansk. Lit.*, p. 65.

arose a fresh, vigorous and illustrious development of it with apparently a strong stimulus to sacrificial worship, as the statements *infra* about the Veda, sacrifice and dharma also indicate. The Ailas Aryanized the brahmans[1] as they did the other peoples, and then the new brahmanism became the stronghold of Aryanism.

Another conclusion follows from this exposition. Bhārgavas and Ātreyas became priests first to Aila kings in W. India, but, broadly speaking, brahmans did not become priests to Aila kings elsewhere until about the time of Duṣyanta and Bharata; and the table on pp. 144–7 shows that by that time the Ailas (Aryans) had dominated the whole of N. India (excluding the three Mānva kingdoms) and the NW. Dekhan, that is, they had reached their full expansion except in distant outlying regions. The brahmans thus had little to do with the Aryan conquest, and in fact it proceeded in great measure against them while they were associated with non-Aryans. It was the Aila kṣatriyas who achieved the whole, and the brahmans joined them when that was practically effected. Hence one reason is clear why, as noticed above (pp. 8, 9), it is kṣatriya genealogies, and they alone, which give an account how the Aryan domination took place, and why the brahmanic literature has really nothing to say about that great transformation. Where the brahmans did claim some credit, as in the story of Māṭhava, king of Videgha (Videha), and his priest Gotama Rāhūgaṇa,[2] it does not refer to the Ailas, for Videha was a Mānva kingdom.

The foregoing sketch has explained the development of brahmanism in its general aspect, and we may now consider what an examination of the reputed authorship of the Rigvedic hymns discloses.[3] A

[1] This may explain the fact that these princes became brahmans and kṣatriyan brahmans without difficulty (p. 245).

[2] Śatapatha Brāhm i, 4, 10–19. See p. 224, note [13]. It is a fable, for it is discredited by tradition about Videha as narrated in chap. XXIV; and, if Agni Vaiśvānara went burning along the earth from the Sarasvatī to Videha, Agni burnt over the Paurava territory (including N. Pañcāla) and the Ayodhyā realm, two of the most famous and best cultivated regions even in early times—which is absurd. If it enshrines any historical truth, it might mean that the reformed brahmanism passed from the Bhārata kingdom to Ayodhyā and then to Videha.

[3] The making of hymns was not confined to brahmans, for it is said that among kṣatriyas Manu and Purūravas Aila were mantra-vādins, and among vaiśyas Bhalandana, Vatsa or Vāsāśva (read *Vatsaprī*?) and Saṅkīla were hymn-makers: Mat *145*, 115–17: Bd ii, *32*, 120–2. See p. 97.

small number are attributed (putting aside seemingly mythological beings such as Triśiras Tvāṣṭra [1] and Ariṣṭanemi Tārkṣya) to very early kings such as Manu Vaivasvata,[2] Nābhānediṣṭha Mānava,[3] Śāryāta Mānava,[4] Vatsaprī Bhālandana [5] and Mandhātṛ Yauvanāśva; [6] or to very ancient rishis who are not free from myth such as Cyavana Bhārgava,[7] Kavi Bhārgava [8] and Uśanas Kāvya; [9] but when hymns are ascribed to truly historical rishis, none are earlier than Viśvāmitra's time. The chronological list (p. 191) shows that the earliest really historical rishi-authors were Viśvāmitra, his sons Madhucchandas, Śunaḥśepa-Devarāta, &c., and Jamadagni. With his time then we enter definitely upon the true Vedic age, and all the other reputed authors who were historical were later, as has been shown with regard to the prominent rishis in that list and the kings in the earlier list (pp. 144 f).

Further, the most ancient kings and rishis above-mentioned, to whom hymns are attributed, were not Ailas. The kings were all Mānvas, and the rishis were connected with the Mānvas or with Daityas and Dānavas. Only one hymn is ascribed to an early Aila, viz. x, *95* to Purūravas, yet it was obviously not composed by him but by some later author, just as were x, *10* and *86*. Not a single other hymn is attributed to any early Aila king until Śivi Auśīnara (x, *179*) and Gāthi or Gādhi (iii, *19* to *22*). The hymns therefore that are said to be the most ancient are ascribed to Mānvas and their rishis, and not to Ailas. Those Mānva kings all reigned at Ayodhyā or in the Vaiśālī realm, that is, in the eastern region, except Śāryāta who was in the west. No hymns are assigned to any one who lived in the north-west until Śivi. These facts supply ground for the declaration that the Vedas were first chanted in the eastern region [10]—not in the north-west. They are significant facts which must be accounted for on the current view, that the Aryans entered India from the north-west and composed the Rigvedic hymns in the Panjab country. They rather suggest that the making of hymns passed with the above described approxima-

[1] Alleged son of Tvaṣṭṛ Bhārgava, p. 196 and MBh v, *8*, 222.
[2] viii, *27* to *31*. [3] x, *61*, *62*. [4] x, *92*.
[5] ix, *68*: x, *45*, *46*? P. 97. [6] x, *134*. [7] x, 19.
[8] ix, *47* to *49*; *75* to *79*? [9] viii, *84*; ix, *87* to *89*?
[10] MBh v, *107*, 3770. Professor Hopkins says no tradition associates the ancient literature with the Panjab (JAOS, xix, 20); and his disillusioned remarks there about the Panjab point towards a more easterly region—as tradition declares.

tion of the brahmans to the Ailas; and it is probable that the Aila Viśvāmitra on becoming a brahman modified the older and perhaps cruder brahmanic character and functions; and, if so, the difference would have accentuated the hostility that Vasiṣṭha (who was a Mānva brahman) showed to his brahmanhood (p. 244). The fact that those earliest Mānva hymns appear now in Sanskrit does not disprove their non-Aila origin, for they would naturally have been Sanskritized in the course of time, as has been noticed above with regard to non-Aryan names.

The next great stage in the composition of the hymns began with the above-mentioned development of brahmanism in connexion with sacrifice after Bharata's time, culminating with the rishis, Nos. 49 &c. in the chronological list (p. 191). The bulk of the Rigvedic hymns date from after that period. His territory included the tract between the rivers Dṛṣadvatī and Sarasvatī, and he sacrificed on the latter,[1] which was a large river then. That region probably had some sanctity before, for on the Sarasvatī was Uśanas-Śukra's tīrtha Kapālamocana,[2] and the river constituted the boundary between the Panjab and the Ganges-Jumna basin,[3] whether it flowed into the Rājputana desert, or especially if the sea extended northwards into that desert then (p. 299). That region was held by Bharata's successors till long afterwards, and the connexion with them and their development of brahmanism apparently made it become specially sacred.[4] This is supported by the general statement (ignoring special māhātmyas) that the most sacred region in the Kṛta age was Naimiṣa forest, in the Tretā Puṣkara, in the Dvāpara Kurukṣetra, and in the Kali age the Ganges.[5] Naimiṣa was on the R. Gomatī[6] in the Ayodhyā kingdom, thus the site of earliest sanctity in India is placed among the Mānvas in the eastern region. So the brahmans whom Purūravas came into special conflict with were the rishis of Naimiṣa as mentioned above. The Dvāpara age began between Divodāsa's and Sudās's times (p. 177), Kuru reigned early in it (p. 148), from him the region of the Sarasvatī obtained the name Kurukṣetra, and so both became

[1] MBh vii, *68*, 2384–5: xii, *29*, 939–40.
[2] P. 197 and MBh iii, *83*, 7005–7.
[3] See geographical remarks by J. Kennedy, JRAS, 1919, pp. 503–5.
[4] Macdonell, *Sansk. Lit.*, p. 174. *Vedic Index* i, 374.
[5] Mat *106*, 57. Kūr i, *37*, 37. &c.
[6] Vā *2*, 8–9. Bd i, *2*, 8–9. MBh iii, *87*, 8301–3: xii, *357*, 13801.

specially sacred in that age.[1] The region was called Brahmāvarta also,[2] though from what time is not clear.

Brahmanism thus appears to have developed in accordance with Aila ideas, and to have owed much of its advance to the influence of kṣatriyas,[3] first, of Viśvāmitra and his sons, and afterwards mainly of the Bhārata princes and kṣatriyan brahmans. It continued to flourish in harmony with later kings of that family, and consolidated its position as a caste, especially in connexion with sacrifice. That such Aila influences did produce modifications is suggested by the remarkable statements made in the Rāmāyaṇa (which can hardly have been the outcome of later brahmanical views); first, that, while eastern and southern kings and kings of the distant Panjab were invited to Daśaratha's sacrifice at Ayodhyā, none of the neighbouring Paurava (Bhārata) and Yādava kings, who flourished then in all the middle region of N. India (pp. 170–2, 276), were invited; and secondly, that Daśaratha called in the help, not of brahmans from Madhyadeśa, but of the rustic Ṛṣyaśṛṅga from Aṅga.[4] It was at that time that the great development of brahmanism had taken place among the Bhāratas. Ayodhyā and the Vasiṣṭhas had no association then with that brahmanically *élite* region. Brahmanism as it took shape under the Bhāratas apparently differed from that at Ayodhyā. Moreover all those brahmans had little in common with the non-Aryan tribes of the Dekhan (though Dekhan kings were invited to the sacrifice), as is suggested by the maltreatment of munis by Rākṣasas in the story of Rāma, for estrangement grew into hostility, which when developed was portrayed in the frequent stories how rishis were afflicted by such folk stigmatized and mythologized as demonic—a view which was carried back into earlier times in later brahmanic stories. Ultimately brahmanism as developed among the Bhāratas became the dominant form.

Tradition supplies some indications touching the compilation of the Veda. Although the later theory was that the Vedas issued

[1] Later brahmanic tales of course ignored this, and carried the river's special sanctity back to the earliest times, e.g. Br *101*.

[2] Manu ii, 17, 19. Other names, MBh iii, *83*, 5074, 7073–8.

[3] *Vedic Index* ii, 87. There is no good reason to doubt that brahmans learnt from princes; see *ante*, p. 96.

[4] For his alleged upbringing and qualifications, see MBh iii, *110*, 9990 f; Rām i, *9* and *10*. See p. 164.

from Brahmā's mouths at the beginning of creation (p. 30), yet other statements occur which betray some recollection of their real commencement. Thus it is said,[1] that the mantras were put together (*saṁhita*) in the Tretā age;[2] that the Vedas were put together at the beginning of the Tretā age and were arranged in the Dvāpara age;[3] and that sacrifice (*yajña*) was instituted at the same time,[4] and so dharma was constituted then.[5] This taken literally is erroneous, because tradition suggests that the Tretā age began about Sagara's time, and most of the rishis who composed the great bulk of the hymns were much later.[6] According to that reckoning Viśvāmitra and his sons (with whom began the real Vedic age, as mentioned above) lived towards the close of the Kṛta age, and so also Jamadagni; Ucathya, Bṛhaspati and Saṁvarta lived at its end; Dīrghatamas and the first Bharadvāja at the beginning of the Tretā, and the earliest Ātreya hymn-makers about the same time. The above statements however would be true to this extent, that the hymns composed by these rishis would have formed incipient collections (*saṁhitās*) among the Viśvāmitras, Bhārgavas, Āṅgirasas and Ātreyas about the commencement of the Tretā age. The alleged institution of sacrifice then agrees with the remarks above about its development soon after Bharata's time.

Those collections would have grown with the fresh hymns composed by later rishis[7] and especially during the great advance of brahmanism under the various branches of the Bhāratas, when and by whom sacrificial rites appear to have been largely

[1] These statements are noteworthy, though they occur in a fanciful description of the Tretā age, Vā *57*, 39 f; Bḍ ii, *29*, 43 f; Mat *142*, 40 f. It is relegated to the Svāyambhuva manvantara, but obviously belongs to historical time, as the introduction of king Vasu Caidya-uparicara shows, see eighth note *infra*.

[2] Vā *57*, 47, 60, 83. Mat *142*, 48, 55, 56, 75. Bḍ ii, *29*, 52, 65, 66, 90.

[3] Vā *57*, 47. Bḍ ii, *29*, 52. Mat *142*, 48. Similarly, Vā *58*, 10–11; Bḍ ii, *31*, 11; (Mat *144*, 10–11 varies). Cf. Lg i, *39*, 56–7: Kūr i, *29*, 43.

[4] Vā *57*, 61, 86, 89. Bḍ ii, *29*, 66; *30*, 1, 5. Mat *142*, 56; *143*, 1, 5. Cf. Lg i, *39*, 51: Gar i, *215*, 8.

[5] Vā *57*, 63, 81. Bḍ ii, *29*, 68, 88–9. Mat *142*, 58, 74. Cf. Vā *58*, 5; Mat *144*, 5: Bḍ ii, *31*, 5 different.

[6] P. 177; and chronological lists, pp. 144–9 and 191–2.

[7] Definitions of *ṛṣi*, *paramarṣi*, *maharṣi*, *ṛṣīka* or *ṛṣiputraka*, and *śrutarṣi*, Vā *59*, 79 f; Bḍ ii, *32*, 86 f; Mat *145*, 81 f.

developed[1] as the hymns show. Tradition does not indicate any marked stage for a long time afterwards, except that it suggests,[2] that in the time of Vasu Caidya-uparicara (pp. 118, 149) the question became acute, whether animals should be offered in sacrifices or only inanimate things. He was the foremost monarch of his day. He was appealed to as an authority on dharma, and declared that the practice of sacrificing animals was quite permissible, and so incurred the anger of brahmans who asserted the doctrine of *ahiṁsā*;[3] though it is said he made a great sacrifice in which nothing living was offered.[4]

The next stage to be noticed is that the division of *ṛc*, *yajus* and *sāman* had apparently come into existence before the time of Hiraṇyanābha, king of Kosala, because he and his disciple, king Kṛta, constructed saṁhitās of sāmans, which were called the 'eastern sāmans',[5] and the chanters of them were called Kārtas (p. 173). Here also appears the influence of kṣatriyas. This and the following compilation were in the Dvāpara age, and the statement above that the Vedas were arranged in that age is true.

By the time of king Brahmadatta of S. Pañcāla (pp. 148, 165) the collections of hymns appear to have been largely constituted, for they were definitely combined into a whole by his two ministers,[6] Kaṇḍarīka (or Puṇḍarīka) and Subālaka (or Gālava) Bābhravya Pāñcāla.[7] Kaṇḍarīka is described as *dvi-veda*, *chandoga* and *adhvaryu*,[8] and as the promulgator (*pravartaka*) of the Veda-śāstra.[9] Bābhravya Pāñcāla was *bahvṛca* and *ācārya*[10] and knew all the śāstras;[11] he

[1] Cf. Vā *57*, 125; Bḍ ii, *30*, 48; Mat *143*, 42; and fourth note above. Rigv iv, *43* and *44* are attributed to Purumīḷha and Ajamīḷha, Sauhotras, who were no doubt king Ajamīḍha and his brother Purumīḍha, p. 112.

[2] Vā *57*, 91–121. Bḍ ii, *30*, 9–48. Mat *143*, 5–37. MBh xiv, *91*, 2828–35. All in fabulous form.

[3] Kūr i, *29*, 41 makes the doctrine begin in the Tretā age.

[4] MBh xii, *338*, 12754–63, in a fable, *337*, 12712 to *339*, 12859.

[5] Here would apply the statement that the Vedas were first chanted in the eastern region (p. 312), if the word 'chanted' be emphatic.

[6] Hv *20*, 1049–50; *23*, 1256–7; *24*, 1303–4. Mat *20*, 24; *21*, 30–1. Pad v, *10*, 69, 116–17. MBh xii, *344*, 13262–4. He, his mother, queen and ministers were all devotees of yoga. The folk-tale (p. 250, note [4]) is told of him and the two ministers.

[7] Called *Pāñcika*, Hv *23*, 1256.

[8] Hv *23*, 1257. Śiv vii, *64*, 10.

[9] Mat *21*, 31. Pad v, *10*, 117 misreading *Vaidya*°.

[10] Hv *23*, 1257. Śiv vii, *64*, 9.

[11] Mat *21*, 30. Pad v, *10*, 116.

composed the Śikṣā[1] and instituted it;[2] he also devised the Krama, mastered it thoroughly and instituted it.[3] This tradition is corroborated by the statement in Vedic literature that Bābhravya Pāñcāla was the author of the Kramapāṭha of the Ṛk-saṁhitā,[4] though it gives no clue to his position or time.

These statements say Rigvedic hymns had been made into a collection by Kaṇḍarīka. His epithets *dvi-veda, chandoga* and *adhvaryu* mean (I take it) that he was specially proficient in the *sāman* and *yajus* departments. Bābhravya, working apparently on that collection, applied himself specially to the Rigveda as his epithet *bahvṛca* suggests, and composed the Śikṣā and devised the Kramapāṭha. Tradition thus declares that the first substantial compilation and study of the hymns of the Veda in its triple departments of *ṛc*, *yajus* and *sāman* were made in S. Pañcāla by these two brahman ministers of Brahmadatta,[5] whose position may be estimated as about a century and a half before the Bhārata battle (pp. 148, 164–5). But Kaṇḍarīka's compilation was not the Veda as we have it now, first, because certain hymns, such as

[1] Hv *20*, 1049; *24*, 1304. [2] *Praṇī*, MBh xii, *344*, 13263.

[3] *Praṇī*, *ibid.* 13262–3: Hv *20*, 1049; *24*, 1304: Mat *21*, 30 and Pad v, *10*, 116 (both which misread *Kāmaśāstra* for *Kramapāṭha*). The *Padapāṭha* would have been older, Macdonell, *Sansk. Lit.*, pp. 50–1.

[4] Weber, *Hist. of Ind. Lit.*, p. 34, showing the error of the above reading *Kāmaśāstra*, it being also inconsistent with the character of these persons as devotees of yoga (ninth note above). The error is explained by Vātsyāyana's statement in his *kāmasūtra* i, that Śvetaketu composed a work on *kāma*, it was abridged by Bābhravya Pāñcāla, and he studied Bābhravya's work. It is shown from many passages (pp. 164–6, and next chap.) that Brahmadatta (and therefore his minister Bābhravya) was long prior to Śvetaketu, and Vātsyāyana's single statement making his Bābhravya posterior to Śvetaketu cannot, by identifying the two Bābhravyas, override that finding; for he wrote eight or nine centuries later than Śvetaketu (*Vātsyāyana—the Author of the Kāmasūtra*; by Haranchandra Chakladar: Journ. of Depart. of Letters, Calc. Univ., vol. IV). His Bābhravya was clearly another, later than Śvetaketu. There is nothing improbable in this, because Babhru was a very common name (see the Index, and also *Vedic Index*), and therefore Bābhravya also; and two Bābhravyas of Pañcāla some four or five centuries apart are nothing surprising after what has been pointed out in chap. XI. The Mat and Pad have confused the two, and altered the earlier Bābhravya's work, the *Kramapāṭha*, to the latter's, a *Kāmaśāstra*. This is only another instance of the confusion of persons of the same name, so often pointed out (pp. 130–4, 203–4, 213, 234, &c.).

[5] He and they are in the transmigrations, p. 250, note [4].

Devāpi's for instance (x, *98*: p. 165), could not have been included since they were later; and secondly, because tradition is unanimous that Vyāsa 'arranged' the Veda, which means a real arrangement of the Veda as it was finally settled.

The final compilation was made after Devāpi's time and not until that of Vyāsa, who followed him by about half a century, because hymns are attributed to Asita or Devala, and Devala was a contemporary of the Pāṇḍavas (p. 233) and so of Vyāsa. Vyāsa[1] must have added all the hymns that were incorporated latest, and completed the canon. Tradition entirely supports this. It says generally that he arranged the Veda,[2] he divided the Veda into four,[3] he divided the four-pāda Veda into four;[4] and there are explicit statements that he compiled the Rigveda.[5] Both tradition and the latest hymns in the Rigveda therefore show the time when the canon was established, and tradition proclaims the man by whom that was done. Only a rishi of commanding ability, knowledge and eminence could have made it a canon accepted unquestioningly thereafter, and that is exactly the character and position which tradition unanimously attributes to Vyāsa, a rishi pre-eminent above all others.[6] He would probably have completed that work about a quarter of a century before the Bhārata battle, that is, about 980 B.C. (p. 182). The priestly literature has suppressed all these facts (p. 10).

There is no definite tradition about the Atharvaveda, but some statements throw light on it.

First, as regards its names. The early mention of its songs occurs under the names *Atharvāṇas* and *Aṅgirasas*, and the oldest

[1] Learning from Jātūkarṇya, p. 217.

[2] Vā *60*, 12; *61*, 77. Bḍ ii, *34*, 12; *35*, 86. Kūr i, *52*, 9–10. Śiv v, *1*, 33. Cf. Bhāg xii, *6*, 49–50: Br *158*, 33–5.

[3] Vā *58*, 11; *73*, 17. Bḍ iii, *10*, 69. Mat *144*, 11. Ag *150*, 23–4.

[4] Vā *1*, 179; *77*, 75. Bḍ iii, *13*, 77. Hv *42*, 2365. Kūr i, *29*, 43. Lg i, *39*, 56–7. Gar i, *215*, 11. Viṣ iii, *4*, 2, 6, 7, 14, 15.

[5] Vā *60*, 19 and Bḍ ii, *34*, 19 say:—

tataḥ sa ṛca uddhṛtya Ṛgvedaṁ samakalpayat.

So also Viṣ iii, *4*, 13, substituting *kṛtavān muniḥ* for *samakalpayat*. Similarly Kūr i, *52*, 16, but corruptly.

[6] He was venerated as an incarnation of Viṣṇu, Vā *1*, 42–3; Kūr i, *30*, 66; Gar i, *87*, 59; &c.: also of Śiva, Kūr ii, *11*, 136: and of Brahmā, Vā *77*, 74–5; Bḍ iii, *13*, 76: and as Brahmā's son, Lg ii, *49*, 17.

name is *Atharvāṅgirasas.*[1] Now tradition calls the earliest certain Aṅgiras *Atharvan Aṅgiras* (p. 218), and these two names and the compound of both are virtually the same appellation. The Atharvāṅgirasa rishis began in the kingdom of Vaiśālī (p. 219), that is, among the Mānvas and not the Ailas. The hymns are also specially connected with the Bhṛgus,[2] who were originally associated with the Mānvas, and so the ancient Bhārgava Uśanas, the teacher of the Daityas (that is, non-Ailas) is called *Atharvaṇāṁ nidhis.*[3] It is said there was a Vasiṣṭha named Atharvan, and the appellation Atharvanidhi is given to two Vasiṣṭhas (p. 207); and the Vasiṣṭhas belonged to the Mānvas of Ayodhyā. All these names therefore connect these songs with the Mānvas and not the Ailas, and mainly with the eastern region (p. 312).

Next, as regards this Veda's character. It is a heterogeneous collection of the most popular spells current among the masses, and its most salient teaching is sorcery.[4] Now the populace was non-Aila (p. 290), and magical power was the particular pursuit of the earliest brahmans, who belonged to the non-Ailas, as shown above. These features indicate that these songs began with and embody the ancient beliefs and practices of the peoples whom the Ailas subjugated, so that naturally the spirit which breathes therein is that of a prehistoric age,[5] of the times prior to the higher development of brahmanism among the Ailas.

Thirdly, may be noticed the word *brahma*. The original thing denoted by it was, as I understand, the magical power, whether incantation, charm or what not,[6] by which a man could exert influence over all natural and supernatural beings—what anthropologists now call *mana.*[7] The Atharvan songs were *brahma*, and the man who employed that was *brahman*, the wizard or medicine-man.[8]

[1] Weber, *Hist. of Ind. Lit.*, pp. 148–9. Macdonell, *Sansk. Lit.*, p. 189. *Vedic Index* i, *18*. Vā *90*, 12. Bd iii, *65*, 12. Hv *25*, 1323.

[2] Weber, p. 148. Macdonell, p. 189. Cf. Vā *29*, 9; Bd ii, *12*, 10; Mat *51*, 10, for a fancied connexion.

[3] Bd iii, *30*, 51–4 with MBh i, *76*, 3188–90 and Mat *25*, 9–11.

[4] Macdonell, p. 185.

[5] *Id.*, p. 185.

[6] MBh xiii, *4*, 260. Weber, p. 149, note. Macdonell, pp. 189–90, 195. Deification of the Pitṛs was *Ātharvaṇa vidhi*, Vā *76*, 1–2; Bd iii, *12*, 1–2.

[7] Even Rākṣasas knew *brahma*, Vā *68*, 36; Bd iii, *6*, 37.

[8] *Brahma-dhānas* are classed with *yātu-dhānas* and *brahma-rākṣasas*, Vā *69*, 130–5; Bd iii, *7*, 95–100.

So the Atharvan books called this Veda the *Brahmaveda*,[1] and claimed that it was the Veda for the *brahman*.[2] They used the words in the earlier sense, and the other Vedic books regarding (I suggest) the words from the later point of view of reformed brahmanism disputed that claim. It is said that in former times only a Vasiṣṭha could act as *brahman*[3]—quite appropriately, since the songs were then Mānva.

Speaking generally therefore, the Atharvaveda was the accumulation of magical beliefs, observances and practices, starting from the non-Aila races and gaining accretions from the Ailas and the people at large; while the Rigveda with its ancillary Yajus and Sāman was the religious expression of mainly the Ailas or Aryans as developed through reformed brahmanism and exhibited in sacrifice.

What Vyāsa did seems to have been this. The statement that he arranged and divided the four-pāda Veda into four suggests (1) that, though ṛc, sāman, and probably yajus and Atharvan[4] were distinguished before, as shown above, yet they had not been treated distinctly, all co-existed as four pādas in one general Veda, and he definitely separated them and constituted them respectively as four distinct Vedas: or (2) that, at any rate, he expressly and formally fixed the fourfold division and completed the canon of each Veda in definite shape, which became final subject to small modifications afterwards.[5] He had four disciples and entrusted to each of them one Veda, viz. the Rigveda to Paila, the Yajurveda to Vaiśampāyana, the Sāmaveda to Jaimini and the Atharvaveda to Sumantu.[6] The priestly literature has suppressed all this just as it has ignored Vyāsa (p. 9), for something of this sort must have taken place on any theory of the compilation of the four Vedas.

[1] Also Vā *65*, 27; Bḍ iii, *1*, 26.

[2] Weber, pp. 123, 149–50. Macdonell, pp. 189, 194–5. So Vyāsa by this Veda constituted the status of the *brahman*, Vā *60*, 18; Bḍ ii, *34*, 18; Ag *150*, 25.

[3] Weber, p. 123.

[4] General remarks about these and mantras and their kinds, Bḍ ii, *33*, 36–46; *35*, 71–3: Vā *61*, 63–4.

[5] Macdonell, *Sansk. Lit.*, pp. 47–50.

[6] Vā *60*, 12–15. Bḍ ii, *34*, 12–15. Viṣ iii, *4*, 7–9. Lg i, *39*, 55–60. Kūr i, *52*, 11–13. Gar i, *215*, 12–13. MBh xii, *329*, 12337–8; *342*, 13025–7 (which substitutes Śuka for the sūta, see p. 21); *351*, 13647–9 (similarly). Bhāg xii, *6*, 51–3.

The Vedic age thus closed roundly at about 1000 B.C.[1] Anteriorly it stretched back for centuries, as the chronological list on pages 191–2 read with pages 144–9 shows. There was a vast difference in time between the earliest hymns and the latest in the Rigveda. Hymns handed down orally during those centuries could hardly have escaped being gradually modified in their diction as the language gradually changed, and when they were at last collected into the canon, their diction would be rather that of the age when the collection was formed than that of the times when they were composed.[2] Hence it is not surprising, if the hymns betray no marked differences of language commensurate with the long Vedic period. They were sacred, but their text would not have attained to fixity and verbal veneration until the canon was completed and closed. Yet even then phonetic changes went on, and the saṁhitā text did not take its final shape till after the completion of the Brāhmaṇas, or about 600 B.C.[3]

CHAPTER XXVII

THE VEDIC SCHOOLS AND TEACHERS AND THE BRĀHMAṆAS

THOUGH the Puranas say very little about secular history after the Bhārata battle, yet the Puranic brahmans incorporated notices of the Vedic schools and later teachers. The development of those schools among Vyāsa's disciples is described best in the Vāyu and Brahmāṇḍa, less fully in the Viṣṇu, and the Bhāgavata has copied less clearly and intelligently.[4] Many of the teachers named[5] are alluded to in Vedic literature, but their assignment in those several schools does not, I believe, always tally with their assignment in that literature; yet there may be truth in both, since teachers were

[1] So estimated also by Macdonell, *Sansk. Lit.*, p. 47.

[2] *Id.*, pp. 47, 66. Weber, *Hist. of Ind. Lit.*, p. 20.

[3] Macdonell, *op. cit.*, pp. 48, 50.

[4] Cf. Kūr i, *52*, 17–18; Vā *1*, 180; *61*, 73–7; Bḍ ii, *35*, 83–6.

[5] Also in Bḍ ii, *33*, 3–17 (not in Vā): Kūr i, *53*, 5–25: Lg i, *7*, 14–52; *24*, 11–132: but the lists are jumbled. There is much variation in many of the lesser names, and Vā is generally followed when they are uncertain.

no doubt masters of more than one Veda. The account in the first two Puranas mentioned was obviously drawn up and added by the Puranic brahmans themselves, and deserves attention, because they had knowledge of those schools, and because the account was endorsed by the brahmanic Viṣṇu and again by the still more brahmanic Bhāgavata.[1] As I have not studied Vedic literature closely, I cannot venture to discuss intricacies, and so merely set out the account briefly here with a few comments. Care must be taken not to confuse different persons of the same name, for the account shows there were many such; thus, as will appear, there were two Sumantus and several Yājñavalkyas, and the Jaimini who taught Pauṣpiṇḍya was great grandson of Vyāsa's disciple Jaimini.[2]

Rigveda.[3] Paila made two versions and gave them to his disciples, one to Indrapramati[4] and the other to Vāṣkala. Vāṣkala made four saṁhitās of his version and gave them severally to his four disciples, Bodhya, Agnimāṭhara, Parāśara[5] and Yājñavalkya. Indrapramati taught his version to Māṇḍūkeya; he taught it to his son Satyaśravas; he to Satyahita; and he to his son Satyaśrī. Satyaśrī had three great disciples, Devamitra Śākalya, Rathītara Śākapūrṇa[6] and Vāṣkali Bharadvāja; and they establishe[d] śākhās. Śākalya made five saṁhitās and taught them to his five disciples, Mudgala, Golaka, Khālīya, Vatsa and Śaiśireya. He was very conceited.[7] King 'Janaka' of Videha performed a horse-sacrifice and a great concourse of rishis attended it. He offered great wealth (including slaves[8]) to whoever should be the greatest among them, so they challenged one another to discussion. Yājñavalkya, son of Brahmavāha, vanquished them all with his questions, and then challenged Śākalya with the penalty that whichever failed should

[1] Weber, *Hist. of Ind. Lit.*, p. 142, note, refers to the Viṣ and Vā accounts, but doubts their trustworthiness—gratuitously.

[2] They are treated as one, Weber, *op cit.*, p. 240, note *.

[3] Vā *60*, 24–32, 63–6; *61*, 1–4. Bḍ ii, *34*, 24–33; *35*, 1–7. Viṣ iii, *4*, 16–26. Ag *150*, 25–6; *258* (a disquisition); *270*, 2–3. Bhāg xii, *6*, 53–60.

[4] To be distinguished from the earlier Indrapramati, p. 214.

[5] To be distinguished from earlier Parāśaras, p. 213.

[6] Śākapūṇi. Weber, *op. cit.*, p. 85.

[7] *Jñānâhaṅkāra-garvita*; hence called *Vidagdha*, Weber, pp. 33, 129: *Vedic Index* ii, 296. Cf. MBh xiii, *14*, 689–92 ?

[8] Videha slaves, *Vedic Index*, ii, 212.

forfeit his life. He answered all Śākalya's questions, but Śākalya could not answer his single question and so perished.[1] Yājñavalkya then carried off the prize.[2] Śākapūrṇa Rathītara made three saṁhitās and also a nirukta. He had four disciples, Ketava, Dālaki,[3] Śatabalāka and Naigama.[4] Vāṣkali Bharadvāja made three saṁhitās, and had three disciples, Nandāyanīya, Pannagāri and Aryava.

Yajurveda.[5] Vaiśampāyana made 86 saṁhitās (27, Viṣṇu) and all his disciples received them except Yājñavalkya, who was discarded because of his presumption. Those 86 disciples fashioned saṁhitās, and comprised three groups distinguished geographically, the northern, the madhyadeśya and the eastern, the chiefs of which were respectively Śyāmāyani, Āsuri and Ālambi. They were all called Carakas and Carakādhvaryus, and (says the Viṣṇu) Taittirīyas. Yājñavalkya, called Brahmarāti,[6] fashioned independently separate yajuses,[7] and had 15 disciples, Kaṇva, Madhyaṁdina, &c. (names given): they were called Vājins. So there were 101 recensions altogether.

All these occurrences and names are explained in a story,[8] which consists largely of fable and grew out of a misunderstanding of names. It says (among other things) that Yājñavalkya Brahmarāti when discarded had to disgorge the yajuses he had learnt from Vaiśampāyana, and the other disciples picked them up; that he then worshipped the sun and obtained his own special yajuses from the sun; and that the name Vājin arose because he was *aśva-rūpa*. Now *vājin* can be synonymous with *vāja-sani*, the name of a

[1] Vā *60*, 32–62, Bḍ ii, *34*, 33–68. Referred to, MBh xiii, *14*, 689 ? Vā adds—Śākalya's disciples on his death incurred the guilt of brahmanicide, but went to Bāḍāditya tīrtha at Pavanapura and were purified (*60*, 67–75 and *59*, 108–30).

[2] This might explain the name *Vājasani* of a Yājñavalkya (Weber, p. 104), except that the name Vājasaneya appears to have arisen earlier; see *infra* under Yajurveda.

[3] Here Vā (*60*, 65–6; *61*, 1) has apparently confused the text and inserted six names wrongly.

[4] Viṣ says, the fourth disciple made a nirukta.

[5] Vā *61*, 5–10, 23–6. Bḍ ii, *35*, 8–13, 26–30. Viṣ iii, *5*, 1–2, 12–13. Ag *150*, 27–8; *259* (a disquisition); *270*, 3–5. Bhāg xii, *6*, 61–74.

[6] Viṣ says, son of Brahmarāta: Bhāg, son of Devarāta.

[7] Called *ayātayāma*, which Vaiśampāyana did not know; so Viṣ. Bhāg copied this.

[8] Vā *61*, 11–23. Bḍ ii, *35*, 14–26. Viṣ iii, *5*, 3–28, embellishing.

Yajñavalkya; this Yājñavalkya was (either Vājasani or) Vājasaneya; hence his disciples, the Vājasaneyas of the White Yajus, were called shortly Vājins: but *vājin* was misunderstood as a 'horse', and so he is styled *aśvarūpa*.[1] Similarly, Tittiri was apparently the chief of the disciples of the Black Yajus,[2] and his followers were the Taittirīyas.

This Yājñavalkya as Vaiśampāyana's disciple would have been prior to Janamejaya III, and his teaching appears to have been adopted by that king, for, it is said, Janamejaya established the Vājasaneyaka school in disregard of a Vaiśampāyana and in spite of his curse, but ultimately abdicated.[3] In other respects this account of the Yajurveda, and especially of the Black Yajus, appears from its brevity and indefiniteness and the large number of disciples and recensions to have contracted the succession of teachers; and the three leaders of the Taittirīyas, Śyāmāyani, Āsuri and Ālambi, should be placed soon after Adhisīmakṛṣṇa's time, if this Āsuri is the same as Pañcaśikha's teacher (see *infra*).

Sāmaveda.[4] Jaimini taught this to his son Sumantu, he to his son Sutvan, and he to his son Sukarman. Sukarman Jaimini made a thousand saṁhitās of it.[5] He had two famous disciples, Pauṣyañji or Pauṣpiñji[6] and Hiraṇyanābha Kausalya. Pauṣpiñji made 500 saṁhitās and taught them to his four disciples, who were called the 'northern sāman chanters'. Hiraṇyanābha made 500 also (15, *Viṣṇu*) and taught them to his disciples, who were called the 'eastern sāman chanters'. Pauṣpiñji's disciples were Laugākṣi (or Lokākṣi), Kuthumi, Kuśītin and Lāṅgali. Laugākṣi had five disciples, and their schools were those of Rāṇāyanīya, Taṇḍiputra, &c. (names given). Kuthumi had his three sons as his disciples, Aurasa,

[1] Viṣ, misunderstanding, makes the sun appear *aśvarūpa*. Bhāg copied.

[2] Weber, pp. 41, 87, 90–1. Viṣ, misunderstanding, turned him and the other disciples into partridges; and so also Bhāg. Tittiri was a name, see p. 105.

[3] Mat *50*, 57–65. Vā *99*, 250–6. This Vaiśampāyana can hardly have been Vyāsa's disciple, chronologically. He may have been the Vaiśampāyana of the MBh (i, *60*, 2227 f.); but there he has been confused with Vyāsa's disciple, and so Vyāsa and the earlier Vaiśampāyana have been wrongly introduced.

[4] Vā *61*, 27–47. Bḍ ii, *35*, 31–55. Partially, Viṣ iii, *6*, 1–8: Bhāg xii, *6*, 75–80: Ag *150*, 28–9; *260* (a disquisition); *270*, 6–8.

[5] Here Vā and Bḍ tell a fable about him and Indra.

[6] *Pauṣyañji* (Vā, Bḍ) is a misreading of *Pauṣpiñji* (Viṣ), i.e. Pauṣpiṇḍya; *Vedic Index*, ii, 27.

Parāśara[1] and Bhāgavitti, and these Kauthumas formed three sections. Śauridyu and Śṛṅgiputra were apparently disciples of Aurasa or Bhāgavitti,[2] and Śṛṅgiputra declared three saṁhitās, those of Caila, Prācīnayoga and Surāla. Pārāśarya Kauthuma declared six saṁhitās, those of Āsurāyaṇa, a Patañjali, &c. (names given). Lāṅgali and Śālihotra[3] each declared six saṁhitās. Lāṅgali's six disciples were Bhāluki, Jaimini, Lomagāyani, &c. (names given); and they promulgated saṁhitās.

Hiraṇyanābha Kausalya's disciple was prince Kṛta. He made 24 saṁhitās, and declared them to his disciples, Rāḍa, Gautama, Parāśara, &c. (names given); and they were the Kārta[4] sāman chanters. Pauṣpiñji and Kṛta were the most famous of all sāman chanters. This statement about Hiraṇyanābha, Kṛta and his disciples is wrongly introduced here, for they belonged to a much earlier period (p. 173): it has been inserted in order to bring them into the scheme of Vedic schools derived from Vyāsa.

Atharvaveda.[5] Sumantu divided it into two and taught it to Kabandha. Kabandha divided it into two again and gave one part to Pathya and the other to Devadarśa (or Vedasparśa). The latter made four versions and taught them to his four disciples, Moda, Brahmabala, Pippalāda and Śaulkāyani. The Pathyas had three divisions, those of Jājali,[6] Kumudādi and a 'Śaunaka'. 'Śaunaka' made two saṁhitās, and gave one to Babhru and the other to Saindhavāyana. Saindhava gave that to Muñjakeśa and it was again made into two. The best *vikalpanas* of the saṁhitās are the Nakṣatrakalpa, Vaitāna, Saṁhitāvidhi, Aṅgiras's kalpa and Śāntikalpa.

This account of the Vedic schools has brought them well into the Brāhmaṇa period, and the chronology of that period may be considered. The great Brāhmaṇas[7] were composed in the country of

[1] To be distinguished from other Parāśaras, p. 213.

[2] The text is defective.

[3] Śālihotra may = Kuśītin, but Bḍ makes him = Lāṅgali.

[4] Vā and Bḍ misread this as *Krānta* (p. 173).

[5] Vā *61*, 49–55. Bḍ ii, *35*, 55–62. Viṣ iii, *6*, 9–15. Ag *150*, 30; *261* (a disquisition); *270*, 8–9. Bhāg xii, *7*, 1–4.

[6] Jājali in Hv *142*, 7999 (if genuine) was much earlier.

[7] Their formation, ten functions (*vidhi*), &c.; Bḍ ii, *33*, 47–58: Vā (incompletely) *59*, 130, 132–41. Their declarers are styled *ṛṣi-putrakas*. Bḍ ii, *33*, 1.

the Kurus or allied Kuru-Pañcālas,[1] hence the fusion of those two peoples is important, which occurred more than a century after the Bhārata battle or about 820 B.C. (p. 285).

The Pañcaviṁśa and Taittirīya Brāhmaṇas are the most archaic of the regular Brāhmaṇas.[2] The Pañcaviṁśa, though its home apparently lay farther east, yet contains a minute description of sacrifices performed on the rivers Sarasvatī and Dṛṣadvatī, and has no allusion to the Kuru-Pañcālas; hence it was apparently composed before the blending,[3] and while the Kurus still reigned at Hastināpura and over Kurukṣetra (say) about 830 B.C. The Taittirīya refers to the united Kuru-Pañcālas,[4] and was therefore composed after the fusion, (say) soon after 800 B.C. 'A more recent group is formed by the Jaiminīya, the Kauṣītaki and the Aitareya Brāhmaṇas. The first of these is probably the oldest, while the third seems, on linguistic grounds at least, to be the latest of the three.' The Śatapatha is posterior to these. Latest of all are the Gopatha Brāhmaṇa and the short Brāhmaṇas of the Sāmaveda.[5] All these would be posterior to the fusion of the Kurus and Pañcālas, and so the Jaiminīya refers repeatedly to the Kuru-Pañcālas, and they are mentioned in the Śatapatha and Gopatha.[6] The Brāhmaṇa period ended apparently before or about 600 B.C.;[7] hence the Śatapatha may be placed somewhat before that date, and it will probably not be far wrong to put the Jaiminīya, the Kauṣītaki and the Aitareya about half-way between the Taittirīya and the Śatapatha, in the last quarter of the eighth century and the first quarter of the seventh, the Jaiminīya first and the Aitareya third.

By the end of the seventh century B.C., the original Puranas had been compiled as shown in chapter IV, and the old traditions became known to a certain extent to the recluse brahmans who composed the Brāhmaṇas (pp. 10, 63): hence the Śatapatha notices much legend, though seemingly with doubtful success.[8] The fact

[1] *Vedic Index*, i. 165.
[2] Macdonell, *Sansk. Lit.*, p. 203.
[3] *Id.*, p. 210. Weber, *Hist. of Ind. Lit.*, pp. 67–8.
[4] *Vedic Index*, i, 165.
[5] Macdonell, *Sansk. Lit.*, p. 203.
[6] The Kuru-Pañcāla dynasty ended about 400 B.C. (p. 180).
[7] Macdonell, *Sansk. Lit.*, pp. 50, 215. Winternitz, in his *Geschichte der Indischen Litteratur* (i, p. 25) makes the landmark the rise of Buddhism, which practically agrees.
[8] e.g. its story of Gotama Rāhūgaṇa, pp. 224, 311.

that the Brāhmaṇas make no reference to the Pāṇḍavas or the Bhārata battle has been explained;[1] and the reason why the Bharatas are not mentioned in the geographical lists of the Aitareya Brāhmaṇa, in Manu, or in the Buddhist texts,[2] is simply that the term Bhārata had become too wide for particular use, as noticed in p. 293. The futility of expecting to find secular history in the Brāhmaṇas, which are purely priestly literature, is emphasized by the fact that they take very little notice even of contemporary kings.

The foregoing succession of teachers of the Vedic schools during the Brāhmaṇa period may be supplemented by notices of various brahmans who were contemporary. Many are mentioned in Vedic literature and in the Mahābhārata and Puranas, but generally in brahmanic statements without definite historical connexions:[3] yet here may be noticed certain of them on whom light can be thrown so as to suggest their mutual, and approximately real, positions.

A near relative probably of the Pāṇḍavas' purohita Dhaumya was Āyoda Dhaumya, who lived in the time of their successor Parikṣit II and his son Janamejaya III.[4] He had three disciples, Upamanyu, Āruṇi Uddālaka Pāñcālya and Veda. Veda became Janamejaya's purohita.[5] Uddālaka[6] was son of Aruṇa Aupaveśi Gautama. Aruṇa had learnt of Upaveśa and of Aśvapati[7] prince of the Kekayas, who instructed also Prācīnaśāla Aupamanyava. Uddālaka learnt also of Patañcala Kāpya (p. 250). He was contemporary with Svaidāyana Śaunaka and Śauceya Prācīnayogya,[8] and he or his

[1] P. 283. See also Macdonell, *Sansk. Lit.*, p. 216.

[2] *Vedic Index*, ii, p. 96.

[3] MBh i, *53*, 2044–50 is a brahmanical jumble.

[4] Dhaumya was a Kāśyapa (p. 233). So Aitar Brāhm (vii, 5, 27) says the Kaśyapas were Janamejaya's hereditary priests.

[5] MBh i, *3*, 673-97, 740–6; *53*, 2047. Weber, *Hist. of Ind. Lit.*, p. 71. An Āruṇi, Var *37*, 7.

[6] He was an Āṅgirasa, Mat *196*, 4, 6, 8. He must be distinguished from Uddāla or Uddālaki, an Ātreya (Mat *197*, 2), whose son was Naciketas, called also Nāciketa. They appear in brahmanical fables; MBh xiii, *17*, 1291–2; *71*, 3486–7: Var *193*, 12 f. *Vedic Index* i, pp. 88–9, 432. Kaṭha Upaniṣad i, 1, 1 and 11; ii, 4, 5 apparently identifies them.

[7] There were more than one Aśvapati, see p. 164, and Mat *208*, 5.

[8] Śatapatha Brāhm xi, 4, 1–9; 5, 3.

son Auddālaka were contemporary with that Prācīnaśāla, four other brahmans and Aśvapati.[1] Uddālaka had a son begotten of his wife by a disciple at his request, Śvetaketu Auddālaki Āruṇeya.[2] He had a favourite disciple Kahoḍa (Kauṣītaki[3]) and gave him his daughter Sujātā in marriage, and their son was Aṣṭāvakra. Kahoḍa was vanquished by Vandin in a controversy before king 'Janaka' and was drowned. Śvetaketu and Aṣṭāvakra, uncle and nephew, were of the same age and were brought up in Uddālaka's hermitage. When Aṣṭāvakra learnt of his father's fate, they both went to Janaka Ugrasena Puṣkaramālin and overcame Vandin.[4] Contemporary with Śvetaketu were the Pañcāla king Pravāhaṇa Jaivala[5] and Jala Jātūkarṇya.[6]

It is said Śvetaketu, who was reckoned a rishi,[7] established strict monogamy for women, in relation to brahman women.[8] It is amazing that such a story should have been fabricated and preserved, if not true; and if true, it would indicate that laxity among brahmans (which various stories suggest in early times) did not disappear till some time later than the Bhārata battle.[9]

Uddālaka had as pupils Yājñavalkya Vājasaneya[10] and Proti Kausurubindi. The Vājasaneya school was established in or by Janamejaya III's time (p. 324). Yājñavalkya had Āsuri as

[1] Chāndogya Up. v, 11–17.

[2] MBh i, *122*, 4724, 4735: iii, *132*, 10599: xii, *34*, 1229: xiii, *165*, 7671. Weber, pp. 71, 137. Called by abridgement, 'son of Gautama,' SBE i, pp. 76–7; *Vedic Index* ii, p. 409. Mentioned, MBh ix, *39*, 2207–9.

[3] *Vedic Index*, i, p. 145.

[4] MBh iii, *132*, 10599 to *134*, 10690. Rām vi, *121*, 16. Fables about Aṣṭāvakra, MBh xiii, *19*, 1390 f.; Br *212*, 72 f.

[5] Chāndogya Up. v, 3, 1. Bṛhadāraṇyaka Up. vi, 2, 1.

[6] *Vedic Index* ii, p. 409. [7] Āpastamba i, 2, 5, 4–6.

[8] MBh i, *122*, 4724–35. Yet the same is attributed far earlier to Dīrghatamas, *104*, 4202–3. Both possibly true.

[9] Cf. the story of Jabālā and her son Satyakāma, who were later (*infra*); Chāndogya Up. iv, 4, 1–2. Cf. *Vedic Index* i, 273, 479–80; ii, 84, 259. As regards polyandry, MBh i, *195*, 7244 to *196*, 7271. Was the description of a brahman by adding *putra* to his mother's name (a practice that prevailed about this period) due to such laxity? Weber, *Hist. of Ind. Lit.*, pp. 71, 131: where Kṛṣṇa Devakīputra, the scholar, is plainly different from Kṛṣṇa the king; so *Vedic Index*, i, p. 184. Kṛṣṇa was a very common name, and Devaka (and therefore the feminine Devakī) an ordinary name.

[10] Bhāg ix, *22*, 38, if correct, would refer to an earlier Yājñavalkya. There were many Yājñavalkyas (p. 237).

pupil.[1] Āsuri's first disciple was Pañcaśikha, who was of Parāśara's gotra, was a bhikṣu,[2] and was called Kāpileya (it is said) after his foster-mother Kapilā and shortly Kapila by the Sāṅkhyas.[3] He went to Janaka Janadeva, king of Mithilā, and the king gave up his hundred teachers and followed Pañcaśikha, who taught him mokṣa according to the Sāṅkhya;[4] and Janaka Dharmadhvaja also was his disciple.[5] Two stages below Āsuri was Āsurāyaṇa, with whom Yāska was contemporary.[6] This Yājñavalkya also taught Madhuka Paiṅgya, he taught Cūḍa Bhāgavitti, he Jānaki Āyasthūṇa, and he Satyakāma Jābāla.[7]

In a chronological succession of teachers are named (downwards)—Upaveśi, Aruṇa, Uddālaka, Yājñavalkya, Āsuri and Āsurāyaṇa:[8] and Voḍhu (or Voḍha), Kapila, Āsuri and Pañcaśikha are mentioned as connected teachers,[9] treating Kapila and Pañcaśikha as distinct.

These particulars yield something like a chronological scheme, and all the more important of these teachers[10] are shown in the following table, which is in continuation of those on pages 148–9 and 192. It starts with teachers contemporary with the Pāṇḍavas, Parikṣit II and Janamejaya III, and nearly all the persons in the first four columns are connected by synchronisms. There are few synchronisms touching the teachers in columns 5–8, yet something may be done to estimate their positions, for the notice of some of them in the Brāhmaṇas would no doubt warrant the inference that such a person flourished well before the Brāhmaṇa which mentions him, at least a quarter of a century prior. The steps are

[1] Weber, *op. cit.*, pp. 128, 131, 235–6. *Vedic Index* i, 72.

[2] MBh xii, *322*, 11875.

[3] Cf. Mat *3*, 29. He is confused with the mythical Kapila, MBh vi, *34*, 1230: xii, *342*, 13078–9; *341*, 12932; *344*, 13254; *351*, 13703: iii, *220*, 14197: Mat *171*, 1–4: story of Sagara's sons (p. 271): Pad ii, *75*, 2—and so called *cira-jīvin*, MBh xii, *218*, 7890.

[4] MBh xii, *218*, 7883–7900; *219*, 7930–4. Fable, *269*, 9600–4.

[5] MBh xii, *322*, 11855, 11875 with *321*, 11839–40.

[6] Weber, pp. 128, 235–6. *Vedic Index* i, 72.

[7] Weber, pp. 130, 134. Bṛhadāraṇyaka Up. vi, 3, 7–11.

[8] Bṛhadāraṇyaka Up. vi, 5, 2–3.

[9] Vā *101*, 338. Bḍ iv, *2*, 273–4. Mat *102*, 18 and Kūr i, *53*, 15 (both placing Voḍhu third). Cf. Vā *23*, 141: Lg i, *7*, 41: *24*, 41: MBh xii, *320*, 11783–4 (which all omit Voḍhu).

[10] Cf. Bḍ ii, *33*, 1–17; which is wanting in Vā. For the references for the following statements see *Vedic Index* generally. The dates of the Brāhmaṇas are those suggested above.

	Kuru-Pauravas	Janakas of Videha	Other kings	Various teachers
92	Vicitravīrya	Dhṛti	... ...	Kṛṣṇa-Dvaipāyana-Vyāsa
93	Dhṛtarāṣṭra	Bahulāśva	... ...	Śuka
94	Pāṇḍavas	Kṛtakṣaṇa	... ...	Bhūriśravas, &c. (p. 214)
95	Abhimanyu	... ...	... ...	Upaveśa
96	Parikṣit II	... ...	Aśvapati of Kekaya	Āyoda, Patañcala, Āruṇa, Prācīnaśāla
97	Janamejaya III	... ...	... ...	Uddālaka, Veda, 'Upamanyu,' Svaidāyana, Prācīnayogya
98	Śatānīka	Janaka-Ugrasena	... ...	Kahoḍa, Vandin, Yājñavalkya-Vājasaneya
99	Aśvamedhadatta	... ...	Pravāhaṇa of Pañcāla	Śvetaketu, Aṣṭāvakra
100	Adhisīmakṛṣṇa	... ...	... ...	Yājñavalkya (son of Brahmavāha)
a	.. ..	... ...	... ...	Āsuri, Madhuka
b	... ...	Janaka-Janadeva	... ...	Pañcaśikha
c	... ...	Janaka-Dharmadhvaja	... ...	Cūḍa-Bhāgavitti
d	... ...	... ...	... ...	Asurāyaṇa, Yāska
e	... ...	Jānaki-Āyasthūṇa	... ...	... ...
f	... ...	... ...	... ...	Satyakāma-Jābāla

Of Rigveda	Of Yajurveda	Of Sāmaveda	Of Atharvaveda	
... ...	... ...	... ...	... ...	92
... ...	... ...	... ...	... ...	93
Paila	Vaiśampāyana	Jaimini	Sumantu	94
Indrapramati, Vāṣkala	... ...	Sumantu-Jaimini	Kabandha	95
Bodhya, 'Yājñavalkya,' Parāśara, Māṇḍūkeya	Yājñavalkya-Brahmarāti	Sutvan-Jaimini	Pathya, Devadarśa	96
Satyaśravas	Tittiri	Sukarman-Jaimini	Pippalāda, &c.	97
Satyahita	... ...	Pauṣpiṇḍya	Jājali, Śaunaka	98
Satyaśrī	Madhyaṁdina, Kaṇva, & .	Laugākṣi, Kuthumi, Kuśītin, Lāṅgali	Saindhavāyana, Babhru	99
Śākalya, Vāṣkali, Śākapūrṇa	'Yājñavalkya'	Rāṇāyanīya, Taṇḍiputra, Parāśara, Bhāgavitti, &c.	... ...	100
Pannagāri, Śaiśireya, Vatsa, Śatabalāka	Śyāmāyani, Āsuri, Ālambi	... ...	Muñjakeśa	a
... ...	... ...	Lomagāyani, Pārāśarya, Prācīnayoga	... ...	b
... ...	... ...	... ...	... ...	c
... ...	... ...	Āsurāyaṇa, a 'Patañjali'	... ...	d
... ...	... ...	... ...	... ...	e
... ...	... ...	... ...	... ...	f

numbered as far as 100, but beyond that there are no clear royal synchronisms to mark definite steps.

Thus the Taittirīya Brāhmaṇa shows that Aruṇa Aupaveśi[1] lived well before 800 B.C., and the synchronisms coupled with the date of the Bhārata battle assign him to the early half of the ninth century B.C. Similarly the Jaiminīya shows that Yājñavalkya Vājasaneya lived well before 725, and his position in the table places him more than a century earlier. The Śatapatha notices Uddālaka, Śvetaketu, Śākalya, Āsuri, Madhuka, Prācīnayogya and Satyakāma, and shows that Satyakāma, the latest of them, lived well before 600 B.C. The Kauṣītaki mentions Uddālaka, Śvetaketu and Madhuka, and fixes their time closer in that Madhuka, the latest of these, lived well before 700. The most effective indication is that to the Tāṇḍins belonged the Tāṇḍya or Pañcaviṁśa Brāhmaṇa of the Sāmaveda,[2] so that Taṇḍiputra and all the prior teachers of that Veda in column 7 were anterior to 830 B.C.

If then we work on these inferences according to the sequence in the table and with the scale proposed at page 182, we may estimate the periods when the teachers *flourished*, except as regards those of the Atharvaveda for whom there are no synchronisms. In the ninth century B.C. flourished Uddālaka in the first quarter, Śvetaketu about the middle, and Śākalya and Taṇḍiputra in the third quarter. In the eighth century Āsuri and Madhuka at the beginning, Pañcaśikha in the middle, and Asurāyaṇa and Yāska in the fourth quarter. In the seventh century Satyakāma in the second quarter. This estimate for Pañcaśikha agrees with Buddhist legends, which speak of him as long prior to Buddha.[3]

The account of the Vedic schools shows that Vyāsa's successors exercised individual liberty in dealing with the text of the Vedas as arranged by him, and so there grew up a multitude of modifications which constituted different 'uses'. Five Puranas explain briefly how that happened.[4] The differences arose from the idiosyncrasies (*dṛṣṭi-vibhrama*) of the various teachers, and consisted in their arrangement of the mantras and Brāhmaṇas and in their transposition of tones and syllables (*svara-varṇa*), but the essential text

[1] *Vedic Index* i, 35.

[2] Macdonell, *Sansk. Lit.*, pp. 209–10. Weber, *op. cit.*, p. 63.

[3] Weber, *op. cit.*, p. 236.

[4] Vā *58*, 12–18. Bd ii, *31*, 12–18. Mat *144*, 11–17. Lg i, *39*, 58–60. Kūr i, *29*, 44–6.

itself remained fixed apparently.[1] The multiplicity and variance of the different uses must have worked their own remedy in the gradual selection of the best versions and the elimination of the rest, until at length one use became generally accepted as the established Saṁhitā text.[2] The table shows that the growth of diversities continued during at least eight successions of teachers, that is, nearly two centuries according to the above estimated dates. The reverse process could hardly have taken much less time. The two processes therefore probably occupied nearly four centuries, and this may be suggested as one reason why 'the Saṃhitā text did not come into existence till after the completion of the Brāhmaṇas' or about 600 B.C.[3]

Moreover, when we compare the teachers in column 4 with those in columns 5–8, we notice that there is no agreement between the two classes (except perhaps as regards No. 100, 'Yājñavalkya')[4] until we reach Āsuri and Āsurāyaṇa. This want of agreement is entirely what should be expected, because the Vedic schools could not have dominated all the religious teachers forthwith, and had gradually to make good their special province and authority, each as regards its own Veda. That process would have been slow, not only because of religious conservatism and jealousy,[5] but also because the multiplicity of competing versions would have weakened their prerogative. It would have required a long time; and the table shows that from Vyāsa's disciples to Āsuri (when the influence began to appear), was more than a century and a half. During that period religious teachers of the old order would have continued to flourish independently alongside the growing Vedic schools, and that is what column 4 shows.[6] The two streams of teaching would have persisted, with gradually diminishing difference, even longer than that, and may not have blended till the close of the Brāhmaṇa period. Hence that condition may be suggested as another cause why 'the Saṃhitā text did not come into existence till after the completion of the Brāhmaṇas'.

[1] So Macdonell, *Sansk. Lit.*, p. 49.

[2] Weber, *op. cit.*, pp. 13–14. [3] Macdonell, *op. cit.*, p. 50.

[4] Not certain, because there were several Yājñavalkyas.

[5] Weber, *op. cit.*, p. 13. This would have restricted the citation by one school of teachers of another school.

[6] Such must have been the position that naturally resulted from the establishment of the Vedic schools, however they were established.

Here notice of historical tradition on the religious side closes, for the Puranas and epic contain nothing noteworthy about later teachers. Their account stops with Āsurāyaṇa, who has been assigned to about the end of the eighth century B. C. It was drawn up by the Puranic brahmans as mentioned above, and the fact that they continued the lines of religious teachers, beyond the stage where their secular tradition closed (p. 57), down to about 700 B. C. with precise statements, and allude to nothing later personal except to Buddha curtly or vaguely, indicates that those additions were made then as a second stage while personal knowledge was fresh. Not long afterwards Jainism and Buddhism challenged the supremacy of the brahmans, and no traditions about later teachers were added. Secular chronicles preserved knowledge of the dynasties and kings who reigned in the chief countries, and were incorporated in the Bhaviṣya Purana, and copied later into the Matsya [1] and other Puranas in the third century A. D. and afterwards (p. 50). Religious tradition about the same period would seem to have become too scanty, uncertain or confused amid the religious conflicts to gain admittance into the Puranas.

Ancient tradition was compiled into the original Purana about the ninth century B. C., later religious historical tradition was added till the end of the eighth century B. C., and the chronicles of the kings of the Kali age were incorporated in the Puranas in prophetic guise down to the early part of the fourth century A. D. Such were the three main stages of the compilation of historical tradition in the Puranas.

[1] It existed before (p. 51).

INDEX

The following words have been generally included in this index, but are sometimes omitted when merely descriptive and not materially important, namely, (1) generic names such as Aila, Yādava and Aṅgirasa; (2) proper names used generically such as Vasiṣṭha and Bharadvāja; (3) names of countries, districts, towns, rivers and mountains.

ABBREVIATIONS

aps	apsaras	*metr*	metronymic	*pss*	princess
b	brahman	*mt*	mountain	*q*	queen
c	country, district	*p*	people	*r*	rishi
f	family, gotra	*patr*	patronymic	*riv*	river
g	god, goddess	*pl*	place	*t*	town
k	king	*pr*	prince	*w*	woman
m	man				

CORRIGENDA

P.	l.		for	read
P. 39	l. 26	*for*	Sivi	*read* Śivi
42	32		Avīkṣita	Āvīkṣita
45	22		(or Sāmba)	(or Śāmba)
65	11		Sukas	Śukas
68	14		Urva	Ūrva
69	11		Sataśilāka	Śataśilāka
,,	,,		Saṅkha	Śaṅkha
70	10		Suka	Śuka
85	17		Vipapman	Vipāpman
110	39		Anavas	Ānavas
112	in the Garga line of descent	*for*	Aṅgirasas	*read* Āṅgirasas
117	l. 26	*for*	Nīpas	*read* Nīpa's
,,	30		Jamamejaya	Janamejaya
124	38		Anavas	Ānavas
129	1		Sarūtha	Śarūtha
130	29		*222*	*122*
136	21		Santanu	Śantanu
148	1		S. PAÑCĀ	S. PAÑCĀLA
,,	No. 79		Arādhin	Ārādhin
161	l. 40		Vedarth	Vedārth
163	27		*E. Anavus*	*E. Ānavas*
165	last		Arṣṭiṣeṇa	Ārṣṭiṣeṇa
191	l. 6		Bṛha ati	Bṛhaspati
198	25		hou e	house
204	37		Gaurāś	Gauraś
209	32		Nāṛada	Nārada
211	25		Santanu's	Śantanu's
218	3		Brahmāṅḍa	Brahmāṇḍa
225	24		Martināra	Matināra
234	5		sacrifice	sacrificer
246	25		Aṅgirasas	Āṅgirasas
254	27		aud	and
259	23		Bṛ	Br
260	19		Srāvasta's	Śrāvasta's
262	24		Anava	Ānava
265	11		Sāryāta	Śāryāta
277	last		*insert* [6] *for the note.*	

P.					
280	l. 17	*for*	Vrṣṇis	*read*	Vṛṣṇis
286	36		Siśunāgas		Śiśunāgas
294	4		Anavas		Ānavas
,,	6		Sivis		Śivis
297	37		Ayu		Āyu
308	28		Vạ		Vā
322	12		Pauspiṇḍya		Pauṣpiṇḍya
324	1		Yajñavalkya		Yājñavalkya
330	No. d		Asurāyaṇa		Āsurāyaṇa
331	No. 99		Kaṇva &		Kaṇva &c.
332	l. 24		Asurāyaṇa		Āsurāyaṇa
335	2		dcscriptive		descriptive
,,	3		Aṅgirasa		Āṅgirasa